Perspectives from *Historical Archaeology*
and *ACUA Proceedings*

Maritime Archaeology

Compiled by
Ben Ford and Wendy van Duivenvoorde

No. 7

SOCIETY *for*
HISTORICAL
ARCHAEOLOGY

Compiled by:
Ben Ford and Wendy van Duivenvoorde

Contact Information:
Ben Ford
Department of Anthropology
Indiana University of Pennsylvania
Indiana, PA 15701
ben.ford@iup.edu

Wendy van Duivenvoorde
Maritime Archaeology Program
Department of Archaeology
Flinders University
GPO Box 2100
Adelaide SA 5001
Australia
wendy.vanduivenvoorde@flinders.edu.au

Cover:
Synthetic aperture sonar image of the collided schooners *Frank A. Palmer* and *Louise B. Crary* (NOAA/SBNMS and applied signal technology, 2010).

Perspectives from Historical Archaeology is a reader series providing collected articles from the journal of the Society for Historical Archaeology (SHA). Published since 1967, <u>Historical Archaeology</u> is the oldest North American scholarly publication on the archaeology of sites and materials from the historic past, and one of the world's premier publications on this subject. Each volume in the *Perspectives* series is developed on either a subject or regional basis by a compiler, who selects the articles for inclusion and their order. The compilers also provide an introduction that presents an overview of the substantive work on that topic. *Perspectives* volumes offer non-archaeologists a convenient source for important publications on a subject or a region; an excellent resource for students interested in developing a specialization in a specific topic or area; as well as a convenient reference for archaeologists with an interest in the material.

The *Perspectives* series is managed by the SHA's Journal Editor and Co-Publications Editor and is published through the SHA's Print-On-Demand Press. Individuals interested in compiling a volume for publication through this series are encouraged to contact the Series Editors:

J. W. Joseph, PhD, RPA
Journal Editor, SHA
New South Associates, Inc.
6150 East Ponce de Leon Avenue
Stone Mountain, GA 30083
jwjoseph@newsouthassoc.com

Annalies Corbin, PhD
Co-Publications Editor, SHA
The PAST Foundation
1003 Kinnear Road
Columbus, OH 43212
annalies@pastfoundation.org

Formed in 1967, the SHA is the largest scholarly group concerned with the archaeology of the modern world (A.D. 1400-present). The main focus of the society is the era since the beginning of European exploration. SHA promotes scholarly research and the dissemination of knowledge concerning historical archaeology. The society is specifically concerned with the identification, excavation, interpretation, and conservation of sites and materials on land and underwater. Geographically the society emphasizes the New World, but also includes European exploration and settlement in Africa, Asia, and Oceania. To learn more about the SHA and historical archaeology, visit www.sha.org.

Contents

Part I. Introduction

Maritime Archaeology through the Lens of Historical Archaeology and ACUA Underwater Archaeology Proceedings
    Ben Ford and Wendy van Duivenvoorde 9

Underwater Archaeology at the Dawn of the 21st Century
    James P. Delgado 17

Sailing Ships, Air Ships, Star Ships: Into the Millennium
    Toni L. Carrell and Donald Keith 22

A Perspective on the Future of Underwater Archaeology
    Arthur B. Cohn 26

Of Strawberries, Women's Thighs, and Jim Delgado's Paper
    Daniel J. Lenihan 30

Beyond Exploration: Underwater Archaeology after the Year 2000
    Richard A. Gould 32

Part II. Shipwreck and Ship Studies

A Preliminary Analysis of Historic Shipwrecks in Northern Ireland
    Colin Breen, Rory Quinn, and Wes Forsythe 37

The Abandoned Ships' Project: An Overview of the Archaeology of Deliberate Watercraft Discard in Australia
    Nathan Richards and Mark Staniforth 43

Recovering the Past of USS Arizona
    James P. Delgado 63

Three Ironclad Warships—The Archaeology of Industrial Process and Historical Myth
    Ervan G. Garrison 75

A Small Craft Typology: Tool for Archaeological Research
    Michael B. Alford 88

The Comparative Analysis of 18th-Century Vessel Remains in the Archaeological Record: A Synthesized Theory of Framing System
    John W. Morris, III, Gordon P. Watts, Jr., and Marianne Franklin 91

In Search of Unique Iberian Ship Design Concepts
    Filipe Castro 100

Outfitting the Pepper Wreck
　　Filipe Castro, Nuno Fonseca, and Audrey Wells 125

Shipwreck Cargoes: Approaches to Material Culture in Australian Maritime Archaeology
　　Mark Staniforth 146

Part III. Maritime Archaeology Ashore

Were the Communities Living on the East African Coast also 'Maritime' Communities? An Archaeological Perspective
　　Annalisa C. Christie 152

Old Slip and Cruger's Wharf at New York: An Archaeological Perspective of the Colonial American Waterfront
　　Paul R. Huey 163

Wharves and Waterfront Retaining Structures as Vernacular Architecture
　　Molly R. McDonald 186

Training and Ferry Slips are not Sexy Lingerie
　　Celia McCarthy 212

Archaeology of the Strangford Lough Kelp Industry in the Eighteenth- and Early-Nineteenth Centuries
　　Thomas C. McErlean 218

Archaeology of the Cod Fishery: Damariscove Island
　　Alaric Faulkner 234

Followup Notes on the 17th Century Cod Fishery at Damariscove Island, Maine—1622–1676
　　Alaric Faulkner 265

The Archaeology of Crisis: Shipwreck Survivor Camps in Australasia
　　Martin Gibbs 268

Conflict and Commerce: Maritime Archaeological Site Distribution as Cultural Change on the Roanoke River, North Carolina
　　Franklin H. Price and Nathan Richards 286

Part IV. Field Techniques, Recording, and Reconstruction

Wagging the Dog: Technology and Archaeology
　　Kimberly Faulk 308

Shifting Sand and Muddy Water: Historic Cartography and River Migration as Factors in Locating Steamboat Wrecks on the Far Upper Missouri River
　　Annalies Corbin 312

Using Remote-Sensing as a Tool for Middle-Range Theory Building in Maritime and Nautical Archaeology
        Rik Anuskiewicz 321

The Assimilation of Marine Geophysical Data into the Maritime Sites and Monuments Record, Northern Ireland
        Rory Quinn 329

Using Multibeam Bathymetry and Backscatter for Mapping and In-Situ Assessments of Deepwater Shipwreck Sites
        Daniel Warren, Robert A. Church, Robert F. Westrick, and Cheng-Wei Wu 345

Testing the Efficacy of Synthetic Aperture Sonar to Locate Historic Shipwrecks in the Stellwagen Bank National Marine Sanctuary
        Matthew S. Lawrence 351

Integrating Data Sets: Results from the City of St. Augustine Seawall Phase I Archaeology Survey, St. Augustine, Florida
        Bradley A. Krueger and Jean B. Pelletier 357

Shipwreck in a Swimming Pool: An Assessment of the Methodology and Technology Utilized on the Yorktown Shipwreck Archaeological Project
        John D. Broadwater 365

Ship Reconstruction and Antiquities Conservation: Maximum Results from Minimum Remains
        J. Richard Steffy 376

ShipShape: Creating a 3D Solid Model of the Newport Medieval Ship
        Toby N. Jones and Nigel Nayling 378

Maritime Experimental Archaeology: Trying the Impossible
        Albrecht Sauer 385

Part V. Cultural Heritage Management and Legislation

The Second Destruction of the Geldermalsen
        Miller, George L. 390

After the Diving is Over
        George F. Bass 398

The World's Worst Investment: The economics of treasure hunting with real life comparisons
        Peter Throckmorton 402

The Ethics of Collaboration: Archaeologists and the Wydah Project
        Ricardo J. Elia 407

Is it Treasure or a Worthless Piece of Ship?
        Paul F. Johnston 420

State and Their Shipwrecks
    Anne G. Giesecke 426

The Abandoned Shipwreck Act 1988 to 1998
    Anne G. Giesecke 433

Shipwreck Protection: Federal and State Law—A View From Louisiana
    Ryan M. Seidemann 437

Threatened James River Shipwrecks and Historical Sites
    Kevin J. Foster 445

*ARPA and Site Damage Management Assessment Applicability to Offshore Underwater
    Cultural Heritage*
        Martin E. McAllister, Larry E. Murphy, and James E. Moriarty, IV 456

Sovereign Immunity and the Management of United States Naval Shipwrecks
    Robert S. Neyland 461

*Establishing Marine Protected Areas in the Dominican Republic: A Model for Sustainable
    Preservation*
        Frederick H. Hanselmann and Charles D. Beeker 468

Education versus Legislation
    Robyn P. Woodward 478

Innovative Approaches to Marine Heritage Management: A View from Across the Divide
    Mark Dunkley 484

*Cooperative Approaches to Protecting Underwater Cultural Heritage: Emerging Themes and
    Trends*
        Sarah Dromgoole 495

A Note About This Particular Perspectives Volume

This is the first effort to compile a Perspectives volume that represents published articles from both the SHA journal, Historical Archaeology and the ACUA Underwater Archaeology Proceedings. This volume represents a comprehensive look at the field of underwater archaeology from the society's earliest conferences to present. Because this volume is compiled from a compilation of sources produced over the years, there are a range of publication styles, printers, and layouts resulting in a number of inconsistencies that can not be helped even in today's technologically advanced world of printing. Many of the articles only exist as print copies and today are very difficult to find. Thus, a number of the articles are facsimiles of the original paper publications. By creating facsimiles we have been able to accomplish one of the stated goals of the Perspectives series making available previously published articles cost effectively. Facsimiles are not edited and often the quality of the images is low. However, weighed against never having access to these important articles, we chose to publish the facsimiles. We have provided the citations for the original publications for reference. Please enjoy this volume.

Ben Ford and Wendy van Duivenvoorde

Maritime Archaeology through the Lens of Historical Archaeology and *ACUA Underwater Archaeology Proceedings*

ABSTRACT

This introduction summarizes trends in the development of maritime archaeology since the 1960s, discusses the publication of maritime archaeological results in Society for Historical Archaeology publications, and provides an overview of the readings included in this volume.

Introduction

The field of maritime archaeology is bound together by common theoretical and methodological concerns; it includes scholars who work on, under, and near the water, all of whom are dedicated to understanding past peoples maritime adaptations. Maritime archaeology is the study of past water-focused cultures. This definition eschews the traditional definition of "maritime" as dealing only with the sea, and expands it to incorporate rivers, lakes, canals, and other bodies of water that played an important role in human subsistence, trade, conflict, recreation, ideology, and religion. This definition also does not require an archaeological site to be wet in order to be "maritime" nor does it pertain exclusively to shipwrecks. Many ships lost in harbors and rivers are now beneath dry land (Hawley 1998; Delgado 2011), and, more importantly, sailors were sailors whether they were afloat or ashore (Hasslöf et al. 1972; Pieters et al. 2006). The fishing sheds, homes, shipyards, quays, warehouses, chandleries, and other maritime facilities that served seamen and their families are also components of maritime archaeology. Within the bounds of this definition there are an array of theoretical and methodological approaches spanning the globe and human history.

Intellectual Currents

1960 is often marked as the birth of modern mar-

itime archaeology (Bass 2011), with the application of then current terrestrial archaeology standards to sites such as Roskilde in Denmark and Cape Gelidonya in Turkey (Bass 1967; Crumlin-Pedersen and Olsen 2002), but the precursors of the field extend at least into the late 19th century with the excavation of ships on land and pioneering work at port towns such as Bergen, Norway (de Morgan 1895; Herteig 1959; Bruce-Mitford 1975–1983). While many early maritime archaeology investigations did focus on shipwreck sites, there was always an interest in parallel topics such as ports and historical maritime ethnography (Flemming 1971; Hasslöf et al. 1972). Several of the techniques commonly used by maritime archaeologists also developed during the 1960s. The use of water dredges and air lifts to remove sediments mobilized by hand or trowel, as well as the use of remote sensing and informant interviews (in particular of fishermen) to locate sites, were all developed during this first decade (Bass 1972, 2011; Quinn 2011).

Many of these early investigations focused on a single shipwreck, attempting to reconstruct how the vessel was built and used, as well as its origins and destination. While this form of historical particularism was not then in vogue, George Bass (1983) has ably argued that it was necessary foundational work to build the database of maritime adaptations. Maritime archaeology went through this phase for the same reason that terrestrial archaeology had a half century earlier—it is not possible to theorize about why people did things until you have a firm idea of the range of things that they did. While historical and technological questions have remained important in maritime archaeology, since the 1980s the increasing knowledge base about maritime cultures has permitted more anthropological inquiry (Gould 1983).

In many ways maritime archaeology has paralleled terrestrial archaeology. For example, both explored site formation processes in the late 1970s and early 1980s (Muckelroy 1978; Schiffer 1987), and both turned to landscapes as an interpretive framework in the 1990s (Westerdahl 1992; Anschuetz et al. 2001). Similarly, maritime archaeology benefits from the same diversity of excavations as terrestrial archaeology; today there are large multi-year projects focused on nationally significant sites, alongside academic and cultural resource management (CRM) investigations that focus on surveying new areas and recording previously unknown sites. The increasing sources of information, as well as the increasing number of practitioners, have led to a wide array of approaches to understanding past maritime cultures. Maritime archaeology papers at a recent Society for Historical Archaeology conference ranged from predictive modeling to discussions of specific shipwreck sites and ship types, and from heritage management through public training to site formation processes.

In recent years, deep-water sites and submerged terrestrial sites have seen increasing attention from maritime archaeologists. Deep-water sites are those below the depths accessible by SCUBA divers utilizing compressed air. With improved technical diving and advances in remotely operated vehicles (ROV) and autonomous underwater vehicles (AUV), these sites are increasingly accessible at the same time that they are more threatened by human activities such as oil and gas development, bottom trawling, and commercial salvaging (Ballard 2008; Søreide 2011). Improved technology has also fueled increased interest in submerged terrestrial sites. These are sites that were sub-aerial when inhabited but are now inundated. There has been interest in these sites in the Mediterranean and Northern Europe for decades (Flemming 1971; Andersen 1985), but advances in geographic information systems (GIS) and global positioning systems (GPS) have made it possible to model the sea bottom and navigate to specific locations for testing, making it possible to search for more ephemeral sites, such as Native American settlements. As with terrestrial archaeology, these new foci have not replaced existing research interests, but have complemented and augmented them as we slowly increase our understanding of humanity's maritime past.

Maritime Archaeology within the Society for Historical Archaeology

James Deetz (1996:5), not unproblematically, defined historical archaeology as "the archaeology of the spread of European cultures throughout the world since the fifteenth century, and their impact on and interaction with the cultures of indigenous peoples." Within this definition, ships are the vector of the spread of Europeans as well as part of the interaction between Europeans and indigenous peoples, ranging from warfare to the syncretism of boatbuilding techniques. Maritime archaeology also traces the

development of seafaring and maritime adaptations that allowed Europeans to push off from their shores and indigenous peoples to sail or paddle out to meet them. Maritime archaeology has thus been a part of historical archaeology since before either sub-field was formally recognized.

This intellectual connection became corporate in 1970 when the Advisory Council on Underwater Archaeology (ACUA), then the Conference on Underwater Archaeology, held its first joint meeting with the Society for Historical Archaeology (SHA). This relationship was formalized in 1987 when the title of the SHA conference was changed to the SHA Conference on Historical and Underwater Archaeology, and again in 2003 when the ACUA and SHA signed a Memorandum of Agreement structuring their relationship (Fischer 1993; ACUA 2013).

Despite this close relationship in North America, the journal *Historical Archaeology* has not been the primary outlet for maritime archaeology publication. Competing, maritime-specific journals and the international focus of maritime archaeology have often led researchers to publish elsewhere. Consequently, the articles contained in *Historical Archaeology* do not provide an entirely balanced view of maritime archaeology. In compiling this volume we found that the majority of the maritime archaeology articles were contained within a few thematic issues or forums, or were limited to specific authors who saw the value of presenting their work in *Historical Archaeology*. And we would argue that there is a value to publishing maritime archaeology findings in *Historical Archaeology* in terms of reaching a broader audience, especially when the results bear on questions that are regional or temporal, not just maritime. In order to provide a more balanced representation of the field, we have drawn additional chapters from the ACUA *Underwater Archaeology Proceedings*. These volumes include underwater papers presented at many of the combined SHA and ACUA annual conferences between 1978 and 1999 and from 2007 to the present.

Overview of this Volume

Section II includes five chapters selected from the 1999 Plenary Session at the SHA/ACUA annual conference (Delgado 2000; Carrel and Keith 2000; Cohn 2000; Lenihan 2000; Gould 2000). The authors of these papers were asked to offer their thoughts on the future of underwater archaeology based on their decades of experience in the field and in response to James Delgado's opening essay. Despite being written nearly 15 years ago, they have proven to be fairly accurate prognosticators and many of the issues that they raised remain with us in the second decade of this century. This section also introduces many of the themes and debates that run through the other sections.

Shipwreck and ship studies form Section III. This section moves from the general to the specific, with chapters ranging from regional syntheses of shipwrecks (Breen et al. 2007; Richards and Staniforth 2006), to studies specific to a ship or ship type (Alford 1985; Delgado 1992; Garrison 1995; Morris et al. 1995; Castro 2008), to discussions of specific ship components such as rigging and cargo (Staniforth 2009; Castro et al. 2010). This section also demonstrates the international reach of maritime archaeology with chapters from Australia, Portugal, Northern Ireland, and the United States.

The second thematic section (Section IV) deals with maritime archaeology ashore. This section begins with a discussion of what it means to be a maritime community (Christie 2010) before delving into several examples of sites used by maritime adapted peoples. These sites include several examples of port infrastructure (Huey 1984; McCarthy 1999; McDonald 2011), as well as extractive industries such as kelp harvesting and cod fishing (Faulkner 1985, 1985; McErlean 2007). This section also includes an article on shipwreck survivor camps as a specific type of maritime site influenced by crisis (Gibbs 2003). The final article provides an example of a synthetic regional study in which a wide range of archaeological resources are combined to investigate cultural change on the Roanoke River (Price and Richards 2009).

Section V deals with field techniques, recording, and reconstruction by following the components of a maritime archaeological project from beginning to end. The first article introduces the role of technology in maritime archaeology (Faulk 2011). Because maritime archaeology regularly takes place in an environment to which humans are not particularly well adapted, technology is often an important component of finding and recording sites. The next several articles deal with finding sites through the use of historic documents and remote sensing technology (Anuskiewicz 1992; Corbin 1998; Quinn 2007; Law-

rence 2011; Warren et al. 2011; Krueger and Pelletier 2012). These articles range from discussions of specific technologies to the use of remote sensing to develop middle range theory and the integration of terrestrial and submerged geophysical data. The section then turns to an article by John Broadwater (1992) discussing shipwreck recording, before moving onto three chapters concerning ship reconstruction (Steffy 1978; Jones and Nayling 2011; Sauer 2011). In the context of shipwreck studies, reconstruction of the ship's hull as it would have been when afloat is often the basis of interpretation. These reconstructions allow the vessel to be understood as an artifact designed to serve a specific purpose within a specific environment. These reconstructions also often allow for an understanding of how the cargo was loaded and the spaces available for crew life.

The final section (VI) addresses ethics as well as cultural heritage management and legislation. These topics are intertwined in that our discipline-specific ethics influence how archaeologists mange cultural heritage and the legislation for which we lobby. As archaeologists, we believe that the past belongs to all people and, consequently, we work not only to record, interpret, and present that past to and for a wide variety of publics, but we also advocate for legal and cultural structures that protect the physical past for all people. This section begins with George Miller's (1992) classic case study on the destruction of the *Geldermalsen* before exploring the tensions between marine salvage and archaeology through several articles (Bass 1990; Throckmorton 1990; Elia 1992; Johnson 1992). Much marine salvage is conducted under salvage law, a long-standing component of maritime law, leading to the legal destruction of many submerged sites in a way that would not be permitted on land. In response to this situation, many nations have instituted additional laws to distinguish archaeological sites from recent shipwrecks that are open to salvage, and to provide protection for archaeological sites. The chapters by Giesecke (1989, 1998), Seidemann (2011), Foster (1992), McAllister et al. (2011), and Neyland (1996) describe these attempts in the United States, while the article by Hanselmann and Beeker (2008) suggests a model for the Dominican Republic. The section ends with three chapters that discuss alternatives to legislation (Woodward 1996; Dromgoole 2007; Dunkley 2009). These articles argue that education and cooperation between archaeologists and other groups are an effective way to manage cultural heritage. Because it is impossible for archaeologists and enforcement officers to monitor every known site, let alone those that are unknown to archaeologists but well-known to local communities, these articles may well define the future of maritime cultural heritage. By inoculating as many people as possible with an appreciation for the importance of the maritime past and an understanding of the logic behind archaeological ethics, it may be possible to preserve that past for future generations.

References

ADVISORY COUNCIL ON UNDERWATER ARCHAEOLOGY
2013   About the ACUA, Advisory Council on Underwater Archaeology <http://www.acuaonline.org/about-the-acua/>. Accessed 14 April 2013.

ALFORD, MICHAEL B.
1989   A Small Craft Typology: Tool for Archaeological Research. In *Underwater Archaeology Proceedings from the Society for Historical Archaeology*, J. Barto Arnold III, editor, pp. 61–63.

ANDERSEN, SØREN, H.
1985   Tybrind Vig. A Preliminary Report on a Submerged Ertebølle Settlement on the West Coast of Fyn. *Journal of Danish Archaeology* 4:52–59.

ANSCHUETZ, KURT, RICHARD WILSHUSEN, AND CHERIE SCHEICK
2001   An Archaeology of Landscape: Perspective and Directions. *Journal of Archaeological Research* 9(2):157–211.

ANUSKIEWICZ, RIK
1992   Using Remote-Sensing as a Tool for Middle-Range Theory Building in Maritime and Nautical Archaeology. In *Underwater Archaeology Proceedings from the Society for Historical Archaeology Conference: 1492-1992 500 Years of Change*, Donald H. Keith and Toni L. Carrell, editors, pp. 92–99.

BALLARD, ROBERT D. (EDITOR)
2008   *Archaeological Oceanography*. Princeton University Press, Princeton, NJ.

BASS, GEORGE F.
1967   Cape Gelidonya: Bronze Age Shipwreck. *Transactions of the American Philosophical Society* 57(8).

1972   *A History of Seafaring Based on Underwater Archaeology*. Walker, New York, NY.

1983   A Plea for Historical Particularism in Nautical Archaeology. In *Shipwreck Anthropology*, Richard Gould, editor, pp. 91–104. University of New Mexico Press, Albuquerque, NM.

1990   After the Diving is Over. In *Underwater Archaeology Proceedings from the Society for Historical Archaeology Conference*, Toni Carrell, editor, pp. 11–13.

2011   The Development of Maritime Archaeology. In *Oxford Handbook of Maritime Archaeology*, Alexis Catsambis, Ben Ford, and Donny Hamilton, editors, pp. 3–24. Oxford University Press, New York, NY.

BREEN, COLIN, RORY QUINN, AND WES FORSYTHE
2007   A Preliminary Analysis of Historic Shipwrecks in Northern Ireland. *Historical Archaeology* 41(3):4–8.

BROADWATER, JOHN D.
1992   Shipwreck in a Swimming Pool: An Assessment of the Methodology and Technology Utilized on the Yorktown Shipwreck Archaeological Project. *Historical Archaeology* 26(4):36-46.

BRUCE-MITFORD, RUPERT
1975–1983   *The Sutton Hoo Ship-Burial*, 3 vols. British Museum, London, UK.

CARRELL, TONI L., AND DONALD KEITH
2000   Sailing Ships, Air Ships, Star Ships: Into the Millennium. *Historical Archaeology* 34(4):14–17.

CASTRO, FILIPE
2008   In Search of Unique Iberian Ship Design Concepts. *Historical Archaeology* 42(2):63–87.

CASTRO, FILIPE, NUNO FONSECA, AND AUDREY WELLS
2010   Outfitting the Pepper Wreck. *Historical Archaeology* 44(2):14–34.

CHRISTIE, ANNALISA C.
2010   Were the Community Living on the East African Coast also 'Maritime' Communities? An Archaeological Perspective. In *ACUA Underwater Archaeology Proceedings 2010*, Chris Horrell and Melanie Damour, editors, pp. 162–172.

COHN, ARTHUR B.
2000   A Perspective on the Future of Underwater Archaeology. *Historical Archaeology* 34(4):18–21.

CORBIN, ANNALIES
1998   Shifting Sand and Muddy Water: Historic Cartography and River Migration as Factors in Locating Steamboat Wrecks on the Far Upper Missouri River. *Historical Archaeology* 32(4):86–94.

CRUMLIN-PEDERSEN, OLE AND OLAF OLSEN, (EDITORS)
2002   *The Skuldelev Ships I:Ships and Bats of the North.*
        Viking Ship Museum, Roskilde, DK.

DEETZ, JAMES
1996   *In Small Things Forgotten: An Archaeology of
        Early American Life.* Doubleday, New York, NY.

DELGADO, JAMES P.
1992   Recovering the Past of USS *Arizona. Historical
        Archaeology* 26(4):69 –80.

2000   Underwater Archaeology at the Dawn of the 21st
        Century. *Historical Archaeology* 34(4):9–13.

2011   Ships on Land. In *Oxford Handbook of Maritime
        Archaeology,* Alexis Catsambis, Ben Ford, and
        Donny Hamilton, editors, pp. 192–201. Oxford
        University Press, New York, NY.

DE MORGAN, JACQUES
1985   *Fouilles a Dahchour, Mars-Juin 1894.* Adolphe
        Holzhausen, Vienna, AT.

DROMGOOLE, SARAH
2007   Cooperative Approaches to Protecting Underwater
        Cultural Heritage: Emerging Themes and Trends.
        In *ACUA Underwater Archaeology Proceedings
        2007,* Victor Mastone, editor, pp. 57–62.

DUNKLEY, MARK
2009   Innovative Approaches to Marine Heritage Man-
        agement: A View from Across the Divide. In *ACUA
        Underwater Archaeology Proceedings 2009,* Erica
        Laneela and Jonathan Moore, editors, pp. 91–101.

ELIA, RICARDO J.
1992   The Ethics of Collaboration: Archaeologists
        and the *Wydah* Project. *Historical Archaeology*
        26(4):105–117.

FAULK, KIMBERLY
2011   Wagging the Dog: Technology and Archaeology.
        In *ACUA Underwater Archaeology Proceedings
        2011,* Filipe Castro and Lindsey Thomas, editors,
        pp. 29–32.

FAULKNER, ALARIC
1985   Archaeology of the Cod Fishery: Damariscove Is-
        land—1622 to 20th century. *Historical Archaeolo-
        gy* 19(2):57 –86.

1986   Followup Notes on the 17th Century Cod Fishery
        at Damariscove Island, Maine—1622–1676, *His-
        torical Archaeology* 20(2):86 –88.

FISCHER, GEORGE
1993   History of the ACUA. Paper presented at the 26th
        Conference on Historical and Underwater Archae-
        ology, Kansas City, KS <http://www.acuaonline.
        org/assets/2010/09/01/df4677138aee6fd4eb10c-
        66b07ee54cd.pdf>. Accessed 14 April 2013.

FLEMMING, NICHOLAS C.
1971   *Cities in the Sea.* Doubleday, Garden City, NY.

FOSTER, KEVIN J.
1992   Threatened James River Shipwrecks and Historical
        Sites. *Historical Archaeology* 26(4):58–68.

GARRISON, ERVAN G.
1995   Three Ironclad Warships—The Archaeology of
        Industrial Process and Historical Myth. *Historical
        Archaeology* 29(4):26–38.

GIBBS, MARTIN
2003   The Archaeology of Crisis: Shipwreck Survivor
        Camps in Australasia. *Historical Archaeology*
        37(1):128–145.

GIESECKE, ANNE G.
1989   State and Their Shipwrecks. In *Underwater Ar-
        chaeology Proceedings from the Society for His-
        torical Archaeology,* J. Barto Arnold III, editor, pp.
        35–40.

1998   The Abandoned Shipwreck Act 1988 to 1998. In
        Underwater Archaeology, Lawrence E. Babits,
        Catherine Fach, and Ryan Harris, editors, pp. 111–
        114.

GOULD, RICHARD A.
2000   Beyond Exploration: Underwater Archaeolo-
        gy after the Year 2000. *Historical Archaeology*
        34(4):24–28.

GOULD, RICHARD A. (EDITOR)
1983   *Shipwreck Anthropology.* University of New Mex-
        ico Press, Albuquerque, NM.

HANSELMANN, FREDERICK H., AND CHARLES D. BEEKER
2008   Establishing Marine Protected Areas in the Do-
        minican Republic: A Model for Sustainable Pres-
        ervation. In *ACUA Underwater Archaeology Pro-
        ceedings 2008,* Susan Langley and Victor Mastone,
        editors, pp. 52–61.

HASSLÖF, OLOF, HENNING HENNINGSEN, AND ARNE EMIL
CHRISTENSEN, JR. (EDITORS)
1972   *Ships and Shipyards, Sailors and Fishermen: In-
        troduction to Maritime Ethnology.* Copenhagen
        University Press, Copenhagen, DK.

HAWLEY, GREG
1998   *Treasure in a Cornfield: The Discovery and Ex-
        cavation of the Steamboat* Arabia. Paddlewheel
        Press, Kansas City, MO.

HERTEIG, ASBJØRN E.
1954   The Excavation of 'Bryggen', the old Hanseatic
        Wharf in Bergen. *Medieval Archaeology* 3: 177–
        186.

HUEY, PAUL R.
    1984   Old Slip and Cruger's Wharf at New York: An Archaeological Perspective of the Colonial American Waterfront. *Historical Archaeology* 18(1):15–37.

JOHNSTON, PAUL F.
    1992   Is it Treasure or a Worthless Piece of Ship? *Historical Archaeology* 26(4):118–123.

JONES, TOBY N., AND NIGEL NAYLING
    2011   ShipShape: Creating a 3D Solid Model of the Newport Medieval Ship. In *ACUA Underwater Archaeology Proceedings 2011*, Filipe Castro and Lindsey Thomas, editors, pp. 54–60.

KRUEGER, BRADLEY A., AND JEAN B. PELLETIER
    2012   Integrating Data Sets: Results from the City of St. Augustine Seawall Phase I Archaeology Survey, St. Augustine, Florida. In *ACUA Underwater Archaeology Proceedings 2012*, Brian Jordan and Troy J. Nowak, editors, pp. 101–107.

LAWRENCE, MATTHEW S.
    2011   Testing the Efficacy of Synthetic Aperture Sonar to Locate Historic Shipwrecks in the Stellwagen Bank National Marine Sanctuary. In *ACUA Underwater Archaeology Proceedings 2011*, Filipe Castro and Lindsey Thomas, editors, pp. 23–28.

LENIHAN, DANIEL J.
    2000   Of Strawberries, Women's Thighs, and Jim Delgado's Paper. *Historical Archaeology* 34(4):22–23.

MCALLISTER, MARTIN E., LARRY E. MURPHY, AND JAMES E. MORIARTY, IV
    2011   ARPA and Site Damage Management Assessment Applicability to Offshore Underwater Cultural Heritage. In *ACUA Underwater Archaeology Proceedings 2011*, Filipe Castro and Lindsey Thomas, editors, pp. 61–65.

MCCARTHY, CELIA
    1999   Training and Ferry Slips are not Sexy Lingerie. In *Underwater Archaeology*, Adriana A. Neidinger and Matthew A. Russel, editors, pp. 11–16.

MCDONALD, MOLLY R.
    2011   Wharves and Waterfront Retaining Structures as Vernacular Architecture. *Historical Archaeology* 45(2):42–67.

MCERLEAN, THOMAS C.
    2007   Archaeology of the Strangford Lough Kelp Industry in the Eighteenth – and Early-Nineteenth Centuries. *Historical Archaeology* 41(3):76 –93.

MILLER, GEORGE L.
    1992   The Second Destruction of the *Geldermalsen*. *Historical Archaeology* 26(4):124–131.

MORRIS, JOHN W., III, GORDON P. WATTS, JR., AND MARIANNE FRANKLIN
    1995   The Comparative Analysis of 18th-Century Vessel Remains in the Archaeological Record: A Synthesized Theory of Framing System. In *Underwater Archaeology Proceedings from the Society for Historical Archaeology*, Paul F. Johnston, editor, pp. 125–133.

MUCKELROY, KEITH
    1978   *Maritime Archaeology.* Cambridge University Press, New York, NY.

NEYLAND, ROBERT S.
    1996   Sovereign Immunity and the Management of United States Naval Shipwrecks. In *Underwater Archaeology*, Stephen R. James, Jr., and Camille Stanley, editors, pp. 98–104.

PIETERS, MARNIX, FRANS VERHAEGHE, AND GLENN GEVAERT
    2006   Fishery, Trade and Piracy: Fishermen and Fishermen's Settlements in and Around the North Sea Area in the Middle Ages and Later. Flemish Heritage Institute, Brussels, BE.

PRICE, FRANKLIN H., AND NATHAN RICHARDS
    2009   Conflict and Commerce: Maritime Archaeological Site Distribution as Cultural Change on the Roanoke River, North Carolina. *Historical Archaeology* (43)4:75–96.

QUINN, RORY
    2007   The Assimilation of Marine Geophysical Data into the Maritime Sites and Monuments Record, Northern Ireland. *Historical Archaeology* 41(3):9–24.

    2011   Acoustic Remote Sensing in Maritime Archaeology. In *Oxford Handbook of Maritime Archaeology*, Alexis Catsambis, Ben Ford, and Donny Hamilton, editors, pp. 68–89. Oxford University Press, New York, NY.

RICHARDS, NATHAN, AND MARK STANIFORTH
    2006   The Abandoned Ships' Project: An Overview of the Archaeology of Deliberate Watercraft Discard in Australia. *Historical Archaeology* (40)4:84–103.

SAUER, ALBRECHT
    2011   Maritime Experimental Archaeology: Trying the Impossible. In *ACUA Underwater Archaeology Proceedings 2011*, Filipe Castro and Lindsey Thomas, editors, pp. 49–53.

SCHIFFER, MICHAEL
    1987   *Formation Processes of the Archaeological Record.* University of New Mexico Press, Albuquerque, NM.

SEIDEMANN, RYAN M.
2011   Shipwreck Protection: Federal and State Law—A View From Louisiana. In *ACUA Underwater Archaeology Proceedings 2011*, Filipe Castro and Lindsey Thomas, editors, pp. 66–73.

SØREIDE, FREDRIK
2011   *Ships from the Depths: Deepwater Archaeology.* Texas A&M University Press, College Station, TX.

STANIFORTH, MARK
2009   Shipwreck Cargoes: Approaches to Material Culture in Australian Maritime Archaeology. *Historical Archaeology* 43(3):95 –100.

STEFFY, J. RICHARD
1978   Ship Reconstruction and Antiquities Conservation: Maximum Results from Minimum Remains. In *Beneath the Waters of Time: The Proceedings of the Ninth Conference on Underwater Archaeology*, J. Barto Arnold III, editor, pp. 53-54. Texas Antiquities Committee Publication No. 6, Austin, Texas.

THROCKMORTON, PETER
1990   The World's Worst Investment: The economics of treasure hunting with real life comparisons. In *Underwater Archaeology Proceedings from the Society for Historical Archaeology Conference*, Toni Carrell, editor, pp. 6–10.

WARREN, DANIEL, ROBERT A. CHURCH, ROBERT F. WESTRICK, AND CHENG-WEI WU
2011   Using Multibeam Bathymetry and Backscatter for Mapping and In-Situ Assessments of Deepwater Shipwreck Sites. In *ACUA Underwater Archaeology Proceedings 2011*, Filipe Castro and Lindsey Thomas, editors, pp. 17–22.

WESTERDAHL, CHRISTER
1992   The Maritime Cultural Landscape. *International Journal of Nautical Archaeology* 21(1):5–14.

WOODWARD, ROBYN P.
1996   Education versus Legislation. In *Underwater Archaeology*, Stephen R. James Jr. and Camille Stanley, editors, pp. 45–50.

2000. Underwater Archaeology at the Dawn of the 21st Century. *Historical Archaeology* 34(4):9–13.

James P. Delgado

Underwater Archaeology at the Dawn of the 21st Century

The end of the 20th century, and the advent of not just a new century, but a new millennium is upon us. These times, and these events, offer us an opportunity to assess what has come to pass, and perhaps, take a wishful peek at the future.

The 20th century was, in many ways, the century of underwater exploration. Brief forays into the deep in the 19th century were the harbinger of greater, farther, deeper reaching excursions to the bottom of the sea in the 20th century. The 20th century's reach into the depths was inspired by the simple human desire to explore–to see, to touch what hitherto had been denied or not yet achieved by other people. It was also, in time, also driven by the exigencies of war and the quest for riches. It was also spurred by the desire to discover and recover the submerged remains of our past or heritage, as represented by drowned campfires, cities swallowed by the sea, and the sunken remains of once proud ships.

The 20th century, appropriately enough for archaeologists who work under the water, began with an encounter with an ancient shipwreck. The 100th anniversary of the discovery of the *Antikythera* wreck–a 1st century BC Greek site famed for its bronze statues and the fabulous "computer," or intricate clockwork mechanism, will soon be upon us. When that wreck was discovered, in 1900, by sponge divers between Crete and the Greek mainland, and just off the shores of the island that gives the wreck its name, it inaugurated a new discipline, for the *Antikythera* wreck was the first shipwreck to be scientifically studied. What followed, slowly at first, and then with increasing frequency, was the discovery of other wrecks, other sites, and the gradual evolution of a discipline.

As the century progressed and the discipline evolved, so too did the technology. The first great leap forward came in the aftermath of the Second World War and the invention and global adaptation of self contained breathing apparatus–SCUBA-technology. The next great leap forward came when an archaeologist–George Bass–took the radical step of actually putting the gear on himself and taking the literal plunge into the depths. What Dr. Bass ultimately showed was that for all intents and purposes, archaeology, regardless of where you practice it, is still archaeology. Some of the tools, and some of the methods may change because you are now under water, but the principles and practice remain the same.

The late 1950s and the early 1960s were an important time for archaeology practised under the water–a number of significant discoveries were made, generating public interest and support, and, for the first time, a Conference on Underwater Archaeology was organised. The first meeting, the *Premier Congres Internationale d'Archaeologie Sous-Marine* was held at Cannes, France in 1955; it was followed by *Il Congreso Internazionale di Archeologia Sotto-Marine* at Albenga, Italy in 1958. The Third International Congress of Underwater Archaeology was held at Barcelona, Spain in 1961, and was organised in part by a new organisation–the Council of Underwater Archaeology, founded in 1959. The next meeting was the first in North America. Between April 26 and 27th, 1963, the Minnesota Historical Society, in St. Paul, hosted "Diving into the Past: Theories, Techniques, and Applications of Underwater Archaeology." It was the premiere of what since then became a regular meeting that we now, once again congregate to hold, this year in Salt Lake City. This would be the 30th Conference on Underwater Archaeology. Starting in 1971, the conference on underwater archaeology has been held in conjunction with The Society for Historical Archaeology, and in 1987, the two concurrent meetings were integrated to become the SHA Conference on Historical and Underwater Archaeology.

The years and the 30 meetings since 1963 have seen great growth in the discipline. Those first meetings in St. Paul discussed a number of topics, that while they remain very relevant nonetheless over time have evolved, diversified, and matured–in step with new technology, new approaches, and new members of the profession. These are some of those early paper topics:

"Applications of Underwater Archaeology to Classical Studies,"

"Methods of Wreck Excavation in Clear Water,"

"Underwater Photography and Archaeology,"

"Some Legal Problems in the Field of Underwater Archaeology,"

"Treating Wood with Polyethylene Glycol,"

"Excavating a Byzantine Shipwreck,"

"The Viking Ships in Roskilde Fiord, Denmark,"

"The Ghost Ship *Vasa*,"

"Underwater Archaeology and the *Cairo*."

Since then, we have expanded on these topics. The Ninth Conference, for example, was organised into specific categories–the field was gradually organising itself into sub-disciplines and themes: to wit "Shipwreck Archaeology," "Ship Reconstruction and Antiquities Conservation," "Inundated Terrestrial Sites," and "Underwater Cultural Resource Management, Theory, and Application, and Other Topics."

By then, too, some specifics–key sites, technologies, and methodologies were emerging: the Serce Limani wreck, USS *Monitor*, the 1554 Flota wrecks, the Brown's Ferry Vessel, Warm Mineral Springs, and the privateer *Defence* were the subject of papers at the 9th conference, as was Richard Steffy's pioneering paper, "Maximum Results from Minimum Remains," Sonny Cockrell and Larry Murphy's pioneering work on assessing site formation processes, "8 SL 17: Methodological Approaches to a Dual Component Marine Site on the Florida Atlantic Coast," as well as papers on remote sensing and site testing by Richard Anuskiewicz and J. Barto Arnold.

Over time, these and other topics have been finely forged and hammered into shape through decades of field work, scholarly analysis and interpretation, and the informed peer review and professional discourse that comes with each of these annual meetings as we gather to share and learn from one another. Reading through the proceedings of the various conferences, it is amazing to look back as underwater archaeology develops into a complex discipline, utilising new practices and technologies, and with an increasing number of both professional and avocational people involved.

In the last thirty years, we have embraced new technology–early papers introduce us to side scan sonar, the magnetometer, satellite imaging, surveying using GPS, computer imaging, SHARPS, and remotely operated vehicles.

In the last thirty years, we have seen underwater work integrated into various branches of archaeology. In many ways, this perhaps has been one of the greatest leaps forward–underwater sites and data have significantly contributed, at times uniquely, to our understanding of the past. An excellent example of the contributions of archaeology underwater–in this case as practised by the Institute of Nautical Archaeology–were recently summed up by George Bass (1998:49) in the December issue of Archaeology magazine:

> Few if any Bronze Age excavations in the past 50 years have been more important than that of the Uluburun shipwreck that lay 145 to 200 feet deep just off the Turkish coast, with its 18,000 artifacts from nearly a dozen different cultures, precisely dated to within a few years of 1300 B.C. The wreck has provided a wealth of information on the histories of literacy, trade, ideas, metallurgy, metrology, art, music, religion, and international relations, as well as for fields as diverse as Homeric studies and Egyptology.

I cannot think of a better way to show just how much underwater archaeology has matured as a discipline.

We have also seen underwater archaeology branch out into three distinct areas: prehistoric work on inundated sites, nautical archaeology, and maritime archaeology. In particular, and almost entirely due to nautical archaeology, we now have a more sophisticated model for the development of watercraft and ships from prehistory up to the present day. A few gaps remain, among them European ships of the 15th and 16th centuries, most Asian craft, and regional variations and types of small craft, although in the latter case the gap is closing thanks to the work of several dedicated scholars like Mark Wilde Ramsing, Bruce Terrell, Michael Alford, Carl Olof Cederlund, and others. The simple fact remains, however, with more than a thousand ancient wrecks alone catalogued in the Mediterranean by A. J. Parker, for example, that we have made considerable inroads thanks to decades of systematic work in the world's oceans, seas, lakes, and rivers.

We have integrated anthropological theory and method to assess human behaviour inherent in the sites we work–general models as well as a more sophisticated understanding of the "maritime subculture." We have developed projects that work not just on individual sites, but groups of wrecks, studied because they fit within a chronology of development, like INA's work in the Mediterranean, because they fit within a region, like the U.S. National Park Service's work at Fort Jefferson National Monument, or Donald Shomette's work on Chesapeake Bay, or because they fit within a wider historical or cultural theme, like Mark Wilde Ramsing's work on the Cape Fear Civil War Shipwreck District, or Gordon Watts' work on Civil War wrecks in the U.S. and Bermuda. We have also assessed the context of individual wrecks in new ways, analysing them as vessels, as cultural indicators, as dynamic entities that evidence the physical and cultural processes that transformed them from ships to shipwrecks.

We have also increasingly advocated, fought for, and developed better mechanisms for the assessment, protection, and management of underwater sites. From fine tooling the National Register of Historic Places, to lobbying for the Abandoned Shipwreck Act, we have been a force. We have also watched, aided and at times abetted, as a profession, the development of state programs for submerged cultural resources, and one of the hallmarks of these conferences are now the state underwater program manager's meetings. We have also witnessed the growth of significant contributions from the federal government, be they the major work done by the U.S. National Park Service's Submerged Cultural Resources Unit, under the direction of Daniel Lenihan, the significant research and excavations of Parks Canada's Underwater Unit, under the direction of Robert Grenier, the contributions made by the National Oceanic and Atmospheric Administration, at first with the wreck of USS *Monitor*, now managed by John Broadwater, but also in the various national marine sanctuaries, and co-ordinated by Bruce Terrell, the many contributions of the Smithsonian Institution, now under the direction of Paul Johnston, or the increased and significant program of the U.S. Naval Historical Center, directed by William S. Dudley and co-ordinated and achieved by a number of professionals, including over the years David Cooper and Bob Neyland.

We have also increasingly seen, in yet another leap forward, the greater involvement of the public, a greater emphasis on education, and on all forms of outreach. From the pioneering Anthropology 500 course offered by John Mann Goggin at the University of Florida–the first university course on underwater archaeology offered and taught in the United States–we have seen the development not just of courses but of undergraduate and graduate level programs at Texas A&M, East Carolina University, the University of Hawaii at Manoa, Florida State University, and Indiana State University, to name a few, in the United States, as well as major programs abroad like that of St. Andrews University. The measure of the success of these initiatives is the incremental increase in the number of new professionals they produce each year, whose ranks are well represented in the conference proceedings, and who today comprise the heart, soul, and backbone of this profession.

We have done more, however, than just train underwater, maritime, and nautical archaeologists. We have offered these courses to other archaeologists, who even though they do not pursue a solely underwater career, understand the discipline and integrate the findings of their "wet" colleagues into their work–for indeed they have learned, as have we, that regardless of the environment you work in, archaeology is archaeology, and underwater sites have a unique potential to offer significant information.

We have also done more than just educate ourselves as archaeologists. One of the greatest signs of our maturity as a discipline is the growing number of avocational members who work with us, make significant contributions, and attend these meetings. Some of the finest work in the field–in the world–today is being done by the avocational, be they the Nautical Archaeology Society, the Underwater Archaeological Society of British Columbia, MAHS, SOS, POW, MAHRI, the sport divers trained at Indiana State, or the countless other groups. In particular, I would be remiss if I did not highlight the work of three members whose contributions are many, and whose dedication and results impress us all–Art Cohn, Donald Shomette, and Joe Zarzynski. It may amaze some of you who just joined these meetings over the past few years that none of these gentlemen received an advanced degree in archaeology. With all due respect to my academically trained colleagues, these three men–Cohn, Shomette, and Zarzynski–show the rest of us how to do it. Their work in Lake Champlain, Chesapeake Bay, and Lake George offers a model for public participation, regional approach, cultural resources management, education and outreach, and publication.

Some of us have made great strides in outreach and education; Monica Reed in video, KC Smith in the classroom, for example. There is also, of course, David Clark's work on the public sessions of this conference.

We have also done more in publishing–the underwater proceedings of these conferences alone take up half a bookshelf–with hundreds of other titles now available. We have not done enough, however, to reach the general public. The number of books that speak to a general audience about what we do, what we find, why it is relevant, and why the public needs to support us–not looters–remains low. The most recently released titles for the most part, as always, focus on treasure, not necessarily knowledge.

We, as underwater archaeologists, as historical archaeologists, as maritime or nautical archaeologists, have made tremendous strides. This has been our pioneering century, and our proceedings are full of the themes, issues, and controversies that have marked these "frontier times." The arguments over legal protection, over treasure hunting, over what would be presented at these conferences, and by whom, over what role professionals should take in working with–or against treasure hunters–over the role of government–both big and small–and over appropriate uses of new technology have been with us over the past thirty years and will likely continue into the new century and the new millennium. The debate over the UNESCO Charter on underwater resources is just one example.

In fact, as the great dividing line comes, we find ourselves engaged in a more complex challenge as we grapple with the Pandora's box that has been opened in the deep ocean thanks to new technology and the increasing sophistication of treasure hunters and salvors who now with greater regularity "talk our talk." The work over the past decade on the wreck of the *Titanic*, the salvage of the SS *Central America* have generally been deplored in the halls of these conferences and widely accepted and approved by the public.

How do we deal with our responsibilities as archaeologists and as people genuinely interested in the past? The major challenge before us, I believe, is to not simply shout "unclean" and oppose treasure hunting and salvage. Do not mistake what I am saying. We must ethically and professional oppose looting, non-scientific recovery of material from archaeological sites, the marketing of antiquities, and not participate in these activities. But we can do this more effectively if we set a new standard for our own behaviour and our own practice in the years to come.

What is this new standard? It is nothing more than an affirmation of what we have already embarked on, and what we have been doing with increasing success. We must build on our strengths, and on our legacy. We must demonstrate, to as wide and public an audience as possible, that the work we do is important, that it contributes something to our society, and that it offers a positive alternative to "pull it up, sell it off." This means great work with avocationals. It means a greater emphasis on publication–to diverse audiences, to the public at large, to children. It means embracing the new technology–like the Internet and CD ROMS, to reach other audiences. One of the best examples of this was the recent work done on the wreck of LaSalle's ship *La Belle*. The web site for that project, constantly updated, and accessible to a global audience, deserves acclaim; and we all need to copy it.

I would also suggest, as a Maritime Museum director, that we work more closely with Museums, to reach their audiences. Nearly all of the world's maritime museums have some form of display or interaction with underwater and maritime archaeology–some of them, like the Viking Ship Museum at Roskilde, the *Mary Rose* Interpretive Centre, the Lake Champlain Maritime Museum, the Western Australia Maritime Museum, the Shipwreck Museum at Bodrum, and the *Vasa* Museum–are practically shrines. Others, like Ships of Discovery, have forged significant partnerships with non-maritime museums, like Ships of Discovery's work with the Corpus Christi Museum. I would respectfully suggest that we can all learn from what these colleagues have been doing and copy it. There are also travelling exhibitions, like the Australian National Maritime Museum's exhibit on the wreck of the ship *Julia Ann*, now showing in Salt Lake City, which while not on the scale of the great *Titanic* travelling road show, exhibition, and souvenir shop, offers a positive, relevant model.

We are moving, in the next year, from one frontier to another. There is no place on this planet we cannot reach, and sites in the deepest parts of the ocean are becoming increasingly accessible. We need to be there, to forge partnerships with the government agencies, institutes, and technicians who have the tools and resources. It has been argued that this will take great money–and certainly the salvors and treasure hunters have dominated this debate by being the ones who have gone down there to recover monetary riches. But we certainly know that all that glitters is not gold–that knowledge, that pride in our past and our achievements as humanity count for far more than mere dollars. Was raising the *Vasa* a cost efficient move? At first, no. But the pride, the international attention, and the resulting tourism made *Vasa* a Swedish treasure that they share with the rest of the world. The time has come for us, through positive work, to find the *Vasa*'s of the deep and bring them to the surface–and the world's attention. The recovery of *La Belle* last year was an excellent beginning. The raising of CSS *Hunley* in 2001 offers another chance for a well-publicised, positive shipwreck recovery. We need to find other exciting, relevant, and well-funded opportunities. We need to let the screens again be filled with the majesty of a bequest from the past, not just the glimmer of gold coins or bars.

In time, in this new millennium, as we reach to newer frontiers, I have little doubt that the next great leap forward will be a branch of both historical and underwater archaeology. This is the conference where the recent past is assessed archaeologically and where archaeologists who work in hostile, life threatening environments, protected by life supporting suits and vehicles, meet to discuss what they do. I suspect that the best attended paper at the 2099 SHA conference will be a former underwater, now deep space archaeologist, reporting on the first season's field work on the *Apollo* 11 Landing site.

May the new millennium be for all of us an opportunity for a brighter, better, bolder future, firmly rooted in the successes of the past.

ACKNOWLEDGMENTS

This paper was given as the Plenary Address for The Society for Historical Archaeology Conference on Historical and Underwater Archaeology, Salt Lake City, Utah.

REFERENCES

BASS, GEORGE F.
   1998 History Beneath the Sea: The Birth of Nautical Archaeology. *Archaeology*, 51(6):48-53.

JAMES P. DELGADO
VANCOUVER MARITIME MUSEUM
1905 OGDEN AVENUE
VANCOUVER, BRITISH COLUMBIA V6J 1A3
CANADA

Toni L. Carrell
Donald H. Keith

Sailing Ships, Air Ships, Star Ships: Into the Millennium

"Space . . . the final frontier." Those words evoke images of a future in which humanity is exploring vast uncharted reaches, encountering new peoples, cultures, and very likely the remains of long since vanished empires. Whether the peoples humanity will encounter traveled in star ships, air ships, or sailing ships, whether they are a thriving civilization or their remains are hidden beneath layers of dust, buried in ice, or concealed beneath some liquid medium, it will be archaeologists who are tasked with the job of understanding the structures that ancient peoples built, the remains they left behind, and the ships in which they traveled.

In Gene Roddenberry's future the archaeologists and explorers will be striving for personal satisfaction and wisdom. Their ethic is one that reveres knowledge and rewards enlightenment that benefits humankind. In Jim Delgado's musings about the future he envisioned that "the best attended paper in at the 2099 SHA conference will be a former underwater, now deep space archaeologist, reporting on the first season's field work on the *Apollo* 11 Landing site." The technology is actually available now to undertake such an excavation. But how would it be handled today? What ethic would be applied? If presented with the opportunity to excavate any of the moon landing sites or if archaeological remains were discovered on Mars, would we treat the ships, temples, ruined cities, hunting sites, or objects as important relics of cultural heritage or would we exploit them for financial gain? Would the people we send seek knowledge for its own sake or would we choose to send those who would search for and excavate for personal or corporate profit? Would the information and collections be kept together for humanity's edification or be disbursed to the mantelpiece and safe deposit boxes of private collectors? Would we choose to sell off a portion of the collection to finance the excavation, keep only the duplicate items, or split

the collection with a commercial salvage group? Given the current debate between archaeology for public benefit and archaeology for private gain the answer to those questions may not be as simple as one would think.

If past performance is a predictor of future behavior, then it is worthwhile to examine briefly what that performance has been with one segment of the cultural resources spectrum, shipwrecks. This component, however, is clearly one of the most contentious. More often than not underwater sites have been and continue to be considered fair game for commercial treasure salvage even when similar sites on land have long been recognized as something governments should hold in common for their citizens, if not for all mankind. In the past, a shipwreck site's principal protection was its anonymity, but improvements in remote-sensing and in navigation technology have stripped that away. Ownership of underwater sites is more at issue than ownership of terrestrial sites as a consequence of the laws and regulations governing maritime affairs and waterways that predate the awareness that those bodies may cover important archaeological sites. In most parts of the world underwater sites have no real protection against human intervention.

The manner in which shipwrecks are perceived and valued differs from group to group: treasure hunters see them as a source of marketable valuables, curio seekers just want to take a memento or two, industry representatives try not to see them at all lest they cause potential delays in construction schedules, engineers seek to eradicate them with dredging and clearing to keep waterways navigable, cultural resource managers try to keep them just the way they are, and archaeologists covet them as precious time capsules filled with invaluable information about our collective past. These views are clearly in conflict and the ultimate disposition of the resource by each of these groups is dramatically different.

There is good reason to believe that there are more people interested in locating and using shipwrecks now that ever before; certainly the remote-sensing equipment used to find sites is much more widely available and affordable than is was in the past. Whereas most treasure

Historical Archaeology, 2000, 34(4):14—17.
Permission to reprint required.

hunting groups were based in first-world countries where the necessary technology and expertise was available, today they are global in distribution, frequently clustering in areas where there is an offshore oil industry requiring divers and underwater inspection equipment. Improvements in ROV (Remotely Operated Vehicle) technology have pushed the frontier of exploration into deep, cold, and dangerous waters previously off limits to divers and even submersibles. This move to deeper water supports a trend detected by Carrell: "In the face of increasing regulation, depletion of the resource, and a more critical public, treasure hunting is mutating by changing its appearance, approach, and pitch. It is migrating to new habitats beyond the borders of the U.S., and adapting by moving into deep water" (Carrell 1996:75).

How well and efficiently have we used shipwreck sites? Are we handling the resource more wisely now, or continuing to make the same mistakes? Are we making decisions about their use based upon scarcity, commercial value, or inherent significance? A review of hundreds of site discoveries since 1952 reveals that efficient use of the shipwreck resource–one that maximizes return for what is consumed–has seldom been practiced, partly because of a lingering perception that the supply of good sites is inexhaustible. This erroneous perception is constantly reinforced by the ability of improved technology to compensate for the decreasing size of the resource by locating new sites in remote areas, under difficult conditions.

How should cultural resources be allotted? It is not controversial what to do with sites of great national appeal like Sweden's *Vasa* (1628), or undeniable historical significance like CSS *Alabama* (1864), or importance as a national shrine like USS *Arizona* (1941), however these represent a small minority of the sum total of shipwreck sites. Attempts to apportion the majority of the resource usually involve legal actions that seek to prove a site is "in peril" or a particular party has the "right" to claim it, rather than who will put the resource to its best use. Whether one would agree that much more has been lost through the actions of indiscriminate salvage, inadvertent curio seeking, or the inevitable passage of time, it is the responsibility of resource managers and government officials to determine their ultimate

fate. The decision making process is hampered by the absence of a critical piece of information. How many shipwrecks sites are there and how many are left? It would seem that a critical first step before continuing to write drafts on our underwater resources bank is to determine the total amount held in our account, what has been withdrawn and spent, and what remains in balance.

A federal government attorney recently observed that the legal perspective on submerged cultural resources globally is to treat them like mineral resources, offshore oil, and gas deposits, when in reality it would be much more appropriate to see them in the same light as an ever-diminishing endangered marine species, e.g. whales. Carrying the mineral resources analogy one step farther, attempting to estimate the total number of sites in the underwater cultural resource bank is similar to the problem petroleum engineers have when trying to determine how much oil is left in known reserves and unproven new fields. The patterns exhibited by exploration geologists and those who search for shipwrecks are essentially the same: the best and most easily extracted sites are discovered and exploited first. The first oil wells were drilled in localities in Pennsylvania and Wyoming where deposits were so close to the surface that they actually seeped out onto the ground. Similarly, "coin beaches" in Florida and Texas signaled the presence of easily accessible shipwrecks close to shore, sparking commercial treasure salvage projects. With the passage of time, sites become progressively more difficult and costly to find–and less productive. Plotting the effort expended to find new sites against the productivity of the sites discovered through time yields an indication of the relative abundance of the resource. High productivity in return for low investment indicates abundance. Low productivity in return for high investment indicates a dwindling resource. The fact that salvors are increasingly willing to front the tremendous costs of deep-water searches and recoveries–published figures for the *Central America* salvage indicate that the equipment and personnel costs for field work alone were well over 14.5 million dollars (Kinder 1998:501-502)–is an ominous indication of the growing scarcity of significant shipwreck sites. The fraction of the total number of sites already discovered undoubtedly includes a higher proportion of the "best" sites–the largest, the most famous, the best preserved, and certainly the richest.

Whether one believes that the shipwreck resource should be used for research and education or commercial salvage, evaluating its condition is a necessary first step. The action proposed here is a simple audit of the shipwreck resource using a method that has served the oil industry well, but may be new to archaeologists. The product of such an audit will be the equivalent of a financial statement indicating the health of the shipwreck account. The audit may be applied to existing small-scale databases by sorting site records according to date of discovery and present status–"extracted" or "in reserve." The results could in the future be combined with other similarly-sorted databases to develop patterns on a larger, even global, scale. However, at the heart of the audit is the assumption that the best indication of how many shipwrecks are left is the pattern revealed by plotting the number of shipwrecks discovered per year over time. This basic method has proven its value numerous times in exploration geology and oil field management (Campbell and Laherrère 1998). The pattern is a curve that rises gradually and, all other factors being equal, peaks and begins to decline. The complete process creates a bell-shaped curve, and the question for shipwreck resource managers is where are we on that curve? Is the resource still on the rise, or already in decline? Like petroleum geologists, shipwreck archaeologists should recognize that ultimately it is production, not just the number of wells discovered per year that is important, and that production always lags behind discovery. When will we "run out" of shipwreck sites depends both on how many are left and how rapidly they are being depleted. The answer to this question is critical if we are to use the resource wisely. The simple method suggested here to evaluate our cultural resources account could make a dramatic difference in how we view and use shipwreck sites in the future. It is particularly important in countries where shipwrecks have already been heavily exploited.

Currently, the shipwreck resources in developing countries are at the greatest risk because they are taking the full brunt of experienced, well-equipped and financed First World-based commercial salvage operations spreading out across the globe looking for rich new hunting grounds. Sadly, many sites will be discovered and exploited before the nations in whose waters they lie are aware of their existence or of alternatives to commercial salvage. The second area at great risk is international waters. The discovery of *Titanic* in 1985 brought to the fore the question: who has jurisdiction over shipwrecks in international waters? Located well offshore in deep water, such sites have no legal protection nor mechanism to develop cooperative international programs for study rather than exploitation. In response to these concerns, the International Council on Monuments and Sites (ICOMOS) appointed a committee to develop guidelines for the responsible management of shipwreck sites. The result was the International Charter on the Protection and Management of Underwater Cultural Heritage (1996). This charter is an integral element of an international agreement, the Convention on the Protection of the Underwater Cultural Heritage (1998), currently being drafted by the United Nations Educational, Scientific, and Cultural Organization (UNESCO). This convention proposes to remove shipwrecks in international waters from the jurisdiction of salvage law and create a procedure for international reporting, study, and preservation of shipwrecks that are of historical or archaeological significance. If this convention is passed and implemented, it could be the basis of a new ethic for the management of underwater cultural heritage.

Jim Delgado closed his remarks with the hope that "the new millennium . . . [may be] an opportunity for a brighter, better, bolder future, firmly rooted in the successes of the past." Certainly our successes or failures in the past will be carried with us. Today the debate places us at a fork in the road. If we don't act now to preserve what is left, however much or little that might be, human nature being what it is, excessive consumption and inefficient use will be the rule rather than the exception. It could be that in 2099 the best attended paper at the SHA will not be a report on an off-earth site, but a retrospective on how the resource was squandered in the 20th century and that we did too little too late to save it.

REFERENCES

CAMPBELL, COLIN JOHN, AND J. H. LAHERRÈRE
1998 The End of Cheap Oil. *Scientific American,* 278(3):78-83.

CARRELL, TONI L.
1996 Mutate, Migrate, Adapt or Die. In *Common Ground: Archeology and Ethnography in the Public Interest,* 1(3-4):72-75. National Park Service, Washington, DC.

INTERNATIONAL COUNCIL ON MONUMENTS AND SITES (ICOMOS)
1996 *ICOMOS International Charter on the Protection and Management of Underwater Cultural Heritage.* International Council on Monuments and Sites, Paris, France.

KINDER, GARY
1998 *Ship of Gold in the Deep Blue Sea.* Atlantic Monthly Press, New York, NY.

UNITED NATIONS EDUCATIONAL, CULTURAL, AND SCIENTIFIC ORGANIZATION
1998 *Draft Convention on the Protection of the Underwater Cultural Heritage.* CLT-96/CONF.202/5. UNESCO, Paris, France.

TONI L. CARROLL
SHIPS OF DISCOVERY MUSEUM
1900 N. CHAPARRAL STREET
CORPUS CHRISTI, TX 78401

DONALD H. KEITH
SHIPS OF DISCOVERY MUSEUM
1900 N. CHAPARRAL STREET
CORPUS CHRISTI, TX 78401

2000. A Perspective on the Future of Underwater Archaeology. *Historical Archaeology* 34(4):18–21.

Arthur B. Cohn

A Perspective on the Future of Underwater Archaeology

Underwater archaeology is still a very young field, one that has spent most of its formative years defining itself. Much time has been spent grappling with some very basic yet intrinsic questions: What is the value of submerged archaeological sites to society? How should underwater sites be studied? What justifies the recovery of submerged artifacts? Who controls access to submerged sites, and who should be permitted to study them? Jim Delgado has effectively identified many of the important current perspectives, trends, and issues within underwater archaeology, most importantly that we have now reached a pivotal point in the development of the field. It is time to evaluate the lessons that have been learned and to move forward with confidence into a new era of research, technology, public interpretation, and cultural resource management.

My career as a professional diver and museum director evolved from the study of sociology and law. With such a background, I have benefited from having one foot in academia and the other firmly planted in the real world. Twenty years ago I was privileged to enter a long-term collaboration with Dr. Kevin Crisman of the Institute of Nautical Archaeology at Texas A&M University, a fellow Vermonter whose love for the history of the Lake Champlain region complemented my own. Our study of Lake Champlain has produced prolific documentation of one of the most well-preserved collections of wooden watercraft in the New World. Along the way we established the Lake Champlain Maritime Museum dedicated to sharing the region's maritime history with the public, and we contributed to the development of the Lake Champlain Underwater Historic Preserves, one of the nation's first underwater historic preserve programs. Additionally, in response to threats from treasure hunters in recent years, Dr. Crisman and I are working with the Portuguese archaeologists and the government of the Azores Islands to develop a strategy for managing that region's rich underwater archaeological resources.

Lake Champlain is a great lake—a long, narrow, deep body of fresh water that served as a vital corridor of transportation from prehistoric times well into the twentieth century. Today, from an underwater archaeologist's point of view, it is a treasure trove of archaeological and historical information. More importantly for the purposes of this paper, Lake Champlain is a microcosm of many of the issues now facing the field of underwater archaeology. It has a history of salvage, usually to the detriment of the vessels that were recovered. It has hundreds of submerged archaeological resources, with more being discovered every year. It has experienced an uncontrollable invasion of zebra mussels. It has sites preserved in shallow water, and it has sites hidden at depths well below safe diving limits. It has an active sport diving community, and it has a large population of diving and non-diving citizens who want to experience, learn about, see, and touch the region's maritime heritage. The challenges we face here are unquestionably universal.

The challenges facing underwater archaeology in Lake Champlain and the rest of the world may be many, but the resources available to counter these inherent difficulties are equally powerful. I believe that three specific components of the field will either make us or break us in the next century: technology, public interpretation, and cultural resource management. No one of these aspects is effective without the other two; our success in the years ahead will depend upon our ability to carefully balance and advance all three.

Advances in underwater technology have already had a profound impact on the world's submerged cultural resources. The majority of submerged sites were formerly protected by their inaccessibility, but the underwater frontier is dwindling almost daily. Fifty years ago, who could have predicted that humans would be able to locate, image, and recover objects from *Titanic*, or salvage tons of gold from the 19th-century steamer *Central America* 9,000 ft. (27,500 m) below the ocean's surface, or systematically survey vast areas of underwater terrain? Similar leaps in technology are certain to occur in the next century, a fact that generates both promise and concern for the future.

We are already starting to witness the positive applications of cutting-edge technology, especially with regard to the interface of computers, sonar, and navigational positioning systems. For example, the Lake Champlain Maritime Museum (LCMM) is currently undertaking a systematic survey of the bottom of Lake Champlain that even a decade ago would have been beyond our means. Driven by the threat of zebra mussels, we have so far examined 120 square miles of lake bottom and are preparing for our fourth field season. We have located 25 previously undocumented shipwreck sites to add to the inventory of the hundreds already known. We have discovered intact 19th-century sailing vessels, canal boats built for towing and canal boats built for sailing, a steam tugboat, a World War II-era military vessel, and one pristine gunboat from Benedict Arnold's Revolutionary War fleet, which engaged the British at the Battle of Valcour Island in 1776. By the time the survey is complete, we expect to have an accurate inventory of Lake Champlain's sites, which will allow us to develop management strategies for the future study and preservation of the collection.

One important part of LCMM's Lake Survey has been the constant challenge of sharing the process and its results with the public. As these underwater sites are found, the shield of inaccessibility that formerly protected them is stripped away. If our assemblage of submerged cultural resources–not just in Lake Champlain, but also in the rest of the world's lakes, rivers, and oceans–is viewed as a "public collection" in storage, then the sites' sudden accessibility could result in their being exploited for private gain. Technology can and will bring fragile submerged archaeological sites into the public domain, and consequently the development of new protective strategies is essential.

Throughout the history of seafaring, the ownership of underwater properties has always been in question. Finders keepers. First come, first served. As the field of underwater archaeology has grown, it has confronted longstanding definitions of salvage law and attempted to redefine them. In the United States, the redefinition took the form of the Abandoned Shipwreck Act of 1987. This important debate is now taking place in the

world's oceans through UNESCO's Convention on underwater cultural heritage. The last few decades have seen a concurrent struggle to create a new academic discipline while changing the definition of a class of resource, so it is understandable that the one thing that brings the argument full circle has been only modestly accomplished: Engaging the public of every nation in the discussion to make them informed advocates for the preservation of their own cultural heritage.

Perhaps one of the most effective tools for protecting submerged cultural resources may prove to be public education, through the media and through museums, a simple process that can develop a wide network of allies, advocates, and support. The issues surrounding the protection and management of submerged cultural resources are complex, and today's public has no choice but to draw conclusions from what is heard and seen in the media. The subtleties of archaeological ethics are often not apparent to the cameras, however, and it can be difficult for many people to differentiate between treasure hunters and archaeologists. If the world's submerged cultural resources are indeed "public" resources, then it is imperative that the public understands the value of these sites, as well as the nature of the threats and issues that surround them.

It is the responsibility of the archaeological community to engage its public constituency and to demonstrate that the irreplaceable reward offered by shipwrecks is enlightenment about our own past. We must create exhibits about our work and write books accessible to mainstream audiences. We must speak at sport diver conferences and at local historical societies, at scout troop meetings and at elementary schools. We must encourage nautical archaeology students to reach out to the public, then give these students training and practice in this important task. We must offer training to sport divers, and we must actively seek their input and participation. One hundred years of scholarly dedication have gone into the creation of this discipline, and we must now make sure that the world knows about it and values its results.

As Delgado points out, one natural avenue for reaching a wide audience among the public extends from the world's maritime museums, although I firmly believe that this resource is still greatly under-utilized. In May 1998, I gave a presentation to the Council of American Maritime

Museums (CAMM). I assumed that I would be preaching to the choir in my discussion of the partnership between archaeological research and maritime museums, but I quickly realized that my audience was skeptical. Composed primarily of museum professionals rather than archaeologists, the group had been turned off by the apparent contentiousness with which topics related to underwater archaeology had been presented to them over the past decade. As a group, they have therefore shied away from dealing with the positive opportunities for public interpretation. Maritime and regional museums are our natural allies–but if we cannot convince them of the worth of scholarly archaeological research, then how can we hope to convince the public.

Clearly at cross-purposes with the goals of scholarly archaeological research is the work of the traditional treasure hunter. To date, the archaeological community's response to the threat of treasure hunting has been to deny treasure hunters access to archaeological conferences, to place prohibitions on museums that acquire or exhibit collections gathered through their enterprises, and to shun members of the archaeological fraternity who collaborate with them. Such sanctions seemed a logical reaction, but now is the time to evaluate the effectiveness of these strategies. Are treasure hunters truly affected by this condemnation, or are we injuring ourselves more by refusing to engage them in dialogue?

Ignoring treasure hunting activities will obviously not make them go away, and by distancing ourselves in this manner we lose the opportunity to salvage information. Sites where treasure hunters operate are usually perceived as "tainted," and the ships, their histories, and the artifacts that are recovered are relegated to the treasure hunt dumpster. The ships, however, are not at fault, and each has an important story to tell. It is true that the archaeologist has an unshakable responsibility to oppose looting, the non-scientific recovery of archaeological materials, and the marketing of antiquities. But is it not also our duty to pursue, preserve, and disseminate non-renewable archaeological information to the best of our abilities?

I feel that it is in our best interests to find common ground with well-meaning avocationals whose interest in underwater archaeology might outweigh their lack of archaeological credentials. This issue arises often at the Lake Champlain

Maritime Museum, where open communication with the local sport diving community is cultivated and valued. The divers are often our eyes and ears, and we would not succeed without their talents, insight, and contributions. Even on the world arena, avocationals such as Bob Ballard have crossed disciplinary boundaries to pursue archaeological research. Ballard, in fact, makes every effort to link archaeologists to his projects, and he articulates to his wide public audience many of the messages that the established archaeological community embraces. Will underwater archaeologists improve the field by criticizing efforts such as Ballard's, or by instead seeking to assist and guide these endeavors and therefore benefit from complementary expertise?

Oceanographic technology, research, and exploration will continue to advance in the years ahead, and the opportunities that will inevitably arise with regard to archaeological studies are challenging yet thrilling. I do believe, however, that the archaeological community will need outside help to keep up, especially in the area of cultural resource management. The Abandoned Shipwreck Act of 1987 was a magnificent landmark in the field, setting a huge precedent for ownership and responsibility, but it admittedly had certain shortcomings–it established no sources of funding, and it was, of course, limited to the waters of the United States. Since its passage, the states have for the most part been left to fend for themselves in providing management resources. Federal funding is erratic and minimal, and even programs such as the Navy Legacy Program and the National Heritage Preservation Act must fight for recognition from the government on a year-to-year basis.

Across the board, the archaeological community has been resourceful in attracting private funding to achieve its goals, but state and federal governments have a responsibility to this issue that can no longer be denied. Just like national forestlands, wildlife, and historic sites, underwater archaeological sites are a public resource (finite, non-renewable) and they must be protected, studied, and preserved. The wealth of information at stake–be it related to regional and international commerce, human conflict, or the evolution of technology–is beyond calculation, but today's public cannot be expected to realize its value without our assistance. We are the natural advocates of the worth of submerged cultural resources, and we must be articulate and persuasive on their behalf.

Shipwrecks are exciting stuff, and the weapons that we have on hand to raise public consciousness of their historical, rather than material, worth are formidable. *Vasa, Mary Rose, Monitor*, the Uluburun wreck, *La Belle, Philadelphia, Hunley*. These and the other sites we study all have behind them incredible tales of human ingenuity, courage, fallibility, and loss–by no means is *Titanic* the only vessel that deserves household recognition. As Delgado observes, "We need to let the screens again be filled with the majesty of a bequest from the past, not just the glimmer of gold coins or bars." Yes, a well-executed, well-funded, well-publicized shipwreck recovery would give us the opportunity to present the case for underwater archaeology in living rooms around the globe. On the other hand, we also have a long list of case studies that can illustrate what happens when a ship is raised in haste or with inadequate long-term funding. What ships should be raised, and why? Who determines if the value of a recovered ship outweighs the worth of an intact site? Who should pay for the project?

At this very moment, I find myself squarely in the middle of this debate. Sitting on the bottom of Lake Champlain in approximately 200 feet of water is an intact Revolutionary War gunboat, one which Benedict Arnold was forced to abandon in 1776 as his ragtag American fleet fled south after engaging the British at Valcour Island in a valiant and successful attempt to slow the British advance into the heart of the colonies. For 221 years this vessel has been unlocated and undisturbed–its bow cannon is still poised to fire, and its mast still standing. In finding it, we have assumed responsibility for its well-being. As the Lake Champlain Maritime Museum works with the Naval Historical Center, state agencies, and appropriate private organizations to decide the future of the site, we wrestle daily with deepwater technological advances, public interpretation, and cultural resource management issues.

The world's collection of submerged cultural resources belongs to the world's citizens, and bringing these sites to public attention will be the key to their effective management, study, and funding. The archaeological process must include steps that will connect the public, both here and abroad, to its own past and its own cultural resources. Private citizens must understand and care about these issues, because the archaeological community needs their assistance and support in order to manage the sites, to preserve them, to lobby for state and federal recognition, and to fund their documentation. Concerned public advocacy will give us our best opportunity to preserve, document, interpret, and learn from our ever more accessible submerged heritage.

ARTHUR B. COHN
LAKE CHAMPLAIN MARITIME MUSEUM
4472 BASIN HARBOR ROAD
VERGENNES, VT 05491

Daniel J. Lenihan

Of Strawberries, Women's Thighs, and Jim Delgado's Paper

There is little to criticize in Jim Delgado's paper. It is articulate, upbeat, and pokes at the whimsy center of our brains–a place that could use a bit more stimulation these days. In the same spirit, we should look for further inspiration on this issue of temporal transitions; wonderful abstractions like the "millennium" according to the Gregorian Calendar. Not from archaeologists however, but rather from philosophers of world-shaping influence. People of the stature of Georg Hegel, John Steinbeck, and Clint Eastwood; individuals whose writings and utterances really capture the human imagination.

Passing a wrinkle in time encountered only every hundred years, not alone thousand, induces us to conjure up equal but conflicting reactions of nostalgia and cynicism. Something Hegel might have seen in his more whimsical moments (if he ever had them) as an emotional dialectic. Consider for example, Steinbeck's plaintive musing over what would be lost in the new century at the turn of 1900. In *East of Eden*, he states "Oh but strawberries will never taste so good again and the thighs of women have lost their clutch"–as poignant a comment on the passing of milestones (if not the most gender-sensitive) as has ever been made.

But, lest that give one the impression JS was just sloppy sentimental over the close of a century, mere paragraphs further in that narrative he soliloquizes that "a man will have clean hands once we get the lid shut on that stinking century," and "any man who deals seconds from this new deck of years–why we'll crucify him head down over a privy."

Jim, in his paper, adopted more the strawberry/ thigh perspective than that of the privy which has among other advantages, that of (dare I say it?) less hindered hindsight. Let me therefore offer a measure of privy-based balance to the equation.

I know it would disappoint Jim, my friends, and my enemies if I were to do otherwise.

Jim writes of the "incremental increase in the number of new professionals" produced by the academic institutions in the U.S. The obvious question from the privy perspective is: has there been an incremental increase in meaningful jobs in this profession to accommodate these young men and women who inarguably do comprise as Jim states, "the heart, soul and backbone of this profession."

Might it be that many who would ordinarily be fiery young standard bearers ready to protect their profession from transparent attacks on the ethics front are driven by necessity to look for "compromise and reasonable alternatives." Jim is correct when he warns of "the increasing sophistication of treasure hunters and salvors who now with greater regularity 'talk our talk'." Those who would argue for collaborating with antiquity traffickers are helped immensely by our inability to provide suitable occupation for these young minds in projects that are scientifically sound and scientifically motivated. As Clint would have warned us "you all simply have got to know your limitations."

Delgado sees the last century as being "frontier times" in our discipline. Perhaps; but for how long does the coon-skin hat image avail us? Until when can we justify often mediocre archaeology on the excuse that we are, after all, a "nascent discipline." We are, in fact, well past our metaphorical birth pangs and should be quickly shedding the remnants of intellectual adolescence. Is it really acceptable that many of the practitioners in this field and their students are still totally out of the mainstream of anthropological method and theory? That they have never devised a research design–not because they are incompetent or unintelligent but because they were never exposed to a single moment of such training on their way to a degree?

Is it just because we are pioneers, asks the privy set, that many terrestrial archaeologists don't take seriously the products of underwater archaeology projects, in fact see the term "underwater archaeology" as an oxymoron? True, this may be partly due their own arrogance and narrow-mindedness, but can all the antipathy of the dry landers be chalked off to the fact that archaeologists may, in general, not always be the sharpest tools in the shed? How many papers on submerged sites were delivered at the SAA this year? How many historical archaeologists went to a single underwater paper at the SHA conference and vice versa for those of the nautical persuasion? Remember, we are not talking about the sharing of information among disciplines, this is all supposed to be part of the *same* discipline. If this appears to be a minor problem, it is only because we have gotten used to the state of affairs--this is a *big* problem, it begs the question of whether what we do is really part of the cumulative gathering of knowledge in the service of the comparative study of humankind.

Jim further tells us, in a strawberry/thigh clouded vision of the future, of the exciting new challenges the discipline faces. He sees deep-sea technology as the first of successive frontiers, reaching eventually to the *Apollo* 11 landing site. But the privy view brings us back to earth as privies are want to do. I would suggest that Jim is confusing engineering problems with archaeological problems. It has not been established to my satisfaction that there exists a mind-blowing assortment of sites available to robots far superior to those within diving depths that should become the prime focus of archaeological efforts in the new millennium. I believe it is incumbent upon us to first more fully address the challenges presented us by sites in shallow water. Develop the questions, the methodologies and the scholarly rigor to integrate our findings meaningfully into the full field of study of the human past before we spend too much time worrying about the heavenly spheres.

The lure of lunar landscapes notwithstanding, we should be paying much more attention to notions of "cultural landscapes" closer to home. It is an eminently useful and promising way in which to organize our thinking about human systems. Cultural landscapes, maritime landscapes, underwater landscapes, seascapes--wherever this conceptual yellow brick road takes us, it is worth

following. The ultimate merging of values of the "natural" and the built environments, be they wet or dry, will result eventually in paradigms around which to construct research that will be fruitful on planes of meaning we have not yet imagined.

We sorely need to put the robotics and computer software aside for the moment and concentrate on the grayware between our ears. The challenge echoing from the privy people is not to develop more sophisticated methods for extracting data but for asking the right questions, so that data becomes information.

And lastly, Jim, you say that "the major challenge before us . . . is not simply to shout 'unclean' and oppose treasure hunting and salvage." No, but that is certainly part of it. This profession needs to quit wallowing in pseudo-intellectual wrist-wringing over being "fair and balanced" in identifying and fighting those who would destroy the material record for personal gain.

Maybe there will come a time when we shake the fuzz off our brains and start talking like archaeologists and preservationists and not apologists for antiquity harvesters and merchants. Most of the people out there trying to become rich on the finding and selling of shipwreck remains are richer, slicker, smarter and more articulate than me and most of you. They don't need our help, they are the enemy.

But Delgado has written a good paper and I have come not to bury him, but to praise him. He has freed us of one of our worst sins in his discussion--that of taking ourselves too seriously. He has given us a therapeutic dose of whimsy and I hope this commentary is taken in the same vein. I will close by seconding his wish that "the new millennium be for all of us an opportunity for a brighter, better, bolder future, firmly rooted in the successes of the past." It would make my day.

May you also take some time to stop and sniff the strawberries.

DANIEL J. LENIHAN
NATIONAL PARK SERVICE
SUBMERGED CULTURAL RESOURCES UNIT
PO BOX 728
SANTE FE, NM 87504

Richard A Gould

Beyond Exploration: Underwater Archaeology after the Year 2000

James Delgado's survey of underwater archaeology provides a useful review of past accomplishments but is strangely silent about the future prospects for the discipline. I agree with Delgado that the century of underwater exploration is over. But where do we go from here? What, if any, new directions should the field of underwater archaeology take without giving up features of the discipline that have already proven their value? The turn of the century is an excellent time to consider new approaches as well as priorities for the future.

One way to begin is to look to neighboring disciplines for lessons–both good and bad–that can clarify the goals of underwater archaeology and direct our efforts toward useful results. One of these neighboring disciplines is marine science, including such specialties as oceanography and marine biology. Another is social science, especially anthropology. Underwater archaeology is still strongly influenced by a discovery-mode orientation acquired from underwater exploration and from land archaeology conducted in a similar manner. Anecdotal, descriptive historical interpretations based on discovery-mode archaeology are capable of producing imaginative, internally coherent, and plausible stories about past human activities. But how credible are such stories? Archaeologists, operating both on land and under water sometimes claim to have made discoveries, and these are often garnished with superlatives cherished by the media (the oldest this, the biggest that) but offer little in the way of scholarly credibility. Many of the examples cited by Delgado are affected by this problem and may need to be re-evaluated critically by future underwater archaeologists.

Recent experience in archaeology on land provides a guide for this process of critical evaluation, and it can be used to review earlier work as well as to design archaeological research in the future. For example, land archaeologists are already accustomed to the use of controlled sampling methods in regional surveys and in site excavations. Scholars like Nance (1983) and Dunnell and Dancey (1983) have confronted the issue of representativeness in regional surveys on land and provide useful frameworks for designing surveys that offer probabilistic results about how characteristic or typical whatever was found in the survey may be for the region as a whole.

Physical sampling methods are widely accepted today in land archaeology, and they enable archaeologists to evaluate their finds at whatever level they survey–whether at the macro-level of entire regions or at the micro-level of particular sites. With some notable exceptions, such as the National Park Service Submerged Cultural Resources Units survey and documentation of the Dry Tortugas National Park (Murphy 1993), underwater archaeologists have generally been slow to adopt these kinds of controls in their research.

Cultural sampling is a related issue for future underwater archaeology. Here I am referring to the celebrity shipwreck fixation that has characterized much of the field in the past. Of course we would all like to know more about the *Titanic*, USS *Monitor*, USS *Arizona*, *Mary Rose*, *Vasa*, and other, similar icons of maritime history. But how representative were these ships of their period or maritime cultural traditions? In many cases these ships were famous precisely because they were unique or unusual. Good regional sampling can often capture less famous ships that were more typical of the maritime technologies and uses of watercraft of their time and place. This is especially important when we find technologies like shell-first wooden construction that appeared early–by at least 1300 B.C. in the eastern Mediterranean–but persisted and were important much later–for example, in Holland during the 17th Century, A.D. What accounts for the longevity of this shipbuilding tradition in certain quarters, even after frame-first hull construction was firmly established? Instead of attempting to shoehorn archaeological shipwrecks into linear, progressionist sequences of technological evolution, underwater archaeologists will need to consider the relative importance of these and perhaps other techniques at different periods and locations.

How typical, for example, was shell-first ship construction in the context of Roman maritime commerce? Was it reserved primarily for coast-hugging vessels engaged in tramping? To what extent may frame-first methods have been applied to large, long-distance bulk carriers, such as appears to be the case for the *Madrague de Giens* wreck near Toulon (Parker 1980)? Perhaps shipbuilders of that period were more eclectic and resourceful than we have imagined. Shell-first and frame-first methods of construction may have been part of a larger repertoire of techniques that were used as needed by the same individuals, depending upon the circumstances. We shall need to understand those circumstances better in order to explain the archaeological and historical occurrences of these methods. This kind of question can never be answered by focusing exclusively on famous or historically unique ships.

In the case of a more recent example, how widespread was the use of steam-powered machinery aboard the first generation of ironclad naval ships? The wreck of the USS *Monitor* might lead us to believe that it was typical. Except for other American turreted monitors, however, it was more common to encounter hand-operated machinery for tasks like raising and lowering anchors, screw propellers, and sails. Underwater archaeology based on controlled approaches to cultural sampling can test the historical reality of much of the received wisdom applied to our ideas about our maritime past. In other words, the ancestry of the battleship may be more complicated than many historians have thought.

If underwater archaeologists have been sluggish in accepting controlled physical and cultural sampling as frameworks for evaluating their finds, the same cannot be said for their recognition of post-depositional factors that affect the archaeological record at shipwreck and submerged terrestrial sites. This approach was ushered in by maritime archaeologist Keith Muckelroy (1978) when he distinguished between extracting filters and scrambling devices as mechanisms to control for post-depositional effects of different kinds on shipwreck sites. Muckelroy's approach introduced a new level of analytical sophistication that has since been matched—possibly even surpassed—by land archaeologist Michael Schiffer's (1987) concept of post-depositional transformations in the archaeological record. Muckelroy's and Schiffer's contributions compel us to recognize and evaluate the impact of different natural and cultural factors that can intervene to alter the physical associations at archaeological sites following the shipwreck or the abandonment of that site. Failure to control in this way can lead to serious misinterpretations of site remains, especially when patterning due to natural factors is mistaken for patterning that resulted from past human behavior.

Critical post-depositional reviews are now widely used by underwater archaeologists as part of their analyses of site remains, especially in regional or public-archaeology programs where cultural-resource management is also an issue. This process of critical review and testing will improve in the future as new undersea technologies also come to play a wider role in archaeology. The results of these efforts so far show that underwater archaeology, while embracing new technologies, must not itself become technologically driven.

Here we need to look to the marine sciences for guidance–but carefully. For the first time, underwater research in archaeology can be carried out effectively at depths below the practical limits imposed by SCUBA. Mini-submersibles, ROVs, AUVs (still experimental, but improving quickly), remote sensing, GPS and DGPS, exact underwater positioning systems, and computerized data-management systems like GIS, have all been used successfully, either operationally or on a trial basis. The appearance of these technologies has created a new kind of blue-water archaeology which operates in a manner that is fundamentally different from doing it the old fashioned way entirely with SCUBA. To suggest that these new technologies were developed specifically for underwater archaeology would be like claiming that the trowel and shovel were invented for archaeology on land. As always, underwater archaeologists are called upon to adapt technologies to their specific needs, and their ability to do this intelligently will be an important priority during the coming century.

Although divers using SCUBA will continue to provide the core of underwater archaeological research for the foreseeable future, the outlook of the discipline cannot be limited to the application of what are essentially land-based techniques under water. New research designs will be needed in which underwater archaeologists take charge and adapt new marine technologies to the unique requirements of their discipline. For example, in the marine sciences generally there is no strict requirement for exact underwater positioning. In most cases, oceanographers and marine biologists can obtain their samples from generalized locations in the water column or on the sea bed. For archaeology, however, it is essential to record physical associations more accurately, which places special demands on these new technologies. Our future research designs will need to drive these technologies to a level of resolution beyond what is considered adequate for most marine science in order to obtain archaeologically useful results.

All of these issues apply to submerged terrestrial-site archaeology as well. This specialty has come a long way since the rampant artifact-oriented, discovery-mode excavations of the Swiss Lake Dwellers and the Sacred Cenote of Chichen-Itza during the late 19th and early 20th centuries. Today we are seeing underwater archaeological surveys and excavations in places like Florida's Big Bend continental shelf and the adjacent Aucilla River (Dunbar, Webb, and Faught 1992). This research is proceeding on a firm scientific basis, in which the investigators have performed controlled surveys to record the submerged geography of the study area. As archaeological sites are encountered, they are evaluated in relation to their geological and paleontological associations. These kinds of approaches to archaeological research design can apply new underwater technologies as needed, and we should expect to see more of this kind of theoretically-driven, as opposed to technology-driven, research in underwater prehistory in the next century.

For underwater prehistorians there is a special challenge. The underwater world abounds with material remains of past human activities that were the residues of extinct cultural systems with no modern counterpart. Land-based prehistorians are already familiar with this problem. For example, how did our hominid ancestors (*Australopithecus* and the early genus, *Homo*) survive as hunter-gatherers for millions of years without the use of fire? All historic and ethnographic hunter-gatherers made use of fire, so modern-day examples cannot provide an accurate analogue for explaining past behavior. Ethnographically-documented examples of pedestrian big-game hunting behavior are also exceedingly rare and tell us little directly about such archaeological cultures as the pre-horse Indians of the American Great Plains.

This issue has already arisen for underwater archaeology in Australia. Geological and pale-ontological evidence indicates that the mainland of Australia-New Guinea was separated from Southeast Asia by a deep-sea trench for millions of years, which means that the original ancestors of the Australian Aborigines must have voyaged out of sight of land to get there. Radiocarbon and thermoluminescence dating currently suggest that this migration took place at least 40,000 and perhaps as much as 60,000 years ago (Morwood and Hobbs 1995), making this the earliest known oceanic voyage in human prehistory. It also required fairly sophisticated watercraft to transport the necessary critical mass of colonists and provisions–not to mention the need for return voyaging.

Ethnographic sources indicate, however, that there were no historic Australian Aboriginal watercraft that were convincingly capable of making such a voyage. We lack any modern counterpart to explain Pleistocene voyaging to Australia. Controlled underwater surveys will be needed to identify submerged terrestrial sites in locations that relate to likely migration routes and points of entry, such as submerged rock art sites. As one such possibility, ancient rock engravings appear commonly along the northwest coast of Australia and may also occur at locations that were submerged by post-Pleistocene sea level rises. The lesson here for submerged terrestrial-site archaeology is that we must avoid assuming the very thing we are trying to find out. Instead of attempting to infer the past by extrapolating from ethnographic Aboriginal watercraft, archaeologists will need to use controlled scientific research designs coupled with new marine technologies to take a fresh look at the situation, without any prior assumptions about how these ancient voyagers should have behaved. Ethnographic information about traditional methods of boatbuilding and use, for example, may be more helpful for contrasting the present with the past instead of as a source of present-day analogues for past behavior.

Among historians of science, this problem is referred to as the fallacy of affirming the consequent. It can arise in different ways, and it applies to the study of historic shipwrecks and related maritime sites like harbors and docks, too. Historic documents are invaluable but can never be accepted at face value for reasons having to do with bias and incompleteness. Such documents must be compared and tested against the archaeological record whenever possible. Archaeology in the presence of historic documents always serves as a reality check based on the circumstantial evidence provided by material associations. But this only works if archaeologists are willing to test the contents of historic documents instead of merely seeking confirmation of the historical record.

For example, over reliance upon the writings of the Roman architect and engineer Vitruvius could lead to serious errors of interpretation in our understanding of ancient Roman harbor construction and the Roman use of hydraulic concrete. As recent studies at have shown (Oleson and Branton 1992; Brandon 1996), there are measurable dissonances between Vitruvius' instructions and the specific characteristics of the Roman breakwater at the Herodian harbor of Caesarea Maritima. Thanks to underwater archaeology, we are gaining a better approximation of actual Roman methods of harbor construction, especially in relation to the problems posed by local topography and by the economic conditions of the period.

Even more recently we have the matter of wrought-iron ship construction during the mid-to-late 19th century. This technology played a key role in the transition from sail to steam propulsion, yet it is no longer extant anywhere in the world as an industrial-scale technology. Historic documents abound describing the manufacturing processes and applications of this technology in shipbuilding, but unanswered questions remain about socio-economic factors that affected its adoption for naval and maritime commercial use during the late Industrial Revolution. We still do not fully understand how a hand-craft technological tradition like wrought iron achieved an industrial scale of production. Unlike steel, which could be mass produced easily and in huge quantities, wrought-iron production was amazingly labor intensive and required both micro- and macro-organization and specialized skills which are still not well known. Underwater archaeologists are in a good position to study the products of this phase of technological history and to test and evaluate the character of these products relative to the historical documentation about them.

As we move into the 21st century, underwater archaeology will need to disengage from discovery-mode approaches based upon the anecdotal and uncontrolled confirmation of dominant assumptions about human prehistory or received wisdom derived from historical documents. Instead, we must exercise a willingness to use archaeological methods to test our ideas about the human past in a scientifically controlled and convincing manner. None of these scholarly goals will mean anything, however, if we fail to confront the dangers posed by treasure hunting.

For trained archaeologists, the threat posed by treasure hunting is obvious and immediate. Underwater recovery of antiquities by treasure hunters for purposes of commercial gain, either through direct sale of artifacts or indirectly through media exploitation, is arguably the single most destructive influence on the underwater archaeological record. For people who are not trained in archaeology, however, the distinction between archaeology and treasure hunting is not always clear, and treasure hunters have effectively fostered this fuzziness to their advantage. There often seems to be little difference between archaeologists who excavate and treasure hunters who remove remains from submerged sites. After all, they all dig don't they? So what's the difference? Archaeologists have always had a hard time explaining the difference, and it just got harder. The fuzziness of public perceptions of underwater archaeology always increases whenever underwater archaeologists ally themselves with treasure hunters by claiming that they can cooperate. Since the interests of underwater archaeology and treasure hunting are diametrically opposed, this kind of alliance always ends badly and leads to the loss of irreplaceable cultural resources.

Underwater archaeologist Toni Carrell (1996) recently pointed out that treasure hunting has recently embraced the same new undersea technologies that have been leading in the direction of blue-water archaeology. Now treasure hunters are moving farther offshore, into extreme deep-water environments, beyond the reach of effective legal restraints. This has opened the door to a heightened form of undersea strip mining, with nothing to impede wholesale site destruction except high capital costs and logistical difficulties. It has never been more important for underwater archaeologists to clarify their own scholarly goals and to communicate these clearly to the public than it is now. One way to answer the treasure hunters effectively when this issue comes up is for underwater archaeologists to make more extensive use of non-destructive methods of site recording and documentation. Such methods are already proving their value in a variety of localities ranging from Bermuda to Pearl Harbor. Since they do not involve the permanent recovery of objects and involve minimal impact to the physical associations at the site, there is no way these approaches can be confused with treasure hunting. They will also have the effect of making underwater excavation more selective and better designed to answer questions and test hypotheses about past human behavior in relation to the marine environment. Whatever solution they choose to resolve this problem, underwater archaeologists must act promptly if there are to be significant cultural resources left for study in the next century.

REFERENCES

BRANDON, C.
  1996 Cements, Concrete, and Settling Barges at Sebastos: Comparisons with Other Roman Harbor Examples and the Descriptions of Vitruvius. In *Caesarea Maritima*, Avner Raban and Kenneth G. Holum, editors, pp. 25-49. E. J. Brill, Leiden, Netherlands.

CARRELL, TONI L.
  1996 Mutate, Migrate, Adapt, or Die. *Common Ground*, 1:72-75.

DUNBAR, JAMES S., S. DAVID WEBB, AND MICHAEL FAUGHT
  1992 Inundated Prehistoric Sites in Apalachee Bay, Florida, and the Search for the Clovis Shoreline. In *Paleoshorelines and Prehistory*, Lucille Lewis Johnson, editor, pp. 117-146. CRC Press, Boca Raton, FL.

DUNNELL, ROBERT, AND WILLIAM S. DANCEY
  1983 The Siteless Survey: A Regional Scale Data Collection Strategy. In *Advances in Archaeological Method and Theory*, Vol. 6, Michael B. Schiffer, editor, pp. 267-287. Academic Press, New York, NY.

MORWOOD, M. J., AND D. R. HOBBS
  1995 Themes in the Prehistory of Tropical Australia. In Transitions: Pleistocene to Holocene in Australia & Papua New Guinea, J. Allen and James F. O'Connell, editors, pp. 747-768. *Antiquity*, Special No. 265.

MUCKELROY, KEITH
  1978 *Maritime Archaeology*. Cambridge University Press, Cambridge, England.

MURPHY, LARRY E. (EDITOR)
  1993 Dry Tortugas National Park. National Park Service, Santa Fe, NM.

NANCE, J. D.
  1983 Regional Sampling in Archaeology: The Statistical Perspective. In *Advances in Archaeological Method and Theory*, Vol. 6, Michael B. Schiffer, editor, pp. 289-356. Academic Press, New York, NY.

OLESON, J. P., AND G. BRANTON
  1992 The Technology of King Herods Harbour. In Caesarea Papers, Robert Lindley Vann, editor, pp. 49-67. *Journal of Roman Archaeology*, Supplementary Series No. 5. Ann Arbor, MI.

PARKER, A.
  1980 Roman Wrecks in the Western Mediterranean. In *Archaeology Under Water*, Keith Muckelroy, editor, pp. 50-61. McGraw-Hill, New York, NY.

SCHIFFER, MICHAEL B.
  1987 *Formation Processes of the Archaeological Record*. University of New Mexico Press, Albuquerque.

RICHARD A. GOULD
DEPARTMENT OF ANTHROPOLOGY
BROWN UNIVERSITY
BOX 1921
PROVIDENCE, RI 02912

2007. A Preliminary Analysis of Historic Shipwrecks in Northern Ireland. *Historical Archaeology* 41(3):4–8.

Colin Breen
Rory Quinn
Wes Forsythe

A Preliminary Analysis of Historic Shipwrecks in Northern Ireland

ABSTRACT

Recent marine survey programs have generated a GIS (geographic information system) distribution of historic wreck sites around the coast of Northern Ireland. These data lead to an understanding of the nature and extent of submerged cultural resources and provide statistical information on the spatial and temporal distribution of historic wrecks, allowing for the reconstruction of past maritime activity. This is important baseline data used for the production of integrated research and management plans for the protection of the resources.

Introduction

Ireland, as an island on the edge of northwest Europe, has been a focus for cultural maritime activity for at least 9,000 years. Its temperate climate and damp, mountainous terrain, combined with its extensive coastline and inland waterways, mean that boats and ships have historically been the most important mode of communication. Shipping provided access to trade and settlement networks and facilitated exploitation of marine resources. Such extensive activity over millennia has invariably left considerable evidence in the form of shipwrecks and abandoned vessels on the foreshore and in rivers and lakes. A modern, contemporary expression of this activity in the landscape is manifested in vernacular and traditional boat forms. Surviving vessels, such as the curraghs of the west coast and double-ended clinker-built boats of the north and east coasts, all testify to this activity.

Recent technological advances have equipped archaeologists with access to the sea floor to study these remains (Lenham et al. 1998). Academic research, combined with extensive media coverage of both professional and treasure-hunting activities, culminated in an increasing awareness of the resource at national and international levels. This awareness is reflected in legislative protective provisions in individual countries and also internationally, exemplified by the inclusion of cultural material in the United Nations Law of the Sea and with the production of the recent UNESCO convention on the protection of underwater archaeological remains (Fletcher-Tomenius and Williams 1999).

Many of the current international legislative provisions oblige states to develop a strategy for the mapping and management of underwater resources. A number of countries addressed these issues by instigating formal mapping and survey programs. In 1993, the Department of the Environment for Northern Ireland started a program of mapping underwater archaeological sites. It is currently engaged in a geophysical survey of seabed sites in association with the Centre for Maritime Archaeology at the University of Ulster, Northern Ireland (Breen 1996). Governments in both jurisdictions in Ireland have been involved with mapping and protecting archaeological sites on land since the 1960s, but it was only with the establishment of the underwater surveys that sites below the high-water mark began to be addressed. The initial phase of the project is now complete. One of the primary outcomes has been the development of a GIS-based inventory of coastal historical shipwrecks.

Methodology and Rationale

Development of the inventory is based upon historical cartographic and documentary material dating back to the 7th and 8th centuries A.D. (Breen and Forsythe 2004). The combination of this material with contemporary marine survey data allows for plotting wreck sites on digital base maps. Bathymetric features, seabed contours, and bottom type are also combined within this package, which generates detailed base survey maps of wreck distribution and can produce wreck predictive models through the combination of natural and cultural data.

Known historical sites can be plotted, and targeted survey strategies are created to locate and map earlier historic and prehistoric sites. The baseline maps also help place sites in context with the maritime landscape and allow for creation of management and research plans aimed at protection of submerged cultural resources.

Wreck Distribution through Time

Analysis of the data sets allows a number of observations on the nature and extent of wreck resources around Northern Ireland's coast. Chronologically, the wreck record is heavily biased towards the postmedieval period, which postdates the 16th century (Figure 1). This bias

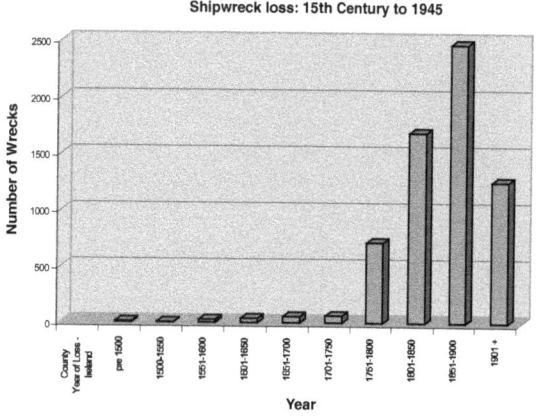

FIGURE 1. Extent of ship loss in Northern Ireland, shown in 50-year periods from the 15th century to 1945. (Graph by authors.)

is largely due to the nature of archival sources and to what cultural material survives on the seabed. Of the more than 3,000 sites recorded in northern Irish waters, 3% predate the 18th century, 11% date from 1751 to 1800, and 66% date to the 19th century. The remaining 20% date to before 1945, with the majority of 20th-century vessels lost during both world wars. Many of these war wrecks were lost ships that were engaged in Atlantic supply convoys passing between Ireland and Great Britain. These convoys were prime targets of the German submarines that patrolled both Irish and British waters. The high percentage of records from the

postmedieval period not only marks a concerted effort on behalf of the authorities to record ship loss but also marks the significant upsurge in shipping and coastal trade after the 1600s. Much of this activity is associated with the industrial revolution in the 19th century.

The bias in records towards the postmedieval period can be attributed to the nature of wreck-site preservation and the history of marine mapping and research. Most wreck sites in Irish waters disintegrate to a fraction of their original form through processes of physical, chemical, and biological breakdown. The harsh environment dictates that many pre-17th-century wrecks have not been located during the charting and mapping of the coast, either because they are buried or were unrecognizable on the seabed. The majority of these sites reach a state of semi-equilibrium with the underwater environment, ranging from a cannon and anchor spread in a rocky gully to a partially preserved hull buried in muddy sediments. It is possible to list a number of types of wreck sites that survive around Ireland, and a tentative categorization is included below. These types are very general and can only be properly defined when local environmental and topographical conditions have been taken into account. A wreck lost off the dynamic north Antrim coast and exposed to the Atlantic Ocean will undergo very different site formation processes from a wreck lost in sheltered Lough Foyle, with its muddy substrate and enclosed environment (Table 1).

Spatial Distribution of Wrecks

Spatial distribution of wrecks is a reflection of shipping activity, routeways, and the presence or absence of natural hazards. Examination of the data provides valuable insights into the nature of wreck distribution around the northern Irish coast (Figure 2). The majority of wrecks are located on the County Down coast. Almost 8% of the total wrecks off the coast of Ireland as a whole occur off this coastline. This percentage reflects the county's importance as a trade and communications route, having a number of major ports located on its coast. County Antrim accounts for 3% of the overall total, with the majority lost in the northern part of Belfast Lough and along Island Magee near Larne Lough. The coast off County Derry accounts

TABLE 1
GENERAL CLASSIFICATION OF SHIPWRECK TYPES IN IRELAND

Type	Description
A	Recent iron or wooden wreck, lost within 50 years of the present, almost wholly complete but beginning the process of disintegration.
B	Iron or composite wreck, lost within the last 50 to 100 years, its hull partially or wholly collapsed.
C1	Iron or composite wreck, lost 100 to 200 years ago, wholly collapsed and represented by a barely definable tangle of metal on the seabed.
C2	Iron or composite wreck, lost 100 to 200 years ago, represented by recognizable but broken wreckage on the seabed.
C3	Iron or composite wreck, lost 100 to 200 years ago, represented by a number of isolated structural features like beams or plates.
D1	Wooden wreck, lost within the last 200 years, exposed on the seabed and in good condition.
D2	Wooden wreck, exposed on the seabed and broken down to the lowermost part of its hull.
E1	Historic wooden wreck, wholly or partially buried in sediment with much of its hull preserved.
E2	Historic wooden wreck, wholly or partially buried in sediment with little preserved.
F1	Artifact spreads of material on low-energy seabed.
F2	Artifact spreads of material on a high-energy site, e.g., shallow, exposed rock.
G1	Hulk, lying on the foreshore either wholly or partially intact.
G2	Hulk, lying on the foreshore and eroded to the lowermost hull.
G3	Hulk, lying buried on the foreshore and being occasionally exposed.

for less than 1% of wrecks, which is unsurprising given its shorter coastline and lesser role in mercantile traffic.

The large number of wrecks around County Down is explained by a combination of the heavy volume of shipping and a number of natural hazards off the coast. A large number of offshore shoals, banks, and rocks that pose a major threat to shipping are present, and it has few natural landfalls. Various localities such as North and South Rocks and the Copeland Islands are scattered with hundreds of wrecks. The coastlines of Down and Antrim have witnessed extensive shipping with a number of prominent medieval harbors, including Ardglass, Strangford, and Carrickfergus, and prime fishing grounds that have attracted fleets for centuries (Wilson 1997). In addition, the more sheltered nature of the northeast coast of Ireland possibly contributes to the higher percentage of preserved wrecks. The exposed shores of the north coast, on the other hand, mitigate against large-scale survival, but as noted previously, each section of the coast and its individual environmental attributes have to be treated separately.

Causes of Wrecking

Vessels are wrecked for many reasons. Conflict can be a major cause, especially during politically volatile periods. Wars generally witness an increase in wrecks. Peaks in the Irish wreck record are apparent during the postmedieval Anglo-Spanish and Anglo-French wars and during the major conflicts of more recent years. Human error can also contribute to the loss of a vessel, particularly if the crew is inexperienced or otherwise incapable of controlling its ship. Numerous references describe instances in which a captain and crew were intoxicated and unable to save the ship when it got into trouble (Breen and Forsythe 2004). Meteorological conditions, however, are the biggest single contributor to shipping loss and loss of life at sea. Certain instances of large-scale weather events have produced a sudden, dramatic loss of shipping. Of the 53 recorded great storms that have affected Ireland (Lamb 1991), 27 have produced at least 254 incidents of wreckage. On 6 January 1839, 42 vessels were lost in a ferocious westerly storm; the distribution of these vessels suggests

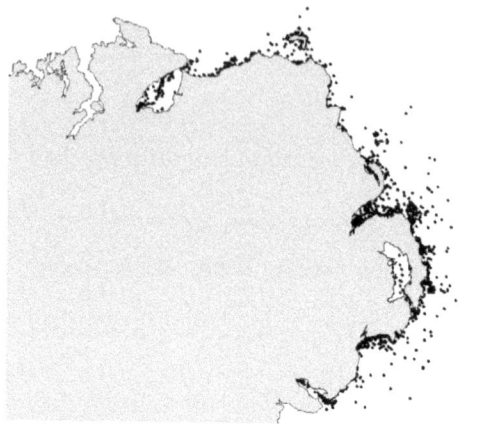

FIGURE 2. Spatial distribution of ca. 3,000 wrecks around the coast of Northern Ireland, dating from the 16th century to 1945. Clusters of wrecks can be seen around ports and areas of natural hazard. (Map by authors.)

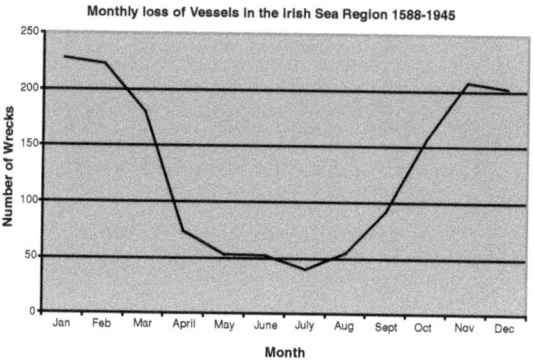

FIGURE 3. Monthly occurrence of wrecks along the Irish seaboard. This data represents information on wrecking over a 357-year period from 1588 to 1945. (Graph by authors.)

that many were simply blown onto the western seaboard by prevailing gales. The direction of the prevailing wind is a recurring influential factor on the distribution of inshore wreckage. The large-scale storms, despite their great losses at the time, account for only a small percentage of those lost due to inclement weather. The majority of vessels have been lost in smaller squalls associated with winter weather each year from October through March (Figure 3).

A direct correlation exists in the wreck database between storm events and the incidence of wrecking. A statistical examination of the wreck record shows 53% of all losses were recorded in the four winter months of November through February, with 15% of the overall total lost in January. This percentage of winter losses contrasts sharply with the 10% of wrecks lost during the summer months of June, July, and August. Moreover, a closer examination of this percentage reveals that half of these vessels were lost as a result of conflict at sea, further highlighting the role of weather in loss.

Socio-Economic Analysis

A valuable aspect of this data as a representative sample of historical shipping is its application to socio-economic analysis of past maritime activity. Insights into the nature and extent of mercantile trade can be ascertained through examination of cargoes, ports of origin, and destinations of

the ships lost in these waters (Figure 4). One striking statistic is the high number of wrecked vessels that originated in English ports. The available port of origin data indicates that 29% of wrecks originated in England, highlighting the extent of cross-channel trade. Only 21% of wrecks were destined for England with Irish cargoes, demonstrating the predominance of the English export trade to Ireland. Of the vessels lost, 35% were carrying coal, a major import commodity in the postmedieval period and a natural resource that is virtually absent from Ireland. Most of this coal was destined for the ports along the eastern seaboard where much of the heavy indigenous industry and commercial activity was concentrated. Foodstuffs and livestock accounted for 18% of cargoes, while 14% of vessels lost off the Antrim and Derry

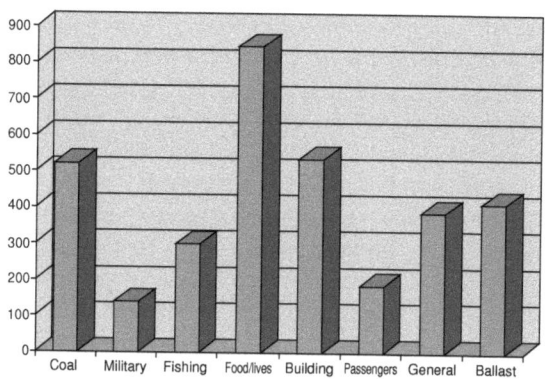

FIGURE 4. Shipwreck cargo types from Northern Ireland, 1588 to 1945. (Graph by authors.)

Perspectives from *Historical Archaeology* and *ACUA Proceedings*

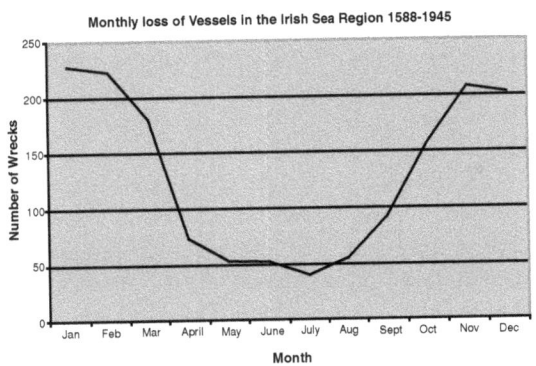

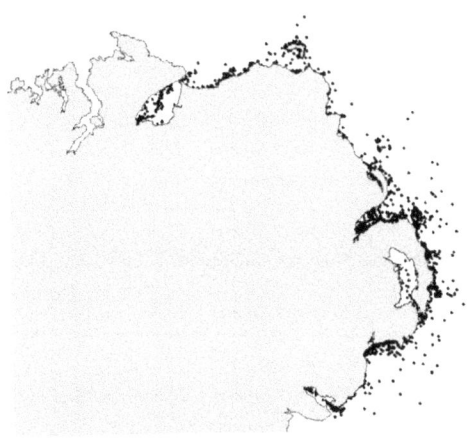

FIGURE 2. Spatial distribution of ca. 3,000 wrecks around the coast of Northern Ireland, dating from the 16th century to 1945. Clusters of wrecks can be seen around ports and areas of natural hazard. (Map by authors.)

FIGURE 3. Monthly occurrence of wrecks along the Irish seaboard. This data represents information on wrecking over a 357-year period from 1588 to 1945. (Graph by authors.)

that many were simply blown onto the western seaboard by prevailing gales. The direction of the prevailing wind is a recurring influential factor on the distribution of inshore wreckage. The large-scale storms, despite their great losses at the time, account for only a small percentage of those lost due to inclement weather. The majority of vessels have been lost in smaller squalls associated with winter weather each year from October through March (Figure 3).

A direct correlation exists in the wreck database between storm events and the incidence of wrecking. A statistical examination of the wreck record shows 53% of all losses were recorded in the four winter months of November through February, with 15% of the overall total lost in January. This percentage of winter losses contrasts sharply with the 10% of wrecks lost during the summer months of June, July, and August. Moreover, a closer examination of this percentage reveals that half of these vessels were lost as a result of conflict at sea, further highlighting the role of weather in loss.

Socio-Economic Analysis

A valuable aspect of this data as a representative sample of historical shipping is its application to socio-economic analysis of past maritime activity. Insights into the nature and extent of mercantile trade can be ascertained through examination of cargoes, ports of origin, and destinations of

the ships lost in these waters (Figure 4). One striking statistic is the high number of wrecked vessels that originated in English ports. The available port of origin data indicates that 29% of wrecks originated in England, highlighting the extent of cross-channel trade. Only 21% of wrecks were destined for England with Irish cargoes, demonstrating the predominance of the English export trade to Ireland. Of the vessels lost, 35% were carrying coal, a major import commodity in the postmedieval period and a natural resource that is virtually absent from Ireland. Most of this coal was destined for the ports along the eastern seaboard where much of the heavy indigenous industry and commercial activity was concentrated. Foodstuffs and livestock accounted for 18% of cargoes, while 14% of vessels lost off the Antrim and Derry

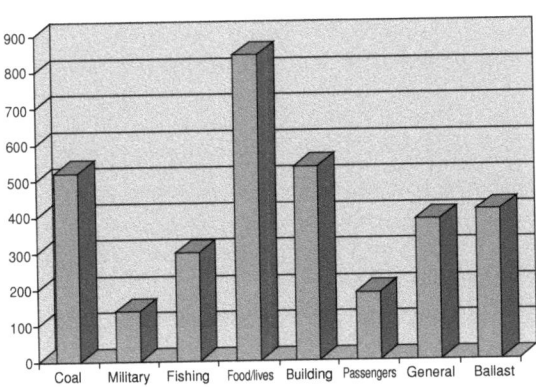

FIGURE 4. Shipwreck cargo types from Northern Ireland, 1588 to 1945. (Graph by authors.)

coasts were engaged in fishing. Only 3% of vessels lost were of a military nature, indicative of the lack of an Irish naval force until the 20th century and the neutrality of the then Irish Free State during World War II.

An examination of ports of registry and ports of origin for Northern Ireland wrecks can also offer insights into where vessels were originating in their trade with the region. The majority of vessels came from northwest England and from western Scotland. A surprisingly small percentage came from what are now the counties of the Republic of Ireland, with only 9% of vessels wrecked on the County Down coast originating from southern Ireland. Wales also has a low percentage represented in both ports of registry and origin. This analysis suggests that a clearly defined economic zone was evident in the north Irish Sea area encompassing southwest Scotland, northwest England, and northeast Ireland.

Port of destination data indicate that 52% of vessels were bound for Irish ports while 21% were bound for England, 4% for Scotland, and 3% for Wales. Where origin data were available, they indicated that 30% of wrecks originated in Ireland, 29% in England, 11% in the United States, 7% in Wales, and 6% in Scotland. Interpretation of these data needs to be approached with caution, as wrecking, by its very nature, is and was random and unpredictable. Many vessels were wrecked while passing Ireland *en route* to somewhere else, while peaks of activity may occur during particular periods or events.

Conclusion

The northern Irish wreck record offers valuable insights into the nature of wrecking in northwest Europe. The record shows a direct correlation between the incidence of wrecking and the economic and climatic conditions. Wreck material is a cultural resource that has now been quantified and characterized. Government agencies use the record to develop integrated management and research plans for historic wreck sites, and it has been incorporated into commercial development plans. This work has also highlighted the importance and extent of the submerged cultural resource as an indicator of past maritime activity. It is the physical evidence of the role of shipping in shaping the economic base of postmedieval Ireland.

References

BREEN, COLIN
1996 Maritime Archaeology in Northern Ireland: An Interim Statement. *The International Journal of Nautical Archaeology* 25(1):55–65.

BREEN, COLIN, AND WES FORSYTHE
2004 *Boats and Shipwrecks in Ireland: An Archaeology.* Tempus Press, Stroud, England, UK.

FLETCHER-TOMENIUS, PAUL, AND MICHAEL WILLIAMS
1999 Draft UNESCO/DOLAS Convention on the Protection of Underwater Cultural Heritage and Conflict with The European Convention on Human Rights. *International Journal of Nautical Archaeology* 28(2):145–153.

LAMB, HUBERT H.
1991 *Historic Storms of the North Sea, British Isles, and Northwest Europe.* Cambridge University Press, Cambridge, England, UK.

LENHAM, JOSEPH, JOHN BULL, JUSTIN DIX, AND BRIAN WILLIAMS
1998 Surveying Submerged Sites: Remote Sensing at Strangford Lough, Co. Down. *Archaeology Ireland* 42(4):18–20.

WILSON, IAN
1997 *Shipwrecks of the Ulster Coast*, 3rd edition. Impact Printing, Coleraine, Northern Ireland, UK.

COLIN BREEN
CENTRE FOR MARITIME ARCHAEOLOGY
SCHOOL OF ENVIRONMENTAL SCIENCES
UNIVERSITY OF ULSTER
COLERAINE BT52 1SA
NORTHERN IRELAND, UK

RORY QUINN
CENTRE FOR MARITIME ARCHAEOLOGY
SCHOOL OF ENVIRONMENTAL SCIENCES
UNIVERSITY OF ULSTER
COLERAINE BT52 1SA
NORTHERN IRELAND, UK

WES FORSYTHE
CENTRE FOR MARITIME ARCHAEOLOGY
SCHOOL OF ENVIRONMENTAL SCIENCES
UNIVERSITY OF ULSTER
COLERAINE BT52 1SA
NORTHERN IRELAND, UK

2006. The Abandoned Ships' Project: An Overview of the Archaeology of Deliberate Watercraft Discard in Australia. *Historical Archaeology* (40)4:84–103.

Nathan Richards
Mark Staniforth

The Abandoned Ships' Project: An Overview of the Archaeology of Deliberate Watercraft Discard in Australia

ABSTRACT

The Abandoned Ships' Project (ASP) was a research initiative of the Department of Archaeology at Flinders University, South Australia, and carried out in conjunction with the doctoral research of one of the authors (Richards 2002). The project involved the compilation of a database of more than 1,500 discarded and partly dismantled watercraft sites, including information from the archaeological inspection of more than 120 deliberately discarded ships. Researchers used this data to assess the degree of correlation between discard activities and economic, social, and technological issues. The logistics of discard were also examined as reflected in commentaries describing discard processes and as seen in the archaeological signatures of these events. This information illustrated the causal relationships among processes (landscape, economic trends, regulatory frameworks, and cultural site formation) associated with harm minimization, placement assurance, salvage, and discard activities.

Introduction

Deliberately abandoned ships are watercraft discarded by their owners in a purposeful, non-catastrophic manner. In this respect, they are substantially different from shipwrecks. Whereas a shipwreck event usually involves the partial (if not complete) loss of control over the fate of a vessel, the deliberate discard of a vessel represents veritable total control over this process. Consequently, these two categories of maritime archaeological sites exist at opposite ends of a behavioral spectrum. Abandoned vessels stand apart from their wrecked counterparts in historical records due to the fragmentary or nonexistent reports of their discard, which is largely due to the lack of reporting about disposal of vessels and the often-clandestine abandonment of vessels without the knowledge of port and coastline management authorities. As Jonathan Moore (1995: 3) commented,

Unlike the fanfare of their launch, the disposal of ships at the end of their working lives was often gradual and received little public attention. If not completely broken up, ship-breakers invariably stripped the vessels of machinery, and scuttled them in deep water, whether alone or in marine graveyards. Invariably they faded from sight, their disappearance easily forgotten, unlike memorable shipwrecks.

From an examination of previous studies concerned with the deliberate discard of watercraft from around the world, these sites belong in two main categories: isolated abandonment sites and, secondly, discard accumulation sites, or so-called ships' graveyards. Additionally, the theme of deliberate abandonment exists within many areas of traditional maritime archaeology. These include examination of ships in antiquity, incorporating both the study of grave ships and boat graves deposited for funerary reuse throughout Northern Europe (Muller-Wille 1974:187) as well as vessels discarded as votive offerings (Christensen 1987:86,114). Other examples include the transformation of intact hulls into building foundations, reclamation devices, artificial reefs and buildings, and the reutilization of disarticulated timber remnants (Meiggs 1960:155; Delgado 1979:316–317; Reiss 1987:185–187; Marsden 1994; Lemee 1997; Arnold et al. 1998; McGrail 1998:41; O'Keefe 1999, 2001). This abridged list of case studies also illustrates that abandonment often entails the discard of ships for disposal as well as the discard of ships for subsequent use.

In Australia, a number of studies were carried out on both isolated and accumulated ship-discard sites. In contrast to the themes of abandonment elsewhere, these sites represent almost exclusively the theme of economic and technological obsolescence (Richards 2003a: 13–21 for a comprehensive list of Australian studies). All of these studies can be linked to the pioneering work of Michael McCarthy, who was the first to carry out the examination of a deliberately discarded watercraft (the ex-whaler *Day Dawn*) and a ships' graveyard (the Jervoise Bay Ships' Graveyard) from the mid-1970s (McCarthy 1979a, 1979b, 1980, 1983a, 1983b). McCarthy was also the first to acknowledge the untapped potential and need to record the resource for future research (McCarthy 1983a:291). The work pioneered by McCarthy influenced two interrelated projects commenced at Flinders University in the late 1990s: the Garden Island Ships' Graveyard Project, focused on a collection of abandoned vessels in Port Adelaide, South Australia, and the nationally focused Abandoned Ships' Project, which emerged from the theoretical and methodological lessons of the Garden Island project. With few exceptions, these two projects are a departure from previous studies of discarded and abandoned watercraft because of the importance that they place on the act of discard as a source for analysis and discussion.

Garden Island Ships' Graveyard Project, 1997–1999

In 1996, author Mark Staniforth of the Department of Archaeology at Flinders University began using the vessels at the Garden Island Ships' Graveyard as a component of undergraduate training for a range of archaeology topics. Over the ensuing years, students produced a number of vessel inspection reports on a large number of sites (on file at the Department of Archaeology at Flinders University). Since 1997 Garden Island was also the subject of a number of honors and postgraduate student dissertations (Richards 1997, 2002; Matthews 1998). This same year, researchers created the Garden Island Ships' Graveyard project, a heading subsuming all of the aforementioned individual investigations of the site.

The Garden Island Ships' Graveyard in South Australia is the state's most documented, investigated, and material-rich watercraft abandonment area. The first investigations of this site began with the study of one of the vessels in this ships' graveyard, the iron barque *Santiago* (Figure 1). This vessel is the most prominent abandoned ship and the only legislatively protected abandoned watercraft in South Australia

FIGURE 1. Remains of the *Santiago* in the Garden Island Ships' Graveyard, Port Adelaide, South Australia. (Photo by N. Richards.)

(Jeffery 1979:24, 1983:84–85; Department of Environment and Planning 1983:7; Marfleet 1988:55; Kentish 1995). *Santiago* has attracted attention for many years due to its unique technical details and status as an early iron sailing ship (built in 1856). It is reputed to be the earliest example of a restorable iron sailing ship (Brouwer 1999:33). In the late 1980s and early 1990s, the Society for Underwater Historical Research published reports on Garden Island that focused on the identification of individual watercraft and an examination of their methods of construction (Brown 1989a, 1989b, 1989c, 1990a, 1990b; Samuels 1989; Christopher 1990). Later, coauthor Nathan Richards (1997, 1998, 1999b) investigated the archaeological and comparative nature of the site, concentrating on a range of site formation issues, and suggested that a more comprehensive interpretation of vessel discard and maritime refuse areas could be elucidated through an approach that went beyond the examination of individual ship histories. This suggested that there may be ways of using primary source historical documentation to examine and expose cultural transformation processes of a maritime nature, and that ship abandonment areas are some of the best sites to communicate cultural site formation. Richards endorsed a broad comparative and anthropologically oriented approach as a way to uncover and better understand behavioral and cultural aspects of maritime sites. Following the conclusion of the Garden Island Ships' Graveyard project, the authors established a new project with expanded scope and objectives called the Abandoned Ships' Project.

Abandoned Ships' Project, 1999–2003

The Abandoned Ships' Project (ASP) arose from the understanding that abandoned watercraft had not been a major focus of maritime archaeological research. The authors established it as a comparative, nondisturbance analysis of discarded watercraft, intended to shed light on the many aspects of history that caused their discard. Additionally the project would examine the cultural forces that have changed the face of discard over time and investigate how these changes are a reflection of cultural behavior. Pivotal to all of these assumptions and positions was the conscious re-evaluation of what ships represent.

Watercraft have been seen by many historical and archaeological researchers as objects or "artifacts" imbued with rich ethnic, cognitive, hierarchical, and technological traits (Throckmorton 1970:31–32, 1987:211; Muckelroy 1978; Shomette 1995:6–7; Valdaliso 1996:95; Lenihan and Murphy 1998:235; Gibbins and Adams 2001:281; Martin 2001:393). McCarthy (1996:22) has asserted that ships are not simply monochronic units but are objects sensitive to cultural conditions and cultural transformations and have traits that illustrate their diachronic nature. This is as much the case for wrecked watercraft as it is for abandoned ones. Indeed, just as researchers like Patty Jo Watson (1983:31) and Daniel Lenihan (1983:63) talk about the potential empirical, anthropological, idiographic, and nomothetic studies that may emerge from the "extraordinary database" of shipwrecks, the authors contend that this potential also exists for the study of abandoned watercraft.

Furthermore, abandoned vessels have much potential for the development of nomothetic and comparative approaches to maritime archaeological materials that have potential to open maritime archaeological research up to new perspectives. Larry Murphy (1983:84) noted, "[t]he shift from considering ships as discrete time capsules to viewing them as integral aspects of a larger parent culture can produce methodological and theoretical developments heretofore not readily apparent." He has also stated (Murphy 1983:67), "Shipwrecks can properly contribute much to the study of human behavior in many areas, and the only limits are imposed by the nature and scope of the questions developed by researchers."

ASP aimed to assemble another "extraordinary database." The basis for the project was the premise that much can be learned from abandoned watercraft if they are considered as complex, composite artifacts representative of the changing designs and technologies of ship construction that can allude to or explain certain trends in economies and technologies. This view perceives the resources as allowing researchers to clearly gauge the effect of economic or historical change and better understand certain incidental changes that had wide repercussions in legislative and bureaucratic aspects of communities around the world.

ASP also took into consideration the discard behaviors and other cultural processes that contributed to the spatial patterning of dumping areas; the historical, economic, and technological causes of abandonment; and the archaeological signatures of such events and activities. Its aim was to show the remains of discarded vessels as significant cultural resources that have the potential to illuminate aspects of the past that other kinds of cultural resources cannot. In particular, this project planned to illustrate that when archaeologists use appropriate comparative methods, the importance and archaeological potential of many aspects of hitherto undervalued maritime heritage may have considerable light shed on them.

To some degree the theoretical framework and methods of analysis outlined by ASP were also a challenge to the traditional theoretical orientation of maritime archaeology in Australia, which (much like the rest of the world) has tended to be "historical particularist" (Green 1990:235; Veth and McCarthy 1999:12; McCarthy 2000: 1,191–192), lacking what Staniforth (2000:90) has termed "theoretical sophistication." While the authors acknowledge historical particularism as having an important place in maritime archaeology, they are also of the opinion that there is a need to be more open to other approaches. Although the researchers consider this theoretical expansion particularly important in the study of watercraft abandonment, they also believe that this is true of maritime archaeology generally. In particular, a broadened thematic basis to studies is needed as well as increased attention to the comparative aspects of research. Arguably, a continued adherence to historical particularist approaches will not facilitate such expansion. The third stage in the "3-stage approach" advocated by Lawrence Babits and Hans Van Tilburg (1998:2) reflects this need for a movement towards comparative analysis where sites must be "presented within interdisciplinary and regional, if not global, perspectives to allow determinations of importance and provide better understanding of each individual site." This research is also a response to the views of researchers (Veth and McCarthy 1999:12; McCarthy 2000:1; Martin 2001) who endorse the "de-particularizing of the particular" and the increased integration of generalizing approaches into all kinds of archaeological research. In this way, the investigation was also a part of the movement towards regional and generalist

analyses undertaken by Australian researchers since the late 1980s, beginning with the work of Leonie Foster (1987, 1988, 1989, 1990) and expanded by other Australian researchers (Jeffery 1989, 1992; Coroneos 1991, 1997; Jordan 1995; Kenderdine 1995; Coroneos and McKinnon 1997). While it may be true that behaviorally focused, anthropological studies have been relatively scarce in Australian maritime archaeology, this has begun to change relatively recently, as demonstrated by the work of researchers such as McCarthy (1996), Staniforth (1997, 2003), Richards (1997, 2002, 2003a, 2003b, 2004), Rebecca O'Reilly (1999), Coleman Doyle (2000), and Bradley Duncan (2000). These studies are good examples of the evolution and development of new theoretical and methodological tools in Australian maritime archaeology and represent an "opening up" towards comparative approaches.

Nevertheless, some studies fundamentally have not moved beyond small-scale regional settings concerning the nature of shipwreck remains to wider geographical and thematic environments. In Australia, as elsewhere, the resistance to pursue comparative aspects of research is partly the result of the tendency to view individual shipwreck sites as isolated time capsules. Richard Gould (2000:13) commented, "The drama of a shipwreck focuses attention on the event, but the conditions that produced the wreck and the consequences arising from it are as significant as the event itself." This insight clarifies what Watson (1983:31) called the "perpetual tension between the idiographic (particularist) and nomothetic (generalist) approaches," which is also fundamentally a tension between the notion of the event and the notion of process.

The researchers confined the ASP study geographically within Australian jurisdictional boundaries and aimed to incorporate data from as many deliberately discarded vessels as possible. While there had been some attempts to compile lists of abandoned vessels previously in Australia (Stone and Loney 1983; Parsons and Plunkett 1995; Plunkett 2003), there was still limited historical literature dedicated to watercraft abandonment. Nevertheless, candidate selection occurred through historical research, in particular where documentary sources noted that a ship owner had discarded the vessel. A small number of candidates were also included

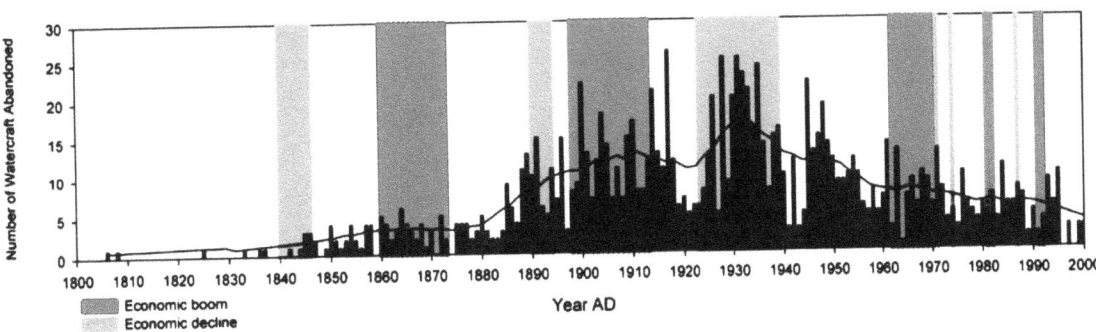

FIGURE 2. Watercraft abandoned in Australia 1800–2000 by number of watercraft (n=1,246 watercraft). (Drawing by N. Richards.)

after they were found in association with other abandoned watercraft (which often occurred when ships' graveyards were inspected). The discovery of vessels in the historical and archaeological records also defined the temporal extent of the study. The abandoned vessels ranged in date from 1806 to 2001 (the year of the earliest vessel abandoned and the final complete calendar year of the study) (Figure 2). The ships belonged to many functional categories, predominantly representing surface commercial craft (excluding aircraft) but also including large pleasure craft and military ships (including a small number of submarines). The database that emerged from archaeological and historical investigation became the Australian National Abandoned Vessel Database (ANAVD). At the conclusion of data collection in February 2002, the database comprised 6,082 individual primary and secondary historical sources collated from various research institutions in every state and territory of the nation. In all, researchers located information regarding 1,542 abandoned ships across Australia (Figure 3).

The archaeological component of the research concentrated on two areas: the location of ships' graveyards and vessel dumping sites and the investigation of the logistics of the abandonment act and salvage. The focus of the investigation was to visit as many vessels as possible, emphasizing sites that reflected the different types of abandonment uncovered by the historical research. In this way, researchers were able to inspect ships' graveyards and individual abandonment sites as well as investigate sites that reflected distinctive post-abandonment uses. Likewise, wide varieties of environmental

conditions, ranging from deep water to intertidal sites, were a part of the survey. Researchers inspected sites by either diving on the archaeological remnants of watercraft or by accessing them at convenient tides if in an intertidal setting. In the case of beached vessels, inspection and survey occurred with a combination of wading, snorkeling, and diving. At all sites, written observations and photographs or site measurement and detailed site description

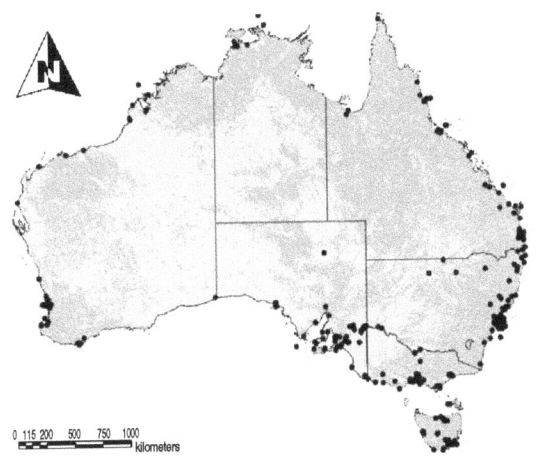

FIGURE 3. Map showing the distribution of abandoned watercraft in association with the Australian coastline and river systems. Circles denote locations of official Commonwealth dumping areas defined under the *Beaches, Fishing Ground and Sea Routes Protection Act*, 1932 (Commonwealth Government 1932). Spatial data is from a variety of sources; GPS locations from archaeological inspection, official nomenclature lists of places names, and scuttling locations known by government authorities (see also Richards 2002). (Drawing by N. Richards.)

were the predominant techniques for recording archaeological remains. All data were entered onto a two-page standardized form similar to that employed by Gustav Milne, Colin McKewan, and Damien Goodburn (1998) to record abandoned watercraft on the Medway River, United Kingdom. At the conclusion of the site-inspection phase of research, more than 120 separate beached and submerged abandoned watercraft had been visited (precise numbers are hard to determine due to the disarticulated nature of some remains).

The underlying theoretical precept represented by ASP is in line with the assertions of researchers such as Ian Hodder (1999) and Staniforth (1997, 1999, 2003). They have suggested that there are many ways of doing archaeology and that there is value in "diverse, complex and ambiguous" archaeological theory within the discipline (Staniforth 1997:159). Consequently, ASP used approaches and methods from many diverse theoretical perspectives. Other aspects of theory used in ASP included an examination of the technological paradigms that have predominated in archaeological theory (Trigger 1995:15) and maritime archaeology in particular (Basch 1972:9; Johnston 1996:231). Additionally, site formation theory as expounded by Michael Schiffer (1972, 1996; Schiffer et al. 1981) and Keith Muckelroy (1978) were central to site interpretation.

One of the main aims of ASP was to use the abandoned vessel resource to make a number of general statements about the degree of correlation among discarded vessels, historic events, and technological, economic, and social change. To do this, a process of extracting statistics from the completed database and testing them against the accepted view of the nature and effect of events and processes in Australian history was undertaken. These analyses were attempts to understand the interaction between national or regional events and archaeological phenomena in relation to highly specific Australian historical contexts. Researchers also used these analyses to question current views concerning the evolutionary nature of technological change. What follows is a synopsis of the major findings of ASP as represented in the four headings: (1) the discard trend and economic cycles, (2) abandonment and landscape, (3) the archaeological signatures of use, and (4) the archaeological signatures of discard.

Discard Trend and Economic Cycles

Maritime historical and archaeological literature has tended to examine the nature of redundancy and discard in a simplistic manner (Loney 1980:86, 1991:138). Normally it is simply noted that a vessel was abandoned because it had become "nail sick" (worn out), economically redundant, or technologically obsolete. Often the assertion that a ship owner has abandoned the vessel for any one of these reasons was sufficient not to warrant further investigation into the causes of its discard. An analysis of the discarded watercraft abandoned in Australia over time illustrates that there is a high degree of correlation between nationally significant economic and historic events and trends in the frequency of watercraft abandonment. Information on abandoned watercraft illustrates these processes since abandoned vessels were engaged in trade until they were no longer required, and catastrophic loss never artificially shortened their working lives. In effect, the use life of a ship is a representation of the health of the trade in which it was engaged. Owing to this, the tendency to discard watercraft (the discard trend) may correlate to historical events such as economic and technological change in a particular community, society, or nation.

Examination of general Australian economic trends over the period covered by this research illustrates that only a few events have had discernible influence on ship abandonment. There are four categories: periods of economic expansion, periods of economic decline, periods of war (a special economic event), and the aftermath of war with the transition into economic reconstruction. There also seems to be significant regional variation in the discard trend caused by unique events and specific responses to national economic crises. For example, changes in ports (such as the addition and modification of port infrastructure) often acted as a source of change in the abandonment trend of regions due to the ramifications these actions had on regional economies. Other factors such as the growth of alternative networks of transportation (rail, road, and air) and communication led to downturns in maritime trade and increased discard events due to increased competition. Data show that environmental change and catastrophe (floods and fires) brought about no discernable change in the discard trend.

The discard trend is also conditioned by the effect of legislative and regulatory frameworks that either change the nature of ship use (changing the ability to use a particular kind of vessel for a longer or shorter period) or have direct ramifications on the protocols of abandoning watercraft. Such systems of cultural constraint, which are normally government controlled, change or multiply the stresses on ship owners in relation to the utilization of their vessels. An example of a *passive* system includes the adoption of strict vessel inspection regulations, which may shorten the use life of a vessel by increasing the costs associated with its use. Other forms include marine insurance clauses and international trade agreements that dictate what types or nationalities of vessels may operate in particular waters. *Active* controls, on the other hand, concern the protocols dictating discard itself, including "rules of salvage." From an archaeological perspective, such constraints have relevance to both pre- and postdepositional aspects of ship disposal. Constraints are primarily concerned with the location of abandonment areas and the treatment of remains before reaching the discard location, as well as with dictating the appropriate treatment of structural remains after abandonment. They are also intimately associated with controlling salvage and ownership rights and responsibilities. In Australia the first national legislation to control the dumping of watercraft in the Australian waters under Federal jurisdiction was the Commonwealth *Beaches, Fishing Ground and Sea Routes Protection Act 1932* (Commonwealth Government 1932). This legislation would control the discard of watercraft in Australian waters until the late-20th century when issues relating to environmental hazards led to the formulation of legislation to control all kinds of sea dumping. Some states also enacted legislation to control the dumping of watercraft within state jurisdiction.

Abandonment and Landscape

Such legislation and regulation illustrates the connection between discarded objects, the perception of the ocean as a dumping ground of infinite capacity, and the human awareness of landscape. The deliberate abandonment of watercraft revolves around a singular and funda-

mentally important point: an abandoned vessel should never be a navigation hazard. For this reason, ship-disposal areas are usually located peripheral to shipping to ensure that there are no navigation hazards that would impede commercial activities. In this regard, the location of ship-disposal areas occurs because of a socially organized use of space that is comparable to deciphering the human patterning of the landscape in other archaeological studies (Portnoy 1981:213; Rathje 1981:52). Ships' graveyard sites occur in very shallow, unused areas or in very deep water. Due to high transport costs, deep-water scuttling areas were only successful when they were not too far away from the main port. In the age of steam, high costs were associated with the use of steam tugs to move vessels out to sea for scuttling. The dangers and costs associated with the abandonment of vessels at sea would increase with distance. All of these factors mean that there is a large degree of predictability in the location of abandonment areas in relation to major ports. On a broader level, ships' graveyards occur at places where there is a concentration of watercraft-based commercial activities in a particular port (an exception to this is military weapons testing against target ships in areas distant from civilian populations). In inner harbor environs, ships' graveyards generally occur in disused or "abandoned" stretches of waterway.

Other factors are also evident in the location of discarded watercraft. First, the locations of major areas of ship discard (including ships' graveyards) tend to congregate adjacent to main or premier ports. These ports are the places where trades change, where people introduce and test technologies, and where unwanted, unused, or unsuitable vessels are laid up. With the exception of military or recreational vessels, abandonment at these locations relates to the concentration of trade at major ports and the fact that major ports were more likely to have remnant trade opportunities in times of economic depression or recession. Abandonment areas can also correspond with certain inner harbor functions. Examples from the historical literature suggest a link between areas of ship breaking (areas that often coincide with dumping areas) and shipbuilding. Additionally, the increased centralization of shipbuilding resources and facilities over time mirrors the increased centralization of ships' graveyard locations. Approximately 30% of the Australian discard resource exists in ships' graveyards. These dense accumulations of what is often a diverse cross-section of vessel types are particularly suited to the examination of the archaeological signatures of use and discard.

Archaeological Signatures of Use

As with shipwrecks, the archaeological remnants of vessel function and proof of vessel function transformation are often evident on abandoned watercraft. All are indicators of change in the behaviors of those who utilized the vessels. As archaeological signatures, researchers can distinguish site-formation processes related to the use, modification, and discard of these vessels. Use and modification processes are important because they have direct influences on discard processes and influence the time and nature of the transformation of a vessel from an operational to an archaeological context. In cases of deliberate abandonment, use has many meanings. In the first instance, the design and construction of a vessel is a signature of intended function as well as evidence of consumer choice in ship purchasing. It is a representation of the adherence or resistance to technological norms. Next, indications of the modification of a vessel's design or construction as seen in the archaeological remains of watercraft are indications of changing technological and economic situations and the reuse processes that accompany them. In some cases, the indications of functional post-abandonment uses are evident. All of these stages in the evolution of an individual vessel's life are significant because they can shed light on economic conditions at the time as well as the reasons behind the vessel's discard. The stages are also important because the types of technologies represented at the time of a vessel's construction have a direct influence on the inclination for certain vessels to be discarded or be utilized for post-abandonment functions (adaptive reuse).

Modifications of many varieties occur to watercraft. The main types of modification are those made to the method of propulsion and to hull dimensions or materials. These alterations will normally bring about a change from a primary (original) to secondary (subsequent) mercantile context (use). Since modifications occur to watercraft when their owner wants a vessel to continue to operate within a trade, or to enable its transfer to a new trade, it is implicit that there are correlations between modification activities and fluctuations in abandonment trends. The modification of a vessel to make it more suitable or commercially competitive is a mechanism designed to save a ship from being discarded (it is in effect a *curation behavior*). For example, there is often a correlation between the modification of the hull of a vessel and the addition and modification to its propulsion. Modifications to propulsion normally serve the purpose of technological augmentation or "upgrade" of a propulsion system to a new, more efficient type that will delay the replacement of the entire vessel. Where a conversion from one use, or from one source of propulsion, to another occurs, the term *retrofit* is more appropriate. This term distinguishes types of conversion and more adequately resembles the process of adaptation in vessels that are undergoing modification to suit the economic climate or new technological developments. Propulsion modification processes are largely a reaction to the introduction of new technologies, especially ones that threaten to overtake and replace old vessel types (for example when a sail vessel undergoes conversion into a steamship).

A comparison of the earliest configuration of ANAVD vessels and their final configuration indicates that only around 3.4% underwent changes to their propulsion system. Of these, most changes occurred to unassisted sailing vessels, followed by side-wheel paddle steamers and single-screw steamships. This is not surprising considering that newer technologies replaced all of these propulsion systems at some time and that these three categories are the most statistically dominant propulsion types in the ANAVD (about 65% of the entire database). If each transition in propulsion systems is examined, it appears that change occurred to particular methods of propulsion over other ones. One other interesting observation is that in some cases, when these changes are compared to the accepted histories of technological change, ship owners appear to be taking retrograde technological steps (Table 1). When the types of activities that these changes represent

TABLE 1
INDIVIDUAL CHANGES TO PROPULSION TYPES IN ANAVD VESSELS
WITH MODIFICATIONS MADE TO THEIR METHOD OF PROPULSION

Original Propulsion	Final Propulsion	Number.	%
Sail (unassisted)	Sail (auxiliary motor)	11	58%
	Steam (single screw)	4	21%
	Sail (auxiliary steam)	2	11%
	Motor (single screw)	1	5%
	Motor (twin screw)	1	5%
Paddle (side-wheel)	Steam (single screw)	5	36%
	Paddle (stern wheel)	3	22%
	Steam (twin screw)	2	14%
	Sail (unassisted)	2	14%
	Sail (auxiliary motor)	2	14%
Steam (single screw)	Motor (single screw)	4	50%
	Sail (unassisted)	2	25%
	Sail (auxiliary steam)	1	12.5%
	Paddle (stern wheel)	1	12.5%
Paddle (stern wheel)	Paddle (side wheel)	5	83%
	Steam (single screw)	1	17%
Steam (twin screw)	**Paddle (side wheel)**	1	50%
	Motor (single screw)	1	50%
Sail (auxiliary motor)	**Sail (unassisted)**	1	50%
	Motor (twin screw)	1	50%
Motor (single screw)	**Steam (single screw)**	2	100%

Note: Bolded items indicate retrograde propulsion amendments; values rounded up to nearest half-percent (n=53).

are considered, hypotheses can be made about the possible economic causes and repercussions. Such modifications, for instance, may represent technological augmentation emerging from economic issues related to fuel costs, fuel efficiency, or changes in trade profitability. For example, some early motor vessels, operating on a benzene fuel, were converted to steam power because of the prohibitive costs of fuel and poor fuel availability.

Modifications to a ship's hull chiefly concern changes to its dimensions and hull material. An analysis of ANAVD shows that historical references to changing the material of a vessel's hull (for example, a change from a wooden to an iron hull) are very rare (under 0.5% of cases). Instead, the modifications of ships' hulls normally constitute an extension (expansion) or contraction (reduction) of their dimensions and tonnage. ANAVD statistics suggest that an increase to a vessel's length with no change to breadth or depth dimension was the most common modification made to deliberately discarded watercraft. Where changes to the breadth of a vessel where made, substantial changes to its depth dimension normally occurred also. Arguably, this suggests that ship owners do not modify their watercraft for the purposes of increasing their capacity to carry more goods or transport more passengers but to modify them for other purposes. Potentially these modifications may occur due to a change in trade that requires a vessel's operation in a new location with certain environmental constraints or may indicate that modifications occur to increase efficiency.

These alterations also have consequences on the duration of use of a vessel. In relation to the use life of abandoned watercraft, the data suggest that modified vessels lasted 9 to 10 years longer than unmodified craft. This substantial cost saving for ship owners is further compounded if many vessels were "hulked" or converted following the completion of their mercantile career for reutilization in support functions (for example as a repository for goods and cargo or as a hull that would be towed). The conversion of a vessel to a support role occurred for a range of economic reasons. Normally a vessel had become unwanted because of its condition and age (tied to an inability to gain marine insurance) or its representation of an old technology that was no longer economical to run. In other cases, it may be because a particular trade disappeared or ceased to be viable. For a ship owner to transform the vessel into a hulk, there needed to be a demand for the fulfillment of such a role, and

the ship needed to be of an appropriate type for this new function. For example, wooden hulls were not preferred as gunpowder hulks (vessels used for storing gunpowder) because TNT sweats nitroglycerine that may soak into timbers and increase the likelihood of explosion (Richards 2002:292).

The demands for hulked vessels varied over time and were themselves related to economic and technological issues. Where demand for hulks was very high, shipbuilders would build vessels to fulfill these specific functions. For instance, the use of hulks was at its highest during the age of the coal-fired steamer, where coal hulks were used to "bunker" or store coal for use. With the growth and popularity of the oil-fired and diesel-powered vessel, the need for such bunkering facilities ceased, thus causing a new wave of discard to occur (Stone and Loney 1983:9; Cairns and Henderson 1995:179).

In other cases vessels were used for special support roles and may have had new and non-traditional functions assigned to them. A short list of examples includes residences, bathhouses,

FIGURE 4. An example of the functional post-abandonment utilization of unwanted watercraft, the Tangalooma Ships' Graveyard and breakwater, Moreton Island, Queensland. (Photo by N. Richards.)

bridges, and breakwaters (Richards and May 2003) (Figure 4). The hulking of a vessel had substantial economic ramifications for a ship owner. While a ship owner may have preferred the vessel to be in use forever, this was not likely. The next preference was to use a vessel for some purpose other than its original function, providing it with a very long lifespan. The analysis of the ANAVD illustrated that the economic advantages to hulking a vessel were substantial, adding up to 12 years to the time that a vessel could be used (Figure 5). This

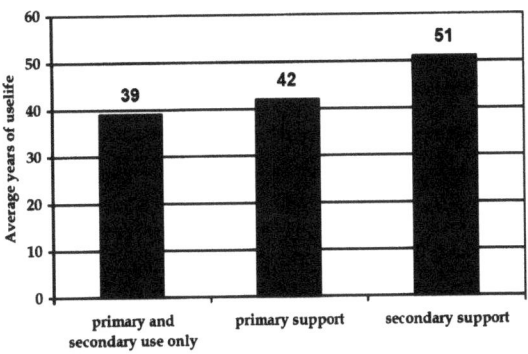

FIGURE 5. The average lifespan of un-hulked and hulked watercraft (rounded to nearest whole number; n=1,059 watercraft). (Drawing by N. Richards.)

is even more significant when considering that many authors contend that the average lifespan of a vessel is only around 20 years. These figures confirm those presented by Richards (1997: 110) regarding the average age of abandoned

vessels in the Garden Island Ships' Graveyard. Additionally, a diachronic analysis shows that across time, and despite technological innovation, watercraft use life decreased drastically between 1790 and 1990 (Figure 6). This trend may indicate the influence of the steam engine in replacing sail vessels in the early-19th century and the replacement of steam technologies in the 1920s and 1930s, which brought about the replacement of coal-bunkering support vessels (coal hulks) as did the transition towards the mass production of watercraft and the increasing perception of ships as throwaway items with limited use-by dates.

Archaeological Signatures of Discard

As with the use of vessels, the discard of watercraft leaves behind unique archaeological signatures, categorized as (1) structural remains that can be generally intact, (2) the absence of rigging and other evidence of propulsion, and (3) a scarcity of portable material culture (if not artifact sterility). Generally, watercraft are not designed to be easily dismantled and are not constructed to be deconstructed. Their very nature reflects the human desire to create improved tools of commerce. A shipbuilder imbues a ship with certain abilities that make it a difficult object to disassemble or destroy, and for this reason, it is both a hardy and an expensive item. A large part of the destruction of a ship involves the dismantling and salvage of a vessel, whether it is to be scuttled, beached, or demolished.

It is clear from historical sources in Australia and abroad that certain processes in the

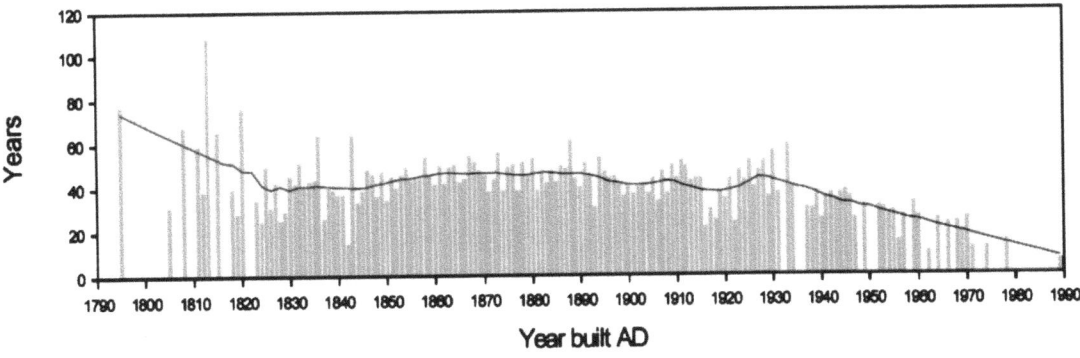

FIGURE 6. The average lifespan of abandoned watercraft, 1790–1990 (n=1,059 watercraft). (Drawing by N. Richards.)

deliberate abandonment of watercraft illuminate the psychology of disposal. While such processes can tell us much about how a ship-breaker may perceive a vessel's hull, it can also outline some of the archaeological signatures that the archaeologist may find on sites in the form of marks and modifications on the ships' hulls. All marks and modifications from the actions taken leading up to and after a dumping event have some relation to the location of disposal and to the processing of the unwanted hull. These processes also relate to the most practical way of disposing unwanted vessel remains and shed light on the technology and economics of disposal and the socio-economics of those people carrying out such activities. Moreover, transitions in the methods of vessel disposal give insight into the economic health of regions and nations, showing to what degree the technology used in dismantling a vessel follows the technology used in its initial manufacture.

An important aspect of the logistics associated with the abandonment of unwanted vessels comes in the form of *harm minimization*. In an abandonment context, harm minimization takes the form of the systematic destruction of a vessel via a series of processes that allow for the reduction of the hull to its smallest size, as dictated by technological, temporal, economic, and environmental constraints. *Structure minimization* or *hull reduction* are the terms used for this process, referring to the strategies of systematic reduction that are required when authorities deem vessels a threat to navigation. When it came to the abandonment of ships, port authorities invariably believed the more a ship's hull was minimized, the less potential harm it could do to other vessels. Ship owners engaging in this activity ultimately had to look on such activity as a precautionary measure for minimizing future potential costs because of their unwanted vessels doing damage to other people's property. This aspect of vessel abandonment also serves to highlight a range of problems for ship owners. On one level, harm minimization is required to enable the safe abandonment of a vessel and ensure that there are no ongoing costs in the control of vessel remains. On another level, the costs associated with harm minimization strategies can be substantial. Every aspect of abandonment is economically driven and has economic consequences.

A number of well-documented hull-reduction techniques are described in the historical and archaeological literature, such as setting a vessel on fire (Figure 7) or diminishing a vessel via salvage and scrapping (McCarthy 1983b:361; Shomette 1996:247–252). Salvage can take the form of pre- and postdepositional salvage. This distinction is an important one since they are indicative of different behaviors, and both types can theoretically be detected in different forms in the archaeological record. Vessel salvage is not simple or straightforward, and the dismantling of watercraft is often as technologically dependant as vessel construction. In many cases, ship owners undertake hull-reduction strategies in order to defray the costs of disposal or to make money from disposal when scrap or ship-fitting prices are high.

This study suggests that there are three main phases in the salvage of abandoned vessel remains: *primary salvage* (predepositional), where salvage occurs before final deposition or abandonment; *secondary salvage* (first-stage postdepositional), where salvage occurs soon after final discard; and *tertiary salvage* (second-stage postdepositional), where salvage occurs intermittently and opportunistically through time after abandonment. Many times, a vessel may not go through all three phases. In situations where

FIGURE 7. The remains of the Norwegian barque *Margaret* burning, Albany, Western Australia. (Courtesy of the Department of Maritime Archaeology, Western Australian Maritime Museum, Richard McKenna Collection, Fremantle, Western Australia.)

the appropriate infrastructure for ship breaking is lacking, very little or no primary salvage activity will occur, and people may discard the vessel relatively uninjured. Likewise, a ship-breaker may undertake substantial primary salvage activities, cease further demolition of the hull, and subsequently leave it alone after discard.

While on most discarded ship hulls it is obvious that some type of salvage has occurred, often evidence of predepositional salvage will not be detectable because postdepositional salvage activities will remove any evidence of the activity. In other cases, evidence of predepositional salvage may not be clear because it has become confused with phases of postdepositional salvage. Indeed, the line between pre- and postdepositional salvage, from an archaeological perspective, is blurred. Since salvagers often need to keep a vessel in a floating condition in order to get it to a final resting place (move it from ship-breaking yard to ships' graveyard), the only evidence of postdepositional salvage may be the absence of material from areas crucial in maintaining vessel flotation. In this way, postdepositional salvage activities are noticeable where ship-breakers have removed structural material

from below the turn of the ship's bilge, towards its keel and garboard strake (lowest section of outer plating or planking), so that the vessel can no longer float. This is illustrated in case of the steamer *Grace Darling* where photographs show major differences in the vessel following its abandonment in 1931 (Figure 8) and also in 1997 (Figure 9). Whereas the first clearly illustrates the sections of hull removed by ship-breakers at another location before the discard of the vessel (primary salvage), the second shows the effect of subsequent (secondary and tertiary) salvage activities undertaken on the ship. In its final salvaged form, the vessel retains no characteristics of flotation.

Hull-reduction strategies can also be a form of *placement assurance*, a term referring to the strategies used to ensure that a discarded vessel remains discarded. The scuttling or sinking of vessels at sea has often been the preferred option for the disposal of watercraft. This has traditionally been because of a desire not to litter the coastline with old wrecks and the "out of sight, out of mind" mentality that has predominated in human sea-dumping activities. Whether someone has scuttled or beached

FIGURE 8. Remains of the *Grace Darling* ca. 1931 showing evidence of predepositional salvage. Its intact nature shows the degree to which the hull was dismantled by ship-breakers before its final movement to the Garden Island Ships' Graveyard. (Courtesy of the South Australian Maritime Museum, Port Adelaide, South Australia.)

FIGURE 9. Remains of the *Grace Darling* showing evidence of postdepositional salvage. The vessel has been salvaged to the point that it may no longer float, indicating the degree to which postdepositional dismantling of the hull has occurred. (Photo by N. Richards.)

Whereas an insurance payout may compensate the owner of a shipwreck (thereby transferring ownership to the underwriter), there is usually no agency that would seek to own an unwanted vessel, unless promised substantial rewards and returns from its salvage (the one exception being "state-owned" vessels). From this perspective, although owners may salvage or abandon a vessel, they are still ultimately responsible for the remains of a vessel, despite its condition and whether they want it or not. In some cases, owners may want to retain the ship if there are post-abandonment uses or if they have subsequent plans for dismantling. In order to dispose of such a vessel owners need to ensure that the vessel will not cause monetary loss by floating off or moving and causing damage to other ships or port structures. This placement assurance, in its multiple forms, exists in two categories: the appropriate treatment of the hull and the choice of an appropriate environment for discard.

Obviously, the easiest method of breaching a vessel in order to inundate a hull is to open it to the sea. Predominantly, the use of explosives is the most common method of doing this (as shown in Figure 10). Likewise, historical literature and archaeological evidence attest to the filling of a salvaged hull with material to add weight. This will work against any residual buoyancy the salvaged and breached hull may retain. Rocks, cement, and gravel were just some of the mate-

a ship, the issue of placement assurance is an important one, especially in an examination of the cultural aspects of site formation. The methods used in ensuring the appropriate abandonment of a vessel, whether it relates to the burning, salvage of materials, or hull perforation activities will leave certain archaeological signatures behind that will enable interpretations to be made on other sites less adequately described in historical sources. This has been a neglected area within maritime archaeology, although most archaeologists would take it for granted that such a process occurs.

In Australia, placement assurance has always been an issue when abandoning a vessel because of the legalities of ownership. In this case, the ownership of an abandoned vessel is much the same as that of a shipwreck because an owner can only extinguish his or her title through sale.

FIGURE 10. Exploded metal plates in the bow of *Garthneill*, Garden Island, Port Adelaide, South Australia. This shows an example of hull-perforation activities concerned with placement assurance. (Photo by M. Staniforth, courtesy of Flinders University.)

rials used to fill abandoned watercraft. Wooden piles are also often associated with abandoned vessels either to delineate disposal areas (ensuring safe navigation, and "penning" ships in), as the remnants of structures once designed to assist with salvage activities, or to pin the ship to the underlying substrate (Figure 11). Additionally the appropriate environment of abandonment is a crucial factor in ensuring the placement assurance of beached vessels. Certain environmental conditions may also adversely affect particular hull-treatment procedures. At beached abandonment locations, ship-breakers who did not thoroughly breach a discarded hull (with explosives or some other procedure) or who do not adequately weigh it down may see it move or eventually float away. Two environmental factors, substrate (which may or may not fasten a ship in position) and tide (which may or may not lift a ship from its position), play important roles in determining how much time, effort, and foresight are required to ensure that there will be no complications following abandonment. The method of beaching and the speed and orientation at which the vessel has been beached may also negate or accentuate the effects of substrate or tidal fluctuation.

Conclusion

Shipbuilders construct watercraft to particular technological standards within the economic parameters dictated by a potential ship owner. Standards exist within a flux of diverse, changing conditions that see watercraft pass through an array of systemic, techno-economic reassignments. As tools of commerce, vessels invariably come to their end within a causal and behavioral spectrum—at one end, catastrophically lost and, at the other, deliberately discarded. This research has suggested that discarded vessels require different theoretical models than shipwrecks, since catastrophe plays no role in making them a part of the archaeological record. The array of decision-making processes that structures the abandonment makes these vessels, more than shipwrecks, reflections of changing techno-economic circumstances.

FIGURE 11. An example of a placement assurance technique as seen in the remains of *Jupiter,* Mutton Cove, Port Adelaide, South Australia, showing a wooden pile driven through the bow of the vessel. (Photo by N. Richards.)

For this reason, discarded watercraft are mirrors to the events and processes that bring about their disposal, and they provide an extremely rich database for shedding light on the effect of technological and economic change on economic and social circumstances (Richards 2003a, 2003b, 2004). The analytic potential of abandoned watercraft relate to how researchers use discard behaviors to inform their views of the archaeological formation process. On one level, discard is seen as a process with a myriad of interconnected causes and, on another, discard is seen as an event that culminates in a number of consequences for the use and reuse of watercraft.

This project has also suggested that the signatures of use and discard have major temporal components. The placement assurance, hull reduction, and salvage mechanisms that are detectable in an examination of archaeological remains are often as technologically dependant as the processes of ship construction. Although this research does not assert that the abandoned watercraft resource is as good a representation of technological innovation as the shipwreck resource is, these findings do indicate that watercraft abandonment is an excellent indicator of technological change. The small numbers of vessels that have undergone major technological transformations through their use-life reflect this. Certain processes that act upon watercraft while in a systemic context, such as conversion and modification activities, have a direct influence on their passing into an archaeological context by artificially extending their use-life. In this way, certain technologies are "flexible" in that they are more open to functional renovation and use-life extension.

Indeed, the fate of all of the abandoned vessels mentioned here is the direct consequence of the types of vessels that they were. Whether in the context of changing economic or technological circumstances, at their most fundamental level they are a reflection of choice. Moreover, as the embodiment of human decision-making processes, they are reflections of the consequences of economic, historical, and technological pressures. By considering the interaction between vessel design (a reflection of technological and economic development and change) and particular historical contexts (itself a reflection of these same processes),

these discard sites have the potential to reveal the human response to the events and processes of human history.

Understanding the history of deliberate watercraft abandonment does much to encourage appreciation of the potential of this understudied resource. Looking at this history through the lens of archaeological theory, transitions are clearly seen in discard activities and in the formation of archaeological sites as guided by shifts in human behavioral responses to economic and technological change. Moreover, it becomes clearer that a high level of continuity exists within the political, technological, and economic causes and consequences of such discard behavior in relation to old, obsolete, or unwanted watercraft. Unwanted ships are not just abandoned; their owners abandon them for any number of reasons that tell much about the people who used them. As has been demonstrated, the benefit of archaeological methods and assumptions, coupled with the wealth of historical literature on the Australian experiences of deliberate vessel abandonment, serves to confirm the potential of this resource. The authors also ask the question: if we can extract meaningful data from such an innocuous archaeological resource through a combination of applied theory and comparative methodology, what research potential exists for many other kinds of maritime archaeological sites?

Acknowledgments

The authors would like to thank all of the staff and students at Flinders University who participated in the fieldwork component of the Abandoned Ships' Project. A Small Grant from the Australian Research Council in 2000 and a Flinders University Small Grant in 2001 funded the Abandoned Ships' Project.

References

ARNOLD, J. BARTO III, JENNIFER L. GOLOBOY, ANDREW W. HALL, REBECCA A. HALL, AND J. DALE SHIVELY
    1998   *Texas Liberty Ships: From World War II Working-Class Heroes to Artificial Reefs.* Texas Parks and Wildlife, Austin, TX.

BABITS, LAWRENCE E., AND HANS VAN TILBURG
1998 Introduction. In *Maritime Archaeology: A Reader of Substantive and Theoretical Contributions*, Lawrence E. Babits and Hans Van Tilburg, editors, pp. 1–3. Plenum Press, New York, NY.

BASCH, LUCIEN
1972 Ancient Wrecks and the Archaeology of Ships. *The International Journal of Nautical Archaeology and Underwater Exploration* 1:1–58.

BROUWER, NORMAN J.
1999 *The International Register of Historic Ships.* Sea History Press, Peekskill, NY.

BROWN, ADRIAN
1989a And Cedric Saw You!: At the North Arm, Port River. *Soundings: The Newsletter of the Society for Underwater Historical Research Inc.*, November: 9–13.
1989b Graveyard Tour. *Soundings: The Newsletter of the Society for Underwater Historical Research Inc.*, August:3–7.
1989c The Ships Graveyard. *Soundings: The Newsletter of the Society for Underwater Historical Research Inc.*, April:22–26.
1990a The North Arm Graveyard. *Soundings: The Newsletter of the Society for Underwater Historical Research Inc.*, February:13–21.
1990b North Arm Graveyard Visit: 18th February. *Soundings: The Newsletter of the Society for Underwater Historical Research Inc.*, April:7–10.

CAIRNS, LYNNE, AND GRAEME HENDERSON
1995 *Unfinished Voyages: Western Australian Shipwrecks 1881–1900.* University of Western Australia Press, Nedlands.

CHRISTENSEN, ARNE EMIL
1987 *Guide to the Viking Ship Museum.* Universitetets Oldsaksamling, Oslo, Norway.

CHRISTOPHER, PETER
1990 *South Australian Shipwrecks: A Database.* Society for Underwater Historical Research, Adelaide, South Australia.

COMMONWEALTH GOVERNMENT
1932 *Beaches, Fishing Ground and Sea Routes Protection Act 1932.* Commonwealth Government, Australian Capital Territory, Canberra, Australia.

CORONEOS, COSMOS
1991 One Interpretation for the Short Working Lives of Early Australian Wooden Sailing Vessels in Victorian Waters. *The Bulletin of the Australian Institute for Maritime Archaeology* 15(2):7–14.
1997 *Shipwrecks of Encounter Bay and Backstairs Passage.* Australian Institute for Maritime Archaeology and Australian National Centre of Excellence for Maritime Archaeology, Adelaide, South Australia.

CORONEOS, COSMOS, AND ROBERT MCKINNON
1997 *Shipwrecks of Investigator Strait and the Lower Yorke Peninsula.* Australian Institute for Maritime Archaeology and Australian National Centre of Excellence for Maritime Archaeology, Adelaide, South Australia.

DELGADO, JAMES P.
1979 No Longer a Buoyant Ship: Unearthing the Gold Rush Storeship *Niantic*. *California History* 63(4): 316–325.

DEPARTMENT OF ENVIRONMENT AND PLANNING
1983 *Conserving Our Historic Shipwrecks.* Department of Environment and Planning, Adelaide, South Australia.

DOYLE, COLEMAN
2000 An Examination of Associations between Significant Historic Events and the Loss and Discard of Vessels in the Townsville Catchment, 1865–1981. Master's thesis, Department of Anthropology, Archaeology and Sociology, James Cook University, Townsville, Queensland, Australia.

DUNCAN, BRADLEY
2000 Signposts in the Sea: An Investigation of the Shipwreck Patterning and Cultural Seascapes of the Gippsland Region, Victoria. Honor's thesis, Department of Anthropology, Archaeology and Sociology, James Cook University, Townsville, Queensland, Australia.

FOSTER, LEONIE
1987 *Port Phillip Shipwrecks Stage 1: An Historical Survey.* Victoria Archaeological Survey, Melbourne, Victoria, Australia.
1988 *Port Phillip Shipwrecks Stage 2: An Historical Survey.* Victoria Archaeological Survey, Melbourne, Victoria, Australia.
1989 *Port Phillip Shipwrecks Stage 3: An Historical Survey.* Victoria Archaeological Survey, Melbourne, Victoria, Australia.
1990 *Port Phillip Shipwrecks Stage 4: An Historical Survey.* Victoria Archaeological Survey, Melbourne, Victoria, Australia.

GIBBINS, DAVID, AND JONATHAN ADAMS
2001 Shipwrecks and Maritime Archaeology. *World Archaeology* 32(3):279–291.

GOULD, RICHARD A.
2000 *Archaeology and the Social History of Ships.* Cambridge University Press, Cambridge, England.

GREEN, JEREMY N.
1990 *Maritime Archaeology: A Technical Handbook.* Academic Press, London, England.

HODDER, IAN
1999 *The Archaeological Process: An Introduction.* Blackwell Publishers, Oxford, England.

JEFFERY, WILLIAM

1979 Santiago. *Annual Report of the Society for Underwater Historical Research*, p. 24. Society for Underwater Historical Research, Adelaide, South Australia.

1983 The Development of Maritime Archaeology in South Australia. In *Proceedings of the Second Southern Hemisphere Conference on Maritime Archaeology*, William Jeffery and Jennifer Amess, editors, pp. 83–92. Department of Environment and Planning and the Commonwealth Department of Home Affairs and Environment, Adelaide, South Australia.

1989 Research into Australian-Built Coastal Vessels Wrecked in South Australia, 1840–1900. *The Bulletin of the Australian Institute for Maritime Archaeology* 13(2): 51–56.

1992 Maritime Archaeological Investigations into Australian-Built Vessels Wrecked in South Australia. *The International Journal of Nautical Archaeology and Underwater Exploration* 21(3):209–219.

JOHNSTON, PAUL F.

1996 The End of the Age of Sail: Merchant Shipping in the Nineteenth Century. In *Ships and Shipwrecks of the Americas: A History Based on Underwater Archaeology*, George F. Bass, editor, pp. 231–250. Thames and Hudson, London, England.

JORDAN, DEIRDRE J.

1995 *East Coast Shipwrecks: A Thematic Historical Survey.* Heritage Victoria, Melbourne, Victoria, Australia.

KENDERDINE, SARAH

1995 *Shipwrecks 1656–1942: A Guide to Historic Wrecksites of Perth.* Western Australian Maritime Museum, Fremantle, Western Australia.

KENTISH, PETER

1995 Stabilization of *Santiago.* University of South Australia Report, No. MET 1291, Part 1, Department of Environment and Natural Resources, Adelaide, South Australia.

LEMEE, CHRISTIAN

1997 A Ship Cemetery on the B&W Site in Christianshavn. *Maritime Archaeology Newsletter from Roskilde Denmark* 9(December):29–34.

LENIHAN, DANIEL J.

1983 Rethinking Shipwreck Archaeology: A History of Ideas and Considerations for New Directions. In *Shipwreck Anthropology*, Richard A. Gould, editor, pp. 37–89. University of New Mexico Press, Albuquerque.

LENIHAN, DANIEL J., AND LARRY E. MURPHY

1998 Considerations for Research Designs in Shipwreck Archaeology. In *Maritime Archaeology: A Reader of Substantive and Theoretical Contributions*, Lawrence E. Babits and Hans Van Tilburg, editors, pp. 233–239. Plenum Press, New York, NY.

LONEY, JACK K.

1980 *Jack Loney's Maritime Australia: Short Tales of Ships and Men.* Quadricolor, Melbourne, Victoria, Australia.

1991 *Australian Shipwrecks Update, Volume 5: 1622–1990.* Marine History Publications, Portarlington, Victoria, Australia.

MARFLEET, BRIAN

1988 Iron and Steam Shipwrecks in South Australia. In *Iron Ships and Steam Shipwrecks: Papers from the First Australian Seminar on the Management of Iron Vessels and Steam Shipwrecks,* Michael McCarthy, editor, pp. 55–58. Western Australian Maritime Museum, Fremantle, Western Australia.

MARSDEN, PETER

1994 *Ships of the Port of London: First to Eleventh Centuries.* English Heritage, London, England.

MARTIN, COLIN

2001 De-Particularizing the Particular: Approaches to the Investigation of Well-Documented Post-Medieval Shipwrecks. *World Archaeology* 32(3):383–399.

MATTHEWS, SHIRLEY

1998 The North Arm Ships' Graveyard, Port Adelaide, South Australia: Some Historical Perspectives of the Ships and Associated Maritime Activity and an Examination of the Artifact Assemblage. Honor's thesis, Department of Archaeology, Flinders University, Adelaide, South Australia.

MCCARTHY, MICHAEL

1979a *Jervoise Bay Shipwrecks.* Department of Maritime Archaeology, Western Australian Museum, Perth, Western Australia.

1979b The Jervoise Bay Study. *The Bulletin of the Australian Institute for Maritime Archaeology* 2(1):36–39.

1980 Industrial Development and the Jervoise Bay Wrecks. *Australian Maritime Archaeology Newsletter* 4: 28–32.

1983a Salvage Archaeology: A Case Study. In *Proceedings of the Second Southern Hemisphere Conference on Maritime Archaeology*, William Jeffery and Jennifer Amess, editors, pp. 283–291, Department of Environment and Planning and the Commonwealth Department of Home Affairs and Environment, Adelaide, South Australia.

1983b Shipwrecks in Jervoise Bay. *Records of the Western Australian Museum* 10(4): 335–373.

1996 *SS Xantho: Towards a New Perspective. An Integrated Approach to the Maritime Archaeology and Conservation of an Iron Steamship Wreck.* Doctoral dissertation, Department of Anthropology, Archaeology and Sociology, James Cook University, Townsville, Queensland, Australia.

2000 *Iron and Steamship Archaeology: Success and Failure on the SS Xantho.* Kluwer Academic/Plenum Publishers, New York, NY.

McGRAIL, SEAN
    1998 *Ancient Boats in North-West Europe: The Archaeology of Water Transport to AD 1500*. Addison Wesley Longman, New York, NY.

MEIGGS, RUSSELL
    1960 *Roman Ostia*. Oxford University Press, Oxford, England.

MILNE, GUSTAV, COLIN McKEWAN, AND DAMIEN GOODBURN
    1998 *Nautical Archaeology on the Foreshore: Hulk Recording on the Medway*. Royal Commission on the Historical Monuments of England, London.

MOORE, JONATHAN
    1995 The Boneyard below the Bridge. *Freshwater: A Journal of the Marine Museum of the Great Lakes of Kingston* 11(1–4):3–28.

MUCKELROY, KEITH W.
    1978 *Maritime Archaeology*. Cambridge University Press, London, England.

MULLER-WILLE, MICHAEL
    1974 Boat-Graves in Northern Europe. *The International Journal of Nautical Archaeology and Underwater Exploration* 3(2):187–204.

MURPHY, LARRY E.
    1983 Shipwrecks as a Data Base for Human Behavioral Studies. In *Shipwreck Anthropology*, Richard A. Gould, editor, pp. 65–90. University of New Mexico Press, Albuquerque.

O'KEEFE, MARY
    1999 The Shipwreck under the City: The *Inconstant*, Wellington, New Zealand. *The Bulletin of the Australian Institute for Maritime Archaeology* 23:121–125.
    2001 Looking at the Ship under the City: The *Inconstant* and the ICOMOS Cultural Tourism Charter. *The Bulletin of the Australian Institute for Maritime Archaeology* 25:109–111.

O'REILLY, REBECCA
    1999 An Assessment of Australian Built Wooden Sailing Vessels (Constructed between 1850–1899) Operating the South Australian Intrastate Trade: Methods and Materials. Honor's thesis, Department of Archaeology, Flinders University, Adelaide, South Australia.

PARSONS, RONALD H., AND GEOFF PLUNKETT
    1995 *Scuttled and Abandoned Ships in Australian Waters*. Ronald H. Parsons, Adelaide, South Australia.

PLUNKETT, GEOFF
    2003 *Sea Dumping in Australia: Historical and Contemporary Aspects*. Commonwealth of Australia, Canberra, Australian Capital Territory.

PORTNOY, ALICE W.
    1981 A Microarchaeological View of Human Settlement Space and Function. In *Modern Material Culture: The Archaeology of Us*, Richard A. Gould and Michael B. Schiffer, editors, pp. 213–224. Academic Press, New York, NY.

RATHJE, WILLIAM
    1981 A Manifesto for Modern Material-Culture Studies. In *Modern Material Culture: The Archaeology of Us*, Richard A. Gould and Michael B. Schiffer, editors, pp. 51–66. Academic Press, New York, NY.

REISS, WARREN
    1987 The Ship beneath Manhattan. In *History from beneath the Sea: Shipwrecks and Archaeology*, Peter Throckmorton, editor, pp. 185–187. RD Press, Melbourne, Victoria, Australia.

RICHARDS, NATHAN
    1997 The History and Archaeology of the Garden Island Ships' Graveyard, North Arm of the Port Adelaide River, Port Adelaide, South Australia. Honor's thesis, Department of Archaeology, Flinders University, Adelaide, South Australia.
    1998 Inferences from the Study of Iron and Steamship Abandonment: A Case Study from the Garden Island Ships' Graveyard, South Australia. *The Bulletin of the Australian Institute for Maritime Archaeology* 22(1): 75–80.
    1999a Garden Island Ships' Graveyard: Maritime Heritage Trail. *Heritage South Australia Newsletter* 15(July): 14–15.
    1999b The Garden Island Ships' Graveyard: Results and Findings of Archaeological Fieldwork 1996–1998. *Proceedings of the National Archaeology Students Conference (NASC)* 1998 1:11–18.
    2000 Ships Graveyard. In *The Port River*, Jane Marr and Cate Kelly, editors, p. 33. City of Port Adelaide Enfield, Port Adelaide, South Australia.
    2002 Deep Structures: An Examination of Deliberate Watercraft Abandonment in Australia. Doctoral thesis, Department of Archaeology, Flinders University, Adelaide, South Australia.
    2003a An Overview of Deliberate Watercraft Discard, Tasmania: 1808–1997. Manuscript, Tasmanian Heritage Office, Hobart, Tasmania, Australia.
    2003b The Role of Isolation in Cultural Site Formation: A Case Study from Strahan, Tasmania. *The Bulletin of the Australasian Institute for Maritime Archaeology* 27:77–84.
    2004 The Role of Geo-Politics in Cultural Site Formation: A Case Study from the Northern Territory. *The Bulletin of the Australasian Institute for Maritime Archaeology* 28:97–106.

RICHARDS, NATHAN, AND SALLY K. MAY
    2003 South Australia's "Floating Coffin": The Diseased, the Destitute and the Derelict *Fitzjames* (1852–c.1900). *The Great Circle* 25(1):19–39.

SAMUELS, BRIAN
1989 The North Arm Project: National Estate Grants Programme. *Soundings: The Newsletter of the Society for Underwater Historical Research Inc.* September: 5–6.

SCHIFFER, MICHAEL B.
1972 Archaeological Context and Systemic Context. *American Antiquity* 37:156–165.
1996 *Formation Processes of the Archaeological Record.* University of Utah Press, Salt Lake City.

SCHIFFER, MICHAEL B., THEODORE E. DOWNING, AND MICHAEL MCCARTHY
1981 Waste Not, Want Not: An Ethnoarchaeological Study of Reuse in Tucson, Arizona. In *Modern Material Culture: The Archaeology of Us*, Richard A. Gould and Michael B. Schiffer, editors, pp. 67–86. Academic Press, New York, NY.

SHOMETTE, DONALD G.
1995 *Tidewater Time Capsule: History beneath the Patuxent.* Tidewater Publishers, Centreville, MD.
1996 *Ghost Fleet of Mallows Bay: And Other Tales of the Lost Chesapeake.* Tidewater Publishers, Centreville, MD.

STANIFORTH, MARK
1997 The Archaeology of the Event—The Annales School and Maritime Archaeology. *Underwater Archaeology Proceedings*, pp. 159–64.
1999 Dependent Colonies: The Importation of Material Culture and the Establishment of a Consumer Society in Australia before 1850. Doctoral thesis, Department of Archaeology, Flinders University, Adelaide, South Australia.
2000 A Future for Australian Maritime Archaeology? *Australian Archaeology* 50:90–93.
2003 *Material Culture and Consumer Society: Dependant Colonies in Colonial Australia.* Kluwer Academic/ Plenum Publishers, New York, NY.

STONE, PETER, AND JACK K. LONEY
1983 *High and Dry: Visible Wrecks and Wreckage in Australian Waters.* Neptune Press Pty., Newtown, Sydney, Australia.

THROCKMORTON, PETER
1970 *Shipwrecks and Archaeology: The Unharvested Sea.* Victor Gollancz, London, England.
1987 Bones on a Beach. In *History from beneath the Sea: Shipwrecks and Archaeology*, Peter Throckmorton, editor, pp. 210–214. RD Press, Melbourne, Victoria, Australia.

TRIGGER, BRUCE G.
1995 *A History of Archaeological Thought.* Cambridge University Press, Cambridge, England.

VALDALISO, JESÚS M.
1996 The Diffusion of Technological Change in the Spanish Merchant Fleet during the Twentieth Century: Available Alternatives and Conditioning Factors. *The Journal of Transport History, (3rd Series)* 17(2):95–115.

VETH, PETER, AND MICHAEL MCCARTHY
1999 Types of Explanation in Maritime Archeology: The Case of the SS *Xantho. Australian Archaeology* 48(June):12–15.

WATSON, PATTY JO
1983 Method and Theory in Shipwreck Archaeology. In *Shipwreck Anthropology*, Richard A. Gould, editor, pp. 23–36. University of New Mexico Press, Albuquerque.

NATHAN RICHARDS
PROGRAM IN MARITIME STUDIES
EAST CAROLINA UNIVERSITY
ADMIRAL ERNEST M. ELLER HOUSE
GREENVILLE, NC 27858

MARK STANIFORTH
DEPARTMENT OF ARCHAEOLOGY
FLINDERS UNIVERSITY
GPO BOX 2100
ADELAIDE, SOUTH AUSTRALIA, 5001
AUSTRALIA

1992. Recovering the Past of USS *Arizona*. *Historical Archaeology* 26(4):69 –80.

JAMES P. DELGADO

Recovering the Past of USS *Arizona*: Symbolism, Myth, and Reality

ABSTRACT

Archaeological investigation of the battleship USS *Arizona* at Pearl Harbor provided the first assessment of a shipwreck that included its mythic and symbolic importance. The study of *Arizona* also demonstrated material evidence of anticipatory recycling and a sense of strategic vulnerability, while also demonstrating the influence of alternative views of the past.

Introduction

In his recent book on anthropological reconstruction of the past, Richard Gould (1990) cogently points to the problems archaeologists and historians face in their recovery and interpretation of human events of the distant or not-so-distant past. Even when the recent past is involved, there are alternative versions of the past reconstructed by historians and archaeologists alike. The belief in the alternative past at times attains a near-religious fervor, particularly when dealing with cultural icons or sanctified places, such as battlefields (Linenthal 1983). This is certainly the case with the most recent of American battlefields on U.S. soil, Pearl Harbor, and with its most visible symbol, USS *Arizona* (Figure 1).

USS *Arizona* and The *Arizona* Memorial

The Japanese attack on Pearl Harbor and the cataclysmic sinking of the battleship *Arizona* was a violent, controversial event (Figure 2). While viewed at the time in Japan as a great victory in the tradition of "surprise strategic attack" that had secured a Japanese victory over the Russian fleet in 1904, Pearl Harbor was viewed in the United States as a cowardly "sneak attack" and termed a "day that will live in infamy." Like other places where great loss of life has occurred in defense of country or other political goals, Pearl Harbor became a national shrine, with much of the attention focused on the battle-scarred and submerged remains of *Arizona* (Figure 3), now the focal point of a shrine erected by the people of the United States to honor and commemorate all American servicemen killed on 7 December 1941, particularly *Arizona*'s crew. *Arizona*'s burning bridge and listing masts and superstructure—photographed in the aftermath of the attack and sinking, and emblazoned on the front pages of newspapers across the land—epitomized to the nation the words "Pearl Harbor" and formed one of the best-known images of World War II in the Pacific. Indelibly impressed into the national memory, the *Arizona* Memorial is visited by millions who quietly file through the structure. Visitors toss flower wreaths and leis into the water and watch the iridescent slick of oil that leaks, a drop at a time, from *Arizona*'s ruptured bunkers after 50 years on the bottom, before reading the names of *Arizona*'s dead carved in marble on the Memorial's walls. Just as important as the shrine, now embodied in the form of the modern memorial that straddles *Arizona*, is the battleship itself. Intact, only partially salvaged, and resting in the silt of Pearl Harbor, USS *Arizona* is an in situ major artifact of the attack.

Following 1980 legislation authorizing the National Park Service to operate the USS *Arizona* Memorial, the National Park Service (NPS) and the U.S. Navy worked cooperatively to preserve and interpret the story of *Arizona* and the Pearl Harbor attack as well as Pacific forces' wartime actions through the Battle of Midway in 1942. A modern visitor center, managed by the National Park Service, houses major exhibits, including attack artifacts, and models and graphics of the battleship as it was and as it now sits beneath the arched Memorial's gleaming white walls. The partnership between the Navy and the National Park Service has also provided a much more detailed view of the aftermath of the Pearl Harbor attack through the archaeological investigation of the battle. The Submerged Cultural Resources Unit

FIGURE 1. USS *Arizona* heads down the East River from New York City on its way to sea trials in 1918. (Courtesy of the USS *Arizona* Memorial, NPS.)

of the NPS was initially asked to survey the remains of *Arizona*. The unit's chief, Daniel Lenihan, worked with archaeologists Larry Murphy and Larry Nordby and scientific illustrator Jerry Livingston to capture *Arizona* on video, slide film, and mylar images, documentation that provided the first comprehensive understanding of the ship since its loss. The NPS drawings and photographs, and a model of the sunken hulk done by Robert F. Sumrall, now present a more graphic view of *Arizona* to the visiting public (Lenihan 1989).

The Submerged Cultural Resource Unit's study also allowed for an assessment of how *Arizona* came to be the major focal point and shrine of the attack. In a strict sense, the survey of *Arizona* was not battlefield archaeology while the later survey of all of Pearl Harbor, including USS *Utah*, plane crash sites, and a search for a Japanese midget submarine, would qualify as such. It was not just a particularistic focus on a famous ship, such as *Titanic*. And yet it was also not an intensive study of an instructive lesser-known ship that epitomized specific behaviors, like Gould's (1990) example of HMS *Vixen* in Bermuda. Rather, the archaeology of USS *Arizona* in large part was a study of how it became a wreck and of how becoming a wreck made it culturally significant. This approach is unique in shipwreck archaeology.

Perspectives from *Historical Archaeology* and *ACUA Proceedings*

FIGURE 2. USS *Arizona* burns after its forward magazines have exploded. The wreck is the tomb of several hundred men who died aboard on 7 December 1941. (Courtesy of the USS *Arizona* Memorial, NPS.)

The Archaeology of USS *Arizona*

When Lenihan and Murphy first planned their survey of *Arizona*, the goal was an understanding of the resource beneath the Memorial, its condition, and factors affecting its preservation. In answering these queries, Lenihan and Murphy also posed a higher order of questions about the battleship and what it demonstrated. In answering the simple question of what was left of the ship, they came face-to-face with the shadow realm of the mythic world and alternative views of the past. There are most assuredly different perspectives on Pearl Harbor, the most famous being the so-called "revisionist" history propounded by many, nota-

bly John Toland, who insists that Franklin Roosevelt knew in advance Pearl Harbor was to be attacked and allowed it to happen in order to push the nation into a war he wanted.

There are also the alternative Japanese and American views of the attack. Even when not considering such lofty matters as different national perspectives, there is a "fantasy" or "fable" history of Pearl Harbor, in part "myth" and in part founded on imperfect memory and recollection. The best example of this perspective was the story that *Arizona* had been destroyed by a bomb down its stack. The U.S. Navy in 1942 and Lenihan and Murphy in 1983 found evidence to the contrary. The stack gratings were intact. In another exam-

FIGURE 3. The *Arizona*, fires out, rests in 40 ft. of water, a complete wreck. (Courtesy of the USS *Arizona* Memorial, NPS.)

ple, a survivor standing atop turret No. 4 at the ship's stern claimed it was hit a glancing blow by a bomb that "scooped out the side of the turret with a big mound of molten steel" (Murphy 1987). No archaeological evidence of such damage was found when documenting the mount of the now-removed turret. Salvage of the turret might have extracted archaeological evidence of the bomb damage, but a 1942 salvage photograph of the turret in question clearly shows no such damage. However, the historical record that aided archaeological interpretation of the No. 4 turret was, on the other hand, a complete failure in terms of what to expect with the No. 1 turret. Based on the extensive surviving documentation of salvage of the

battleship, the on-site managers and the archaeologists assumed that no guns remained. Yet on the first dive the NPS discovered the still-mounted No. 1 turret with its three 14-in. guns.

One of the major questions of the survey was the extent of damage done by Japanese torpedoes. One of the most daring aspects of the attack was the use of aerial torpedoes that were successfully dropped to run in shallow water and detonate after short runs. Much time and effort had gone into preparation of specially modified torpedoes, and extensive practice in a new technique for aerial torpedo attack had honed the skills of the Japanese pilots. Survivors claim that *Arizona* was hit by at least two torpedoes, one of which passed beneath the repair ship *Vestal*, which was moored alongside the battleship. *Arizona* was also hit by several aerial bombs one of which is generally credited by historical accounts as the agent of the battleship's destruction (Prange et al. 1981). The missile in question was an armor piercing 16.1-in. shell from either the battleship *Nagato* or its sister *Mutsu* that was modified into an aerial bomb. Navy divers assessing the battle damage in 1942 found evidence that the 1,760-lb. projectile had hit near *Arizona*'s No. 2 turret, penetrated several decks, and detonated near the forward magazines, touching off nearly a million pounds of powder that demolished the forward sections of the ship, pushed out the casemates and hull above the waterline at the bow, lifted decks vertically, and collapsed the No. 1 turret and its barbette some 28 ft. No discussion of torpedo damage was made, and recent archaeological investigation has proved fruitless because the ship has sunk into the harbor mud and silt has built up, covering the underwater hull areas and effectively masking any possible torpedo damage. This situation is unfortunate, for it is also possible that a well-delivered torpedo hit forward could have touched off the magazines. A material argument for the 16.1-in. shell theory recently surfaced with the discovery at the Aberdeen Proving Ground Museum in Maryland of the base plate from a 16.1-in. Japanese naval shell recovered from the forward area of *Arizona*. It is indeed tempting to identify it as the shell, for it would then be as one historian claimed as important "as the bullet that killed Lincoln." Yet there is insufficient archaeological evidence to assess the question. Archaeology cannot conclusively determine what sank *Arizona*. There remains the Navy's conjecture, which the NPS has as yet found no evidence to refute. The question might be resolved by excavating the silt and mud from the hull to investigate the battleship's port side, where the torpedoes would have hit.

More instructive than the battle damage is what was done to *Arizona* after the battle. In the aftermath of the Pearl Harbor attack, the United States Navy commenced repair and salvage work and succeeded in raising all the sunken vessels with the exception of USS *Arizona* and USS *Utah*. Of the vessels raised, all were salvaged and returned to duty except USS *Oklahoma*, which sat at Pearl Harbor through the war, was sold for scrap, and sank while under tow to the mainland in 1947. The Pearl Harbor salvage was one the most comprehensive and costly maritime salvage operations of modern times. The first priority was the recovery of anti-aircraft guns and gun directors for them, a logical first order of business for a fleet subjected to devastating aerial assault, and was then followed by other armament, ammunition, and complete ships. Those ships that were lightly damaged were repaired and rushed into service, while more difficult jobs—such as completely capsized battleships and the destroyer *Shaw*, with its bow blasted off—were the next priority. Despite an emphasis on salvaging ships from apparently hopeless circumstances, early on it was decided not to pursue complete salvage of *Arizona* (Wallin 1968:267–268).

While *Arizona* was investigated and surveyed, the Navy decided only to remove its topsides, which stuck above the water, and salvage the battleship's armament. Six days after the attack, the senior surviving officer from *Arizona* forwarded the ship's action report to Adm. Husband Kimmel, Commander-in-chief of the Pacific Fleet, and noted: "The USS *Arizona* is a total loss except the following is believed salvageable: 50-caliber machine guns in maintop, searchlights on aftersearchlight platform, the low catapult on quarterdeck, and the guns of numbers 3 and 4 turrets" (cited in Lenihan 1989:34). Removal of the ship's safes, personal belongings and valuables, and classified and sensitive documents was the first order of business in early 1942. Around this time, as many as 105 bodies were recovered. Salvage of the masts and the superstructure followed. The toppled foremast was cut free on 5 May 1942, followed by the mainmast on August 23. The stern aircraft crane and conning tower were removed in December 1942. Portions of the forecastle and the forward sections of the hull were cut free and raised, and holes were cut into the hull to remove equipment and permit access for salvage crews. The ship was not completely salvaged, however. As early as June 1942, the commandant of the Navy

Yard recommended abandoning work on *Arizona* because it was a task of great magnitude entailing the diversion of large numbers of men and equipment from other work. The facility of salvage was the deciding factor since time and expenses mounted as the Pacific Fleet was raised from the mud of Pearl Harbor. *Arizona*'s damage was such that the only option considered by the salvage officers was building a cofferdam, but "examination of the harbor's coral bottom concluded that it was too porous" (Martinez in Lenihan 1989:34). As early as December 1942, the decision not to raise or salvage *Arizona* was made, and on the first of the month, the battleship was stricken from the Navy Register of commissioned ships.

Despite this decision, more of the ship was salvaged. With the exception of the No. 1 turret, which was severely damaged by the blast—so that its gun trunnions appear to have sheared, depressing the gun barrels at an unnatural angle, all other ordnance and ammunition was removed in 1943. The 14-in. guns in turrets no. 2, 3, and 4, and all 5-in./51-cal. and 5-in./25-cal. secondary batteries were salvaged from *Arizona*. The aft sections were partially dewatered and ammunition was removed from the ship's magazines. The salvage of the no. 3 and 4 mounts included the armored turrets themselves as well as the guns, their rotating parts, and hoisting mechanisms (Figure 4). This work appeared to Lenihan to fit a behavior described by Gould in an early work, *Shipwreck Anthropology*, that he found evidence of both in the wrecks of the Spanish Armada of 1588 and in airplane crashes during the Battle of Britain in 1940: "The greater the defensive isolation of the combatants, the greater will be the efforts by that combatant to salvage and recycle items and/or materials of strategic value from any wrecks that fall within its territory" (Gould 1983:106). The salvaged no. 3 and 4 turrets from *Arizona* are specific evidence of anticipatory recycling. The turret mechanisms, armor, and guns were used to equip two coastal defense batteries, one at Mokapu Head and the other up the slopes of the Wianae Mountains on Oahu's western shore.

As part of a plan that envisioned ringing Oahu with battleship turrets, the turrets from *Arizona*

FIGURE 4. Removing projectiles from turret No. 4. (Courtesy of the USS *Arizona* Memorial, NPS.)

were to be augmented with the four 14-in. turrets from the battleship *Oklahoma*—which had been hit by at least five torpedoes, had capsized, and was a total loss at Pearl Harbor. While *Oklahoma*'s turrets proved unsalvageable, the work to clean, repair, and reassemble *Arizona*'s turrets proceeded. This work included building new ammunition hoists and mounting the guns in 70- by 50-ft. concrete barbettes nine to 15 ft. thick (Kirchner and Lewis 1967:430–433). The installation at Mokapu, Battery Pennsylvania, was completed and test-fired in mid-August 1945, four days before the Japanese surrender. After the war, both batteries were abandoned and the guns and machinery cut up for scrap. Nonetheless, these installations, regardless of their ultimate fate, were built and armed with *Arizona*'s guns in anticipation of a Japanese battleship assault by sea, in which case battleship gun to battleship gun (U.S. being on land, of course) would slug it out. It was not an unusual concept. On the mainland, 16-in. guns destined for battleships never built were mounted in casemated concrete and earth batteries on the mainland near San Francisco. On Oahu, however, the placement of such batteries was clear evidence of strategic vulnerability and anticipatory recycling.

Arizona as Relic and Symbol

It is interesting to note that at this time the salvage of certain items from *Arizona* filled the national need for a source of relics. Before the ship itself became a relic, pieces of it were shipped across the nation to serve as icons testifying to the sacrifice of the ship and crew. Anchors, the ship's bells, a section of a mast, even bulkhead hatches and smaller items—like a bugle and clocks from the hulk—made their way onto patriotic displays, museum collections, and War Bond drives. It was a response that echoed earlier memorialization tributes to lost or famous ships. When Drake's *Golden Hinde* foundered after rotting on display on the Thames after its famous voyage of piracy and circumnavigation, it was broken up and its timbers used to make souvenirs, including a chair now at Woburn Abbey. Pieces and parts of the ill-fated USS *Maine* were sent around the country for memorials and exhibits, including bitts, the captain's bathtub, and the foremast, which now marks the graves of the crew at Arlington National Cemetery. Tons of scrap steel from *Maine* were even cast into memorial plaques and sent throughout the country to appease those who did not receive an appropriate relic (Prioli 1990). This process of relic-collecting started with *Arizona* but stopped short of raising the entire ship.

It is interesting to note that in comparison USS *Utah* was not as intensely salvaged. Daniel Lenihan states that "many of the easily salvaged items of ship's apparel, armament, and groundtackle on *Utah* were left in place," which he feels possibly indicates the "very nature of the *Arizona* and its symbolic significance" (Lenihan 1989:10). One could construct an argument for this and for strategic vulnerability and the interaction of both behaviors, as well as pointing to a decision reached at a certain point, regardless of behaviors, simply to leave both ships where they were, salvage written off or indefinitely postponed because it was simply too expensive to continue with either vessel for the limited possible returns. This raises the question of whether *Arizona* as a sunken ship became a relic and shrine as a convenient answer to the question of salvage. Salvage was entertained after the war, in 1948, in large measure explained as a means of recovering the dead, but the idea was discarded.

Arizona is now unique in the world as a naval memorial and relic, the nation's only major naval memorial associated with disaster (Figure 5). Although destruction of USS *Maine* propelled the nation into war in the last century, only pieces are displayed. Other sunken warships lie unmarked in the ocean, with only plaques ashore to commemorate their loss. As one naval officer noted, *Arizona* was the only warship lost during World War II whose wreckage still remained in sight when the war ended; all others were in deep water where "their bones rest in unknown lands beneath the sea" (cited in Friedman et al. 1978:n.p.). *Arizona*, with the remains of its crew aboard, serves as a tomb as well as a cenotaph for them, for the 1,177 men killed aboard the battleship are not all there now. Yet even the number of bodies aboard is subject to question. At least 105 bodies were recovered in early 1942, while other bodies—some complete, others merely parts blown across the harbor—were recovered floating in the waters around the ship in the days after the attack. Yet others were completely consumed by the inferno. Historian Gordon Prange notes that such was the case with the ship's captain:

> Some time after the attack, when the *Arizona* had cooled off, a party boarded her, found a pile of ashes on deck, and in the ashes an Academy class ring. They took it ashore and had a goldsmith clean it. Inside they could then read the name, Franklin Van Valkenburgh. The command sent it to his wife (Prange et al. 1988:422).

Others, sealed in the collapsed forward sections of the ship, remain aboard. There are probably several hundred of the ship's dead aboard, and the ship, once deemed unraisable, then became a war grave and a tomb, a necessity borne not only out of sentiment but also of pragmatism. In 1947, the Navy's final decision to not recover bodies from

FIGURE 5. USS *Arizona* Memorial. (Courtesy of the USS *Arizona* Memorial, NPS.)

the wreck was made after weighing two factors. First, the costs of salvage were deemed too costly; and secondly, the bodies, if recovered, would be "medically unrecognizable." The same pragmatism emerged with shipwrecks in the deep sea where bodies were irretrievable, and thus the usual efforts to recover a body were abandoned and the only comfort available was the concept of burial at sea. *Arizona*, even in shallow waters and accessible, became such a site not only for those whose bodies do lie there, but also as a cenotaph for those whose bodies were completely consumed or recovered and buried unidentified ashore. In its more recent history, *Arizona* has even become the receptacle for the urns of cremated survivors of the ship's company who expressed a desire to be buried at sea with their shipmates. They are placed inside the barbette of the No. 4 turret, now an open well that leads into the ship's interior.

It is interesting to note, however, that the rusting visible hulk of the battleship was not unanimously viewed as an appropriate resting place. In 1955, the commander of the 14th Naval District at Pearl Harbor wrote the Secretary of the Navy of his determination that the Navy do something because "this burial place for 1,102 men is a rusted mass of junk" (Slackman 1984:57). The continued existence of *Arizona* as a visual vault for the dead was disturbing to others. Proposals ranged from dismantling the ship and burying its dead with other war casualties at the National Memorial Cemetery of the Pacific to burying the ship beneath landfill and building a memorial park over the site. *Arizona*'s initial pragmatic role as a war grave and the later need to memorialize the ship and the attack gave rise to a new material expression at the site. During the war, the Navy discussed plans to make *Arizona* a war memorial. Even then, divergent views on a memorial's nature and purpose reflected its symbolic value. While ultimately the wreck is a war grave, the Navy's primary interest in *Arizona* was an obligation to memorialize "what had been one of the fleet's proudest ships and the sailors that went down with her" (Slackman 1984:47). Yet in time the ship itself did not serve as a war memorial. That distinction belongs to the concrete arched structure that spans the sunken ship but does not touch it. The *Arizona* Memorial, built in 1962, supposedly dips in the middle to symbolize the initial low point of U.S. fortunes after the attack and rises at both ends to symbolize the nation's rise to victory. It would therefore be less a memorial to *Arizona* than a memorial to the great experience of America in World War II. An alternative view is that the Memorial's shape is constrained by the structural requirements of a concrete "bridge-like" structure.

Yet, the original design concepts of Memorial architect Alfred Preis reflected the site as a grave. In 1950, Preis envisioned a floating "eternal flame." The first design he submitted for the actual memorial was similar to European crypts he had visited in his youth. It included a submerged viewing chamber open to the sky with portholes where visitors would "view the underwater remains of the ship, encrusted with the rust and marine organisms that reminded the architect of the jewelled imperial sarcophagi" (Slackman 1984:73). That design, with its stark confrontation of death, met with a lack of enthusiasm from the Navy. In time, these and other political considerations actually drew the memorial purpose away from the ship itself to become a statement on war, with the ship and its crew serving as a metaphor. The *Arizona* Memorial is now interpreted to emphasize the war experience at Pearl Harbor. This gives a new meaning to why the Memorial does not touch the ship. Is it an engineer's desire to not rest a permanent structure on a rusting, unstable hulk? Or, is it purposeful distancing? The clean, pristine white concrete and marble of the Memorial is a stark contrast to the rusty and fouled remains of the ship.

Sections of the ship "blocking" the Memorial's construction were actually cut away in 1961 and now rest, unmarked and overgrown with weeds, in a scrap pile on the Waipio Peninsula. This wreckage is in itself an interesting archaeological statement. While in the way of the Memorial, and discarded, it was not, and apparently could not be, scrapped. A painted sign on the rusting steel notes it is "not for sale." While seemingly bothersome for memorialization efforts, the *Arizona* remains at Waipio could not be treated as garbage given their sacred nature as relics, in part reflected by the admonition they are not for sale. Ironically, one of the Navy's reasons for cooperating with the archaeological survey of the ship in 1983 was to seek a place to bury the Waipio scrap "at sea" next to the hulk.

The Memorial, by not touching the ship, remains clean, and offers a sanitized, alternative view of death and disaster. What is most interesting is the apparent discrepancy of the Memorial's message in later memorialization efforts. If the *Arizona* Memorial is indeed, as Congress decreed in 1961, "in honor and commemoration of all the members of the Armed Forces of the United States who gave their lives to their country during the attack," then why are only the names of *Arizona*'s dead carved on a white marble wall inside the Memorial? This led to two other material expressions of this discrepancy, the 1972 memorial to USS *Utah*, at the other side of Ford Island, and recent plans for a "Remembrance Exhibit" ashore that will list the names of everyone else killed at Pearl Harbor on 7 December 1941. Left unresolved is whether the new memorial will list the names of Japanese airmen and submariners killed in the attack. Clearly, the *Arizona* Memorial is not a memorial to everyone killed on that day. Why then the need to separate the Memorial from the ship?

Arguably, *Arizona* has now become the centerpiece, and the major focal point for visitors to Pearl Harbor. By the 1960s, the ship and the Memorial had become a vehicle for personal reflection on war's causes, conduct, and results. When the shock and initial anger of 7 December had diminished, *Arizona* transmuted into a symbol of what could happen if the nation were again caught unaware. The battleship stood for the need for military preparedness, for not underestimating potential foes, for alertness, and for mutual understanding and respect (Prange et al. 1986: 629). To most Americans, the Memorial and ship are a major shrine that reflects the basic truths of how people perceive and deal with war. It remains a potent symbol, meaning many things to many people. For those survivors of the event, and the families whose dead are entombed in the ship, *Arizona* is a place to come to confront the past and perhaps come to terms with it. For many Americans alive on 7 December 1941, Pearl Harbor was a symbol of the nature of the enemy they fought. Propagandists often employ emotion-laden terms, and for war-generation Americans, Japanese military conduct is summed up in phrases like the "Rape of Nanking," the "Bataan Death March," "Kamikaze," and "Pearl Harbor" (Dower 1986:28). For some people, *Arizona* symbolizes the sinister character of the enemy attack. While not suggesting that this perspective is wrong, it is an alternative view to that of the Japanese, and thus even the archaeological study, conducted by Western scientists and explained by Western interpreters, is colored by this perception. The author often wonders what the archaeological study of Pearl Harbor would offer if it was done by Japanese scientists in some alternative world in which they won the war.

Conclusions

Archaeology like all science is a social process, never practiced in pure isolation, and includes the real world and its mythic perceptions. The archaeologists at Pearl Harbor came face to face with this phenomenon. The Navy initially insisted no dives could be made because people had been killed diving on the wreck during salvage operations. Three different versions of the tale were even offered (Murphy 1990, pers. comm.). The record is clear, however. There were no diving fatalities on USS *Arizona*. Thus Daniel Lenihan and his colleagues were confronted at the very beginning of their project with the mythic past. The nature of the ship of the war grave—and symbolically laden terms like "desecration"—also affected their work, for one of the first concessions they made was a commitment not to enter the ship. Even the data they gathered were appropriated for the symbolic values

and alternative views of the past. Thus the video-taped tour of the ship produced from their work in 1983 notes that an awning stands open as it did on 7 December 1941, invoking yet again the image of unpreparedness and sneak attack on a peaceful Sunday morning. Fire-hose nozzles scattered on deck could be appropriated for the theme of sacrifice, or of "they died with their boots on." (The Errol Flynn movie of "Custer's Last Stand" with the same title was one of Hollywood's most popular offerings of December 1941.) Even crockery scattered on the galley floor can serve as a reminder of a Sunday morning breakfast forever interrupted by Japanese perfidy (Murphy 1990, pers. comm.).

It is perhaps for these reasons that some people may be critical of studying the archaeology of the recent past, or the archaeology of such a well-known vessel, a "great" ship. As archaeologists look at other "great ships," or warships in particular, the symbolism is so powerful that even scientists are drawn into responding solely to the mythic values, as was the case with *Monitor* and *Titanic* (Delgado 1988). Only a few meaningful anthropological inferences have been gleaned from *Monitor*. All other approaches to the ironclad have placed little emphasis on anthropological returns, or analyzed the role and context of mythic or "relic" value and its connotations. Researchers should be looking at these "great ships" for just that reason, among others, to delve into the how and why of mythicization. Archaeology is, after all, often viewed as only the recovery of lost or forgotten information from the past. In truth, archaeology should function as a systematic scientific tool that extracts meaningful human behavior from the material record regardless of its age. Given an event of the magnitude and emotional impact as Pearl Harbor and *Arizona*'s loss, perceptions and memory, even the historical record, are clouded by what the participant or historian chose to see or thought they saw. People see the same events differently, based on their unique psychology and cultural experiences prior to the event, hence alternative views of the past abound.

Archaeologists suffer from the same "behavioral baggage'' in their analysis, and their work is often colored by social processes of the present in which they are immersed, including the intrusion of the mythic world into the real world, including perceptions of battlefields and wrecks like *Arizona* as ''reservoirs of sacred power'' (Linenthal 1991). However, when archaeologists practice their science as systematic minimalists they work not from imperfect memory or selective documentation and perceptions but rather from a wide range of physical remains. The study of *Arizona* offers first-level impressions of what happened and what survives, and provides the means for assessing reality against subjective perception while accounting for differences in human behavior. Hence, the archaeology of *Arizona* is in part a laboratory for analyzing American society's myths, symbols, and images—the expression of what makes people what they are. It is also the means for anthropological assessments of the ships, crews, and events of 7 December 1941. It is even the anthropological assessment of reactions of people to the archaeological study, as demonstrated here. In the end, it all reflects the basic truth that *Arizona* is a very sacred place that reflects the cultural beliefs as Americans at this place and time, and that this view may not be compatible with the material evidence of the archaeological record.

ACKNOWLEDGMENTS

This article in part incorporates portions of an earlier work, a chapter entitled "Significance: Memorials, Myths and Symbols," which was published as part of Lenihan (1989). I wish to acknowledge the hours of discussion and critical thinking provoked by my colleagues Larry E. Murphy (National Park Service, Submerged Cultural Resources Unit) and Edward Tabor Linenthal (Department of Religious Studies, University of Wisconsin, Oshkosh). Carmine Prioli (University of North Carolina, Chapel Hill) shared his thoughtful analysis of *Maine*'s postwar fate. Daniel J. Lenihan (Chief of the Submerged Cultural Resources Unit) provided the opportunity to participate in the last field season of the Pearl Harbor survey and to prepare the significance chapter of his final report. Daniel A. Martinez (Park Historian, USS *Arizona* Memorial) provided historical citations and clarified discrepancies in the written record.

REFERENCES

DELGADO, JAMES P.
1988   *A Symbol of American Ingenuity: Assessing the Significance of USS* Monitor. U.S. Government Printing Office, Washington, D.C.

DOWER, JOHN W.
1986   *War Without Mercy: Race and Power in the Pacific War.* Pantheon Books, New York.

FRIEDMAN, NORMAN, ARTHUR D. BAKER III, ARNOLD S. LOTT (LCDR, USN [RET]), AND ROBERT F. SUMRALL (USNR)
1978   *USS* Arizona (BB39). Leeward, Annapolis, Maryland.

GOULD, RICHARD A.
1990   *Recovering the Past.* University of New Mexico Press, Albuquerque.

GOULD, RICHARD A. (EDITOR)
1983   *Shipwreck Anthropology.* University of New Mexico Press, Albuquerque.

KIRCHNER, D. P., AND E. R. LEWIS
1967   The Oahu Turrets. *The Military Engineer*, November–December:1.

LENIHAN, DANIEL J. (EDITOR)
1989   *Submerged Cultural Resources Study: USS* Arizona *Memorial and Pearl Harbor National Historical Landmark.* National Park Service, Santa Fe, New Mexico.

LINENTHAL, EDWARD TABOR
1983   Ritual Drama at the Little Bighorn: The Persistence and Transformation of a National Symbol. *Journal of the American Academy of Religion* 51(2):267–281.
1991   *Sacred Ground: Americans and Their Battlefields.* University of Illinois Press, Urbana.

MURPHY, JOY WALDRON
1987   Diving into the Past: A Rare View of Pearl Harbor. *Impact/Albuquerque Journal Sunday Magazine*, March 10:3. Albuquerque, New Mexico.

PRANGE, GORDON W., DONALD M. GOLDSTEIN, AND KATHERINE V. DILLON
1981   *At Dawn We Slept: The Untold Story of Pearl Harbor.* McGraw-Hill, New York.
1986   *Pearl Harbor: The Verdict of History.* McGraw-Hill, New York.

1988   *December Seventh, 1941; The Day the Japanese Attacked Pearl Harbor*. McGraw-Hill, New York.

PRIOLI, CARMINE
1990   The Second Sinking of the *Maine*. American Heritage 42(1). New York.

SLACKMAN, MICHAEL
1984   *Remembering Pearl Harbor: The Story of the USS
Arizona Memorial. Arizona* Memorial Museum Association, Honolulu, Hawaii.

WALLIN, VADM HOMER N.
1968   *Pearl Harbor: Why, How, Fleet Salvage, and Final
Appraisal*. U.S. Government Printing Office, Washington, D.C.

JAMES P. DELGADO
VANCOUVER MARITIME MUSEUM
1905 OGDEN AVENUE
VANCOUVER, BRITISH COLUMBIA V6J 1A3

1995 Three Ironclad Warships—The Archaeology of Industrial Process and Historical Myth. *Historical Archaeology* 29(4):26–38.

ERVAN G. GARRISON

Three Ironclad Warships— The Archaeology of Industrial Process and Historical Myth

ABSTRACT

Three ironclad warships, C.S.S. *Georgia*, U.S.S. *Cairo*, and U.S.S. *Monitor*, are discussed as examples of industrial process in the United States Civil War period. In their archaeological study the author and others have relied principally on explanatory methodologies that stress their definition within social and technological contexts. This explanatory protocol is examined within concepts of technology which involve the function, and functioning, of manufactured things both within their own era as well as in present-day life. This consideration examines the mythologization of historic things, particularly shipwrecks, and cites the need to identify and account for this occurrence within the archaeological and historical analysis of these or any other industrial sites.

Introduction

A history of technology can be simply described as: (1) a history of objects or things; and (2) a history of processes that involve objects and things. Now, before this simple description begins to sound comedic—full of objects, things, and stuff—this article will point out some past difficulties in discussing technology per se before moving to the archaeological study of it. For instance to the Greco-Roman world, and indeed up until 17th-century France, the term "technology" was used to describe the production of speech or the art of speaking. It was not until the 18th century that the term was expanded to include the study of arts and crafts and thus, by extension, the products of arts and crafts—i.e., objects and things—technological objects and technological things (Perrin 1990:7). Beckman, in 1777, defined technology to include the notion of process, e.g., "the science which deals with the processing of raw material and the knowledge of crafts" (Guillerme and Sebestik 1966:72). In the 20th century, technology has widened its semantic domain to include technique and applied science.

An archaeology of technology, and one specific to maritime industrial technology, begins with the study of the object. The object can be simple or complex. Inherent in the study of simple or complex objects is the notion of the complexity of the processes that produced them. For instance, the wooden ship and the iron ship reflect distinctly different historical contexts and concomitant technological, economic, and social processes.

Indeed it has been said by historians of technology that the Industrial Revolution deeply changed the content of technology. By extension one can argue that any archaeology that attempts to study industrial technology must be cognizant of the complexity of industrial objects and the processes that produced them. The technology of wood is not that of iron, neither in terms of the things fashioned from these materials nor in the processes attendant to them. One term for technology is the German word *technik* whose definition involves the functioning of natural and manufactured things, including the set of principles according to which the artifacts work and the methods used in making them (Fores and Rey 1977:2). Any archaeology of technology would do well to incorporate these ideas in its methodology as well.

But, as Moella (1989:93) writes, important modern commentaries on technology by Mumford and others (Giedion 1948; Usher 1954[1929]; Ellul 1964; Veblen 1992[1899]) held "technique" (Mumford's—*technic*) apart from technology or the rational study of industrial arts. Another view is that of Robin Ridington (Dickason 1992) portraying non-European technology as "consist(ing) of knowledge rather than tools." This interpretation has relevancy for industrial archaeological studies as well as those of primitive technology; "tools" or industrial objects are the result of knowledge, simple and complex. As archaeology, in the main, seeks the function of objects, this article will argue that function arises from both historical place and technology, but its meaning's origin is less surely placed.

This study examines three cases of the archaeology of ironclad warships. Each will be seen to be the product of social and industrial settings such that their final form and function expresses the technological possibilities of a specific time and place. As such, they inform one about the specific historical era—the United States Civil War—and reflect both a model of technology and society that is part past, part present. The archaeology of technology in this context has embedded within it an eye toward the meanings objects carry of their function in the past and the present.

Whatever their meaning within their milieu only that which has intellectual—and cultural—meaning today takes priority in discussions and interpretations of these industrial objects. To a large degree, these objects become tokens of the reading one places on their history—relics with stories and meanings we give them for our own purposes. The specific case of the U.S.S. *Monitor* especially emphasizes this point; what is history and what is icon is difficult to discern. All the cases presented here reflect this point to one degree or another.

The Ironclad Ship as Archaeology

Of all the warlike technology of the zenith of the Industrial Revolution and the Age of Progress, none has loomed more impressively, generated more controversy, or captured the general imagination of powers with naval pretention, than the ironclad warship.

—Baxter (1933:3)

Ironclad warships were one culmination of the period termed the Industrial Revolution which, by the mid-19th century, was nearly two centuries old. They were superweapons of their day. American armorclads of the U.S. Civil War, such as the U.S.S. *Monitor,* C.S.S. *Virginia,* and their no less famous heirs, were not the first iron warships. European naval powers like Great Britain and France had commissioned the first ironclads in the *La Gloire* in 1858 and H.M.S. *Warrior* in 1859 (Baxter 1933: 110, 158; Garrison 1991). By 1860 more than 40 of this class of ship had been built or authorized in Europe (Delgado 1988:11). The historically significant difference between these and American ironclads lay in the fact that the latter were the first to be used in ship-to-ship warfare.

One thesis of this work is that the ironclad war-ships of the American Civil War were as much products of industrial process and place as the historic persons who conceived them. Here, I refer mainly to John Ericsson, designer of the U.S.S. *Monitor,* implying if there had been no "Ericsson," that particular time and place would have produced another individual like him. As such, the study of the ironclads' archaeological remains can reveal much about the indigenous industrial base, available technology, and resources as well as society. This point of departure views these American ironclads as maritime industrial sites which, by their technological attributes, reflect much of their cultural milieu. By comparing and contrasting these sites one can learn much of what was in the "realm of the possible" (Braudel 1981) in mid-19th-century America. An important facet of this line of inquiry involves the regional differences and consequences in industrialization at the time of the Civil War.

Iron, Steam, and Marine Technology

The 19th century found the United States rapidly adopting and innovating technology in the larger context of the period termed the Industrial Revolution. This was particularly true for the northeastern section of this country. Politically separated from Great Britain in the late 18th century, the United States, nonetheless, was linked culturally and thus technologically to that mother country of industrialization. By the mid-19th century, in terms of mechanization, the United States was a mirror of British and western European technological society (Habakkuk 1962:5, 168).

Britain in the 17th and 18th centuries had laid the groundwork for the Industrial Revolution by maximizing the potential of prime movers, e.g., animal, wind, and water power. Animal power was utilized in horse mills and gins with gearing using ratios of 100:1 for rotary power. Wind power came in the form of post, smock, and power mills whereby Britons pumped water and ground cereal grains. Waterwheels were used where sufficient hydraulic resources could be harnessed such as in the hill counties of England and Scotland. All were coupled with changes in English agriculture and deforestation due to increased fuel and building demands. These power sources bridged England's change to a coal-based technology, which, in turn, led to what H. G. Wells (1971:4) termed the "Mechanical Revolution."

Britain was richly endowed with coal deposits, producing over 3 million tons of mined coal annually by the 17th century. As these mines went deeper, the damage by water increased and dewatering became critical. Horses and overshot waterwheels to run pumps were expensive. Horses ate costly fodder, and waterwheels required feedstock which, in turn, necessitated expenditures for dams and reservoirs. This requirement for mine dewatering and later needs of the burgeoning factory system led to the development of steam power. Coupled with concomitant advances in ironmaking, these seemingly disparate developments paved the way for the ironclad warship.

The first steam engines, of the late 17th and early 18th centuries, were pumping engines to keep the water out of the mines. The great advances in English machine tools from 1775 to 1850 came from attempts to improve mining equipment, steam engines, rails, and ships (Habakkuk 1962:168). The efficiency of these large, low pressure (40–50 psi) engines was increased by James Watt in the late 18th century. He also created the first rotative designs to be used in industry such as the Nottingham cotton mills in 1785 (Wells 1971:800). Still the steam engine, even the primitive Savery or Newcomen pumping engines, could not have developed before sheet iron was available. It was not until 1728 that rolled sheet iron appeared; bars and rods in 1738 (Wells 1971:801). These were the results of improvement of refractory furnaces using forced air blast in the reduction of iron ores. These furnaces first consumed charcoal made from wood and, by the 18th century, coke produced from more abundant coal.

Seagoing steamships followed the S.S. *Savannah* in 1819 which crossed the Atlantic using steam-driven side paddle wheels for part of the voyage and sails for the remainder. The propeller-driven steamship was first developed by the great British civil engineer Isambard Kingdom Brunel with the S.S. *Great Britain* in 1845. Almost all of the elements for the iron warship were present in the *Great Britain*'s design—steam power, iron plating, screw propeller (Kemp 1978:153). All that was needed was the shell gun or rifled cannon.

It was the latter technological innovation that paradoxically slowed the acceptance of the ironclad ship into the world's navies. Invented in the 1820s, the shell gun was supplemented by rifled ordnance capable of hurling 100-lb. projectiles accurately well over a mile. Naval authorities were concerned about the brittleness of early iron plate and the effect of this ordnance upon it. Only after the addition of thick wooden backing to cushion the impact of the shells, heavier armor thicknesses, and watertight compartments did the world's admiralties begin to add ironclad ships to their fleets. These vessels remained untested as to their ultimate purpose—combat—until the outbreak of the American Civil War.

Ironclads and the American Civil War

At the outbreak of war, in April 1861, the North had a superior sail navy. The South, by comparison, had almost none. The man who realized this discrepancy most acutely was the Confederate Secretary of the Navy, Stephen Mallory:

> Inequality of numbers may be compensated by invulnerability. Not only does economy, but naval success dictate the wisdom and expediency of fighting with iron against wood (in Still 1985:10).

Mallory's subsequent actions over the next four years led to the building of the C.S.S. *Virginia* and over a score of ironclad vessels. These ironclads were quite diverse in size and design, but all the Southern armorclads shared a certain overall commonality in concept attributed to Confederate Naval Constructor John Porter. Porter's design was for what he termed a "harbor defense vessel" (Still 1985:94). Its salient feature was a heavily armored casemate shield that protected a heavy battery of shell and rifled guns. The vessel's hull, submerged in combat by controlled ballasting, was of wood and contained the steam propulsion machinery, stores, magazines, and quarters for the officers and crew.

FIGURE 1. Artist's drawing of C.S.S. *Georgia*, published in *Harpers New Monthly*, 1863.

Single or multiple screw propellers were generally fitted to the respective designs with the rare exception with paddle wheel propulsion—e.g., C.S.S. *Louisiana* used screws and paddle wheel. One example of these Southern vessels is the C.S.S. *Georgia,* an archaeological site, on which this author conducted studies, located in the Savannah River of coastal Georgia (Garrison and Anuskiewicz 1984).

C.S.S. *Georgia*

The *Georgia* (Figure 1) was the product of an Antebellum planter society whose industrial base, such as it was, served agriculture. Hawke (1988: 120) comments on this fact: "The South, for the most part, turned its back . . . and plowed its money into land." Eaton (1961:246) echoes this perspective: "The agrarian ideal that permeated all classes of Southern society undoubtedly hampered growth." Hawke (1988:120) further states that, "even if the incentive existed, the chance that industry could flourish in the South was slim. It lacked a pool of trained, discipline workers."

The southern Georgia economy utilized its industry for the processing of the staple crop—cotton. Industrial sites in Georgia, and the deep South in general, were relatively few in number. Richmond, Atlanta, Columbus, Selma, and Chattanooga were notable exceptions. The South in time may have overcome its resistance to the new technology and the people—the immigrants, inventors, and entrepreneurs—who were spreading about the nation, but Diane Lindstrom (1978:34) maintains that the region faced a serious deficiency in what she terms "growth poles" or industrial cities and towns. These centers "enjoyed a well-developed business system, relatively under-employed labor and capital, (and) a high level of artisan and mechanical skills," Lindstrom (1978:34) writes. Lindstrom's point is reiterated by Hawke (1988:121): "None of the four Southern towns that were receptive to technological innovations and that contained an embryonic industrialism—Richmond, New Orleans, Charleston, and Louisville—satisfied all of these requirements, particularly the last one, an accessible and prosperous hinterland that could buy what a growth pole produced." It was not until after the Civil War, in the late 19th century, that a true industrial center arose in the South at Birmingham, Alabama (Greenberg 1980:209–242).

Much of the industrial base that did exist served the railroads of the South. The region paid dearly for this decentralized industrial base with its smallish, scattered iron furnaces and rolling mills connected by a non-standardized rail gauge infrastructure. At the beginning of the Civil War at least a dozen gauges were in use (De Camp 1961:53) Construction of the *Georgia* was funded by donations from the "Ladies Gunboat Association," comprised of women from towns and cities of Georgia (*Southern Recorder* [*SR*] 1862:2). The total cost of the ironclad was just over $115,000 (Lawrence 1961:134). No working plans or builder's model were used in the construction, and only artists' sketches of the ironclad exist (Figure 1). Consequently, there are significant discrepancies as to its exact dimensions (Garrison and Anuskiewicz 1984). Various sources place the *Georgia*'s length between 150 and 260 ft., a considerable disparity. An 1863 newspaper correspondent described the ironclad as "a monstrous creature" . . . à la *Merrimac* . . . "with sides and ends sloping to the water at an angle of 45 degrees . . . and covered with long slabs or strips of railroad iron" (Nordoff 1863:115–116).

The superstructure was armored with 500 tons of iron fitted together in such a manner to provide a defensive armor shield about 8 in. thick backed with 2 ft. of oak and pine. The *Georgia* carried a crew of 13 officers and 109 men, captained most of its career by Lt. Washington Gwathmey, who earlier served aboard the *Virginia*. *Georgia* fought no battles and passed its career as a stationary floating battery, together with the other vessels of the Savannah Squadron, blocking Union thrusts on the port of Savannah. With Sherman's capture of Savannah, by land forces, the *Georgia* was scuttled on 20 December 1864.

Throughout 1979–1981, and at short intervals until 1984, the archaeological study of this ironclad confirmed its resting place, aided in its preservation and provided data to amend or correct historical omissions or errors. Although badly damaged in its upper works by removal attempts in 1868, by dynamiting and later dredging of the harbor channel, a formidable amount of the ship remains—case-mate, hull, machinery, and ordnance. Combined with archival data these studies developed a picture of a casemated ironclad, approximately 150 ft. in length, 50 ft. in width, propelled by twin propellers, and mounting four heavy guns at the time of its sinking. The vessel's iron shield was grouted with concrete to help protect the iron armature from corrosion and provide a stronger overall structure. This concrete, coupled with burial in relatively anaerobic sediments, has aided in the preservation of large portions of casemate.

Engineering studies of metal and samples recovered from the wreckage provided insights into the metallurgy and materials of its manufacture (Garrison and Anuskiewicz 1984:95–96). The ironclad's shield was made of wrought iron backed by heartwood yellow pine indigenous to the coastal Pine Barrens of Georgia. Its iron was most probably a product of Atlanta or Columbus mills. These places of iron manufacture, over 200 miles away, combined with the general lack of rail standardization in southern railroads, contributed to delays in *Georgia*'s building. Armor, ready for mounting, languished on rail sidings, for want of adequate or proper gage rail transport.

U.S.S. *Cairo*

The midwestern United States was still frontier in many ways at the time of the Civil War. Nonetheless its industrial development had been fueled by a riverine infrastructure built around the Mississippi, Missouri, and Ohio Rivers. The agricultural products of the midwestern farmers, together with manufactured goods, moved eastward via the Erie Canal, the Great Lakes, and the wide inland rivers. Industry moved westward to Buffalo, Pittsburgh, Wheeling, Louisville, Duluth, Chicago, and centers like St. Louis, as well as to numerous smaller but important sites. Unlike the South, the Midwest's technological base was more diversified in kinds of products and services it supplied to its region. In particular, Illinois and Kentucky could provide coal while southeastern Missouri had rich reserves in iron and lead. Additionally these areas had tremendous forests available for charcoal furnaces that flourished in the first quarter to the mid-19th century. Steam navigation provided demand for industrial goods for the boat building yards such as Cincinnati, Lexington, Anderson (Indiana), and St. Louis. Boilers, engines, and fittings were built and utilized in the region.

Oliver (1956:142), in his assessment of the spread of American technology, states that, "the settlements along the Atlantic coast no longer had a monopoly on Yankee ingenuity." The Midwest or "western country" was attracting skilled artisans, inventors, and mechanics (Oliver 1956:142). Emigrants, following the close of the War of 1812, poured into the old Northwest and Southwest territories in numbers to cause five states to be admitted to the Union: Indiana (1816), Mississippi (1817), Illinois (1818), Alabama (1819), and Missouri (1821).

Frontier expansion led to conflicting influences on industrial development. Habakkuk (1962:40) writes on the seeming contradiction regarding industrialization and agriculture with: "the high returns of American (Midwestern) agriculture . . . (imposing limitations on) . . . the industrial investment." To Habakkuk, it was only after the frontier closed that industrial growth became rapid. To his economic analysis of American industry in the 19th century, the "abundant land and scarce labor was obviously greater on the plains of Ohio," and only the machine enabled the land to be cultivated at all (Habakkuk 1962:40).

Another aspect of the industrialization of the Midwest, "insufficiently stressed," is that the technology of the 19th-century Midwest was a "resource-intensive" technology, substituting, where it was possible, abundant natural resources for "either labor or capital" (Rosenberg 1975:54). This same trade-off characterized the development of the high-pressure steamboats on the western rivers. Hunter, in his 1949 treatise on the technology of western steamboats, points out the highly wasteful nature of their engines but their considerably cheaper costs compared to low-pressure engines (Hunter 1949:130–133). The lighter weight, horizontal cylinder designs of Daniel French were more suitable for the western shallow-draft designs. French's engines weighed less than the flywheels of

FIGURE 2. Restored U.S.S. *Cairo*, Vicksburg National Military Park. (Photo by author.)

Fulton's engines and employed neither walking-beam nor flywheel, acting directly on the paddle by means of connecting rods and pittman arms (Oliver 1956:194).

Along with French were men like Henry M. Shreve and James B. Eads. Shreve is credited with the design standard for all subsequent western steamboats with his construction of the *Washington,* a 400-ton vessel built in 1816 (Hunter 1949: 193). Shreve built his boat to sail *on* the water and not *in* it. He designed a vessel of shallow draft and low, flat hull with a towering superstructure. Eads elaborated the Shreve and the earlier Fitch designs into the successful river ironclad U.S.S. *Cairo* and sister vessels. When faced with the need for warships adapted to the unique conditions of riverine warfare, the Union combined the ideas of John Lenthall, Chief of the Naval Bureau of Construction and Repairs, with those of Samuel Pook, Naval Constructor, and James Eads, a St. Louis engineer. The result of this synthesis was a vessel that differed significantly from that seen in the *Georgia.*

The U.S.S. *Cairo* (Figure 2) was classified as one of the City-Class gunboats, nicknamed "Pook's Turtles" (Milligan 1965). The vessel was 175 ft. long and 50 ft. wide, drawing 7 ft. Its casemate carried 122 tons of armor, which reduced its armament from a designed 20 cannon to 13. The flat-bottomed, wooden hull was divided into 15 watertight compartments by longitudinal and lateral bulkheads. The high-pressure boilers (150 psi) and twin engines drove a large paddle wheel in a central raceway protected by the casemate. The designers felt that use on the narrow nature of inland rivers and in the siege of shore fortifications required the casemate to be heavily armored only in the front and along the sides over the boilers and engines. This left the stern and top either lightly or non-armored, which later proved to be a costly supposition that cost the loss of two of the City-Class vessels to stern bombardment and plunging fire. Seven of the class were built at a cost of $89,600 each. Ead's contract originally called for construction of all seven within 64 days but supplies were slow in arriving, adding over a month to the original schedule (Gaden 1994: 29).

Cairo's thin, unarmored wooden hull, typical of river steamers, proved its undoing as it was sunk by a Confederate mine in the Yazoo River, during the Vicksburg Campaign in 1863. The vessel was not studied archaeologically, which was perhaps more damaging to it than the mine that sank it. Salvaged in 1963–1964 using wire cable lifts, the process cut an intact vessel into three pieces, destroying forever many important features and artifacts (Bearrs 1974). The raised remains languished for 13 years before the National Park Service took charge of them and began a preservation program (McGrath 1981). The project took the form of an archaeology of a well-meant but botched salvage. The National Park Service's careful work resulted in a display of the remnants of the vessel at Vicksburg National Military Park. Lost sections such as the hurricane deck, after casemates, stacks, the ship's boats, and wheelhouse have been mocked up or "ghosted in" and original fabric, where possible, have been restored. The iron machinery and ordnance survived, less scathed.

U.S.S. *Monitor*

Built after the *Cairo,* the U.S.S. *Monitor* (Figure 3), when stripped of its weighty cloak of national myth and legend, represents a technological watershed in ironclad vessel design. The vessel, together

FIGURE 3. Launch of the U.S.S. *Monitor,* September, 1862. (Courtesy of U.S. Naval Historical Center Washington, D.C.)

with the C.S.S. *Virginia,* proved the vulnerability of wooden ships to ironclad vessels mounting modern ordnance as well as demonstrating the difficulty such vessels had in combat with one another.

Carl Bridenbaugh (1961:31, 46) says that on the eve of the American Revolution there "was almost a complete dearth of skilled artisans in the United States . . ." and that those that were here found it particularly hard to flourish in the South where "for wont of towns, markets, and money they were inexorably drawn into planting and farming." In the North they prospered. In Connecticut, for instance, lay "the village precursors of the great industries located today in Bridgeport, New Haven, New Britain, Wallingford, and Meriden" (Bridenbaugh 1961:46). By the eve of the American Civil War, William Tecumseh Sherman could warn a Southern colleague:

> The North can make a steam engine, locomotive or railway car; hardly a yard of cloth or a pair of shoes can you make. You are rushing into a war with one of the most powerful, ingeniously mechanical and determined people on earth— right at your own doors. You are bound to fail (in Gaden 1994:24).

The *Monitor* was a product of this industrial heartland of mid-19th-century America. The North-east was the most populated and technologically developed of the regions. It was a consumer of resources, natural and agricultural commodities. Its industrial process was predicated on the production of excess goods for export rather than just local consumption. The Northeast had abundant water power, water distribution systems, canals, and railroads, as well as a major inland water route in the Hudson River. Massachusetts and New York led the region in industry. The oldest ironworks were at Saugus, Massachusetts; major textile works at Lowell, Massachusetts; and a "Newcastle-like" industrial complex flourished at Troy, New York. Nearly 60 percent of the United States iron ore in 1860 came from Pennsylvania, followed by Ohio, and New York (Still 1988:7). These mills produced nearly 75,000 tons from 15 furnaces which allowed the state to supply 195 establishments producing bar, sheet, and railroad iron (Sullivan 1927:206–208; Hogan 1971:12–13). Troy and New York City led in iron and steel fabrication (Neu 1960:54).

Utilizing these facilities and his own genius, Ericsson was able to create a seminal design combining earlier concepts of design and improvements in iron hulls, armor, steam screw propulsion, shell guns, and turrets (Watts 1975:4). *Monitor* was a true product of modern industrial production processes. Drawing on the natural resources and technological and manufacturing base of the Northeast, John Ericsson, the ironclad's designer, was able to build and assemble his vessel in 100 days. Moreover, the *Monitor* was, as Nicholas D. Ward (1974:4) has noted, an anticipation of modernity, "the blending and harmonizing of methods of construction with design to achieve desired goals." Much as today, Ericsson's contractors and subcontractors had a clear idea of what their individual product would be but less of the complete, assembled ship. This in itself separated the *Monitor* out as a unique departure in naval architecture and a break with traditional ship manufacturing methods.

Monitor was 173 ft. long; 41 ft., 4 in. wide; drawing 10 ft., 4 in.; and displaced 987 gross tons. Its freeboard was only 18 in. On its deck was a single turret mounting two 11-in. Dahlgren smoothbore guns, a pilot house, and smoke and blower stacks. The hull was wrought iron surrounded by a 32-in.-wide iron armor belt of 27 in. of oak and pine covered by five layers of 1-in. iron plates. The turret was 9 ft. high, 20 ft. in diameter, and turned by the two steam engines through a gear train. The power units were two Ericsson vibrating-lever engines driving a single four-bladed propeller, 9-ft. in diameter. Its designed service speed was 6 knots (Webber 1969:3).

Monitor survived its only combat by nine months, sinking in a storm off Cape Hatteras, North Carolina, on New Year's Eve, 1862. The ironclad was relocated in 1973 in 230 ft. of water 16 miles southwest of Cape Hatteras Light. Since 1975, the vessel has been protected in this nation's first National Marine Sanctuary. It has been the subject of major archaeological studies in 1977, 1979, 1983, 1985, and 1987. Over the years 16 scientific missions to *Monitor* have yielded much in terms of a visual record of the wreckage. Using photogrammetric techniques, digital-image analysis, and limited in situ measurements, much of the details of the *Monitor,* at the time of its loss, have been ascertained (Arnold et al. 1991). In addition the *Monitor* has given underwater archaeology a better understanding of the technical difficulties of studying a deep-water shipwreck.

The National Oceanic and Atmospheric Administration (NOAA), the agency charged with the protection of *Monitor,* began annual assessments in 1990. As the agency's archaeologist, I participated in three of these photo/videographic surveys, which were designed to compile a year-to-year record of the present condition of the wreck. They have been conducted with submersibles and divers. Over this time a few small artifacts—lamp shroud and some case bottles—have been recovered from the wreck to prevent their loss to the Gulf Stream's currents that swirl around the site. In the main, the vessel lies upside down, pedestalled at an oblique angle, on its detached turret, slowly deteriorating in the salt water of the Atlantic Ocean (Figure 4).

Discussion

These three examples of the early American ironclad warship represent products of U.S. regional expressions of the 19th century's phase of the Industrial Revolution. In their designs and construction are seen shared elements combined in manners

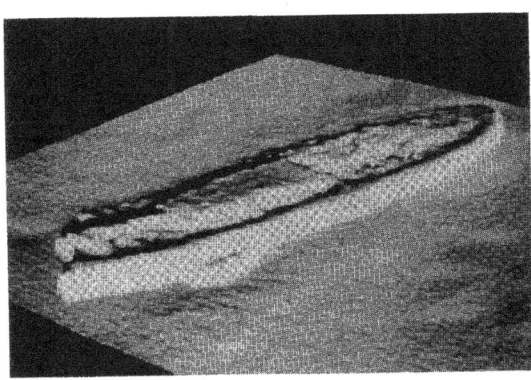

FIGURE 4. Computer-generated, isometric view of the wreck of *Monitor* produced from sonar data taken by the 1987 NOAA study and created by W. Kenneth Steward, Woods Hole Oceanographic Institution. (Courtesy of the National Oceanic and Atmospheric Administration, Washington, D.C.)

that reflect constraints of the industrial potential of their particular place. C.S.S. *Georgia* was a flawed copy of the earlier *Virginia,* fabricated out of used, low-pressure engines, mounting a massive armor casemate and heavy battery which hopelessly limited its speed and maneuverability. The vessel was a local, less successful expression of Porter's general concept of the Confederate armorclad. The southern, lowland marine industry that produced it used familiar elements in armor, engines, and hull design which resulted in an extemporaneous composite of innovative design hampered by an inadequate industrial base.

U.S.S. *Cairo* was a more successful adaptation of existing technology to the ironclad concept. Still, the *Cairo* was essentially an armored riverboat, produced within the capabilities of a regional maritime industrial technology. This midwestern regional industrial base was more greatly influenced and developed by the more advanced northeastern section than that of the lowland South, and its product—*Cairo*—reflects this origin.

U.S.S. *Monitor* is rightly termed a true innovation in warship design. Flawed in that it and its immediate successors were not true seagoing vessels, *Monitor* was the direct lineal ancestor of the modern surface warship. While not truly original in the individual parts of its design, the total assemblage was indeed more than the sum of them. H.G. Wells has succinctly described this in his appraisal of the iron ship:

> The great ship . . . is not, as they imagine, a magnified version of the small ship..of the past; it is a thing different in kind, more lightly and strongly built, of finer and stronger materials; instead of being of precedent and rule of thumb, it is a thing of subtle and intricate calculation. In the old ship, matter was dominant—the materials and its needs had to be slavishly obeyed; in the new, matter has been captured, changed (and) coerced (Wells 1971:80).

The examples given here were three attempts to accomplish this process. Likewise, this study has shown how historical and archaeological study can illuminate what success each achieved and some of the social and technological factors responsible for that level of success. Archaeology, coupled with social, economic, and technological history, comfortably supports the hypothesis of a fundamental disparity in regional structures, social and industrial, directly affecting wartime expansion in volume and kinds of goods (Oliver 1956:286–292). A northern industrial base, in place by the 1840s, merely required an increase in tooling and production. Naval and civilian engineers of the North simply stepped up an already established trend toward a large steam navy. The American Midwest, lacking the Northeast's industrial mass, still shared enough of its technological capacity to fashion innovative designs such as *Cairo*. The South, in contrast, could do neither because of an agrarian-oriented industrial plant. It lacked, as well, the infrastructure, in terms of railroads and canals, to compensate for this dispersed industrial plant. That the South was able to lay down 32 ironclads, compared to 49 for the North, speaks more to a crisis-driven innovativeness than a calculated usage of an in-place capability.

The triumph of the ironclad ship did not come without detractors, as seen in this post-war comment by Lieutenant James I. Waddell, commander of the last Confederate commerce raider, C.S.S. *Shenandoah:*

> The worst of the iron plated vessel is that the black ugly armor has no such vitality and cannot be christened with the

pretty old-fashioned names which helped the sailor's superstition out, we cannot answer for such hideous monsters. They were created out of dull mineral which came from the bowels of the earth, and should they not all come to grief like the *Monitor,* the black-smith will some day turn them into pots and pans, iron railings and boilers (in Horan 1960:189).

Much of Waddell's prejudice against the "hideous monsters" can be understood by most readers. Many will share his sentiments about technology. Although it pervades the reader's life, technology is not completely comforting. The example of the computer is simple enough proof. Commentators on the relation of humans and technology, Lewis Mumford and Sigfried Giedion, have identified this tension with the machine (Hughes 1989:111–113). Hughes notes that "the mechanical environment is appropriate for rational man, although it can destructively repress the emotional" (Hughes 1989: 113)—a reprise of Giedion's (1948) apprehensions of technology seen in *Mechanization Takes Command.* Both Giedion and Mumford see a continued need for a balance between the organic and the mechanical.

The recognition of technology's importance, and its attendant "otherness," raises the question that is important in discussion of the study of the remains of these three ironclad warships. How important would these broken, rusty hulks be if technology—and war—in their time were not important also today? If technology (Mumford's *megamachine*) is a metaphor for our society then we should identify ourselves with and within these objects. Strandh (1979:6) likens this to the ancient talmudic saying, that we do not see things as they are, but as we are. As students of the past, archaeologists recognize that archaeology conjures history. The history of these objects is constructed by researchers just as reconstructions of these vessels are attempted in models and fact. Delgado (1992; cf. Kelly 1992) has addressed this issue in the case of another famous American warship, the U.S.S. *Arizona.* Here the vessel has been vested with meaning less of technological history than that of a historical disaster and aroused nationalism.

The U.S.S. *Monitor* shares a similar role in the country's national consciousness. At issue is the ability of those involved—researchers and administrators alike—to separate *Monitor,* the object from *Monitor,* the myth. Imbued with a patina of folk legend and national lore, *Monitor* is a syncretic construction of history and myth without equal in any United States shipwreck. To many involved with its rediscovery, artifacts recovered from the vessel seemed more in need of a reliquary than a museum (Delgado 1988:12).

Reduced by currents and corrosion and even World War II depth bombs, the rusting remnants of *Monitor* can hardly measure up to the fanciful images constructed about the ironclad. This was poignantly illustrated during the 1987 expedition to the site, which obtained high-resolution photo and acoustic images of the wreckage. A technical advisor, who had written and lectured extensively on the *Monitor,* struggled, when looking at TV monitors of the actual shipwreck, to find "his" *Monitor* in the reality before him. The coral-encrusted wreckage, shimmering with schools of small tropical fish, was not the "historical" ideal held in the mind of that observer.

The same is basically true for the restoration of the raised *Cairo* (Figure 2). Even without the icon-like stature of the *Monitor,* the *Cairo* presents a skeleton-like caricature of the warship it once was. This disparity is apparent to even the most marginally informed or disinterested visitor. The *Georgia* stirs even less passion. None cannot begin to measure up to the historical ideal the present creates—or accepts from the past—for these vessels.

A well-worn phrase for shipwrecks is that of "time capsules." Perhaps this description has some merit but not in the sense in which it was originally intended. The time within the capsule may be more our own than that of the object. Lt. Waddell may have had it partially right—his iron-plated "hideous monsters" stir a certain fascination. Their oddness and uniqueness are only enhanced by the historical role—technological and symbolical—assigned them.

Delgado (1992:69), echoing Gould (1990), points out that even when the recent past is involved, there are alternative versions of the past reconstructed by historians and archaeologists. Castleden (1993:3–4) makes the same point in his *Making of Stonehenge.* He suggests that the giant stones have no single meaning or purpose, and even their ancient reality has been lost to continual mythologization. In the case of the *Monitor,* as seen with the perplexed 1987 observer, the symbolism of the vessel is so powerful that even scientists are drawn into responding to the mythic values (Delgado 1992:78). This, more than formidable logistical and economic hurdles, has resulted in the few meaningful inferences, historical or anthropological, gleaned from the archaeological studies of the *Monitor.*

There are ways to remedy this situation. Alison Wylie (1993:14) calls for a debunking of scholarly and popular mythologies of the past by rigorous empirical demonstrations of their distortion and incompleteness. Historic technological objects, such as *Monitor, Cairo,* and *Georgia* are embedded in these "invented pasts" (Wylie 1993:14) just as are the R.M.S. *Titanic,* S.S. *Edmund Fitzgerald,* and U.S.S. *Arizona.* Gould (1995, pers. comm.) calls these wrecks "celebrity shipwrecks." Without this status, they lose some of their inherent appeal. As students of technology, past and present, able to expose and critique these myths, archaeologists must first recognize them by doing their best with the enigmatic and fragmentary evidence that archaeology offers. Researchers must read it for rigorous empirical evidence and historical context while not losing sight of society's needs for myths and symbols.

Revisiting these three ironclads, archaeologically and historically, removes some of the patina of myth and symbol with which society has imbued them. It situates them within a less subjective frame of reference where they, as industrial objects, can be dispassionately assessed and appreciated. Much can be appreciated in terms of particular technological detail as well as sociohistorical context. This study of three ironclads has attempted to revise and clarify their roles within the emergence of U.S. industrial technology as a regional phenomenon. Moreover, it has looked at them as symbols for this industrial emergence—metaphors for revolution, nationhood, and technology, itself.

In this effort, this article has followed Ellul, Giedion, Mumford, Usher, and others on machine as symbol. If technology is a metaphor for modern society—mechanical and mechanistic—then the objects of this technology symbolize values for that society. The study of industrial technology, maritime of otherwise, through both textual and archaeological data, is unique in that the industrial object directly influences the reading of it. A strict history of the technological does not have this aspect. Citing Ferguson, quoted in Gordon and Malone's (1994) excellent synthesis on industrial archaeology, *The Texture of Industry,* "Even when the authors took pains to describe industrial processes . . . written language was not equal to the task. Mechanical techniques involve a large component of nonverbal thinking that is not easily recorded in words or even in drawings" (Ferguson 1977:827–836). The industrial object allows one to investigate and even reproduce these implicit techniques, which aids in the even more elusive construction of meaning for the object itself. A dynamic is present in this archaeology that is unique in both scale and context.

REFERENCES

ARNOLD, J. BARTO III, MICHAEL G. FLEISCHMAN, DINA B. HILL, CURTIS E. PETERSON, W. KENNETH STEWART, STEPHEN R. GEGG, GORDON P. WATTS, JR., AND CLARK WELDON
1991 *1987 Expedition to the* Monitor *National Marine Sanctuary.* Sanctuaries and Reserves Division, National Oceanic and Atmospheric Administration, Washington, D.C.

BAXTER, JAMES P. III
1933 *The Introduction of the Ironclad Warship.* Harvard University Press, Cambridge, Massachusetts.

BEARRS, EDWARD
1974 *Hardluck Ironclad.* Louisiana State University Press, Baton Rouge.

BRAUDEL, FERNAND
1981 *Civilization and Capitalism, 15th–18th Century.* Vol. 1, *The Structures of Everyday Life.* Harper and Row, New York.

BRIDENBAUGH, CARL
1961 *The Colonial Craftsman.* University of Chicago Press, Chicago, Illinois.

CASTLEDEN, RODNEY
1993 *The Making of Stonehenge.* Routledge, London.

DE CAMP, L. SPRAGUE
1961 *The Heroic Age of Invention.* Doubleday, New York.

Delgado, James P.
 1988 "A Symbol of American Ingenuity": Assessing the Significance of the U.S.S. Monitor. U.S. National Park Service, Washington, D.C.
 1992 Recovering the Past of U.S.S. Arizona: Symbolism, Myth, and Reality. Historical Archaeology 26(4):69–80.

Dickason, Olive Patricia
 1992 Canada's First Nations: A History of Founding Nations from Earliest Times. University of Oklahoma Press, Norman.

Eaton, Clement
 1961 The Growth of Southern Civilization, 1790–1860. Harper, New York.

Ellul, Jacques
 1964 The Technological Society. Alfred A. Knopf, New York.

Ferguson, Eugene S.
 1977 The Mind's Eye: Nonverbal Thought in Technology. Science 197:827–836.

Fores, M., and I. Rey
 1977 Technik: The Relevance of a Missing Concept. Nature 269:2.

Gaden, Elmer L., Jr.
 1994 Eads and the Navy of the Mississippi. Invention and Technology 9(4):24

Garrison, Ervan G.
 1991 Artful Methods: A History of Engineering and Technology. CRC Press, Boca Raton, Florida.

Garrison, Ervan G., and Richard J. Anuskiewicz
 1984 An Archaeological and Engineering Evaluation of the C.S.S. Georgia. Historical Archaeology 21(1):74–100.

Giedion, Siegfried
 1948 Mechanization Takes Command: A Contribution to Anonymous History. Oxford University Press, New York.

Gordon, Robert A., and Patrick M. Malone
 1994 The Texture of Industry. Oxford University Press, New York.

Gould, Richard A.
 1990 Recovering the Past. University of New Mexico Press, Albuquerque.

Greenberg, Stanley
 1980 Race and State in Capitalist Development. Yale University Press, New Haven, Connecticut.

Guillerme, J., and J. Sebestik
 1966 Les commencements de la technologie. Thales 12:72.

Habakkuk, H. John
 1962 American and British Technology in the Nineteenth Century: The Search for Labour-Saving Inventions. Cambridge University Press, Cambridge, U.K.

Hawke, David Freeman
 1988 Nuts and Bolts of the Past: A History of American Technology, 1776–1860. Harper and Row, New York.

Hogan, William T.
 1971 An Economic History of the Iron and Steel Industry in the United States. Five volumes. Heath, Lexington, Massachusetts.

Horan, James D. (editor)
 1960 C.S.S. Shenandoah. The Memoirs of Lieutenant Commanding James I. Waddell. Crown, New York.

Hughes, Thomas P.
 1989 Machines, Megamachines and Systems. In Context: History and the History of Technology; Essays in Honor of Melvin Kranzberg. Research in Technology Series 1:108. Stephen H. Cutcliffe and Robert C. Post, editors. Lehigh University Press, Bethlehem, Pennsylvania.

Hunter, Lewis C.
 1949 Steamboats on Western Rivers; An Economic and Technological History. Harvard University Press, Cambridge, Massachusetts.

Kelly, Roger E.
 1992 The Archaeology of an Icon. Archaeological Studies of World War II, Monograph 10, edited by Raymond W. Wood. University of Missouri, Columbia.

Kemp, Peter K.
 1978 The History of Ships. Two Continents Publishing, New York.

Lawrence, Alexander A.
 1961 A Present for Mr. Lincoln. Ardivan Press, Macon, Georgia.

Lindstrom, Diane
 1978 Economic Development in the Philadelphia Region, 1810–1850. Columbia University Press, New York.

McGrath, H. Thomas, Jr.
 1981 The Eventual Preservation and Stabilization of the U.S.S. Cairo. International Journal of Nautical Archaeology and Underwater Exploration 10(2):79–94.

Milligan, John D.
 1965 Gunboats Down the Mississippi. U.S. Naval Institute Press, Annapolis, Maryland.

Moella, Arthur P.
 1989 The First Generation: Usher, Mumford, and Giedion. In Context: History and the History of Technology; Essays in Honor of Melvin Kranzberg. Research in

Technology Series 1:93. Stephen H. Cutcliffe and Robert C. Post, editors. Lehigh University Press, Bethlehem, Pennsylvania.

MUMFORD, LEWIS
  1934   *Technics and Civilization.* Harcourt and Brace, New York.

NEU, IRENE D.
  1960   *Erastus Corning, Merchant and Financier, 1794–1872.* Cornell University Press, Ithaca, New York.

NORDOFF, CHARLES
  1863   Two Weeks at Port Royal. *Harpers Weekly Magazine* 27:115–116.

OLIVER, JOHN W.
  1956   *History of American Technology.* Ronald Press, New York.

PERRIN, JACQUES
  1990   Technology and Work Organization. *History and Technology* 7(1):7.

ROSENBERG, NATHAN
  1975   America's Rise to Woodworking Leadership. *America's Wooden Age: Aspects of Its Early Technology,* edited by Brooke Hindle, pp. 54–55. Sleepy Hollow, New York.

SOUTHERN RECORDER [Savannah] (*SR*)
  1862   No title. *Southern Recorder,* July 15:2.

STILL, WILLIAM N., JR.
  1985   *Iron Afloat.* University of South Carolina Press, Columbia.
  1988   Monitor *Builders: A Historical Study of the Principal Firms and Individuals Involved in the Construction of the U.S.S.* Monitor. National Maritime Initiative, U.S. National Park Service, Washington, D.C.

STRANDH, SIGVARD
  1979   *A History of the Machine.* A&W Publishing, New York.

SULLIVAN, JAMES (EDITOR)
  1927   *History of New York.* Six volumes. V. Lewis Historical Publishing, New York.

USHER, ABBOTT P.
  1954   *A History of Mechanical Invention.* Reprint of 1929 edition. Harvard University Press, Cambridge, Massachusetts.

VEBLEN, THORSTEIN
  1992   *The Theory of the Leisure Class.* Reprint of 1899 edition. Transactions Publishers, New Brunswick.

WARD, NICHOLAS D.
  1974   Reflections on the Finding of the *Monitor. Loyal Legion Historical Journal* 30(3):4.

WATTS, GORDON P., JR.
  1975   Monitor of a New Iron Age: The Construction of the U.S.S. *Monitor.* Unpublished M.A. thesis, Department of Sociology and Anthropology, East Carolina University, Greenville, North Carolina.

WEBBER, RICHARD
  1969   *Monitors of the U.S. Navy, 1861–1937.* Naval Historical Division, U.S. Navy Department, Washington, D.C.

WELLS, H. G.
  1971   *The Outline of History.* Doubleday, New York.

WYLIE, ALISON
  1993   Invented Lands/Discovered Pasts: The Westward Expansion of Myth and History. *Historical Archaeology* 27(4):1–19.

ERVAN G. GARRISON
DEPARTMENTS OF ANTHROPOLOGY AND GEOLOGY
UNIVERSITY OF GEORGIA
ATHENS, GEORGIA 30602

1989 A Small Craft Typology: Tool for Archaeological Research. In *Underwater Archaeology Proceedings from the Society for Historical Archaeology,* J. Barto Arnold III, editor, pp. 61–63.

MICHAEL B. ALFORD

A Small Craft Typology: Tool for Archaeological Research

Three common questions facing archaeologists in the field upon confronting the remains of a small craft or larger vessels are: "What is it?", "How old is it?", and "Is it significant?". As presumed experts in the area of marine vessel evolution and history, the maritime staff at North Carolina Maritime Museum is frequently approached for assistance in obtaining answers to those questions.

These questions are not necessarily easily answered, identification and evaluation are complex issues. Most often, the vessels in question are situated in underwater sites, and the archaeologist has gathered what little data as was possible under the most trying of conditions. The combination of limited visibility, hazardous currents, physical hardship, and poorly preserved, usually largely obscured structural components conspire to prevent accurate observation of critical features.

Finding answers to these questions is made even more difficult if there happens to be no common language between the asker and the hopeful responder. Nomenclature of ship structures is often vague and ambiguous. In some aspects of vernacular boat types there may be no recognized standard nomenclature. Boat building practices can vary widely from region to region, or even within the same general locale. Often, the questions come over the telephone, with each party groping for descriptive phrases that will somehow transform murky images into concise identities. Inevitably, the tables are turned and the hunter of information becomes the hunted, the brunt of questions rather than the recipient of answers.

This is a frustrating situation for everyone involved. The archaeologist in the field needs immediate answers. Often, a contractor or government agency is complaining of needless delays and escalating construction costs. Analysis of data and reluctance to make decisions based on sketchy observations

may be viewed as incompetence or intolerable regulatory quagmires.

Although archaeologists are on the "front line," and thus take most of the "heat" in these situations, it is unrealistic to expect them to be specialists in all the fields they encounter on a dig, or a dive. That is particularly true in the case of boat and ship structures, for which we are now still gathering the data (for regional vessels) that will enable the teaching of what is a fragmented and difficult subject. But since the specialist in this case also may not be a diver, and cannot (or will not) go on site, (I freely confess to being a terrestrial being; I am not and have never been aquatic or even semi-aquatic in the sense that the acronym "scuba" suggests.) and because in most cases the "object" cannot be delivered to the expert's laboratory, the underwater archaeologist becomes the "eye" of the specialist. In order to "see," the archaeologist must know what to look for, and must be able to communicate back to the specialist the observations that will lead to answers.

This is the function to which the small craft typology attempts to contribute. It is designed to reduce a maze of types, and variations within types, to a manageable number of related groupings, with the key characteristics by which they may be identified. The idea has sprung from the urging of state Underwater Archaeology Unit personnel, who needed a guide to North Carolina's diverse historical small craft. After years of collecting data from abandoned boats, from boats stored in barns, from pieces of boats lying in marshes or behind fish houses, by examining fragments of boats raised from underwater graves, and from repeated efforts to combine, or reconcile field work with historical accounts, records and documents, the unwieldy nature of this mountain of data had become obvious. Work was begun on a scheme to classify known examples of vernacular North Carolina boat building techniques into a simplified checklist that would provide assistance to divers who needed to make quick, on-site assessments relating to identification and historical significance of submerged resources. Patterns and relationships emerged when examples were grouped by similarity of major structural elements, and when those elements were given a hierarchical status.

The system is based on the premise that structural systems are a more reliable indicator of origin and related cultural aspects than is shape, and what we usually refer to as the "lines of a boat." This concept may not be universally accepted as yet, but at least in the present situation it has removed several blocks that had continually proved troublesome previously.

Acceptance of a typology based on structural morphology does not eliminate shape as a consideration. In the first place, boat shape is very much related to the methods and materials selected for construction. However, shape can and does vary within a type, within limits, and is also, like fad and fancy, subject to the whims of taste and the winds of change. A shape typology would probably have to begin with a classification separating hulls into the traditional three classes: round-bottom, vee-bottom, and flat-bottom. Immediately, this invokes artificial criteria which will prejudice many future decisions regarding classification. True evolutionary lines, if present, will be camouflaged and may go undetected. There are other instances in which inconsequential factors conspire to confuse the issue when shape is used as a classification device.

The structural system recognizes the role of boat-building technology in the social and economic development of a societal group. As boat use and economic factors change in a community, shape, size, and arrangement of the boat and its equipment may alter, but the basic structural elements will evolve more slowly, because of the dependency of the building on the technology "status quo" in a vernacular setting.

A structural typology has the added advantage of being based on tactile, definitive objects that are readily recognizable and readable in the field. It must be emphasized that the present typology is based on data collected to date and is thus limited. It is still undergoing testing in the field and also with accumulated file data.

The structural elements incorporated into the typology are planking style, keel morphology, and the system of transverse frames. It is helpful if the diver or observer can determine the general structural class, designated as "plank on frame," or "skiff," etc., but at this point the system is not so cumbersome as to prevent starting in the middle and then eliminating the obvious disparities.

The designation "flat-bottom," "deadrise," and "round-bilge" are used in the sense of construction types, and are not descriptions of shape. Many times, any of these three construction types can be flat or relatively flat in shape over some portion of the bottom, leading to confusion and misinterpretation. There is an apparent allusion to shape in the descriptives "square both ends" and "sharp stern," but the reference is intended for structural features, transverse structures truncating each end in the first instance, and planking terminating at the stem and stern post in the second.

Boats hollowed from logs or incorporating log shells in their construction occupy a separate major category. In a system based on "round," "vee," and "flat" bottoms, these clearly distinct boats usually get tucked away in irrelevant or inappropriate categories. Log boats derive essential strength from the monolithic nature of their shells. When logs or log parts are joined, however, and in some lightly constructed single log boats, additional stiffening and strength is achieved through the use of transverse frames and sometimes longitudinal devices. In the more sophisticated form of log boats, we may see techniques applied to "extend" the capacity of these craft. In North Carolina this consists of either raising the freeboard through the use of a strake or strakes installed along the upper edges of the log shell, or by separating the port and starboard portions of the log shell and combining them with a centerline structure resembling the stem, keel, deadwood, and sternpost of plank-built boats. The two techniques are often seen in the same example.

Apparent limited success with the typology suggests that eventually it may lead to a dichotomous key by which, through a series of simple choices between paired structural features, identification of vessels at the specific level may be accomplished. Such a key is a tool ideally suited to the needs of the archaeologist who may lack the specialization required for identification and evaluation of the wide variety of vessels of diverse origins potentially residing in underwater sites.

There are some negative aspects to this typology. It has previously been stated that it is limited and experimental. I suspect also that it is oversimplified, thus resulting in the risk that field operators may assume a vessel is insignificant if a vessel's remains do not immediately settle into a niche in the typology outline. The typology does not directly address significance, admittedly one of the initial objectives. On the other hand, it does say that vessels or remains which can be placed on the outline match certain minimum criteria for vernacular craft historically used in North Carolina. Every boat of vernacular origin is unique; each has significance of greater or lesser degree. Identification is nine-tenths of the significance questions, and the typology is a step toward identification.

An extremely troubling deficiency in this typology is its lack of application for boats whose origins lie outside the boat-building techniques historically practiced in North Carolina. Boats are obviously mobile and, by purpose, move about and may operate some distance from their points of origin. Some of these will obviously come to rest in foreign ports. Application to vessels which have come from outside the implied geography may result in misleading conclusions, or may fail to register at all. Hopefully, though, observations which are made within the scope of this typology will result in data that will be helpful in arriving at a valid identification of any vessel type for which there is available documentation. Its success ultimately lies with the experience of the user and his or her willingness to pursue matters to fruition.

The references in this paper provide a guide to literature relating to small craft typologies.

Remarks to Accompany Typological Outline

The typology suggested in this outline is an evolving system based on limited information. The structural features on which the categories, as they are presently configured, were established represent concepts based on a combination of field observation and historical records; none are speculative. They are valid only when applied to the vernacular boat types native to North Carolina and, specifically, to those generally not more than 40 ft in length. The typology is further limited, for the most part, to boats and methods used prior to about 1920.

The author makes no claim that this system is either accurate or complete at this time, only that it appears to work as a device to classify boat types within its scope and to indicate possible relationships. Further testing and evaluation in light of recent and forthcoming data will enable a continued honing process to increase the reliability and effectiveness of the typology.

Typology of North Carolina Indigenous Boat Types for the Period 1790 - 1920

Draft Outline December, 1988

TYPOLOGICAL HULL CLASSIFICATION

I. HOLLOWED LOG SHELL (dugout, canoe, canoe-boat, kunner [coll.], periagua)
    A. Single log, simple, trough-form or rudimentary
    B. Single log, simple, modeled form
    C. Single log, complex (inserted frames, modeled form)
    D. Split log, complex (inserted frames), extended, modeled form
    E. Multiple log, complex, extended, modeled form (unconfirmed verbal report)

II. PLANK-ON-FRAME
    A. Round bilge, molded cross-section keel
        1. Transom stem
        2. Fantail stem
        3. Staved round stem
    B. Round bilge, flat keel (or hog)
        1. Transom stem
        2. Round staved stem
    C. Round bilge, lapstrake
        1. Sharp stem
        2. Transom stem
            a. Skiff
            b. Deep keel, decked or partially decked
    D. Deadrise bottom, longitudinally planked bottom, molded cross-section keel
        1. Transom stem
        2. Fantail stem
        3. Staved round stem
    E. Deadrise bottom, bottom planked longitudinally, flat or plank keel, or keel-less
        1. Transom stem
        2. Fantail stem
        3. Staved round stem
        4. Log forefoot
        5. Staved forefoot
        6. Planked forefoot
    F. Flat bottom, longitudinally planked, more or less rockered bottom
        1. Transom stem
        2. Staved round stem
        3. Sharp stem
        4. Square both ends
        5. Side frames molded
        6. Side frames straight
        7. Side planked
        8. Sides molded cross-section
    G. Plate bottom and knee, little or not bottom rocker
        1. Sharp stem or transom stem
            a. Side frames molded
            b. Side frames straight

III. SKIFF CONSTRUCTED (slab or post)
    A. Flat bottom skiff, bottom planked transversely
        1. Transom stem
        2. Sharp stem
        3. Swim head (square both ends)
    B. Deadrise skiff, bottom planked longitudinally small angle of deadrise (modified skiff const.)
        1. Log forefoot
        2. Staved forefoot

IV. FLATS, FLATBOATS AND SCOWS (square both ends)
    A. Essentially skiff-built but larger and heavier construction
        1. Bottom planked transversely
        2. Bottom planked longitudinally
    B. Archaic form (molded side construction)

REFERENCES

CHAPELLE, HOWARD I.
    1951   *American Sailing Craft.* W.W. Norton, New York.

GREENVILLE, BASIL
    1976   *Archaeology of the Boat.* Wesleyan University Press, Middletown, Connecticut.

JOHNSTONE, PAUL
    1980   *The Seacraft of Prehistory.* Harvard University Press, Cambridge, Massachusetts.

MCKEE, ERIC
    1983   *Working Boats of Britain.* Conway Maritime Press, London.

PHILLIPS-BIRT, DOUGLAS
    1979   *The Building of Boats.* W.W. Norton, New York.

MICHAEL B. ALFORD
NORTH CAROLINA MARITIME MUSEUM
315 FRONT STREET
BEAUFORT, NORTH CAROLINA 28516

1995. The Comparative Analysis of 18th-Century Vessel Remains in the Archaeological Record: A Synthesized Theory of Framing System. In *Underwater Archaeology Proceedings from the Society for Historical Archaeology*, Paul F. Johnston, editor, pp. 125–133.

JOHN W. MORRIS III
GORDON P. WATTS JR.
MARIANNE FRANKLIN

The Comparative Analysis of 18th-Century Vessel Remains in the Archaeological Record: A Synthesized Theory of Framing Evolution

Introduction

The evolution of ship design and construction is a dynamic process which began the moment man first floated across a stream on a tree limb. The roots of this change across time and space can be found in the changing economic demands on waterborne transport. These demands would eventually create the rise of vessel specialization by functional necessity. This paper does not examine this process as an entity, nor does it provide a seamless theorem without exception. What it does offer is a synthetic view of design and construction shifts as evidenced by archaeological data spanning the 18th century. It should be considered a point of departure for additional research and consideration.

A pattern of vessel specialization by economic necessity is demonstrable in diverse cultures throughout history. The 18th century was chosen due to the wealth of information available from archaeological sites, as well as the large volume of documentary resources. Archaeology has provided excellent design and construction examples often contradicting contemporary documents. This is attributable to the nature of technical documentation, which tends towards the idealized or perfected design concept rather than the resulting reality. A finished vessel is probably never as perfect as the paper record suggests. Far more vessels have been constructed than documented, and countless localized variations and permutations of designs were never recorded at all.

The differences are plainly evident in the shift in framing patterns in the run of the hull and radical variations found in framing the ends. Obviously, changes in hull forms, rigging, and technological innovations accompany this evolutionary process. However, this paper is confined to framing changes in the archaeological record from 1692 to 1853. The examples cross spatial boundaries as well as functional applications. The sites presented are not all those available for this synthesis. However, all vessels discussed in this article have been examined, documented, or excavated by the authors. This presentation format also limits the detail included in individual vessel descriptions.

The vessel remains selected include those from Port Royal, Jamaica (1692); Rose Hill, North Carolina (1725-1750); Otter Creek, North Carolina (post-1772); Readers Point, Jamaica (post-1765); British Site, Bermuda (post-1770); *Betsy*, Yorktown, Virginia (1772); Vessel 20, Savannah, Georgia (late 18th century); Vessel 2, Savannah, Georgia (late 18th or early 19th century); and *Scuppernong*, Elizabeth City, North Carolina (1853). The basic data for these hulls are presented in Figure 1.

Framing Evolution

The general theory of the transition in framing patterns is graphically illustrated in Figures 2 and 3. Figure 2 addresses the frames in the flat run of the hull and covers the following shifts. Single, non-linear frames shown in Figure 2.1 are supplanted by single linear frames (Figure 2.2). Single frames give way to the double frame (consisting of a floor paired with the associated first futtock) and the subsequent rising futtocks, which remain in a linear orientation. In its earliest form the double frame has no horizontal fasteners, a longitudinal space between each frame's components, butt scarfs, tight frame spacing, a large offset from the centerline of the vessel to the heel of the first futtock (Figure 2, space "A"), and sided dimensions exceeding molded dimensions (Figure 2.3). The transition

VESSEL/ LOCATION, NATION, DATE	LOA, BREADTH P- PRESERVED	FRAME TYPE	CANT TYPE	FUTTOCK OFFSET CL	AVG. MOLDED VS. AVG. SIDED DIMENSION
Port Royal, Jamaica Pre-1692	74'P est. 25'	# 3	None	1'8"	M" ‹ S"
Rose Hill, NC 1725-1750	61'9"P 16'P	# 4	None	11"	M" ‹ S"
Otter Creek, NC Post 1772	58'P 16'P	# 4	None	13"	M" - S"
Reader's Pt., Jamaica Colonial Built, post 1765	57'P 15'P	# 4	# 3	6" from Ksn Edge	M" - or ‹ S"
Bermuda, British, Post 1770	69'9"P 24'P	# 4	None	6-8 1/2" from edge of Hogging Piece	M" › S" Floors M" › S" Futtocks
Betsy, Yorktown,VA British, 1772	73'P 23'P	# 5	# 3	10 3/4"	M" › S"
Vessel 20 Savannah,GA, last 1/4 18th c.	77'4"P 21'4"P	# 4	# 3	6" from Ksn Edge	M" - S"
Vessel 2 Savannah, GA, U.S. Built, late 18th c. or early 19th c.	67'9"P 19'7"P	# 4/ # 6	# 4	Heels Under Ksn Do Not Butt	M" ‹ S"
Scuppernong, Elizabeth City NC, Carolina Built, 1853	75'9"P 17'P	# 6	# 4	Heels Butt CL	M" › S"

FIGURE 1. Vessel data.

continues with the heels of the first futtocks moving toward the centerline of the vessel, frame components moving closer to one another (Figure 2, space "B"), an increase of space between frames, the use of horizontal longitudinal fasteners between frame components, the advent of chock scarfs, and an increase of the molded value relative to the sided value (Figure 2.4–2.5). The culmination of this transition is the eventual butting of the heels of the first futtocks over the centerline of the vessel beneath the keelson (Figure 2.6). At this point the frame spacing has also increased and the molded value exceeds the sided, with notable exceptions such as coastal schooners, shoal draft vessels, and other craft grounding in the course of their trade.

Cant Frames

Figure 3 illustrates the shifting frame arrangement in the bow of the vessel. Forming a ship's bow is a complex and difficult task seldom documented in the archival sources and poorly preserved in the material record. The technical nomenclature for these frames is diverse and varied; the term cant frame itself cannot rightly be applied to frames perpendicular to the centerline at a vessel's extreme ends. Figure 3.1 shows the final frames in the pattern still squared with the hull. The outer molded surface of these frames was heavily beveled to impart shape to the vessel end, and the timbers of the frames are relatively heavy. These frames were both floors and half-frames, with the heels always on the vessel centerline. Even with the evolution of the pattern of bow frames, stern framing generally retained frames perpendicular to the hull. The subsequent pattern type (Figure 3.2) has canted half-frames, still heavily beveled but with the forwardmost frame heels butting against the forward half-frame rather than against a timber on the vessel centerline. The next pattern type (Figure 3.3) is referred to as a radial cant frame pattern (Morris 1991). Radial cants vary not only in pattern but also can be used to form stern and bow with a framing pattern radi-

ating from the vessel's centerline timbers (Figure 4). These timbers are often segmented and variegated to produce the necessary foundation for the heels of the framing timbers. In the bow these timbers are in the form of a segmented apron; in the stern they are transom chocks (Morris 1991). Radial cants in the bow are also possible while the framing timbers in the stern remain square to the centerline. Variations of this pattern generally differ in the arrangement along the centerline, in the degree of angle relative to the keel and in the extent of the use of filler frames. The culmination of this progression is seen in Figure 3.4, where all bow frames are canted, all still touch the centerline, and filler frames are utilized. This arrangement is codified and fairly well standardized by the 19th century, although variations abound.

Vessel Descriptions

A construction technique common to all of these sites is the use of master (or loft) frames. Although frame spacing between masters varies considerably from vessel to vessel, it is present regardless of vessel size or function. Master frame use is generally indicative of the technique of whole molding, with, the vessel's hull form created by these master frames and a series of ribbands or battens. Framing and planking in this construction method occur simultaneously and can be traced as far back as the 16th century in both the archival and archaeological records; it is still employed in wooden ship construction. Beyond this similarity, all the vessels described in this work vary somewhat.

Another element considered is the placement of floors relative to the associated first futtock. Convention says that the first futtock is forward of the floor forward of the mid-ship bend (master couple). Aft of this couple, the first would fall abaft the floor. However, archaeological evidence suggests that this is seldom the case, so variations are included in this discussion. Although there is no discernible chronological sequence to this placement, it is a viable consideration in the framing theory.

Lost in 1692, the vessel remains at Port Royal provide a point of departure for this theory (Clifford 1993). Although the structure is badly degraded with no extant cant frames, the framing pattern in the run of the hull is obviously early double-frame construction (similar to Figure 2.3). Each first futtock is associated with a floor timber, although substantial gaps exist between these components. The first futtocks' heels are offset 1 ft. 8 in. from the centerline and the floors are placed on 2 ft.-6 in. centers. The molded value is 8 in. and is exceeded by the sided dimension of 9 in., with a substantial space between frames. In this vessel the master frames would have been single, consisting of the floors and their organic or linearly associated futtocks. Due to site preservation, it is not possible to establish the floor/first futtock relationship relative to the bow and stern.

The next two sites are both from North Carolina and are similar in size and framing. The Rose Hill site has a date range of 1725 to 1750 (Wilde-Ramsing et al. 1992). The double frames have the first futtock fayed closely to the associated floor (Figure 2.4). These futtocks are offset by 11 in. and are not fastened to the floors. The sided dimension is 11 in., slightly greater than the molded value of 10-1/2 in. No cant frames were present at the site and the floor/first futtock pattern was not recorded. The second site at Otter Creek, North Carolina, dates to post-1772 and has a framing pattern almost identical to the Rose Hill site (Jackson 1992). Other similarities include an apparent lack of fasteners between frame components and the use of whole molding. The first futtocks at Otter Creek are offset 13 in. and the floors have equal molded and sided values. The first futtocks, however, have a greater molded dimension relative to the sided. On this hull, the first futtock is always forward of the floor.

The next site is a colonial vessel dated to post-1765 at Readers Point, Jamaica (Cook and Rubenstein, this volume). Its framing pattern is shown in Figure 2.4, with tightly-fitted floors and futtocks. Despite this close fit, horizontal fasteners are used only in the nine master frame

pairs. The first futtocks are offset 6 in., with the average sided value equal to or greater than the average molded value. Additionally, cant frames were preserved, clearly representing a variation of the radial pattern illustrated in Figure 3.3.

The next three sites also have framing patterns somewhat similar to Readers Point in both the cant framing and hull run. Two of them appear to have been in the coal trade at some time in their careers. *Betsy*, a collier built in 1772 at Whitehaven, England, was lost at

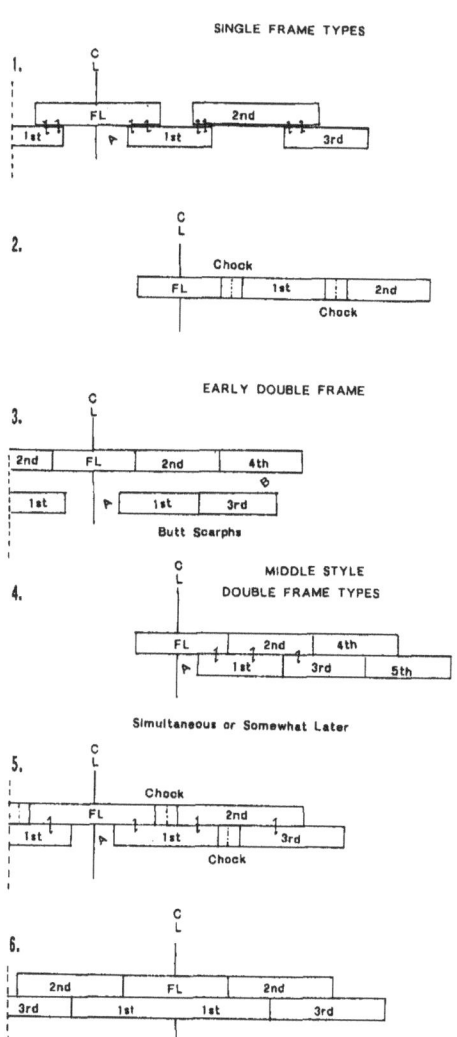

FIGURE 2. Basic 18th-century framing pattern evolution.

1.

PERPENDICULAR FRAMES, BOTH 1/2 AND FLOORED, WITH BEVELED OUTBOARD MOULDED SURFACE TO SHAPE VESSEL ENDS

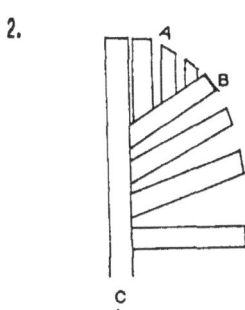

2.

CANTED BUT STILL HEAVILY BEVELED WITH (A) KN, HP,etc. BUTTING (B) 1/2 FRAME

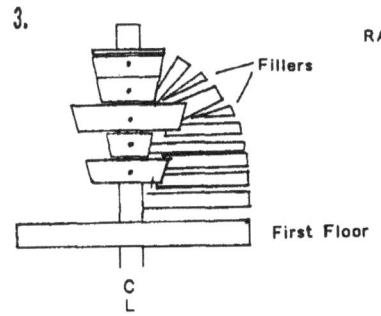

3.

RADIAL CANTS W/ SEGMENTED APRON CHOCK

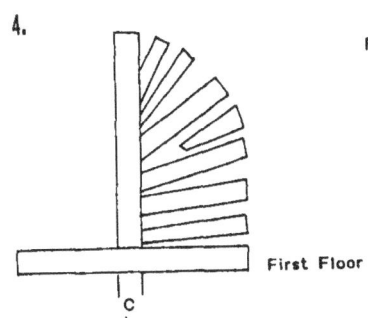

4.

RADIAL VARIATIONS PERSIST UNTIL THIS PATTERN

FIGURE 3. Basic evolution of bow cant frames.

Yorktown, Virginia, in 1781 (Morris 1991). It is a heavily-framed vessel, with the first futtocks always abaft their associated floors. The framing pattern is shown in Figure 2.5, although slight gaps appear on some frames between components. Seven bolted master frames were employed in the construction—the only frames on the vessel with components actually fastened together. Frame spacing is tight, with the first futtocks offset 10-3/4 in. Molded values actually exceed sided values but the latter dimension is still massive. The increase in molded values was therefore not accomplished at the expense of the sided dimension, creating a very heavy frame. Extensive use was made of fillet pieces on the heels of the first futtocks and beneath the floors adjacent to the keel. *Betsy* has radial cant frames in the bow and the stern, with segmented centerline timbers variegated to accept the frame heels (Figures 3.3 and 4).

The site off of Bermuda's west coast has all of the construction signatures of a collier, as well as extensive coal residue in the bilges (Watts and Krivor 1995). Dated to the last quarter of the 18th century, this vessel was heavily framed in a pattern similar to *Betsy* (Figure 2.5). Like the Yorktown collier, this vessel has heavy, irregularly-sided timbers with a slightly greater molded dimension. First futtocks are offset 6 to 8-1/2 in. from the edge of the hogging piece, and fillet pieces were used on the heels of the firsts and beneath the floors adjacent to the keel. Room and space is very tight, also like *Betsy*.

The third vessel grouped with these two heavily-framed merchantmen is Vessel 20 at Fig Island, in Savannah, Georgia (Tidewater Atlantic Research 1994). The greatest similarity is in the radial cant frame variant with a segmented apron. There are five master frames forward of the master couple and seven masters aft. Only the master frames are longitudinally fastened. Forward of the midships bend, the floor is forward of the first futtock. Aft of the bend, the floor is abaft the first futtock. All firsts are offset by 6 in. and molded values are roughly equal to sided. Frame spacing is greater than the previous sites and varies considerably (Figure

2.4). Accurate values were precluded by the degraded remains.

The final two sites bring the pattern into the 19th century. Vessel 2 at Fig Island was most likely built in the last quarter of the 18th century and may be representative of coastal trading vessels from the period (Tidewater Atlantic Research 1993). The framing pattern resembles Figure 2.4, but the heels of the first futtocks pass under the keelson without quite butting on the centerline, as in Figure 2.6. Eight master frames are all longitudinally fastened and arranged with the floor always abaft the first (with one exception). Butt scarfs were employed in forming the frames and the gaps between components were shimmed. Spacing between frames varies but is not as tight as in previous examples. Although the bow cants are degraded, they are closest in appearance to Figure 3.4. The full shape of the bow imparts a radial appearance, but construction is somewhat more linear with a finer entry. In the stern are half-frames squared to the centerline, with beveled outer molded surfaces forming the after underbody.

The vessel chosen to conclude this study is the coastal schooner *Scuppernong*, built in North Carolina in 1853 (Turner, this volume). *Scuppernong* has a framing pattern with the first futtocks butting heels on the vessel centerline (Figure 2.6). The molded value for individual frame components is 6 in. with a sided value of 5 in. All frame elements are fayed closely together with a substantial space of 13-1/2 in. The cant frames are canted from the centerline timbers to form a sharper bow and lack a segmented apron (Figure 3.4).

Summary

The sites described in the text and illustrated in the figures clearly illustrate the shift in framing patterns in both the flat run of the hull and the cant frames. As they replaced single frames, double frames started with separate but paired components, with the heels of the first futtocks far offset from the centerline and room being equal to space. This practice, as illustrated by

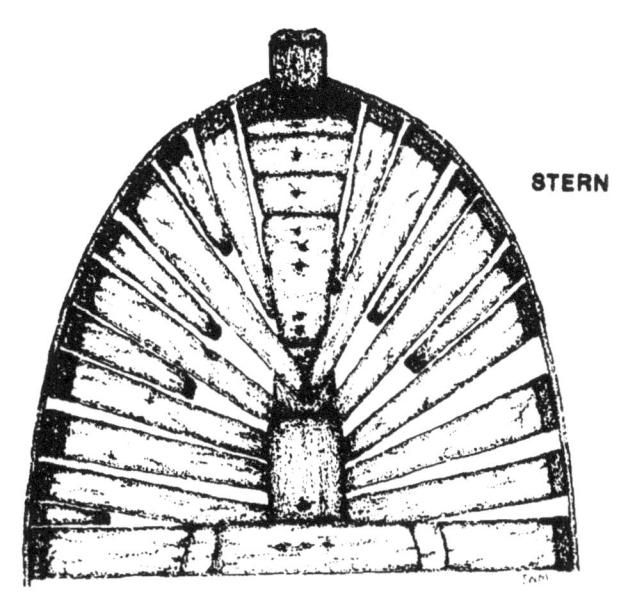

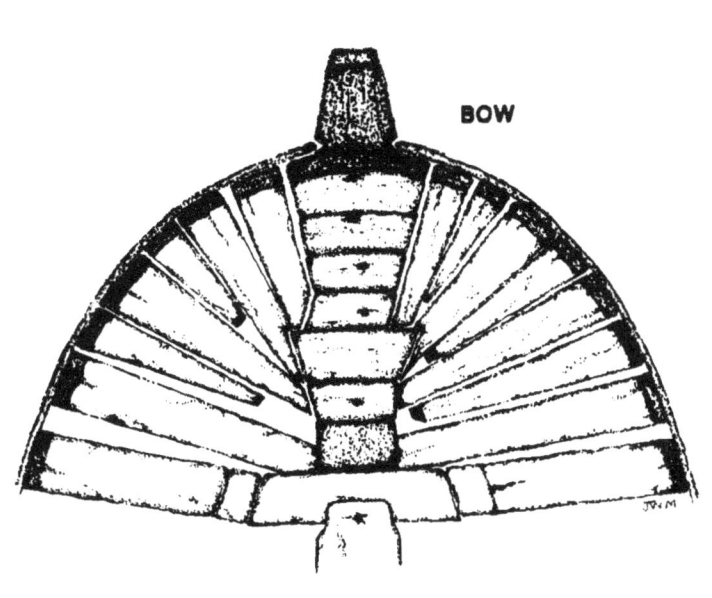

FIGURE 4. Bow and stern cant frames on *Betsy* (Morris 1991:98).

the Port Royal site, was described by Deane (1670). As the framing pattern evolved, the heels of the first futtocks moved toward the center, the components of individual frames moved closer together, and molded values increased (not always at the expense of sided values). This is most clearly demonstrated by the collier *Betsy* and the vessel off Bermuda. As the frame components underwent these shifts, space between frames also usually increased. However, even as the heels of the first futtocks drew closer, space was still needed to allow "breathing," prevent rot, aid in pumping out the bilge, and maintain a dry cargo area (Steele 1805; Morris 1991; Wilde-Ramsing et al. 1992). Eventually, as typified by *Scuppernong*, the firsts would butt on the centerline and the molded and sided values would either be equal or the molded value would become greater. Additionally, space would exceed room. Cant frames also evolved, and the shift in the cant framing pattern probably reflects a shift in hull form and material availability as much as anything else.

Conclusions

The shifts in framing patterns presented here result from several factors. The most significant is economic demand, giving rise to the technological response of vessel form specialization by functional necessity. Construction advances would naturally follow a demand for vessels that were more seaworthy, better suited to specific tasks, and profitable. Other considerations are environmental variations from trade pattern shifts, availability of construction materials, advances in associated technology, and demographic shifts changing specific maritime practices.

Although the proposed theory is chronological in nature, it is neither seamless nor free of exceptions. Framing patterns do shift across the 18th century as the sites described indicate. It should be explained that the list of exceptions to the evolutionary steps presented here is too lengthy to include. However, the typologies presented here, synthesized from numerous archaeological investigations, provide a point of departure for future research on 18th-century wreck sites. Additionally, beyond the specific typological information in this work, there is a conceptual consideration to be made. The application of synthetic data analysis from vessel sites is applicable to other time periods, as vessel specialization is not confined to the 18th century.

REFERENCES

CLIFFORD, SHEILA A.
1993 An Analysis of the Port Royal Shipwreck and its Role in the Maritime History of Seventeenth-Century Port Royal, Jamaica. Unpublished Master's Thesis, Department of Anthropology, Texas A & M University, College Station, Texas.

COOK, GREGORY, AND AMY L. RUBENSTEIN
1995 The Reader's Pt. Project: The Excavation of an Eighteenth-Century Sloop in St. Ann's Bay, Jamaica. In *In The Depths Defined: 1995 Underwater Archaeology Proceedings From The Society For Historical Archaeology Conference On Historical And Underwater Archaeology*, this volume. Edited by Paul Forsythe Johnston. Society for Historical Archaeology, Washington, D.C.

DEANE, ANTHONY
1670 *Deane's Doctrine of Naval Architecture*. Conway Maritime Press (1981 reprint), Greenwich, London.

JACKSON, CLAUDE V. III
1992 *Historical and Archaeological Investigations of a Sunken Federal Period Vessel Near Oriental, North Carolina*. Underwater Archaeology Unit, Division of Archives and History, North Carolina Department of Cultural Resources, Kure Beach, North Carolina.

MORRIS, JOHN W. III
1991 Site 44YO88, The Archaeological Assessment of the Hull Remains at Yorktown, Virginia. Master's Thesis in History, East Carolina University, Greenville, North Carolina.

STEEL, DAVID
1805 *Naval Architecture*. London, England.

TIDEWATER ATLANTIC RESEARCH
1993 (Vessel 2) Archaeological Data Recovery Area I, Fig Island Channel Site, Savannah Harbor, Georgia. Prepared for the U.S. Army Corps of Engineers, Savannah District.

1994   (Vessel 20) Phase II Archaeological Data Recovery, Area I, Fig Island Channel Site, Savannah Harbor, Georgia. Prepared for the U.S. Army Corps of Engineers, Savannah District.

TURNER, ALEXANDER
1995   A Preliminary Report on the Scuppernong: A Mid-Nineteenth Century North Carolina Built Centerboard Schooner. In *In The Depths Defined: 1995 Underwater Archaeology Proceedings From The Society For Historical Archaeology Conference On Historical And Underwater Archaeology*, this volume. Edited by Paul Forsythe Johnston. Society for Historical Archaeology, Washington, D.C.

WATTS, GORDON P. JR., AND M. C. KRIVOR
1995   Investigation of an Eighteenth Century English Shipwreck in Bermuda. *The International Journal of Nautical Archaeology*. In press.

WILDE-RAMSING, MARK U., W. ANGLEY, R. W. LAWRENCE, AND G. J. SCOFIELD
1992   *The Rose Hill Wreck, Historical and Archaeological Investigations of an Eighteenth Century Vessel at a Colonial River Landing near Wilmington, North Carolina*. Underwater Archaeology Unit, Division of Archives and History, North Carolina Department of Cultural Resources, Kure Beach, North Carolina.

JOHN W. MORRIS III
P.O. BOX 13512
MELROSE, FLORIDA 32666

GORDON P. WATTS JR.
P.O. BOX 2494
WASHINGTON, NORTH CAROLINA 27889

MARIANNE FRANKLIN
P.O. BOX 13512
PENSACOLA, FLORIDA 32591

2008. In Search of Unique Iberian Ship Design Concepts. *Historical Archaeology* 42(2):63–87.

Filipe Castro

In Search of Unique Iberian Ship Design Concepts

ABSTRACT

Defining 15th- and 16th-century Iberian shipbuilding traditions related to European expansion overseas is a difficult task. Scarce documentary evidence and the systematic destruction of Spanish and Portuguese shipwrecks by those with a purely monetary agenda make the task even more complex. In spite of these obstacles, data suggests that a distinctive shipbuilding tradition existed on the Iberian Peninsula. Through careful mining of the documentary and archaeological evidence, the concepts behind Iberian ship design can be articulated as well as compared and contrasted to other European shipbuilding traditions.

Introduction

The study of nautical archaeology is only a half-century old. Although a sizeable overall sample of shipwrecks has been studied around the world, there is no one type with a sample large enough to approximate the principle of redundancy practiced in terrestrial archaeology. From an history of technology perspective, synthesis of broad interpretive schemes and conceptual modalities is not possible from shipwreck data alone. Furthermore, ships are like fingerprints: they share conceptual characteristics, but each differs slightly, producing a unique construction set with distinctive sailing and handling qualities. There is only one *Kyrenia* and there is only one *HMS Victory*, but if either of these ships were compared to a number of contemporary examples, the shared conceptual designs and features of their individual cultures would be obvious. It is important to first examine the wider context of the European history of shipbuilding and its influence on Iberian shipbuilding. To do this, historical documents regarding the economical, political, and social contexts in which ship designs were conceived, built, and operated must be consulted, along with iconographic and ethnographic materials. This is an arduous task since documentary evidence, both textual and iconographic, is dispersed, scarce,

and often vague for the first 150 years of the Age of Exploration. Researchers know caravels sailed southwards along the western coast of Africa from the first quarter of the 15th century, and yet no treatise on shipbuilding exists until the 1570s (Domingues 2005:13). Ethnographic data are scarce and relate largely to a different type of working craft, smaller, built by eye in coastal settlements for their population's everyday work, as opposed to the ocean-going vessels produced during the state-driven shipbuilding revolution of the 15th and 16th centuries under analysis. The combined textual and ethnographic evidence suggests, nevertheless, that Iberian ship design and construction was strongly influenced by imported Italian shipwrights, following a conceptual model that is believed to originate in Mediterranean galley construction, although archaeological proof of this is inconclusive. Arab influence may also have been important, although it is even more difficult to prove because there is an almost complete lack of evidence.

Spanish scholars led the first scientific studies in Iberian naval archaeology in the late-19th century, during the decade that preceded the 400th anniversary of the Columbus voyages in 1892. This Spanish interest in the "Ships of Discovery" triggered research and studies in Portugal. In the century that followed, scholars from both countries produced a series of thorough studies that entailed a meticulous combing of the archives, in both countries and abroad (Domingues 2000:13–56). These works are historical in nature since the scientific study of shipwrecks had not yet begun. Moreover, human carelessness and Mother Nature had already reduced the reservoir of documentary evidence through fires, natural decay, earthquakes, and tidal waves. Yet, 19th-century scholars diligently studied and analyzed what remained, including the existing iconography. Although a systematic analysis of the surviving iconography still awaits comprehensive study, the majority of the existing iconography from the 15th and 16th centuries is published (Barata 1989:15–102; Casado Soto 2001:131–161). Now, little more than a century since the first scholarly studies of the

Iberian ship designs were published, it is fair to state that further understanding of Iberian shipbuilding of the period under analysis rests almost exclusively on the study of ship archaeological remains (Alves 2001).

Given the rate of systematic destruction of Spanish and Portuguese shipwrecks for economic gain, without giving thought to the knowledge carried within the remnant ship structure, the odds are not in favor of nautical archaeology. Historical archaeologists need to evaluate and organize the information available and use future finds to compare, contrast, and fill in the gaps in knowledge about these amazing artifacts, perhaps the most expensive and sophisticated ships that were built in their time. This paper looks at what is known, archaeologically and through historical documentation, and sets the groundwork for comparison in the hopes that the study of Iberian ship design will reach the enviable status of redundancy in the future.

Beginning with archaeologically recovered data, all Iberian shipwrecks that have been found and of which some information has been somehow published are listed in tables 1 through 5. Table 6 shows the hull remains that have been found bearing characteristics that are commonly associated with Iberian construction but that are known or at least suspected to have been built elsewhere. Although detailed recording and technical descriptions of each ship's construction characteristics admittedly do not make very exciting reading, this information is of paramount importance for future comparative studies. Despite the fact that these ships made possible European exploration and expansion overseas during the 15th and 16th centuries and were arguably the equivalent to today's space shuttles, scholarly monographs often reduce ships to dry and uninspiring sets of tables and numbers, geometrical algorithms, and timber assemblage arrangements.

Ships resulted from a number of factors, many of which were contingent upon the ever-changing social, economic, and political landscape. The most important thing about ships is undoubtedly the people that ordered, thought about, planned, and executed their construction. Their final shape, size, and performance depended on the availability of materials, tools, knowledge, and personal skills, which may have been combined with fashions and perceptions of a reality that is unknown. The study of the ideas and the people behind the revolution in ship design, which made possible the discovery of new continents and the exploration of new seas, islands, and continents, is important and exciting. Such study will certainly make a relevant contribution to the history of science and technology. Articles about ship design can and sometimes do make captivating reading. One can only hope that when more scholars produce exciting papers, acknowledging the people behind the artifacts, the value of shipwreck remains will exceed the economic gain associated with salvage in the minds of journalists, politicians, antique dealers, and the public.

Research Questions and Parameters

To fully address ship design concepts, it is relevant to ask a series of questions. Is there a set of unique artifactual components or characteristics that can be identified in the archaeological remains of a ship, marking it as Iberian? How different is Iberian shipbuilding from other contemporary shipbuilding traditions? Was there an Iberian shipbuilding tradition during the Age of Exploration (15th–17th centuries) or is this just a cultural myth?

All of these questions must be couched in the parameters of the time. First, there were no international standards for shipbuilding and there were no national standards until the beginning of the 17th century. Second, shipbuilding was an art based on oral tradition and learned through apprenticeship (Dell'Amico 2002:21–25). Third, since there were only vague unit standards and the concept of precision was much different, it is difficult to look for standard measurements or precise proportional relations among ships' parts.

Not even the advent of the printing press transformed shipbuilding from tradition to replicable science until much later. Although the earliest treatises often aimed at codifying cultural concepts, these were not printed and did not circulate outside very small and generally national circles of interested people. Most shipbuilding treatises remained in manuscript forms, although a Spanish merchant authored the first printed naval architectural treatise and lawyer named Diego García de Palacio and was printed in Mexico in 1587.

TABLE 1
NEW WORLD ROUTES: SIXTEENTH-CENTURY SHIPWRECKS

Shipwreck	Date	Location	Timber remains	Data[1]
Molasses Reef Shipwreck	Early-16th century	Bahamas	Small portion	Salvaged/Excavated (1)
Highborn Cay Shipwreck	Early-16th century	Bahamas	Part of the bottom	Salvaged/Excavated (1)
Bahia Mujeres Shipwreck	Early-16th century	Mexico	None	Surveyed (1)
Playa Damas Shipwreck	Early-16th century	Panama	Part of the bottom	Surveyed/Salvaged (2)
San Esteban	1554	Texas	Stern heel	Salvaged/Excavated (1)
Espiritu Santo	1554	Texas	Unknown	Salvaged (1)
Santa Maria de Yciar	1554	Texas	Unknown	Destroyed by dredges (1)
La Condesa	1555	Portugal	Unknown	Looted? (3)
Emanuel Point Shipwreck	1559	Florida	Extensive	Partially excavated (1)
Saint John's Bahamas Shipwreck	Mid-16th century	Bahamas	Part of upper works	Excavated (1)
Mystery Wreck of MAREX	Mid-16th century	Bahamas	Unknown	Salvaged (1)
Caio Nuevo Shipwreck	Mid-16th century	Mexico	None	Surveyed (1)
Francisco Padre	Mid-16th century?	Cuba	Unknown	Salvaged? (4)
Galera	Mid-16th century?	Cuba	Unknown	Surveyed (5)
San Juan	1565	Canada	Extensive	Excavated (1)
San Pedro	1596	Bermuda	Unknown	Salvaged (1)
Western Ledge Reef Shipwreck	Late-16th century	Bermuda	Extensive	Excavated (1)
Spanish Wreck	Late-16th century	Bermuda	Yes	Salvaged (1)
Ines de Soto Shipwreck	Late-16th century	Cuba	None	Excavated (1)
San Cayetano	Late-16th century?	Cuba	Unknown	Excavated (5)
Basque galleon 1	16th century	Canada	Yes	Surveyed (6)
Basque galleon 2	16th century	Canada	Yes	Surveyed (6)
Basque galleon 3	16th century	Canada	Yes	Surveyed (6)
Saona Site 1	16th century	Dominican Republic	Unknown	Salvaged/Surveyed (7)
Saona Site 2	16th century	Dominican Republic	Unknown	Salvaged/Surveyed (7)
Saona Site 3	16th century	Dominican Republic	Unknown	Salvaged/Surveyed (7)
West Turtle Shoal	16th century?	Florida	Part of the stern	Salvaged/Surveyed (8)
Angra B	16th century	Azores	Part of the bottom	Surveyed (1)
Angra D	16th century?	Azores	Extensive	Excavated (1)

[1] Data sources: (1) Castro 2005b:193–202; (2) Castro 2005c; (3) Toja 1990; (4) Alejandro Mirabal <http://arq.de/downloads/curriculos/eng_alejandro_mirabal.pdf> on 20. Oct. 2005; (5) López Pérez and Díaz Pelegrín 2005; (6) Robert Grenier 2003, pers. comm. ; (7) Turner 1994; (8) Roger Smith 2005, pers. comm.

TABLE 2
NEW WORLD ROUTES: SEVENTEENTH-CENTURY SHIPWRECKS

Shipwreck	Date	Location	Timber remains	Data[1]
Fuxa Shipwreck	Early-17th century	Cuba	Extensive	Excavated (1)
Green Cabin Shipwreck (*San Martin*)	1618	Florida	Part of the bottom	Surveyed (1)
San Antonio	1621	Bermuda	Unknown	Salvaged (1)
Nuestra Señora de Atocha	1622	Florida	Part of the bottom	Salvaged/Partially recorded (1)
Shot Wreck	1622	Florida	Unknown	Salvaged (1)
Santa Margarita	1622	Florida	Part of upper works	Salvaged/Partially recorded (1)
Dry Tortugas Shipwreck	1622	Florida	Extensive	Salvaged (1)
Nuestra Señora del Rosario	1622	Florida	None	Surveyed (1)
Urca La Viga	1639	Bermuda		Salvaged (1)
Nuestra Señora de la Concepción	1641	Dominican Republic	Unknown	Salvaged (1)
Stonewall Shipwreck	Mid-17th century	Bermuda	Part of the bottom	Salvaged/Surveyed (1)
Nuestra Señora de las Maravillas	1656	Bahamas	Unknown	Salvaged (1)
Jesús M.ª de la Limpia Concepción	1654	Ecuador	Unknown	Salvaged (1)
Santíssimo Sacramento B	1668	Brazil	Extensive	Excavated (1)
San Francisco Wreck	1650–1660	Cape Verde	Unknown	Salvaged (9)
Los Lingotes	Late-17th century?	Cuba	Unknown	Surveyed (5)

[1] Data sources: (1) Castro 2005b:193–202; (5) López Pérez and Díaz Pelegrín 2005; (9) From <http://www.arq.de/english/sanfrancisco. htm> accessed 20 Oct. 2005.

TABLE 3
MANILA GALLEONS: SIXTEENTH- AND SEVENTEENTH-CENTURY SHIPWRECKS

Shipwreck	Date	Location	Timber remains	Data[1]
San Felipe	1575	Baja California	None	Surveyed (10)
San Diego	1600	Philippines	Extensive	Salvaged/Partially recorded (1)
Nuestra Señora de la Concepción	1638	Guam	Unknown	Salvaged (1)
Santa Margarita	17th century?	Guam	Unknown	Salvaged (1)
Nuestra Señora del Pilar	1690	Guam	Unknown	Salvaged? (11)

[1] Data Sources: (1) Castro 2005b:193–202; (10) Edward van der Porten 2003, pers. comm.; (11) From <http://www.maritimeinvestment. com.au/pilar.html> accessed 20 Oct. 2005.

TABLE 4
EUROPE: SIXTEENTH- AND SEVENTEENTH-CENTURY SHIPWRECKS

Shipwreck	Date	Location	Timber remains	Data[1]
Corpo Santo	Late-14th century	Portugal	Stern heel	Excavated (1)
Ria de Aveiro A	Mid-15th century	Portugal	Part of the stern	Excavated (1)
Cais do Sodré	Late-15th century?	Portugal	Extensive	Excavated (1)
Studland Bay	Early-16th century	England	Unknown	Excavated (1)
Baleal 1	16th century	Portugal	Unknown	Looted (12)
Arade 1	Late-16th century	Portugal	Extensive	Excavated (13)
Santa Maria de la Rosa	1588	Ireland	Part of the bottom	Excavated (1)
Capitana de Ivella	1596	Spain	None	Surveyed (1)
Ponta do Altar B	Early-17th century	Portugal	None	Surveyed (1)

[1] Data sources: (1) Castro 2005b:193–202; (12) Castro 2004; (13) Castro 2005a.

Shipbuilding treatises began appearing in the Iberian Peninsula in the final quarter of the 16th century but were not written *by* shipwrights and do not seem to have been written *for* shipwrights. They seem, rather, to be a consequence of a Renaissance taste for collecting and organizing knowledge, and eventually using it in enlightened discussions of learned men. Neither the Spanish nor the Portuguese texts contradict the idea of a typical, unique Iberian oceangoing merchantman type, but these texts are far from codifying such ships. The texts seem to aim at a standard vessel for the Portuguese India route, the *nau* with a capacity of 500 to 600 tons and echo a known state trend to standardize and organize its affairs. It is relevant that in some ways the standardization of shipbuilding in written treatises worked against the concept of unique, cultural shipbuilding designs and accelerated the concept of a universal design, undistinguishable by cultural characteristics. If there was a unique Iberian shipbuilding concept, the later years of the Age of Exploration mark the beginning of its terminus.

Iconographically, ships were loosely captured, prior to the rise of the Dutch middle class, in architectural motifs and the rare model. Although ships were ubiquitous, it was not until the rise of the merchant class that portraits of ships were commissioned regularly. The genre of marine art can be traced to the Netherlands where Dutch artists began capturing ships of the merchant class on canvas. In keeping with other contemporary genres of Dutch art, marine art was extremely accurate, often the work of painters who had gone to sea during their careers (Taylor 2004). This art form followed the rise of the merchant class throughout Europe and England. In the late-16th century, the work of Hendrick Cornelisz. Vroom (ca. 1566–1640) gained some admiration in Spain but did not seem to have established a school of maritime painting. A few of his paintings seem to have been purchased in Portugal during his stay (on the way to Holland, from Italy, after a shipwreck), but there is no serious marine art in Portugal until much later (Russell 1983:3).

European shipbuilding raced to keep up with the changing geopolitical landscape of the 16th century. It was a dynamic time, and ship types and ship construction changed rapidly along with all other facets of European cultures. Fernando Oliveira, a Portuguese priest who wrote some of the best ship treatises of his time, noted that "less than forty years ago the names *zabra* and *lancha* were not known on this land [Portugal] and now they are common." After explaining further how some boat names were recently introduced and others completely forgotten, he continued: "The boats from Santarém [a village

TABLE 5
PORTUGUESE INDIA ROUTE: SIXTEENTH- AND SEVENTEENTH-CENTURY SHIPWRECKS

Shipwreck	Date	Location	Timber remains	Data[1]
Portuguese Shipwreck	Early-16th century	Mayotte	Unknown	Looted (14)
Portuguese Shipwreck	Early-16th century	Madagascar	None	Surveyed (24)
S. João	1552	South Africa	Unknown	Surveyed (1)
S. Bento	1554	South Africa	Unknown	Surveyed (1)
Fort San Sebastian Shipwreck	Mid-16th century?	Mozambique	Extensive	Salvaged (15)
Santiago	1585	Bassas da India Atoll	Unknown	Salvaged (1)
Sto. António	1589	Seychelles	Small portion	Looted/Surveyed (1)
Sto. Alberto	1593	South Africa	Unknown	Surveyed (1)
Cochin Shipwreck	Late-16th century	India	Unknown	Looted? (14)
Wan-Li Shipwreck	Early-17th century	Malaysia	Unknown	Salvaged (15)
Nossa Senhora dos Mártires	1606	Portugal	Small portion of the bottom	Looted/Excavated (1)
Espiritu Santo	1608	South Africa	Unknown	Surveyed (1)
Madre de Deus	1610	Japan	Unknown	Destroyed by dredge works (16)
Nossa Senhora da Luz	1619	Azores	None	Surveyed (1)
S. João Baptista	1622	South Africa	Unknown	Surveyed (1)
Sao Joseph	1622	Mozambique	Unknown	Salvaged? (17)
S. Gonçalo	1630	South Africa	Unknown	Survivor's camp excavated (1)
Santa Maria Madre de Deus	1643	South Africa	Unknown	Surveyed (1)
Santíssimo Sacramento	1647	South Africa	None	Salvaged (1)
N.ª S.ª da Atalaia do Pinheiro	1647	South Africa	Unknown	Survivor's camp excavated (1)
Sunchi Shipwreck	Mid-17th century	India	None	Excavated (17)
Sto. António de Tana	1697	South Africa	Extensive	Excavated (18)

[1] Data sources: (1) Castro 2005b:193–202; (14) Patrick Lizé 2006, pers. comm.; (15) From <http://www.mingwrecks.com/wanli.html> accessed 20 Oct. 2005; (16) Reis 2002:81; (17) Tripati et al. 2006; (18) Piercy 1977, 1978, 1979, 1981; (24) A. Rosenfeld 2006, pers. comm.

located on the margins of the Tagus River, 70 km upstream from Lisbon] raise now their heads further, and change their names from *cervilhas* to *muletas*; and this is from four days ago to the present; imagine the change that will occur in one hundred, or two hundred years from now" (Oliveira 1580:76).

Maritime World of the Iberian Peninsula

Units of Measure

Beginning with the most basic pieces of information for comparison, it is immediately apparent that even the units of measure were

Shipwreck	Date	Location	Timber remains	Data[1]
Cattewater	Early-16th century	England	Extensive	Excavated (19)
Lomelina	1512	France	Extensive	Excavated (20)
Rye A	16th Century	England	Part of a mast step	Surveyed (21)
B&W 7	Late-16th century	Denmark	Part of the bottom	Excavated (23)
Calvi	Late-16th century	France	Extensive	Excavated (22)
Saint Honorat I	17th century	France	Unknown	Surveyed (1)

[1] Data sources: (1) Castro 2005b:193–202; (19) Redknap 1984; (20) Guérout et al. 1989; (21) Lovegrove 1964; (22) Villié 1989, 1990, 1991; (23) Lemée 2006.

not consistent throughout the Iberian Peninsula. Spanish shipwrights used one of two *codos* (or cubits), measuring approximately 55.7 cm in Andalusia (*codo castellano*) and 57.5 cm in the Basque country (*codo cantábrico*). This Basque *codo* was eventually adopted for the whole country after 1590 (Casado Soto 1988:102–104). Portuguese counterparts used the *rumo*, thought to be Genoese in origin and equivalent to 154 cm, the height of a Portuguese *tonel*. These values were broken down into *palmos and dedos* (Table 7). The Portuguese *tonel* was also a unit of volume, measuring 1.275m^3. A Spanish *tonel* was 20% larger measuring 1.521 m^3. One Spanish *tonel* equaled 8 cubic *codos cantábricos*. Considering that both units of volume were used, the Iberian *tonelada* of burden ranged between 1.7 and 2.2 modern metric tons of displacement (Castro 2005b:189–192).

Ship sizes

Early in the 17th century the Habsburg kings, who ruled both the crowns of Spain and Portugal between 1580 and 1640, issued legislation to standardize the construction of oceangoing ships (Serrano Mangas 1985; Vicente Maroto 1998). It is not clear how effectively these rules were enforced, but it is a fact that commissions of experts from both Spain and Portugal seriously discussed the size and shape of Iberian ships and that there was a convergence on ship design and construction throughout Europe during this century (Barcelos 1899). Following the development of the firearm, which helped centralize power, Gutenberg's invention of the printing press in the 15th century slowly transformed all of Europe. By 1570 the appearance of a

TABLE 7
SPANISH AND PORTUGUESE SHIPBUILDING UNITS IN THE SIXTEENTH CENTURY

Unit	Metric System Equivalent	Country
Codo castellano	55.7 cm	Spain
Codo cantábrico	57.5 cm	Spain
Vara castellana	83.6 cm	Spain
Palmo	20.9 cm	Spain
Dedo	1.74 cm	Spain
Tonelada de carga	1.382 m^3	Spain
Tonel macho	1.521 m^3	Spain
Rumo	154 cm	Portugal
Goa	77 cm	Portugal
Palmo de goa	25.667 cm	Portugal
Vara	220 cm	Portugal
Palmo de vara	22 cm	Portugal
Dedo	1.83 cm	Portugal
Tonel	1.275 m^3	Portugal

Sources: Casado Soto 1988; Castro 2005.

number of texts and treatises on shipbuilding documented the variety of typical oceangoing vessel for each major route (Table 8). Again, these texts suggest that there were several common traits to Spanish and Portuguese (Iberian) oceangoing ships.

The descriptions of *naos*, caravels, and galleons are similar for both geopolitical sovereignties. Sizes vary within each type but cluster around several functional standard sizes, which are in turn closely aligned to a particular route or function within the fleets.

Small Coasting Craft Designs vs. Oceangoing Ship Designs

Small Craft

Throughout history, shipbuilders conceived, designed, and constructed vessels for diverse purposes, using available resources, traditional knowledge, and cultural exchange. Under the broad aegis of maritime trade and warfare, vessels of many different sizes and shapes were built for many different purposes. Not all ves-

TABLE 8
SPANISH AND PORTUGUESE TEXTS ON SHIPBUILDING
IN THE LATE-SIXTEENTH AND EARLY-SEVENTEENTH CENTURIES

Date	Author and Title	Bibliography
ca. 1570	Fernando Oliveira, *Ars nautica*	Ms. Voss. LAT. F. 41, Leiden University Library, Leiden, Netherlands. Unpublished.
1575	Juan Escalante de Mendoza, *Ytinerario de navegación de los mares y tierras occidentales*	Codice in Sec. Ms., Biblioteca Nacional, Madrid, Spain. Reproduced in facsimile in a CD Rom edition by the Fundación Histórica Tavera. Published in Cesáreo Fernández Duro, *Disquisiciones nauticas* (1880), 5 Vols., by Instituto de Historia y Cultura Naval, Madrid, Spain,1996, vol. 5, pp. 413–515.
ca. 1575–1625	Anonymous, *Livro náutico e o memorial das várias coisas importantes*	Ms. F.464; F. 889; F. 7241, Biblioteca Nacional, Lisbon, Portugal. Published in Francisco Contente Domingues, *Os navios do mar oceano* by Centro de História dos Descobrimentos, Lisbon, Portugal, 2005.
ca. 1580	Fernando Oliveira, *Livro da fabrica das naus*	Ms. 3702, Biblioteca Nacional, Lisbon, Portugal. Published as *O Livro da fabrica das naos.* Facsimile, transcription, and English translation by Academia de Marinha, Lisbon, Portugal, 1991. *O Liuro da fabrica das naos.* Facsimile, transcription and translations into English and Chinese, Macau by Museu Marítimo de Macau, 1995.
1587	Diego García de Palacio, *Instrucción nauthica para el buen uso y regimiento de las naos, su traza y goviero,*	Palacio, Diego García de, *Instrucción nauthica para el buen uso y regimiento de las naos, su traza y goviero*, Pedro de Ocharte, Mexico,1587. Reproduced in facsimile in a CD Rom edition by the Fundación Histórica Tavera. Partially reproduced in Cesário Fernandez Duro, *Disquisiciones nauticas* (1880), 5 vols., by Instituto de Historia y Cultura Naval, Madrid, Spain, 1996, vol. 5, pp. 5–36. Available in English translation by J. Bankston, Terrence Association, Bisbee, AZ, 1988.
1607	*Ordenanzas*	Ms. ? Reproduced in Martín Fernandez de Navarrete, *Colección de documentos y manuscriptos compilados por Fernandez de Navarrete* by Kraus Thomson Organization Ldt., Nendeld, Liechtenstein, 1971, vol. 23, pp. 575–592.

Date	Author and Title	Bibliography
1607	*Ordenanzas*	Ms. ? Reproduced in Martín Fernandez de Navarrete, *Colección de documentos y manuscriptos compilados por Fernandez de Navarrete* by Kraus Thomson Organization Ldt., Nendeld, Liechtenstein, 1971, vol. 23, pp. 575–592.
ca. 1608–1610	João Baptista Lavanha, *Livro primeiro de arquitectura naval*	Cod. 63; Fls. 41-78, Col. Salazar, Library of the Real Academia de Historia, Madrid, Spain. Published as *Livro Primeiro de Architectura Naval*, Facsimile, transcription and English translation by the Academia de Marinha, Lisboa, Portugal, 1996.
1611	Tomé Cano *Arte para fabricar, fortificar y aparejar naos de guerra merchante*	Tomé Cano, *Arte para fabricar, fortificar y aparejar naos de guerra merchante*. Luis Estupiñan, Seville, Spain, 1611. Reproduced in Cesário Fernandez Duro, *Disquisiciones nauticas*, 5 Vols., (1880), by the Instituto de Historia y Cultura Naval, Madrid, Spain, 1996, vol. 5, pp. 36–97.
1613	*Ordenanzas*	Archivo General de Indias, Seville, Indiferente, 2595. Reproduced in Fernando Serrano Mangas, *Función y evolución del galeón en la carrera de Indias*, Madrid, Spain, 1992, pp. 211–239.
1616	Manoel Fernandez, *Livro de traças de carpintaria*	Cod. Manoel Fernandez, Biblioteca do Palácio Nacional da Ajuda, Lisbon, Portugal. Published as Manoel Fernandez, *Livro de traças de carpintaria*, 1616. Facsimile by the Academia de Marinha, Lisboa, Portugal, 1989; Transcription and translation into English by the Academia de Marinha, Lisboa, 1995.
ca. 1630	Gonçalo de Sousa, *Coriosidades de Gonçalo de Sousa*	Ms. 3074, Biblioteca Geral da Universidade de Coimbra, Coimbra, Portugal. Published as Francisco Contente Domingues, *Os navios do mar oceano*. Centro de História dos Descobrimentos, Lisbon, Portugal, 2005.
1618	*Ordenanzas*	*Recopilación de Leyes de los Reynos de las Indias* (1680), 3 vols. Edited in 1943 by Gráficas Ultra, Madrid, Spain. Reproduced in José Luis Rubio Serrano, *Arquitectura de las Naos y Galeones de las Flotas de Indias*, 2 Vols. Ediciones Seyer, Malaga, Spain, 1991.
1631–1632	Pedro Lopez de Soto (?), *Diálogo entre un vizcaíno y un montañés*	Ms. 2593, Library of the University of Salamanca, Salamanca, Spain. Published as Maria Isabel Vicente Maroto, *Diálogo entre un Vizcayno y un Montañéz sobre la Fábrica de Navíos*, Ediciones Universidad de Salamanca, Spain, 1998.
1640–1641	Marcos Cerveira de Aguilar, *Advertências de navegantes*	Cod. 13390, Biblioteca Nacional, Lisboa, Portugal. Unpublished.

sels were large or partook in transoceanic trade. Many performed smaller, humbler activities such as transporting people and animals; participating in general riverine traffic between the coast and hinterlands; plying coastal trade; facilitating fishing, piloting, and messenger service.

Designs of small craft were as diverse as the people who created them. Although the

Iberian Peninsula is not exceptionally large geographically, a minimum four different distinctive coastal regions can be identified: the Bay of Biscay westwards to Galicia; the Atlantic coast of Portugal; the Algarve and Andalusian coast (the old Western Arab coast); and, beyond Gibraltar, the Mediterranean coast, encompassing Catalonia and its formidable seafaring tradition. Visitors and invaders that established colonies and factories along the Iberian coastlines influenced each one of these indigenous populations. Phoenicians, Greeks, Carthaginians, Romans, Goths, and Arabs each left their marks in the architecture, language, agriculture, religious beliefs, and many other cultural and technological traits, including shipbuilding traditions. It is not surprising that Iberian craft have a particular look, reflecting many outside cultural influences.

In the 19th century, Admiral Quirino da Fonseca (1915) listed 167 different types of ships and boats mentioned in historical documents for Portugal alone—a sizeable variety of vessel types for a relative small geographic area. Modern research and ethnographical work confirm this diversity of solutions. Some boat types still exist, and their antecedents are traceable. For example, Galicia's *dornas* are lapstrakes, built with a clear northern influence (Romero 1991:107), while the bottom-based *barcos rabelos* from the Douro River in the north of Portugal were built with flush-laid bottoms and lapstrake sides like the medieval cogs (Filgueiras 1992). To the south, the *saveiros* from the city of Aveiro are evolved plank canoes, and they look very similar to a Middle Eastern model from the third millennium B.C. at Ur (Filgueiras 1980:11). On the other hand, the Mediterranean influence is clear along most of the southern part of the Portuguese coast. Algarve's *caíques* are a good example of the Mediterranean *lateeners* (Iria 1963).

Emergence of Three-Masted Ships

It is generally accepted that northern Europe and the Mediterranean were two different worlds, with different trading networks, organizations, and ship designs. Late-medieval maritime trade was carried in both galleys and round ships, which were frame-based, lateen-rigged, carrying one, two, or three masts. In contrast, the workhorses of the Baltic and North Atlantic trade were square-rigged, clinker-built vessels, sometimes referred to as keels, probably descending directly from the 11th-century short sea traders. A well-preserved archaeological example of these is the Skuldelev 1 boat, carrying approximately 25 tons (Crumlin-Pedersen and Olsen 2002:125).

From the 11th century onwards, as cities grew and the trade between them intensified, clinker-built boats like the Skuldelev 1 grew in size and became the hulks depicted on town seals and in historical sources (Crumlin-Pedersen 1991:76–79). Hulks were partially replaced, in the early-14th century, by another type of trading craft: the cog (Adams 2003:51–58). Cogs emerged sometime during the early-12th century and differed from hulks in that they were constructed from sawn planks, with a flat, flush-laid bottom and central rudder. Only the upper sides of the cog were lapstrake. Also rigged with square sails, cogs may have influenced the development of a new type of vessel in the Mediterranean, commonly referred to as *cocca* (*cocche, pl.*). This design may be the direct ancestor of the Italian *carracks*, the Spanish *naos*, and the Portuguese *naus*. *Cocche* had many characteristics of Mediterranean design, including integrated castles and flush-laid planks nailed to a pre-existing frame structure, but unlike other Mediterranean designs, *cocche* mounted a square sail like their northern relatives.

Around this time, at the beginning of the 14th century, the most common Mediterranean design was the nave, a two-masted round ship. This type was used continually from at least the 11th to the 20th centuries, when Portugal had small, two-masted lateeners, named *caíques,* engaged in short sea trade along the country's coast (Iria 1963). A good example of this design dating to the 11th century is *Serçe Limani*, a shipwrecked vessel excavated off the coast of Turkey (Matthews 2005:185). During the 14th century, these ships appear with a square sail on the foremast. As early as 1336 or 1338, *navi* appear in the iconography with a square sail on the foremast, and soon after, images of *cocche* appear with the same rigging (Bellabarba 1999:85). There must have been some practical advantages to this rigging configuration, because its use expanded during the century and eventually evolved into a full-rigged ship with the addition of a third mast before the foremast. A 1409 document from Barcelona is the first to illustrate a *cocca* with a third mast mounted on the forecastle, rigged with a square sail (Mott 1997:146).

Three-masted vessels obviously fulfilled a need, since they were adopted very quickly both in the Mediterranean and along the north-European coasts. The English ship *Grace Dieu*, lapstrake-built in 1418, may have mounted three masts (Friel 1993:7).

Most European nations, including Portugal and Spain, adopted the three-masted ship, built on a framed-first design, during the 15th century. The extension of the frame-based shipbuilding model in northern Europe is relatively well documented in the archaeological record (Adams 2003).

In Portugal and Spain the advent of the three-masted ship is not as well understood. Historical documents clearly indicate that the strategically located Iberian Peninsula was the nexus of two worlds, but how this played out in ship design is not clear. Oliveira wrote in his 1580 treatise on shipbuilding, *Livro da fabrica das naus*, that the vessels in which the Portuguese sailed down the coasts of Africa were not much different from the *trincados* (literally lapstrakes) of Galicia (Oliveira 1580:76; Barker 1992:435). These *barchas*, as they were called, are unknown today and may have been full clinkers such as the keels, bottom-based vessels such as the cogs, or some design in-between.

Oceangoing Ships

Regarding the design of larger oceangoing ships, the landscape was considerably different (Figure 1). Oceangoing ships were conceived, designed, and built during the period after firearms helped consolidate state power and the geopolitical boundaries of the modern state. The monarchs that ordered these ships may have entertained a loose sense of their country's geographical boundaries, perceiving a rather fluid sense of nation, but they quickly developed strict control of the monopolies of taxation and justice within the perhaps still-medieval whole. Sudden access to distant resources generated by the changing geopolitical context triggered a number of shifts in public policy, technological advancement, and

FIGURE 1. Portuguese *nau* from *Livro de Lisuarte de Abreu*, a mid-16th-century manuscript. (Abreu 1558.)

economics, including shipbuilding. Fifteenth-century ships were a product of the state's will, not the private sector. At this time, states had the political capacity to enforce rules and the economic capacity to plan and launch war at a scale unmatched during the previous Middle Ages (Mendes 1993).

During the late-16th century, the Iberian Peninsula was a cosmopolitan region harboring the bureaucracies that ruled over two extensive empires, and it attracted foreign scholars, merchants, and intellectuals to its major cities. Based on naval power, both the Spanish and the Portuguese empires required a steady stream of larger and better ships, and those built in the Basque country and in Portugal were considered among the best in the world (Escalante de Mendoza 1575:450). This boom lasted for more than 100 years until the 17th century, when the Basque economy based on the whaling industry of the North Atlantic collapsed. Basque shipbuilding suffered as well, both in the design quality and construction (Serrano Mangas 1985:11–46).

Historical information for this period, both documents and iconography, reveals that all Iberian oceangoing ships were conceived in a similar way, regardless of region, city, or shipyard.

Following the Mediterranean shipbuilding tradition, ships were built empirically, based on proportion and scale, and did not require plans or drawings (Rieth 1996:39–50). Built in a carvel style with flush-laid planks fastened to the frames, Iberian oceangoing ships followed a construction tradition thought to date back to the time of oared vessels in the Mediterranean. Even the earliest of the carvel hulls used a number of frames with predesigned curvatures. These frames were mounted over the keel prior to planking, thus defining the shape of the hull (Figure 2).

Cultural Influences

Baltic Influence

Portugal and Spain traded with the Baltic starting in the 14th century, exchanging cereals, metals, and textiles for salt, cork, olive oil, wine, and wool. Permanent commercial relations between Lisbon and Danzig were established in 1430, and there is evidence that Portuguese merchants bought vessels in the north, from Galician, Basque, or British origins (Albuquerque 1994:484). Cross-cultural influence undoubtedly took place. Several Portuguese and Spanish shipwrecks from this period have mast steps that show a northern influence when compared with the Mediterranean ones of similar vessels (Rieth 1998:181). Rectangular dovetail joints between floor timbers and first futtocks have also been recorded. These differ from the traditional Mediterranean hooked scarves, also found on shipwrecks, including the early-14th-century *Culip VI*, the 16th-century Ottoman shipwreck of *Yassı Ada*, and the late-17th-century shipwreck *Sardinaux* (Rieth 1998:184).

Italian Influence

It is curious that in England, as in Venice, predesigned frames were placed at regular intervals along the entire axis of the hull, while in Portugal and Spain the predesigned frames were clustered in the central portion of the ship's hull (Adams 2003:124; Bondioli 2003:223–224).

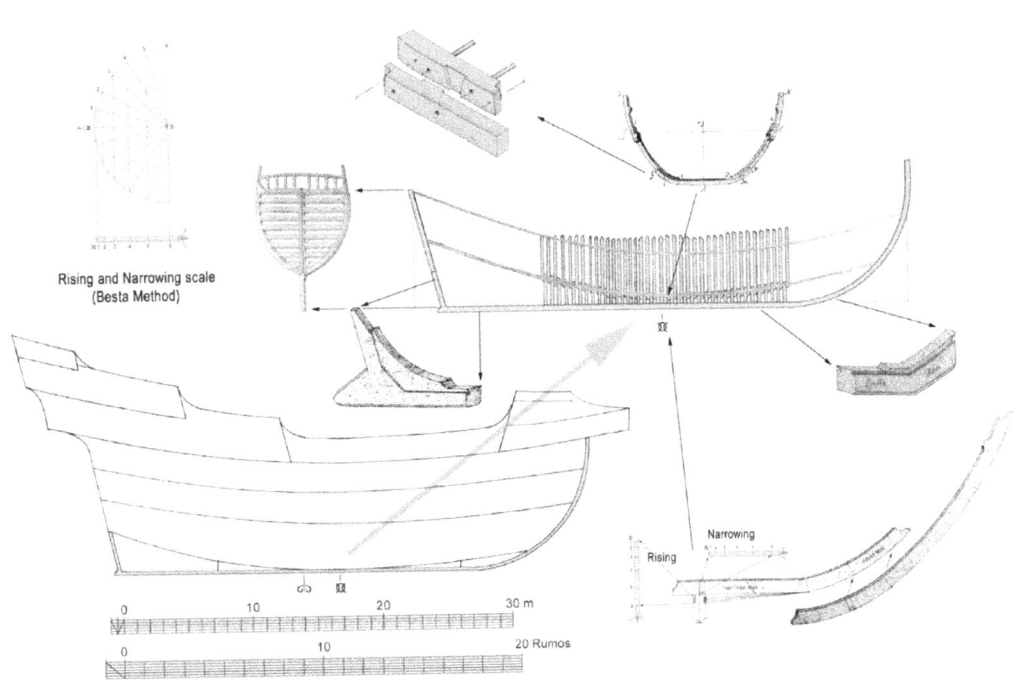

Rising and Narrowing scale (Besta Method)

FIGURE 2. Some of Iberian ships' main traits: a number of predesigned and preassembled central frames; floors and futtocks assembled with dovetail scarves; curved timbers connecting the keel and the posts; rising and narrowing of ship's bottom obtained by the whole molding system. (Drawing by author, 2006.)

Ribbands stretched around the erected frames from stem to stern defined the remaining shape of the hull. The stern frames and bow frames were shaped to conform to the curvature defined by the ribbands (Sarsfield 1991). From the top of the first futtocks upwards, next to nothing is known about the construction sequence and the shipwrights' methods of controlling the hull shape. Documentary sources are vague, and the archaeological evidence is scarce.

Considering the Platonic view of the world that held sway at the time, it has been hypothesized that ships would have been conceived from a number of basic measurements that were all proportionally related, such as keel length, maximum beam, hold depth, and overall length (Barata 1989:212–223). Yet, even with a shared worldview, the construction methodologies and units of measurement were loose enough to ensure inevitable variation.

Contemporary documents and archaeological remains indicate that there was variation in the shapes and sizes of ships during this period (Xavier 1992; Philips 2000). Nevertheless, 16th-century state shipbuilding was among the earliest preindustrial trades that incorporated the complexities and basic characteristics of industrial production: division and specialization of labor, execution of sequential and repetitive tasks, and stock management at a large scale, all carried out within a multilayered hierarchical and bureaucratic organization.

Although this method did not require plans or drawings, rules and practices necessarily were as precise as possible because the ability to create symmetry, the key to a good ship, required extensive control of the shipbuilding process.

The parallel between English and Venetian frame design most likely relates to the employment of Venetian shipwrights by Henry VIII in the mid-16th century (Glasgow 1970:10,24). Mediterranean influence on Iberian shipbuilding is explained by a long and continuous economic relationship with the city-state of Genoa, documented as early as the 12th century, when Bishop Gelmirez invited Italian shipwrights from Pisa to build and operate a fleet of galleys charged with protecting the Galician coast (Filgueiras 1989:543–544).

By the late-13th century, Genoese ships began visiting the Bay of Biscay's coast, setting up intermediate trading points for their commercial enterprise in the northern Atlantic. Already trading with Muslim Seville, the Genoese established a permanent presence in the city soon after it capitulated to Alfonso X in 1248. By the second half of the 15th century, the Genoese community in Seville had grown quite large (Pike 1966).

The relations among and influence by the Genoese and Portuguese sailors and shipwrights are fairly well documented and reflected in the shift of units of measure. By the 16th century, Portuguese shipwrights used the *goa* (77 cm) and the *palmo de goa* (25.67 cm) for shipbuilding. Both of these units of measure have a perfect parallel in Genoese units of measure (Ciciliot 1998:27; Barker 2001:214).

Italian influence on Spanish and Portuguese courts was continuous from the 13th to the 15th centuries. Evidence for this tight relationship is seen in recorded relations of private individuals, the documented voyages to the Canaries of Lanzaroto Malocello, Niccoloso da Recco, and Angiolilo del Tegghia de' Corbizzi, as well as the contracted services of the Italians Antoniotto Usodimare and Alvise Cadamosto by Portugal's Infante D. Henrique to sail his caravels down the coast of Africa (Albuquerque 1994:535–536).

These contacts continued into the 15th and 16th centuries, even under the Habsburg rule. In February 1513 Pantaleone Queirolo, a shipwright from the small village of Varazze, appears to have left his homeland in Italy for Portugal with a group of shipwrights contracted to construct and operate galleys for the King of Portugal (Ciciliot 2000). Throughout the 15th and 16th centuries, evidence of similar contracts for Italian shipwrights to work in Portuguese shipyards exists (Viterbo 1988:280,425,452,458,521).

The Italian connections certainly had an important impact on Spanish and Portuguese state-driven shipbuilding industries. Italian merchant cities such as Naples, Genoa, and Venice were home to highly developed shipbuilding industries, having highly organized shipyards where craftsmen were divided into specialized groups: woodcutters, sawyers, carpenters, and caulkers working within the enclosed shipyard complex. Organized shipyards with specialized sets of labor were able to construct the ships quickly in a reliable and repetitive fashion (Lane 1934a, 1934b).

Arab Influence

Arabs were great shipbuilders who may have used frame-based vessels since the 8th century. The author of The Book of Animals, Gahiz (or al-Jahiz) (born A.D. 776), mentions an Umayyad governor of Iraq named al-Haggag, who died in A.D. 714 and is reputed to have built the first vessels "nailed and caulked." Other Arab references from the 10th century onwards mention the construction of vessels built with planks nailed to the frames, as opposed to the Indian Ocean and Red Sea vessels in which the planks were sewn together (Darmoul 1985). It is fair to assume that the Arab world was another source of influence on Iberian shipbuilders. Iberian Muslims were a major naval power in the Mediterranean. Arab warships helped make the conquest of the Iberian Peninsula possible. Arab navies fought Viking invaders and later sacked coastal villages with regularity when the Christian leaders started the push against Muslim rule. Reconquista, as the Arab occupation of the Iberian Peninsula is known, lasted more than 10 generations, from the 12th to the 15th century, and encompassed periods of peace and cooperation as well as substantial sharing of cultural ideas.

After the Reconquista, the Arab population in the southern Iberian Peninsula was not expelled. Christianized Arabs went on building boats and ships under the new Christian rulers. The shipbuilding industry appears to have remained robust, possibly because of the widespread piracy in the region. It is likely that the southern Iberian Christianized Arabs were engaged in seasonal piratical incursions into the Maghrib, Arabic for the northwest area of Africa. These raids had to be carried out by sea. Because Arabs remained along the southern Iberian Peninsula, Arab influence permeated the region's culture. People in this area adopted Arab values, practices, and vocabulary. For instance almogama, the Portuguese word for tail frame, literally translates as "meeting point" in Arabic. Since there was no lack of Italian designations for this specific timber, the fact that Portuguese shipwrights adopted an Arab word reveals how closely integrated the cultures were within the shipbuilding profession. This is further substantiated by the writings of Father Oliveira who wrote about his visits to harbors and shipyards of Spain, France, Italy, England, and "some in the lands of the Moors" where he observed how they built their ships. He also wrote about how he "practiced with their carpenters, and learning their styles, and carpentry customs, and construction traditions." Known for his candor, Oliveira mentioned the Maghrib harbors and shipyards together with the Italian and the Spanish counterparts without expressing any particular criticism. It is very likely that shipbuilding in the Maghrib was as good and sophisticated as in any other major seafaring country of the time (Oliveira 1580:56).

The Iberian Ship

One of the questions asked previously is whether there is a unique artifactual component or characteristic in ships that can be identified as wholly Iberian. First, it is important to note that Iberian Atlantic ships, as these ships are sometimes called, were built on the Atlantic coast of Iberia primarily to sail on the Atlantic Ocean.

From the discussions on units of measurement, type, size, and cultural influence, it is apparent that Iberian ship designs shared similarities with their other European and Mediterranean contemporaries. Even with limited documentation and iconography, it seems clear that three-masted, carvel-built vessels in the Mediterranean, the Iberian Peninsula, and England during the 16th century were not that different from one another. There were certainly regional differences, differences in units of measurement, and differences in many details but not in the overall style and basic design. If one excludes the Portuguese India naus, much larger than all the other merchantmen of their time, fit for the six- to eight-month voyage to the Indian subcontinent, most small or medium-sized oceangoing ships must have looked similar to the nonprofessional eye. Once again turning to the accounts of Oliveira, it is not evident in his writings that he found these small and medium-sized merchant craft fundamentally different. In fact, he appears to have been more inclined to create a Rosetta Stone, as it were, of ship terminology. In his 1580 writings, he states that the ships that the Spanish and Portuguese called naos, the Italian called carracas, and the German called urcas were equivalent (Oliveira 1580:76). Evidence from the north of Europe suggests that the differences between Iberian and Mediterranean ships were either less important or less apparent since Portuguese ships are frequently referred to as *carracks*.

Since at the macro level there does not appear to be significant differences for Iberian ships, the next step is to examine particular construction traits. Clusters of specific traits with regard to construction provide indications of cultural signature. Any individual trait might be shared with other cultures, but clusters will be unique. The problems with this type of analysis stem from the ability to differentiate among overall Iberian and specific regions as well as the shifting patterns of clustered traits over time.

Thomas Oertling has proposed the existence of an Iberian shipbuilding tradition based on a cluster of 11 traits (Table 9) (Oertling 1989, 2001, 2005). His hypothesis is based on archaeological evidence found on several shipwrecks. There are scholars who support Oertling's findings and those who do not. The detractors argue that although the sample shipwrecks were engaged in Iberian trade, there is no way to confirm that they were all actually built in Iberia.

Eric Rieth (1998:178–180) argues that when common traits appear in a large enough number of shipwrecks from the same cultural horizon, they comprise "architectural signatures" that constitute the defining characteristics of a shipbuilding tradition. The Oertling Trait Cluster is the "architectural signature" of Iberian shipbuilding (Figure 2).

Iberian Trait Cluster Signature

The first trait is a given number of preassembled and predesigned central frames. Dovetail scarves are recorded on all Iberian ships, varying only in shape. Both the Pepper Wreck and *Atocha* had rectangular scarf joints (Castro 2005b) (Brian Jordan, 1998, pers. comm.), while the early 16th-century Genoese shipwreck from Villefranche, thought to be the *Lomelina*, had both dovetail and hooked scarf joints (Rieth 1998:183–184).

The second trait relates to the way hull planks are fastened to the frames, specifically the use of iron fastenings. In contrast, the use of treenails varies. The shipwrecks of Cais do Sodré and the *Nossa Senhora dos Mártires* exhibited only iron fastenings (Rodrigues et al. 2001:375–377; Castro 2005b:136).

The third and forth traits pertain to the use of a curved timber (*couce*) at the juncture between the keel and sternpost. The *couce* is reinforced with a curved stern knee. Over the paired *couce* and stern knee sit the y-shaped frames called *picas*. In all instances, save one, that of the Emanuel Point shipwreck, thought to be one of

---

TABLE 9

IBERIAN ATLANTIC VESSELS: CHARACTERISTICS PROPOSED BY THOMAS OERTLING (2001)

1	A given number of pre-assembled central frames bearing dovetail joints.
2	Carvel planking fastened with a combination of nails and treenails.
3	A knee joining the after end of the keel and the sternpost (*couce*).
4	A single piece deadwood knee over the *couce* upon which sit the y-frames (*coral*).
5	Y-frames tabbed into the deadwood knee.
6	Keelson notched over the floors.
7	Mast step is an expanded portion of the keelson, part of which is cut to seat the ship's pump.
8	Buttresses supporting the mast step against the footwale.
9	Ceiling extending only over the floors, the last strake notched to receive filler planks.
10	Teardrop-shaped iron strop accepting a deadeye attached to two or three lengths of chain, the last link through an eyebolt.
11	Flat transom with proud sternpost.

the 1559 Tristan de Luna's ships, this combination was observed (Smith et al. 1995:35).

The fifth trait pertains to the carved tabs on the upper face of the stern knee. The tabs receive the y-shaped *picas*. This trait is not universal, only occurring in about 40% of the shipwrecks recorded. This trait, besides occurring in Iberian shipwrecks, also occurs on a few Mediterranean shipwrecks, such as the Calvi I shipwreck (Villié 1990:103).

The sixth trait is a notched keelson, which is widespread across many traditions. The *Mary Rose*'s keelson is notched to receive frames (Marsden 2003:95), as is the Woolwich shipwreck (Salisbury 1961:85).

The seventh and eighth traits pertain to the mast-step assemblage. On Iberian ships, the keelson widens at the mast step and is buttressed. The buttresses lock against bottom stringers. This seems to be a solution common to other shipbuilding traditions, specifically in the north of Europe. The Newport ship, a clinker-built vessel dated to the second half of the 15th century has such a mast step. In contrast, Mediterranean examples exhibit a mast-step arrangement that rests between two sister keelsons. This is the case in the Genoese *Lomelina* shipwreck (Guérout et al. 1989:72–77,86; Rieth 1998:181).

The ninth trait pertains to the ceiling arrangement. Filler planks are inserted between the futtocks sealing the lower bilge underneath the ceiling planking. The only other example of fillers come from the Calvi I shipwreck, built in the Mediterranean in the late-16th century (Villié 1989:27, 1990:95–96).

The tenth trait is the use of teardrop-shaped, iron strops. Although this is a prevalent characteristic among Iberian ships, the deadeyes of the *Mary Rose* are also teardrop shaped (Marsden 2003:108).

The eleventh trait calls for flat stern panels. These first appear in the Basque iconography in the last quarter of the 15th century and then again around 1500 in a view of the port of Venice by Jacopo Barbari (Taras Pevni 2002, pers. comm.) (Casado Soto 1995:40; Bash 2000). In the mid-16th century, flat panels appear on a Basque whaling ship at Red Bay, Labrador, but at the same time, contemporary iconography shows what seems to be both round and flat sterns (Figure 3) (Grenier et al. 1994). This may be an example of a trait that shifts through time or of a specific style of vessel.

To these 11 traits might be added another specific feature that does not show up with any regularity in the archaeological record. Written sources suggest a distinctive amidships section on Iberian ships that is neither common to the contemporary ships of the Mediterranean nor northern Europe. Iberian amidships sections are round and full, appearing to derive from a single

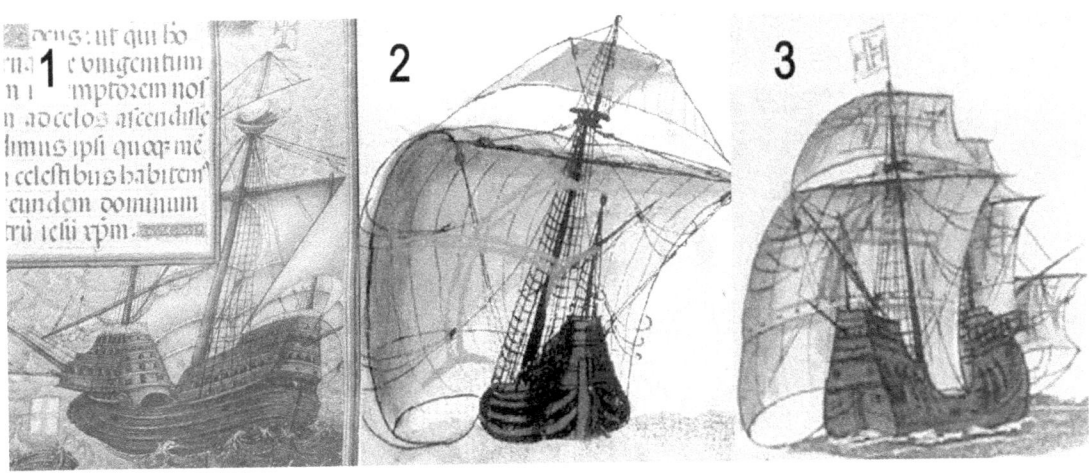

FIGURE 3. Round and square sterns of Portuguese ships after mid-16th-century manuscripts: (1) Livro da Condessa de Bertianos (anonymous, codex from library of Lisbon's Science Academy); (2) *Livro de Lisuarte de Abreu* (Abreu 1558); (3) Livro da Memória das Armadas (anonymous, codex from library of Lisbon's Science Academy).

arc. Mediterranean manuscripts from 150 years earlier exhibit a similar amidships section; however, 15th- and 16th-century Mediterranean and English amidships sections are often depicted as a composite of several arcs (Figure 4).

An argument can also be made for the presence of combined traits being an indicator of Iberian ship designs. The Iberian Peninsula was a nexus of Mediterranean and European cultures, and there are three of Oertling's Iberian shipbuilding traits that potentially reflect this unique area's ability to absorb and integrate diverse ship design components into hybrids. The presence of scarved frames, exhibiting both dovetail and hooked scarves, reflects influence from two sources of shipbuilding design, as does the presence of flat-panel sterns and round sterns. In addition, the ability of an Iberian ship to pass in the North Atlantic as a *carrack* and at the same time pass in the Mediterranean as another type of vessel may reflect the Iberian ship's hybrid nature. Thus, it may be just as important to look for the hybrid as a distinctive look that incorporates multiple traits.

Looking at other forms of evidence, there is some support for the existence of particular subtypes, although samples remain so small as to be inconclusive. For example, there is little information regarding the types of wood used to build Iberian ships. Portuguese treatises recommend cork oak for the structure of the Indiamen and pine for the planking. This was exactly what was found on the Pepper Wreck, an early-17th-century Portuguese Indiaman thought to be the *Nossa Senhora dos Mártires*, lost near Lisbon in 1606. All other vessels whose timbers were sampled and identified exhibit a range of Iberian oak species and a few other types of hardwood, but nothing conclusive. To date, there are no dendrochronological series for the Iberian Peninsula. Finally, a comparison of contemporary iconography shows some typical features, such as an almost complete lack of decorations, especially in the Portuguese long-sea merchantmen. On the other hand, most early-16th-century depictions of Portuguese ships show a red cross painted on the fore and mainsails.

Iberian Ship Types

Since the portion of hull preserved on most shipwrecks is usually small, it is difficult to separate typologies from archaeological evidence. Documentary evidence shows there were three main types of sailing ships: naos, galleons, and caravels.

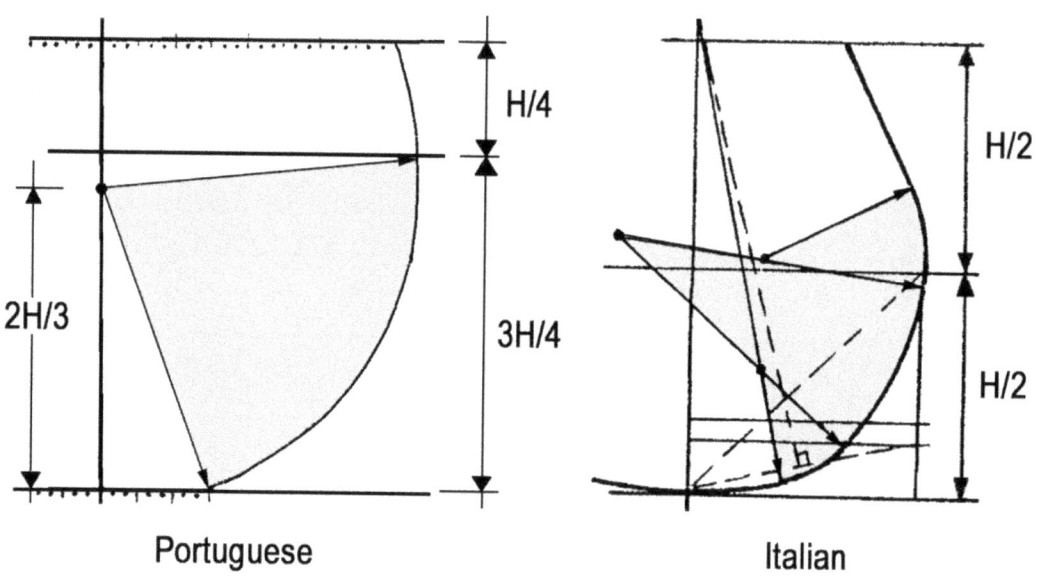

FIGURE 4. Midship sections: Portuguese after Fernando Oliveira (ca. 1580); and Italian after Matthew Baker (ca. 1570). (After Barker 1986.)

The Spanish word nao (in Portuguese *nau*) means vessel but refers to a ship with two, three or four decks and fully integrated fore and stern castles, bearing three masts and a bowsprit, all rigged with square sails, except the mizzenmast. The mizzenmast, intended for steering, was rigged with a lateen sail. As mentioned above, the first depiction of a three-mast, full-rigged ship appears in a Catalan drawing dating to 1409 (Mott 1997:146). The length-to-breadth ratio of the vessel in the Catalan drawing appears to have been around 3:1. This is a common ratio for Mediterranean round ships. Where iconography differentiates between other styles and naos, it is clear that naos have both square and round sterns (Figure 3).

Galleons are mentioned in the first decade of the 16th century and primarily functioned as warships with two or three decks, fully integrated fore and stern castles, three or four masts, and a bowsprit. The fore and main masts were rigged with square sails, and the mizzen and bonaventure masts were rigged with lateen sails. The length-to-beam ratio appears to have been slightly higher than that of the naos, around 3:5. Contemporary galleon scantling lists show a much sturdier vessel with thicker masts and spars (Domingues 2005:366–373). Flat stern panels seem to be a characteristic of these ships, understandably, since a square stern allows for more deck space during military operations, specifically in regard to the movement of stern guns.

Caravels were originally lateen-rigged ships with one or two masts. Generally thought to have developed in the Mediterranean during the 12th century, caravels were mainly employed in fishing activities in Portugal, in the 13th century (Fonseca 1934; Pires 1985, 1986, 1988, 1990; Domingues 1989; Ciciliot 1999). Absent from original documents throughout the 14th century, caravels reappear in the beginning of the 15th century as the preferred "Ships of Discovery," sometimes bearing painted eyes on both sides of the bow, a trait paralleled in the Mediterranean since ancient times (Marques 1998). No doubt, this preference reflects the vessel's swiftness and maneuverability (Pico 1964:73–83). Towards the end of the 15th century, there are references to three-mast, ship rigged caravels, and the 16th century witnessed the development of the *caravela de armada* with four masts and rigged on

all masts with lateen sails, except the foremast, which bore square sails. Caravels were still in use in the 17th century, as reported in the 1616 Manoel Fernandez treatise, and sailing around Cape Horn (Fernandez 1616; Vaughan 1913; Vicente Maroto 2001), and they continue to be mentioned in the 18th century (Domingues 2005:259). All vessels of the time were armed and traveled in fleets for added protection. A number of smaller vessels, such as *patachos*, *zabras*, and *galizabras* sailed regularly with the fleets, as supporting craft, and may have been conceived and built in the same way as the larger ships.

Treatises on Iberian Ships

Although this discussion has focused on an Iberian design concept, it is important to note that two major geopolitical entities, Spain and Portugal, inhabit the same mass of land. Their languages, although similar, are recognizably different. Their units of measure are different, and thus the manuscripts and treatises that describe shipbuilding differ. To fully understand an Iberian concept, it is important to understand the similarities and differences of the manuscripts describing shipbuilding.

Spanish Ships Described in Shipbuilding Treatises

Spanish ships are described in several late-16th and early-17th-century texts, of which some contain detailed information. The best descriptions are collectively presented in the three manuscripts by Juan Escalante de Mendoza, *Itinerario de Navegación de los Mares y Tierras Occidentales* (1575), Tomé Cano's *Arte para Fabricar, Fortificar y Apareiar naos* (1611), and Diego García de Palacio, *Instrucción nautica para el buen uso de las naos, su traça, y gobierno conforme à la altura de México* (1587). García de Palacio's work was the first ship treatise ever printed. The later work, *Dialogos entre un vizcaino y un montañez*, dates to 1631 or 1632 and is attributed to the experienced shipbuilder Pedro Lopez de Soto (Vicente Maroto 1998). These manuscripts in combination with the codified three sets of legislation, known as the *Ordenanzas* and issued in 1607, 1613, and 1618, form the main reservoir of Spanish ship architectural documentation (Philips 1987, 1993).

Although modern calculation of early Spanish ship tonnage is a difficult subject, ship's sizes were well documented, both in Spain and in Portugal (Casado Soto 1988). The sizeable sample of registered ship sizes reveals that Spanish *naos* for the *Carreira da Índia* during the first half of the 16th century averaged around 100 metric tons burden, close to 200 metric tons displacement, and doubled their size, on average, during the second half of that century (Pérez-Mallaína 1998:93). The trend towards growth of the merchantmen's sizes, felt during the 16th century, seems to have encountered opposition in the beginning of the 17th century, and efforts were made to standardize ship shapes and sizes (Barcelos 1899; Costa 1997).

Escalante de Mendoza (1575) mentions in his treatise on navigation that *naos* of 500 tons burden were the best fit for the New World route. Soon after, García de Palacio (1587) states that 400 tons burden is a good size for commerce and war.

The *Ordenanzas* of 1607 created legislation that applied to both Spanish and Portuguese merchantmen with capacities between 150 and 250 tons burden. The *Ordenanzas* also defined the functions of larger vessels: *galeonzetes* of approximately 300 to 500 tons were intended as ships of war, as were galleons with capacities between 550 and 750 tons. Cano (1611) described a *naos* measuring 12 *codos* in breadth as having a capacity of 232 tons. The important factor is that the proportions of these vessels did not change much, in spite of any change in size (Philips 1993).

In Spain, formulas were used to calculate a ship's capacity since the middle of the 16th century, and it is likely that it was the same in Portugal (Casado Soto 1988:102–109). Historical documents, however, mention a practical system in use in Portugal in which officers would come aboard with a number of hoops and gauges and estimate the real number of barrels that would effectively fit in the ship's hold (Costa 1997:64).

Portuguese Ships Described in Shipbuilding Treatises

In Portugal, where the Indiamen were designed for a voyage of six to eight months across three oceans, ships were necessarily larger than their Spanish equivalents. Yet, both shipbuilding traditions appear to have consistently increased vessel size during the first part of the 16th century (Costa 1997:437–439). By 1571 the capacity of Indiamen was fixed between 350 and 500 tons burden, but how this capacity was calculated is unknown.

Portuguese shipbuilding treatises describing vessels in the late-16th and early-17th centuries contain detailed illustrations and information. The most extensive are the two treatises of Oliveira, *Ars nautica* (1570) and *Livro da fabrica das naus* (1580). The works of João Baptista Lavanha's *Livro primeiro de arquitectura naval* (ca.1610), and Manoel Fernandez's *Livro de traças de carpintaria* (1616) are also important and informative documents (Domingues 2005; Philips 2000). They all indicate that a capacity between 500 and 600 tons burden was the optimum size for the India route or *Carreira da Índia* ships.

Historical records clearly indicate that the ships intended for the India route were consistently larger than the ships built and sailed in the European, Mediterranean, and African trade. Sailing routes between the Iberian Peninsula, northern Europe, the Mediterranean, the western coast of Africa, and Brazil were generally shorter than routes to the East Indies. Despite the continuous stream of state incentives for the construction of ships over 100 *toneladas* for the Atlantic and Mediterranean trade routes, some dating back as far as 1470, small traders still averaged between 40 and 100 *toneladas* as late as the mid-16th century.

Conclusion

Considering the issue of Iberian ship design from both the macro and the micro points of view and taking into consideration all the available knowledge in historical documents, iconography, and the archaeological record, a consistent image of Iberian vessels emerges, making a compelling argument for the existence of an Iberian Atlantic shipbuilding tradition. No single argument, trait, or point of view conclusively settles the question. It is the combination or sum of the parts, seen as a whole, that provides a compelling argument: at the nexus of European and Mediterranean shipbuilding on the Iberian Peninsula, a unique cultural tradition in shipbuilding evolved. It was the rounded midship, the presence of dovetail scarves, the proportions, and the basic measurement units that all melded to create the Iberian ship design, what Reith refers to as *"un air de famille"* (Xavier 1992; Philips 2000; Alves 2001).

One can only hope that at least some Iberian shipwrecks found in the future will be scientifically studied, adding to the sample of collected data and possibly solving some of the ongoing questions. Questions about the tangent of stemposts to keels, consistent proportional arcs in the stempost and bow, the rake of sternposts, low length-to-beam ratios, and fully integrated fore and stern castles are just a few of the issues awaiting answers. Many other issues also beg further research: the question of the *dentes* or little protrusions in the frames drawn in Lavanha and Fernandez's treatises; the arrangement of the bottom stringers, ceiling, pump sumps, and mast-step buttresses; the number and arrangement of reinforcements such as standing and hanging knees, riding timbers; or the illusive *entremichas* mentioned in the documents— all need to be checked and criticized against archaeological data.

Only further scientific research of archaeological remains of ships across many nationalities from the same cultural horizon will provide further evidence as to how particular or homogeneous the Iberian shipbuilding tradition was during the Age of Exploration.

For all these reasons, the question of the protection of the Iberian shipwrecks is a pressing one. As I write these last lines, the court trials of a number of prominent antique dealers and museum conservators are unfolding and showing, perhaps for the first time, the enormous extent of the destruction inflicted by looters, fueled by the antiques market, on the archaeological record worldwide (Watson and Todeschini 2006). Portuguese and Spanish shipwrecks have been systematically destroyed by treasure hunters worldwide, sometimes with the cooperation of professional archaeologists (Bound 2004; Castro and Fitzgerald 2006). Perhaps this article will contribute to a better understanding of the importance of these ships and their protection against looting and treasure hunting.

References

ABREU, LISUARTE DE
1558   *Este livro que he de Lisuarte de Abreu* (This Book That Is of Lisuarte de Abreu). Manuscript 525, Pierpont Morgan Library, New York. Facsimile printed in 1992 by Comissão Nacional para as Comemorações dos Descobrimentos Portugueses, Lisbon, Portugal.

ADAMS, JONATHAN
2003   *Ships, Innovation, and Social Change: Aspects of Carvel Shipbuilding in Northern Europe 1450–1850.* Stockholm Studies in Archaeology 24. Stockholm Marine Archaeology Reports, No. 3. Universitet Stockolm, Stockholm, Sweden.

ALBUQUERQUE, LUÍS DE
1994   *Diccionário de História dos Descobrimentos Portugueses* (Dictionary of the History of the Portuguese Discoveries). Editorial Caminho, Lisbon, Portugal.

ALVES, FRANCISCO (EDITOR)
2001   *Proceedings: International Symposium on Archaeology of Medieval and Modern Ships of Iberian-Atlantic Tradition*, Lisbon, September 1998. IPA, Lisbon, Portugal.

BARATA, JOÃO DA GAMA PIMENTEL
1989   *Estudos de Arqueologia Naval* (Studies in Naval Archaeology), Vol. 1. Imprensa Nacional Casa da Moeda, Lisbon, Portugal.

BARCELOS, CHRISTIANO SENNA
1899   Construcções de naus em Lisboa e Goa para a carreira da Índia no começo do século XVII (Construction of Naus at Lisbon and Goa for the India Route in the Beginning of the Seventeenth Century). *Boletim da Sociedade de Geographia de Lisboa* (1898–1899) 17(2):13–72. Lisbon, Portugal.

BARKER, RICHARD
1986   Fragments from the Pepysian Library. *Revista da Universidade de Coimbra* 32:161–178.
1992   Shipshape for Discoveries and Return. *Mariner's Mirror* 78(4):433–447.
2001   Sources for Lusitanian Shipbuilding. *Proceedings: International Symposium on Archaeology of Medieval and Modern Ships of Iberian-Atlantic Tradition*, Lisbon, September 1998, Francisco Alves, editor, pp. 213–228. IPA, Lisbon, Portugal.

BASH, LUCIEN
   2000   Les navires et bateaux de la Vue de Venise de Jacopo
          Barbari (1500) (The Ships and Boats of the View
          of Venice by Jacopo Barbari [1500]). Lucien Bash,
          Brussels, Belgium.

BELLABARBA, SERGIO
   1999   Note Sull'Origine della Nave a Tre Alberi (Note on
          the Origin of the Three-Masted Ship). Archeologia
          delle Acque, Nucleo Archeologia Subacquea del
          Veneto 1(2):81–93.

BONDIOLI, MAURO
   2003   The Art of Designing and Building Venetian
          Galleys from the Fifteenth to the Sixteenth Century:
          Boats, Ships, and Shipyards. Proceedings of the
          Ninth International Symposium on Boat and Ship
          Archaeology, Carlo Beltrame, editor, pp. 222–227.
          Università Ca' Foscari, Venice, Italy.

BOUND, MENSUN
   2004   The Fort San Sebastian Wreck: A Sixteenth-Century
          Portuguese Porcelain Wreck off the Island of
          Mozambique. In Christie's catalog, The Fort San
          Sebastian Wreck. Auction Held on May 19, 2004,
          Amsterdam, Netherlands.

CANO, TOMÉ
   1611   Arte para fabricar, fortificar y apareiar naos de guerra
          merchante, con las reglas de arquearlas reduzido
          a toda cuenta y medida, y en grande utilidad de la
          navegación (The Art of Building, Strengthening,
          and Rigging Naos of War and Trade, with the Rules
          to Find Their Capacity Simplified to Their Basic
          Measurements, and of Great Utility for Navigation).
          In Disquisiciones nauticas (Nautical Disquisitions),
          5 vols., pp. 36–97, transcribed by Cesário Fernandez
          Duro in 1880. Reprinted in 1996 by Instituto de
          Historia y Cultura Naval, Madrid, Spain.

CASADO SOTO, JOSÉ LUÍS
   1988   Atlantic Shipping in Sixteenth-Century Spain and
          the 1588 Armada. In England, Spain and the Gran
          Armada 1585–1604, M. J. Rodriguez-Salgado and
          Simon Adams, editors, pp. 95–132. Barnes and Noble
          Imports, London, England, UK.
   1995   El País Vasco y el mar. Desde los orígines hasta el
          siglo XVIII (The Basque Country and the Sea from
          Its Origins to the Eighteenth Century). In El País
          Vasco y el mar a traves de la história (The Basque
          Country throughout History), José Luís Casado
          Soto, Monserrat Gárate, José Ignacio Tellechea, and
          Juan Pardo, editors, pp. 15–77. Museo Naval, San
          Sebastian, Spain.
   2001   The Spanish Ships of the Oceanic Expansion:
          Documentation, Archaeology, and Iconography from
          the Fifteenth and Sixteenth Centuries. Proceedings:
          International Symposium on Archaeology of Medieval
          and Modern Ships of Iberian-Atlantic Tradition,
          Lisbon, September 1998, Francisco Alves, editor,
          pp. 131–161. IPA, Lisbon, Portugal.

CASTRO, FILIPE
   2004   Os naufrágios do Baleal (Shipwrecks of Baleal).
          Mundo Submerso 7(91):68–72.
   2005a Archaeology and Dredges: The Arade River
          Archaeological Complex. International Journal of
          Nautical Archaeology 34(1):72–83.
   2005b The Pepper Wreck: A Portuguese Indiaman at the
          Mouth of the Tagus River. Texas A&M University
          Press, College Station.
   2005c Playa Damas Project: Artifact Inventory—ShipLab
          Report 9. Manuscript, Nautical Archaeological
          Program Library, Texas A&M University, College
          Station.

CASTRO, F., AND C. FITZGERALD
   2006   The Playa Damas Shipwreck: An Early-Sixteenth-
          Century Shipwreck in Panama. In Heritage at Risk:
          Underwater Cultural Heritage at Risk: Managing
          Natural and Human Impacts, special edition, Robert
          Grenier, David Nutley, and Ian Cochran, editors, pp.
          38–41. ICOMOS Heritage at Risk Series. UNESCO,
          Paris, France.

CICILIOT, FURIO
   1998   Metrologia delle imbarcazioni genovesi medievali
          e postmedievali (Metrology of Medieval and
          Postmedieval Genoese Watercraft). In Navi di legno.
          Evoluzione tecnica e sviluppo della cantieristica
          nel Mediterraneo dal XVI secolo a oggi (Ships of
          Wood: Technical Evolution and Development of the
          Shipbuilding Industry in the Mediterranean from the
          Sixteenth Century to the Present), Mario Marzari,
          editor, pp. 27–30. Servizio Cultura, Comune di Grado,
          Grado, Italy.
   1999   Note sulle caravellae medievali mediterranee (Notes
          on Mediterranean Caravels). Atti e Memorie della
          Società Savonese di Storia Patria (1998–1999)
          34–35:71–82. Savona, Italy.
   2000   Genoese shipbuilders in Portugal and in Asia (Early
          Sixteenth Century). In Fernando Oliveira e o seu
          tempo. Humanismo e arte de navegar no Renascimento
          Europeu (1450–1650), Actas da IX Reuniao
          Internacional de História da Náutica e da Hidrografia
          (Fernando Oliveira and His Era: Humanism and the Art
          of Navigation in Renaissance Europe (1450–1650):
          Proceedings of the Ninth International Reunion for
          the History of Nautical Science and Hydography),
          Inacio Guerreiro and Francisco C. Domingues, editors,
          pp. 153–161. Patrimónia, Cascais, Portugal.

COSTA, LEONOR FREIRE
   1997   Naus e Galeões na Ribeira de Lisboa (Naus and
          Galleons in Lisbon Royal Shipyard). Patrimónia,
          Cascais, Portugal.

CRUMLIN-PEDERSON, OLE
   1991   Ship Types and Sizes. In Aspects of Maritime
          Scandinavia, A.D. 200–1200, Ole Crumlin-Pederson,
          editor, pp. 69–82. The Viking Ship Museum, Roskilde,
          Denmark.

CRUMLIN-PEDERSON, OLE, AND OLAF OLSEN
  2002 *The Skuldelev Ships I*. Centre for Maritime Archaeology of the National Museum of Denmark, Roskilde.

DARMOUL, ALI
  1985 Les épaves sarrasines (The Sarracine Wrecks). In *L'homme mediterranéen et la mer* (The Mediterranean Man and the Sea), M. Galley and L. Ladjini Sebai, editors, pp. 157–158. Editions Salammbô, Tunis, Italy.

DELL'AMICO, PIERO
  2002 *Costruzione navale antica* (Ancient Shipbuilding). Edizioni del Delfino Moro, Albenga, Italy.

DOMINGUES, FRANCISCO CONTENTE
  1989 A caravela quatrocentista nas fontes da arqueologia naval portuguesa (The Caravel of the 1400s in the Historical Sources of Portuguese Naval Archaeology). In *Actas do Congresso Internacional Bartolomeu Dias e a sua Época* (Proceedings of the International Congress on Bartolomeu Dias and His Time), Vol. 2, Humberto B. Moreno, editor, pp. 515–538. Comissão Nacional para as Comemorações dos Descobrimentos Portugueses, Universidade do Porto, Porto, Portugal.
  2000 *Os navios da expansão: O "Livro da fabrica das naus" de Fernando Oliveira e a arquitectura naval portuguesa dos séculos XVI e XVII* (The Ships of the Expansion: "Livro da Fabrica das Naus" from Fernando Oliveira and Portuguese Naval Architecture of the Sixteenth and Seventeenth Centuries). Dissertação de doutoramento em História da Expansão Portuguesa apresentada à Faculdade de Letras da Universidade de Lisboa, preparada sob a orientação do Professor Doutor António Dias Farinha. Universidade de Lisboa, Lisbon, Portugal.
  2005 *Os navios do mar oceano* (The Ships of the Ocean Sea). Centro de História dos Descobrimentos, Lisbon, Portugal.

DURO, CESÁRIO FERNANDEZ
  1880 *Disquisiciones nauticas* (Nautical Disquisitions), 5 vols. Reprinted in 1996 by the Instituto de Historia y Cultura Naval, Madrid, Spain.

ESCALANTE DE MENDOZA, JUAN
  1575 *Itinerario de Navegación de los Mares y Tierras Occidentales* (Itinerary for Navigation of the Seas and Western Lands). In *Disquisiciones nauticas* (Nautical Disquisitions), 5 vols., pp. 413–515, transcribed by Cesário Fernandez Duro in 1880. Reprinted in 1996 by Instituto de Historia y Cultura Naval, Madrid, Spain.

FERNANDEZ, MANOEL
  1616 *Livro de Traças de Carpintaria* (Book of Carpenter's Designs). Reprinted in 1989 by Academia de Marinha, Lisbon, Portugal.

FILGUEIRAS, OCTÁVIO LIXA
  1980 The Decline of Portuguese Regional Boats. *Maritime Monographs and Reports*, No. 47. National Maritime Museum Greenwich, London, UK.
  1989 Gelmirez e a reconversão da construção naval tradicional do NW Sec. XI-XII: Seus prováveis reflexos na época dos Descobrimentos (Gelmirez and the Reconversion of Traditional Naval Shipbuilding in the Northwest, Eleventh and Twelfth Centuries: Its Probable Effects in the Period of the Discoveries). *Actas do Congresso Internacional Bartolomeu Dias e a sua Época* (Proceedings of the International Congress on Bartolomeu Dias and His Time), Vol. 2, Humberto B. Moreno, editor, pp. 539–576. Comissão Nacional para as Comemorações dos Descobrimentos Portugueses, Universidade do Porto.
  1992 *Arquitectura do rabelo* (Architecture of the Rabelo). Rozès, Porto, Portugal.

FONSECA, HENRIQUE QUIRINO DA
  1915 Memórias de arqueologia marítima portuguesa (Memoirs of Portuguese Maritime Archaeology). *Separata dos anais do Clube Militar Naval* (Annals of the Naval Military Club, Independent Vol. J. F. Pinheiro, Lisbon, Portugal.
  1934 *A caravela Portuguesa e a Prioridade Técnica das Navegações Henriquinas* (The Portuguese Caravel and the Technical Priorities of Prince Henry's Navigations). Imprensa da Universidade, Coimbra, Portugal. Re-edited in 1978 by Ministério da Marinha, Lisbon, Portugal.

FRIEL, IAN
  1993 Henry V's Grace Dieu and the Wreck in the River Hamble near Burlsdon, Hampshire. *International Journal of Nautical Archaeology* 22(1):3–19.

GARCÍA DE PALACIO, DIEGO
  1587 *Instrucción Nautica para el buen uso de las Naos, su traça, y gobierno conforme à la altura de México* (Nautical Instruction for the Good Use of Naus, Their Design, and Governance at the Latitude of Mexico). In *Disquisiciones nauticas* (Nautical Disquisitions), 5 vols., pp. 7–37, transcribed by Cesário Fernandez Duro in 1880. Reprinted in 1996 by the Instituto de Historia y Cultura Naval, Madrid, Spain.

GLASGOW, TOM
  1970 Maturing the Naval Administration. *Mariner's Mirror* 56(1):3–26.

GRENIER, R., B. LOWEN, AND JEAN-PIERRE PROULX
  1994 Basque Shipbuilding and Technology c. 1560–1580: The Red Bay Project. In *Proceedings of the Sixth International Symposium on Boat and Ship Archaeology* Roskilde 1991, Christer Westerdahl, editor, pp. 137–142. Oxbow Monograph, No. 40. Oxbow Books, Oxford, England, UK.

GUÉROUT, MAX, ERIC RIETH, AND JEAN-MARIE GASSEND
  1989 Le navire génois de Villefranche. Um naufrage de 1516? (The Genoese Ship of Villefranche: A 1516 Shipwreck?) *Archaeonautica* 9:1–165. Centre National de la Recherche Scientifique, Paris, France.

IRIA, ALBERTO
  1963 *As Caravelas do Infante e os Caíques do Algarve: Subsídios para o Estudo da Arqueologia Naval Portuguesa* (Prince Henry's Caravels and the Caíques from Algarve: Subsidies for the Study of Portuguese Naval Archaeology). Associação dos Arqueólogos Portugueses, Lisbon, Portugal.

LANE, FREDERIC C.
  1934a Naval Architecture about 1550. *Mariner's Mirror* 20:24–49.
  1934b *Venetian Ships and Shipbuilders of the Renaissance.* The Johns Hopkins Press, Baltimore, MD.

LEMÉE, CHRISTIAN P. P.
  2006 *The Renaissance Shipwrecks from Christianshavn: An Archaeological and Architectural Study of Large Carvel Vessels in Danish Water, 1580–1640.* Ships and Boats of the North Series, Vol. 6. The Viking Ship Museum, Roskilde, Denmark.

LÓPEZ PÉREZ, ALESSANDRO, AND IVÁN DÍAZ PELEGRIN
  2005 Arqueología Subacuática en Cuba. Reseña Histórica (Underwater Archaeology in Cuba: Historical Summary). Manuscript, Oficina del Historiador de la Ciudad de La Habana, Havana, Cuba.

LOVEGROVE, H.
  1964 Remains of Two Old Vessels Found at Rye, Sussex. *Mariner's Mirror* 50(2):115–122.

MARQUES, A. H. DE OLIVEIRA
  1998 *A Expansao quatrocentista* (Expansion of the 1400s). Editorial Estampa, Lisbon, Portugal.

MARSDEN, PETER
  2003 *Sealed by Time: The Loss and Recovery of the Mary Rose.* The Mary Rose Trust, Portsmouth, England, UK.

MATTHEWS, SHEILA D.
  2004 Evidence for the Rig of the Serçe Limanı Ship. In *Serçe Limanı. An Eleventh-Century Shipwreck,* Vol. I, *The Ship and Its Anchorage, Crew, and Passengers,* George F. Bass, Sheila D. Matthews, J. Richard Steffy, and Frederick H. van Doorninck, Jr., editors, pp. 171–188. Texas A&M University Press, College Station.

MENDES, ANTÓNIO ROSA
  1993 A vida cultural (Cultural Life). In *História de Portugal* (History of Portugal), Vol. 3, pp. 375–421. José Mattoso. Circulo de Leitores, Lisbon, Portugal.

MOTT, LAWRENCE V.
  1997 *The Development of the Rudder: A Technological Tale.* Texas A&M University Press, College Station.

OERTLING, THOMAS J.
  1989 The Few Remaining Clues. In *Underwater Archaeology Proceedings for The Society for Historical Archaeology Conference,* J. Barto Arnold III, editor, pp. 100–103. Society for Historical Archaeology, Baltimore MD.
  2001 The Concept of the Atlantic Vessel. *Proceedings: International Symposium on Archaeology of Medieval and Modern Ships of Iberian-Atlantic Tradition,* Lisbon, September 1998, Francisco Alves, editor, pp. 213–228. IPA, Lisbon, Portugal.
  2005 Characteristics of Fifteenth- and Sixteenth-Century Iberian Ships. *The Philosophy of Shipbuilding,* Frederick M. Hocker and Cheryl A. Ward, editors, pp. 129–136. Texas A&M University Press, College Station.

OLIVEIRA, FERNANDO
  1580 *O Livro da Fabrica das Naos* (The Book of Naus Construction). Reprinted and translated in 1991 by Academia de Marinha, Lisbon, Portugal.

PÉREZ-MALLAÍNA, PABLO E.
  1998 *Spain's Men of the Sea.* The Johns Hopkins University Press, Baltimore MD.

PHILLIPS, CARLA RAHN
  1987 Spanish Ship Measurements Reconsidered: The *Instruccion nautica* of Diego Garcia de Palacio (1587). *The Mariner's Mirror* 73(3):293–296.
  1993 The Evolution of Spanish Ship Design from the Fifteenth to the Eighteenth Century. *The American Neptune* 53(4):229–238.
  2000 Manuel Fernandes [sic] and His 1616 *Livro de Tracas de Carpintaria. The American Neptune* 60(1):7–29.

PICO, MARIA ALEXANDRA TAVARES CARBONELL
  1964 *A terminologia naval portuguesa anterior a 1460* (Portuguese Naval Terminology prior to 1460). Sociedade de Língua Portuguesa, Lisbon, Portugal.

PIERCY, ROBIN
  1977 Mombasa Wreck Excavation: Preliminary report, 1977. *International Journal of Nautical Archaeology* 6:331–347.
  1978 Mombasa Wreck Excavation: Second preliminary report, 1978. *International Journal of Nautical Archaeology* 7:301–319.
  1979 Mombasa Wreck Excavation: Third preliminary report, 1979. *International Journal of Nautical Archaeology* 4:303–309.
  1980 Mombasa Wreck Excavation: Fourth preliminary report, 1980. *International Journal of Nautical Archaeology* 10:109–118.

PIKE, RUTH
1966 *Enterprise and Adventure: The Genoese in Seville and the Opening of the New World.* Cornell University Press Ithaca, NY.

PIRES, ANTÓNIO TENGARRINHA
1985 *As caravelas dos descobrimentos: IIA: Mareação de bolina* (Caravels of Discoveries: IIA: Sailing Close to the Wind). Academia de Marinha, Lisbon Portugal.
1986 *As caravelas dos descobrimentos: IIB: Uso da bolina* (Caravels of Discoveries: IIB: Use of Close-Hauled Sailing). Academia de Marinha, Lisbon Portugal.
1988 *As caravelas dos descobrimentos: IIC: Bolina na costa portuguesa* (Caravels of Discoveries: IIC: Close-Hauled Sailing along the Portuguese Coast). Academia de Marinha, Lisbon Portugal.
1990 *As caravelas dos descobrimentos: IID: Caravela de meados do séc. XV* (Caravels of Discoveries: IID: The Caravel of the Mid-Fifteenth Century). Academia de Marinha, Lisbon Portugal.

REDKNAP, M.
1984 *The Cattewater Wreck: The Investigation of an Armed Vessel of the Early Sixteenth Century.* BAR no. 131, Series no 8. London, England, UK.

REIS, ANTÓNIO ESTÁCIO DOS
2002 *Astrolábios náuticos* (Nautical Astrolabes). Edições Inapa, Lisbon, Portugal.

RIETH, ÉRIC
1996 *Le Maître-gabarit, la Tablette et le Trébuchet. Éssai sur la conception non-graphique des carènes du Moyen-Âge au XXe siècle* (The Maitre-Gabarit, the Tablette, and the Trebuchet: Essay on the Nongraphic Conception of Hulls from the Middle Ages to the Twentieth Century). Comité des Travaux Historiques et Scientifiques, Paris, France.
1998 Construction navale à Franc-Bord en Méditerranée et Atlantique (XIVe–XVIIe siècle) et "Signatures Architecturales" Une Première Approche Archéologique (Caravel Naval Construction in the Mediterranean and the Atlantic [Fourteenth to Fifteenth Centuries] and "Architectural Signatures": A First Archaeological Approach). In *Méditerranée antique. Pêche, navigation, commerce* (Ancient Mediterranean: Fishing, Navigation, and Commerce), Eric Rieth, editor, pp. 177–188. Comité des Travaux Historiques et Scientifiques, Paris, France.

RODRIGUES, P., F. ALVES, E. RIETH, F. CASTRO
1998 L'épave dun navire de la moitié du XV.ème siècle/ début du XVI.ème, trouvée au Cais do Sodré (Lisbonne). Note Préliminaire, (The Shipwreck Dating to the Middle Fifteenth/Early Sixteenth Century Found at Cais Do Sodré [Lisbon]). In *Proceedings: International Symposium Archaeology of Medieval and Modern Ships of Iberian-Atlantic Tradition,* Lisbon, September 1998, Francisco Alves, editor, pp. 347–380. IPA, Lisbon, Portugal.

ROMERO, FERNANDO ALONSO
1991 Traditional Clinker and Carvel Techniques in the Northwest of Spain. In *Carvel Construction Technique: Skeleton-First, Shell-First: Fifth International Symposium on Boat and Ship Archaeology,* Amsterdam 1988, Reinder Reinders and Paul Kees, editors, pp. 103–111. Oxbow Monograph, No. 12. Oxbow Books, Oxford, England, UK.

RUSSELL, M.
1983 *Visions of the Sea: Hendrick C. Vroom and the Origins of Dutch Marine Painting.* Leiden University Press, Leiden, NL.

SALISBURY, W.
1961 Woolwich Ship. *Mariner's Mirror* 47(2):81–91.

SARSFIELD, JOHN P.
1991 Master Frame and Ribbands. In *Carvel Construction Technique: Skeleton-First, Shell-First: Fifth International Symposium on Boat and Ship Archaeology,* Amsterdam 1988, Reinder Reinders and Kees Paul, editors, pp. 137–145. Oxbow Monograph, No. 12. Oxbow Books, Oxford, UK.

SERRANO MANGAS, FERNANDO
1985 *Los galeones de la Carrera de Indias, 1650–1700* (The Galleons of the West Indies Route, 1650–1700). Escuela de Estudios Hispano-Americanos de Sevilla, Seville, Spain.

SMITH, R. C., J. R. BRATTEN, J. COZZI, AND K. PLASKETT
1998 *The Emanuel Point Ship: Archaeological Investigations, 1997–1998, Preliminary Report,* Florida Bureau of Archaeological Research, Pensacola.

SMITH, R. C., J. SPIREK, J. BRATTEN, AND D. SCOTT-IRETON
1995 *The Emanuel Point Ship: Archaeological Investigations, 1992–1995, Preliminary Report,* Florida Bureau of Archaeological Research, Pensacola.

TAYLOR, JAMES
2004 *Marine Painting: Images of Sail, Sea, and Shore.* National Maritime Museum, Greenwich, England, UK.

TOJA, MARCELLO
1990 Quei tesori dimenticati (Those Forgotten Treasures). *Mondo Sommerso* 342:56–65.

TRIPATI, SILA, S. GAUR, A. S. SUNDARESH
2006 Exploration of a Portuguese Shipwreck in Goa Waters, Western Coast of India. In *Bulletin of the Australasian Institute for Maritime Archaeology* 30:127–136.

TURNER, SAM
1994 Saona Artillery: Implications for Inter-Island Trade and Shipboard Armaments in the First Half of the Sixteenth Century. Master's thesis, Department of Anthropology, Texas A&M University.

VAUGHAN, H. S.
   1913   The Nodal Caravels of 1618. *Mariner's Mirror* 3(2):171–176.

VICENTE MAROTO, MARIA ISABEL
   1998   *Diálogo entre un vizcayno y un montañés sobre la fábrica de navíos* (Dialog between a Viszcayno and a Montañes about the Construction of Ships). Ediciones Universidad de Salamanca, Salamanca, Spain.
   2001   La expedicion de los hermanos Nodal y del cosmógrafo Diego Ramirez de Arellano (The Expedition of the Nodal Brothers and the Cosmographer Diego Ramirez Arellano. *Revista de Historia Naval* 19(73):7–28.

VILLIÉ, PIERRE
   1989   L'épave Calvi I (The Calvi I Shipwreck). *Cahiers d'Archéologie Subaquatique* 8:19–56.
   1990   L'épave Calvi I (The Calvi I Shipwreck). *Cahiers d'Archéologie Subaquatique* 9:83–130.
   1991   L'épave Calvi I (The Calvi I Shipwreck). *Cahiers d'Archéologie Subaquatique* 10:69–108.

VITERBO, SOUSA
   1988   *Trabalhos náuticos dos portugueses* (Nautical Works of the Portuguese). Imprensa Nacional Casa da Moeda, Lisbon, Portugal.

WATSON, P., AND C. TODESCHINI
   2006   *The Medici Conspiracy: The Illicit Journey of Looted Antiquities: From Italy's Tomb Raiders to the World's Greatest Museums.* Public Affairs Books, London, England, UK.

XAVIER, HERNANI AMARAL
   1992   *Novos Elementos para o Estudo da Arquitectura Naval Portuguesa Antiga* (New Elements for the Study of Ancient Portuguese Naval Architecture). Academia de Marinha, Lisbon, Portugal.

FILIPE CASTRO
NAUTICAL ARCHAEOLOGY PROGRAM
105 DEPARTMENT OF ANTHROPOLOGY
TEXAS A&M UNIVERSITY
COLLEGE STATION, TX 77843-4352

2010. Outfitting the Pepper Wreck. *Historical Archaeology* 44(2):14–34.

Filipe Castro
Nuno Fonseca
Audrey Wells

Outfitting the Pepper Wreck

ABSTRACT

This article is part of a series of papers on the attempts to reconstruct and understand an early-17th-century Portuguese Indiaman based on the archaeological remains of the presumed *Nossa Senhora dos Mártires*, a Portuguese *nau* that sank at the mouth of the Tagus River, Portugal, in September 1606. With the help of 3-D computer software, the authors try to understand how the interior space of this ship was used and occupied, and propose a plausible size, weight, and configuration for the cargo storage, which will be tested in terms of the fully loaded ship's intact stability. The result is intended as a theoretical model of a ca. 1600 Portuguese *nau*. Only further archaeological probing will tell whether it is an accurate model or not.

Introduction

The Portuguese Indiaman tentatively identified as the *Nossa Senhora dos Mártires*, whose remains were found at the mouth of the Tagus in the early 1990s, was the product of more than a century of evolution (Figure 1). Named the "Pepper Wreck" due to the considerable amount of pepper found on its bottom, this shipwreck was excavated and partially reconstructed during the last decade (Castro 2003, 2005a, 2005b; Castro and Fonseca 2006; Santos et al. 2007).

It is difficult to reconstruct a ship of this period due to the scarcity of documentary, archaeological, and iconographic data. There are some good images, dated to earlier and later periods, but the evolutionary process that led to the design and construction of the *Nossa Senhora dos Mártires* sometime between 1600 and 1605 is not clear. From at least the second decade of the 16th century onwards there is a clear differentiation between *naus* and galleons in written documents. As the 16th century unfolded, the capacity of *naus* tended to increase, castles became lower (on both galleons and *naus*), and the differences in size between main courses (the lower sails of the main- and foremasts) and

topsails diminished considerably. In the beginning of the 16th century, iconographical sources showed large main courses and small trapezoidal topsails on the main- and foremasts. A century later this difference was less pronounced. This fact was taken into account when the rigging of the Pepper Wreck was reconstructed. It is not known at this time whether these changes in rigging arrangement were accompanied by relevant changes in hull design.

The reconstruction attempted was based on the measurements obtained from the Pepper Wreck ship remains, analyzed in light of a small number of shipbuilding treatises and manuals dating from around the time of the supposed *Nossa Senhora dos Mártires* shipwreck in September 1606 (Castro 2003, 2005a). As when shooting at a moving target, many of the choices made in the reconstruction took into account the evolution in dimensions and basic design features that occurred during the time which elapsed between the dates of the different documents consulted (Figure 2).

It is difficult to reconstruct all the steps of this evolutionary trend, given the lack of data, and perhaps even more difficult to identify and isolate the factors that triggered each one of these changes. The 16th century saw the consolidation of the modern state, and was marked by a fierce competition among nations for new lands and markets, complicated by religious dissent and war.

One of the research directions of this project was the study of life aboard and the way it may have influenced ship size, shape, and functionality. To be sure, it seems that other factors, such as the depth and accessibility of the ports of call, may have played equally important roles in shaping these ships' hulls and rigging arrangements. Toward the end of the 16th century a shallow draught seems to have been a particularly important design feature for Portuguese *naus*, given the shallow depth of the water at both the Goa and Cochin anchorages on the Indian subcontinent, partly due to continued dumping of ballast over the decades (Barcelos 1898–1899:17–18,62). This design restriction must have posed some interesting challenges to the shipwrights, which should

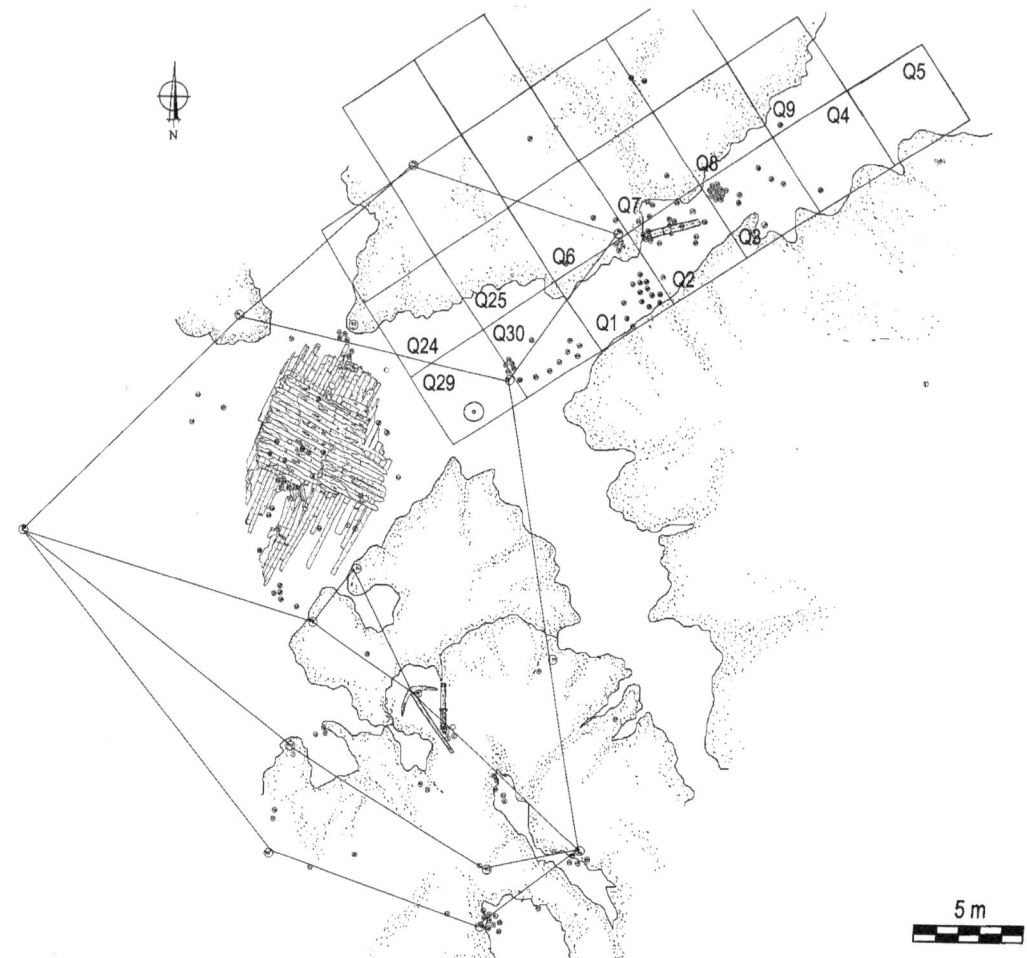

FIGURE 1. Pepper Wreck site plan. (Image by Filipe Castro, 2001.)

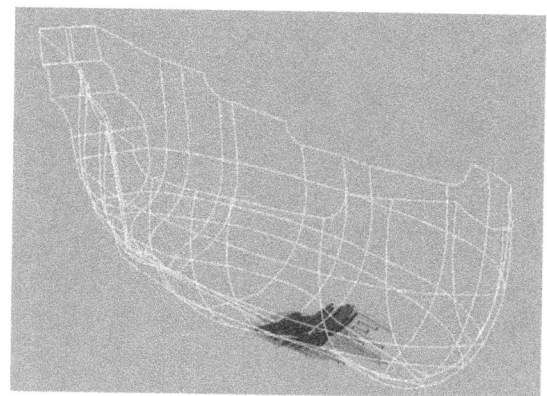

FIGURE 2. Reconstruction scheme. (Image by Kevin Gnadinger, 2008.)

be studied in the future, mostly considering the light weight of the peppercorns that filled most of these ships' holds, and the necessity to carry heavy artillery on the upper deck for protection.

Be that as it may, life aboard remains a relevant factor in the reconstruction of any long-distance sailing ships. Their inhabitants, "the big children who people those dark and wandering places of the earth," as novelist Joseph Conrad described them in his own time, were the engines of such complicated machines (Conrad 1914:20).

The process of evolution of India *naus* throughout the 16th century is an interesting subject, but one whose analysis requires far more data than is presently available. Some surviving documents call for changes in ship design, but it is not known how the perceived necessities for change and improvement were conveyed and filtered through the Portuguese bureaucracy, or which changes in hull shape and rigging were actually implemented and which were not. Most of the records that had survived the inclemencies of time were destroyed on 1 November 1755, when Lisbon was hit by a terrible earthquake, a series of tidal waves, and a fire that lasted for several weeks.

One of the most useful tools that has been used in the reconstruction of the Pepper Wreck was a virtual model, patiently developed by Audrey Wells—co-author of this paper—at Texas A&M University's Department of Visualization Sciences (Wells 2008). The virtual reconstruction of the Pepper Wreck was an iterative process in which every step provided a better image of the complex spaces that composed the ship's inner space, and at the same time showed new problems and raised new questions (Figure 3). It

was both an exciting and humbling process which allowed the proposal of a preliminary arrangement for the cargo. In many ways, it can be said that every step taken toward understanding the way in which the space was appropriated leads to a realization of how much work still needs to be done. Archaeology is ultimately about people, and this paper is an attempt to reconstruct a plausible scenario aboard the conjectural model of *Nossa Senhora dos Mártires*.

The main purpose of the reconstruction presented here is to try to reach the people that thought, built, and sailed these ships. It is known that sailing conditions improved throughout the 16th century because mortality rates diminished consistently as experience was gained. On the way back from his first trip (1498–1499), not knowing the wind patterns in the Indian Ocean, Vasco da Gama lost almost half of his men trying to sail

FIGURE 3. Pepper Wreck model. (Image by Audrey Wells, 2008.)

Maritime Archaeology

against the prevailing monsoon winds. Nearly a century later, Cornelis Houtman, leading the first Dutch expedition to the Far East, would lose 153 of his 240 men. In the 16th century, experience was almost everything. In 1606, *Nossa Senhora dos Mártires* sailed to India in six months without the loss of a single person. In fact, nobody in the entire fleet died (de Azevedo 1964:155).

Many of the problems, however, could not be solved. Ships were always too crowded at departure to prevent a future lack of hands should the ship be hit by disease or be becalmed around the equator. Living space was minimal, and sanitary conditions must have been miserable. In addition, despite all improvements, until the advent of steam sailing ships only went where the wind took them.

Lack of wind or contrary winds plagued some of the voyages throughout the century. As a result, food and water were at times scarce and their quality could degrade rapidly, chiefly when ships were becalmed in the tropical heat. If ships were immobilized for too long, vitamin deprivation generated diseases such as scurvy, which could cost many lives. For these reasons provisioning was a serious matter that nobody took lightly (Neves 2004). Food was carefully stored in the holds of Portuguese India *naus*, protected in compartments specially built and locked under careful supervision.

When reconstructing the Pepper Wreck the problems related to space appropriation and storage arrangements became paramount to the understanding of life aboard, the ship's stability and trim, and its sailing performance. Moreover, every study of the ship's structure, its strength, and resistance to fatigue is closely tied to a good understanding of the nature and number of its crew and passengers, as well as the nature and quantity of its cargo and storage conditions.

To better understand such a complex and compact floating city, for the purposes of this discussion it has been divided into thirteen separate components: hull; ballast; masts and spars; sails; rigging; water and provisions; firewood; anchors and fittings; armament; spare parts, tools, and materials for repairs at sea; crew, soldiers, and passengers; personal belongings; and cargo.

Hull

The reconstruction of the ship's hull is an iterative process. The ship's shape has been tentatively recreated based on the archaeological data and following late-16th-century and early-17th-century guidelines (Castro 2003, 2005a), and refined using engineering tools (Castro and Fonseca 2006; Santos et al. 2007).

A study of the structure of an India *nau* (Hazlett 2007), as well as the construction sequence (Hazlett 2007; Castro and Fonseca 2008), has been done at Texas A&M University based on a document from the *Livro náutico* codex.

The division of the interior spaces is a difficult task. The only known Portuguese *naus* preserved well enough to provide information on the positions of bulkheads or on the distribution of cargo seem to have been destroyed by treasure hunters off Mozambique (Mirabal 2007). While there is almost no information on the excavation or salvage methods of these shipwrecks, it is unlikely that treasure hunters recorded in detail the nail marks that could indicate the existence of bulwarks on the inner surface of the framing structure and ceiling planking.

Documentary sources are scarce. There is one document dating to 1607 that shows the distribution of the cargo in a two-decked *nau*, and some accounts of voyages and of shipwrecks mention cargo storage, but seldom in detail or in a systematic way (Castro 2005a:20). One unsigned and undated document at the Ajuda Library, Lisbon, mentions in detail the allowances of cargo granted to each crew member (Guinote et al. 1998:362–370). Although the Ajuda document refers to a larger ship than the 1607 two-decker, it describes a space arrangement coherent with the 1607 drawing in many points, clearly establishing a pattern.

As a general rule, these ships were divided horizontally: the upper and weather decks, as well as both castles, were occupied by persons and animals, while the lower decks were filled with cargo (Castro 2005a:64). The upper classes occupied the aft area of the main deck (*convés*), the area under the quarterdeck, and the stern castle, namely the lodgings on the quarterdeck (*tolda*) and sometimes a small poop deck above it (*chapitéu*). The boxes and bales with their personal belongings were stored in their cabins, and in some cases on the lower decks. Livestock would be stalled abaft of the mainmast, birds and rabbits in cages carefully piled and tied, and sheep and goats, together with other large mammals, in boxes built on the deck.

The remaining area on the main deck was probably clear most of the time. Ship's boys would bundle to sleep in the forward area, under the forecastle. The lodgings of the crew and soldiers were underneath the weather deck and on the gun deck together with their private belongings, the ovens, part of the firewood and victuals, and the ship's boat. Abaft the main hatch, to starboard, were the lodgings and storage areas of the captain, master, pilot, second pilot, clerk, and purser. The corresponding areas to port side, together with the central area situated before these two, were used for storage. Towards the bow, to starboard, were the lodgings of the boatswain and boatswain's mate, and to port side were lodged the carpenters, caulkers, and cooper (Castro 2005a:64). At the bow, under the foremast step, slept the sailors and remaining ship's boys.

The hold was used for drugs and spices, of which pepper was the main cargo, stored in small magazines built for that purpose. Evidence suggests that the precious peppercorns were stored in holds built on the lower deck, atop the ballast. These holds were closed and carefully caulked to withstand the six-month voyage with a minimum of humidity (Castro 2005a:64).

A preliminary structure has been designed based on the timber list of the *Livro náutico* and the scantlings observed on the Pepper Wreck and the Seychelles shipwreck, possibly the remains of the India *nau Santo António*, lost between Mozambique and India in 1589 (Blake and Green 1986; Patrick Lizé 2002, pers. comm.; Hazlett 2007).

The weight of the hull was estimated at 398 metric tons (t) (Santos et al. 2007).

Ballast

Inspecting two *naus*—both larger than the Pepper Wreck—being built in 1623 at Lisbon's shipyards, shipwright Valentim Themudo stated that the minimum amount of ballast these ships would take on in India for the voyage home was 9 *palmos* (*de goa*), or 2.31 m of height in the hold. This study has estimated that the nature of the main cargo—peppercorns—made it necessary to keep around 175 t of ballast in the hold of the reconstructed Pepper Wreck (Santos et al. 2007). The ballast consisted, probably, of broken limestone (1.55 t/m^3) and was carried directly above the keel inside the lower hold. The 175 t of ballast occupies roughly 113 m^3 and would have filled the lower hold up to a height of 1.46 m. This height of ballast would have left a substantial portion of the lower deck available for cargo, with a usable free height of around 2 m, after taking into account that a layer of wood—an orlop deck—would be added on top of the ballast to create a surface for proper cargo storage. The beam positions of this orlop deck can be seen in the pictures of a shipwreck salvaged by treasure hunters in Mozambique, named IDM-003, and believed to have been lost there in 1607 (Alejandro Mirabal 2008, pers. comm.).

The objective of ballasting these ships was to increase their stability, and in this way safely oppose the inclining moment induced by the wind on the sails. The authors have concluded that with 175 t of ballast the ship would be safe in terms of stability, even complying with modern stability criteria for large sailing vessels (Santos et al. 2007). This conclusion seems to be validated by the analysis of ship losses on the Indian route. In fact, several causes have been identified for ship loss, and poor stability was not among them.

The estimated amount of ballast that a ship like the Pepper Wreck carried on its inbound voyage will nevertheless be refined upon further analysis. As mentioned above, according to the data available, peppercorns were stored in the hold and lower deck (*primeira coberta* in Portugal), and the water and wine must have occupied part of the upper and weather decks, because the area of the hold indicated by 16th-century traveler Jan Huygen van Linschoten (1997)—from the mainmast forward, under the area of the main hatch—was too small for all the water and wine necessary for a six-month trip. How high the orlop deck was laid remains a relevant question. It is likely that India *naus* sailed to India with more ballast than this. Typically, outbound *naus* would carry cargos of silver coins, copper ingots, and soldiers. In 1627, João Pereira Corte Real complained that over the previous century the piles of ballast dumped in the anchorage in front of the city of Goa were making it very difficult to bring the large *naus* closer to land (Barcelos 1898–1899:62). Only further analysis will help to improve the current reconstruction.

Masts and Spars

A tentative reconstruction of the ship's masts and spars has been proposed (Castro 2005b; Castro and Fonseca 2008), based on a number of documents from the period. One of the main sources for this reconstruction is a manuscript dated to the late 16th century and titled *O livro náutico* (Biblioteca Nacional [1590b]; Domingues 2004:351–361). The sizes and diameters of the masts and spars obtained through different methods seem plausible, and fall within the ranges expected from the analysis of other documents as well as the iconographic record.

The total weight of the model's masts and spars was estimated at 25.62 t, to which must be added the weight of the mast tops (crow's nests), estimated at 2.35 t (Castro 2005b).

Sails

The sails stretched from yardarm to yardarm and their height was dependent on the space allowed by the mast size and arrangements (Garcia de Palacio 1880:25–30). A tentative sail plan has been developed based on the following documents: (1) the rigging section of Garcia de Palacio's treatise, *Instrucion Nautica para el buen uso de las Naos, su traça, y gobierno conforme à la altura de Mexico*, dated to 1587 (Garcia de Palacio 1880); (2) the list "Aparelhos de um galeão" from the Portuguese manuscript "Coriosidades de Gonçalo de Sousa" at the Library of Coimbra University), dated to about 1620 (de Sousa [1620]); and (3) two lists—folios 38 to 41 and 178 to 181—from the first of the three volumes of the Portuguese codex of D. António de Ataíde (de Ataíde 1588–1633), known as "Collecção de varios documentos e papeis régios e administrativos respectivos as armadas e expedições marítimas," dated to 1624 and ca. 1630.

A review of the best contemporary iconography helped solve a few problems, although only a handful of images have been drawn or painted with enough detail to allow the observation of ships' rigging arrangements. Other than a small number of reliable Portuguese images, the best contemporary images consulted include etchings by Frans Huys (1522–1562) after drawings by Pieter Brueghel the Elder (1525–1569) (Gunn-Graham 1998), the late-16th-century frescoes from the Spanish palaces Escorial and Viso del Marques, and two paintings by Hendrick Cornelisz. Vroom (ca. 1562–1640).

The plausibility of the sail plan developed has raised more questions than that of the hull reconstruction, and only further research may contribute to a better understanding of late-16th-century Portuguese sail making. The sizes and weights of all sails have nevertheless been estimated with some degree of certainty at 1.7 t (Castro 2008). We have considered the total weight of all sails, including spares, at 3.5 t.

Rigging

The rigging has not yet been fully reconstructed. Its study is still underway. Again, there are few contemporary written sources for this period, and most need to be tried and tested against the iconographic record. Four documents with relevant information have been found so far: (1) "Medidas para fazer hũa Nao de Seicentas Tonelladas," from *Livro náutico*, ca. 1590 (Biblioteca Nacional [1590b]); (2) a list from a document titled "Conta das medidas de uma nau da India," from "Coriosidades de Gonçallo de Sousa," ca. 1620, (de Sousa [1620]); (3) "Advertências de navegantes," from Marcos Serveira de Aguilar (ca. 1640) (de Aguilar [1640]); and (4) a list from the first volume of the "Collecção de varios documentos e papeis régios e administrativos respectivos as armadas e expedições marítimas" collected by António de Ataíde (de Ataíde 1588–1633).

A reconstruction of the standing rigging configuration does not pose many serious problems because some of the documents consulted are quite specific about the size and position of the chain plates, and therefore allow an almost perfect reconstruction of the shrouds' positions. The paths of the basic running rigging are rather simple, and the questions remaining are mainly related to the positions of the standing ends and belaying points of the running rigging on the reconstructed deck. In any case, these factors do not bear too much importance in the overall testing of the model.

The total weight of the rigging has been estimated at 5 t (Santos et al. 2007).

Water and Provisions

Foodstuffs occupied an important part of the ship's space. While the "haves" brought impressive amounts of food, both for their own consumption and that of their servants and slaves, the "have nots" generally ate the daily rations supplied by the ship, complemented by whatever they had brought in their boxes.

Common sailors would be supplied with a daily diet of hardtack, which was soaked in a mixture of wine and water before it was consumed, and some salted meat together with beans, rice, or lentils. Personal supplies supplemented this diet, as did fishing when there was time and the bottoms allowed it. Depending on where they were in the trip, personal supplies could consist of fresh water, olive oil, and smoked ham or sausages, as well as pickled vegetables, onions, garlic, and a small portion of fruits and sweets, which were generally finished long before the trip was over (de Matos 1998).

The rich brought a long list of foodstuffs aboard, and ate very well by any standards, old or contemporary (de Matos 1998; Castro 2005a:66–69). Judging by some priests' accounts, the meals consisted of a "stove breakfast" taken in the morning, between 8:30 and 9:30 a.m., a substantial dinner around 2:00 p.m., and later a supper consisting of fresh fruits, dried grapes or figs, cheese, olives, and almonds, which could be followed by cold meats from dinner, such as ham, sausages, or pork.

Although these have been better described elsewhere, it is difficult to resist mentioning here a few of the foodstuffs brought aboard by the upper classes (Castro 2005a:67). In 1576 a Jesuit priest's personal food list consisted of around 75 L of wine, 4 barrels of water, 4 barrels of hardtack, 1 smoked pig, 30 kg of salted beef, 100 chickens, 50 pork sides (spareribs), 60 sausages, 20 hakes, 100 dried dogfish, 15 pumpkins, 10 bales of rice, 1 barrel of vermicelli, and 3 baskets of onions. Also included in his luggage was a long list of different types of peas, beans, sweets, dried fruits, spices, and condiments, all in small quantities, including chickpeas, beans, lentils, sugar, quince jam, dried raisins, plums, dates, mustard, garlic, pickled roots (achar), saffron, coriander, "one pound of each spice," olive oil, vinegar, and butter (Guerreiro 1998:428). In 1631 Captain António de Saldanha embarked on his trip from Lisbon to Goa with the impressive quantity of 275 kg of sweets, consisting of jams and jellies, sweet yellow paste—a mousse made of egg yolks and sugar syrup—and several sorts of sugars and honeys.

A list of the basic rations on the India route is indicated below, in Table 1. These items were packed in bags (sacas), jars, boxes, chests, and barrels for storage purposes, and distributed throughout the ship. It is believed that barrels were used in three main standard sizes. There were tonéis, pipas, and quartos, the pipas having half of the capacity of tonéis and the quartos half the capacity of pipas. Richard Barker has done the most extensive research on this subject to the knowledge of this article's authors. For lack of precise data, this study has adopted the sizes determined by that investigator from precise data from about 1800: tonéis with a capacity of 1,140 L, pipas containing 570 L, and quartos 285 L (Barker 1994, 2007, pers. comm.). Regarding the barrel sizes, the dimensions indicated by Fernando Oliveira for the tonéis (1.54 m high, 1.02 m in diameter), and Barker's values for pipas (1.23 m high, 0.82 m in diameter) and quartos (0.98 m high, 0.64 m in diameter), have been adopted, even though Barker has expressed some reservations regarding this solution (Barker 2008, pers. comm.).

No information about the sizes of the chests has been found. Box sizes were regulated, and varied between 1.10–1.32 × 0.44 to 0.55 × 0.66 cm (Guinote et al. 1998:363; Neves 2004:113). There were countless jars of all sorts and sizes, of which a fair number have survived in the archaeological record. It is difficult to determine average sizes for those. Contemporary texts refer to a multitude of baskets, small boxes, bags, and bales, whose sizes may also have varied immensely. For the purpose of simulating the cargo arrangement, this study has standardized the dimensions of baskets (base diameter 0.60 m, and height 0.80 m), bags (1.50 × 0.40 × 0.60 m), and bales and chests (1.50 × 0.50 × 0.70 m). The total weight of the water and provisions was estimated at 292 t.

Firewood

Briefly mentioned by the late-16th-century traveler van Linschoten (1997), firewood consumption must have been an important matter. Assuming a total of 450 people including crew and passengers cooking for 120 days, it is estimated that to warm a half liter of water per person from 20° to 100° C every day, the ship needed to carry around 3 t of firewood,

TABLE 1
AVERAGE DAILY RATIONS ON THE INDIA ROUTE[a]

Quantities on the List	Totals in Metric Units	Rations (Average of 362 people × 180 days)[b]	Storage
1,074 *quintais* of hardtack	64.44 t	989 g per person per day	1,289 *sacas*
115 *pipas* of wine	65.550 m³	1.006 L per person per day	115 *pipas*
1,086 *arrobas* of meat	16.29 t	250 g per person per day	35 *pipas*
150 dozen hakes	1800 units	5 fish per person for the whole trip	18 *pipas*
315 *quartilhos* of olive oil	157.5 L	0.435 L per person for the whole trip	1 *pipa*
13 *pipas* of vinegar	7.410 m³	0.796 L per person per week	13 *pipas*
313 *pipas* of water	178.410 m³	2.738 L per person per day	313 *pipas*
25 *moios* of salt	19.5 m³	0.3 L per person per day	20 *tonéis*
130 *arrobas* of sardines	1.950 t	5.387 kg per person for the whole trip	13 *quartos*
14 *alqueires* of chickpeas	182 L	0.5 L per person for the whole trip	1 *pipa*
10 *alqueires* of almonds	130 L	0.36 L per person for the whole trip	1 *quarto*
10 *alqueires* of plums	130 L	0.36 L per person for the whole trip	1 *quarto*
10 *alqueires* of lentils	130 L	0.36 L per person for the whole trip	1 *quarto*
2 *alqueires* of mustard	26 L	0.07 L per person for the whole trip	1 large jar
724 *cabos* (braids) of garlic	—	2 braids per person for the whole trip	20 baskets
724 *cabos* of onions	—	2 braids per person for the whole trip	70 baskets
8 *arrobas* of sugar	117.52 kg	325 g per person for the whole trip	8 large jars
8 *arrobas* of honey	117.52 kg	325 g per person for the whole trip	48 jars

[a]Castro (2005a:66).

[b]Falcão (1859:200). Merely indicative, since it is known that the soldiers' portions of hardtack, wine, olive oil, vinegar, salt, sardines, chickpeas, plums, lentils, mustard, sugar, and honey were generally about one-third smaller than those of the crew.

considering the efficiency of the ovens at around 0.3. This amount of firewood would have taken about 12 m³ of space, perhaps in a small storage compartment near the ovens.

Anchors and Fittings

The best Portuguese treatises don't mention a standard number and size of anchors for an Indiaman. Several other Portuguese and Spanish contemporary texts address this subject, although generally referring to ships smaller than the reconstructed Pepper Wreck. In 1575 Escalante de Mendoza stated that ships should carry four large anchors (one sheet and three bowers), one smaller anchor (kedge) for maneuvering, and the two ship's boats' anchors (Escalante de Mendoza 1985:43–44). The weights should be calculated in this way: ships with a capacity of 100 t should have anchors (bowers) of 10 *quintales* (ca. 460 kgf), and for each 100 t of increase in capacity add three *quintales* to the anchor's weight (1 Spanish *quintal*=46.04 kgf). Following Escalante's

rule, a 600-tonner like the reconstructed Pepper Wreck should have anchors of 25 *quintales*, or ca. 1,150 kgf. A few years later, in 1587, Garcia de Palacio prescribed five large anchors (one sheet and four bowers), one smaller anchor (kedge) for maneuvering, and the two anchors of the ship's boats (Garcia de Palacio 1880:32–33). Referring to a ship of 400 t, Garcia de Palacio claimed that the weight of the sheet anchor should be between 16 and 18 *quintales* (737 and 835 kgf), not far from the value obtained with Escalante's rule.

In England, a rule for finding the weight of the sheet anchor dates to ca. 1582 and is known as "hawkyns rule" (Tinniswood 1945:88). It stipulated that the circumference of the anchor cable, given in inches, should be squared and divided by 16, the result giving the weight of the sheet anchor in hundredweights of 112 lb. (1 cwt.=50.8 kgf). The circumference of the anchor cable should be 0.5 in. per foot of the ship's beam. The reconstructed Pepper Wreck's beam being 12.32 m (Castro 2003:22), or slightly above 40 ft., this would make the weight of the anchor equal to:

$$Weight = (40 \times 0.5)^2/16 \times 50.8 = 1{,}270 \text{ kgf}$$

Tinniswood (1945:89) shows ranges of values obtained for 1602 and 1640 suggesting that English anchor weights were slightly above those indicated by Spanish authors (Table 2).

A late-16th-century list from *Livro náutico* transcribed by Contente Domingues mentions eight anchors per ship consistently: four of 17 *quintais* (999 kgf), two of 16 *quintais* (940 kgf), and two spare anchors also of 16 *quintais* (Domingues 2004:437–458).

For this model, four anchors of 1,000 kgf, four anchors of 950 kgf each, and one small anchor for the ship's boat of 150 kgf, totaling 7,850 kgf, have been adopted. All anchors were stored on the lower decks, except the two bowers, which were placed at the bow of the ship.

Anchor cables, weighing typically as much as the respective anchors, were stored inside the ship's boat or in compartments on the lower decks. Anchors and cables weighed a total of 15,700 kgf. For the storage of both the anchors and cables, an area near the center of gravity of the ship has been considered, and the total weight value rounded to 16 t.

Armament

It is difficult to estimate the number and size of the guns carried on these ships throughout the 16th century and during the early decades of the 17th century. To determine a configuration for the ship's guns this study has used the following armament list from the manuscript "Memorial das várias cousas importantes" (Biblioteca Nacional [1590a]:folio 1,126v.), titled "Rol da artilharia e munições de hua nao pa India de quinhentas e cinquenta até seiscentas toneladas" (List of Artillery and Ammunition of a *Nau* to India of Five Hundred Fifty to Six Hundred Tons):

Two *esperas* with all fittings
One *camelo* with all fittings
Four *pedreiros* with all fittings
Four *falcões* with three chargers each
Twelve *berços* with three chargers each
Stone cannon balls for the *espera*, sixty
Stone cannon balls for the *camelo*, thirty
Stone cannon balls for the *falcão*, one hundred and twenty
Stone cannon balls for the *berço*, three hundred
Powder ladles and swabs, twelve
Leather bags, four

TABLE 2
NUMBER AND WEIGHTS OF ANCHORS INDICATED FOR A 600-TON SHIP

	Escalante's Rule	1602[a]	1640[a]	Livro náutico
Sheet Anchor	—	—	25–28 cwt.[b] 1,270–1,422 kgf	17 *quintais*[c] 999 kgf
1st and 2nd Bowers	25 *quintales*[d] 1,151 kgf	22¼ cwt. 1,130 kgf	24–26 cwt. 1,219–1,312 kgf	16 *quintais* 940 kgf
3rd and 4th Bowers	25 *quintales* 1,151 kgf	—	23–25 cwt. 1,168–1,270 kgf	16 *quintais* 940 kgf
Spare Parts	—	—	—	16 *quintais* 940 kgf
Kedge	—	—	3.5 cwt. 178 kfg	

[a]Tinniswood (1945:89).
[b]English hundredweight (cwt.) = 50.80 kgf.
[c]Portuguese *quintal* = 58.754 kgf.
[d]Spanish *quintal* = 46.04 kgf.

Crowbars, four
Spears, 200
Pikes, 50
Darts for the tops, 100
Harquebuses with all fittings, 60
Gunpowder for canon, 10 *quintais*
Gunpowder for handguns, 1 *quintal*

Nuno Rubim, a Portuguese specialist in artillery of this period, advised against generalizations, given the fact that nomenclatures, sizes, and weights of guns changed during this period (Rubim 2008, pers. comm.). This gun list is only tentative, however, and its importance in this phase of the study lies with the total weight of guns, ammunition, and remaining arms and implements.

The significance of these designations is indicated below, in light of the documents available (do Valle 1962; Barker 1996). *Esperas*, or *terços de canhão*, would throw a stone with a diameter of around 12 cm, and had bores of 18 to 20 diameters (ca. 2.4 m). One *espera* could weigh around 22 *quintais* (1,293 kgf).

Camelos, or *meios canhões*, would throw a stone with a diameter of around 19.5 cm, and had bores of 12 diameters (ca. 2.34 m). One *camelo* could weigh as much as 28 *quintais* (1,645 kgf).

Pedreiros, or more appropriately *canhões pedreiros*, would throw stones with diameters between 27 and 49 cm, and had bores of around 6 or 7 diameters. The larger *pedreiros*, named *espalhafatos*, were not used aboard ships, and it is likely that this list refers to the smaller ones, or *selvagens*, which threw stones with diameters of 27 cm and had bores of around 7 diameters (ca. 1.89 m). One *pedreiro* could weigh as much as 13 *quintais* (764 kgf).

Falcões were small culverins, sometimes breech-loading guns. "Memorial das várias cousas importantes," the same codex from which this list was taken mentions *falcões* of 7.5 *quintais* each (440 kgf).

Berços were smaller breech-loading guns, throwing a stone with a diameter around 5 cm, and having a weight of around 2 *quintais* (118 kgf).

To these must be added the weight of the respective gun carriages, which were probably all two-wheeled carriages, as shown in Figure 4 (Salgado 2000:279).

The storage of small weapons and armor on India *naus* may have followed the rule set in 1576 for the ships which composed the fleets that protected the Portuguese coast and the Atlantic

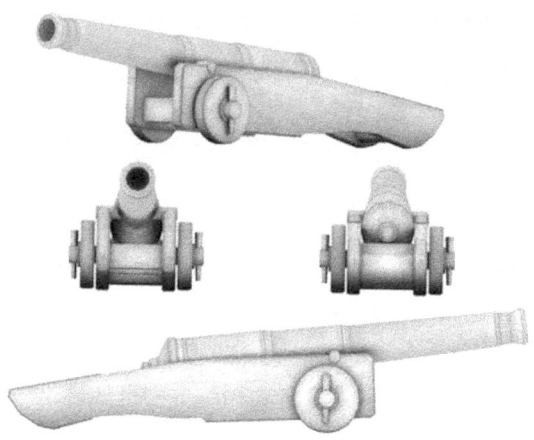

FIGURE 4. Gun carriages. (Image by Audrey Wells, 2008.)

Ocean between Portugal and the Azores and Madeira islands. Helmets, cuirasses, and small weapons were stored on deck in barrels, sealed and protected as much as possible from moisture. Pikes, spontoons, or partisans were stored under the stern castle in boxes built to the purpose, near the boxes built for the muskets. Cannon balls were stored in wooden boxes on the main deck (Neves 2004:194–195).

The total weight of guns, carriages, and all armament items was estimated at 30 t, slightly below previous estimations (Santos et al. 2007).

Spare Parts, Tools, and Materials for Repairs at Sea

There are several lists of spare parts and equipment necessary for the six-month voyages of these ships. Because spare parts, materials for repairs, and tools do not take much space in comparison with other items, the authors of the present article have opted to leave them for a more refined analysis, to be carried out later after testing a set of more basic research questions relative to the plausibility of the model. Documents indicate that care was taken to store lanterns, candles, shrouds, cables, and sails in compartments built especially for that purpose and locked away from the crew and passengers (Neves 2004:144). A document from the late 16th century states that sails, shrouds, and anchor cables should be stored in a compartment on the second deck, counting from below (Guinote et al. 1998:366).

The total weight of all spare parts, tools, and materials for repairs at sea has been estimated at 15 t.

Crew, Soldiers, and Passengers

In spite of the destruction of the Casa da Índia's archives in the earthquake of 1755, there is some information about the crews, soldiers, and passengers that sailed on these vessels around 1600 (Domingues 1989; Castro 2005a).

Although no comprehensive study of life aboard Portuguese Indiamen of the 15th through the 17th centuries—focusing on the age, social status, social mobility, and economic status of crews, passengers, and soldiers—has been published, there are enough documents and a small number of good studies pertaining to this subject to allow a reconstruction of the composition of the crew, passengers, and soldiers that would have sailed from India to Lisbon in 1606 (Castro 2005a:61–64).

Although there are probably differences between the kinds of people transported by galleons and *naus*, and between outbound and inbound voyages, it is fair to assume that these vessels could carry between 400 and 500 persons. The great galleon *São João*, a 900-tonner built in Lisbon in 1550, was said to have over 500 people aboard—200 Portuguese and 300 slaves—when it sank off the coast of South Africa in 1552 on the return trip from India to Portugal (de Brito 1735[1]:14,19; Costa 1997:439). The *São Bento*, of similar size, built in Lisbon one year after the *São João*, was carrying around 500 people—148 Portuguese and a little over 344 slaves—at the time of its loss in 1554, also off the coast of South Africa on the return trip to Portugal (de Brito 1735[1]:61,71; Costa 1997:439). In 1559 the naus *Águia* and *Garça*, both on their return trip to Portugal, were carrying together a total of 1,137 people, among them gentlemen, soldiers, sailors, slaves, women, and children (de Brito 1735[1]:240). The *nau Santiago*, lost on its way to India at Bassas da India Atoll in 1585, was carrying 450 people (de Brito 1735[2]:79).

Contente Domingues cites the galleon *S. Bartolomeu*, which left for India with a crew of 150, plus 250 soldiers in 1589 (Domingues 1998:64). Figueiredo Falcão mentioned a crew of 124 people in 1607, and described their wages and benefits (Falcão 1859:198), as did an experienced admiral,

João Pereira Corte Real, in 1619, in a letter to King Philip III of Spain, the II of Portugal. The jobs and numbers of people performing each role also varied, as did the designations of their functions, but only slightly, as shown in Table 3 below.

To the crew must be added the passengers, generally businessmen and nobles with their slaves and servants, as well as a small group of priests, and frequently a number of soldiers that could vary between 50 and 250 persons. Their figures, as shown in Figure 5, were modeled after the sketches of Luca Cambiaso (1527–1585) and their stature established between 1.50 and 1.65 m.

As mentioned above, this crowd was lodged on the upper and weather decks and in the castles, sharing the weather deck with a number of animals brought by the wealthier for consumption during the trip, usually including cows, sheep, and pigs, together with the ubiquitous chickens, ducks, and rabbits.

The crew of the present model was estimated at 150 people (including 50 apprentices, or deck boys), to which were added 200 slaves, 50 gunners and soldiers, and 50 passengers, weighing a total of 30 t (about 66 kgf per person).

Personal Items

Almost everybody brought cargo to and from India. Even food was sold upon arrival in India, although after having been stored six months or more in the hold of a ship it is hard to imagine its condition.

It is difficult to say what the size of a sailor's sea chest was, although judging by other examples it seems fair to imagine a range of sizes around 1.10–1.32 × 0.44 to 0.55 × 0.66 cm (Guinote et al. 1998:363; Neves 2004:113). Together with some personal possessions and clothes, Portuguese sailors were known to bring some food to complement the diet supplied by the captain. On their way back to Portugal it is likely that everybody tried to bring as many things to sell in Lisbon as possible, from small amounts of spices to cotton cloth, silks, and drugs (Figure 6). After filling their chests with whatever they considered worth bringing, the normal procedure would be to store the remaining merchandise in bundles, boxes, or barrels, which were numbered and inventoried, and pay a tariff upon safe arrival at port (Arquivo Histórico Ultramarino 1616).

TABLE 3
COMPOSITION OF THE CREWS ON THE INDIA ROUTE[a]

Galleon *S. Bartolomeu*, 1589	India *Nau*, 1607	India *Nau*, 1619	English Equivalent
1 Capitão	1 Capitão[b]	1 Capitão	Captain
—	—	6 Criados[d]	Servants
1 Escrivão	1 Escrivão[b]	1 Escrivão	Clerk
1 Capelão	1 Capelão[b]	1 Capelão	Chaplain
1 Mestre	1 Mestre	1 Mestre	Master
1 Piloto	1 Piloto	1 Piloto	Pilot
1 Contramestre	1 Contramestre	1 Contramestre	Boatswain
1 Guardião	1 Guardião	1 Guardião	Boatswain's mate
1 Sota-Piloto	1 Sota-Piloto	1 Sota-Piloto	Second Pilot
—	2 Estrinqueiros	2 Estrinqueiros	Sailors[c]
2 Carpinteiros	2 Carpinteiros	2 Carpinteiros	Carpenters
2 Calafates	2 Calafates	2 Calafates	Caulkers
1 Tanoeiro	1 Tanoeiro	1 Tanoeiro	Cooper
1 Despenseiro	1 Despenseiro	2 Despenseiros	Purser
1 Meirinho	1 Meirinho	1 Meirinho	Bailiff
1 Barbeiro	—	1 Barbeiro	Barber
50 Marinheiros	45 Marinheiros	40 Marinheiros	Seamen
50 Grumetes	48 Grumetes	60 Grumetes	Ship's boys
4 Pagens	4 Pagens	4 Pagens	Pages
1 Condestável	1 Condestável	1 Condestável	Constable
29 Bombardeiros	11 Bombardeiros	20 Bombardeiros	Gunners
250 Soldados	—	—	Soldiers
Total: 400 people	126 people	150 people	

[a]Barcellos (1898–1899:19); Castro (2005a:63).

[b]Not mentioned by Figueiredo Falcão, but obviously always part of the crew.

[c]Sailors in charge of the windlass that operated the mainsail and the foresail in the *naus*. There were no *estrinqueiros* aboard the galleons, since the sails were operated from the capstans.

[d]Captain's servants (*criados do capitão*).

The weight of a personal sea chest has been estimated at around 50 kgf, for a total of about 22.5 t for the entire ship.

Cargo

The main cargo carried by these ships, the very reason for their existence, was peppercorns, which seem to have been stored in bulk in the vessel's hold, in boxes (*paióis*) built and caulked for that purpose (Figure 7). These boxes were built over the ballast, possibly over an orlop deck, and were probably around 2.5 m or 10 *palmos de goa* high. After being filled from the deck above through a small aperture opened for that purpose, the small square holes were closed and caulked (Barcelos 1898–1899:50; van Linschoten 1997:310–311). The amount of pepper carried varied with the size of each

ship, as well as with other factors, such as the number of passengers and slaves brought back to Portugal. We know that in 1601 three galleons—*São Francisco*, *Conceição*, and a third vessel whose name is not referenced—arrived at Lisbon with 9,914 *quintais* of pepper, the equivalent to 580 t more or less (1 *quintal* = 58.754 kgf). In 1602 two ships arrived at Lisbon bringing 7,598 *quintais* of pepper (around 446 t). In 1603 four vessels arrived with 21,349 *quintais* of peppercorns, the equivalent to 1,250 t (Castro 2005a:69–70). The average cargo during this period seems to be around 250 t of peppercorns per ship, corresponding to a volume around 500 m³, considering a specific gravity for the more-or-less dry peppercorns of around 0.5.

It was decided to load only around 172 t of peppercorns in the holds of the reconstructed Pepper Wreck to save space for other cargo in

FIGURE 5. Figures of the crew, soldiers, and passengers. (Image by Audrey Wells, 2008.)

FIGURE 6. Barrels (*tonéis, pipas,* and *quartos*), boxes, bales, baskets, and pots. The main storage containers were individually designed and sized according to the data available, mainly written sources. (Image by Audrey Wells, 2008.)

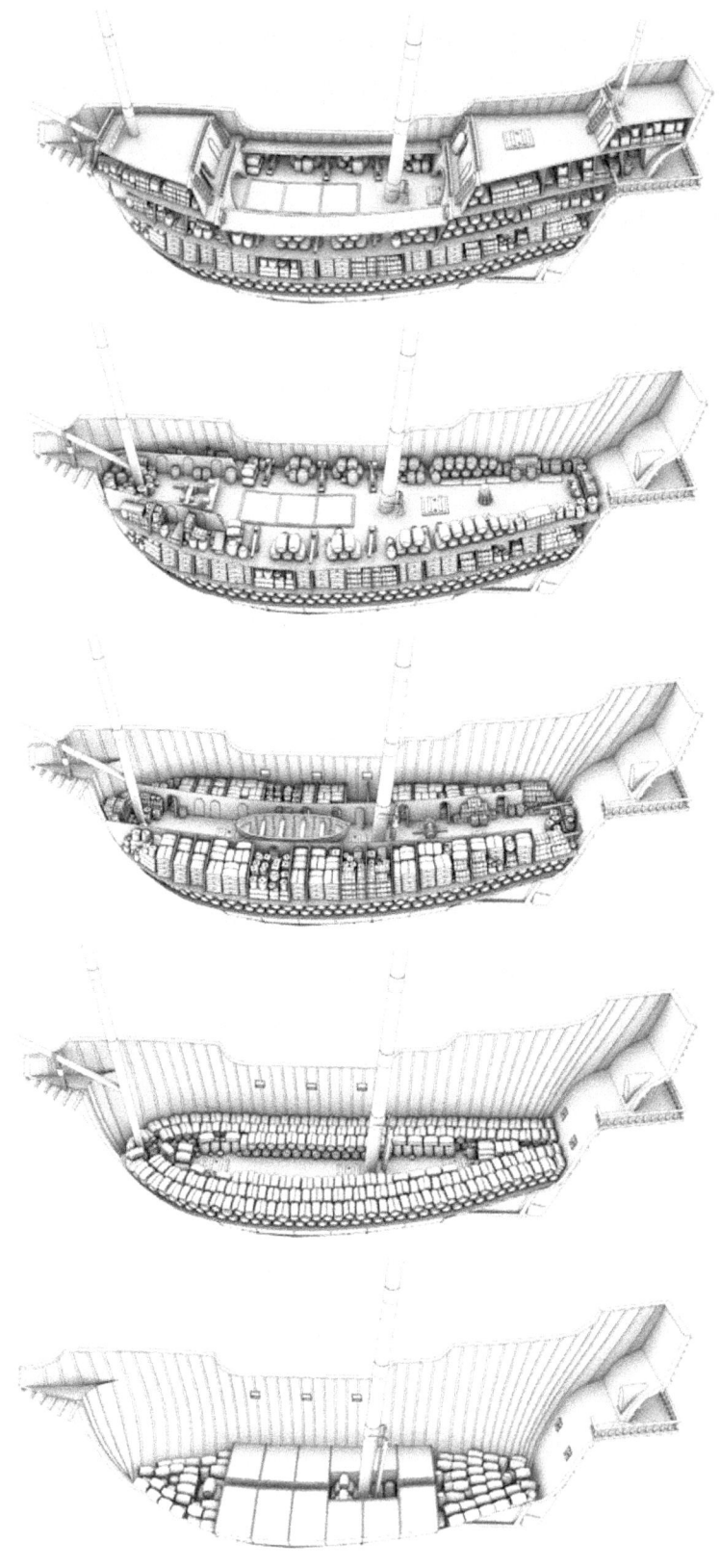

FIGURE 7. Pepper holds (*paióis da pimenta*) with the capacity to carry 172 t of peppercorns. (Image by Audrey Wells, 2008.)

the lower hold. As built in the model, the peppercorn holds (*paióis da pimenta*) have a capacity of 345 m³.

The cargo of these ships was large and diversified, and divided into four major categories for custom purposes: *drogas*, *fazendas*, *miudezas*, and *pedraria* (Castro 2005a:13–16). *Drogas* (drugs) included all the spices—pepper, cinnamon, ginger, cloves, nutmeg, and mace—along with indigo, lacquers, resins, borax, camphor, chinawood, sandalwood, incense, ebony, and ivory. *Fazendas* (cloth) included bales of cotton cloth, silk, and thread, but it also included other items, such as slaves. *Miudezas* (odds and ends) comprised miscellaneous products from chests and writing desks to musk oil, and included inlaid boxes, statuettes, fans, porcelain, lapis lazuli, azurite, amber, gold, and jewelry. Finally *pedraria* (gems) referred to all semiprecious and precious stones, such as diamonds, pearls, and rubies.

All these items were stored in boxes and pots, or bags and bales. Again, there is not much information about their sizes, colors, and materials of manufacture. The best iconographical evidence for *miudezas* is perhaps the small collection of Japanese screens dating to the late 16th and early 17th century representing the arrival of Portuguese ships at Nagasaki (Pinto 1993). Following the shipwreck of the *nau Nossa Senhora da Luz* in 1615 at Faial Island, Azores, a detailed list of the cargo salvaged has been elaborated, mentioning each item and the way in which it was found, together with the way in which it was shipped to Lisbon (Arquivo Histórico Ultramarino 1616; Paulo Monteiro 2002, pers. comm.; José Bettencourt 2007, pers. comm.). There were basically three types of container: *caixões*, or boxes measuring 6 × 2.5 × 3 *palmos de vara* (1 *palmo de vara*=22 cm), the equivalent to 1.10–1.32 × 0.44–0.55 × 0.66 cm (Guinote et al. 1998:363; Neves 2004:113), *fardos*, or bundles, and *pipas*, which were, as mentioned previously, small barrels with half the capacity of a *tonel*, a barrel 1.54 m high and 1.02 m in diameter.

There is not yet a maximum number computed for boxes loaded aboard the reconstructed Pepper Wreck, but law determined that sailors, gunners, and officers could each bring one box free of custom charges, and soldiers and deck boys half a box each (Neves 2004:156,162). Given the profitability of the Asian trade it is fair to assume that officers brought more than one box each. Nevertheless, considering the lists from Table 2, the minimum number of boxes that would come aboard with the crew with European merchandise to be sold in India, and then later with Asian goods to be sold in Portugal is 253 boxes (106 single-owner boxes plus 147 shared boxes) for the galleon *S. Bartolomeu* of 1589, 100 boxes (74 single-owner plus 26 shared) for the 1607 *nau*, and 115 boxes (80 single-owner plus 35 shared) for the 1619 *nau*.

It has been determined that a total of 225 boxes for the Pepper Wreck model, 200 single-owner, and 25 shared between two deck boys each, would weigh a total of around 15 t. The remaining cargo of cotton bales, silk, precious woods, a large number of jars with drugs and spices, exotic furniture, porcelains, and stonewares, has been estimated at 120 t, occupying around 240 m³.

Space Use and Appropriation

As mentioned above, the process of loading the ship was an iterative one, and the results presented here are only tentative (Figure 8). An off-the-shelf 3-D computer graphics and 3-D modeling software package (Autodesk Maia) was used to attempt to define all spaces and fit all the cargo, fittings, and people inside. Volumes and weights are indicated in Table 4 below.

The total weight obtained was about 1,335 t, roughly 12% above the maximum displacement calculated from the first set of line drawings produced in 2001 (Castro 2005a). The highest possible waterline would allow a displacement of 1,600 t, well above the value obtained in the first trial. In this phase of the project only a possible cargo arrangement was calculated to avoid losing time with details. Pending a series of engineering tests, the model will be refined and tested in future archaeological investigations.

A few small discrepancies between this first stability model and the refined model are expected to occur, once everything and everybody are fitted inside the ship. A few documents survive that describe the chambers and spaces assigned to every officer, and point out the problems raised by excess cargo. The image that emerges from these documents is far from clear, but when read in view of the reconstruction—a

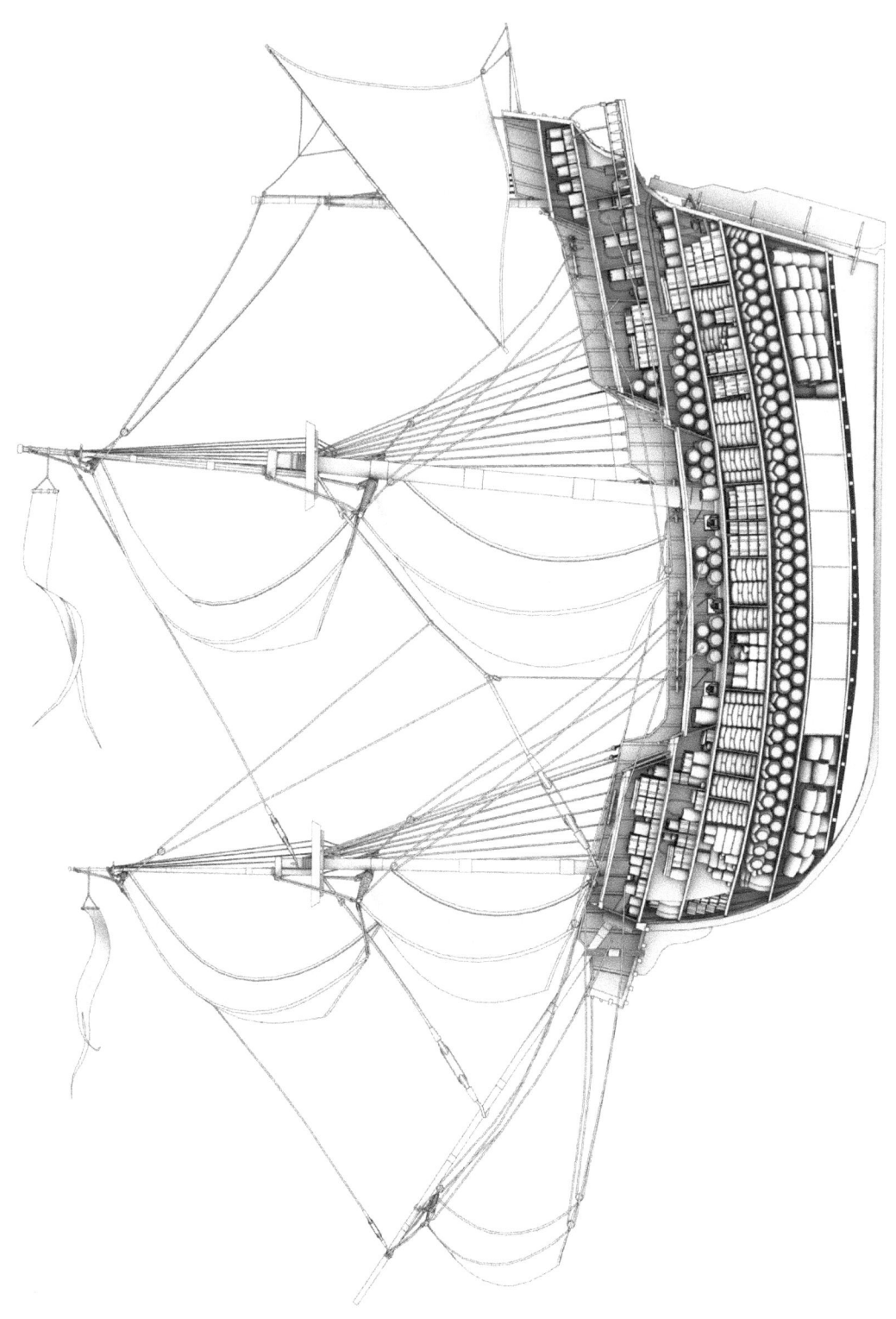

FIGURE 8. The Pepper Wreck model fully loaded. (Image by Audrey Wells, 2008.)

TABLE 4
ESTIMATED WEIGHTS AND VOLUMES

Item	Weight (kgf)	Volume (m³)	Containers
Hull	398,000	—	—
Ballast	175,000	113	In the hold, below the orlop deck
Masts and spars	28,000	—	—
Sails	3,500	—	—
Rigging	5,000	—	—
Water and provisions	292,000		1,289 *sacas*, 20 *tonéis*, 496 *pipas*, 16 *quartos*, 90 baskets, 9 large jars, and 48 small jars
Firewood	3,000	12	In a compartment next to the ovens
Anchors and fittings	16,000	—	—
Armament	30,000	—	—
Spares and tools	15,000	—	—
Crew, soldiers, and passengers (450 people)	30,000	—	—
Personal belongings	22,500	—	450 boxes
Cargo—peppercorns	172,000	345	Holds specially built
Cargo—other	135,000	—	Boxes, bales, and barrels
Two small boats called *batel* and *esquife*	10,000	—	—
Total	*1,335,000*		

three-decker—they shed some light into many doubts and information gaps. The stern castle, perhaps presenting only two pavements in the late 16th century, was occupied by the captain and passengers, their food, and their servants and slaves. The space of the quarterdeck between chambers was reserved for the gunners when the weather was cold and wet. Sailors and apprentices were supposed to sleep in the forecastle and on the space before it, over the beak head. Officers had their chambers below deck, where they slept and kept their food, belongings, and cargo for personal trade.

The remaining space was occupied with ballast, provisions, and cargo. When the fully loaded model is examined, the first impression is one of low efficiency: the total volume of peppercorns, 345 m³, is around 17% of the total space below the weather deck (Table 5). Even if 250 t of peppercorns had been loaded instead of the 172 t of this model, that percentage would have been around 25% of the total space and 19% of the total weight. The weight of the remaining cargo were estimated at this time to be around 135 t, accounting for 10% of the total. Only further studies will allow the detailing of the spaces available, namely after fitting in the entire crew and passengers.

TABLE 5
INTERIOR SPACES

Zone	Area (m²)	Volume (m³)
Weather deck	391	—
Upper deck	401	716
Lower deck	351	641
Hold	250[a]	692

[a]Orlop deck area.

In the present configuration the option has been taken to make this ship a three-decker after Fernando Oliveira's 1580s model, rather than a four-decker after the 1616 model of Manoel Fernandez. The reasons are explained elsewhere and fall outside the scope of this paper (Castro 2005a). The lower portion of the hull, beneath an orlop deck, was filled with 175 t of ballast up to a height of 1.46 m. Built above the orlop deck, which the model has partially planked, were the peppercorn holds (*paiós da pimenta*) occupying a central portion of the hull and leaving space for water and heavy spare parts. The total area of the orlop deck is 250 m² and the volume of the hold is 692 m³. In this version space was not included in the hold for the anchors and anchor cables because there was no evidence for it. The spaces left empty in the hold, however, are sufficient to store the spare anchors, should evidence be found that anchors and cables were stored in the hold. In this model 13 heavy barrels (tonéis) with water have been placed in the free hold spaces, together with other minor food containers, such as baskets and pots, all for personal use. A corridor was left in the middle of the peppercorn holds as suggested in the 1607 drawing by Figueiredo Falcão, the only drawing in existence showing a division of the spaces (Falcão 1859:200a).

The lower deck, above the hold, measuring 351 m² and delimiting a volume of 641 m³, was fully loaded with water and wine. The amount of water and wine necessary to supply the needs of the crew and passengers during the six-month trip—115 pipas of wine and 313 of water—determined this solution. Since it was decided to use pipas (570 L) instead of tonéis (1,140 L), a certain amount of free space was obtained above them, and it was filled with sacks of hardtack. At this stage it was decided not to nest the barrels atop one another, with the booge (widest section) of the upper cask resting in the hollow where the heads of the four lower barrels meet. This arrangement implies the use of a number of smaller barrels used to occupy the space in the back of the second row, over the heads of the lower barrels, introducing a layer of unnecessary complexity to the cargo distribution. It is likely that this deck was divided into locked compartments to avoid unauthorized consumption of foodstuffs, and that the barrels were stacked in a more stable configuration, but at this stage of the project the positions of these divisions and the exact sizes and positions of the barrels are unknown.

The middle deck, above the lower deck and below the weather deck, measured 401 m² and defined a space of 716 m³. It housed the windlass and the ship's boats, generally two, the smaller nested inside the larger and full of spars, cables, sails, and some if not all spare anchor cables. Only the larger ship's boat has been placed. The free area was divided into small compartments with transverse walls in which most of the hardtack was held. Among these compartments two probably housed the ovens—of which there were

perhaps two, one to starboard and one to port side—and one small compartment of around 12 m³ used to store 3 t of firewood.

The upper decks were occupied mainly with personal possessions, and at this stage no arrangement has been proposed. The area of the upper deck, including the spaces beneath the fore (70 m²) and after castles (112 m²), is 391 m² in the model. The remaining barrels, bales, jars, baskets, and boxes have been distributed throughout this space. All the cargo, passengers, and victuals were placed inside the ship's model, and not much was made of the extra 12% weight at departure, because it is known that the first leg of every trip was completed with an overcrowded ship.

Fitting in the 450 people that may have travelled in such a ship from Lisbon to the Indian subcontinent during a six-month voyage was not easy. The entire free space encompasses six areas: the stern castle (tolda) with 110 m², the weather deck with 211 m², the forecastle area (70 m²), the pavement covering the stern castle (around 100 m² and designated alcáçova), the pavement covering the forecastle area (70 m²), and the second pavement of the stern castle, covering the alcáçova (about 40 m² and designated chapitéu). The total area available adds up to around 600 m², which divided by 450 persons leaves 1.3 m² of living space per capita at departure.

Conclusions

Perhaps one of the most interesting outcomes of this project was the use of virtual reality to help detail, inventory, and position the intricate web of spaces that composed such a ship, and that cannot be defined in the abstract from the documentary evidence alone. The virtual model developed by Audrey Wells at the Texas A&M University Visualization Sciences Department proved to be an invaluable tool in helping to understand the complex spaces of the volume of an India nau's hull (Figure 9). Moreover, when "visited" with the immersion equipment known as the "Cave," a vivid idea of the space available in which to move around during the long voyage was provided (Parke 2005).

In this phase of the project the objective was to develop one possible configuration of the cargo arrangement, and this has been fully achieved. The basic question was whether it was possible to store all the goods and people mentioned

FIGURE 9. Virtual reality as a way to help understand complex spaces. Audrey Wells in Dr. Frederic Parke's "Cave." (Image by Audrey Wells, 2008.)

in the documents in such a small space, and provide an environment in the remaining space in which 450 people could live for six months. Further analysis will help to refine this study and produce a more reliable virtual hypothesis of a late-16th-century India *nau*.

Acknowledgments

We are indebted to Richard Barker, who showed us the second list of Ataíde's manuscript, Augusto Salgado, who shared with us his impressive collection of pictures of the Escorial and Viso del Marques frescoes, Javier Lopez Martin, Nuno Rubim, and again Richard Barker for their help with the interpretation of the gun list, Paulo Monteiro for showing us the "Nossa Senhora da Luz" manuscript, and to José Bettencourt for informing us of the existence of a published transcription.

References

ARQUIVO HISTÓRICO ULTRAMARINO
 1616 Inventários de Manuel Pacheco de Lima e João Correia de Mesquita da pedraria e fazendas salvadas do naufrágio Nossa Senhora da Luz (Inventories by Manuel Pacheco de Lima and João Correia de Mesquita of the Precious Stones and Merchandise Salvaged from the Nossa Senhora da Luz Shipwreck). Manuscript, Caixa 1, Doc. 12, Arquivo Histórico Ultramarino, Azores, Portugal.

BARCELOS, CHRISTIANO SENNA
 1898–1899 Construcções de Naus em Lisboa e Goa para a Carreira da India no Começo do Século XVII (Construction of Naus in Lisbon and Goa for the India Route in the Beginning of the 17th Century). *Boletim da Sociedade de Geographia de Lisboa* 17(1):5–72.

BARKER, RICHARD
 1994 Barrels at Sea: Water, Stowage, and Guns on the Portuguese Ocean. In *Procedings of the First Symposium on Maritime History: As Navegações Portuguesas no Atlântico e o Descobrimento da América* (Portuguese Navigations in the Atlantic and the Discovery of America), pp. 365–379, 431–432. Academia de Marinha, Lisbon, Portugal.
 1996 A Gun-list from Portuguese India, 1525. *Journal of the Ordnance Society* 8:52–71.

BIBLIOTECA NACIONAL
 [1590a] Memorial das várias cousas importantes (Memory of Several Important Things). Manuscript, Codex 637, Secção de Reservados, Biblioteca Nacional, Lisbon, Portugal.
 [1590b] *O livro náutico* (Nautical Book). Manuscript, Codex 2257, Secção de Reservados of the Biblioteca Nacional, Lisbon, Portugal.

BLAKE, WARREN, AND GREEN, JEREMY
1986 A Mid-XVI Century Portuguese Wreck in the Seychelles. *International Journal of Nautical Archaeology* 15(1):1–23.

CASTRO, FILIPE
2003 The Pepper Wreck. *International Journal of Nautical Archaeology* 32(1):6–23.
2005a *The Pepper Wreck.* Texas A&M University Press, College Station.
2005b Rigging the Pepper Wreck. Part 1—Masts and Yards. *International Journal of Nautical Archaeology* 34(1):110–122.
2008 Rigging the Pepper Wreck. Part 2—Sails. *International Journal of Nautical Archaeology* 38(1):105–115.

CASTRO, FILIPE, AND NUNO FONSECA
2006 Sailing the Pepper Wreck: A Proposed Methodology for Understanding an Early 17th-Century Portuguese Indiamen. *International Journal of Nautical Archaeology* 35(1):97–103.
2007–2008 A bordo de uma nau da India: "The Pepper Wreck" (Aboard an India Nau: "The Pepper Wreck"). *Actas de la 13.o Reunión Internacional de Historia de la Nautica y de la Hidrografía* (Proceedings of the 13th International Reunion of the Commission for the History of Nautical Science and Hydrography). *Cuadernos de Estudios Borjanos* 50–51:199–235.

CONRAD, JOSEPH
1914 *The Nigger of the* Narcissus. Doubleday and Company, Garden City, NY.

COSTA, LEONOR FREIRE
1997 *Naus e Galeões na Ribeira de Lisboa.* Patrimónia, Cascais, Portugal.

DE AGUILAR, MARCOS SERVEIRA
[1640] Advertências de navegantes (Notices to Mariners). Manuscript, Codex 13390, Secção de Reservados, Biblioteca Nacional, Lisbon, Portugal.

DE ATAÍDE, ANTÓNIO
1588–1633 *Codices of D. António de Ataíde,* 3 vols. Microfilm, Biblioteca Central de Marinha, Lisbon, Portugal.

DE AZEVEDO, MARIA DE FÁTIMA FERROS
1964 Uma viagem da India para o reino em 1605–1607 (A Voyage to the Kingdom, 1605–1607). Doctoral dissertation, Department of History, University of Lisbon, Lisbon, Portugal.

DE BRITO, BERNARDO GOMES
1735 *História Trágico-Marítima* (Tragic History of the Sea), 2 vols. Officina da Congregação do Oratório, Lisbon, Portugal.

DE MATOS, ARTUR TEODORO
1998 Quem vai ao mar em terra se avia. Preparativos e recomendações aos passageiros da Carreira da Índia no século XVII (He Who Goes to the Sea Prepares Himself on Land. Preparations and Recommendations to the India Route Passengers in the 17th century). In *A Carreira da Índia e as Rotas dos Estreitos, Actas do VIII Seminário Internacional de História Indo-Portuguesa* (The India Route and the Routes of the Straits, Proceedings of the 8th International Seminar on Indo-Portuguese History), Artur Teodoro de Matos and Luis Filipe Thomaz, editors, pp. 377–394. Angra do Heroísmo, Azores, Portugal.

DE SOUSA, GONÇALLO
1620 Coriosidades de Gonçallo de Sousa (Curiosities of Gonçallo de Sousa). Manuscript, No. 3074, Biblioteca Geral, Universidade de Coimbra, Coimbra, Portugal.

DOMINGUES, FRANCISCO CONTENTE
1989 Viver a bordo (Living Aboard). *Oceanos* 2:37–60.
1998 *A Carreira da Índia* (The India Route). CTT Correios de Portugal, Lisbon, Portugal.
2004 *Os navios do mar oceano* (The Ships of the Ocean Sea). Centro de História dos Descobrimentos, Lisbon, Portugal.

DO VALLE, HENRIQUE PEREIRA
1962 Nomenclatura dos Bocas de Fogo Portuguesas do Século XVI (Portuguese Gun Nomenclature of the 16th Century). *Revista de Artilharia,* 439–440:381–390.

ESCALANTE DE MENDOZA, JUAN
1985 *Itinerario de navegacion de los mares y tierras occidentales* (Itinerary of Navigation on the Western Seas and Lands). Museo Naval, Madrid, Spain.

FALCÃO, LUIZ DE FIGUEIREDO
1859 *Livro em que se contem toda a fazenda e real patrimonio dos reinos de Portugal, India, e ilhas adjacentes e outras particularidades, ordenado por Luiz de Figueiredo Falcao, secretario de el rei Filippe II ... 1607* (The Book of All the Royal Wealth and Patrimony of the Kingdoms of Portugal, India, and Adjacent Islands, and Other Particularities, Ordered by Luiz de Figueiredo Falcão, Secretary of King Philip II ... 1607). Imprensa Nacional, Lisbon, Portugal.

GARCIA DE PALACIO, DIEGO
1880 *Instrucion Nautica para el buen uso de las Naos, su traça, y gobierno conforme à la altura de Mexico, 1587* (Nautical Instruction for the Right Use of Naos, their Design, and Handling at the Height of Mexico, 1587). In *Disquisiciones Nauticas* (Nautical Disquisitions), Vol. 5, Cesário Fernandez Duro, editor, pp. 7–36. Reprinted 1996 by Instituto de Historia y Cultura Naval, Madrid, Spain.

GUERREIRO, INÁCIO
1998 A Vida a Bordo na Carreira da Índia. A Torna-Viagem (Life Aboard in the India Route. The Return Voyage). In *A Carreira da Índia e as Rotas dos Estreitos, Actas do VIII Seminário Internacional de História Indo-Portuguesa* (The India Route and the Routes of the Straits, Proceedings of the 8th International Seminar on Indo-Portuguese History), Artur Teodoro de Matos and Luis Filipe Thomaz, editors, pp. 415–432. Angra do Heroísmo, Azores, Portugal.

GUINOTE, PAULO, EDUARDO FRUTUOSO, AND AFONSO LOPES
1998 *Naufragios e Outras Perdas da Carreira da India* (Shipwrecks and Other Losses of the India Route). Grupo de Trabalho do Ministério da Educação para as Comemorações dos Descobrimentos, Lisbon, Portugal.

GUNN-GRAHAM, TORQUIL IAIN
1998 The Marine Engravings of Peter Bruegel the Elder. *American Neptune* 58(4):329–341.

HAZLETT, ALEXANDER
2007 *The Nao of the* Livro Nautico: *Reconstructing a Sixteenth-Century Indiaman from Texts*. Doctoral dissertation, Department of Anthropology, Texas A&M University. University Microfilms International, Ann Arbor, MI.

MIRABAL, ALEJANDRO
2007 *Interim Report on Underwater Archaeological Excavations off the Island of Mozambique and Mogincual, from March to November 2006*. Arquenotas Worldwide, Funchal, Portugal <http://www.arq-publications.com/html/mozambique.htm>. Accessed March 2008.

NEVES, BRUNO
2004 A legislação da Carreira da Índia, caracterização e análise da sua evolução 1500–1580 (The Legislation of the India Route, Characterization and Analysis of Its Evolution 1500–1580). Masters thesis, Department of History, University of Lisbon, Lisbon, Portugal.

PARKE, FREDERIC I.
2005 Lower Cost Spatially Immersive Visualization for Human Environments. *Landscape and Urban Planning* 73(2–3):234–243.

PINTO, MARIA HELENA MENDES
1993 *Biombos Namban* (Namban Screens). Museu Nacional de Arte Antiga, Lisbon, Portugal.

SALGADO, AUGUSTO
2000 Portuguese Galleons' Armament at the End of the Sixteenth Century. In *Actas IX Reunião Internacional de História da Náutica e da Hidrografia* (Proceedings of the 9th International Reunion of the Commission for the History of Nautical Science and Hydrography), Inácio Guerreiro and Corrente Domingues, editors, pp. 277–292. Patrimónia, Cascais, Portugal.

SANTOS, TIAGO, NUNO FONSECA, AND FILIPE CASTRO
2007 Naval Architecture Applied to the Reconstruction of an Early XVII Century Portuguese Nau. *Marine Technology* 44(4):254–267.

TINNISWOOD, J. T.
1945 Anchors and Accessories 1340–1640. *The Mariner's Mirror* 31(2):84–105.

VAN LINSCHOTEN, JAN HUYGEN
1997 *Itinerário, Viagem ou Navegação de Jan Huygen van Linschoten para as Índias Orientais Portuguesas* (The Voyage of Jan Huyghen van Linschoten to the East Indies). Comissão para as Comemorações dos Descobrimentos, Lisbon, Portugal.

WELLS, AUDREY
2008 Virtual Reconstruction of a Seventeenth-Century Portuguese Nau. Master's thesis, Department of Visualization Sciences, Texas A&M University, College Station.

FILIPE CASTRO
NAUTICAL ARCHAEOLOGY PROGRAM
DEPARTMENT OF ANTHROPOLOGY
TEXAS A&M UNIVERSITY
COLLEGE STATION, TX 77843-4352

NUNO FONSECA
UNIT OF MARINE TECHNOLOGY AND ENGINEERING
TECHNICAL UNIVERSITY OF LISBON
INSTITUTO SUPERIOR TÉCNICO
AV. ROVISCO PAIS
1049-001 LISBON, PORTUGAL

AUDREY WELLS
VISUALIZATION LABORATORY
TEXAS A&M UNIVERSITY
C418 LANGFORD CENTER 3137 TAMU
COLLEGE STATION, TX 77843-3137

2009. Shipwreck Cargoes: Approaches to Material Culture in Australian Maritime Archaeology. *Historical Archaeology* 43(3):95 –100.

Mark Staniforth

Shipwreck Cargoes: Approaches to Material Culture in Australian Maritime Archaeology

ABSTRACT

What has been learned from the detailed study of cargo material found on merchant shipwreck sites in Australia? Some extensive collections of shipwreck cargo material have resulted from archaeological excavations by maritime archaeologists over the past 30 years or so. Other collections have been created by SCUBA divers, primarily before the introduction of the Commonwealth (Federal) Historic Shipwrecks Act in 1976. Many of these have now been documented as a result of the 1993 amnesty. The relationship between cargo artifacts from archaeologically excavated shipwrecks and similar artifacts found on terrestrial historical archaeological sites is explored through a consideration of the meanings attached to these objects, suggesting ways that artifact studies focused on shipwreck cargo material can contribute to understandings of colonial societies, the nature of capitalism, and the rise of consumerism. It is argued that successful colonial settlement was only possible where there was a regular supply of suitable consumer goods for the newly arrived colonists.

Introduction

Merchant shipwreck sites in Australia are examined here, describing what has been learned from the detailed study of archaeologically excavated cargo material and some of the important artifact studies that have been conducted in Australian maritime archaeology over the last three decades. The relationship between artifacts from merchant shipwrecks and similar artifacts found on terrestrial historical archaeological sites are briefly examined by considering some of the meanings of these objects while also acknowledging that "the meanings of objects may change as they move into new contexts" (Hodder 1989:73). Some ways that artifact studies can contribute to understandings of colonial societies, the nature of capitalism, and the rise of consumerism are suggested. Finally, it is

argued that colonialism was only possible where there was a regular supply of appropriate consumer goods for the newly arrived colonists.

Susan Lawrence (1998:8) has suggested that material culture studies can be divided into three broad types. The first type is empirical studies involving the construction of artifact catalogs and databases, using techniques like seriation to establish accurate chronologies of artifact types. Shipwrecks, of course, often provide securely dated contexts for artifacts, while the same artifacts from terrestrial sites can sometimes be difficult to date precisely. Furthermore, the inventory of imported colonial goods as recovered from terrestrial sites can be skewed for a variety of behavioral and taphonomic reasons, so the study of wrecked cargoes provides a unique opportunity to examine artifact assemblages. Unfortunately, only a few merchant shipwreck artifact catalogs have ever been published in Australia, despite their potential use for detailed comparative studies. One early example was Sarah Kenderdine's (1991) South Australian study, *Artifacts from Shipwrecks in the South East 1851–1951*, and another example is discussed later in this paper (Stanbury 2003). Such catalogs are essential tools for developing interpretations of large-scale artifact assemblages from shipwreck sites. In recent years, computerized artifact catalogs that use relational database software programs such as Microsoft Access have become increasingly accessible. For some years, there have been proposals regarding the establishment of a national artifact database, but to date this has yet to become a reality.

Lawrence's second type of material culture studies is ethnographic studies of material life that are aimed at revealing aspects of everyday life. She suggests that these have been more common in American historical archaeology than in Australian, despite considerable potential for such studies to illuminate the ways in which convicts, immigrants, or the poor lived. Indeed, it has been asserted that "Ultimately maritime archaeology seeks to provide information about the way in which people lived in past times whether this is through technological, economic, social or cultural information" (Staniforth

1991:21). Despite this goal, virtually no serious studies have been conducted in Australian maritime archaeology of, for example, the everyday lives of working seamen through their material culture. Possibly the site with the best potential for such a study was, and still remains, the HMS *Pandora*.

The third category deals with the cognitive aspects of material culture that involve the consideration of the social and cultural meanings of objects. Lawrence has made use of Bourdieu's concept of *habitus*, which she defined as "the understanding of the behaviors and practices appropriate to one's place in society" (Lawrence 1998:8). Artifacts can have multiple meanings as well as meanings that change over time. Meanings are attached by people to the shape, texture, color, decoration, use, and discard of the object. These meanings arise from historical associations and may have emotional connections. Furthermore, meanings are not fixed and will vary according to chronological and geographical location as different cultures and individuals attach different meanings to a particular object at different times over the life history of an artifact (Kopytoff 1986).

One of the problems sometimes faced by maritime archaeologists is being able to tell the cargo items that were destined for sale upon arrival from personal belongings that were carried by individuals. Sometimes the numbers of identical objects suggest cargo, while location and context can sometimes indicate the personal nature of objects. Nevertheless, personal belongings can be difficult to positively identify, as material such as clothing (buckles, buttons and fabric) and shoes found on wreck sites in Australian waters (including both *Sydney Cove* and *Eglinton*) may be cargo, or personal objects, or even a mixture of the two (Stanbury, 2003:167–177).

Cargo Artifacts

Often maritime archaeologists have focused on the transport stage in the life history of artifacts by examining the cargo that is being transported from one port to another. This focus can provide valuable archaeological evidence about the nature and extent of trade, specifically about precisely which objects were being carried as well as exactly when and to where they were being transported. As Lorna Weatherill (1996:197) has argued, the increasingly widespread availability of consumer goods in the 18th century was central to the rise of the consumer society, and she has suggested that for Britain, at least, "Trade with the Far East brought attractive consumer goods on to the market at modest cost."

It is often claimed that trade has been well documented during recent centuries, that written records of shipping movements and detailed cargo lists are both available and comprehensive. In contrast, it has been argued that, while the available documentary sources are sometimes extensive, they are frequently not comprehensive, and they often lack the detail necessary to draw supportable conclusions about past societies (Staniforth 2003:17). Furthermore, it has been argued that taking a cultural perspective to examine economic activity can often illuminate different aspects of the past and that it is necessary to interpret the material culture (in the form of the cargo) in terms of the societies for which it was bound (Staniforth 2003:21–26).

A number of wreck-based artifact studies have been completed in the Australian state of Victoria over the past two decades, with particular attention paid to the *William Salthouse* (1841) and the *Loch Ard* (1878) (Staniforth 1987; English 1990; Morgan 1990; Stuart 1991; Peters 1996; Fielding 2003). The earliest of these studies was an examination of the cask (barrel) component of the cargo of the trading vessel *William Salthouse*, which sank at the end of a voyage from Montreal in Canada to Melbourne in 1841 (Staniforth 1987). This work illustrated some of the shortcomings of written evidence, as the archaeological assemblage contained a number of casks that were not listed in the "official" cargo manifest. It also demonstrated that according to the brands and stencil markings on the cask heads, the quality of the salted pork and flour in the casks that were being imported into the newly established colony of Victoria were neither the best nor the worst quality available at the time.

Part of the contents of the salted meat casks from *William Salthouse* was the subject of an archaeological analysis of 19th-century butchering patterns by A. J. English (1990). This study focused on the archaeologically derived bone material from beef (*Bos taurus*) and pork

(*Sus scrofa*) casks, using a comparison with 19th-century archival material and evidence from terrestrial archaeological sites (primarily in Sydney, New South Wales). English (1990:63) concluded "the Canadian butchering pattern used, except in the case of beef limb division, was indistinguishable from patterns used by Australian retail butchers selling fresh meat last century." The analysis also clearly demonstrated that "salted meat cuts need not necessarily comprise only boned pieces" as some historical archaeologists working on the First Government House site in Sydney had previously assumed.

In another study, Peter Morgan (1990) examined the morphology and traced some of the origins of the glass bottles from the *William Salthouse*. This study revealed three distinctly different styles of bottles, many of which were complete and with their contents still intact. Nearly half of the "French Champagne" style bottles, for example, had corks stamped on the bottom surface with the letters *AY* in a circle; this proved to be a village in the Champagne region of France (Peters 1996:64). Subsequent research demonstrated that direct trade between France and what had been French Canada had almost entirely ceased with the British takeover after 1760 (Staniforth 1999). The restrictions arising from the Navigation Acts meant that the movement of goods such as French Champagne to Canada always involved trans-shipment at some intermediate British port. Interestingly, the final voyage of the *William Salthouse* represented an attempt to circumvent those same Navigation Acts by conducting trade directly from one British colony (Canada) to another (Australia) without making port in the mother country (Britain). Another study of 19th-century glass bottles, conducted by Iain Stuart (1991), involved the examination of some of the bottles from the *Loch Ard*. Stuart, like Morgan, emphasizes the usefulness of shipwreck cargoes in the study and accurate dating of artifacts, where both the date of the wreck and the nature of the cargo are well established.

Morgan's work was subsequently followed up by research involving the analysis of some of the *William Salthouse* bottle contents (primarily wines) conducted by Sera Jane Peters (1996). This research included sensory analysis of the wine in the form of wine tasting that was conducted by knowledgeable and experienced wine tasters. Peters (1996:65) concluded, "Although not all archaeological wines can be tasted due to excessive salt and micro-biological spoilage, a tasting exercise, used in conjunction with chemical analysis, can provide a valuable qualitative as well as quantitative description of the wines."

The efforts of historical and maritime archaeologists have had limited effect on the wider discipline of Australian history. Archaeologists have regularly made claims about the importance of the vast quantities of broken bits of ceramics and glass that come from archaeological sites, but many historians (and even, one suspects, some archaeologists) fail to see the point of using material culture to understand, or tell stories about, the past. In a departure from the accepted norms, historian Kate Fielding has used material culture from the *Loch Ard* shipwreck to examine some of the meanings of the *Loch Ard* "tragedy," where all but two of those on board died in the wrecking event. Fielding (2003:7) argues that archaeologically excavated artifacts can be seen as "embodiments of contemporary fascination with the wreck drama."

One of the best and most comprehensive artifact catalogs produced on cargo objects excavated from an Australian shipwreck is the *Eglinton* report (Stanbury 2003). The 462-ton barque *Eglinton* was lost on 3 September 1852 while approaching the coast of Western Australia, bound for the port of Fremantle. Intended for the recently settled Swan River Colony (established in 1829), *Eglinton* was carrying a large, diverse, and valuable general cargo that was only partly salvaged at the time of sinking (Stanbury 2003:5–7). The wreck site was discovered in 1971 and excavated by maritime archaeologists from the Western Australian Maritime Museum during two short seasons in 1972 and 1973 (Stanbury 2003:15). The *Eglinton* report provides a comprehensive artifact catalog (complete with a large number of high quality photographs and line drawings) of the remaining cargo items, in particular the ceramics, glassware, ironmongery, and tinware. Unlike the earlier *Sydney Cove* wreck (1797), with its Chinese porcelain, the majority of the ceramics in the *Eglinton* cargo were British transfer-printed earthenwares. These included many of the common mid 19th-century patterns (including Anemone, Canton, Rhine, Willow, and Trellis & Plants) made by Staffordshire potters such as Minton, Spode, Thomas Fell and Co., and Enoch Wood and Sons (Stanbury 2003:79–130).

Myra Stanbury places the *Eglinton* artifact assemblage in its historical context through an extensive exploration of the available historical documentation. Stanbury (2003:33) suggests that the ship and its cargo "could equally represent any one of a number of merchant vessels travelling to destinations in the eastern settlements of Australia at this period" which "provide(s) a fascinating indicator of the range of manufactured and consumer goods being imported into Australia." Studies from terrestrial archaeological sites have allowed for a tentative identification of the range of imported consumer goods available in Australia. Ship cargoes are important in this developing knowledge because they were actively selected by British merchants with particular colonies in mind and reflect both conscious choice and shared cultural values (Staniforth 2003:5).

One important theme-based artifact study has involved the detailed comparative analysis of the historical and archaeological data from four Australian shipwrecks: *Sydney Cove* (1797), *James Matthews* (1841), *William Salthouse* (1841), and *Eglinton* (1852) (Staniforth 1995, 1996, 1997, 1999 and 2003; Staniforth and Nash 1998). The earliest of these papers touches on aspects of the bottles, casks, and ceramics recovered from the wrecks of the *Sydney Cove* and *William Salthouse*. This paper also suggests that it will be through a comparison of intact cargoes and (partial) assemblages recovered from terrestrial sites that will ultimately allow researchers to reconstruct how the socio-economic status of colonists was maintained and more importantly (in a neo-Marxist sense) communicated (Staniforth 1995).

Chinese porcelain has been commonly found on historical archaeological excavations on sites dating before about 1830 in Sydney, New South Wales (Staniforth 1996:16). Initial suggestions were that porcelain artifacts were indicative of direct trade between Canton and Sydney in this period, but research into shipping arrival records revealed that only two vessels actually made the direct voyage between Canton and Sydney in the 30 years before 1820. This trade was, in fact, carried on aboard vessels that were owned or chartered by British merchants (often Scots) who were resident in India, involved in what was known as the "country trade." It involved shipment from Canton to India (usually Calcutta), trans-shipment, and subsequently transport to Sydney. Artifact analysis of the Chinese porcelain component of the country trade vessel *Sydney Cove* (1797) revealed the differing forms and probable functions of the materials, including teawares, toiletry wares, and dinnerwares (Staniforth 1996; Staniforth and Nash, 1998). A subsequent study focused on late-18th-century notions of personal hygiene and the presence of toiletry sets, washing water bottles, and associated bowls on board the *Sydney Cove*. This research examined the link (in terms of prevailing social thoughts) between personal hygiene, infectious disease, the practice of personal cleanliness, and possible remedial action in the face of a hot and "inhospitable" climate (Staniforth 1997).

Overall, this research has been a work of synthesis conducted in order to examine "the ways in which a consumer society became established in the Australian colonies between 1788 and the middle of the 19th century" (Staniforth 1999:iv). It has illustrated some of the changing encoded meanings and symbology in material culture over time, as informed by the works of researchers like Grant McCracken (1988) and John Brewer and Roy Porter (1993). The research argues that such meanings came out of the desire of colonists to maintain cultural continuity through distinguishing themselves from indigenous peoples, stabilizing their relationships with their new home via familiar links (through recognizable material culture), reinforcing social order and relations, and structuring social hierarchies (Staniforth 2003:2). This exploration of "the concepts and meanings that underlie the material world" (Staniforth 1999:xxi) brings to light many of the behaviors that were associated with the colonial expansion and colonization of Australia, based on the cultural preferences and attitudes of the colonists themselves. This research has considered different aspects of the colonial experience, including cultural appropriateness, the growth of capitalism and consumerism, the cultural meaning of objects, and social differentiation. It maintains that consumption plays an important role in the negotiation of social position (Staniforth 2003:1–9) and concludes that

> The archaeology of the *Sydney Cove* is an example of the archaeology of the event. The wreck was an important historical incident in the early settlement history of Australia. However, material culture from the wreck site also represents an opportunity to incorporate the archaeology of the event into larger scale issues such as capitalism, consumption and colonisation as well as changing cultural attitudes associated with dining, tea drinking, and personal hygiene (Staniforth 1997:163)

Conclusion

In order to better understand the development of a consumer society in the early Australian colonies, it is necessary to examine the food, drink, and other consumer goods that were actually being imported into those colonies. The study of shipwreck cargoes provides researchers with opportunities to look in detail at cargoes that failed to make it to their destination. By extension, and by careful comparison with what has been found on terrestrial archaeological sites, it is possible to gain a better appreciation of the ways in which cultural behaviors and attitudes were transported, established, communicated, maintained, and mediated in the early Australian colonies through the use of imported material culture. Wreck sites and their associated archaeological assemblages represent an opportunity to consider wider issues and themes, such as consumption and colonization, as well as to reflect on the transfer of cultural attitudes associated with such activities as dining, tea drinking, and personal hygiene.

References

BREWER, JOHN, AND ROY PORTER
  1993 *Consumption and the World of Goods.* Routledge, London, England, UK.

ENGLISH, ANTHONY J.
  1990 Salted Meats from the Wreck of the *William Salthouse*: Archaeological Analysis of Nineteenth-Century Butchering Patterns. *Australian Historical Archaeology* 8:63–69.

FIELDING, KATE
  2003 A Pane in the Past: The *Loch Ard* Disaster and a Few Bits of Glass. *The Bulletin of the Australasian Institute for Maritime Archaeology* 27:1–8.

HODDER, IAN (EDITOR)
  1989 *The Meaning of Things: Material Culture and Symbolic Expression.* One World Archaeology, No. 6. Harper Collins, London, England, UK.

KENDERDINE, SARAH
  1991 *Artifacts from Shipwrecks in the South East 1851–1951.* State Heritage Branch, Department of Environment and Planning, Adelaide, South Australia.

KOPYTOFF, IGOR
  1986 The Cultural Biography of Things: Commodification in Process. In *The Social Life of Things: Commodities in Cultural Perspective*, Arjun Appadurai, editor, pp. 64–91. Cambridge University Press, Cambridge, England, UK.

LAWRENCE, SUSAN
  1998 The Role of Material Culture in Australasian Archaeology. *Australasian Historical Archaeology* 16:8–15.

McCRACKEN, GRANT
  1988 *Culture and Consumption: New Approaches to the Symbolic Character of Consumer Goods and Activities.* Indiana University Press, Bloomington.

MORGAN, PETER
  1990 Glass Bottles from the *William Salthouse*: A Material Culture Analysis. Bachelor honours thesis, Department of Archaeology, La Trobe University, Melbourne, Australia.

PETERS, S. JANE
  1996 Archaeological Wines: Analysis and Interpretation of a Collection of Wines Recovered from the *William Salthouse* Shipwreck (1841). *Australasian Historical Archaeology* 14:63–68.

STANBURY, MYRA
  2003 *The Barque* Eglinton*: Wrecked Western Australia 1852.* Special Publication 13, Australasian Institute for Maritime Archaeology, Fremantle, WA.

STANIFORTH, MARK
  1987 The Casks from the Wreck of the *William Salthouse*. *Australian Historical Archaeology* 5:21–28.
  1991 The Maritime Archaeology of Immigration. *The Bulletin of the Australian Institute for Maritime Archaeology* 15(2):21–24.
  1995 Dependent Colonies: The Importation of Material Culture into the Australian Colonies (1788–1850). In *Underwater Archaeology: Proceedings from the Society for Underwater Archaeology Conference*, Paul E. Johnston, editor, pp. 159–164. Washington, DC.
  1996 Tracing Artifact Trajectories: Following Chinese Export Porcelain. *The Bulletin of the Australian Institute for Maritime Archaeology* 20(1):13–18.

1997 The Archaeology of the Event: The Annales School and Maritime Archaeology. In *Underwater Archaeology Proceedings from the Society for Historical Archaeology Conference 1997*, Denise A. Lakey, editor, pp. 159–164. Corpus Christi, TX.

1999 Dependent Colonies: The Importation of Material Culture and the Establishment of a Consumer Society in Australia before 1850. Doctoral thesis, Department of Archaeology, Flinders University, Adelaide, Australia.

2003 *Material Culture and Consumer Society: Dependent Colonies in Colonial Australia*. Kluwer Academic/Plenum Press, New York, NY.

STANIFORTH, MARK, AND MIKE NASH
1998 *Chinese Export Porcelain from the Wreck of the Sydney Cove (1797)*. Special Publication 12, Australian Institute for Maritime Archaeology.

STUART, IAIN
1991 Glass Bottles from the *Loch Ard* Shipwreck (1878): A Preliminary Study. *Australian Historical Archaeology* 9:31–36.

WEATHERILL, LORNA
1996 *Consumer Behaviour and Material Culture in Britain 1660–1760*. Routledge, London, England, UK.

MARK STANIFORTH
DEPARTMENT OF ARCHAEOLOGY
FLINDERS UNIVERSITY
ADELAIDE, SOUTH AUSTRALIA 5001, AUSTRALIA

2010. Were the Community Living on the East African Coast also 'Maritime' Communities? An Archaeological Perspective.
In *ACUA Underwater Archaeology Proceedings 2010*, Chris Horrell and Melanie Damour, editors, pp. 162–172.

Were the Communities Living on the East African Coast also 'Maritime' Communities? An Archaeological Perspective

Annalisa Charlton Christie
PhD Research Student
University of York
C/O The Kings Manor, Exhibition Square
York, YO1 7EP   United Kingdom

Several archaeological studies indicate that communities living on the East African coast exploited maritime resources – with the implication that they were maritime *societies; however, few historical sources refer to these activities or to how the sea influenced social organization. Anthropological studies within maritime societies suggest that beyond a maritime subsistence economy, the question 'what constitutes a maritime society?' is more complex. Here, the maritime nature of the Swahili is evaluated within an anthropologically informed maritime framework using data collected from recent work Kua and the submerged settlement site of Kisimani Mafia, both in the Mafia Archipelago, Tanzania.*

Introduction

Numerous archaeological studies along the East African Coast follow anthropological and historical literature by referring to the Swahili as 'maritime' (Sheriff 1981; Horton 1996a, 1996b, 1997a, 1997b; Abungu 1998). Although, the focus of this research has been either on examining how their geographical position influenced the role of the Swahili as cultural brokers between the Indian Ocean trading networks and the African interior (Horton and Middleton 2000:89), elucidating the nature and impact of this trade (Kusimba 1999), or understanding Swahili identity (Breen and Lane 2003:472). By contrast, the implications of using the term 'maritime' in reference to the Swahili will be examined using an anthropologically informed maritime framework to question what archaeologists mean when they describe a society as maritime. This is illustrated with examples drawn from the Southern Swahili, with particular reference to recent work conducted in the Mafia Archipelago, Tanzania. The importance of integrating maritime orientated terrestrial studies with underwater research will be highlighted and some of the challenges of conducting sub-tidal research within East Africa will be discussed.

Situated approximately 21 km (13 miles) off the Tanzanian coast opposite the Rufiji Delta, the Mafia Archipelago (comprising Mafia, Chole, Juani and Jibondo islands) (Figure 1) represented a small enough research area to examine the influence of the sea on the socio-cultural and ideological organisation of communities living there. The project applied a maritime cultural landscape approach, which combined intertidal zone and foreshore surveys with shovel test pit excavations and ethnographic interviews. Research concluded with a small-scale excavation at the 13th – 18th century settlement site of Kua, which aimed to evaluate the social complexities of maritime interactions through the detailed analysis of faunal assemblages in the context of associated archaeological and structural remains. Each of these strategies (survey, ethnography and excavation) provides different narratives about the communities living in the archipelago, and these are evaluated in the light of considerations from maritime anthropological studies.

Theoretical Frameworks

To address whether the Swahili were a maritime society, it is important to evaluate how these societies have been considered and defined within the archaeological and anthropological literature. Archaeologically, although numerous studies drawn from an extensive geographic range indicate that they are investigating maritime societies; few have stated explicitly what they consider to constitute maritime culture. In the early years of maritime archaeology, when maritime archaeological research was focused almost exclusively on sub-tidal remains such as shipwrecks and submerged settlements, defining maritime societies was considered less important. As Muckelroy (1976:6) indicated "...concern with coastal communities which derive their livelihood predominantly from the sea is excluded since... [they]... will display their maritime connections only marginally." Based on this definition, there is no such thing as a maritime society – these are simply coastal communities

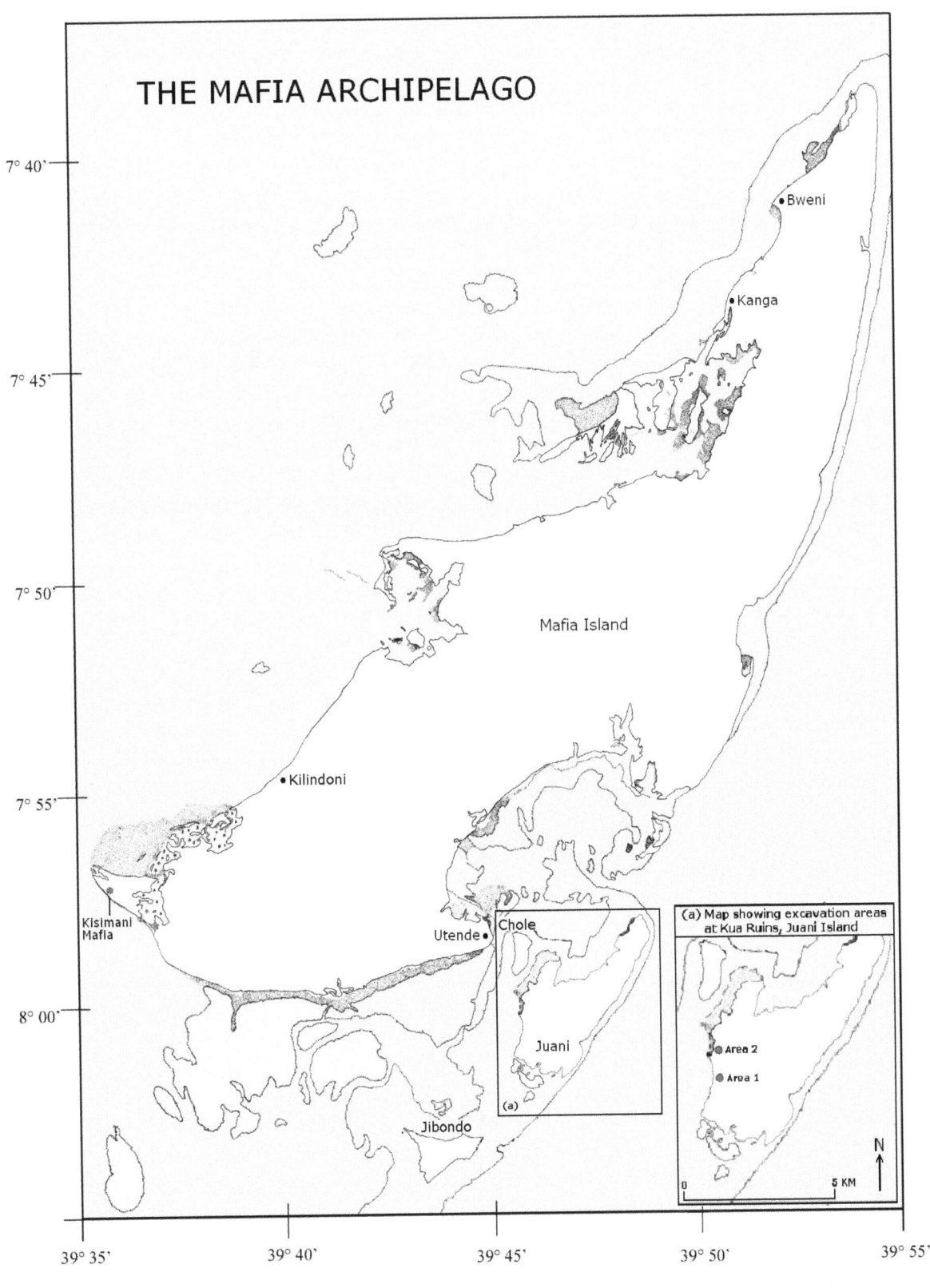

THE MAFIA ARCHIPELAGO

• Bweni

• Kanga

Mafia Island

• Kilindoni

Kisimani
Mafia

Utende •   Chole

Juani

Jibondo

(a) Map showing excavation areas
at Kua Ruins, Juani Island

• Area 2

• Area 1

N

0   5 KM

7° 40'
7° 45'
7° 50'
7° 55'
8° 00'

39° 35'   39° 40'   39° 45'   39° 50'   39° 55'

FIGURE 1: MAP SHOWING THE MAFIA ARCHIPELAGO (A) MAP SHOWING EXCAVATION AREAS AT KUA RUINS, JUANI ISLAND (DRAWING BY AUTHOR, 2010).

for whom the sea is merely another resource. Over the years, the importance of these terrestrial remains has come to the fore, with concepts such as the 'maritime cultural landscape' (Westerdahl 1992) highlighting the necessity of situating sub-tidal archaeology in the context of the surrounding landscape. The incorporation of terrestrial remains into the remit of maritime archaeology has been on one hand a change for the better. The sub-tidal remains that were the focus of studies forty or fifty years ago were created and utilized by communities living on the coast, and in turn, these communities interacted with and manipulated the marine environment. Although, the incorporation of terrestrial remains has also complicated maritime archaeology by encouraging debate into how these maritime cultures should be considered and defined. After all, as Westerdahl (1998) highlights "if you do not possess a population attuned to maritime preoccupations, even if the current population is residing on the seashore, there is no maritime culture" (Westerdahl 1998:1).

Those studies that have attempted to define maritime cultures have normally taken one of two perspectives. The first perspective considers maritime cultures as unique entities, proposing a general list of components that should be present for a society to be considered maritime. One concept that attempted to create a generalized list of maritime cultural traits is the 'maritime cultural landscape'. First used from an interpretative viewpoint by Westerdahl in 1992, the maritime cultural landscape is defined as "the human utilisation (economy) of maritime space by boat: settlement, fishing, hunting, shipping and its attendant sub-cultures" (Westerdahl 1992:5). As part of this maritime cultural landscape, Westerdahl (1992) proposed five features that should be present for a society to be considered 'maritime'. Specifically, these included: shipwrecks, geomorphological processes affecting the coastal environment, maritime influenced place names, the "tradition of usage" defined as "...the mental map of coastal people in general based on the existence of well used havens and routes on the influence of local winds and currents" (Westerdahl 1992:8) and land-based remains. Initially these land-based remains were restricted to "ancient monuments preserved on the waterfront" (Westerdahl 1992:8), however this has since been expanded to incorporate the "physical remains of maritime communities' technologies and practices" (Lane 2005:96) including aspects of a marine subsistence economy. This includes, the remains of shellfish exploitation – such as shell middens, the archaeological remains of fishing

tools used in this exploitations (hooks, lines, nets, net weights shore-based fish traps), and the actual remains of this exploitation represented by fish processing sites and fish bone assemblages (Pollard 2007:246). Recently, Westerdahl (2005, 2007) and others (McNiven 2003, Van de Noort 2003, Chapman and Geary 2004) have started to explore the influence of the sea on the cognitive and ideological organization of maritime societies, through the investigation of, amongst others, the "ritual landscapes at sea" (Westerdahl 2005:2). Despite these developments, many maritime cultural landscape studies still tend to focus on the technological and economic aspects of maritime exploitation. As Westerdahl (1994) himself suggests, "maritime culture implies maritime economies... a combination of fishing, hunting and shipping" (Westerdahl 1994:267). This has lead to the underlying implication that a maritime society is one that lives by the sea and exploits maritime resources. The second perspective taken in the attempt to define maritime cultures suggests that rather than being a unique entity, maritime culture is just one facet of a broader cultural system (Hunter 1994). This is more culturally specific, but some generalisation is still required to identify the 'maritime cultural traits' that comprise this maritime component. The author suggests that this is the perspective of those who have classified the Swahili as a maritime society in the past. One aspect of research along the East African coast has been the attempts to establish the origins of the Swahili. Initial interpretations (in the 1960s and 1970s) tended to emphasize the presence of exotic pottery and other imported materials to suggest a foreign genesis for the Swahili (Chittick 1984). Conversely, later approaches (ca. 1980s onwards) tended to examine coastal-hinterland connections, utilizing a more detailed analysis of local pottery, and historical linguistics (Nurse and Spear 1985; de Vere Allen 1981; Willis 1992), to emphasize the local origins of the Swahili (Horton 1996b; Chami 1998). By focusing on Swahili origins (either exotic or local), the Swahili Coast has often been perceived as a cultural offshoot to a larger non-maritime social system, rather than as a distinct maritime-orientated cultural system in its own right.

Given temporal and geographical variation of cultures included in the remit of maritime archaeology, a generalized definition of maritime cultures or a checklist of 'maritime cultural traits' is likely to be ineffective. Different societies will have their own unique set of maritime traits that will be manifested in a culturally specific way. Therefore, each maritime culture must be examined in a culturally specific context. In this way, maritime culture is actually an archaeological construct, rather than a means by which a society might define itself.

Firth (1993) argues for examining maritime societies rather than maritime cultures indicating the definition of maritime societies (i.e. the range of beliefs, norms, and practices that need to be present for a society to be considered maritime or to have a maritime component) should be "a conclusion towards which progress is directed rather than a starting point that determines which things... [should be studied]" (Firth 1993:3). Unlike maritime cultural landscape approaches, the characteristics Firth (1993) suggests for maritime societies are rooted in social theory. Specifically, he characterizes maritime societies utilizing Giddens' (1981) definition of societies, which explores the relationship between a social system and its surrounding landscape, or if applied to maritime communities, their relationship to the marine environment (Firth 1993:2). Giddens' definition includes four aspects all of which have to be influenced by the marine environment for a social system to be considered as a maritime society. These are: defined locale, legitimized prerogatives, shared institutions, and inclusive identities (Giddens 1981:45). When defining maritime societies, the incorporation of other aspects of social systems beyond 'defined locales' is useful as it acknowledges that 'maritime-ness' is more than an environmental construct; by which if a community lives by the sea then it is implicitly assumed to be maritime.

Examining maritime societies in this way is useful, and the influence of the sea on the four aspects of Giddens' definition is well demonstrated in several of the ethnographic studies conducted amongst known maritime communities – demonstrated in this paper by D'Arcy's evaluation of identity and environment in 'Remote Oceania' (D'Arcy 2006:1). In this study, the marine environment influences defined locale not only because the communities live by the sea, but also on a smaller scale, specific zones of particularly the near-shore marine environment were controlled by specific kin groups within the society (D'Arcy 2006:98). Following Giddens' definition (Giddens 1981:45), the boundaries of these zones are identified by these groups using natural features both on land and at sea (D'Arcy 2006:101). Additionally, coastal peoples were considered distinct from those living on the island interior (referred to as "bush people" by those living on the coast) (D'Arcy 2006:29). Legitimized prerogatives in which societies "lay claim to...occupied space... [particularly]...the use of the material environment to provide sources of

food...." (Giddens 1981:45) is also clearly applicable in D'Arcy's example. This is in part demonstrated by the fact that access to specific zones of the marine environment, and thus the resources within those zones, was controlled by kin groups. It is also demonstrated by the fact that in Tahiti, "only members of the chiefly class... could own canoes. This gave them control over fishing as well as sea travel" (D'Arcy 2006:59). The influence of the marine environment on shared institutions or "an 'institutional clustering' of practices among the participants in the social system" (Giddens 1981:45) and inclusive identities are also demonstrated in Oceania, first, by the clear marine influence of religious beliefs (D'Arcy 2006:40-49). Second, by the fact that he suggests, "the waters of the Pacific were cultural seascapes rich in symbolic meaning, crowded with navigational markers, symbols of tenure, fishing and surfing sites, and reminders of gods and spirits in the form of maritime familiars and sites of their exploits... [Furthermore]... the sea was important for livelihood and sustenance, social networks, and assertion of chiefly and community *mana*. It also shaped identity" (D'Arcy 2006:169).

By rooting his classification of maritime societies in social theory, Firth's (1993) approach goes beyond the environmental and economic definition of maritime societies as those that live by the sea and exploit marine resources, indicating that for a society to be truly maritime, the marine environment should actively influence, and be influenced by, the overall social organization of that society. This perspective is more reflective of how maritime societies are understood within anthropological frameworks.

Anthropological studies within maritime societies have highlighted that maritime interactions such as exploitation, navigation, and even seafaring are socially complex, often involving a plethora of underlying beliefs and ritual practices that are culturally specific. They indicate that in many cases the sea has the potential to influence social, political, and sometimes ideological organization, playing an important role in the construction of maritime identities (Sather 1997, Cooney 2003, Conte 2006, D'Arcy 2006). As Cordell (1984) highlights, "the seascape is a living history with associated myths, stories and legends that provide moral and cultural guidelines. It is the storehouse of social identity..." (Cordell 1984:307 cited in Hviding 1996:233). Ethnographic studies have been utilized in within maritime archaeology, however their application has tended to be restricted to the exploration of the social and technical aspects of boat building (McGrail

2001; McGrail and Blue 2003), or to exploring the techno-economic aspects of marine resource exploitation (D'Arcy 2006:1). The use of maritime ethnography as an interpretative tool for exploring the socio-cultural contexts of maritime interactions is less frequent. While the author recommends that maritime archaeologists look to anthropological studies to elucidate the social complexities of maritime interactions, it is not suggested that it is possible to use these studies as direct analogies for archaeological materials. Instead, the examination of critically evaluated anthropological studies challenges archaeologists to question these interactions from a more socio-cultural perspective, and to provide alternative questions that could be asked of the archaeological record (McGrail 2001:3). Such questions could include is there any, evidence of gendered division of labor in maritime exploitation?; is there evidence of differential access to, or control of, resources or knowledge of maritime techniques?; what, if any are the embedded social meanings within maritime activities?; and what is the influence of maritime interactions on wider social and ideological organization? Such questions are often overlooked as in many cases the socio-cultural context of maritime activities are considered too difficult to access archaeologically.

Regional Context

Having established how maritime societies have been defined archaeologically and anthropologically, the following sections present some of the existing data collected from research along the East African coast, and data collected during the recent studies in the Mafia Archipelago to evaluate whether it is possible to classify the Swahili as a 'maritime' society.

Many archaeological projects within the region have considered the sea as a conduit for the exchange of goods and ideas examining the involvement of the Swahili in long-distance maritime trade networks. This has often formed the basis for the interpretation that the Swahili were a maritime society (e.g. Sheriff 1981; Horton 1996a; Abungu 1998) and numerous studies have examined the importance of maritime trade and the influence of external contact (facilitated by this trade) on architectural styles, religion, linguistics, and social organization (Kusimba 1999: 61, 64). The focus of existing research on long distance trade and exchange only indicates that the Swahili are a mercantile rather than maritime society. As mentioned previously, maritime archaeology acknowledges that there are other

factors beyond maritime trade that need to be examined if the maritime nature of that society is to be fully understood.

One component of maritime societies that has until recently, been largely under-researched in this region is the nature of maritime exploitation. This is partly due to the research aims and research designs of archaeological projects along the coast. The focus on exploring the influence and spread of Islam has meant that many of the excavations within large stone-town sites have tended to focus on the excavation of the mosques rather than domestic spaces. Those projects that have looked at domestic space (such as Donley-Reid 1982) have tended to take a more theoretical perspective to examine the use of space and place within the house organisation, rather than focusing on the excavation of dump deposits and faunal assemblages.

Over the last ten to fifteen years, there has been an increasing emphasis on the importance of examining the nature of Swahili subsistence economy through the analysis of both archaeobotanical (Walshaw 2010) and faunal remains (Horton and Mudida 1993; Horton 1996b; Van Neer 2001). Such studies have demonstrated conclusively that the Swahili had an active and complex maritime subsistence economy, primarily based on small-scale artisanal fisheries (Horton 1996b:384), supporting the assertion that the Swahili were a maritime society based on maritime archaeological definitions. On the other hand, studies such as Van Neer's examination of the faunal assemblages from Kizimkazi on Zanzibar or Horton and Mudida's work on the assemblages from Shanga, have tended to take an economic perspective, exploring diet rather than the social aspects of exploitation (Horton and Mudida 1996:393; Van Neer 2001:391). The following section suggests how a detailed investigation of faunal assemblages within a spatial framework can be used to examine the socio-cultural context of maritime exploitation, demonstrating this with data collected from recent work at Kua.

Recent Research

Situated on the southwest coast of Juani Island (Figure 1), Kua is a large settlement site comprising several complex structures. These include the remains of a 'palace' structure; evidence of more than forty houses, normally represented by surrounding walls; seven mosques; several cemetery areas; and numerous latrines. The site is now considerably overgrown in areas; however, the standing remains are extensive enough to

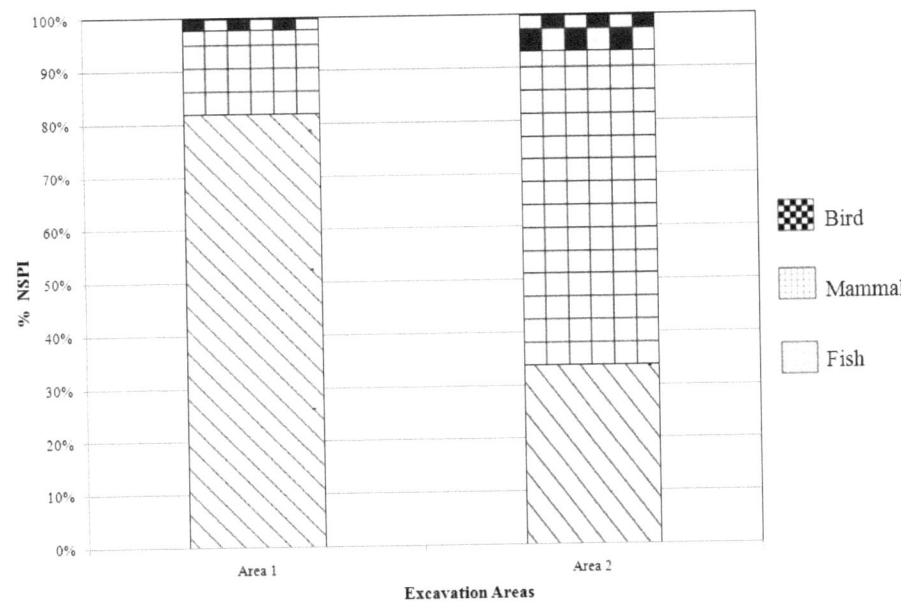

FIGURE 2: CHART SHOWING THE % NSPI OF FISH, MAMMAL AND BIRD BONES RECOVERED FROM THE EXCAVATION AREAS (CREATED BY AUTHOR, 2010).

the location of each house in proximity to the main palace structure. This has since been supported archaeologically by the presence of prestige items like beads and iron slag exclusive to the deposits associated with the higher status household and a higher proportion of imported pottery from the same unit compared to the unit associated with the lower status household.

The spatial analysis of the faunal assemblages indicated that there were differences in patterns of resource exploitation. Specifically, material from Area 1 comprised primarily fish bones from much larger fish taxa, whereas the assemblage from Area 2 comprised mostly mammal bones (categorized as large ungulate – likely cow; medium ungulate – likely goat; and small ungulate – likely dik dik) with a few much smaller fish bones (Figure 2). This suggests that the majority of marine resource exploitation was conducted by individuals of lower social status.

In terms of the terrestrial species: although the proportions of large, medium, and small sized ungulates were not perceptibly different (Table 1), there was a considerable difference between the two units in elements represented, particularly in the large ungulate category (Figure 3). Specifically, in Area 1 these elements were all from the skull and mandible or the forelimbs (Figure 3a), whereas in Area 2, the represented elements were more varied, with the majority of fragments coming from the hind limbs (Figure 3b). While the individuals of the lower status household had access to terrestrial species, the presence of hind limb bones in Area 2 suggests that the higher status household had access to better cuts of meat.

As the stratigraphy recorded in Area 1 was less temporally defined, only the stratigraphic analysis of Area 2 is presented here. As part of this analysis, the

give a clear suggestion of settlement organization. This provided an opportunity to make interpretations about household status based on the nature of the structural remains. Ethnographic data collected during the field season indicated that, at least at Kua, rubbish disposal was done on a house-by-house basis, with refuse disposed near the house compound. The surface remains of these midden deposits are visible in several areas across the site, represented by dense concentrations of local and imported pottery, beads, marine shells, and faunal remains. It was hypothesized that by excavating the midden deposits associated with two households of differing social status, the faunal assemblages collected during excavation could be examined both spatially and stratigraphically to elucidate the influence of social status on resource accessibility and to evaluate changing patterns of resource exploitation.

Two 2m x 3m (6.6 ft. x 9.8 ft.) excavation units were opened at the site. The first was placed over the midden deposit associated with a lower status house (referred to as Area 1), while the second was opened across the midden deposit of a higher status household (referred to as Area 2 (Figure 1a).

Status differences between the two households were initially determined based on three factors: first, ethnohistorical data collected from local community members who still maintain close linkages with the site; second, differences in the scale of the associated architecture; and third,

Resource	% NSPI of ungulate remains recovered	
	Area 1	Area 2
Large Ungulate	69.9	67.41
Medium Ungulate	28.64	32.18
Small Ungulate	1.46	0.41

TABLE 1: PROPORTIONS OF UNGULATES RECOVERED FROM AREAS 1 AND 2.

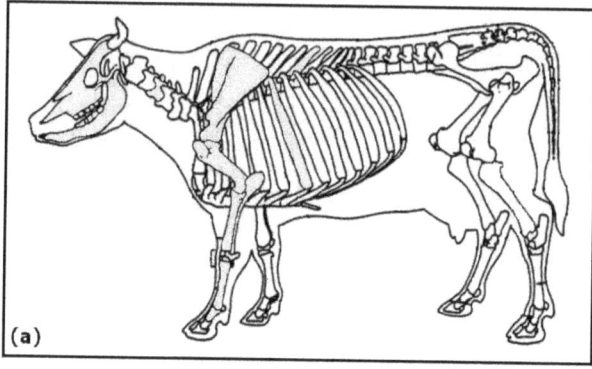

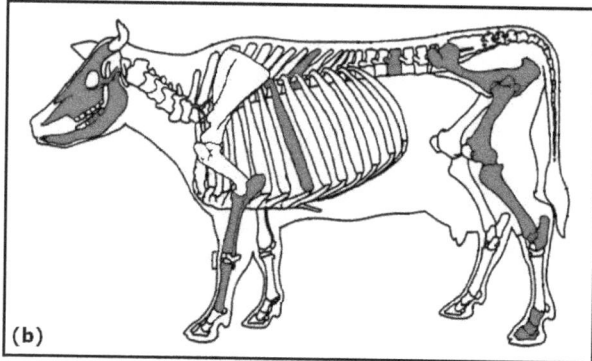

FIGURE 3: LARGE UNGULATE SKELETONS HIGHLIGHTING THE LOCATIONS OF ELEMENTS (A) RECOVERED FROM AREA 1 AND (B) RECOVERED FROM AREA 2 (DRAWN BY AUTHOR, 2010).

subsistence molluscs representing approximately 60% of the exploited resources in the initial phases of midden deposit compared to their contribution of only 30% in the final phases. The difference is made up by an increase in edible shellfish consumption over time rather than a decrease in fish resources (Figure 4). By proceeding with the hypothesis that maritime exploitation is primarily conducted by individuals of lower social status, then these changes could be indicative of a decline in the social or economic status of the individuals living in the associated household. Further analysis and excavation (to increase the sample size) would be required to test this hypothesis, possibly by examining whether the element representation from the terrestrial species of a larger sample changes over time. Based on the spatial patterns identified earlier, one might expect to find that the elements represented in the later deposits of Area 2 would be comprised primarily of forelimb or skull bones.

Discussion

Analysis of the Kua data has highlighted that maritime interactions were socially complex, but, based on maritime archaeological definitions, it also raises the question: If the higher status household was, at least initially, not actively engaged in maritime consumption, was the community living at Kua a maritime one? Provisionally, this indicates more strongly that they were a maritime community. The fact that the higher status individuals exploited a higher proportion of terrestrial

proportions of exploited resources (fish and mammals - both calculated based on the % NSPI of identifiable elements excluding fragments; decorative molluscs, and subsistence molluscs - both calculated based on number of complete shells, or right side valves for bivalves) recovered from each recorded context were compared. During the excavations at Area 2, midden formation was recorded over four contexts (1000 – 1004 inclusive), with 1000 representing the most recent deposition and 1004 representing the initial formation of the midden (Figure 4). It should be noted that the assemblages from contexts 1001 and 1002 have been grouped together as post-field analysis indicated they were the same deposit. Within Area 2, the consumption of marine resources gradually increases over time with terrestrial resources and non-

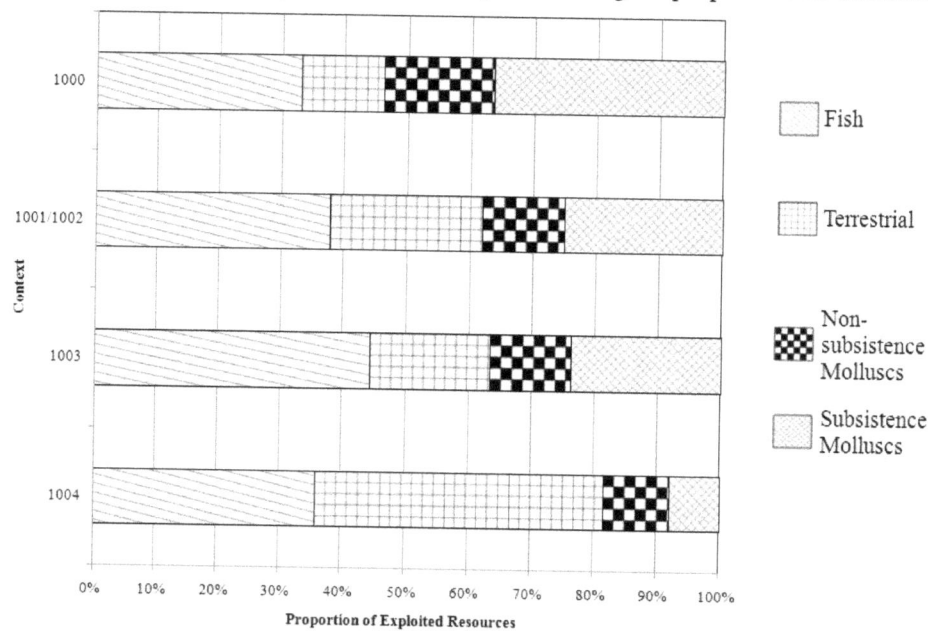

FIGURE 4: STRATIGRAPHIC ANALYSIS OF FAUNAL REMAINS FROM AREA 2 (CREATED BY AUTHOR, 2010).

species rather than large fish and marine mammals could be interpreted as a mode of signifying their status. If the sea was commonplace within the society (as one would expect within a maritime society), the consumption of terrestrial species may have been a form of distanciation whereby the elite differentiated themselves from the ordinary. When considered in the context of settlement organization in which the higher status individuals tend to live closer to the sea than those of lower status, their proximity to the sea could also be seen as a reiteration of this status because, although they are not actively exploiting marine resources, they still control access to the sea.

The demarcation of status through the use of differential patterns of resource use has parallels in other ethno-archaeological studies. Of particular note is Moss's (1993) ethnographic study of shellfish consumption amongst the Tllingit society. In addition to challenging the assumed gender roles within shellfish collection and use (Moss 1993:626), she also highlights that the consumption of shellfish was influenced by social status. She suggests that the consumption of shellfish was generally associated with lower social status indicating that "the aristocrat, was encouraged to avoid eating shellfish as part of a larger strategy to achieve wealth and status." (Moss 1993:646).

Maritime Approaches: Integrating Terrestrial and Sub-Tidal Investigations

Kua would have played a key role in the sociopolitical organisation of the Mafia Archipelago; however, its importance should be evaluated in the context of its interactions with the nearby contemporary site of Kisimani Mafia (Figure 1). Unlike Kua, where very little previous archaeological reconnaissance had been conducted, Kisimani Mafia was excavated by Neville Chittick in the late 1950s (Chittick 1961), and the site is mentioned in several historical sources (King 1917; Revington 1936; Piggott 1941). These sources suggest that Kisimani Mafia would have been founded in the late 11th century when Mafia was under the nominal control of the Sultanate of Kilwa (King 1917:118; Chittick 1961:1).

Within the broader context of the sociopolitical organization of the archipelago, numerous sources have suggested a close, if tumultuous, relationship between Kisimani Mafia and Kua. These local histories tell of the collapse of Kisimani Mafia, indicating that following a long-term feud between the two sites "... the town of Ras Kisimani was inundated by the sea" (Revington 1936:36). The record of the inundation of Kisimani Mafia by the sea is of particular relevance to maritime archaeologists, in part because whilst it may not have been the direct result of retaliation from Kua, it can provide proxy evidence to suggest the nature of coastal processes in the area – possibly indicating a rise in sea levels. The historical sources also highlight the potential for submerged remains in the area (Piggott 1941:27). Even though Piggott (1941) remains unconvinced by the potential for submerged structural remains, preliminary surveys conducted during the recent project and previous surveys conducted by Chami (2000) have indicated that there are certainly extensive sub-tidal archaeological scatters extending from Kisimani Mafia to as far as Bwejuu Island (Chami 2000:210). Future work at the site needs to integrate the investigation of both sub-tidal and terrestrial remains uniting them under the umbrella of maritime archaeology, as the remainder of the terrestrial remains are threatened by coastal erosion and modern development. Despite having been excavated previously, Chittick's (1961) report focuses almost exclusively on the coins and pottery uncovered during excavation, with a primary emphasis on the imported pottery. Details of any faunal or shell assemblages recovered are not recorded, and it remains unclear whether any such assemblages were even collected. Preliminary archaeological reconnaissance at the site in 2009, recorded considerable deposits of marine shell and other faunal remains interspersed with local and imported pottery. These deposits have the potential to indicate the nature of resource exploitation at the site, which could be compared to the data collected from Kua to determine whether the patterns identified at Kua are replicated at other sites in the archipelago.

The importance and friability of maritime heritage within East Africa has been increasingly recognized over the last ten to fifteen years, with explicitly maritime-focused studies such as Breen and Lane's work around Mombasa, and Pollard's work around Kilwa (Breen et al. 2001; Breen and Lane 2003; McConkey and McErlean 2007; Quinn et al. 2007; Pollard 2007, 2008), playing a fundamental role in highlighting the variety of both terrestrial and sub-tidal maritime heritage that needs to be recorded, investigated, and monitored. Breen and Lane's (2003) work incorporated a significant sub-tidal survey using acoustic scanners to identify anomalies on the seabed, identifying numerous cultural anomalies from shipwrecks to fishing technologies, and isolated finds to submerged settlements (Breen and Lane 2003:482).

Maritime cultural landscape approaches have encouraged research into the terrestrial remains of maritime societies (the importance of which are highlighted by the research at Kua); however, it is important to not go to the other extreme and overlook the importance of the submerged remains that formed the cornerstone of maritime archaeology at its conception. Sub-tidal remains have an important story to tell that should be integrated into the broader narratives of foreshore and intertidal studies. Unfortunately, the development of maritime projects (both terrestrial and sub-tidal) within the region, particularly those conducted by local archaeologists, has been hindered by several factors; first, there is a lack of trained local maritime archaeologists working in the region. Second, it is often incorrectly assumed that because archaeologists are working on the coast they are conducting maritime archaeology. As argued above, maritime archaeology is as much a social construct as it is an environmental one. If archaeologists working on the coast do not engage with the theoretically established set of maritime cultural indicators, then they are not conducting maritime archaeology. Finally, maritime archaeology, and particularly sub-tidal investigations, in the region is restricted by the common perception that the techniques and equipment are expensive and that it is just about 'fishing or boats' (Wertz 1997:558). To a certain extent, these challenges are starting to be overcome, with several training courses on maritime archaeology aimed specifically at local archaeologists within the region. Courses such as the one run by the British Institute in Eastern Africa on Zanzibar in 2006, were designed to aid in the recognition, recording, monitoring, and management of the rich maritime heritage in their respective countries.

Concluding Remarks

To conclude, whilst the Swahili have heretofore been considered a maritime society, much of this interpretation has been based on their involvement in long distance trade. Recent research into Swahili subsistence economy has begun to make a more convincing case for this; however, this research needs to be expanded to evaluate maritime exploitation from a social perspective, on a regional scale. As the data collected from Kua indicates, resource exploitation is socially complex and the marine environment influences amongst others, settlement organization. Whether these patterns of resource exploitation are replicated at other sites within the archipelago remains to be seen through further research,

as the site did not exist in isolation. The potential for submerged remains at other sites within the archipelago and indeed within the broader region indicates that further research should integrate both coastal and underwater approaches, not least because these sites are threatened by both natural processes and, in some cases, modern development. To maximize the understanding of the Swahili as a 'maritime' society, it is important that future research within the region should be conducted within a framework rooted in maritime anthropology that acknowledges the social complexities of maritime interactions and recognizes the role of the sea in the construction of maritime identities.

Acknowledgments

I would like to thank my supervisor Dr Paul Lane both for his constructive criticism during early drafts of this paper, and for his advice throughout this project. Thanks also to the Arts and Humanities Research Council and the University of York for giving me the opportunity to conduct this research. Finally 'Asante Sana' to my research assistants and government organisations within Tanzania who helped facilitate my project - specifically the Tanzanian Commission for Science and Technology (COSTECH), the District Commissioners Office in Mafia, and the Mafia Island Marine Park. Thank you all.

References

ABUNGU, GEORGE HO
1998   City States of the East African Coast and their Maritime Contacts. In *Transformations in Africa: Essays on Africa's later past,* Graham Connah, editor, pp. 204-218. Leicester University Press, London and Washington.

BREEN, COLIN., AND PAUL J. LANE
2003   Archaeological approaches to East Africa's changing seascapes. *World Archaeology* 35(3):469-489.

BREEN, COLIN., WES FORSYTHE, PAUL LANE, TOM MCERLEAN, ROSEMARY MCCONKEY, ATHMAN L. OMAR, RORY QUINN AND BRIAN WILLIAMS
2001   Ulster and the Indian Ocean? Recent maritime archaeological research on the East African coast. *Antiquity* 75:797-798.

CHAMI, FELIX A.
1998   A Review of Swahili Archaeology. *African Archaeological Review* 15(3):199-218.

CHAMI, FELIX A.
2000   Further Archaeological Research on Mafia Island. *Azania* XXXV:208-214.

CHAPMAN, HENRY P., AND BENJAMIN R. GEARY
2004   The Social Context of Seafaring in the Bronze Age Revisited. *World Archaeology* 36(4):452-458.

CHITTICK, NEVILLE
1961   *Kisimani Mafia: Excavation at an Island Settlement on the East African Coast.* Antiquities Division, occasional paper, Dar es Salaam.

CHITTICK, NEVILLE
1984   *Manda: Excavations at an Island Port on the Kenyan Coast.* British Institute in Eastern Africa, Nairobi.

CONTE, ERIC
2006   Ethnoarchaeology in Polynesia, In *Archaeology in Oceania,* Ian Lilley, editor, pp. 240-259. Malden, Oxford and Victoria.

COONEY, GABRIEL
2003   Introduction: Seeing Land from the Sea. *World Archaeology* 35 (3):323-328.

CORDELL, JOHN C
1984   Defending Customary Inshore Sea Rights, In *Maritime Institutions in the Western Pacific,* Kenneth Ruddle and Tomoya Akimichi, editors, pp. 301-326. Senri Ethnological Studies 17, Osaka: National Museum of Ethnology.

D'ARCY, P
2006   *The People of the Sea: Environment, Identity and History in Oceania.* Honolulu.

DE VERE ALLEN, JAMES
1981   Swahili Culture and the Nature of East Coast Settlement. *The international Journal of African Historical Studies* 14(2):306-334.

DONLEY-REID, LINDA W
1982   House power: Swahili space and symbolic markers, In *Symbolic and Structural archaeology,* Ian Hodder, editor, pp.63-73. Cambridge University Press, London and New York.

FIRTH, ANTONY
1993   Three Facets of Maritime Archaeology: Society, Landscape and Critique, University of Southampton, University of Southampton, Southampton <http://www.arch.soton.ac.uk/research/firth/>; republished in April 2010 at http://splash.wessexarch.co.uk/wp-content/uploads/2010/04/Firth-1995-Three-Facets-of-Maritime-Archaeology-140410.pdf.

GIDDENS, ANTHONY
1981   *A Contemporary Critique of Historical Materialism Vol. 1: Power, Property, and the State.* Macmillan, London.

HORTON, MARK
1996a   Early Maritime Trade and Settlement along the Coasts of East Africa. In *The Indian Ocean in Antiquity,* Julian Reade, editor, pp. 439-459. Kegan Paul International, London and New York.

HORTON, MARK
1996b   *Shanga: the archaeology of a Muslim trading community on the coast of East Africa.* British Institute in Eastern Africa, London.

HORTON, MARK
1997a   Mare Nostrum – a new archaeology in the Indian Ocean. *Antiquity* 71:753-755.

HORTON, MARK
1997b   Eastern African Historical Archaeology. In *Encyclopaedia of Precolonial Africa,* Joseph O Vogel, editor, pp. 549-554. Altimira Press, Walnut Creek, London and New Delhi.

HORTON, MARK AND JOHN MIDDLETON
2000   *The Swahili: The social landscape of a mercantile society.* Blackwell Publishers, Oxford and Massachusetts.

HORTON, MARK AND NINA MUDIDA
1993   Exploitation of maritime resources: evidence for the origin of Swahili communities of East Africa. In *Archaeology of Africa: Foods, Metals and Towns,* Thurstan Shaw, editor, pp. 673-693. Routledge, London and New York.

HUNTER, JR
1994   'Maritime Culture': Notes from the Land. *The International Journal of Nautical Archaeology* 23(4):261-264.

HVIDING, EDVARD
1996   *Guardians of Marovo Lagoon: Practice, place and politics in maritime Melanesia.* Honolulu.

KING, NORMAN
1917   Mafia. *Geographical Journal* 50:117-125.

KUSIMBA, CHAPURUKHA M.
1999   *The Rise and Fall of Swahili States.* Altimira Press, Walnut Creek, London and New Delhi

LANE, PAUL J
2005   Maritime Archaeology: A Prospective Research Avenue in Tanzania. In *Salvaging Tanzania's Cultural Heritage.* Bertram, B,B, Mapunda and Paul Msemwa, editors, pp. 96-132. Dar es Salaam University Press, Dar es Salaam.

MCCONKEY, ROSEMARY,. AND THOMAS MCERLEAN
2007   Mombasa Island: A Maritime Perspective. *International Journal of Historical Archaeology* 11(2):99-121.

McGRAIL, SEAN
2001   *Boats of the World: from the Stone Age to Medieval times.* Oxford University Press, Oxford.

McGRAIL, SEAN,. AND LUCY BLUE
2003   *Boats of South Asia.* Routledge, London and New York.

McNIVEN, IAN J
2003   Saltwater People: Spiritscapes, Maritime Rituals and the Archaeology of Australian Indigenous Seascapes. *World Archaeology* 35(3):329-349.

MOSS, MADONNA
1993   Shellfish, gender and status on the Northwest coast: reconciling archaeological, ethnographic and ethno-historical records of the Tlingit. *American Anthropology* 95(3):631-652.

MUCKELROY, KEITH
1978   *Maritime Archaeology.* Cambridge University Press, Cambridge.

NURSE, DEREK, AND THOMAS SPEAR
1985   *The Swahili: reconstructing the history and language of an African society 800-1500.* University of Pennsylvania Press, Philadelphia.

PIGGOTT, DWI
1941   Mafia – History and Traditions (collected by Kadhi Amur Omar Saadi). *Tanganyika Notes and Records* 11:35-40.

POLLARD, EDWARD J.
2007   An Archaeology of Tanzanian Coastal Landscapes in the Middle Iron Age (6th – 15th centuries AD). Doctoral dissertation, University of Ulster.

POLLARD, EDWARD J.
2008   The maritime landscape of Kilwa Kisiwani and its region, Tanzania, 11th to 15th century AD. *Journal of Anthropological Archaeology* 27:265-280.

REVINGTON, TM
1936   Some notes on the Mafia Island Group. *Tanganyika Notes and Records* 12:23-27.

QUINN, RORY, WES FORSYTHE, COLIN BREEN, DONAL BOLAND, PAUL LANE, AND ATHMAN L. OMAR
2007   Process-based models for port evolution and wreck site formation at Mombasa, Kenya. *Journal of Archaeological Science* 34:1449-1460.

SATHER, CLIFFORD
1997   *The Bajau Laut: adaptation, history and fate in a maritime fishing society of St Sabah.* Oxford University Press, New York and Kuala Lumpur.

SHERIFF, ABDUL MH
1981   The East African coast and its role in maritime trade. In *Ancient Civilisations of Africa,* G Mokhtar, editor, pp. 551-567. UNESCO, California.

VAN DE NOORT, ROBERT
2003   An Ancient Seascape: The Social Context of Seafaring in the Early Bronze Age. *World Archaeology* 35(3):404-415.

VAN NEER, WIM
2001   Animal remains from the medieval site of Kizimkazi Dimbani, Zanzibar. In, *Islam in East Africa: New Sources (Archives, Manuscripts and Written Historical Sources. Oral History. Archaeology),* BS Amoretti, editor pp.385-410. Herder, Rome.

WALSHAW, SARAH C.
2010   Converting to rice: urbanization, Islamization and crops on Pemba Island, Tanzania, ad 700-1500. *World Archaeology* 42(1)137-154.

WERTZ, BRUNO EJS
1997   Maritime Archaeology. In *Encyclopaedia of Precolonial Africa,* Joseph O. Vogel, editor, pp. 558-560. Altimira Press, Walnut Creek, London and New Delhi.

WESTERDAHL, CHRISTER
1992   The Maritime Cultural Landscape. *The International Journal of Nautical Archaeology* 21:5-14.

WESTERDAHL, CHRISTER
1994   Maritime Cultures and Ship Types: Brief comments on the significance of Maritime Archaeology. *The International Journal of Nautical Archaeology* 23(4):265-270.

1998   The Maritime Cultural Landscape: On the concept of the traditional zones of transport geography, Nordic Underwater Archaeology <http://www.abc.se/~m10354/publ/cult-land.htm>.

2005   Seal on Land, Elk on Sea: Notes on the Applications of the Ritual Landscape at the Seaboard. *The International Journal of Nautical Archaeology* 34(1):2-23.

2007   'Horses are Strong at Sea': The liminal aspects of the Maritime Cultural Landscape, Global origins and development of seafaring. pp 139-153. Cambridge.

WILLIS, JUSTIN
1993   *Mombasa, The Swahili and the making of the Mijikenda.* Clarendon Press, Oxford.

1984. Old Slip and Cruger's Wharf at New York: An Archaeological Perspective of the Colonial American Waterfront. *Historical Archaeology* 18(1):15–37.

PAUL R. HUEY

Old Slip and Cruger's Wharf at New York: An Archaeological Perspective of The Colonial American Waterfront

ABSTRACT

In 1969 the removal of an entire block of filled land adjacent to Old Slip in Manhattan during construction of a new building revealed a sequence of soil deposits dating from about 1690 to 1800. Sampling of these soil layers indicated deposition during successive periods of land filling in the area, before and after the construction of Cruger's Wharf at this location in 1739 and 1740. Old Slip provides an example of a type of Dutch-influenced waterfront development beginning in the late 17th century that contrasts with development of the waterfront in Boston, Philadelphia, and other cities initially settled by the English. Colonial American city waterfront development differed distinctively, on the other hand, from English precedents.

Old Slip and the New York Waterfront

For years after its capture by the English in 1664, New York city retained many of its Dutch characteristics. As a major colonial trading port, the city developed a distinctive system of slips, or inlets, along its shoreline. A road or street usually ran inland from each slip so that the slip served as a canal-like extension of the street (Figure 1). As the blocks of intervening land along the shoreline were filled in, a heavy log cribbing was built in line with the slips to hold back the fill. Thus, as the shoreline was filled, the slips were extended as inlets between the blocks of new land. Usually the slips were maintained for no more than one block inland in length.

The shoreline of lower Manhattan in the area that later became the southwest side of Old Slip was settled probably as early as 1655 by Abraham Martens Clock, who was previously a carpenter in Rensselaerswyck, located up the Hudson River near Albany. In 1656, Clock was granted a water lot that extended into the river. By the summer of 1660, he had built a large house facing the river as well as a smaller house for his son facing the present-day Hanover Square (Stokes 1916:II, 323).

On the maps of 1728 and 1735 (Figures 1 and 2), the original shore line and house of Abraham Martens Clock were approximately one block inland northwest of Old Slip. The formation and extension of the slip by means of land fill on each side of it had commenced by 1695, as shown on Miller's map of that year (Figure 3). By 1716 the additional block of filled land was virtually complete between Dock [Pearl] Street at Hanover Square and Water Street. The view drawn about 1716 by William Burgis (Figure 4) shows a row of new houses overlooking the quay along Water Street, with a large house at the south corner of the Old Slip inlet and Water Street. The quay along Water Street, including "Hunters Key," ran in a nearly straight northeast-southwest direction (Figure 1). It is within this block of filled land that excavations were directed by Arnold Pickman, Diana Rockman, and Nan Rothschild in 1981 (Rothschild 1982:26–27).

In 1739 Henry Cruger, Henry Cuyler, and their partners hired an Albany builder named Adam van Alen to construct a huge wharf of 30-foot timbers along the waterfront beginning 170 feet from Clock's corner at Old Slip and extending southwestward parallel to Water Street. Every 20 feet a cedar post was set into the wharf for tying up ships (Stokes 1916:IV, 561). Cruger's Wharf was finished in 1740 (Figure 5), and it enclosed an area that was subsequently filled between it and the shore at Water Street. In 1754 Cruger widened the Wharf about four feet, and a map made in 1755 shows this area enclosed and partly filled (Stokes 1916:IV, 649; Stokes 1915:pl. 34). The plan surveyed in 1765 and 1766 by John Montresor shows the block entirely enclosed and filled (Figure 6) (Montresor 1775).

Henry Cuyler, one of the partners, died in 1770, and from 1771 to 1773, Henry Cruger petitioned with little success to receive water lots extending from the Wharf southeast into the river (Anon.

FIGURE 1. Detail of the Manhattan shoreline from "Plan of the City of New York In the Year 1735," showing the system of slips and the location of Old Slip (Stokes 1915 pl. 30). The circle is drawn around locations of the houses of Abraham Martens Clock and his son in the 17th century. I.N. Phelps Stokes Collection, Art, Prints and Photographs Division, The New York Public Library, Astor, Lenox and Tilden Foundations.

1905:324, 332, 339–40, 362–63, 410, 438–39; Scott 1970:105, 108). Henry Cruger was closely associated with Bristol merchants and had extensive interests in the West Indies. His son, Henry, served in Parliament for Bristol with Edmund Burke from 1774 to 1780. It is recorded that during one of Henry Cruger's campaign speeches, a New Yorker happened to be present and shouted "huzzah for Old Slip!" (Van Schaack 1859:34). Henry, Sr., went to England in 1775, and he died in Bristol in 1780 (Van Schaack 1859). In 1778, a fire in the area of his Wharf had consumed 64 houses,

three ships, storehouses, and at least one dwelling (Scull 1882:126, 508).

Front Street eventually replaced Cruger's Wharf. The filling of Old Slip had commenced by 1784, and in 1791 "Persons in the neighborhood" proposed in a petition to continue Front Street across it (Anonymous 1917:34–38, 75, 97, 99, 106, 161, 310, 641, 643). Finally, by 1797 filling had continued along the shore southeast of Front Street, and the new waterfront was characterized by the numerous piers and wharves that projected into the river and replaced the old slips and the

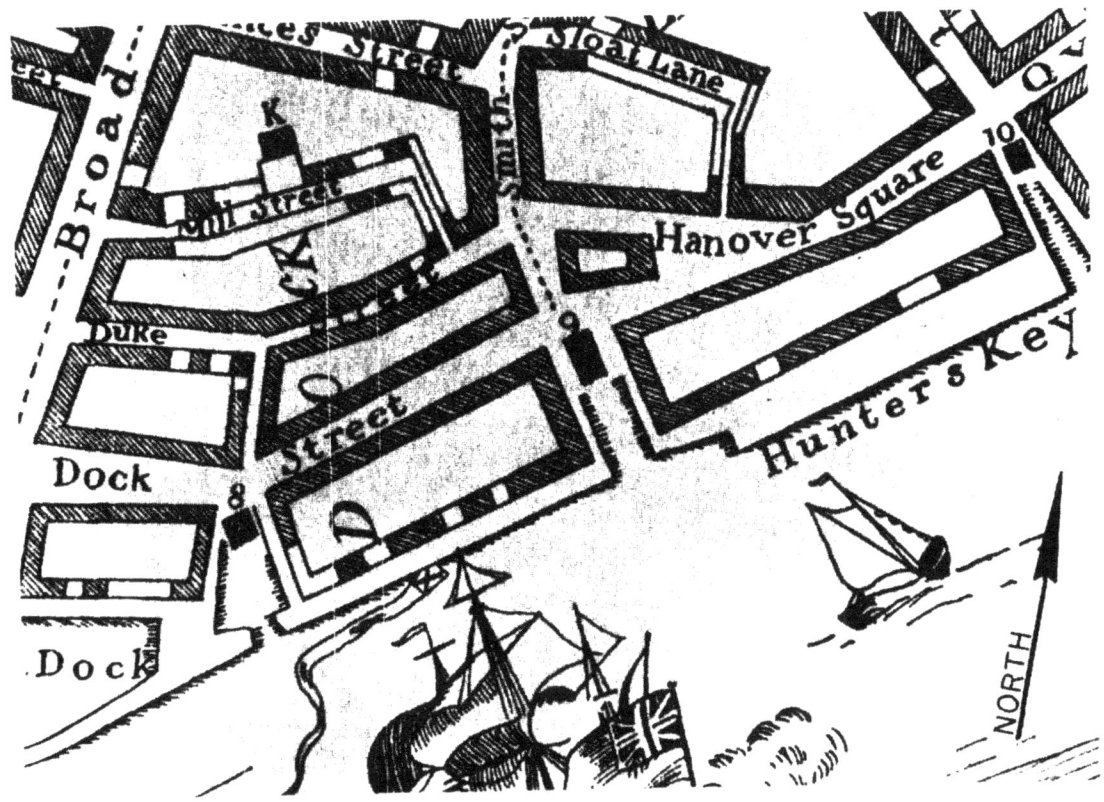

FIGURE 2. Detail of Old Slip (at number 9) from a plan of New York City about 1728 (Anon. 1898:262–63)

wharves that had paralleled the shoreline (Stokes 1915:pl. 64).

Archaeological Investigation of the Cruger's Wharf Area

When a new building was constructed by the Uris Corporation at Old Slip and Water Street in 1969, a large area of historic landfill was excavated to an immense depth, below the original bottom of the river. Workmen and relic collectors began finding a variety of artifacts including a bow of a small boat. Bottles were discovered that included types produced from about 1675 through the 19th century. One large round bottle bore a seal impressed with the words "Henry/Cuyler/Iun.'/1750." Another bottle seal fragment was inscribed

"16 . . . /A. Schuyler." Intact bottles included one example made probably between about 1685 and 1715 and an even earlier bottle dating ca. 1675–1690, based on its form (Noël Hume 1961:99, nos. 4 and 7).

Fortunately it became possible in September 1969 to make arrangements with the Uris Corporation to allow the New York State Historic Trust (now the Division for Historic Preservation in the New York State Office of Parks, Recreation and Historic Preservation) to conduct limited archaeological work at the site. The entire block southeast of Water Street contained vast quantities of significant colonial material that were rapidly destroyed by the construction work. By the time arrangements for archaeological salvage were made, only one access ramp into the hole remained

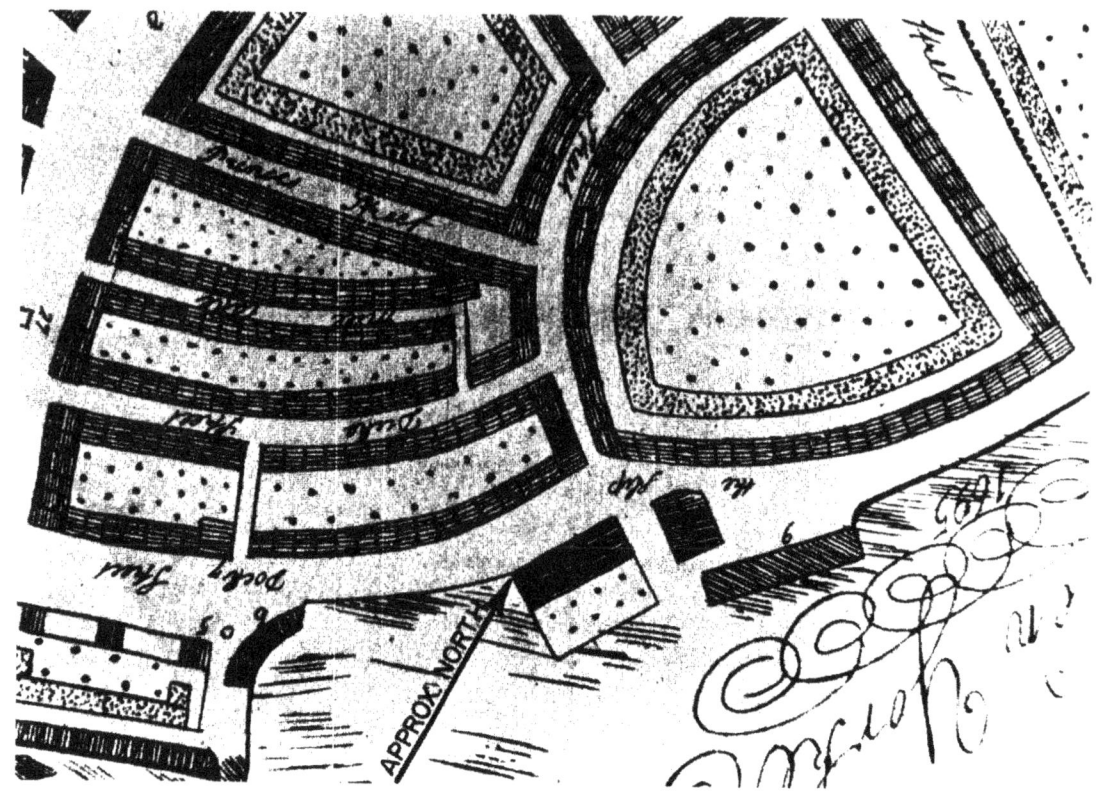

FIGURE 3. Detail of Old Slip ("the Slip") from the map of New York drawn in 1695 by Reverend John Miller (Valentine 1853:226–27)

where the original layers of the soil profile could still be observed and recorded.

In the process of cleaning and measuring this profile, many artifacts in stratigraphic association were unearthed. The original log crib footing under the northeast end of Cruger's Wharf built in 1740 at Old Slip was clearly visible (Figure 7). Measurement of the site revealed that this footing extended to a point 175 feet southeast from Water Street along the original line of Old Slip. The 20-foot section of profile exposed through the fill was immediately southwest of the footing (Figure 8). Until the land filling between 1740 and ca. 1765, the area to the northwest was under water, and ships were moored here. The view in Figure 7 gives some idea of the scale of the Cruger's Wharf

pier footing and the scope of the excavated soil profile area on the ramp immediately to the right. A temporary datum level for the profile was established at the base of the nearby log pier footing (Figure 9).

Most noticeable in the soil profile was the reddish sand that represents the original river bottom. The same natural reddish sand deposit was visible to the northwest in the construction cut along Water Street, closer to the original shore and where the upper surface of the red sand had sloped up to 9 feet 6 inches above the datum level measured from the base of the log cribbing. The drawing of the soil profile reveals a series of strata that can be dated on the basis of historical documentation and associated artifacts. The gray sand dates

FIGURE 4 Detail from the "South Prospect" view of New York by William Burgis, ca. 1716 1718. Courtesy of I.N. Phelps Stokes Collection, Art, Prints and Photographs Division, The New York Public Library, Astor, Lenox and Tilden Foundations.

probably ca. 1650–ca. 1700 and represents deposition on the harbor bottom while the shore line was expanding from Dock Street to Water Street. Above this, the dense gray clay dates probably ca. 1700–ca. 1740, or until Cruger's Wharf was constructed if not slightly later. The wood chips deposited on the surface of this layer probably date from this construction. Until 1740, the area remained a harbor bottom. The next deposit is dense black clay and in part represents the gradual filling of the block inland from Cruger's Wharf, ca. 1740–ca. 1765 or later. These two layers, the dense gray clay dating from about 1700 to 1740 and the dense black clay dating from about 1740 to 1765, yielded a useful sequence of artifacts.

The many artifacts from the dense gray clay included a scratch blue white salt glazed stoneware saucer. The floral design on this saucer somewhat resembles that on scratch blue white salt glazed stoneware saucer fragments from Fort Ligonier (ca. 1758–1766) in Pennsylvania and at Wormslow Plantation in Georgia (ca. 1737–1790), but it is most similar to the design on a fragment from a mid-18th century British military site southwest of Fort Ligonier (Grimm 1970:156; Kelso 1979:118, nos. 3 and 4; Miller and Stone 1970:123, no. e). Another white salt glazed stoneware saucer from the same stratum is undecorated. Other artifacts included a nearly intact medicine bottle of pale green glass, the spout from a Jackfield ware teapot, and sherds of buff-bodied earthenware decorated with combed brown slip and lead

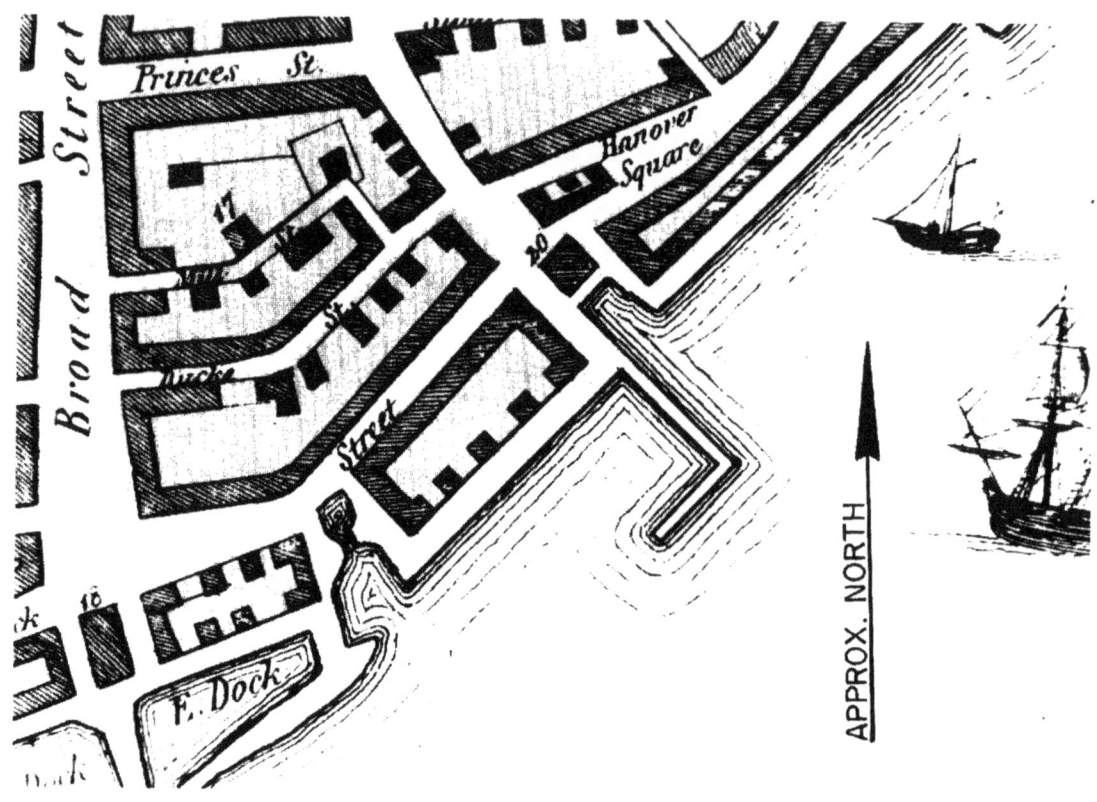

FIGURE 5. Detail from a plan of the city and environs of New York in 1742–1744 showing Cruger's Wharf (Grim n.d.).

glazed. Two types of this decorated "yellow ware" occurred: one type was decorated by means of combing through a buff slip coating to a brown slip layer, and the other type was decorated by direct application of brown slip prior to the lead glazing. While dated examples of this combed ware exist from as early as the 1680s, in 1750 it was being imported to New York directly from Liverpool and Bristol. Gerard Beekman wrote in 1750 from New York that "it Cost 8/6 in Bristol but the Same Sort of Yeallow ware with Small black dashes on it Comes also from Liverpool at 2/ Sterling a Crate less then they Cost at Bristol and the Crates Larger" (Hodgkin and Hodgkin 1973:16; White 1956:115). The medicine bottle was slightly conical in form and probably represents a transition from the type illustrated by

Noël Hume from a context of ca. 1660 and the type also recovered from the wreck of a British warship sunk in 1703 (Noël Hume 1970:73, no. 7; Perkins 1979:Fig. 6, no. 15). The scratch blue white salt glazed stoneware saucer and the Jackfield ware probably date very shortly before or about 1740, at the end of the dense gray clay deposition time period (Godden 1965:xiv; Mayes 1972:71; Mountford 1971:48). They are among the most recent dateable objects in this deposit and thus provide a *terminus post quem* date no earlier than ca. 1740 which, however, closely coincides with the documentary record.

The next stratum above was dense black clay, a deposit largely associated with Cruger's Wharf. The dense black clay was very thick and sticky and smelled of decaying organic matter. Artifacts in-

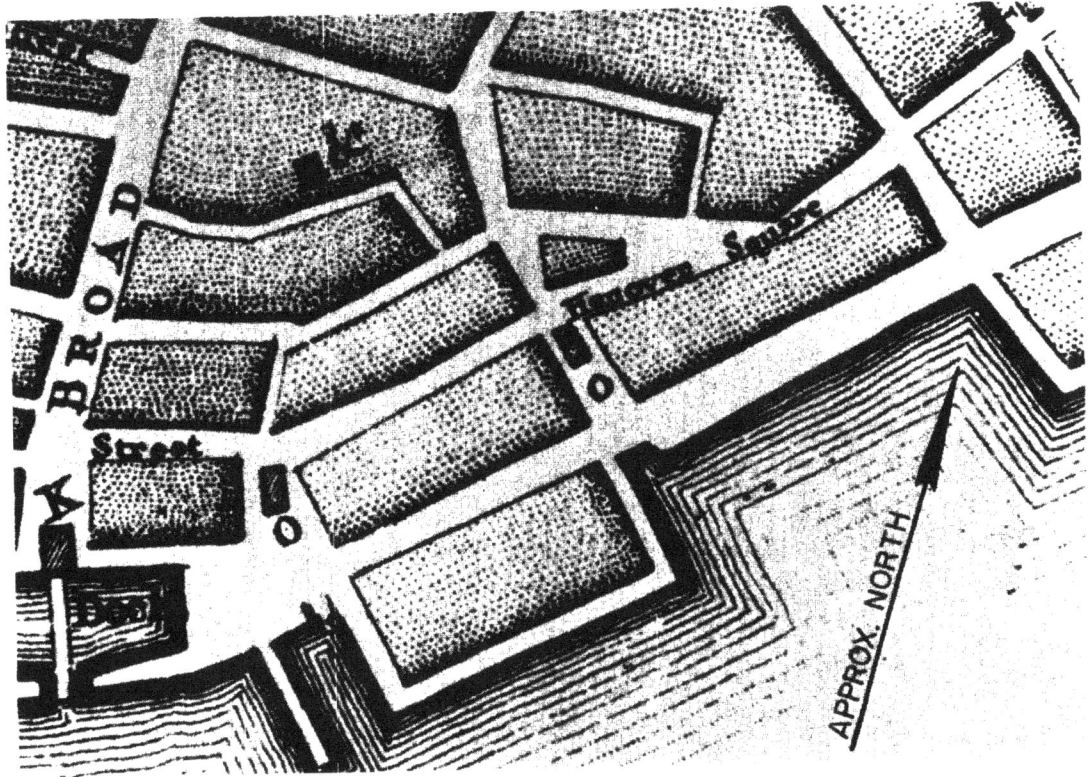

FIGURE 6. Detail from the plan by John Montresor. surveyed in 1765 and 1766 and published in London in 1775 (Montresor 1775).

cluded glass, ceramics, and preserved pieces of ship rigging such as bits of rope and pulley sheaves. The lead glass was frequently discolored to a smokey black because of its contact with the strong, caustic soil. Some of the ceramics were manufactured probably earlier than 1740. One sherd is a buff earthenware plate fragment decorated with "joggled" buff, tan, and brown slip (Goring 1981:10, 14). This plate had once been crudely mended with a black tar-like substance applied along a broken edge. It dates probably from within the first four decades of the 18th century. Similar examples have been found in England at Burslem in Staffordshire (Mountford 1967:22, 25) and at a warehouse site in Norwich, Norfolk (Jennings 1981:104–05). In other American ports it has appeared in contexts predating

1740 at Brunswick Landing, New Jersey, and at Port Royal, Jamaica (Grossman 1982:IV-51, 52, VII-8, 9, pl. V.1.1-10b, pl. V.1.1.-18d; Mayes 1972:53, 76–77, nos. 27, 29). Sherds have been found in the Hudson Valley at the Van Wyck house in Fishkill, built in 1732 (Cartwright n.d.:47), and at the Schuyler Flatts site in an 18th century stratum and at the De Ridder-Vandenburgh house in an occupation zone dating ca. 1720–1790, both excavated by the author and both located in Albany County. A broken Chinese porcelain bowl from the dense black clay dates probably from the 1720s or 1730s (Frank 1969:62–63). Duplicates have been excavated in Kenya on the east African coast (Sassoon 1978:128–29), and in New York state at the early 18th century Requa House site in Tarrytown (Brennan 1980) and at

FIGURE 7 View of the Uris construction site in September 1969 looking eastward from beside Water Street toward Old Slip and the log cribbing for Cruger's Wharf.

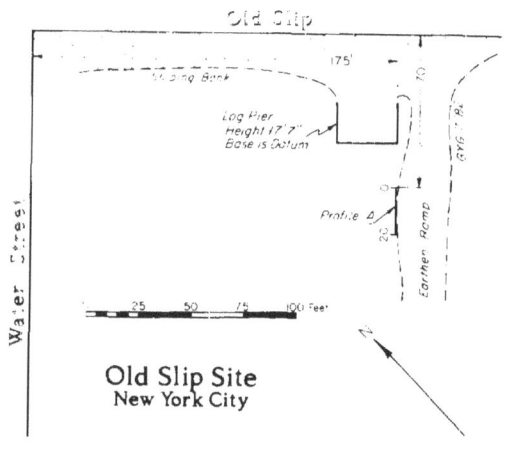

FIGURE 8. Plan of the Old Slip site in September 1969

Crown Point in Fort St. Frédéric. built by the French in the 1730s and now a State Historic Site. On the other hand. a larger blue decorated Chinese porcelain bowl that was also found seems perfectly typical of the period 1750 to 1775 (Jolliffe 1973:14, no. 7; Miller and Stone 1970:85, no. a).

The artifacts in the dense black clay demonstrate the introduction and first appearance of molded white salt glazed stoneware plates at this site after 1740. These were probably parts of shipments sent to Cruger's Wharf from England. Included are examples of the bead and reel pattern and the dot. diaper. and basket pattern. as well as a variety of the barley pattern (Noël Hume 1970:116. nos. 1 and 2). The barley pattern variation is an alternating seed with basket and wavy line rim pattern. It appears on an oval dish modelled by Aaron Wood

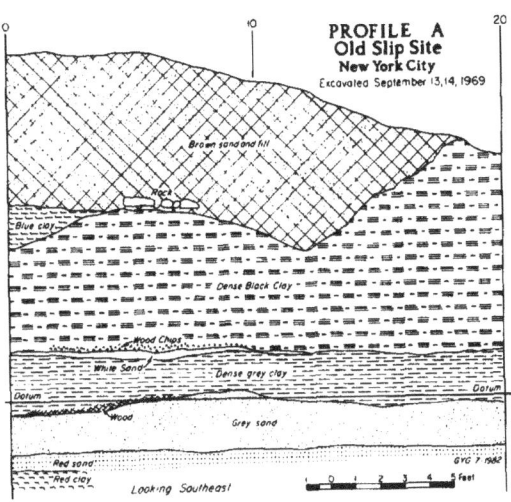

PROFILE A
Old Slip Site
New York City
Excavated September 13,14, 1969

FIGURE 9. Exposed and cleaned northwest face of the soil profile at Old Slip, September 1969.

of Burslem in 1760 (Mountford 1971:47, pl. 152). White salt glazed plate fragments with this pattern have been excavated at Burslem, at Port Royal, Jamaica, at Fort Stanwix and at Johnson Hall both in the Mohawk Valley of New York, and at Fort Montgomery in the Hudson River Highlands (Hanson and Ping Hsu 1975:32, 121, no. e; Mountford 1967:22, no. 6; Mayes 1972:69, no. 13). Sir William Johnson built and occupied Johnson Hall in 1763, but in 1769 his agent at New York advised him to purchase the "new fashioned" creamware rather than the "Common White" wares that were neither any longer fashionable nor available in the quantity Johnson had ordered (Flick 1931:173). The Fort Stanwix specimen is from a context dating after 1764. Excavations by John H. Mead at Fort Montgomery, built by the Americans in 1776 and destroyed in 1777, have produced numerous ceramics, including this type and pattern, that must have been "old fashioned" by 1776.

Colonial trade patterns are also suggested by many of the other artifacts at the site, such as a clay pipe bowl perhaps made by John Bryant of Bristol (Walker 1977:1073–75) or some other Bristol maker with the same initials who also supplied similar pipes that were excavated at Port Royal, Jamaica (Mayes 1972:113, no. 30). These artifacts represent not only part of a definite, dateable material sequence observed at this site, but many can be associated with historic Cruger's Wharf and the goods that were shipped there in the 18th century.

The material at Cruger's Wharf and Old Slip clearly suggests a predominant trade connection with Bristol and the west of England. Cruger's Wharf was constructed at the beginning of the War of the Austrian Succession, following a period of vastly increased demand worldwide for English manufactured goods and products (Kroll 1971: 145, 153, 166; O'Callaghan 1855:559–61; Rogers 1970:144, 163; Shelvocke 1930:118–19). Actively protected and cultivated by Queen Anne and Governor Hunter during the previous French war, the import of English-made goods to New York had grown in an atmosphere of sharp trade rivalry that involved the colonies of France and Spain (Bonomi 1971:81–87; Brown 1935:321–22, 328; O'Callaghan 1855:559–61). It is with this increased concentration of English goods, perhaps, that there had occurred by 1730 what Bonomi has characterized as a sectional realignment in which landed merchants elsewhere in the colony relied less on partnerships with a few large New York importers and more often imported directly from England using agents or sometimes family members located in New York (Bonomi 1971:101). The question remains whether New York interests, instead, may have been increasingly represented by the growing number of free traders with sloops and small land holdings that extended up the Hudson Valley in this period.

Waterfront sites in New York City such as Cruger's Wharf and Old Slip, as archaeological resources, include not only landfill deposits but also deeper strata that were evidently deposited on the harbor bottom before and perhaps during the initial land filling process. The numerous unbroken bottles, intact or nearly intact ceramic vessels, pieces of ships' rigging, intact leather shoes, and other complete objects suggest that portions of imported cargoes as well as personal items were frequently lost or discarded overboard during usual waterfront activities. The remarkably high artifact density revealed in the scraping of a single profile cut not only indicates the intensity of activity at Cruger's Wharf and in the harbor but also indicates the need for carefully controlled excavation and sampling procedures at all levels. If such sites are properly studied, they may hold the key to understanding New York not only as a colonial distribution center reaching far inland but also its relation to other ports along the eastern seaboard. Through careful analysis of types and specific attributes of artifacts retrieved from stratified, dateable river bottom layers such as under or near Cruger's Wharf, it may be possible to determine changing patterns of trade involving the goods imported to New York by geographical distribution based on comparison with data from other sites.

FIGURE 10. Village of Goedereede on the Island of Goeree in South Holland. Courtesy of Consulate General of The Netherlands

The Colonial American Waterfront: Origins and Development

Dutch Seaports

The waterfront of New York typified by slips in the colonial period may represent Dutch influence. Nearly every slip was located at a street that led into the city from the waterfront, suggesting the channeling of water into developed areas that is also typical of Dutch land use (Figure 10). An English traveller in Rotterdam in 1668 noted "The Heads or Keyes between which we entred the towne by water are handsome, and Ships of great burden are received into the middle of divers streets without difficulty, (their Channels being deep and large)" (Brown 1677:2–3). When John Smeaton toured South Holland in 1755, he observed at Brielle that "The Heads of Jettys at the mouth [of the port] are wood piles, drove near each other, as is done every where in the Low Countries; the whole port being a canal, as is generally the case in Holland. . . ." Around Zaandam in North Holland he noted that "the ground is in general laid out in long slips" so that small vessels carrying goods had access to mills. Between Haarlem and Amsterdam in the River Ij he saw "a little harbour for fishing Boats, constructed in the form of a T; so that let the wind come which way it would the boats would lay quiet on one side or

other. It was composed of 2 Rows of piles, & filled between with light seaweed" (Smeaton 1938:35–36, 40, 53). In Gelderland, at Culemborg, Blaeu's engraving of 1648 shows, in addition to a town harbor, a small square slip for ships cut into the bank of the River Lek directly opposite a main city gate that faced the river (Bacon 1967:149).

The view of Amsterdam in 1544 by Cornelis Anthoniszoon (Figure 11) shows canals such as the Oude Zijds Voorburg Wal leading into the heart of the city and providing maximum access to the waterfront. The harbor front was cut off from the Ij by a double row of pilings interrupted with several openings for ships to pass through. Creation of new land was a continuous process in Amsterdam, and by 1605 the quiet harbor of the Lastage shipyard shown in the 1544 view had become land. By 1625 additional new blocks of land in the form of islands separated by canals were created; Realen Island (Figure 12) was an example of such a block. In some cases delays resulted from land speculation. The new land was contained within quay walls constructed at private expense by the owners under supervision of the city. The city shared expenses for bridgeheads and the streets which appeared along the quays (De Roever n.d.:31; Reinders 1981:256–57).

A double row of pilings continued to be used to close off the harbor at the time of Smeaton's visit in much the same fashion as it had 200 years ear-

Perspectives from *Historical Archaeology* and *ACUA Proceedings*

FIGURE 11. Detail from the view of Amsterdam in 1544 by Cornelis Anthoniszoon, showing the Oude Zijds Voorburg Wal, Schreierstoren, and part of the Lastage shipyards.

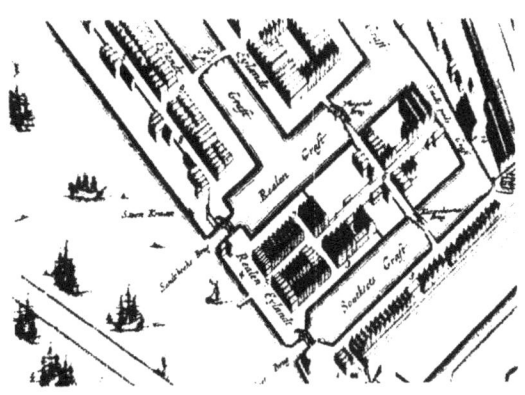

FIGURE 12. Detail of the Realen Island from a map of Amsterdam engraved about 1725 by Gerred de Broen. Reprinted by Bureau Voorlichting Amsterdam de V.V.V. Amsterdam.

lier. The double piling curtain evidently offered shelter and protection for the unloading of goods, but the quiet water also caused sediment to settle and fill the harbor. Although by 1674 the situation had become so serious that special studies and dredging projects were initiated (Reinders 1981:257), in 1755 Smeaton recorded that

> The Shipping lays wholy out of the Town in the Tye, no vessels of size being capable of getting into the canals within the Town. . . . All along the Key, at a small distance from the Shore, are drove double rows of piles to which the Ships fasten; and some lay within and some without; and also serve as some sort of defence from the surf which in some Winds troubles them not a little.

He explained that large ships not only were prevented from entering the city canals by the shallowness but also because of the maximum 26-foot length of the sluice locks (Smeaton 1938:38).

New Amsterdam and New York

The town of New Amsterdam had soon emulated its Old World namsake with its development of a canal in the 17th century. Some time before 1633 the Heere Gracht was constructed as a canal in present Broad Street (Stokes 1916:IV, 78). The sheet piling with which it was lined had to be replaced in 1654, but it was not filled in until 1676. The Heere Gracht extended in a broad curve from the waterfront to about present Beaver Street, and from there it was continued to Wall Street with the pretentious name of Prinsen Gracht, also borrowed from old Amsterdam (Stokes 1915:122, 153, 210).

Stuyvesant, meanwhile, in 1648 or 1649 had constructed a small projecting wooden pier at Schreyers Hook near the tip of Manhattan (Stokes 1915:122), and by 1660 a second pier had been built just to the east, at the Custom House. Between the two a basin was formed, and in January 1676 plans were made to enlarge it as "The Great Dock." Completed by 1679, the Great Dock consisted of two curving quay walls of wood that enclosed a basin divided into a West Dock and an East Dock by a central projecting pier. The Great Dock remained a prominent water-front feature through the remainder of the colonial period (Stokes 1915:pl. 13, pl. 17, 209, 225).

The projecting piers of the Great Dock were connected to a linear quay wall of sheet piling that had been commenced as early as 1656 along the eroding beach (Stokes 1915:pl. 17, 121, 225). The Danckaerts view of 1679 shows the Heere Gracht completely filled, and the quay wall continues northeast to a point beyond Old Slip. Already the formation of Old Slip had begun, as a deliberate break in the quay wall opening into a narrow inlet possibly in the process of being excavated as a short canal or as a sloping ramp to the water's edge (Stokes 1915:pl. 17).

Construction of the Great Dock in the 1670s coincided with the entry of London merchants into the New York market and the arrival of ships direct from London (Ritchie 1977:114–15). Archdeacon

has shown, however, that economically the Dutch continued to dominate New York City through the 1670s (Archdeacon 1976:40). The city nevertheless underwent a transformation in the 1680s and 1690s. French Huguenot refugees joined the English, whom they resembled socially and with whom they allied themselves politically, and they established important trade connections with family members in places such as Boston and Bristol. By 1703 the English and their French Protestant allies had replaced the Dutch as the economically dominant group (Archdeacon 1976:41, 48, 57, 73). Reverend John Miller on his map in 1695 clearly documented some of the major changes that were occurring in the 1680s and 1690s. Showing the Great Dock as "The Old Dock," he recorded "The New Docks" as large, regular block areas enclosed within new wharves or quay walls built out from the old shore line in the area northeast of Old Slip. Narrow channels remained between each block, continuing the streets on land (Stokes 1915:pl. 23, 235). With Old Slip as the first, construction of other slips soon followed along the waterfront in the 1690s:Coenties Slip, Van Clyff's (Burling) Slip, Theobald's Slip, Fly Market Slip, Broad Street Slip. More slips were then built during the first four decades of the 18th century. The increasingly wealthy English merchants as well as landed merchants of Dutch background rushed to acquire land in the large new blocks. By 1703 the English and French in these new areas were in the majority, except at Burger's Path (Old Slip) which nevertheless ranked as the wealthiest street in 1703. In 1703 the Dutch inhabitants of more ordinary wealth filled the older, inner blocks of land (Archdeacon 1976:83–89).

This process of creating new land along the waterfront repeated itself through most of the 18th century, although maintenance of the slips often created problems. Cadwallader Colden explained in 1745 that

all along the shoar from one end of the Town to the other there is a continuation of wharfs to which the ships lay their sides except at the ends of those streets which run nearly perpendicular to the river & terminate upon the river where the wharfs are discontinued & Gaps left called Slips into which the Periaguas & small Vessels enter & unload & here at the ends of these streets the Market places are built. These slips are likewise the common shores into which all the filth & nastiness of the town & streets is emptied . . . (Colden 1937:329).

In 1757 William Smith observed, also, that "The City has, in reality, no natural bason or harbour. The ships lie off in the road, on the East side of the town, which is docked out, and better built than the West side . . . " (Smith 1972:201).

Maps from 1766 and 1767 reveal the beginnings of New York's final phase of waterfront development. Since the time of Smith's description, a new type of feature had begun to appear. These were projecting piers or wharves in the northeast corner of the town, extending from the shore along Water Street beginning northeast of Burling Slip but not built in line with the existing slips (Stokes 1915:pl. 34, pl. 40, pl. 42). Finally, as the process of land creation continued, the slips were mostly filled in the 1780s and 1790s, and the old slips became lost among the narrow, projecting piers between docks that dominated the entire waterfront by 1797.

Other American Ports

The waterfront that was typical of most of New York in the 18th century until the Revolution is unlike the distinctive waterfront development pattern of many other American port cities and towns that were initially settled by the English, where projecting piers or wharves were built into the harbors. Only in the 1790s did New York begin more closely and fully to conform to the pattern established elsewhere. Plans of Newport, Rhode island, for example, as early as 1758 show many projecting wharves in the harbor, crowded along the waterfront (Downing and Scully 1967:34) (Figure 13). Boston had similar wharves in the 17th and 18th centuries (Figure 14), as did Philadelphia (Figure 15). The wharves of Norfolk, Virginia, in 1728 were built of long pine logs laid from the shore to the edge of the channel and tied together with cross beams (Boyd 1967:36–37). Projecting wharves were built in the harbor of Canso in Nova Scotia, established between 1732 and 1742 by Edward How, a Boston merchant (Ferguson, et al.

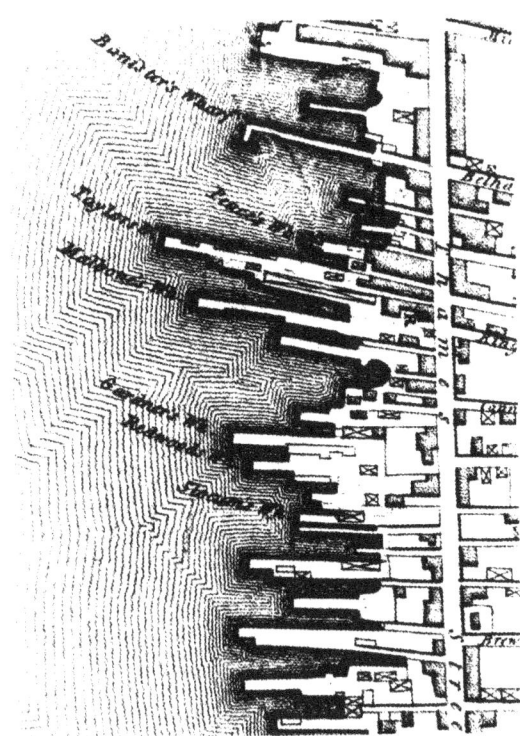

FIGURE 13. Detail from the plan of Newport by Charles Blaskowitz (1777). Courtesy of New York State Library, Albany, New York.

1981:13). One, which was destroyed by the French in 1744, was "built with stone and timber ninety feet long and fifty feet wide at the front" (Flemming 1977:130).

Carl Bridenbaugh has carefully documented the history of waterfronts and wharf construction in Philadelphia, Boston, Newport, New York, and Charleston (Bridenbaugh 1966:23–24, 170–74, 325–28). Boston, he notes, surpassed other colonial ports in terms of activity and development. Surrounded by shallow water and marshy ground, Boston rapidly expanded as wharves were built and land was filled. The grant to Captain Benjamin Gillam in 1668 "to wharfe before his owne ground adjoyninge to his dwelling house" was typical of many. By 1671 the houses along the waterfront were "for the most part raised on the Sea-banks and wharfed out with great industry and cost, many of them standing upon piles, close together

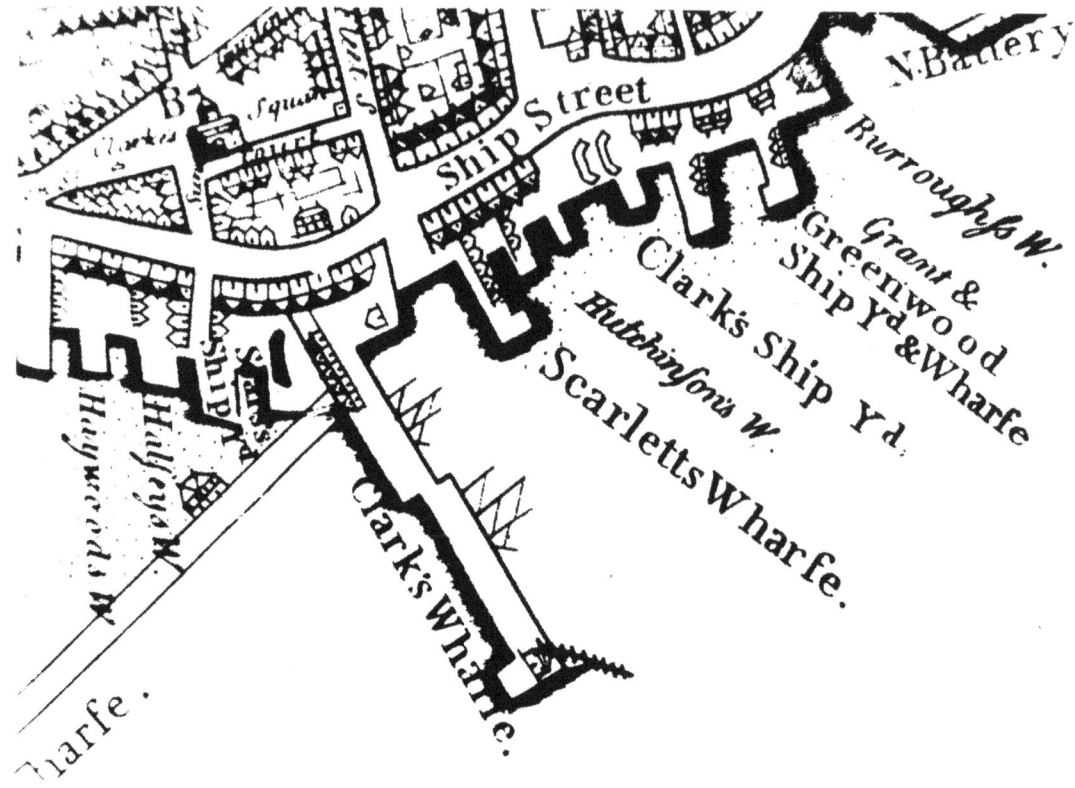

FIGURE 14. Detail of the Boston waterfront from the map by Captain John Bonner in 1722 (Bonner 1835).

FIGURE 15. Detail of the Philadelphia waterfront, ca. 1760, by George Heap (Heap ca. 1760). Courtesy of New York State Library, Albany, New York.

on each side of the streets as in London . . . '' (Whitehill 1963:11, 15, 18).

The irregular shoreline of Boston wharves attested to its rapid development. While most of the docks were created between the narrow, irregular projecting wharves and piers such as appear on the Bonner map of 1722, the Town Dock served as a large slip or inlet extending to Dock Square and was developed probably as early as 1641. South of this a second cove was dug in 1643 and apparently still existed inland from Oliver's Dock in 1769 (Bridenbaugh 1966:23; Whitehill 1963:11, 45). In the 1730s ''Town Slips'' also existed at the foot of Wood Lane and of North Street. The Town Slip at North Street became a ferry landing in 1734, and in 1738 the Town Slip at the foot of Wood Lane was filled in and a wharf built across it (Anon. 1885:85, 168, 191, 202).

The crowded, projecting wharves and piers that characterized most American seaports except for New York in the 17th and 18th centuries appear to have been a uniquely American innovation. English harbors, large and small, rarely if ever developed such a waterfront system. Excavations in London have revealed massive timber quays built by the Romans in the 1st, 2nd, and 3rd centuries that ran parallel to the river bank for great distances. One section of quay consisted of open timber framed boxes, planked over, that must have floated up and down with the tide. In other areas the quay wall was anchored to the old foreshore with timber tiebacks. The archaeological evidence of cargoes indicates that one area was used by ships unloading Rhenish pottery. In two locations the traces of small jetties that projected (one at least 16 feet) into the river have been found, and at another place the quay turned inland, perhaps forming an inlet, but in each case the evidence is fragmentary (Anon. 1982; Bateman and Locker 1982:204; Miller 1977:50; Miller 1982:143–45, 147; Schofield and Miller 1976:392–95; Tatton-Brown 1974:155–57).

Medieval revetments of the 12th to the 15th centuries in London also varied in construction but generally paralleled the previous shoreline. Some of these timber revetments were braced front and back, while other sections were braced only in front, into the river (Hillam and Herbert 1980:439, 444). The waterfront in this period became structurally more varied and less regular than in Roman times as each occupant built his own section of wharf with stairs leading down to the foreshore at low tide. The quay wall of ca. 1440, however, was built of stone. A quay wall excavated in Amsterdam from the first half of the 14th century was also constructed of stone, and in London at Blackfriars a 14th century stone-lined dock or inlet in the waterfront that was filled ca. 1480 has been found (Baart, et al, 1977:58; Bloice 1974:133; Schofield and Dyson 1980:50–53).

The Medieval London waterfront included a number of inlets that functioned as docks of various sizes where one or two ships could enter at high tide. Of the three such inlets, or water gates, of major significance, only Billingsgate and Queenhithe were the principal docks by 1600, and Billingsgate had surpassed Queenhithe in importance, according to Stow. Billingsgate, dating from the 15th century, is shown in a drawing about 1544 with two ships fitted tightly in it. The map by Braun and Hogenburg about 1580 shows Billingsgate and Queenhithe as the two noteworthy docks indented into an otherwise more or less continuous waterfront quay wall (Figures 16 and 17). The Ogilby and Morgan map of London in 1677 still shows Billingsgate as a rather spacious dock for large ships (Figure 18) (Anon. 1982; Schofield and Dyson 1980:52; Stow 1970:38–39, 41, 185, 314, 319–22).

The *Seaman's Grammar* of 1627 defines a wet dock as ''any place where you may hale in a ship into the oze out of the tides way, where shee may dock her selfe.'' A 1758 description of the Thames explained that ''Docks are small Harbours cut into the Land,'' and a dictionary of 1766 simply repeated the 1627 definition of dock (Anon. 1971:779–80; Bailey 1766). Docks were places where large ships could settle into the harbor bottom mud at low tide, and the extreme tidal range was thus the major factor that affected development of the English waterfront. A drawing by Hol-

FIGURE 16. Detail of the Queenhithe Dock from the map of London by Braun and Hogenburg about 1580. Greater London Council Publication 171.

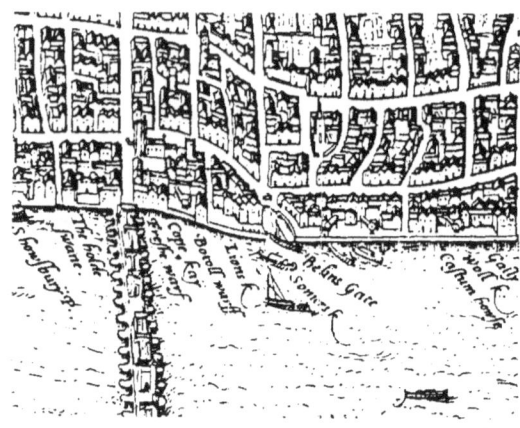

FIGURE 17. Detail of the Billingsgate Dock from the map of London by Braun and Hogenburg about 1580. Greater London Council Publication 171.

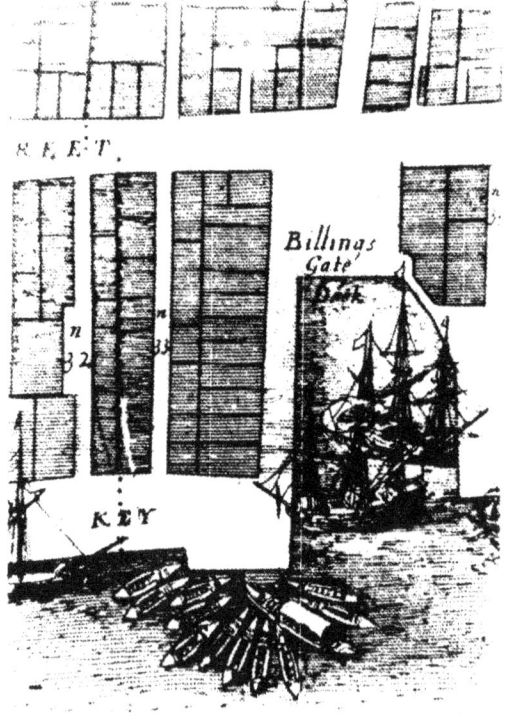

FIGURE 18. Detail of the Billingsgate Dock from the map of London by Ogilby and Morgan in 1677 (Anon. 1982)

lar in the 1640s shows the quay wall at Lambeth with a narrow, projecting, stationary wooden pier or jetty constructed across the river foreshore sloping down to the water's edge at low tide (Figure 19). Hollar also drew a view of the Milford Stairs, an example of the permanent steps that were frequently constructed from the quay wall to provide access to the foreshore at low tide (Hind 1972:pl. IX, pl. X). Such structures, of course, were covered as the tide returned, and they were of limited utility except for access to very small boats. They may nevertheless have provided a limited precedent for the development of American wharves.

With its single quay wall and in the absence of a system of projecting wharves, the harbor of Torquay, Devon (Figure 20), is in many ways typical of small English harbors, and its harbor bottom is completely exposed at low tide (Doone 1950:29). Such harbors were typically surrounded by a wall or quay to which vessels were tied. At the port of Bristol, ships tied to the quay tilted outward at an inconvenient angle at low tide (Little 1967:163). In most harbors ships were allowed to rest on the harbor bottom, in the mud flats. At a few British ports, such as Glasgow situated on a tidal river near its tidal limit or Southampton where the tidal range is sufficiently moderate, it is possible for open docks and river quays to serve for the accommodation of larger vessels (Vernon-Harcourt 1910:354). Glasgow and Southampton were not fully developed until the 19th century, however. In the 1830s the River Clyde at Glasgow was only three feet deep, and it was subsequently dredged to 28 feet (Baedeker 1901:524). Defoe in the 18th century found that despite its prosperous trade with America, Glasgow suffered from the extremes of disastrous floods to almost the complete dryness of the Clyde, depending on the season (Defoe 1971:604–06). Southampton as a port declined steadily in its maritime trade through the 16th and 17th centuries, and in describing Southampton's continuing decay in the 1720s, Defoe mentioned only its "spacious quay." The town revived with the opening of the Docks in the 19th century (Defoe 1971:154; Winbolt 1955:99).

It is remarkable that the first enclosed dock

FIGURE 19. View of the quay at Lambeth House by Wenceslaus Hollar, ca. 1646. Original drawing in The British Museum (Hind 1972:pl. IX).

FIGURE 20. View of the harbor at Torquay, Devon, ca. 1935.

lems and difficulties and severely limited the capacity of English harbors, while the lesser tides in America made it much easier to load and unload ships at dockside at all times.

Improvements in small English harbors usually consisted of quays along the shore line and one or two projecting masonry piers which also acted as breakwaters (Andrews 1973:119–21; Couch 1871:33–34) (Figure 21). While such piers in deep harbors obviously permitted large ships to stay afloat, they were expensive and difficult to construct, and because of the extreme range of the tide, difficulty of access to boats in deep water tied to a projecting pier at low tide is often evident (Figure 22).

While the scarcity of timber in England such as that used to construct Cruger's Wharf in New York or the wharves in Boston was probably also a major factor in the separate development of American and English ports, Defoe in the 1720s described gentlemen's estates in the immediate area of Southampton "so full of large full grown timber, that it seemed as if they wanted sale for it, and that it was of little worth to them" (Defoe 1971:153). Sailing past Margate in 1755, Smeaton observed

where ships could remain afloat was not built in England until 1715 at Liverpool (Anon. 1919:13, 99–100). Tides at New York rise only four or five feet, while tides in England are commonly 10 or 12 feet and sometimes 20 feet in the Thames and Mersey rivers (Albion 1970:220). The range of tides at London Bridge is about 16 or 17 feet (Bosworth 1913:21). The great height of tides and force of tidal currents in England caused endless prob-

FIGURE 21. View at low tide of the old harbor of Whitby, North Yorkshire, a major English seaport in the 18th century and home of Captain James Cook, R.N., F.R.S. Courtesy of the British Tourist Authority, London.

FIGURE 22. The harbor at Boscastle, Cornwall. *Country Life*, July 11, 1963.

that the port "seems chiefly formed by a Pier or Jetty of Wood" (Smeaton 1938:1). At Ostend, in present Belgium, he reported that the piers consisted of three rows of large piles, spaced and bolted together with cross beams, filled with rock to the low water mark, and paved on the top with sloping sides. This type of pier, he observed, resisted the force of waves much better than those of masonry (Smeaton 1938:12–13). He saw the same type of piers at Flushing (Smeaton 1938:20). Smeaton was particularly impressed by what he

saw in Belgium and the Netherlands, and such construction was apparently quite similar to the techniques used in New York and other American port cities in building quay walls and wharves. That such projecting piers also served as wharves is suggested by an English description of the Dutch colonial city of Batavia (in Indonesia) in 1713:

> There are also two large Peers, that run out about half a Mile into the Sea, and serve to drain all the Canals and Inland Water that run through the City. They are likewise very useful for small Vessels that lie along the Piles, where they load or unload their Cargoes (Beeckman 1973:24–25).

Summary and Conclusions

Emergency excavations at Old Slip in 1969 revealed a sequence of dateable fill layers from the original harbor bottom extending from the late 17th century until after the American Revolution. The artifacts and soil deposits can be correlated with episodes of land filling as well as harbor activity in neighboring areas and within the large block partially encompassed by Cruger's Wharf, built in 1739 and 1740.

The landfilling process demonstrated at New York, Boston, and many other American and European port cities is a nearly universal one. From the 12th to the 16th century, the London shoreline advanced in a series of roughly parallel quay walls distances of as much as 300 feet (Schofield and Dyson 1980:50). At Bergen, Norway, by the end of the Medieval period, the timber framed quay wall lay over 200 feet beyond the original shore line. Between ca. 1250 and 1550 more than 300 feet of land was reclaimed behind sheeted abutments and a jetty at Dordrecht (Baart, et al., 1977:28, 38–39). These distances were dwarfed by the scale and rate of landfill expansion that occurred in American colonial port cities, particularly Boston. Moreover, the relatively straight and continuous timber and stone quay walls parallel with the shore line at Amsterdam as at London and elsewhere are in many ways most similar to the type of waterfront that developed at New York. London had a limited number of docks that roughly correspond to New York's later slips, but the great regularity and control in the development of the expanding New York waterfront and its land areas would seem more closely to resemble the land development process in Amsterdam. Amsterdam in the 17th century greatly expanded in size with its creation of large blocks of new land such as Bickers, Realen, and Prinsen Islands in addition to the large new urban areas developed and divided into blocks by canals.

The landfill process and the rapid creation of slips in New York in the 1690s roughly corresponds to the ascendancy of English and French Huguenot mercantile interests over the mostly Dutch pro-Leisler interests (Archdeacon 1976:141–42). The limited but controlled sample from the Cruger's Wharf soil profile provides an abundance of English artifacts that attest to the full impact of English manufacturing and trade upon New York as elsewhere by the early 18th century. The mystery of New York's atypicality as a port among most other American seaports is perhaps not easily explained. Equally curious are some of the striking differences between English ports and those harbors developed in other American cities that were settled initially by the English. Klein has observed that contrasting with the South's dominantly bilateral and New England's heavily triangular trade patterns, the commerce of the Middle Colonies was partly triangular but more largely direct with Europe. The central focus of the question of New York's uniqueness, however, Klein believes is the great diversity of its population. It was this cultural diversity that tended to encourage moderation. There is historical evidence, nevertheless, that in the late 17th century New York was more highly stratified economically than either Boston or Philadelphia (Ritchie 1977:136). While the range of wealth was much more concentrated and less extreme in Philadelphia than in New York, both cities developed common councils that tended to be regarded as "exclusive and privileged" and were governed after the manner of English cities, according to Bridenbaugh (1966:145). In Boston, economic stratification had emerged by 1771 that was equal to that of New York in 1676. Despite the continuity of maritime enterprise in Boston, town government had entered into the hands of the elite after 1750 with the emergence of a new type of social system (Henretta 1965:81–83, 89–90).

New York's more highly stratified distribution of wealth by the late 17th century, combined with its strong common council that was established by charter in 1686, may be factors which directed its distincitve form of waterfront development during the late 17th and 18th century colonial period. The common council continued to seek powers not authorized in the 1686 charter, and in 1731 Governor Montgomerie granted a new charter which secured for the common council the extension of the city's borders to 400 feet beyond low-water mark on the Hudson and East rivers (Ellis, Frost, et al.:46). It is quite possible that New York's uniqueness and atypicality among other cities resulted, in part, from the ability of particular economic groups to maintain tight control through land development policies favorable to their own interests. In other cities a more open attitude may have prevailed, with less restraint on development. Additional historical as well as archaeological research and comparison will be necessary before these and other questions of cultural differences and relationships within New York and between New York and other port cities can be more fully studied and understood.

ACKNOWLEDGMENTS

The author extends special thanks to those individuals who have been of particular assistance in the preparation of this paper. Budd Wilson assisted with the maps, as did Jim Corsaro and other always-helpful staff members of the New York State Library. The late Ralph D. Phillips provided information on Henry Cruger and on English harbors. Nan Rothschild of Barnard College offered helpful suggestions and supplied information on excavations in 1979 and 1981 at Hanover Square, Pearl Street, and the Stadt Huys block, not far from Old Slip. John H. Mead of the Palisades Interstate Park Commission at Bear Mountain State Park generously shared data from his excavations at Fort Montgomery. Charlotte Wilcoxen, Research Associate at the Albany Institute of History and Art, helped identify the porcelain. In addition, many staff members of the Bureau of Historic Sites in the Division for Historic Preservation of the New York State Office of Parks, Recreation and Historic Preservation provided helpful suggestions and assistance. Gwyn Gillette prepared the drawings, Joe McEvoy and Jon Jameson assisted with photographs, and Kathleen Benac typed the manuscript. The site was initially reported by George Demmy of South Street Seaport, who also loaned equipment to the project, and Clayton Pauley assisted with the excavations and recording.

This paper in its original form was presented at the annual meeting of the Council for Northeast Historical Archeology held in October 1982 at Amherst, Massachusetts.

REFERENCES

ALBION, ROBERT GREENHALGH
1970 *The Rise of New York Port [1815–1860]*. David & Charles, Newton Abbot, Devon.

ANDREWS, JOHN H.
1973 The Thanet Seaports, 1650–1750. In *Essays in Kentish History*, edited by Margaret Roake and John Whyman, pp. 119–26. Frank Cass, London.

ANONYMOUS
1885 *A Report of the Record Commissioners of the City of Boston, Containing the Boston Records from 1729 to 1742*. Rockwell and Churchill, City Printers, Boston.
1898 *Third Annual Report of the State Historian of the State of New York, 1897*. Wynkoop Hallenbeck Crawford Co., State Printers, New York.
1905 *Minutes of the Common Council of the City of New York: 1675–1776* (Vol. VII). Dodd, Mead and Company, New York.
1917 *Minutes of the Common Council of the City of New York: 1784–1831* (Vol. I). Published by the City of New York, New York.
1919 *A Pictorial and Descriptive Guide to Liverpool, Birkenhead, Wallasey, The Wirral, Etc.* (Twelfth Ed.—Revised). Ward, Lock & Co., Limited, Warwick House, Salisbury Square, London.
1971 *The Compact Edition of The Oxford English Dictionary* (Vol. I). Oxford University Press, New York.
1982 Billingsgate Excavation. Museum of London folder. City of London Archaeological Trust, London.

ARCHDEACON, THOMAS J.
1976 *New York City, 1664–1710: Conquest and Change*. Cornell University Press, Ithaca.

BAART, JAN, WIARD KROOK, ET AL.
1977 *Opgravingen in Amsterdam*. Fibula-Van Dishoeck, Amsterdam.

BACON, EDMUND N.
1967 *Design of Cities*. The Viking Press, New York.

BAEDEKER, KARL
1901 *Great Britain*. Karl Baedeker, Publisher, Leipsic.

BAILEY, N.
1766 *An Universal Etymological English Dictionary*. Printed for T. Osborne, et al., London.

BATEMAN, NIC, AND ALISON LOCKER
1982 The Sauce of the Thames. *The London Archaeologist* 4 (8):204–07.

BEECKMAN, DANIEL
1973 *A Voyage to and from the Island of Borneo*. Barnes and Noble Books and Dawsons of Pall Mall, Folkestone, England.

BLASKOWITZ, CHARLES
1777 A Plan of the Town of Newport in Rhode Island. Publish'd by Willm. Faden, Charing Cross Septr. 1st. (New York State Library No. 7457).

BLOICE, BRIAN
1974 Excavation Round-up 1973. *The London Archaeologist* 2 (6):133–35.

BONNER, JOHN
1835 The Town of Boston in New England by Capt. John Bonner 1722. Engraved from a copy in the possession of Wm. Taylor Esq. and published by George G. Smith, Engraver, No. 91 Washington, opposite State Street, Boston.

BONOMI, PATRICIA U.
1971 *A Factious People: Politics and Society in Colonial New York*. Columbia University Press, New York.

BOSWORTH, G. F.
1913 *Cambridge County Geographies: Middlesex*. At the University Press, Cambridge.

BOYD, WILLIAM K. (EDITOR)
1967 *William Byrd's Histories of the Dividing Line Betwixt Virginia and North Carolina*. Dover Publications, Inc., New York.

BRENNAN, LOUIS A.
1980 The English Ceramic Sequence from the Requa Site, Philipse Manor, New York. Paper presented at the 64th Annual Meeting, New York State Archeological Association, Syracuse, New York, April 18, 19, and 20.

BRIDENBAUGH, CARL
1966 *Cities in the Wilderness: The First Century of Urban Life in America, 1625–1742*. Alfred A. Knopf, Inc., New York.

BROWN, BEATRICE CURTIS (EDITOR)
1935 *The Letters and Diplomatic Instructions of Queen Anne*. Cassell and Company Ltd., London.

BROWN, EDWARD
1677 *An Account of Several Travels Through a Great Part of Germany*. Printed for Benj. Tooke, and are to be sold at the Sign of the ship in St. Paul's Church-yard, London. (Reprinted in 1971 by Arno Press & The New York Times, New York.)

CARTWRIGHT, JULIETTE J.
  n.d. *Report of the 1974 Excavation at the Van Wyck Homestead, Fishkill, New York.* Fishkill Historical Society, Fishkill (?).

COLDEN, CADWALLADER
  1937 *The Letters and Papers of Cadwallader Colden* (Vol. VIII). Printed for The New York Historical Society, New York.

COUCH, JONATHAN
  1871 *The History of Polperro, a Fishing Town on the South Coast of Cornwall.* W. Lake, Boscawen Street, Truro; Simpkin, Marshall, & Co., Stationers' Hall Court, London.

DEFOE, DANIEL
  1971 *A Tour through the Whole Island of Great Britain.* Penguin Books Ltd., Harmondsworth.

DE ROEVER, N.
  n.d. *De kroniek van Staets.* n.p., Amsterdam.

DOONE, VAL
  1950 *We See Devon.* George G. Harrap and Company Limited, London.

DOWNING, ANTOINETTE, AND VINCENT J. SCULLY, JR.
  1967 *The Architectural Heritage of Newport, Rhode Island: 1640–1915.* Clarkson N. Potter, Inc., Publisher, New York.

ELLIS, DAVID M., JAMES A. FROST, HAROLD C. SYRETT, AND HARRY J. CARMAN
  1962 *A Short History of New York State.* Cornell University Press, Ithaca.

FERGUSON, ROBERT, SCOTT FINLEY, JOE LAST, SUZANNE PLOUSOS, AND BIRGITTA WALLACE
  1981 Report on the 1979 Field Season at Grassy Island, Nova Scotia. Parks Canada *Research Bulletin* 152.

FLEMMING, DAVID B.
  1977 *The Canso Islands: An 18th Century Fishing Station.* Parks Canada Manuscript Report Number 308.

FLICK, ALEXANDER C. (EDITOR)
  1931 *The Papers of Sir William Johnson* (Vol. VII). The University of the State of New York, Albany.

FRANK, ANN
  1969 *Chinese Blue and White.* Walker and Co., New York.

GODDEN, GEOFFREY A.
  1965 *An Illustrated Encyclopedia of British Pottery and Porcelain.* Bonanza Books, New York.

GORING, RICH
  1981 European Ceramics in 17th and 18th Century New York. *The Bulletin and Journal of Archaeology for New York State* 80 and 81:1–18.

GRIM, DAVID
  n.d. A Plan of the City and Environs of New York as they were in the Years 1742, 1743, and 1744. Drawn by D. G. in the 76th year of his age. . . . Cedar Street. August 1813. Copied from an Original Drawing by David Grim in the possession of the N.Y. Historical Society. Lith. G. Hayward, 120 Water Street, New York.

GRIMM, JACOB L.
  1970 *Archaeological Investigation of Fort Ligonier: 1960–1965.* Carnegie Museum, Pittsburgh.

GROSSMAN, JOEL W.
  1982 *Raritan Landing: The Archaeology of a Buried Port.* Four volumes. Rutgers Archaeological Survey Office, New Brunswick, New Jersey.

HANSON, LEE, AND DICK PING HSU
  1975 *Casemates and Cannonballs.* U.S. Department of the Interior, National Park Service, Washington.

HEAP, GEORGE
  ca.   East Prospect of the City of Philadelphia; taken by
  1760 George Heap from the Jersey shore under the direction of Nicholas Scull. T. Jefferys, London. (New York State Library No. 74811.)

HENRETTA, JAMES A.
  1965 Economic Development and Social Structure in Colonial Boston. *The William and Mary Quarterly* 22 (1):75–92.

HILLAM, JENNIFER, AND PAUL HERBERT
  1980 Tree-Ring Dating: The Mermaid Theatre, City of London. *The London Archaeologist* 3 (16):439–444.

HIND, ARTHUR M.
  1972 *Wenceslaus Hollar.* Benjamin Blom, Inc., Publishers, New York.

HODGKIN, JOHN ELIOT, AND EDITH HODGKIN
  1973 *Examples of Early English Pottery Named, Dated, and Inscribed.* E. P. Publishing Limited, East Ardsley, Yorkshire.

JENNINGS, SARAH
  1981 *Eighteen Centuries of Pottery from Norwich.* East Anglian Archaeology Report No. 13. Norwich Survey in collaboration with Norfolk Museums Service, Norwich.

JOLLIFFE, SUSAN
  1973 Chinese Porcelain from the Shipwreck *Machault.* Parks Canada *Research Bulletin* 14.

KELSO, WILLIAM M.
  1979 *Captain Jones's Wormslow.* The University of Georgia Press, Athens.

KLEIN, MILTON M.
  1974 New York in the American Colonies: A New Look. In *Aspects of Early New York Society and Politics,* edited by Jacob Judd and Irwin H. Polishook, pp. 8–28. Sleepy Hollow Restorations, Tarrytown.

KROLL, MARIA (TRANSLATOR AND EDITOR)
1971   *Letters from Liselotte*. The McCall Publishing Company, New York.

LITTLE, BRYAN
1967   *The City and County of Bristol: A Study of Atlantic Civilisation*. Republished by S. R. Publishers Ltd., East Ardsley, Wakefield, Yorkshire.

MAYES, PHILIP
1972   *Port Royal, Jamaica Excavations 1969–70*. Jamaica National Trust Commission, Kingston.

MILLER, J. JEFFERSON, II, AND LYLE M. STONE
1970   *Eighteenth-Century Ceramics from Fort Michilimackinac*. Smithsonian Institution Press, Washington.

MILLER, LOUISE
1977   New Fresh Wharf: 2, The Saxon and Early Medieval Waterfronts. *The London Archaeologist* 3 (2):47–53.
1982   Miles Lane: the Early Roman Waterfront. *The London Archaeologist* 4 (6):143–47.

MONTRESOR, JOHN
1775   A Plan of the City of New-York & its Environs. . . . Sold by A. Dury. Dukes Court St. Martins Lane, London.

MOUNTFORD, ARNOLD R.
1967   Greenhead St., Burslem (SJ 867499). *City of Stoke-on-Trent Museum Archaeological Society Reports No. 2: For 1966*. City of Stoke-on-Trent Museum Archaeological Society, Hanley.
1971   *The Illustrated Guide to Staffordshire Salt-Glazed Stoneware*. Garrie & Jenkins. London.

NOËL HUME, IVOR
1961   The Glass Wine Bottle in Colonial Virginia. *Journal of Glass Studies* 3:90–117.
1970   *A Guide to Artifacts of Colonial America*. Alfred A. Knopf, New York.

O'CALLAGHAN, E. B. (EDITOR)
1855   *Documents Relative to the Colonial History of the State of New-York* (Vol. V). Weed, Parsons and Company, Printers, Albany.

PERKINS, D. R. J.
1979   *Wreck of a British Man-of-War discovered on the Goodwin Sands*. Interim Report. The Isle of Thanet Archaeological Unit.

REINDERS, H. R.
1981   Het uitdiepen van de haven van Amsterdam in de zeventiende eeuw. *50 jaar onderzoek*. Rijksdienst voor de Ijselmeerpolders, Lelystad.

RITCHIE, ROBERT C.
1977   *The Duke's Province: A Study of New York Politics and Society, 1664–1691*. The University of North Carolina Press, Chapel Hill.

ROGERS, WOODES
1970   *A Cruising Voyage Round the World*. Dover Publications, Inc. New York.

ROTHSCHILD, NAN A.
1982   Recent Archaeological Field Work in New York City. *PANYC Newsletter* 8:26–27.

SASSOON, CAROLINE
1978   *Chinese Porcelain Marks from Kenya*. BAR International Series (Supplementary) 43. British Archaeological Reports, Oxford.

SCHOFIELD, JOHN, AND TONY DYSON
1980   *Archaeology of the City of London*. City of London Archaeological Trust, London.

SCHOFIELD, JOHN, AND LOUISE MILLER
1976   New Fresh Wharf: 1, The Roman Waterfront. *The London Archaeologist* 2 (15):390–95.

SCOTT, KENNETH (EDITOR)
1970   Genealogical Data from the New-York Gazette; and the Weekly Mercury. *The New York Genealogical and Biographical Record* 101 (2):104–11.

SCULL, G. D. (EDITOR)
1882   *The Montresor Journals. Collections of the New-York Historical Society for the Year 1881*. Printed for the Society, New York.

SHELVOCKE, GEORGE
1930   *A Privateer's Voyage Round the World*. Jonathan Cape & Harrison Smith, New York.

SMEATON, JOHN
1938   *John Smeaton's Diary of his Journey to the Low Countries: 1755*. Printed for the Newcomen Society by the Courier Press, Leamington Spa.

SMITH, WILLIAM, JR.
1972   *The History of the Province of New-York* (Vol. I). Edited by Michael Kammen. The Belknap Press of Harvard University Press, Cambridge.

STOKES, I. N. PHELPS
1915   *The Iconography of Manhattan Island: 1498–1909* (Vol. I). Robert H. Dodd, New York.
1916   *The Iconography of Manhattan Island: 1498–1909* (Vols. II, IV). Robert H. Dodd, New York.

STOW, JOHN
1970   *Stow's Survey of London*. J. M. Dent & Sons Ltd., London.

TATTON-BROWN, TIM
1974   Rescue Excavations on the Old Custom House Site, Part 2.—Roman. *The London Archaeologist* 2 (7):155–59.

VALENTINE, DAVID T.
1853   *History of The City of New York*. G. P. Putnam & Company, No. 10 Park Place, New York.

Van Schaack, Henry C.
1859 *Henry Cruger: The Colleague of Edmund Burke in the British Parliament, A Paper Read Before the New York Historical Society, January 4th, 1849.* C. Benjamin Richardson, 348 Broadway, New York.

Vernon-Harcourt, Leveson Francis
1910 Dock. *The Encyclopaedia Britannica* (Vol. VIII). Encyclopaedia Britannica, Inc., New York.

Walker, Iain C.
1977 *Clay Tobacco-Pipes, with Particular Reference to the Bristol Industry.* National Historic Parks and Sites Branch, Parks Canada, Department of Indian and Northern Affairs, Ottawa.

White, Philip L. (editor)
1956 *The Beekman Mercantile Papers, 1746–1799.* The New-York Historical Society, New York.

Whitehill, Walter Muir
1963 *Boston: A Topographical History.* The Belknap Press of Harvard University Press, Cambridge.

Winbolt, S. E.
1955 *Hampshire and the Isle of Wight.* Penguin Books Inc., Harmondsworth.

Paul R. Huey
New York State Office of Parks,
    Recreation and Historic Preservation
Bureau of Historic Sites
Peebles Island
Waterford, New York 12188

2011. Wharves and Waterfront Retaining Structures as Vernacular Architecture.
Historical Archaeology 45(2):42–67.

Molly R. McDonald

Wharves and Waterfront Retaining Structures as Vernacular Architecture

ABSTRACT

This paper examines timber landfill-retaining structures built prior to the mid-19th century in both Europe and North America. It focuses on the timber building traditions in which these wharves, quays, slips, and bulkheads were constructed, viewing them as examples of historical carpentry that fit within a known historical and cultural framework of vernacular construction. These now-buried waterfront structures are increasingly the focus of archaeological investigations. It is argued that a revised approach to documenting and understanding landfill-retaining structures may yield greater insight into the specific cultural influences exercised historically on landmaking and landmaking technology in the New World.

Introduction

Early timber landfill-retaining structures, including wharves, quays, and shoreline walls, are now often buried within the fast land of American and European towns and cities and are increasingly the focus of archaeological study. This paper examines the methods used to build these structures, identifies the drawbacks of prevailing archaeological classification systems, and emphasizes the importance of viewing landfill-retaining structures as part of the history of vernacular carpentry. By reviewing American and European archaeological examples through the lens of vernacular architecture, this paper argues that most early timber landfill-retaining structures in the United States were influenced more strongly by log building traditions originating in portions of present-day Scandinavia and Germany than by those of England or the Netherlands.

Wood was the most common material used to build landfill-retaining structures in North America during the period on which this study focuses: the 17th, 18th, and early 19th centuries. This preference for wood is clearly reflected in the archaeological record and can likely be attributed to the relative abundance of timber in North America. Even in locations such as New York City, where local timber stocks were depleted during the colonial period, transportation of lumber from forested areas farther north had become an established industry by the late 18th century (Fox 1902). While stone was used with some frequency in cities such as Boston, on the whole, timber was the material of choice (Seasholes 2003).

Previous Classification Systems and Their Difficulties

Archaeological investigations of the 1980s pioneered the documentation of buried wharves and bulkheads in America and first tackled the interpretation of their cultural contexts. These and subsequent studies have tended to classify retaining structures according to the following four "construction types."

Crib construction has been described as timbers arranged in a relatively loosely constructed "crib," alternating courses of horizontal "headers and stretchers" aligned perpendicular to each other (Figure 1). The terms "header" and "stretcher" are traditionally used to describe brickwork, but have also been used to denote the perpendicular alignments of horizontal logs in landfill-retaining structures. The joinery used in cribs is described as being "notched together in 'Lincoln Log'-type construction to form a box-shaped frame," with transverse and longitudinal crossties (Louis Berger & Associates [LBA] 1990:V-2). Cribs are often described as containing floors to help retain the cobbles, gravel, and other types of fill within them (Heintzelman 1985).

The solid-filled construction category is described as being built in a boxlike form constructed of headers and stretchers, corner notched in much the same way as the crib type described above. The solid-filled type, however, is more tightly constructed and therefore able to retain finer fills such as sand, soil, and refuse (Heintzelman 1985:9; LBA 1990:V-2). Other sorts of retaining structures have also been put in the solid-filled category, such as "vertical piles with horizontal planking or load-bearing stone walls"

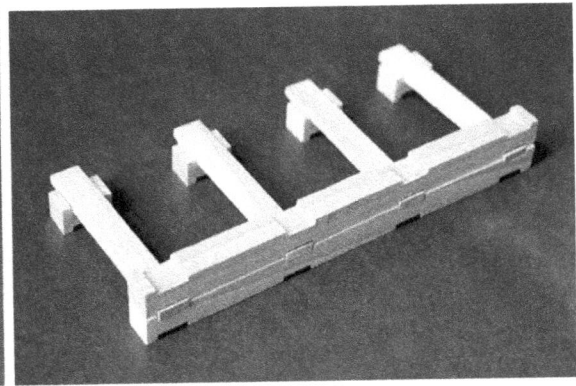

FIGURE 1. Models illustrating the crib form (*left*) and wall form (*right*) of timber landfill-retaining structures. (Photo by author, 2010.)

(Heintzelman 1985:9). Norman defines solid-filled retaining structures as "freestanding, load-bearing retaining walls or bulkheads, usually filled behind with dredged materials" (Norman 1987:13). Despite the identification of the "solid-filled" type with fine fills, Heintzelman notes, "cobbles and/ or ballast stone ... were sometimes also used" (Heintzelman 1985:9).

Cobb construction is generally described as consisting of an "open work" box; or as "an open work version of the crib, using cobblestones to fill up and sink the timber crib" (Heintzelman 1985:10; LBA 1990:V-3). Due to the large gaps between courses of stacked logs, they are only able to contain large cobbles and other ballast-type fills. The details of the construction method are not clearly defined, but, it is clear that the term refers to a framework of headers and stretchers forming a cell or crib unit. Wharves identified as cobb have been constructed of either squared timbers or logs in the round.

The fourth type, grillage construction, has been described as "several layers of logs laid alternately at right angles and intermittently weighted with stone rubble fill" (Norman 1987:26). Grillage structures are distinct in that the perpendicular courses of horizontal timbers are continuous, creating a raftlike form that contains no central boxlike void (Figure 2). Joan Geismar, principal investigator at the 175 Water Street site in New York, coined the term "grillage" as applied to wharves, distinguishing it from the engineering term "grillage," which denotes sunken caissons or foundations for bridges and other structures isolated in water (Geismar 1983). Multiple grillage

rafts could be floated out to the location desired and sunk with stone and ballast (LBA 1990:V-3).

As is evident from the above descriptions, the classification system currently used for retaining structures (particularly the crib, solid-filled, and cobb categories) engenders considerable vagueness and confusion. All of the types are described primarily as timber structures built in a manner similar to log houses. Only the "solid-filled" construction category allows for other types of construction method and form, such as timber-framed bulkhead walls or masonry seawalls; yet the solid-filled category may also refer to a tightly constructed timber crib. Solid-filled cribs are distinguished from cobb cribs in that cobbwork is more openly constructed and can only retain large-aggregate fills. It logically follows, then, that the initial category of "crib" construction should be a general term embracing the cobb and solid-filled subcategories, rather than the three types being distinct and parallel categories.

Additional confusion has arisen from the multiple definitions or unclear meanings characterizing certain important typological terms. The term "solid-filled" has been used to describe a construction method, form, or fill material. The word "crib" is used by some to define one of the four "construction types," denoting the product of a construction method using alternating perpendicular timbers notched together at the corners. "Crib" has also been used, however, to denote the boxlike form. According to the existing typology, one might refer to the "crib" form of a cobb or solid-filled wharf. When the word "crib" is used in isolation, it is unclear if the

FIGURE 2. A grillage structure encountered at the South Ferry Terminal site in Lower Manhattan. (Photo by Dewberry-Goodkind, Inc., 2006; courtesy of MTA Capital Construction, New York, NY.)

word is meant to describe a construction method or a built form.

While the established typology makes a distinction between "crib" and "cobb" wharves, some historians and archaeologists imply that "cobb" wharves were a subtype of crib wharves, and that the only defining feature of the cobb subtype was its containment of cobbles (Small 1941:8). In her study of historical New England wharf-construction types, Mary Jane Brady admits, "the distinction between cobbwork and cribwork is a fine one" and ultimately "may be strictly semantic." The term cobbwork may have been an older usage that was gradually replaced by the term cribwork (Brady 1978:10A). Norman, in his study of Baltimore wharf construction, considers the term cobb to be a New England dialect term for crib construction (Norman 1987). These commonly used categories may have hampered archaeological inquiry in part because archaeologists are compelled to fit the structures that they encounter into categories that lack meaning or clarity. Furthermore, in adhering to these categories, the emphasis is shifted from more meaningful descriptions and classifications.

A New Approach to Landfill-Retaining Structures

Rather than applying a blanket typological term, archaeologists should focus attention on describing the basic attributes of a feature, making clear distinctions between the various aspects of construction, such as structure material, fill material, form, structure type, and construction method. Consideration of these discrete aspects, defined below by the author, will help ensure the collection of clear and comprehensive data and will refocus analysis on attributes that can be more meaningfully contextualized.

Structure material refers to the wood, masonry, or other material of the retaining feature. In timber construction, one should identify the wood type, the way the wood was processed, and whether any tooling marks are evident. The fill material should also be described. Documented fill materials range from large-aggregate fill (such as cobbles or cordwood) to fine fill (such as sand, clay, and silt), and may be relatively clean or contain refuse.

The *form* of a retaining structure refers to its units of construction. Three common form examples are cribs, grillage complexes, and walls. The term crib has been used in a number of ways in the past, as discussed above, but it is defined here specifically as a boxlike form with an interior space. A set of cribs (or "cribbing") with multiple subdivisions created by crossties or partitions should be called a "block," and its subdivisions "cells." In some cases, cribbing does not take the form of a block with cell divisions. Instead, the structure may be either one large box, or a box braced with crossties that do not immediately overlay each other. The term crib should be used to refer to either a block-and-cell construction or to a box-shaped structure without clear cell divisions. The grillage form differs from the crib form in that each perpendicular course of stacked logs is continuous, creating a more solid raftlike structure rather than a boxlike crib with a void in the center. Typically a grillage complex is held together with a minimum of joinery or other fasteners (Kilkenny 2002:6.43). Walls represent a third example of a form type. Walls (also called bulkheads or revetments) are essentially a linear form, which may or may not be braced from either or both sides, and may be constructed of timber, stone, or other materials. Sunken ships have also been used as a form of landfill-retaining structure. Vessels that appear to have been intentionally scuttled for the purpose of landmaking have been found at a number of sites, including 175 Water Street in New York City and Keith's Wharf in Alexandria, Virginia (Geismar 1983; Engineering-Science, Inc. 1993). A vessel was also recently found by AKRF, Inc. archaeologists in a ca. 1800 landfill context at the World Trade Center site in Manhattan. While these finds are interesting and are relevant to the topic of landfilling in general, they will not be explored in detail in this paper, which focuses on timber features built specifically for retaining fill.

Structure type refers to the overall structure to which these structural units belong. Continuous linear shorelines, which regularized and extended the waterfront, might be created using bulkhead walls, cribbing, or other forms. Wharves, slips, and quays were structure types associated with docking vessels and could also be created using various forms, including retaining walls or cribbing. It should be noted that a wharf generally refers to a structure that is connected to fast land and juts into the water at an angle roughly perpendicular to the shore. In contrast, a quay extends into the water but is oriented parallel to the shoreline (Norman 1987:7). A slip describes a water-filled basin, often formed by two parallel wharves or quays. A number of different cribbing configurations have been used to create wharves. In "block-and-bridge" configurations, the spaces between blocks of timber cribbing are "spanned by plank bridges" (LBA 1990:IV-25). Alternatively, cribs or other forms could be arranged in two parallel rows, and the gap between the two rows could be filled, forming a land surface (Small 1941).

Lastly, *construction method* refers to the vernacular building tradition in which a given structure is built. The next section of this article will closely examine this category as it applies to "landbound" structures, such as houses and barns. This review of vernacular timber building traditions in Europe and North America will set a framework in which to evaluate wharves and bulkheads as examples of vernacular carpentry.

Identifying the Vernacular Construction Method of Landfill-Retaining Structures

A limited number of vernacular traditions, including log construction, timber-frame construction, and plank construction, among others, were used historically to build timber structures of various sorts. These traditions have been likened to languages, and each carries with it a specific history and set of cultural influences (Harris 1978). Like houses, barns, and other types of landbound structures, it is argued that early timber retaining structures were built in a specific vernacular building tradition. By locating a retaining structure within a vernacular tradition, the structure is meaningfully contextualized within a specific cultural and historical framework. The primary building traditions using timber are reviewed below, with particular attention to the European origins of these traditions. It should be noted that, particularly in North America, where influences from many traditions and locations came together in new social and environmental conditions, some hybrids and localized traditions did occur.

As distinct from other wood-based building techniques, timber framing implies the use of timbers to create a frame made up of vertical and horizontal members tied together by various carpentry joints and without the use of nails or other methods of structural support (Brown 1986:22) (Figure 3). Most important of the timber-frame carpentry joints are the pegged mortise-and-tenon joint, the scarf joint, the lap joint, and their variations (Figure 4). A great number of different carpentry joints are used to create a frame, some of which are quite complex and require extensive skill and craftsmanship

to master (Harris 1978; Sobon 2002). Within Britain, timber framing represented the most common form of wood construction for roughly five centuries. It is believed to have developed in the 12th or 13th century, replacing a tradition in which timber buildings were constructed using earthfast posts inserted directly into the ground rather than connecting into wood sill beams. The scarcity of lumber in Britain resulted in the decline of the tradition by the 18th century (Brown 1986:22).

Extensive research by British buildings archaeologists has shown that the joints used in the construction of timber-framed buildings can be used as indicators of construction date as well as region (Hewett 1980). Furthermore, Richard Harris, a scholar of British timber framing, argues that a specific "grammar of carpentry" existed in Britain. The framing styles of the nation, like a language, consisted of certain unique rules with

FIGURE 3. An example of a timber-framed barn in New York State with the roof and cladding removed. (Photo by Randy Nash, 2009.)

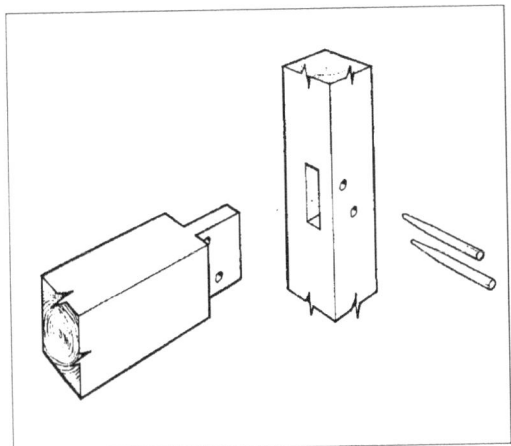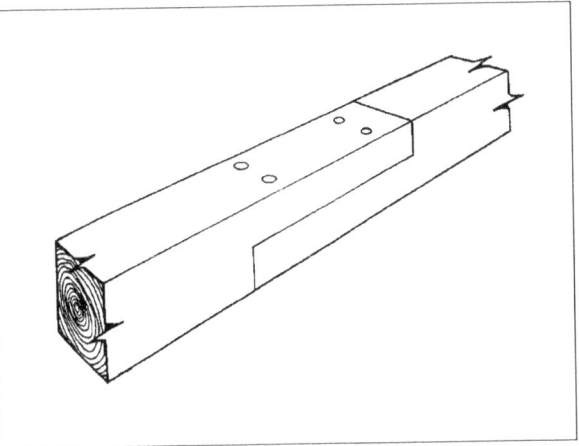

FIGURE 4. Basic timber-frame joinery: a mortise-and-tenon joint with wood pegs (*left*); and a halved or "half lap" scarf joint with four wood pegs (*right*). Scarf joints are used to splice two timbers together in the same alignment (Sobon 2002). (Courtesy of Jack Sobon and the Timber Framers Guild, Alstead, NH.)

which British carpenters would become fluent. Certain framing characteristics, therefore, are to be found only in Britain; and although many British carpenters would have been familiar with French or Dutch techniques, he argues, the retention of the unique British tradition related to a certain sense of cultural identity (Harris 1978).

Timber framing was a common approach to building in the American colonies, and British carpenters brought their distinctive approach to timber framing to the New World. While basic roots in British framing techniques continued to be manifested in most North American buildings, certain joints and assemblies changed, diverging from the British "grammar of carpentry" (Harris 1978).

The timber-framing traditions of other European countries follow the same basic principles as English timber framing, but with distinctive variations. Dutch timber-framed houses and barns are framed using a series of H-bents, for example, and there are differences in the manner in which building roofs are framed. In terms of joinery, several joint types are recognized as being distinctly Dutch, including the through-tenon common in barns. In this joint, the tenon (often rounded at the end) extends through an open mortise and is typically held in place with a wedge on the outer side of the mortise, as well as pegs through the mortise (Sobon 2002). In North America, Dutch-influenced framing traditions were more common and longer enduring

in areas where Dutch-descendant populations and cultural influences persisted, such as northern New Jersey, western Long Island, and the Hudson Valley.

Log construction, also called stacked log construction or corner-timbered construction, is typified in North America by log cabins and houses constructed on the American frontier with wide regional dispersal (Figure 5). Log-construction houses tend to be made of timber from coniferous tree species, which can be either squared or left in the round. "The basic strategy for constructing a log house is to stack logs one on top of the other and notch them to interlock at the corners. Logs in perpendicular walls are offset in height by one half-log diameter in order to allow the corner joints to lap" (Allen 2006:514). The term "scribing" in log construction refers to the method of shaping each timber so that its surface perfectly fits the logs above and below it. This is achieved by tracing the contours of one log onto the log above it using a special template. The tradition of log building was a long one in Norway, Sweden, and Finland, as well as Germany, Switzerland, Eastern Europe, and elsewhere. Log building was rarely, if ever, used in Britain (Jordan 1978).

A wide variety of corner-notching styles can be found in the log tradition (Figure 6). One of the simplest corner notches is the saddle notch, which is "fashioned by hollowing out a

FIGURE 5. An example of a log house in New York State with dovetail corner notching. (Photo by William Krattinger, 2008.)

saddle-shaped depression near the end of the log, shaped to fit the rounded contour of the adjacent log or another saddle" (Jordan 1978:58). Myriad other notch types have also been used, including square, half-square, dovetail, semilunate, and lock notches (Jordan 1978). A single dowel was sometimes inserted vertically into a hole bored in the center of a notch to reinforce the joint. Scarf joints and mortise-and-tenons, more common in timber framing, occur in modified forms and with less frequency in log construction. Perpendicular partition walls and floor joists were notched into the main walls using a variety of flush or protruding lock notches (Phleps 1982).

Several scholars have researched the origins of the American log house. There is some evidence for the use of log building techniques in early French Canada among the Acadians. Documentary evidence suggests that Swiss soldiers may have erected log structures in the first decades of the 17th century in Port Royal in Nova Scotia

(Wonders 1979:193). None of these early Canadian log structures survive, and evidence comes in the form of written accounts that paint too generalized a picture of the structures to provide any real insight into their character. True corner-notched log structures do not appear to have been erected in French Canada. Likewise, log buildings do not appear to have been used in early Dutch settlements in the New World (Mercer 1967).

The first American log houses in North America were likely constructed by the Scandinavian settlers in the New Sweden colony in the year 1638. The New Sweden colony was composed of Swedish, Finnish, and Dutch settlers, and was located along the Delaware River in an area that now includes portions of Delaware, New Jersey, and Pennsylvania. It was organized by the New Sweden Company, a joint-stock company that received financial and administrative support from the Swedish government and from Swedish and

FIGURE 6. Examples of log-construction corner notching, including saddle notching (*top left*), dovetail notching (*bottom left*), half-lap (or half-square) notching with dowels (*top right*), and lock notching (*bottom right*). (Courtesy of AKRF, Inc., after Phleps 1982.)

Dutch investors. In a study of the origins of various features of American log dwellings, T. G. Jordan argues that the New Sweden colony, though small in population, had a widespread influence on log construction in America. This was due in large part to the fact that the Finns and other Scandinavians who settled New Sweden were among the few European American groups whose homelands were still heavily forested. Their vernacular building traditions were particularly well suited to the American colonies, such that non-Scandinavian settlers who passed through the New Sweden vicinity en route to other regions picked up and disseminated log-construction techniques. Certain corner notches such as the V notch, which would become common in North American log buildings, can be specifically traced to Finnish settlements in Scandinavia (Jordan 1995). During the first half of the 18th century, settlers from portions of what is now Germany and Switzerland began to settle in Pennsylvania and brought with them their own log building traditions. As with the earlier Scandinavian traditions, and perhaps still more pervasively, these log-construction methods spread from the mid-Atlantic region to other parts of North America (Jordan 1978).

The first known log building in New England was a meetinghouse built in Portsmouth, New Hampshire, in 1659. A few examples of log houses have been documented in Maine and New Hampshire from the 1660s onwards, mostly garrisons intended for refuge during periods of hostility with Native Americans. Log houses were extremely rare in New England until the 1720s, however, when large numbers of Scotch Irish migrated to the area from the south. Throughout the 18th century in New England, log structures probably tended to be seen as temporary or inferior, and were often demoted to the status of outbuildings when a timber-framed or masonry dwelling would eventually be built (Garvin 2001). Log-construction dwellings were never common in what is now New York City. Most of the wood vernacular buildings constructed there in the 18th and 19th centuries were timber framed, in the English and Dutch framing traditions. The 1860 *Gazetteer of the State of New York* records the number of dwellings per county and their construction method. The only five counties in New York State that were devoid of log-construction dwellings were the counties that now comprise New York City (French 1860).

Plank construction is considered a distinct vernacular construction method, but due to a relative lack of scholarship on the tradition, its origins, development, and geographical distribution are not well understood. Most plank buildings are covered with clapboards and cannot be easily recognized from the exterior, compounding the difficulty of inventorying them. Plank construction was a relatively common form of vernacular

architecture in certain parts of North America, however, particularly in the 19th century. Plank construction typically uses vertical planks let into the sill beam and wall plate to form building walls. The planks themselves act as structural members, and therefore can take the place of posts, studs, braces, and sheathing. Planks were let into the sills and plates using a variety of methods: some were tenoned, often using wood pins or dowels; some were rabbeted into the sill, often using spikes; and some were spiked into the exterior of the sill and plate. Vertical-plank examples were observed in Vermont from the 18th century to ca. 1900 (Lewandowski 1995:45), and conformed to a similar timeframe in New York. Examples of horizontal-plank construction, or "plank-on-edge" construction, have also been documented in central New York State and elsewhere (Kevlin 1986:43). A version of horizontal-plank construction, called *piéce-en-piéce*, was in use in French Canada in the 17th and 18th centuries (Wonders 1978:196). Plank framing might have been favored in some North American applications because it required less specialized knowledge of complex timber-frame joinery, or it may have gained popularity for aesthetic reasons (Lewandowski 1995). On a more practical level, by the mid-19th century, mill-processed lumber was becoming inexpensive and readily available, making plank construction a low-cost framing alternative (Kevlin 1986).

Plank construction in North America is similar to the European "stave" construction, which was used in Scandinavia, particularly in churches, throughout the medieval period. The basic skeleton of these structures was essentially timber framed: the word stave comes from the Old Norse *stafr*, which referred to the structure's upright posts. The planks that made up the wall and provided structural support were usually vertical and were let into the sills and plates using mortise-and-tenon joints (Jensenius 2003). Stave construction was also employed in medieval England, although few examples are known, and the significance of the construction method in England is not yet well understood (Milne 1991).

Documented Landfill-Retaining Structure Examples

Having reviewed some of the primary vernacular building traditions and defined the other important aspects by which structures may be described (material, form, structure type, etc.), this section will examine archaeologically excavated examples. It begins by describing retaining structures documented archaeologically in portions of Europe, and goes on to review a representative sample of structures from the eastern United States. The areas now known as Britain, peninsular Scandinavia, and the Netherlands were chosen for study within Europe both because of their long and active landfilling tradition, and because early immigration from these areas to North America may have resulted in an influence on the American building traditions in the colonial and postcolonial periods.

Relatively few postmedieval timber wharves appear to have been documented archaeologically in Europe. Therefore, many of the European structures discussed in this section date to the late-medieval period. As discussed earlier, however, the late-medieval carpentry traditions of Europe are relevant to studies of North American carpentry through the early 19th century. Comparison of late-medieval European retaining structures and colonial and postcolonial American retaining structures is equally valid. Early medieval and premedieval approaches will not be addressed in detail because they are considered less relevant to the analysis of influences on North American building.

This section does not represent an exhaustive review of early timber landfill-retaining structures investigated archaeologically. Rather, the following examples were selected with the goal of providing a representative sample of construction types for each geographical area examined. Table 1 summarizes the primary characteristics of the retaining features documented at each of the archaeological sites discussed in this section.

Britain

From 1974 through 1976, archaeological investigations on the London waterfront at Trig Lane along the north shore of the river Thames uncovered a complex set of medieval landfill-retaining structures built in several phases between the mid-13th and late 15th centuries. These structures were revetments (linear retaining walls or bulkheads), behind which fill was placed. They were built in the river, parallel to the shore, for the purpose of reclaiming land. Most were constructed of wood (oak and elm), while others were constructed of stone. The wood revetments encountered at Trig Lane fell into two main categories: timber-frame construction and stave construction. The earliest (13th century) timber-framed revetments at Trig Lane were founded on a principal base plate (sill beam), lengthened by means of scarf joints, and retained by piles (Figure 7). Squared timber posts were set into the base plate using pegged mortise-and-tenon joints. Horizontal boards were affixed along the rear faces of the posts. The resulting wall was reinforced from both the front (river side) and the rear (land side). In the front, a squared-timber shoring member was joined to the top of each post with a chase-tenon, and ran diagonally downwards to meet a pile-retained subsidiary base plate in a bird's-mouth abutment (a V-shaped pocket usually placed at the end of a timber to bear against the inside of another timber—in landbound structures, the joint is most commonly found in rafters, where they connect to wall plates). The revetment was additionally supported from the landward side using perpendicular tiebacks (fixed in place by piles driven at the corners of a small pegged half-lap cross member) and diagonal braces (Milne and Milne 1978:88).

Slightly later timber-framed revetments at Trig Lane differed from those described above in that they were no longer shored from the front. Instead they relied solely on back braces, which were relatively widely spaced and were more complex in construction. Feature G7, for example, dating to ca. 1345, exhibited some similarities to those described above, including a pile-retained base plate into which vertical posts were set using mortise-and-tenon joints. Horizontal boards were affixed to the rear face. No subsidiary base plates or front shores were used, however. Instead, raised cross-shaped tiebacks were secured to the revetment with the use of unusual and effective edge-trenched joinery. This edge trenching consisted of notches cut into each side of the end of the tieback, which were fit into corresponding notches in the posts of the revetment wall (Milne and Milne 1978:91).

Stave (plank) construction revetments at Trig Lane also exhibited complex joinery (Figure 8). The late-14th-century Features G10 and G11 were constructed of pile-retained base plates with mortises or grooves into which continuous walls of tenoned vertical planks were set. The planks were fixed to each other using free tenons (in the case

TABLE 1
REPRESENTATIVE SAMPLE OF LANDFILL RETAINING STRUCTURES

Project	Date	Structure Material	Fill Material	Form	Structure Type	Construction Method
Britain						
Trig Lane, London	13th–15th c.	Oak, elm	Loose fill, gravel, refuse	Wall	Continuous shoreline	Timber frame; plank frame
Custom House site, London	14th c.	Timber (unknown type)	Unknown	Wall	Quay	Timber frame
Seal House site, London	13th c.	Timber (type unknown)	Unknown	Wall	Continuous shoreline	Timber frame
Burford Wharf, Stratford	18th–19th c.	Oak and softwood	Loose fill, some refuse	Wall	Wharf	Modified plank frame
The Netherlands						
Merwede, Dordrecht	13th–16th c.	Timber (type unknown)	Unknown	Wall	Continuous shoreline	Modified plank frame
Waterlooplein site, Amsterdam	16th c.	Timber (type unknown)	Unknown	Wall	Continuous shoreline	Modified plank frame
Norway						
Finnegården 3a and 6a, Bergen	13th c.	Timber (type unknown)	Cobbles, fills, refuse	Crib	Wharf	Log construction
Domkirkegaten 6, Bergen	12th c.	Timber (type unknown)	Cobbles, fills, refuse	Crib	Quay	Log construction
North America						
Cheapside Wharf, Baltimore, MD	Late 18th c.	Southern yellow pine	Clean local sand/ silt	Crib	Wharf	Log construction
Keith's Wharf, Alexandria, VA	18th c.	Timber (type unknown)	Sand, silt, some refuse	Wall	Wharf	Log construction
Meadows site, Philadelphia, PA	18th c.	Oak, pine	Sand, gravel, cobbles	Crib (prob.)	Wharf	Log construction
SUCF Parking Structure site, Albany, NY	18th c.	White pine	Silt, sand, clay, timber ricking	Wall and crib	Linear shoreline	Log construction, grillage, and pile
Site 1 of Washington Street URA, New York, NY	Late 18th–early 19th c.	Timber (type unknown)	Cobbles, sandy silt	Crib	Wharf	Log construction
Telco Block, New York, NY	Mid-18th c.	Pine, sweetgum	Cobbles	Crib (prob.)	Wharf	Log construction
Assay site, New York, NY	18th c.	Timber (type unknown)	Cobbles, silt, some refuse	Crib and wall	Wharf	Log construction and modified plank construction
Town Dock wharves, Charlestown, MA	17th–18th c.	Timber (type unknown)	Loose silt/clay	Wall and crib	Wharf	Log construction and modified plank construction
Mill Pond site, Boston, MA	Early 18th c.	Timber (type unknown)	Unknown	Crib and raft	Wharf	Log construction and grillage
Derby and Central wharves, Salem, MA	18th–early 19th c.	Pine (white and southern yellow)	Silt and cobbles	Crib and wall	Wharf	Log construction

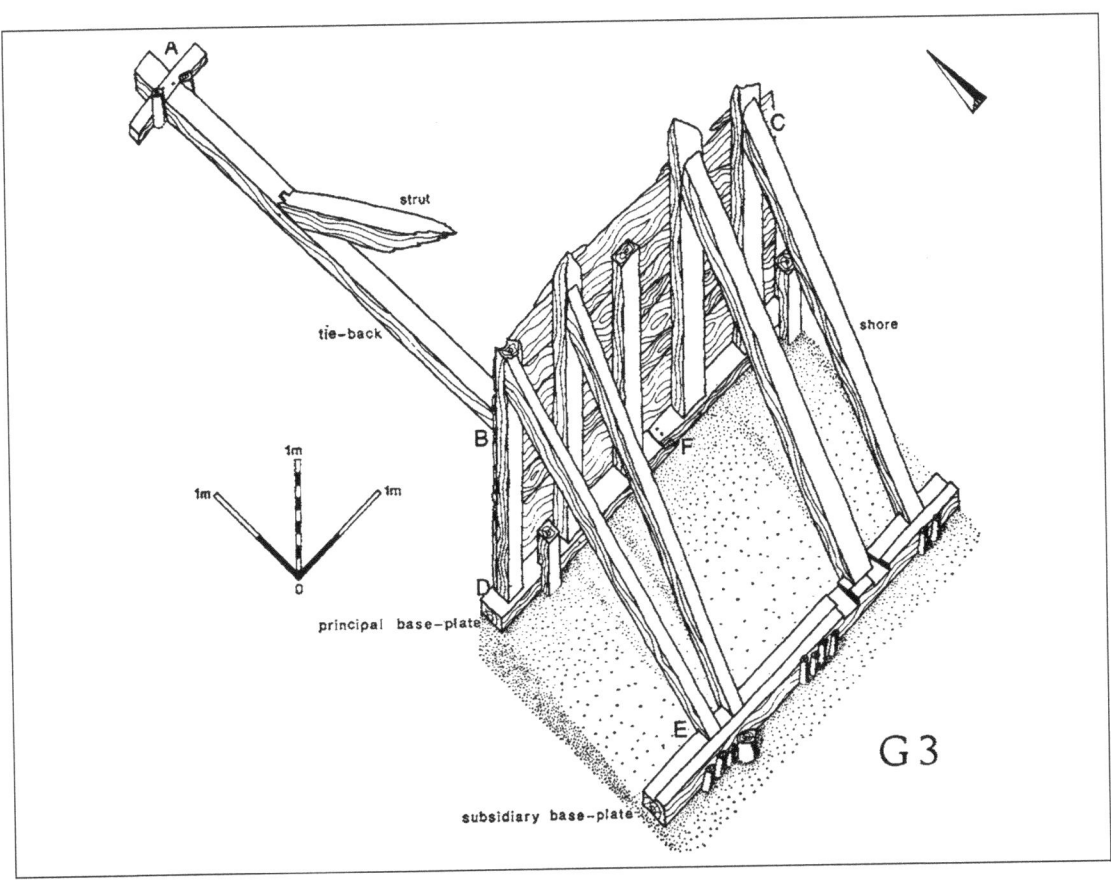

FIGURE 7. Feature G3 from the Trig Lane site in London. The joint types found in the structure are described as follows (Milne and Milne 1978): "A, pegged half lap; B, central face-tenon; C, chase-tenon; D, pegged central tenon; E, bird's mouth abutment; F, half-edged scarf with square vertical butts and two face pegs." (Courtesy of the Society for Medieval Archaeology, Edinburgh, UK, and Maney Publishing, Leeds, UK.)

of G10) or dowels (in the case of G11). Feature G11 also had a top plate, with mortises in both upper and lower faces, suggesting a second level of vertical planks that did not survive. Both of the stave revetments also used edge-trenched tieback systems. These consisted of pile-founded base plates with diagonal braces chase-tenoned at either end and inclined towards each other to create a triangular shape that provided additional support to the upper portion of the revetment (Milne and Milne 1978:93).

In relating the timber joinery used in the revetments to that of other types of vernacular architecture, Milne and Milne (1978) argued that while the techniques generally parallel each other in many aspects, they differ in some. Certain joints used in the landfill-retaining structures were considered anachronistic in contemporaneous landbound vernacular architecture, while others predated frequent use in extant landbound structures. Furthermore, while stave construction was apparently common in revetment construction, it was fairly rare in English buildings of the medieval period (Milne and Milne 1978:102).

At the Custom House site, excavated in 1973, less than a mile east of Trig Lane on the river Thames, several successive campaigns of timber retaining structures were encountered, ranging in date from the 2nd century to ca. 1300. Archaeologists identified a 2nd-century timber quay, which was made of "a series of timber boxes ... built of four or five tiers of horizontal oak beams" (Hobley 1981:2). This was essentially a log-built crib structure made up of blocks and cells, a construction type and form that is rare in Britain and appears to be unique to Roman-period

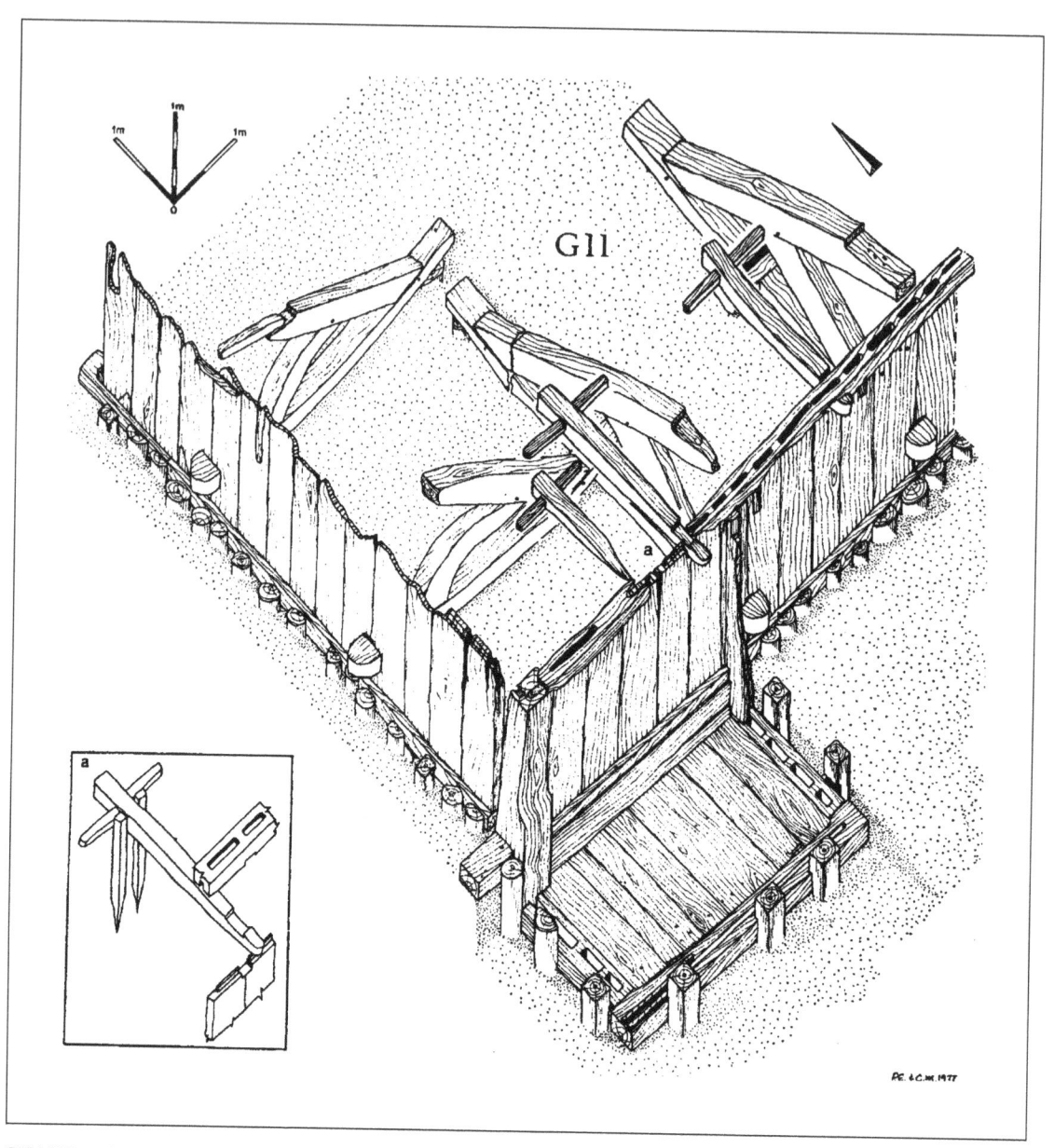

FIGURE 8. Feature G11 from the Trig Lane site in London, a 14th-century stave (plank-construction) revetment wall with complex back braces. The posts and platform pictured at the *bottom right* are believed to have served as the base of a water tank (Milne and Milne 1978). (Courtesy of the Society for Medieval Archaeology, Edinburgh, UK, and Maney Publishing, Leeds, UK.)

sites. Also encountered at the Custom House site was a ca. 1300 revetment wall of timber-frame construction that resembled Feature G3 at Trig Lane. It had upright posts fixed into a base plate. Perpendicular tiebacks positioned at regular intervals along the rear foot of the wall were notched into both the primary base plate and a subsidiary base plate, and were retained by piles. Diagonal braces mortised into the perpendicular plates were chase-tenoned into the tops of the posts, providing additional support. A similar 13th-century timber-framed revetment encountered at the Seal House site (midway between the Custom House site and Trig Lane) lacked a subsidiary base plate; instead the perpendicular tiebacks were retained by piles (Heintzelman-Muego 1983:5–8).

In general, wood was supplanted by stone as the preferred material for landfill-retaining structures in Britain toward the end of the medieval period due to the shortage of timber. Some examples of postmedieval timber revetments have been encountered, however. These tend to break from the patterns Milne recognized for the medieval period. Recently, 18th- and early-19th-century timber wharves were investigated by AOC Archaeology Group at Burford Wharf in Stratford, England, along the former shores of the Channelsea River. Both the 18th- and 19th-century features were linear wood revetment walls aligned to form wharf structures. They consisted of timber posts onto which horizontal planks were nailed. The posts were sawn half- and quarter-round oak and "imported softwood" timbers. No front bracing was present. Back bracing consisted of tiebacks placed at intervals of a few feet, using wrought-iron bolts and straps. Fill deposited on the landward side consisted of sand and gravel; ceramic artifacts were found in the early-19th-century fills. The archaeologists considered the Burford Wharf features to be typical of postmedieval timber retaining structures in Britain (Carew et al. 2009).

The Netherlands

Landmaking was common practice in the Netherlands, as confirmed by documentary sources and historical maps. Paul Huey has examined the similarities between the ubiquity of slips in New York and the slips and canals so common in Amsterdam and other Dutch cities. In port cities in the Netherlands, as in early New York, slips were positioned as canal-like continuations of streets (Huey 1984).

Despite the existence of manmade land in the Netherlands historically, little archaeological information is available to shed light on the methods used to construct landfill-retaining structures in Holland. Baart et al.'s (1977) seminal work on the archaeology of the Netherlands and northern Europe discusses several sites that contained timber underpinnings for buildings constructed on wet or unstable ground in the medieval and postmedieval periods. The only true Dutch landfill-retaining structure discussed in this work, however, is a wood bulkhead along the Merwede estuary in Dordrecht, built in phases between 1250 and 1550. The approximately 109 yd. long

linear bulkhead consisted of a line of wood piles spaced at intervals of a few feet, to which vertical planks had been fixed (the method of affixing was not stated). The linear bulkhead appears to have been stabilized from both the landward side and waterside with perpendicular tiebacks (Baart et al. 1977:39).

From 1981 to 1982, the City of Amsterdam Office of Monuments and Archaeology excavated the Waterlooplein site on the east bank of the river Amstel in central Amsterdam, which yielded 16th-century timber landfill-retaining structures (Ranjith Jayasena 2009, pers. comm.). While no report was ever written on the excavation, photographs of the site appear to depict two parallel timber revetment walls connected with a third perpendicular revetment (Figure 9). One of the parallel walls appears to be constructed of closely spaced vertical squared-timber piles. The other two walls appear to be constructed of stacked planks sandwiched between timber stakes or narrow piles. Like the first Dutch example, this feature was also linear in form and used piles and planks as primary structural elements.

Although the sample size is far too small to serve as the basis for a generalized understanding of Dutch bulkhead construction, the features at the Waterlooplein and Dordrecht suggest that pile (or earthfast-post) construction may have been a common approach. This may indicate that, in contrast to what Milne has argued for medieval Britain, bulkheads in the Netherlands did not mirror other types of land-bound construction. Timber framing was the dominant wood-based vernacular construction method in the Netherlands in the late medieval period, yet no known timber-framed bulkheads have been documented there.

Scandinavia

In contrast to the largely earthfast-post, stave, and timber-framed constructions found in English medieval landfill-retaining structures, examples from Norway are exclusively part of the log-construction tradition. Furthermore, in contrast to both British and Dutch examples, Norwegian retaining features appear to have been built exclusively in crib (rather than wall) form.

In 1981 to 1982, A. R. Dunlop and A. Golembnik excavated the Finnegården 3a and 6a sites, located near the terminus of Vågen Bay, the main harbor of Bergen, on the west coast of Norway.

FIGURE 9. A ca. 1500–1550 wood revetment wall located on the eastern bank of the river Amstel at the Waterlooplein site in Amsterdam. (Photo by Amsterdam Office for Monuments and Archaeology, Amsterdam, the Netherlands, 1982.)

At these sites, a row of timber "caissons," or cribs, were encountered, which were presumed to be the foundations for a 13th-century pier. These 5 × 5 ft. cribs "were corner-timbered, filled with stones, and ... strengthened by vertical lock bars placed through slots in the timbers" (Myrvoll 1991:152) (Figure 10). Similar cribform wharf foundations of a later 14th-century phase were larger, measuring roughly 16 × 16 ft.

In 1987, J. Komber, in coordination with A. R. Dunlop, excavated the Domkirkegaten 6 site, located roughly 1,000 ft. east of the Finnegården site, also along the former waterfront of Vågen Bay. From the earliest phase of the site (12th century), a small (3 × 3 ft.) log-construction crib was encountered. This crib was sitting on what would have been a shoreline beach, just above sea level. A row of piles was encountered in association with the crib, interpreted as a quay frontage. A slightly later 12th-century row of larger cribs (8 × 11 ft.), probably a quay foundation, was also encountered. These corner-timbered cribs were

placed roughly 5 ft. apart along a former beach. Some were almost identical in construction to those found at the Finnegården site, while others had double lock bars rather than single lock bars, to provide additional strength (Myrvoll 1991).

Denmark does not follow this pattern. A number of timber wharves have been documented in Denmark, ranging in date from the 11th century through the 18th century. None of these were built using the log-construction method or the crib form. Instead, they tend to be linear in form and are constructed of timber piles, either closely spaced or used in combination with horizontal planks or wattles (Roland 2005). The difference can be explained by the fact that Denmark lacked both the timber supply and the strong land-bound log-construction tradition associated with peninsular Scandinavia.

No archaeologically investigated landfill retaining structures in Sweden or Finland are known to the author. Log-construction wharves in crib form have been documented in Novgorod in

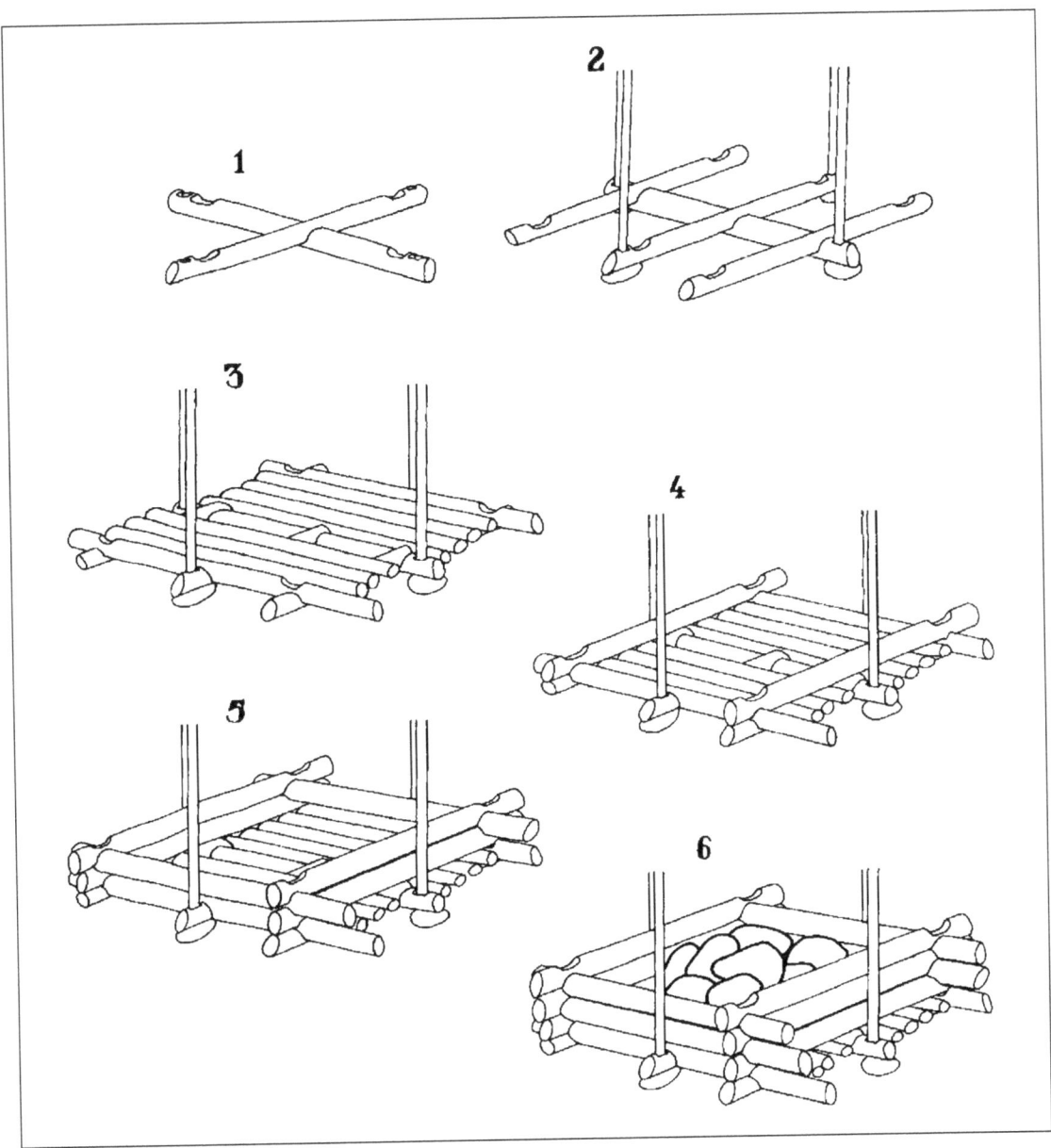

FIGURE 10. The construction sequence of a caisson or crib, based on the medieval log-construction fill-retaining structures found at the Finnegården 3 site in Bergen, Norway (Myrvoll 1991). (Courtesy of Siri Myrvoll and the Council for British Archaeology, York, UK.)

Russia and Gdánsk in Poland (Baart 1977), however, and it is likely that throughout peninsular Scandinavia, as well as parts of eastern Europe where coniferous timber was plentiful and log construction dominated land-bound vernacular building, log-construction crib wharves were standard. A stacked-log riverfront wall reinforced by tiebacks, dating to the 14th or 15th century, was documented in Riga, Latvia (Gläser 2005).

United States

Southeast and Mid-Atlantic

In 1984, the Baltimore Center for Urban Archaeology excavated the late-18th-century Cheapside Wharf in Baltimore, Maryland. It was identified as a crib wharf consisting of lower logs, which would have been built on shore and sunk into place, and topping logs, which would have been constructed in place. The wharf was reportedly constructed largely of southern yellow pine and filled with clean local sands, silts, and clays (Norman 1987:74). The logs on the west side of the wharf were squared timbers, while those forming the east and south walls of the wharf were left in the round (possibly due to their lower visibility). The logs were joined lengthwise with scarf joints secured with wrought-iron pins, and the corners in the structure were notched with lap joints secured with vertical wrought-iron pins (Norman 1987). This technique has parallels in log house construction, in which dowels were sometimes used to reinforce notches (Phleps 1982). White oak anchor piles were driven along the exterior of the bulkheads. Diagonal braces, consisting of smaller-scantling round logs, were found at the corners of the crib. Internal crossties were also present, arranged without regular pattern. The flush dovetail ends of the crossties were often incorporated into scarf-joint assemblies in the wall and were fixed with wood pegs or wrought-iron pins (Norman 1987:80). This type of assembly, also identified at Site 1 of the Washington Street Urban Renewal Area in New York (Geismar 1985), has parallels in log construction.

Archaeological work at Ford's Landing on the Potomac waterfront in Alexandria, Virginia, was carried out by Engineering-Science, Inc. from 1986 to 1993. A complex of 18th-century timber bulkheads associated with the former Keith's Wharf was investigated. The log-construction walls that made up the wharf were not part of crib structures. Rather, they were linear features, arranged to form the three sides of a projecting wharf. The fill sampled within Keith's Wharf was clean clayey sand, apparently redeposited local subsoil. The walls that formed Keith's Wharf consisted of stacked timbers roughly 1 × 1 ft. and either square-hewn or hewn on three sides (the interior face retaining bark). Runs of timber were lengthened using half-lap scarf joints. Both tiebacks and diagonal braces were flush dovetail notched, often pegged into open mortises in the walls, and attached to wood pilings or horizontal deadmen (timber anchors) on the landward side. Along the internal face of the bulkhead wall were long narrow timber "alignment stakes," probably used as guides during construction. These untrimmed wood branches were driven

into the riverbottom every 2 to 5 ft. At the corners of the structure, where two bulkhead walls came together, "cross-lap or saddle cut" corner notching was used. The timbers extended a short distance beyond the corner notches, and were saw-cut on angles. No pegs were incorporated into the notches, but "two rectangular dowels or drift pins" were observed at one end, "reinforcing the horizontal position of the timber" (Engineering-Science, Inc. 1993:159).

In Pennsylvania, archaeologists from John Milner Associates, Inc., and later Louis Berger & Associates (LBA), excavated the Meadows site in the late 1980s. Located just south of the Penn's Landing area in Philadelphia, the project area was historically part of a mid-17th-century Swedish settlement. Portions of several early- to mid-18th-century log-construction wharves were identified (LBA 1991). Thomas Penrose Wharf was constructed of round logs notched together at the corners "in a Lincoln-log-like manner" (LBA 1991:IV-13). The wharf consisted of seven courses of logs, which had been hewn flat only on the upper and lower faces. Half-lap scarf joints along the length of the wall were "secured by wrought-iron barbed spikes" (LBA 1991:IV-15). A number of crossties with flush "dovetail and shoulder" tenons were notched into open housings at the junctions of stacked log courses in the wall face. The far ends of the ties could not be exposed, but it was thought likely that they connected to another parallel wall and that the walls were part of a "crib" structure. Shorter "tie-back braces" extended only 8 ft. into the fill, secured with both horizontal deadmen and wood piles (LBA 1991:IV-21). The fill within the wharf consisted of sand, gravel, and large cobbles. Two sections of Fisher's Wharf were also encountered, one made up of six courses of square-cut oak and southern yellow pine timbers, notched together at the edge in a "Lincoln-log" fashion. The other section was made up of horizontal planks that were fastened to the adjacent timber section with metal spikes. The wharf appeared to be made up of "crib" units, but this could not be confirmed, since only the face of the feature was exposed (LBA 1991).

New York

In 2002 Hartgen Archaeological Associates (with Karen Hartgen as principal investigator) completed data recovery along Albany's Hudson River waterfront at the site of a proposed parking structure for the State University Construction Fund (SUCF). Albany was settled by the Dutch in the 17th century as Beverwyck, located adjacent to Fort Orange on the west bank of the Hudson River. The English assumed control of the town along with the rest of New Netherland in 1664. A number of 18th-century waterfront features were documented including several timber bulkheads forming a linear shoreline along the former Hudson River waterfront. The first set of bulkheads encountered dated to the 1730s, the next parallel set to the 1760s, and a final parallel set to the 1780s (Hartgen et al. 2002).

The 1730s bulkhead walls were identified as being of "grillage" construction. The grillage consisted of stacked continuous courses of logs, each course aligned perpendicular to the one above and below it. Stones filled gaps within and between courses. The grillage form was distinguished from a crib because the timbers were "simply stacked on top of each other with no joinery, no watertight bulkhead wall, and little room for soil fill in between timber layers" (Kilkenny 2002:6.43). In both the 1760s and 1780s bulkheads, two construction types were present, including "stacker construction" (i.e., log construction) and pile construction (Hartgen et al. 2002:6.9). The log-construction features consisted of five to six courses of stacked logs creating a roughly 5 ft. high wall (Figure 11). The round timbers, identified as pine, had slightly flattened upper and lower faces and were joined lengthwise using half-lap scarf joints. The bulkheads were supported internally with timber shores and diagonal braces keyed into the face of the bulkhead using a variety of simple notches. Some were flush-tenoned into open mortises in the top of a single course of timber. Others had sallied (pointed) ends notched into the wall at the junctions of two log courses. The braces were secured with horizontal deadmen in the rear.

Pile-construction bulkhead walls on the site consisted of very tightly spaced vertical timbers. These piles were generally round logs without bark (Figure 12). Where small vertical gaps existed between piles, they were plugged with

FIGURE 11. A mid-18th-century log-construction bulkhead wall along the Hudson River at the SUCF Parking Structure site in Albany (Hartgen et al. 2002). (Courtesy of Hartgen Archaeological Associates, Rensselaer, NY.)

narrow wood planks. Two different methods of pile installation had been used on the site: pile driving and trench excavation. The pile driving method involved the use of piles with pointed ends that had been driven into the river sediment. The trench method involved the excavation of a narrow channel in which a timber sill was laid. The piles stood on this sill, but were not notched into it. Trench excavation was likely used to prevent piles from sinking too far into the silty riverbed. The fill contained within the 1760s and 1780s pile bulkheads included large expanses of "timber ricking," a term used to describe densely stacked small-scantling logs lacking any joinery (Figure 12). The ricking "was probably deposited just before construction of the bulkhead and used to support the pile driver. ... The ricking was then left as fill once the pile driver had completed its task" (Kilkenny 2002:6.49). A small section of "crib" construction was also identified on the site. This was simply a "small diagonally-oriented bulkhead with a crib-style support system," which acted as a connector between two other bulkheads (Kilkenny 2002:6.47).

Site 1 of the Washington Street Urban Renewal Area, located near the Hudson River in Manhattan, was investigated by LBA with Joan Geismar as principal investigator. A buried timber feature on the site was identified as a "cobb wharf" built in a "block-and-bridge" configuration. The wharf blocks consisted of log-constructed cribs (using both squared timbers and round logs) filled with rocks (Geismar 1985:IV-2). The logs were notched at the corners, with square notches, saddle notches, and half-square (lap) notches secured with wood stakes or stabilizing rods. The lower portion of the structure was more tightly constructed than the upper portion; any gaps that existed were filled with thin boards. Half-lap scarf joints were present. Perpendicular braces were notched into the walls of the structure

FIGURE 12. A pile-construction bulkhead at the SUCF Parking Structure Site in Albany (Hartgen et al. 2002). (Courtesy of Hartgen Archaeological Associates, Rensselaer, NY.)

in a variety of ways, including flush L-tenons, square tenons notched into scarf joints, and flush dovetail notches. Piles of small-scantling wood were driven vertically into the river sediment to retain or guide the exterior wall of the structure (Geismar 1985:IV-11).

The Telco block near the East River and Fulton Street in Lower Manhattan was excavated by Diana Rockman, Wendy Harris, and Jed Levin of Soil Systems, Inc., in 1981. Two mid-18th-century wharves, the Van Cortlandt/Berrien Wharf and the Bowne/Byvanck Wharf, were encountered. The exposed wall of the Van Cortlandt/Berrien Wharf consisted of 10 stacked squared timbers identified as pine. Two courses of perpendicular round logs were laid at 3 ft. depth intervals, creating platforms, which helped to contain the stone fill within the cells. These logs were presumed to connect to another wall of timbers parallel to the wharf face, but the supposed location of the rear wall was not excavated. Crossties were notched into the timber wall at random intervals using square notches held with "vertical pegs." The Bowne/Byvanck Wharf was similar in construction and included cells filled with large cobbles. Timber samples from the wharf were identified as sweet gum. A vertical stabilizing rod or "anchoring pile guide" was inserted through a hole in the outermost header in the wall, locking it to the outermost header; an analogous hole suggesting a missing pile guide was located on the other end (Rockman et al. 1983:65). These anchoring pile guides are reminiscent of the "lock bars" found in the multiple sites in Norway. The wharf also featured crossties let into the wall by means of square notches.

Excavations were carried out at the Assay site in the early 1980s by Greenhouse Consultants, led primarily by Diana Wall and Roselle Henn. The results of these excavations and subsequent analyses were put forward in a report by LBA in 1990. The Assay site was at Old Slip near the East River in Lower Manhattan. Several late-18th-century waterfront retaining structures were identified, including east–west oriented Bache's Wharf and two sections of another, north–south oriented wharf (Figure 13). Four bulkhead walls constructed of vertical and horizontal planks and piles were also documented.

Bache's Wharf was described as being constructed with stacked 1 × 1 ft. timbers (both round logs and squared timbers). Although the units of the structure were believed to be cribs, this could not be proven because only the north face of Bache's Wharf was exposed. Smaller cross timbers were tied into the wall every few feet with "half dovetail and shoulder housings" (LBA 1990:IV-25). The ends of the cross timbers were flush with the outer face of the structure. Vertical guideposts were near the ends of the structure. These were let in with a square notch flush with the face of the horizontal timbers. Iron spikes may also have been used to fix these guideposts to the face. The north–south wharf, perpendicular to Bache's Wharf, consisted of two abutting log-construction sections (or cribbing blocks) in the same alignment. Each was roughly 15 ft. (seven to eight timbers) high and was constructed of round and squared corner-notched timbers. The northern cribbing block was one cell wide, while the southern was two cells wide. Within these blocks, saddle-notched cross braces created a series of square cells that varied in dimension from 4 to 8 ft. on a side. Squared wood guideposts secured with metal spikes were used here too. A layer of smaller-scantling wood was laid between the upper three courses of stretchers, "in order to create a floored cell in which to contain the stone fill" (LBA 1990:IV-31). Small split logs that did not extend the full width of the cells were located between the lower two courses of stretchers.

Four shorter timber bulkheads were also encountered at the Assay site. The first consisted of 10 vertical planks retained by a hewn horizontal timber. It appeared that the planks had been driven directly into the riverbed clay, and the timber served only to guide or retain them. Another 23 ft. long section of bulkhead consisted of five horizontal planks retained by square posts or stakes. No further information on fasteners or joinery used in this bulkhead was provided. Two additional bulkheads were constructed of horizontal planks retained on each side by a series of wood stakes or pilings (LBA 1990).

New England

A number of early timber retaining structures have also been investigated in New England. Because British influences were particularly dominant in early New England, examination of wharves constructed prior to the popularization of

FIGURE 13. A view of the crib form of the late-18th-century north–south wharf at the Assay site. (Photo ca. 1984 from the Assay Site Collection; courtesy of the New York State Museum, Albany.)

log building traditions in the early 18th century has the potential to yield insights into the history of carpentry in this region. Most of the 17th-century timber retaining structures investigated in New England lacked sufficient integrity to provide conclusive data, however.

The Institute of Conservation Archaeology and, subsequently, the Public Archaeology Laboratory, Inc. (PAL), investigated Town Dock Wharves/ Dry Dock site in Charlestown, Massachusetts, in the 1980s and early 1990s. The site contained several wharf segments built in phases from 1640 to 1835. The earliest segment encountered appeared to be a wall forming one side of a former wharf. The face of the wharf had been removed or obliterated during subsequent building campaigns, and the construction technique used to build the feature could not be determined. Cruciform tiebacks that had braced the structure from the landward side were still in place, however, and verified that the feature was linear in form. A later, ca. 1813 section of wharf was a log-construction feature in crib form, using

dovetail-notched crossties and containing loose-clay and silt fills. Two sections of plank bulkhead were also found at the site, both dating to the early 19th century. Both consisted of stacked horizontal planks held in place by piles. While a few of the planks were held to the piles with nails, they primarily relied on gravity and the pressure of the fill on the landward side to keep them in place (PAL 1994).

In 2000 John Milner Associates, Inc., with Charles D. Cheek and Joseph Balicki as principal investigators, conducted a data recovery at the Mill Pond site in the North End of Boston. A ca. 1707 wharf that appeared to contain a grillagelike structure consisting of stacked timbers with no joinery was investigated. The waterside edge of the wharf was not clearly defined, and it was speculated that the bulkhead that had originally retained this loose timber complex had been obliterated during subsequent construction. A bulkhead dating to the late 18th century, a later rebuilding episode, consisted of two parallel walls of stacked timbers less than 3 ft. apart, which were tied to each other by short crossties placed at irregular intervals, forming a sort of modified crib form (Cheek and Balicki 2000).

The Derby and Central wharves in Salem, Massachusetts, have been the subject of several studies. They were most recently investigated by University of Massachusetts Archaeological Services (Mitchell T. Mulholland, principal investigator) and the National Park Service (Dana C. Linck, principal investigator) in the late 1990s. Original sections of the 1762 Derby Wharf were identified as a log-construction retaining wall with tiebacks. A late-18th-century addition to the Derby Wharf and the entirety of late-18th-century Central Wharf were also built using log-construction techniques, but in crib form (Garman et al. 1998).

Conclusions

A number of patterns are suggested regarding pre-1850s landfill-retaining structures, particularly when the above examples are reviewed according to their vernacular construction method and other basic attributes, such as form. This approach, rather than the prevailing reliance on the "crib," "solid-filled," and "cobb" typology, sets wharves and bulkheads more meaningfully in the context of cultural and architectural history.

European examples have revealed clear regional distinctions in landfill-retaining structure construction. In Britain, medieval timber retaining structures are typically of timber-frame construction and take the form of a braced retaining wall. Other British examples include retaining walls of earthfast-post (pile) construction, stave (plank) construction, or masonry construction. No log-construction or crib-form structures appear to have been constructed in Britain after the Roman period. In contrast, all known medieval examples in present-day Norway are of log construction and are in crib form. The construction methods used in landfill-retaining structures in medieval England and Norway are consistent with the chief construction methods used in land-bound vernacular structures in those nations during the same period. In medieval England, timber-frame construction was dominant, and in medieval Norway, log construction was dominant.

In North America, log-construction methods were used in the vast majority of pre-1850 timber landfill-retaining structures in all regions along the eastern seaboard. These structures were often, but not always, built in a crib form. Examples of linear log-construction retaining walls with tiebacks have also been documented at sites in New England, New York, and the South. Other kinds of landfill-retaining structures documented in North American sites include vertical- or horizontal-plank bulkhead walls, but these tend to appear in relatively short segments in combination with other types. Timber-pile walls were encountered at the SUCF Parking Structure site along a section of river shoreline. No examples of timber-framed retaining structures appear to have been documented in the United States.

In his analysis of waterfront structures in London, Gustav Milne has argued persuasively that a close connection exists between land-bound vernacular buildings and contemporaneous timber retaining structures. This parallel, he argues, persisted through the three primary developments in historical timber joinery in Britain, consisting of earthfast-post construction, stave construction, and timber-frame construction (Milne 1991). Milne concludes that "both types of structure, although clearly different in function, utilized the same range of techniques. That this approach differs from the methods employed by other specialist carpenters, such as boat builders, is also apparent" (Milne 1991:116). Milne argues that "the waterfront installations in medieval London were erected by the same men who were responsible for timber building elsewhere in the city" (Milne 1991:116).

It is uncertain if American wharf builders, like their British counterparts, were the same individuals who constructed houses and barns. Most likely, construction of wharves in North America was typically performed or overseen by house carpenters until the 19th century, when the specialized profession of "dockbuilder" developed. In their study of the Schermerhorn Row block in Manhattan, Kardas and Larrabee suggest that in New York the transition came around the close of the 18th century, when "rapid growth of the waterfront required greater investment of capital, was accomplished by more standardized construction techniques, and was characterized by the emergence of specialist/contractors, as opposed to the earlier period when general craftsmen/carpenters included waterfront construction among their other building skills (Kardas and Larrabee 1991:26). The physical evidence supports the notion that carpenters were involved in early American wharf construction. The correlation between land-bound buildings and landfill-retaining structures in America, however, does not appear to be as close as that shown by Milne for medieval England. By the 18th century, many American carpenters would have been familiar with both the timber-framing tradition of British and Dutch origin and the log-construction tradition of Scandinavian and German origin. While a preference for timber framing persisted in house and barn construction, however, it appears that log construction was almost always chosen to build wharves and other landfill-retaining structures.

In her 1983 paper on wharf construction, Andrea Heintzelman-Muego (1983:13) states:

> Close comparison of particularly the joinery detail in some of the English structures with that found in excavated wharf structures located along the Atlantic seaboard of the United States bear some uncanny similarities. ... [I]n the crib type wharf construction used in the United States ... we begin to see similarities in material, design, and joinery detail with that found in England. Perhaps then, it can be reasonably deduced that locally excavated wharves are indeed traceable to earlier English architectural and structural designs.

Contrary to Heintzelman-Muego's contention, most historical American waterfront structures along the eastern seaboard differed considerably from medieval English examples in form and construction tradition. Timber waterfront structures in post-Roman Britain consisted primarily of timber-framed or plank-framed revetment walls, while most American examples used log-construction methods and relied heavily on the crib form. While rare examples of plank or pile walls have been encountered, there are no known timber-frame examples in America.

Instead, most American waterfront retaining structures have more in common with the Norwegian features reviewed above. Similarities include the log-construction technique, the crib form, and details of construction such as saddle and half-lap corner notching, wood dowels or spikes driven through the notches, and vertical lock bars inserted into holes in the lower courses of timber to stabilize the structure. The lock bars encountered at the Washington Street Urban Renewal Area and the Telco block, for example, resemble those used in the Domkirkegaten and Finnegården sites in Norway. Still other aspects

of the American retaining structures draw from log-construction techniques such as the joinery assembly encountered in several sites (e.g., the Washington Street Urban Renewal Area and Cheapside Wharf) in which the ends of crossties were incorporated into scarf joints. This assembly was often used in log houses where floor joists or partition walls were fitted into the main walls (Phleps 1982).

There are many examples of linear retaining walls in North America that, while built using log-construction methods, resemble the form of the British and Dutch retaining walls. Their locations range throughout the eastern seaboard and have formed continuous linear shorelines or the sides of a wharf. The use of the log-construction method in combination with the linear form may represent an American adaptation influenced by multiple traditions.

More specific Dutch influences on American wharf and bulkhead building are not evident in general. The closely spaced piles found at the SUCF Parking Structure site in Albany do bear similarities to those found at the Waterlooplein site in Amsterdam, and it is possible that this reflects a Dutch influence. No other examples of this approach being used in North American wharf or bulkhead construction have been found, however.

On the whole, American retaining structures appear to have drawn most heavily from the log-construction tradition, even in parts of North America dominated by British or Dutch culture. This pattern is striking, because the log-construction tradition is not native to Britain or the Netherlands and was not used for land-bound buildings or waterfront retaining structures in those locations. The log-construction tradition applied to landfill-retaining structures in the New World may have originated in the colonial Swedish and Finnish settlements in the Delaware Bay area. Scholars have made compelling arguments linking early colonial American log houses to Scandinavian log building traditions in this region, and the same pattern likely holds true for waterfront structures. Slightly later, log traditions from what are now Germany, Switzerland, and neighboring areas also influenced North American building. The log-construction approach was likely borrowed in English- and Dutch-dominated locations due to its effectiveness, ease of construction, and the availability of softwoods. Furthermore, the predominance of log wharves and bulkheads in areas where the method was rarely used for landbound structures, such as Manhattan, Brooklyn, and parts of New England, appears to support the concept that while the technology for log construction was indeed part of carpenters' vocabularies by the early 18th century, it was considered appropriate only for the most utilitarian of structures.

While Milne has shown close parallels between land-bound buildings and waterfront retaining structures in Britain, the correlation in North America appears to be more complex. Further study of retaining structures from the point of view of vernacular carpentry could yield meaningful insights into both the development of wharf construction and, more broadly, the dissemination of building traditions throughout North America.

Acknowledgments

The author wishes to give special thanks to Diane Dallal of AKRF, Edward Morin and Meta Janowitz of URS Corporation, and Daniel Addey-Jibb of Hamlet Heavy Timberwork. Thanks also to Linda Stone, Randy Nash, Jack Sobon, and Bill Krattinger.

References

ALLEN, EDWARD, AND ROB THALLON
  2006 Fundamentals of Residential Construction. John Wiley and Sons, Hoboken, NJ.

BAART, JAN, WIARD KROOK, AB LAGERWEIJ, NINA OCKERS, HANS VAN REGTEREN ALTENA, TUUK STAM, HENK STOEPKER, GERARD STOUTHART, AND MONIKA VAN DER ZWAN
  1977 Opgraving in Amsterdam: Twintig Jaar Stadskernonderzoek. Fibula-Van Dishoek, Haarlem, the Netherlands.

BRADY, MARY JANE
  1978 The Construction of Marine Structures in New England Prior to 1901. Master's thesis, Department of Historic Preservation, Columbia University, New York, NY.

BROWN, R. J.
  1986 Timber-Framed Buildings of England. Robert Hale, London, UK.

CAREW, TIM, DAMIAN GOODBURN, NIGEL JEFFRIES, AND ANGUS STEPHENSON
  2009 Post-Medieval Wharfs on the Channelsea River: Burford Wharf Calico Printing Works, Stratford E15. London Archaeologist 12(6):163–171.

CHEEK, CHARLES D., AND JOSEPH BALICKI
  2000 Archaeological Data Recovery: The Mill Pond Site (BOS-HA-14), Boston, Massachusetts. Report to Timelines, Inc., Littleton, MA, and the Central Artery Tunnel Project, Becthel/Parsons-Brinckerhoff, Boston, MA, from John Milner Associates, Inc., West Chester, PA.

ENGINEERING-SCIENCE, INC.
  1993 Maritime Archaeology at Keith's Wharf and Battery Cove (44AX119): Ford's Landing: Alexandria, VA. Report to Cook Inlet Region of Virginia, from Engineering-Science, Inc., Washington, DC.

FOX, WILLIAM F.
  1902 History of the Lumber Industry in the State of New York. United States Department of Agriculture, Bureau of Forestry, Washington, DC.

FRENCH, J. H.
  1860 Gazeteer of the State of New York. R. Pearsall Smith, Syracuse, NY.

GARMAN, JAMES C., LESLIE C. SHAW, F. TIMOTHY BARKER, AND MITCHELL T. MULHOLLAND
  1998 Archaeological Investigation at Derby and Central Wharves, Salem Maritime National Historic Site, Salem, Massachusetts. Report to the National Park Service from University of Massachusetts Archaeological Services, Amherst, MA.

GARVIN, JAMES L.
  2001 A Building History of Northern New England. University Press of New England, Hanover, NH.

GEISMAR, JOAN H.
  1983 The Archaeological Investigation of the 175 Water Street Block, New York City. Report to HRO International, New York, NY, from Soil Systems, Inc., Marietta, GA.
  1985 Archaeological Investigations of Site 1 of the Washington Street Urban Renewal Area, New York City. Report to Shearson Lehman/American Express through the New York City Public Development Corporation, New York, NY, from Louis Berger & Associates, East Orange, NJ.

GLÄSER, MANFRED
  2005 Mittelalterliche Hafen: Anlagen in Norddeutschland (Medieval harbors: constructions in Northern Germany). In Bolværker—fra Middelalderen og Nyere Tid (Bulkheads—from the Middle Ages to more recent times), Thomas Roland, editor, pp. 37–48. Næstved Museum, Næstved, Denmark.

HARRIS, RICHARD
  1978 Discovering Timber-Framed Buildings. Shire Publications, Princes Risborough, UK.

HARTGEN, KAREN, J. WILLIAM BOUCHARD, NANCY CLARK, JUSTIN DIVIRGILIO, JASON FENTON, CHRISTOPHER KILKENNY, MATTHEW KIRK, ANDRE KRIERS, MATTHEW LESNIAK, KEVIN MOODY, SCOTT STULL, ADAM TÖKÉS, AND WALTER WHEELER
2002 At the River's Edge: Two-Hundred-Fifty Years of Albany History. Data Retrieval, SUCF Parking Structure, Maiden Lane, Albany, New York. Report to State University Construction Fund, Albany, NY, from Hartgen Archaeological Associates, Inc., Rensselaer, NY.

HEINTZELMAN, ANDREA J.
1985 Late Seventeenth- and Eighteenth-Century Wharf Technology: Historical and Archaeological Investigations of Three Eastern U.S. Examples. Master's thesis, Department of Anthropology, American University, Washington DC.

HEINTZELMAN-MUEGO, ANDREA
1983 Construction Material and Design of 19th Century and Earlier Wharves: An Urban Archaeological Concern. Paper presented at the 16th Conference on Historical and Underwater Archaeology, Denver, CO.

HEWETT, CECIL A.
1980 *English Historic Carpentry.* Phillimore, London, UK.

HOBLEY, BRIAN
1981 The London Waterfront: the Exception or the Rule? In *Waterfront Archaeology in Britain and Northern Europe*, Gustav Milne and Brian Hobley, editors, pp 1–9. Council for British Archaeology, Research Report No. 41. London, UK.

HUEY, PAUL R.
1984 Old Slip and Cruger's Wharf at New York: An Archaeological Perspective of the Colonial American Waterfront. *Historical Archaeology* 18(1):15–37.

JENSENIUS, JØRGEN H.
2003 The Inverse Design Problem in Medieval Wooden Churches of Norway. Paper presented at the 6th Asian Design International Conference, Tsukuba, Japan. Stavekirke.org <http://www.stavkirke.org/artikler/artikkel-japan.html>. Accessed 3 December 2009.

JORDAN, TERRY G.
1978 *Texas Log Buildings: A Folk Architecture.* University of Texas Press, Austin.
1995 The Material Culture Legacy of New Sweden on the American Frontier. In *New Sweden in America*, E. Hoffecker, R. Waldron, L. Williams, and B. Benson, editors, pp. 71–83. University of Delaware Press, Newark.

KARDAS, S., AND E. LARRABEE
1991 Summary Report of 1981–1983 Archaeological Excavation, The Schermerhorn Row Block. Report to New York City Economic Development Corporation, New York, NY, from Historic Sites Research, Princeton, NJ.

KEVLIN, MARY JOAN
1986 Radiographic Inspection of Plank-House Construction. *Bulletin of the Association for Preservation Technology* 18(3):40–47.

KILKENNY, CHRISTOPHER
2002 Harbor at the Headwaters of Prosperity: Albany's Eighteenth-Century Waterfront. In At the River's Edge: Two-Hundred-Fifty Years of Albany History. Data Retrieval, SUCF Parking Structure, Maiden Lane, Albany, New York, Karen Hartgen, J. William Bouchard, Nancy Clark, Justin DiVirgilio, Jason Fenton, Christopher Kilkenny, Matthew Kirk, Andre Kriers, Matthew Lesniak, Kevin Moody, Scott Stull, Adam Tökés, and Walter Wheeler, authors, pp. 6.1–6.88. Report to State University Construction Fund, Albany, NY, from Hartgen Archaeological Associates, Inc., Rensselaer, NY.

LEWANDOWSKI, JAN LEO
1995 Traditional Timber Framing in Vermont, 1780–1850. *APT Bulletin* 26(2&3):42–50.

LOUIS BERGER & ASSOCIATES (LBA)
1990 The Assay Site: Historic and Archaeological Investigations of the New York City Waterfront. Report to HRO International, New York, NY, from Louis Berger & Associates, East Orange, NJ.
1991 The Meadows Site: Historical and Archaeological Investigations of Philadelphia's Waterfront. Report to Urban Engineers, Inc., Philadelphia, PA, from Louis Berger & Associates, East Orange, NJ.

MERCER, HENRY C.
1967 *The Origin of Log Houses in the United States.* Bucks County Historical Society, Doylestown, PA.

MILNE, GUSTAV
1991 Waterfront Archaeology and Vernacular Architecture: A London Study. In *Waterfront Archaeology: Proceedings of the Third International Conference on Waterfront Archaeology, Bristol, 1988*, G. L. Good, R. H. Jones, and M. W. Ponsford, editors, pp. 116–120. Council for British Archaeology, CBA Research Report No. 74. London, UK.

MILNE, GUSTAV, AND CHRISSIE MILNE
1978 Excavations on the Thames Waterfront at Trig Lane, London, 1974–76. *Medieval Archaeology* 22: 84–104.

MYRVOLL, S.
1991 Vågen and Bergen: the Changing Waterfront and the Structure of the Medieval Town. In *Waterfront Archaeology: Proceedings of the Third International Conference on Waterfront Archaeology, Bristol, 1988*, G. L. Good, R. H. Jones, and M. W. Ponsford, editors, pp. 150–161. Council for British Archaeology, CBA Research Report No. 74. London, UK.

NORMAN, JOSEPH GARY
1987 Eighteenth-Century Wharf Construction in Baltimore, Maryland. Master's thesis, Department of Anthropology, College of William and Mary, Williamsburg, VA.

PHLEPS, HERMANN
1982   *The Craft of Log Building: A Handbook of Craftsmanship in Wood.* Lee Valley Tools, Ottawa, ON.

PUBLIC ARCHAEOLOGY LABORATORY, INC. (PAL)
1994   The Town Dock Wharves/ Dry Dock Site and Town Dock Pottery Site, Central Artery North Reconstruction Project, Archaeological Data Recovery, Charlestown, Massachusetts, Volume IV-A. Report to Massachusetts Highway Department, Boston, MA, from PAL, Inc., Pawtucket, RI.

ROCKMAN, DIANA, WENDY HARRIS, AND JED LEVIN
1983   The Archaeological Investigation of the Telco Block, South Street Seaport Historic District, New York, NY. Report to Jack Resnick and Sons, New York, NY, from Soil Systems, Inc., Marietta, GA.

ROLAND, THOMAS (EDITOR)
2005   *Bolværker—fra Middelalderen og Nyere Tid* (Bulkheads—from the Middle Ages to more recent times). Næstved Museum, Næstved, Denmark.

SEASHOLES, NANCY S.
2003   *Gaining Ground: A History of Landmaking in Boston.* Massachusetts Institute of Technology Press, Cambridge.

SMALL, EDWIN W.
1941   *Early Wharf Building.* Eastern National Park and Monument Association, Salem, MA.

SOBON, JACK A.
2002   *Historic American Timber Joinery: A Graphic Guide.* Timber Framers Guild, Becket, MA.

WONDERS, WILLIAM C.
1979   Log Dwellings in Canadian Folk Architecture. *Annals of the Association of American Geographers* 69(2):187–207.

MOLLY R. MCDONALD
AKRF, INC.
440 PARK AVENUE SOUTH
NEW YORK, NEW YORK 10016

1999. Training and Ferry Slips are not Sexy Lingerie. In *Underwater Archaeology Proceedings* 1999, Adriana A. Neidinger and Matthew A. Russel, editors, pp. 11–16.

CELIA MCCARTHY

Training Walls and Ferry Slips are not Sexy Lingerie

Introduction

Ordinary landscapes do not usually attract the attention of the average citizen. Common landscape elements seem to have no intrinsic appeal and convey little meaning beyond their function. Ordinary structures at the water's edge, such as piers, quays, wharves, seawalls, jetties, and pilings are not "sexy" like a shipwreck, a statuesque chateau, or Monticello. To most people, these are infrastructure elements, like sidewalks. How could they possibly be historically significant? To some they are "hysterically significant" and will just get in the way of progress. To these people, the historical significance of obsolete old stone training walls that probably never worked in the first place is unfathomable. Evaluating the concrete foundation walls of demolished ferry slips to determine if they might be eligible for the National Register of Historic Places seems ludicrous. The fear that preservation of such ruins will interfere with the construction schedule of important development projects seems overwhelming. But preservation of structures is not necessarily the point. A cultural resources planner at the Port of Oakland helps to identify and evaluate the historical significance of potential historic properties, assess the effects of development projects on those properties and, if necessary, develop a treatment plan to mitigate those effects and preserve the information those properties contain.

The history of Oakland harbor development dates to the mid-19th century. The Port of Oakland, established in 1927, is an autonomous, financially self-supporting department of the City of Oakland, California, created to develop, manage, and promote the City's waterfront. The Port fulfills these responsibilities as trustee for State tidelands and in accordance with the City Charter. As the manager of most of Oakland's wa-terfront and a major developer of shoreline properties, the Port must comply with local, state, and federal environmental protection laws. These laws oblige the Port to consider the effects of its projects, and those of its tenants, on properties determined to have historical significance.

How do we assess the significance of shoreline resources? Since they are vulnerable and require perpetual maintenance to remain stable under constant tidal action, waterfront structures quickly fall into disrepair and they may deteriorate to the point where public safety is a concern. Along-shore sites and structures are not always attractive and it is most likely that nothing "important" happened there. As a result, historical resources along the waterfront are frequently dealt with as individual elements being affected by separate development projects. They are rarely seen as components of a larger maritime landscape. Disarticulated study, even though it is conducted according to the legal mandate, tends to result in the demolition of these elements without sufficient consideration for the cumulative alteration of the area's historical footprint or the loss of maritime cultural knowledge. One way to comprehend historical significance is to understand the Oakland waterfront as a maritime cultural landscape worthy of scrutiny, the way in which that landscape connects to the greater San Francisco Bay Region, the role of human choice and responsibility in the making of landscapes, and the historical context within which decisions about landscape modification have been made.

What is a Landscape Study?

For the purpose of this paper, the term "cultural landscape" will be used to describe the territory created by human beings—the settings we build for ourselves in relationship to the space that surrounds us—especially those settings that emphasize community and membership (Groth 1997b). Geographer Pierce Lewis (1979) explains that the common usage of the verb "to landscape" generally means to enhance a piece of land with plants in an artful fashion. As the term is used in studies such as this, however, ". . . it is proper and important to think of cultural landscape as nearly everything we see when we go outdoors. Such a common workaday landscape has very little to do to with the skilled work of landscape architects, but it has a great deal to say about the United States as a country and Americans as people" (Lewis 1979). Lewis goes on to explain that our human landscape is our unwitting autobiography, though it may not be easy to read. The cultural landscape may be messy and disorganized, but we can learn to interpret it if we use our eyes and think about what we are seeing.

The study of the American cultural environment, or cultural landscape, can be traced to the work of John Brinckerhoff Jackson, who published the first issue of *Landscape* magazine in 1951. Jackson challenged a whole generation of geographers, architects, planners, archaeologists, folklorists and many others to contemplate the interaction between the landscape and the aspirations and needs of the people who inhabit it. Jackson's interest went beyond looking at extraordinary examples of architecture and landscaping to explore the significance of the common, everyday environment (Groth 1997a).

According to Thomas Carter (1998), study of the historical landscape is a type of research that is becoming increasingly prevalent, whether it goes by the name of vernacular architecture, material culture, or cultural landscape studies. Specific topics and methods may vary, he says, but a growing number of people have embraced the idea that the systematic study of the built environment has enormous potential to provide understanding of both past and present human behavior.

This examination of the Oakland shoreline is based on Paul Groth's articulation of the fundamental principles of the study of cultural landscape, which are included in the introductory lecture of his course on the History of the U.S. Cultural Environment at U.C. Berkeley: (1) nearly all items in the human landscape reflect culture in some way; (2) the evolution and con-

tinuing existence of most cultural landscapes are intimately related to landforms, climate, soil, and plant life; (3) humans are a part of nature, therefore their habitats are a part of nature; (4) history matters when trying to unravel the mystery of the present landscape; (5) often elements of the cultural landscape make little sense if they are studied out of their local context; (6) landscapes are the true reflection of culture and cultural change; people tend to say things in landscape that they would never say in words (Groth 1997b). Groth emphasizes that *ordinary* is a key word in landscape study and that ordinary landscapes are important and worthy of study. What frequently attracts interest is a particularly beautiful example of architectural style (e.g. Italianate, Queen Anne, or Craftsman), a designed landscape (e.g. Golden Gate Park), or buildings associated with prominent people (e.g. Mount Vernon). Observation and analysis of the everyday built environment, however, can reveal profound changes in cultural activities found in an area over time (Carter 1998).

Context

During the last half of the 19th century, the San Francisco Bay Area was developed from a sparsely settled agrarian region into a thriving metropolis. According to geographer James Vance (1964), the initial American period in the Bay Area was characterized by an open-extensive settlement pattern due to the presence of a body of water which permitted the near-instantaneous creation of a regional transportation system. That water-based transportation system extended far into California via the river system. Transportation of passengers and cargo by water was a commonplace event throughout the Bay Area and the general public encountered shoreline structures on a regular basis. This is no longer the case. Since the turn of the century, Bay Area residents have increasingly relied on the automobile for transportation, as has most of the population of the United States. Bridges throughout the Bay region carry daily commuter traffic high above the water and there is little on the landscape of today's superhighway to indicate when one actually leaves the land and ventures out over water. With the advent of regular air travel, the number of ocean-liner passengers has drastically declined. The shoreline landscape has become increasingly alien to the average citizen to the point where only working mariners and small boaters develop any familiarity with it (Stilgoe 1994).

Most of the Oakland waterfront, occupied by Port of Oakland Marine Terminals, Southern Pacific and Union Pacific Railroad Yards, the now-closed Fleet and Industrial Supply Center, and a variety of industrial properties, has become a specialized landscape, shaped by the increasingly specialized spatial requirements of industry and transportation technology of the past and present. A 19th-century resident of Oakland would find nothing familiar about today's landscape and would not even recognize the landforms. Since 1882, hundreds of acres of tidal marsh lands on both sides of the Oakland Estuary have been filled, dramatically altering local geography.

Case Study 1: Oakland Inner Harbor Training Walls

The shipping channel and the training walls that helped to define the basic footprint of waterfront development in Oakland are over 100 years old. They were constructed by the U.S. Ar.ny Corps of Engineers between 1874 and 1896, as part of a federal harbor improvement program, and once extended into open bay waters for almost two miles with no land on either side. As an alternative to dredging in the 19th and early-20th centuries, engineers attempted to harness the power of nature with training walls, two parallel stone or concrete walls, which were built to enhance the natural currents to scour and deepen the shipping channel of a river or estuary.

Jetties, breakwaters, or wave protection structures are usually covered with a layer of loosely-placed large stone, commonly referred to as riprap, with many faces and voids to dissipate wave energy. This kind of shoreline treatment is common: piles of rocks, great granite blocks, and even concrete rubble from a demolished building strewn along the shoreline. The Oakland Inner Harbor training walls are different. They are faced with large stones, hand-set in a dry-masonry technique, which gives them an unusual, smooth appearance.

Before the training walls were constructed, the Oakland estuary was a shallow, silted slough that could only be navigated by boats with a draft of 5 or 6 ft. Ocean-going ships simply could not make it over the bar, even at high water. The training walls were a grand experiment that never really succeeded as a self-flushing operation, and the federal channel between them has always required routine dredging. Nevertheless, the walls were crucial to the harbor improvement program in Oakland and are the oldest surviving remnant of that program. All other improvements, including extensive filling projects, have grown up in reference to the established channel, as delineated by the training walls. The training walls, with their dry-masonry facing, represent an important engineering feat in their own right and, combined with other harbor improvements, contributed significantly to the economic growth and population expansion of Oakland and other East Bay cities and have continued to do so since the last decades of the 19th century (McCarthy and Lerner 1997).

Efforts to evaluate the training walls in anticipation of base transfer and reuse planning of both the Fleet and Industrial Supply Center and the Alameda Naval Air Station illustrate the utility of applying a maritime landscape perspective to shoreline resources. In 1996, when this project began, Richard Lerner, anthropologist at the Army Corps of Engineers, San Francisco District, had been conducting research and was interested in looking at the resources (both north and south walls and the channel) as a system. The Navy conducted its own evaluation of a portion of the south wall. The Port of Oakland's initial survey of the north wall recorded only a fraction of the resource. These site-oriented studies identified only a portion of the resource, largely because survey was conducted from the land only; no view was taken from the water. At Lerner's suggestion, a survey from the channel waters was conducted in July 1997, which clearly showed that although a considerable portion of both walls has been covered with fill or destroyed, significant portions of both the north and south training walls remain. They are visible at most tidal levels and their overall integrity is high. Some sections of the walls have deteriorated and other small areas have been repaired but the large sections of the jetties that are still visible retain a significant portion of their integrity of design, material, workmanship, feeling, and association and are able to convey these qualities, especially when viewed from the water or from the opposite shore of the channel. The State Historic Preservation Officer concurred with the determination that the training walls and federal channel are eligible for the National Register.

Case Study 2: Western Pacific Mole

A second case study involves an assessment of the remains of two ferry slips on the Western Pacific Railroad's Oakland mole, located on the shores of San Francisco Bay at the north side of the western end of the entrance to the Oakland estuary. A mole is a large structure of earth or stone that extends out in the water and has a large, flat surface which can be used for the transfer of cargo and passengers between boats and land-based transportation. The two ferry slips at the Western Pacific mole—one for freight, the other for passengers—were placed into service in 1910. Passenger operations between Oakland and San Francisco continued until mid-1933, when passenger service was terminated at this location and transferred to the Southern Pacific Railroad's mole just to the north. The passenger terminal and train shed were demolished in 1940 but both slips contin-

ued to operate as a transfer point for freight until 1978. An evaluation of the entire complex was made in 1985 and the resource was determined not eligible for the National Register because alteration and demolition had severely impacted its historic character (Wall and Delgado 1985). Shortly after this evaluation, the wooden fender and decking system was demolished. An evaluation of the remnants of the mole foundations in the summer of 1997 reaffirmed the near total loss of integrity of design, materials, workmanship, feeling, and association (McCarthy, Corbett, and Minor 1997). This site, however, is of local importance for two reasons. First, the establishment of the Western Pacific mole at this location set in motion the legal process that enabled the City of Oakland to regain title to a significant portion of its waterfront. Second, the site has evolved into an intermodal transportation facility and thus the setting represents the evolution of transportation technology. While the facility is not eligible for the National Register, one has merely to walk out to the edge of the mole foundations and view the San Francisco skyline in the distance to feel the sense of embarkation that remains. Many sites encountered within the Port's jurisdiction may not possess enough integrity to be eligible for the National Register but they may be of local importance and may meet the standards for recognition under other state and local programs. Sites of local interest that are located in public access areas provide an opportunity for public education. When viewed as part of Oakland's maritime cultural landscape, even concrete retaining walls, the fragments of a once greater facility, can be interpreted and convey the historical significance of the site and the events that occurred there.

Long-Term Management Strategies

What strategies should be used to ensure that shoreline resources are adequately assessed? Essentially, waterfront surveys may require alternative methods of study. Properties located along the shoreline should be viewed from the water as well as on land whenever possible. Surveys should be undertaken at a low tidal levels, in order to ensure that resources that may be partially or wholly submerged at higher tidal levels may be viewed. In addition, viewing shoreline development as a cultural landscape, allows an evaluator to determine significance from a broader, less particularistic point of view. Seemingly useless elements of the transportation infrastructure, when viewed in relationship to the articulation between the water and the land, take on new meaning. An important component of a long-term cultural landscape approach to maritime resources within the Port's jurisdiction is to develop a property typology. The Port's waterfront resources extend from San Leandro Bay along the Estuary to the Outer Harbor in San Francisco Bay and include a wide variety of property types. Development along the shoreline has largely occurred in relationship to the confluence of transportation modes in the area; therefore, as transportation technology has evolved, so have the related features. Significance can be assessed in relationship to the property type and its associated themes. Historical research and field survey indicate that seven historic-period property types may be present within the Port's jurisdiction. These categories are: transportation infrastructure, shoreline stabilization structures, industrial properties, commercial properties, domestic occupation sites, military properties, and submerged sites.

Another primary objective is to develop research themes and pose questions that will assist in determining the historical significance of these property types. Who built this? What was its purpose? Where did the materials come from? Why does it look the way it does? What does it tell us about the development of structure and infrastructure in the Bay Area? Does it reflect the relationship between public attitudes about the environment and the development of public policy? Does its scale demonstrate the efforts of private enterprise or municipal development? Does it aid in the understanding of the impact of transportation technology on local geography? Does it contain information about people who inhabited the shoreline? What does it tell us about the relationship between human beings and water-based transportation? Does it contain evidence of poorly documented or undocumented processes that could add to the body of maritime cultural knowledge? Does it have interpretive potential? Asking questions such as these about the historical materials in the landscape that have survived into the present can help us to construct the past of a community, approach an understanding of how and why things may be different in the present, and incorporate this understanding into our plans for the future.

At the end of the 19th century, most ships were made of wood and were loaded and unloaded by men with hand trucks. Now, at the end of the 20th century, ships are made of steel and are loaded and unloaded by fewer men operating enormous machines. While many other waterfronts languish in obsolescence, Oakland's is dynamic. Planners at the Port of Oakland are completely re-envisioning the Oakland waterfront to accommodate both deep-draft, ocean-going container vessels and the desire for more open space and public access to the shoreline. The shoreline in Oakland is an evolving maritime cultural landscape. The aim is not necessarily to preserve all the material remains of the past, but to document them and to maintain the body of maritime cultural knowledge so people will be able to remember they were there. Recording maritime cultural resources, evaluating their historical significance, and interpreting them in public access areas has become part of the planning process. Establishing thresholds of significance that relate to the whole and enable us to see the ordinary, rather than restricting our vision to disarticulated sites, can only aid in that effort.

ACKNOWLEDGMENTS

Dr. Margaret Purser and Dr. Paul Groth provided invaluable guidance on earlier papers on this subject. Many thanks to Richard Lerner, who would not take no for an answer, to Glenn Simpson for his encouragement, and especially to Kimberly Esser for her support and comments. Opinions expressed in this paper are my own and are not necessarily shared or endorsed by the agency that employs me.

REFERENCES

CARTER, THOMAS
    1998 Building Communities: Pioneering New Ways of Preserving the Western Landscape. *Common Ground* 3(2/3):46-53.

GROTH, PAUL
    1997a Frameworks for Cultural Landscape Study. In *Understanding Ordinary Landscapes*, edited by Paul Groth and Todd W. Bressi, pp. 1-21. Yale University Press, New Haven, Connecticut.
    1997b Reader and Course Guide for History of the U.S. Cultural Environment, 1783-1900. Dated Fall Semester 1997. Department of Architecture and Department of Geography, University of California, Berkeley, California.

LEWIS, PIERCE
    1979 Axioms for Reading the Landscape: Some Guidelines to the American Scene. In *The Interpretation of Ordinary Landscapes: Geographical Essays,* edited by Donald W. Meinig, pp. 11-31. Oxford University Press, New York.

MCCARTHY, CELIA, AND RICHARD LERNER
    1997 National Register of Historic Places Registration Form for Oakland Inner Harbor Training Walls/Jetties and Federal Channel, Oakland and Alameda, California. Manuscript on file, Port of Oakland, Oakland, California.

MCCARTHY, CELIA, MICHAEL CORBETT, AND WOODRUFF C. MINOR
    1997 Record Form, DPR 523 for Marine Facilities Associated with Western Pacific Railroad Mole. Manuscript on file, Port of Oakland, Oakland, California.

STILGOE, JOHN
    1994 *Alongshore*. Yale University Press, New Haven, Connecticut.

VANCE, JAMES E., JR.
    1964 *Geography and Urban Evolution in the San Francisco Bay Area*. Institute of Governmental Studies, University of California, Berkeley, California.

WALL, LOUIS S., AND JAMES P. DELGADO
    1985 Assessment of Eligibility for National Register of Historic Places: Deteriorated Marine Facilities, Western Pacific Railroad, Oakland and San Francisco, California. Report prepared by Historic Preservation Planning, Montara, California. Submitted to Union Pacific System, Stockton, California.

CELIA MCCARTHY
SONOMA STATE UNIVERSITY
PORT OF OAKLAND
ENVIRONMENTAL PLANNING DEPARTMENT
530 WATER STREET
OAKLAND, CALIFORNIA 94607

2007. Archaeology of the Strangford Lough Kelp Industry in the Eighteenth- and Early-Nineteenth Centuries.

Historical Archaeology 41(3):76 –93.

Thomas C. McErlean

Archaeology of the Strangford Lough Kelp Industry in the Eighteenth- and Early-Nineteenth Centuries

ABSTRACT

An archaeological survey of the maritime cultural landscape of Strangford Lough in Northern Ireland found rich and varied remains of structures relating to the kelp industry. Adding this information to historical documentation provided great insight into the rapid rise of an economic asset in the 18th century and its equally rapid decline in the early-19th century. Kelp provided an essential material for major industries of the industrial revolution and was a major source of income in coastal Ireland. This paper traces the imprint left on the foreshore and coastal archaeology of an Irish Sea lough by the exploitation of seaweed for making kelp.

Introduction

An archaeological survey of the maritime cultural landscape of Strangford Lough was undertaken by a contracted team of archaeologists on behalf of the government agency, Environment and Heritage Service, between 1995 and 2000 (Figure 1) (McErlean et al. 2002). The team was subsequently appointed to the staff of the Centre for Maritime Archaeology at the University of Ulster, Coleraine, Northern Ireland. From the outset of the survey, new types of archaeological sites were recorded. Evidence for the economic exploitation of seaweed around the shores of the lough led to the understanding that this was an activity of major importance for the Irish economy in the late-18th and early-19th centuries.

Seaweed was an important coastal resource in past settlement, and its exploitation is one of the many components of the maritime cultural landscape. Its use by people is probably as old as their exploitation of the seashore but is still imperfectly understood and under-researched, even though in historic times its importance becomes apparent. The eating of edible seaweed as a food supplement is still widespread throughout the world today and may be seen as a survival from the diet of prehistoric coastal dwellers. Its exploitation by coastal communities for livestock grazing and as a source for fodder for cattle, sheep, and pigs is well documented. Seaweed was used from an early period in coastal areas as a fertilizer for crops as it contains nitrogen, phosphate, and potash, and its application greatly enhances soil fertility. Because the shoreline has a high density of sandy soils, seaweed supplied a moisture-trapping compost, greatly improving soil texture. Its effects are short lived, and in areas where it was used, fresh applications were added every year. In Ireland, this resource, known as "wrack," was intensively used in coastal areas. With a rising population in the 18th and early-19th centuries, it was also a jealously guarded resource. In the 18th century around large parts of the Irish and Scottish coastlines, seaweed achieved

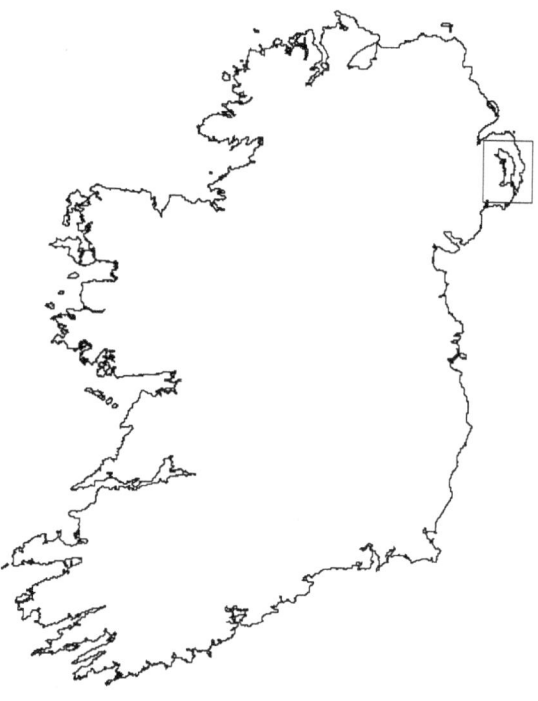

FIGURE 1. Strangford Lough location. (Map by Wes Forsythe, 2001.)

a new importance as the resource base for the production of kelp.

"Kelp" is the commercial name for the burned ashes of seaweed, which in the past was used as source of an impure form of soda (sodium carbonate) and of iodine. The name kelp causes some confusion because of its use both as a name for a family of seaweeds, the kelps (these being mainly the *Laminarias*) and as the name for seaweed slag. In origin, the term originally referred to the slag and later was applied to the plants. Soda, as an alkali, was in great demand in the 18th century for a large number of industrial processes, the most important of which were in the manufacture of glass and soap and as an agent in bleaching linen. Kelp making as a source of soda in the 18th century revolutionized the economy of the northern and western seaboards of Ireland and Scotland, providing a cash crop in an otherwise largely subsistence economy. The intertidal zone, previously exploited for wrack and fishing, now assumed a greater economic importance. The possession of "a kelp shore," as those parts of the coastline supporting suitable growth of seaweed for kelp production were named, was highly valued.

In the soda-ash stage of kelp making, which largely dates to the 18th century and the early years of the 19th century, the best seaweeds were the bladder wracks *Fucus vesiculosus* and *Ascophyllum nodosum*, which grow in the intertidal zone, mainly on the middle and lower shore. In the iodine stage, dating to the 19th and 20th centuries, kelp making turned almost exclusively to the drift weed, the *Laminarias*, or kelps, as they contain a larger amount of iodine (Chapman 1970:24). Because of its abundance on Irish and Scottish coasts, the most important of these was *Laminaria digitata*. As these species grow at extreme low water and in the subtidal zone, the focus of seaweed gathering in the 19th century shifted from the intertidal to the subtidal zone. In Strangford Lough, the great days of kelp making belong to the soda phase of the industry, and little evidence was found for any large-scale activity in the area of iodine production. One of the major discoveries of the survey was that the largest class of artificial structures on the foreshore and coastal edge were those relating to kelp production of the 18th- and early-19th centuries. Future intertidal surveys are likely to demonstrate a similar component in the archaeology of many parts of the Irish and Scottish coastlines.

Kelp Industry in Ireland and Scotland

The use of seaweed slag as a source of soda may have a very ancient origin, but it is not until the 17th century that documentation starts to to demonstrate seaweed's widespread use. For centuries, potash, mainly extracted from wood ashes, had been the main source of alkali. It may have been the growing scarcity of wood that influenced the shift to seaweed as an alternative source of alkali. Much of the published material on Irish kelp making is concerned with the 19th- and early-20th-century iodine phase of the industry. There is little specific literature about Irish kelp production as a source of soda, so that only the broad outlines of its history are currently known. Production for industrial purposes seems well established in Irish coastal areas by the end of the 17th century, as it is recorded as an export item in 1702 (Harper 1974:22). Its origins would seem to lie in developments earlier in that century. During the 17th century, the production of kelp as a source of soda for glassmaking, especially in England and France, stimulated demand for the product (Godfrey 1975:159). In France, kelp making for glass manufacture on the coasts of Normandy and Brittany had become a well-regulated industry by the 1690s (Chapman 1970:25). In the early-17th century, a number of glasshouses were established in Ireland, and kelp is mentioned among the stock of one established by the first Earl of Cork at Ballynegeragh in County Waterford in ca. 1618 (Westropp 1920:25–30).

Another major stimulus appears to have been provided by the Irish linen industry, which was well established, especially in Ulster, by the end of the 17th century. The industry underwent a rapid period of development in the first decade of the 18th century, not least in terms of improved bleaching techniques (Crawford 1980:114–115). In 1698, Louis Crommelin and a group of French Huguenots settled in Lurgan in County Armagh and were one of the contributing forces in the improvement in linen technology, although the importance of their contribution has been questioned (Crawford 1980: 113). It is possible to speculate that, given the French influence in many aspects of the linen industry, the growth of Irish kelp production for bleaching may have been stimulated by French kelp making. In 1711, the Irish Board of Linen and Hempen Manufactures was established to promote and regulate linen production. Rewards and grants were given to develop new processes, amongst which kelp making may have been included (Crawford 1980:113).

There is certainly clear evidence that in County Antrim, kelp manufacture was being encouraged by County Grand Jury presentments (Harper 1974). In 1712, several individuals near Larne Lough and Island Magee were awarded a subsidy of 6s 9d (six shillings and nine pence) per ton for making kelp, and in that year they produced just over nine tons (Harper 1974:23). By 1716, the subsidy had dropped to 2s 6d (two shillings and six pence), perhaps suggesting that kelp making in the Antrim coast region was becoming more widespread. By about 1720, kelp was being made on the west coast of Ireland (O'Neill 1970). The impression is that it became a major activity on parts of the Irish coastline in the following two decades. The western and northern seaboards of Ireland and their offshore islands, with their rocky coastlines, support an abundant growth of seaweed, and it seems that these were exploited relatively quickly.

The story of Scottish kelp making mirrors that of Ireland. Some aspects of it are better documented and can be used to shed light on its Irish counterpart (Rymer 1974a, 1974b). It appears to have commenced in the Orkneys in 1722 and soon became a major industry. An idea of its economic importance can be ascertained from the fact that between 1722 and 1793, the Orkney landlords were calculated to have made £291,976 from kelp (O'Dell and Walton 1962: 194). Later, kelp making commenced in Western Scotland and the Isles and the influence of Irish kelp makers appears strong. Its introduction seems have taken place over a period of about 40 years from about 1730 to 1770. North Uist seems to have been the earliest Hebridean island to commence manufacture. It is believed that in 1735, an Irishman was brought in by MacDonald of Boisdale to teach kelp manufacture to the islanders (McKenzie 1974). By 1746 production had started in Tiree (O'Dell and Walton 1962: 195). In 1748, McLeod of Harris permitted some Irish to make kelp on his shore for the first time (Thompson 1973). In Lewis it started

about 1750 and on Coll, in 1764 (McKay 1980: 171). An Irish manufacturer is said to have introduced it to Jura in 1762 (McKay 1980: 125), followed by Barra in 1763. By about 1770, it would appear that any of the shores in Western Scotland and the Scottish Isles having sufficient seaweed was a site for kelp making. An idea of the scale and importance the industry in the 1760s in the Hebrides is given below in a table extracted from figures given in *The Rev. Dr. John Walker's Report on the Hebrides of 1764 and 1771* (Table 1) (McKay 1980).

The development of the kelp industry in Scotland had a tremendous impact on the marginal economies of the coastal fringe of the highlands and islands and led to considerable economic and social change, being one of the factors influencing the rapid rise in population. By the beginning of the 19th century, Scotland's kelp industry as a whole was producing about 20,000 tons annually. Its collapse had severe effects on coastal society and contributed to a subsequent depopulation and emigration (Rymer 1974a). The market price for kelp can be traced in more detail from the Scottish industry than the Irish one, but as the two industries were to some extent integrated, these are of direct relevance. Following the law of supply and demand, the price of kelp rose steadily throughout the 18th century. From 1740 to 1760, the average price of kelp was about £3 per ton, doubling to about £6 between the years 1760 to 1790. During 1790 to 1800, the price continued to rise, reaching £10, followed by a decline from 1800 to 1805. The years between 1807 and 1810 were the peak period in the price of kelp as the Peninsular War interfered with the import of the Spanish equivalent known as *barilla*. During this time, the price reached £16 per ton and above. From 1810 to 1820, prices dropped dramatically to those of 30 or 40 years previously. By the 1830s, the price had slumped to a level that made kelp making economically unviable, and the soda phase of the industry collapsed. The price of Irish kelp followed a very similar trend but, because of a perceived inferiority to the Scottish product, consistently at a slightly lower market price (Table 1).

During the 18th century, kelp faced a major competitor in the form of Spanish *barilla*, made from the ash of the shore plant, *Salsola sativa*. *Barilla* contained about 20% alkali as opposed

TABLE 1
KELP PRODUCTION IN THE HEBRIDES IN 1764

Island	Kelp Tonnage Produced in 1764 (unless otherwise stated)	Price per Ton	Export Value
Lewis	50	£3.5.0	£162.5.0
Harris	100	£3.5.0	£325.
North Uist	500	£3.5.0	£1625
Benbecula	200	£3.5.0	£650
South Uist	100	£3.5.0	£325.5.0
Barra	60	(£3.5.0)	(£195)
Islay	"some kelp"		
Jura	40 (1762)	(£3.5.0)	(£130)
Colonsay	40	£4	£160
Mull	100	£3.10.0	£350
Coll	40	£4	£160
Tiree	44	£3.5.0	£143.0.0
Skye	200	£3.15.0	£750.0.0
Total	1,384		£4,975.10.0

Note: Figures extracted from McKay 1980.

to 10% in Irish and Scottish kelp (Barker 1977: 488). To protect the home industry, heavy duties were imposed on kelp imports in the mid-18th century. In spite of this, the product was in great demand, and Belfast merchants imported large quantities from Spain to supply the local bleachers in the late-18th century. The pages of the *Belfast News Letter* during this period carried frequent advertisements announcing the arrival of cargoes of *barrilla* to be sold at auction on the quays. In the 1820s, two events took place, which had a direct result on Irish and Scottish kelp making as a source of soda. The first was the reduction of the import duties on *barilla* in Britain in 1822 and in Ireland in 1823 (U.K. Parliament 1824:238–239). The second was the abolition of the salt tax in 1825, which made it commercially viable to make soda chemically using the Leblanc method. During the next 10 years, kelp making for soda went into rapid decline, and its production ceased along major stretches of the coast. In 1812, Curtois discovered iodine as an element in seaweed slag. Its subsequent applications in medicine, dyes, and

later in photography revived kelp making as a coastal economic activity during the 19th century. Some coastal communities continued kelp production to supply the iodine market, but its economic significance and extent was much more limited than that of the soda industry.

Kelp Industry in Strangford Lough ca. 1720 to 1820

Documentary evidence for kelp making in Strangford Lough is sparse and fragmentary, but a general overview can be constructed from brief comments by a number of authors, as outlined below. At present, it is unclear when kelp manufacture started in the Lough, but an early reference to the value of the seaweed resource, suggesting that the production of kelp had commenced, is found in the articles of sale of the Montgomery Estate at Greyabbey in 1717. In addition to the land and islands being transferred, it states, "and all kelp, wreck and sea-weed growing or being or that hereafter shall grow or be on the said manor, towns, lands, rocks and premises, or on the coasts or shores thereof or of any part thereof, or that belong or are reputed to belong to the same" (Hill 1869:420).

By the middle of the 18th century, production was well established, had become a major economic activity, and had produced significant revenue for the owners of the foreshore of the lough. Walter Harris (1744:154) noted, "The greatest and profitable manufacture carried on in these islands, and on the flat stony coasts surrounding the lake, is the burning of seaweed into kelp, which employs upwards of 300 hands, and is said to produce to the several proprietors neat profit upwards of £1000 per annum."

The impact of the introduction of kelp making sometime earlier in the century had, by this date, transformed the local coastal economy and considerably raised the profile of the foreshore as a zone for exploitation. Kelp making had taken precedence over the exploitation of seaweed as manure, and Harris (1744:43) further noted,

> This Peninsula produces large Quantities of Barley, and a kind of Oats, called the Light-Foot-Oats, as well from the Help of Marle abounding in the marshy Grounds, as from Ore-Weed, which they have in great Plenty, both from the Islands in the Lake, and the Eastern Shore. But this Vegetable is too precious to be used much as Manure; for they turn it to a better Account by burning it into Kelp, which they do in great Quantities, that they not only supply the linen manufacturers in this and neighboring counties, but export it in abundance for the use of the glass-houses in Dublin and Bristol, as appears in the custom-house books of Portaferry.

The economic importance of the foreshore affected land values of the adjoining shores. For instance, in 1757 when Judge Ward of Castle Ward was considering purchasing the townland of Audleystown on the southern coast of the Lough, one of the factors to be ascertained was the amount of kelp made over a three-year period (McErlean and Reeves-Smyth 1990:16). In his account of his economic fact-finding tour through the region in 1776, Arthur Young noted (Hutton 1892:139),

> All along the coasts of Ardes and in Strangford Lough sea wrack is collected by the country people with great diligence, for burning into kelp; it yields at present from 40s to 50s a ton, the bleach greens have much

of it, and the rest of it is exported to England. Some gentlemen, who keep their shores in their own hands, pay 20s a ton for collecting and burning: at other times they pay rent for the shore. In loch Strangford the kelp is better than the open shore.

As the demand for kelp rose steadily during the second half of the 18th century, Strangford Lough was advantageously placed near the heart of the Irish linen industry, in northern Down and Antrim, to supply the increasing demand for kelp from the linen bleachers. This branch of the industry had expanded rapidly from 1730 to 1750, and, by the middle of the century, there were local bleach greens around the lough at Newtonards, Comber, Ardmillan, Downpatrick, and Portaferry. The bulk of the Strangford kelp would have been sold locally but, as seen from the reference above, quantities were also shipped further afield to Dublin and Bristol to supply glass houses. On the eve of the rapid decline of the industry after 1823, A. Atkinson (1823) noted in reference to Portaferry:

> The manufacture of a seaweed called box-wrack, into kelp, may be considered as a part of the trade of this place, in common with every other part of the Strangford shore. About 1000 tons weight of this kelp is manufactured in the district just noticed, and disposed of chiefly in the markets of Dublin and Glasgow.

In the late 18th century, in common with much Irish kelp in general, Strangford kelp had acquired a poor reputation for quality in comparison to "highland kelp" as the Scottish product was normally called. One of the main accusations made against Irish kelp makers was that the product was frequently adulterated by the inclusion of stones to raise its weight. In 1802, J. Dubourdieu (1802:240–241) noted in reference to the Strangford kelp that

> A considerable quantity of kelp is made every summer along the coasts, but particularly on the Lough of Strangford; the whole quantity manufactured there ... amounts to between four and five hundred tons, whilst that made on the eastern coast does not amount to more than one hundred tons per annum; that on the shores of the lake is much superior in quality to that on the open shore, but neither the one nor the other are of so good a quality as formerly, owing to the avarice of the labourers employed in making it, who, to increase the weight, mix more than the proper proportion of gravel with the ashes, after they are reduced to a fluid state; the proper proportion is one to twenty,

but, by putting more than that quantity, the kelp is not so much in demand as it formerly was. If I recollect aright, there is a law against the adulteration of kelp, which directs it to be broken in pieces, and thrown upon the fields, excepting, however, the field of the person so adulterating it.

Decline of the Kelp Industry in Strangford Lough

The decline of the industry can be traced through the Ordnance Survey Memoirs of the 1830s for the parishes surrounding the lough (Day and McWilliams 1991, 1992). In 1833, kelp manufacture was still being carried out in Killinchy Parish, on the western side of the lough, where it is recorded (Dubourdieu 1802: 88) that

> Kelp is made on the main shore and on the islands off the parish. From the northern extremity to the road at White Rock 40 pounds per annum is paid for the privilege of burning kelp, not any lease granted. The renter gets 30 tons of kelp, which he sends to Liverpoole and obtains from 3 pounds 10 shilling to 9 pounds a ton according to the quality. From White Rock to the southern extremity of the shore at Ringhaddy the right of burning kelp on it is held by lease for 20 years of the rent of 60 pounds per annum. The same person also rents the adjacent island at 90 pounds per annum and manufactures on an average 120 tons of kelp, which he sends to Liverpoole and obtains the prices stated above.

As stated in the description of Ardglass Parish in 1835 (Dubourdieu 1802:2), the industry was declining rapidly.

> Kelp (an impure kind) mixed with sand and earthy matter was formerly obtained in great quantities from different species of Fucus but the price of article has declined so much of late as scarcely to defray the expense of preparing and bringing it to market. Soap boilers in the neighbourhood use it still in preference to barilla.

Elsewhere around the lough, surviving documentation suggests strongly that kelp making ceased in many areas during the 1830s. The loss of income from kelp making to landowners, tenants, and laborers must have been considerable. The industry was carried on for more than 100 years on its foreshores, and at no time, before or since, has there been so much human activity in the intertidal zone.

Kelp Shores of Strangford Lough

With the exception of the tidal sandflats at its northern end, most of the coast of the lough and its islands support a good growth of foreshore seaweed and were therefore commercially viable for kelp manufacture. The organization of kelp making varied on each estate, with some carrying out production directly. By at least the mid-18th century, others were letting out their shores separately from the adjoining land for kelp making. The *Belfast News Letter* periodically carried advertisements for the letting of kelp shores. For instance in 1754, the Delamont estate advertised the reletting of their shore for any period not exceeding 31 years (*Belfast News Letter* 1754:3). In 1773, James Bailie of Inishargie advertised the letting of the kelp shore at Gransha for three lives or 31 years. and in 1776 the Ardkeen estate advertised their extensive kelp shores on the islands of the middle section of the lough for up to 31 years (*Belfast News Letter* 1773:4). It would seem that it was the practice on many estates to rent out their shores in their entirety. The renter presumably acquired precedence over any traditional shore rights of tenants of the estate to cut seaweed for fertilizer, but one may assume that their rights to the cast weed was still intact. Little information has come to light about the cost of renting a kelp shore, except for the very late details given in the Ordnance Survey Memoirs, which record that in 1833, the renter paid £40 and £60 per annum for different parts of the shore in Killinchy parish. The islands off the shore of the parish, which contained a rich growth of seaweed, were let for £90 per annum (Day and McWilliams 1991:88).

Kelp Production on the Ringdufferin Estate 1779–1807

A search was made through papers of the main estates around Strangford Lough, but this proved disappointing as little of substance was found in reference to kelp-making activities. The survival of a kelp account book covering the period 1779 to 1807 and detailing kelp production on the Ringdufferin Estate over a 30-year time span has proved an extremely valuable source of information on the local organization of the industry. The book has been preserved at Ringdufferin House since the 18th century and was brought to the attention of the survey team by Mr. Paddy Mackie. Permission to use material from it was generously given by the current owners of the Ringdufferin estate, Mr. and Mrs. Martin Hamilton.

The estate is situated in the midsection of the western shore of Strangford Lough and has a long and well-documented history of occupation from medieval times to the present. The Bailie family owned the estate from the early-17th century to the middle of the 20th century. The kelp account book covers the period of ownership of James Bailie who held the estate from 1774 to 1819. He was a prominent man in local affairs, being at one time High Sheriff of County Down and a magistrate, as well as being a diligent landowner and substantial maritime trader. Bailie kept direct control of the kelp production on his shores through all of its stages—harvesting, burning, storing, and marketing. Analyses of his detailed accounts allow many observations to be made on how the industry was conducted at a local level in part of the lough in the late-18th century. The Bailie estate was comparatively small, and funds made from kelp production must have been a major source of income. The demesne, or home farm, consisted of the townland of Ringdufferin and nearby Pawle Island (pronounced "pole"). The shoreline of the island has an extensive boulder foreshore with a good cover of seaweed, which slopes down to an expanse of intertidal mud flats. There is a similar extensive fringe of seaweed-covered boulder foreshore on its eastern side.

Between 1779 and 1799, the accounts are detailed, and information may be extracted concerning the amount of kelp made each year, the location of the seaweed used, who it was sold to, and at what price. From 1799 to 1807, the recorded information is less precise. Table 2 notes some aspects of the accounts covering the period 1779 to 1799. An interesting feature is that for kelp making, the foreshore of the estate was divided into three sections: Warren Point to Grove Point, Castle Island to Danes Point, and Pawle Island (Figures 1, 2, 3).

The important point to emerge is that only one division on the estate was harvested each year. In 1779, for example, Warren Point to Grove Point was cut, followed in 1780 by the

Castle Island to Danes Point division, and in 1781 by Pawle Island. The same three-year cycle of cutting was repeated in 1782–1784, 1785–1787, and 1788–1790, demonstrating that each division was cut only once every three years. The Warren Point to Grove Point shore was cut in 1779, 1782, 1785, 1788, and 1791. This provides clear evidence of a three-year rotational system of cutting being practiced to allow the seaweed on each division three years to recover and grow to a sufficient size to make it economical to harvest. It seems probable that on other kelp shores around the lough a similar rotation system was practiced and that management of the resource entailed a division of the shore to facilitate this system (Table 2).

Using the formula that 20 tons of wet seaweed equals 1 ton of kelp (Chapman 1970: 45), it is possible to gain an impression of how much seaweed was cut annually for the kelp production on the estate by the team of four

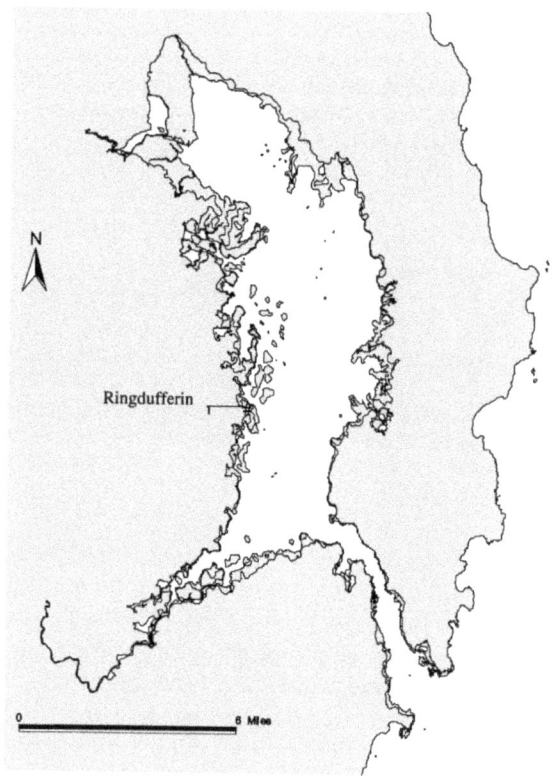

FIGURE 2. The location of the Ringdufferin Estate. (Map by author, 2001.)

TABLE 2
KELP PRODUCTION (IN TONS) ON THE RINGDUFFERIN ESTATE 1779–1799

Year	Warren Point to Grove Point	Castle Island to Danes Point	Pawle Island
1779	31	-	-
1780	-	37.5	-
1781	-	-	26
1782	22	-	-
1783	-	35	-
1784	-	-	20.5
1785	23	-	-
1786	-	35	-
1787	-	-	35
1788	21	-	-
1789	-	30.5	-
1790	-	-	Cut, amount NK
1791	26	-	-
1792	-	-	-
1793	-	40	-
1794	-	-	-
1795	31	-	-
1796	-	-	32
1797	-	36.5	-
1798	29	-	-
1799	-	37	20.5
Average Av. production (to nearest ton)	26 tons over 7 cuts	36 tons over 7 cuts	25 tons over 5 cuts
Probable weight of wet seaweed cut	520 tons per cut	720 tons per cut	500 tons per cut

kelpers who carried out the cutting and burning. Once every three years, some 720 tons of wet seaweed were cut from the Castle Island to Danes Point shore, 520 tons from Warren Point to Grove Point, and 500 tons from Pawle Island. The accounts show that the sale of kelp began in most years in late May or early June, and so, presumably, kelp making commenced in early summer and continued during the summer months. The net profit depended on the current market price and the production expenses. The accounts show that the cost of making a ton of kelp remained static at £1 per ton from 1779 to 1812, but in 1812 rose to £1 5s (one pound and five shillings) per ton. All of this cost appears to have been accounted for by the wages of the kelpers who were paid at £1 per ton. A note in the account book estimates that for the nine years from 1779 to 1787 inclusive, a profit of £1,123 was made from making kelp and that the average yearly profit was £125. On a small estate like Ringdufferin, this figure demonstrates that kelp making provided an important source of income.

The sales accounts show that the market price of the kelp fluctuated over the period covered by the accounts, as shown in Figure 4. Sales were continuous from June to late September but largely ceased during the winter months. Small amounts of the remaining portion of the previous year's production were sold sporadically from February to May and fetched slightly higher prices, presumably as the product was becoming scarce. The accounts start on a high in 1779 and 1780 as a result of the British war with France and the American colonies, which interrupted the import of ashes from abroad and pushed up the price of home-produced

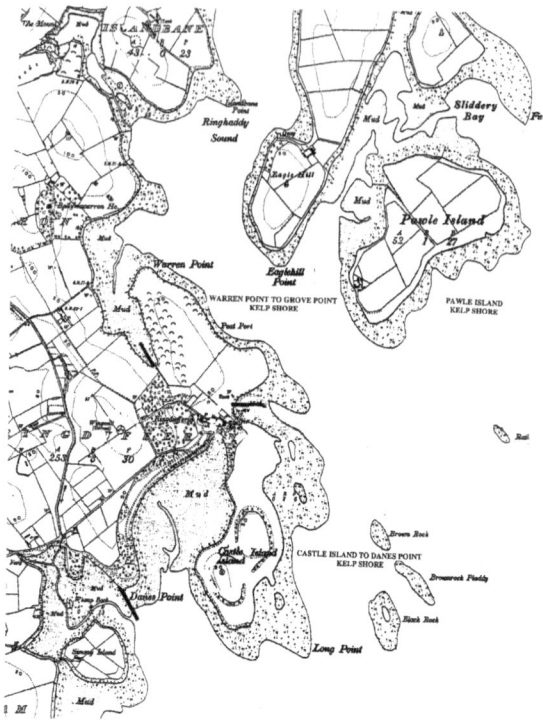

FIGURE 3. The Ringdufferin kelp shores. (Based on Ordnance Survey 6-inch map, sheet 24, Co. Down, 1920.)

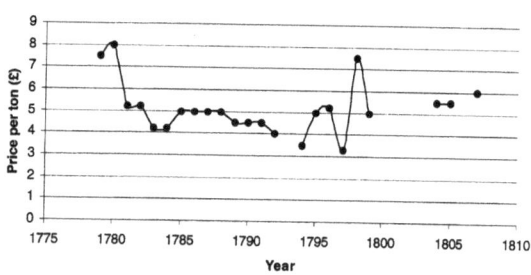

FIGURE 4. Price of kelp from the Ringdufferin accounts 1779 to 1807. (Graph by author, 2001.)

kelp. In 1780 the price reached £8 per ton, and a net profit of £240 was made. The only comparable year with such a high price during the period covered by the account was 1798, when it jumped from £3 10s (three pounds and ten shillings) to £7 10s (seven pounds and ten shillings). The rebellion in that year may have made local kelp scarce or resulted in difficulties in getting ashes from abroad, thus increasing the price.

For the most part, the kelp was sold directly from the estate to the consumers. The local bleachers of Down, Armagh, and South Antrim were major customers with individuals in Tandragee, Dromore, Ballynahinch, Lisburn, Lambeg Belfast, Antrim, and elsewhere referred to in the account. Among those mentioned in the 1780s are Samuel Delacherois, the Mussens of Lisburn, and John Riddle of Comber. Some customers, such as Alexander Finlay of High Street and Mathew Steel of Castle Street in Belfast, were soap boilers. The only obvious glassmaker who can be identified is John Smylie and Co. of Belfast who was a customer in 1788. The kelp was normally sold by the hundredweight and transported inland by carriers who charged £1 for 6 hundredweight, or transported by boat to customers in Down, Strangford, Newry, and Dublin.

Archaeology of Kelp in Strangford Lough

Introduction: Stages in Kelp Making

The process of kelp making consisted of a number of well-defined stages: harvesting the seaweed on the foreshore where it was then dried, burning it in kilns, and storage of the product. Structures relating to all of these production stages have left their mark on the archaeology of the shore. A superb example of this range of activities is to be found at Chapel Island, to the west of Greyabbey, where there are kelp kilns and the ruins of a kelp house. Nearby on the foreshore to the east is a large kelp grid, which artificially extended the seaweed-growing area over a sandy zone near low water. Since kelp making on a large scale appears to have ceased around Strangford Lough before the middle of the 19th century, it is not surprising that there are no contemporary accounts of the process available from folk tradition in the area. There is much information, mostly of 19th-century date, from other parts of the coast of Ireland and from Scotland. A clear outline of how kelp making was carried out can be reconstructed (Evans 1957; Clark 1971; Thompson 1973; Harper 1974; Fenton 1978; Hamond 1991, 1998). Most of these descriptions relate to the production of kelp for iodine extraction in the later 19th century rather than to the production of soda in the 18th century. Nevertheless, apart from the change in the exploitation of the largely subtidal drift weeds, the main outlines of the process were very similar and can be used to throw light on how kelp making was carried out around the lough.

Harvesting the Seaweed and Shore Divisions

It is important to stress that in kelp making for soda, seaweed harvesting took place on the foreshore and was based largely on the bladder wracks. As these plants re-grow from their roots, they were cut rather than pulled. Cutting was carried out during the summer months by teams of kelpers and was a labor-intensive exercise. The removal of many tons of wet seaweed during the relatively short period between the tides would have required a considerable effort. The cut weed was removed from the foreshore in panniers or in carts if the boulder-strewn shore topography allowed. In Strangford Lough, based on the Ringdufferin information, a three-year rotation cycle seems to have been the norm.

The most important impact of kelp making on the coastal archaeology of Stangford Lough is the subdivision of the foreshore by low stone walls, erected to define seaweed rights and probably to regulate rotational cutting. These intertidal walls normally commence at, or just below, the high water mark and continue down the low water mark or else at the junction of the boulder zone with the mud or sand. The walls, which have no corresponding land counterpart and relate only to the foreshore, are not shown on the large-scale Ordnance Survey maps. No awareness was found to exist in local knowledge about their significance or function. All are of dry stone construction and built using double boulders with infill. The walls vary in height from 0.5 m to a maximum of 1.5 m and are on average 1 m wide. Their length is governed by the width of the local boulder zones, which vary considerably. Almost all are in a ruinous state.

Some 150 examples were found during the survey and are mostly concentrated on the western and southwestern parts of Strangford Lough and adjacent islands. They are largely absent on the northern and eastern parts and nonexistent on the sand flats at the northern end of the lough. On a simple level, their overall distribution generally reflects that of the distribution of the seaweed-covered boulder foreshores present in the lough. Their absence on this type of terrain on the east and northeast requires comment. This apparent anomaly probably stems from differences in shore management among the estates around the lough. On those where the seaweed resource was kept directly under their own control, or leased out as a block to an outside contractor, there may have been little need to subdivide the foreshore. In contrast, it was the practice on many estates to give shore rights to tenants who held land on the adjoining shore, and this would have resulted in the need for a well-defined demarcation of the foreshore. On some parts of the coast, where the subdivision of the foreshore is intense with walls spaced closely along the foreshore, it is possible to suggest that an individual tenant would have held a number of these subdivisions, which were cut on a rotational basis.

Burning and Kelp Kilns

Before burning, the cut weed was dried to make it combustible and to prevent rotting, which would render it useless. The drying process for the seaweed appears to have been very similar to haymaking and took place along the shoreline. The weed was spread out on grass or draped on a sea wall and allowed to dry in the sun or wind, then stacked in conical ricks. When sufficient amounts were ready, a kiln was prepared. The burning process took on average 8 to 12 hours and required the constant attention of two to four people. The fire was started using whatever local source of fuel was available—turf, straw, or dried gorse, for example—and this was placed at the bottom of the kiln. The dried seaweed was added slowly to the smoldering fire, as fast burning at a high temperature could ruin the product.

After the initial firing, little or no additional fuel was needed. The residue gathered in the bottom of the kiln in a viscous, porridge-like mass, which had to be stirred frequently by the kelpers from the sides of the kiln using wooden poles (ash being the preferred wood) or iron rods.

During the burning, the kilns gave out large plumes of white, oily smoke, which could be cultivation of seaweed as a crop in the intertidal zone. In order for the larger brown seaweeds to grow, they require stones or boulders to securely anchor their root-like base or "holdfast." Areas of the foreshore or seabed composed of bare, smooth rock or of sand or mud are generally devoid of seaweed growth, but growth can be encouraged by the placement of small boulders. This technique was adopted to extend the zones of natural growth. This practice was remarkable enough in Strangford Lough to merit a comment by Arthur Young on his agricultural tour of the country in 1776 when he wrote, "An instance of industry in this loch deserves to be recorded. It is not uncommon for the men to draw stones from their fields, and spread them on the shores in order to make wrack (fucus) grow; a good crop being only obtained from rocks and stones" (Hutton 1892:139).

Seventeen examples of artificial stone settings or kelp grids for seaweed cultivation were found around the foreshore of the lough (Figure 6). The true number is probably much greater as

their detection is sometimes difficult during field survey. Those now devoid of seaweed growth are easily detected because they are visually prominent on the foreshore as artificial stone settings, by virtue of their geometric plans. Other examples where the stones are set less regularly can be easily missed or dismissed as natural. The greatest problem for detection in many cases is concealment under a dense seaweed cover. Some examples were found almost completely submerged under mud or sand, caused by either sinking or deposition, and many have probably disappeared from view in this way. The distribution of kelp grids revealed during the survey shows a concentration on the northeastern section of the lough, with five good examples found on the western side of the lough in the Reagh Island to Ringneill area. All of the known examples are located on flat, sandy foreshores and are mostly to be found on the middle to lower shore.

Much of the distribution pattern can be accounted for in terms of foreshore terrain. The general absence of grids on the western and southwestern foreshores of the lough can be explained by the high content of mud where stones would sink. No examples were found on the extensive sand flats at the north of the lough, which is puzzling. It is interesting to observe that a relatively large number of the grids are presently devoid of seaweed growth. One explanation for this may be found in the limited information available on known cultivation techniques, which document that it was important to reset and turn the stones at regular intervals, and, since this has ceased, seaweed growth has been inhibited. Probably the most splendid example of a kelp grid in the lough is that at Herring Bay (Ballygarvan) whose outline is best viewed from the air or from the overlooking high ground (Figures 7 and 8).

This little horseshoe-shaped bay has a narrow fringing boulder zone that slopes down to a flat, sandy central area, covered by 2 to 3 m of water at high tide. The depth of water makes it ideal for growing the brown sea weeds of the middle and lower shore, but the absence of stones would have prevented natural growth and was rectified by the creation of a very regular grid of artificially placed stones. The grid occupies an area of some 5.4 acres and is composed of approximately 102 parallel rows

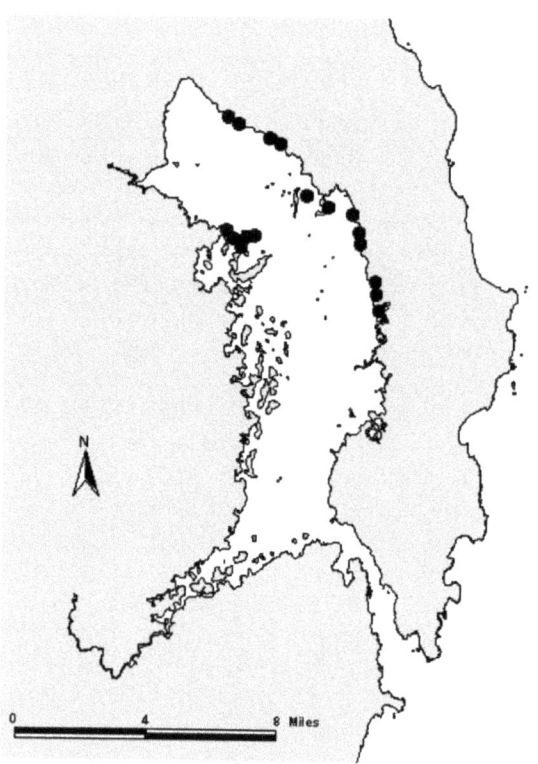

FIGURE 6. The distribution of kelp grids. (Map by Thomas McErlean and Wes Forsythe, 2001.)

FIGURE 7. The Herring Bay kelp grid from the air. (Courtesy of Environment and Heritage Service, Department of the Environment, Northern Ireland, UK.)

FIGURE 8. The Herring Bay kelp grid from the east. (Courtesy of Environment and Heritage Service, Department of the Environment, Northern Ireland, UK.)

of stones. Spacing the rows from 0.9 to 1.7 m apart and placing the stones in adjoining rows in alternate positions allowed each plant to grow without competing with its neighbor.

The other examples of kelp grids around the lough (Figure 9) vary in extent from about 0.6 to 3.7 acres. It is possible that the smaller ones may represent small-scale cultivation by individual tenants, while the larger ones of more than 2 acres may have been created under estate management. The size of the stones used reflects the average size of the local shale and greywacke boulders on the immediate foreshore and are, on average, 0.35 by 0.25 by 0.10 m. The average spacing between stones and rows is about 0.6 m.

From the observation by Young quoted above, it appears that the kelp grids of Strangford Lough were in existence by the middle of the 1770s. This is one of the earliest references to seaweed cultivation in the country, and it is obvious that Young regarded it as something

FIGURE 9. Reagh Island kelp grid (Courtesy of Environment and Heritage Service, Department of the Environment, Northern Ireland, UK.)

quite singular. Another early reference to the practice in Strangford is contained in an advertisement in 1773 to let the kelp shore at Gransha on the southeast of the lough. One of the inducements offered to the prospective tenant was "the liberty to improve at least 50 acres, the bottom hard clay, and the stones very convenient ... If a tenant living at a distance takes the shore, he shall have the duty work of man, horses, and wheel cars to draw stones" (*Belfast News Letter* 1773:4). This suggests that the practice of "improving the shore" was well established by this date and may have commenced in the middle of the 18th century. The origins of this form of cultivation are obscure but are of great interest. One of the best contemporary 18th-century descriptions of the practice was made by Dr. John Walker in his *Report on The Hebrides,* dated 1764 to 1771, in which he advocated its introduction. Although lengthy, this is worth quoting in full:

Besides the making of kelp, there is scarce anything in Sky, that can be called manufacture. The Island produces about 200 ton annually yet this is but a small quantity compared to what it might produce with proper improvement. The planting of sea weeds is the improvement here meant. The most simple of all kinds of cultivation, but if I mistake not, would turn out the most profitable. All submarine plants when burnt produce the lixivial Salt called Kelp, so

necessary in many extensive manufactures, and which already brings a great sum of money annually to the Western Coasts of Scoland. But nine tenths of all the kelp manufactured in the Hebrides, are produced from the three following plants. FUCUS serratus. Linn,. F. vescculosus Linn. F. nodosus. Linn. These three plants cannot grow either upon sand and sleech, but almost always be rooted upon stone. They generally cover all the fast rocks within ordinary Flood Mark, but the greatest crop of them is to be obseerved where a sandy or sleechy shore, is thick covered with loose rocks and stones of such a size, as to be seldom or never moved by the violence of the waters. It is also to be noticed, that they are of quicker and more vigorous growth, according as they are situated near the Mark of the lowest ebb; and gradually from a less luxurient crop, as they approach flood mark. Their growth also is greatly promoted by shelter; for they arrive at a larger size, in a landlocked bay where the water is calm, than upon an exposed shore. To cover the shores, especially near the Mark of Ebb, with loose stones from 50 lb to 200 Weight, is all that is required, to raise these profitable plants in great abundance. The sea is everywhere full of their seeds, and there adhaere to and grow upon every stone, capable of lying in the sea water, without mouldering. There are none of the Hebrides, in which, the quantity of kelp might not be greatly augmented by this improvement and in Sky in particular, it might be prosecuted to a great extent. In the lochs of Fallart, Arnisnisort, Snizort, Bracadale, Slapan, and Eyshort, there are some thousand of acres, on which no sea weeds grow at present, but which might all be planted in this manner for the production of kelp. The sides of these vast locks, like almost all the other shores in the Highlands, are thick covered with loose rocks and stones fit for the purpose, and all the trouble and expence attending this improvement, is to carry them off the ground, a few hundred yards within the Floodmark. The profit attending this simple piece of improvement, must be very extraordinary; yet it could not be exactly ascertained as in all the Islands, I could not find an accurate answer to this question how much kelp is produced from an acre of sea weeds. The Islanders employed in the manufacture have no idea of an acre, and they were as much at a loss, as to the weight of kelp, producible from any certain weight or quanity of sea weeds. I had the pleasure of finding this proposed cultivation of sea weeds, admitted by some of the most intelligent gentlemen in the Western Islands, both as practicable and highly profitable and upon enquiring into the most proper method of carrying it into execution, they all agreed in this. That if the great proprietors of the Islands, and who live all at a distance, did not think proper to engage in the trouble and expence of this improvement: their tenants might plant the shores, with stones, in the manner described above; upon the assurance of receiving from them three crops of sea weeds, rent free which would require about 12 years. In this way the landlords at the expiration of 12 years, might have the rental of their Estates greatly increased, without any trouble or expence whatever (McKay 1980:211–212).

There is very little historic documentation on Irish seaweed cultivation, save for at a few localities. A. D. Cotton (1911) described wrack cultivation on Clare Island, Achill Island, and Clew Bay in County Mayo. He coined the term "*Fucus* Farms" for these intertidal cultivation plots and remarked on the effectiveness of providing an artificial anchorage for certain species of seaweed, as demonstrated by rapid colonization and subsequent luxuriant growth (Cotton 1911:53). On Clare Island these were still in use in the early-20th century and Cotton (1911:153) described them thus:

> Where rocks are present Fucus grows naturally, but where, as is usually the case, the shore is composed of sand, the farmers set to work to obtain a growth of Wrack by artificial means. Stones about a foot square are disposed in rows a yard apart, with paths left between for carting. Sporelings speedily appear on the stones, and during the course of a year develop into good-sized plants. The following season the Wrack is cut. This operation takes place in February and March, was observed by the survey party of Easter, 1910. ... Owing to the symmetrical arrangement of the stones, the artificial plots are at once distinguishable from natural vegetation; but when the weed is in its second season and the plants inclined to overlap, the distinction might not strike the eye of the casual observer.

On Clare Island, the seaweed was cut after two year's growth, and the stones turned over for a new crop to develop. The dominant colonizing species was *Fucus vesiculosus* with only small numbers of *Ascophyllium* and *Fucus serratus*.

Perhaps the best-known and most impressive example of seaweed cultivation on the Irish coast is that at Mill Bay, on the northern shore of Carlingford Lough, County Down (Evans 1957:221–222). The cultivation is at its most impressive on air photographs from which can be seen more than a square mile of the intertidal sand flats, laid out in rectangular plots composed of rows of spaced boulders. In the latter half of the 19th century, there were 1,100 plots, each about half an acre in size. Like the County Mayo examples, the plots were used as a source of wrack and were cut about every two years. Maintenance of the bed was carried out every few years as the stones sank in the sand or were silted up, requiring the row to be raised and reset (Doran [1975]:56). Several hundred local farmers leased the beds from the landlord, and the seaweed was used on the potato crop.

The antiquity of these cultivation plots has not been established, but they were in existence in 1846 and continued in use to about 1940 (Evans 1957:221; Doran [1975]). The important difference between the Clare Island and Mill Bay beds and those of Strangford is that they were being used in the 19th and 20th centuries to grow seaweed as a fertilizer. Estyn Evans (1957: 221) did not think the origin of seaweed cultivation arose out of the kelp industry "as the best species for kelp grow in deeper water." In this, he mistakes the earlier phase of the industry in the 18th century, which concentrated on the *Fucus* species, and the 19th century phase for iodine, which concentrated more on the *Laminaria* species. It seems highly probable that the practice originated in the commercial incentive offered by kelp making in the 18th century and was later used as a source of wrack.

Conclusion

The intertidal zone in Strangford Lough was harvested intensely for seaweed from about 1720 to 1830, and it is interesting to speculate on what the ecological impact of this annual loss of a large volume of algae must have been. There have been a number of proposals in recent times for the commercial harvesting of *Ascophyllum* and other algae in the lough on a relatively large scale, with a commercially viable figure of 3,000 tons per year being suggested. Research suggests that this would be damaging ecologically and that harvesting of key species would cause unacceptable environmental change (Davison and Boaden 1990: 2–8). In 1976, some small-scale cutting of *Ascophyllum* was carried out. Its effect was still observable three years later during quantitative investigation that demonstrated a noticeable ecological change between cut and uncut areas (Boaden and Dring 1980).

The effects included loss of shore cover, a reduction of canopy cover on the shore, an influx of nontarget algae from the upper zones, and changes and impoverishment of the subcanopy and under-boulder fauna—in other words, a reduction in the faunal biomass. It is clear that the brown algae on which the kelp industry was based makes a major contribution to the ecology of the lough. Its intense exploitation over a long period must have modified the ecology of the shore. Harris (1774:247) suggested that one of the reasons for the decline in the herring shoals in the lough may have been kelp burning during the spawning season and that the removal of seaweed in the sheltered bays where they spawned probably contributed to the declining numbers. He proposed, "Therefore seaweed ought not to be burned in the herring bays during the fishing season, nor until the young fish have growth and strength sufficient for their removal."

Others commentators during the 18th century expressed concerns about the environmental effect of kelp manufacture, providing an interesting avenue of future research. The fragmentary historical and archaeological evidence of the long-vanished kelp industry in Strangford Lough demonstrates that this resource was of prime importance in the economy of the region in the 18th and early-19th centuries and that this period witnessed the maximum exploitation of the intertidal zone.

References

ATKINSON, A.
1823 *Ireland Exhibited to England: In a Political and Moral Survey of Her Population*. Baldwin, Cradock, and Joy, London, England, UK.

BARKER, T. C.
1977 *The Glassmakers Pilkington: The Rise of an International Company, 1826–1876*. Weidenfell and Nicholson, London, England, UK.

BELFAST NEWS LETTER
1754 Delamont Estate: Advertisement. *Belfast News Letter*, 25 January:3. Belfast, Northern Ireland, UK.
1773 James Bailie: Advertisement. *Belfast News Letter*, 11 May:4. Belfast, Northern Ireland, UK.

BOADEN, PATRICK J. S., AND M. J. DRING
1980 A Quantitative Evaluation of the Effect of *Ascophyllum* Harvesting on the Littoral Ecosystem. *Helgolander Meersunters* 33:700–710.

CHAPMAN, V. J.
1970 *Seaweeds and Their Uses*, 2nd edition. Methuen, London, England, UK.

CLARK, W.
1971 *Rathlin, Disputed Island, Portlaw*. Volturna Press, Portlaw, Republic of Ireland.

COTTON, A. D.
1911 Algae, Marine, A Biological Survey of Clare Island in the County of Mayo and Adjoining District, Section 1. *Proceedings of the Royal Irish Academy* 31(B): 53–56,151–154.

CRAWFORD, WILLIAM H.
1980 Drapers and Bleachers in the Early Ulster Linen Industry. In *Négoce et Industrie en France et en Irlande aux XVIIIe et XIXe Siècles, Franco-Irish Symposium on Social and Economic History*, L. M. Cullen and P. Butel, editors, pp. 113–119. Éditions du National de la Recherche Scientifique, Paris, France.

DAVISON, A. J., AND PATRICK J. S. BOADEN
1990 The Management of Strangford Lough: A Study of the Marine Environment, Its Conservation, and Its Exploitation. Report to the Department of the Environment (NI), Countryside and Wildlife Branch from the School of Biology and Biochemistry, Environmental and Evolutionary Biology Division, The Queen's University of Belfast, Belfast, Northern Ireland, UK.

DAY, ANGELIQUE, AND PATRICK McWILLIAMS (EDITORS)
1991 *Ordnance Survey Memoirs of Ireland, Volume 7, Parishes of County Down II 1832–4, 1837, North Down and the Ardes*. Institute of Irish Studies, Belfast, Northern Ireland, UK.

1992   *Ordnance Survey Memoirs of Ireland, Volume 17, Parishes of County Down IV 1833–7, East Down and Lecale.* Institute of Irish Studies, Belfast, Northern Ireland, UK.

DORAN, JOSEPH. S.
[1975] *My Mourne.* Mourne Observer Press, Newcastle, Northern Ireland, UK.

DUBOURDIEU, J.
1802   *Statistical Survey of the County of Down with Observations on the Means of Improvement; Drawn up for the Consideration and by Order of the Dublin Society.* Graisburry & Campbell, Dublin, Republic of Ireland.

EVANS, E. ESTYN
1957   *Irish Folk Ways.* Routledge and Kegan Paul, London, England, UK.

FENTON, ALEXANDER
1978   *The Northern Isle: Orkney and Shetland.* Donald Publishers, Edinburgh, Scotland, UK.

GODFREY, E. S.
1975   *The Development of English Glass Making, 1560–1640.* University of North Carolina Press, Raleigh.

HAMOND, FRED
1991   *Antrim Coast and Glens, Industrial Heritage.* HMSO Belfast, Northern Ireland, UK.
1998   Water and Weed: The Exploitation of Coastal Resources. *Ulster Local Studies* 19(2):60–75.

HARPER, DOUGLAS
1974   Kelp Burning in the Glens. *The Glynns, Journal of the Glens of Antrim Historical Society* 2:19–24.

HARRIS, WALTER
1744   *The Ancient and Present State of the County of Down.* Dublin, Republic of Ireland.

HILL, GEORGE
1869   *The Montgomery Manuscripts, 1603–1706.* James Cleeland, Belfast, Northern Ireland, UK.

HUTTON, A. W. (EDITOR)
1892   *Arthur Young's Tour of Ireland, 1776–1779.* George Bell, London, England, UK.

LAWLOR, H. C.
1925   Archaeological Section, 9th Session, 1924–1925. *Proceedings of the Belfast Natural History and Philosophy Society, 1924–1925,* Belfast, Northern Ireland, UK.

MCERLEAN, THOMAS, ROSEMARY MCCONKEY, AND WESLEY FORSYTHE
2002   *Strangford Lough: An Archaeological Survey of the Maritime Cultural Landscape.* Northern Ireland Archaeological Monographs, No. 6, Environment and Heritage Service. Blackstaff Press, Belfast, UK.

MCERLEAN, THOMAS, AND TERRENCE REEVES-SMYTH
1990   Castle Ward Demesne. Manuscript, National Trust Rowallane, Saintfield, County Down, Northern Ireland, UK.

MCKAY, M.
1980   *The Rev. Dr. John Walker's Report on the Hebrides of 1764 and 1771.* John Donald Publishers, Edinburgh, Scotland, UK.

MCKENZIE, W. C.
1974   *The History of the Outer Hebrides, Lewis, Harris, North and South Uist, Benecula and Barra.* Mercat Press, Edinburgh, Scotland, UK.

O'DELL, A. C., AND K. WALTON
1962   *The Highlands and Islands of Scotland.* Thomas Nelson and Sons, London, England, UK.

O'NEILL, T. P.
1970   Some Irish Techniques of Collecting Seaweed. *Folklife* 8:13–19.

ORDNANCE SURVEY
1834   Down sheet 18, Ireland, 6-inch map. Ordnance Survey of Ireland.
1858   Down sheet 11, Ireland, 6-inch map. Ordnance Survey of Ireland.

RYMER, L.
1974a   A Note and Comments, the Kelp Industry in North Knapdale. *Scottish Studies* 18:127–132.
1974b   The Scottish Kelp Industry. *Scottish Geographical Magazine* 90(3):142–152.

THOMPSON, F.
1973   *Harris and Lewis, Outer Hebrides.* David and Charles, Newton Abbot, England, UK.

UNITED KINGDOM (U.K.) PARLIAMENT
1824   Repeal of Duties. *Sessional Papers* (Commons).

WESTROPP, M. S. D.
1920   *Irish Glass.* Herbert Jenkins London, England, UK.

THOMAS C. MCERLEAN
CENTRE FOR MARITIME ARCHAEOLOGY
SCHOOL OF ENVIRONMENTAL SCIENCES
UNIVERSITY OF ULSTER
COLERAINE BT52 1SA
NORTHERN IRELAND, UK

1985. Archaeology of the Cod Fishery: Damariscove Island—1622 to 20th century.

Historical Archaeology 19(2):57 –86.

ALARIC FAULKNER

Archaeology of the Cod Fishery: Damariscove Island

ABSTRACT

In the 17th and 18th centuries, seasonal fishermen from France and England practiced nearly identical methods of dry curing codfish on the coasts of North America. The complex measures taken in cleaning, salting and drying the cod were followed with ritual fidelity. The well-preserved product was exported to the warmer climates of the Antilles and Mediterranean where it found a ready market. Structures for this land based operation were rebuilt annually, each camp requiring a vast area of drying racks and a specific set of wattle walled buildings, roofed with bark and sod or else covered by the ship's sails. These structures should leave diagnostic post mold configurations.

A sedentary fishery, leaving more permanent remains, evolved along with colonization in the 1620s, as at Damariscove Island, off the coast of Maine. In New England, the winter fishery provided employment compatible with agriculture. Damariscove offers an early example of this mixed economy and an opportunity to examine its role in promoting early settlement. Distributions of clay pipes recovered in the initial Damariscove survey indicate a marked shift in settlement focus from the harborside, prior to the Indian Wars of 1676 to ca. 1725, to upland locations thereafter. This most likely reflects abandonment of the cod fishery in favor of sheep raising as the dominant economic pursuit.

Introduction

Damariscove is the last in a series of islands which juts into the sea from the Damariscotta River estuary, about one-third of the way "down east" along the coast of Maine (Figure 1). The islands and peninsulas of this submerged coastline are of particular historic interest, for it was here that the English made their first successful settlements in Maine, based principally on the cod fishery. Damariscove was the earliest of these settlements, supporting in 1622 a year-round population of 13 fishermen employed by Sir Ferdinando Gorges, a member of the Council for New England who was eventually to become sole proprietor of Maine.

Besides supplying fish for export, these men were to keep the island "farmed out in Sir Ferdinando's name to such as shall there fish." For their protection against the French and Indians, they had built "a strong palisado of spruce trees of some ten feet high, having besides their small shot, one piece of ordnance and some ten good dogs" (James 1963:15–16). With the hope of learning more of this occupation and its successors, the author directed an intensive survey of Damariscove in the summers of 1979 and 1980, sponsored by the Maine Historic Preservation Commission. The documentary and archaeological research at this and related fishing stations in Maine has led him to examine the archaeology of the cod fishery in general.

As it was the lure of the cod fishery which brought Europeans to the Northeast, the history and archaeology of this industry should be of paramount importance in understanding the process of colonization here. Very little archaeological work has been done on the early English fishery, and even less is known of its French and Acadian counterparts. This is not due to any want of sites, for in Maine at least 20 17th century fishing settlements have been located. With growing interest in the role of the cod fishery in promoting settlement, the need for a reliable historical and archaeological model of the industry has become apparent. A prototype, developed here, relies far more heavily on historical information than archaeological data, but this is bound to change. This version should be useful in site identification, and in the recognition of key features and artifacts associated with early cod fishing stations. It also implies specific patterns of refuse disposal which may be tested archaeologically.

Comtemporary records of the cod fishery in the 17th, 18th, and 19th centuries are numerous, and in some instances are remarkably detailed. In describing the layout of a fishing station and the activities which are involved in the processing of the cod, the author has drawn heavily on the best French and English primary sources. These include the writings of Nicolas Denys (Ganong 1908), Duhamel du Monceau (De la Morandière 1962), James Yonge (Poynter 1963), Thomas

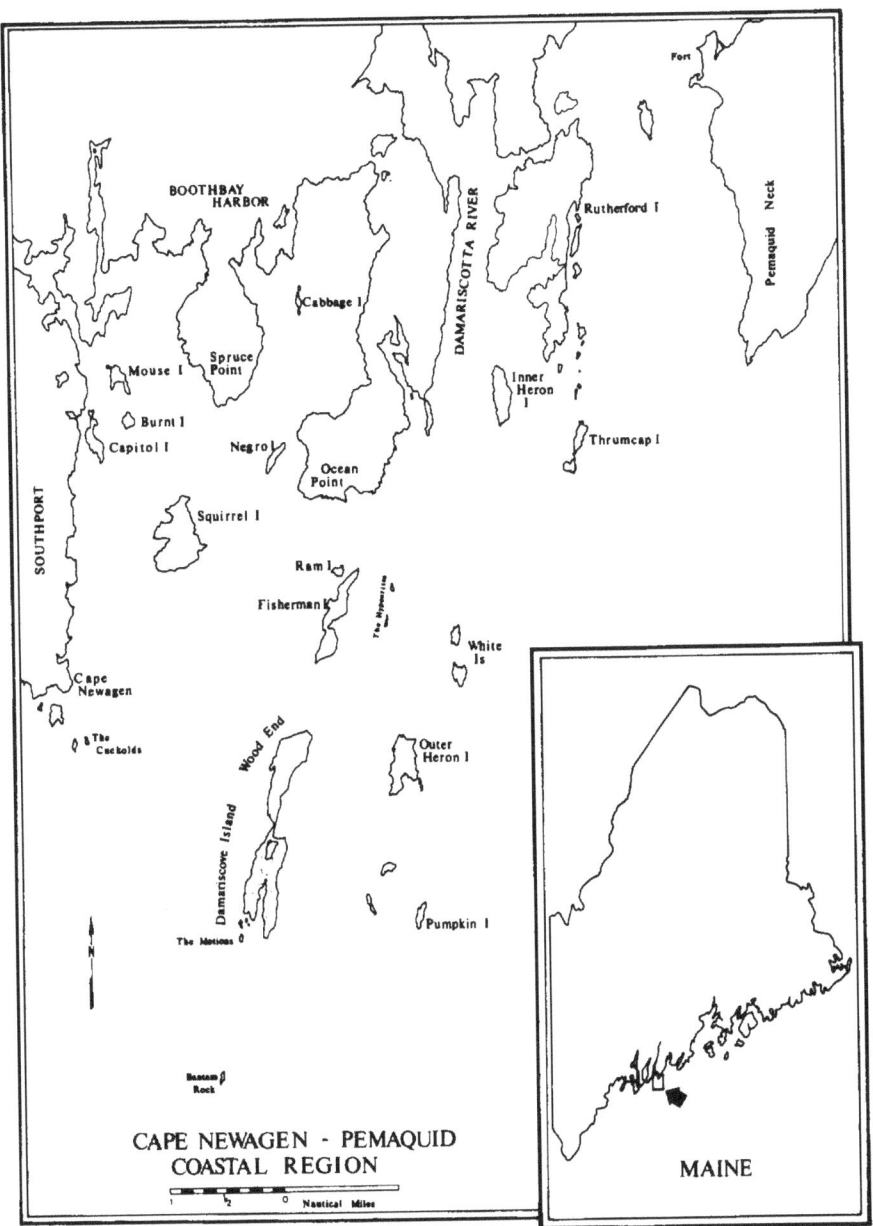

FIGURE 1. Islands near the mouth of the Damariscotta River, mid-coastal Maine.

Knight (1867), John Josselyn (1865), John Downing (Baxter 1889:372–376) and John Winter (Baxter 1884). Illustrations derived from these and other original sources are reproduced here to complete the model.

Early French and English Fishing Strategies

The history of the cod fishery in North America goes back to the early 16th century when the waters off Newfoundland were fished by French,

Portuguese, English, and Spanish Basque crews. By mid-century, the English and French were the principal contestants for this fishery, a rivalry which continued through the 17th century with the expansion of the fishery into Acadia and New England (Innis 1940:13–23). Most fishing sites to be encountered arhcaeologically, then, will be either French or English.

Fishing captains in the cod fishery were equipped to pursue one or the other of two basic processing methods. The catch could be cured *wet* by cleaning and salting it on board ship, or it could be dried on racks or *flakes* on shore. The wet on *green* process, as it was also called, was the simpler of the two strategies, for it involved no shore facilities and a minimal investment in equipment. The fishing was all done from the mother vessel, and the catch was simply cleaned on deck and then salted in the hold (Figure 2). Thus, with a relatively small vessel and crew, it was possible to make a brief voyage to nearby fishing banks and return with a product ready for market (De la Morandière 1962:145–160).

The dry fishery, because it involved establishing base stations on shore, is of particular archaeological interest. Appropriate sites required not only nearby fishing grounds, but also a protected harbor with room for setting up *stages* on which the fish were unloaded and cleaned, *flakes* for drying the catch, shelters for the crew, and a storehouse for

FIGURE 2. Method of the green cod fishery. Seen from the back on deck are the fishermen, behind them the dressers, and below decks the *salter*. In the detail below, working at the splitting table, are at left a *header* and at right a *splitter*. At the far right is a fisherman working behind his spray hood. Aprons over the barrels keep the workers on deck relatively clean and dry (after De la Morandière 1962: Plate VII; courtesy of G. P. Maisonneuve et Larose).

Perspectives from *Historical Archaeology* and *ACUA Proceedings*

provisions. Fishing was done from a number of small boats brought over on the mother vessel and was therefore limited to the waters within a few hours sail of the base station. This precluded fishing for the largest cod along the offshore banks, but smaller cod were best suited to this process anyway, as it took many weeks of curing to dry the flesh thoroughly (De la Morandière 1962:35).

One advantage to the dry cure was that it required only about half the salt of the green process (Ganong 1908:527). This was of consequence to the English, who lacked the port facilities needed to manufacture salt in quantity and were forced to purchase it from the continent (Innis 1940:51). Also, in the dry fishery, any excess salt was stored at the processing site for future use; it therefore did not compete with fish for cargo space on the return voyage (De la Morandière 1962:67).

Dry fishing was also more productive in some respects than was the green fishery. According to Denys, writing of the Acadian fishery of ca. 1670, a 200-ton ship outfitted for green curing required a crew of about 25 men and boys, and it might be expected to return in three or four months with 45,000 fish. A comparable ship in the dry fishery required twice the crew, and the voyage might last twice as long, but the vessel would generally return with 200,000 fish, more than four times that produced by the green cure strategy (Ganong 1908:527). Thus the profitability of the dry fishery depended considerably on labor and provisioning costs, as well as the expense of capital equipment.

The greatest advantage, however, was the superiority of the dried product. The finest grade of *merchantable* cod could be expected to last for years, and regularly commanded high prices in the Mediterranean (Knight 1867:43, 38). Unlike green–cured cod, it could be transported to warmer latitudes without spoiling. Merchantable cod provisioned North American colonists, supplied food for the military and paid for Spanish goods and gold, while *refuse* cod was fed to slaves in the Antilles (Innis 1940:51, 57). This dried cod, then, was primarily an export product, while green–cured cod was generally intended for domestic

consumption (De la Morandière 1962:345, Lounsbury 1934:144).

Prior to 1600, the French and English practiced both techniques in the Newfoundland fishery. The French fishermen, however, were based in numerous scattered ports with substantial local markets, and they preferred the green process. Any attempt to dry the cod was conducted after the return, but the results did not compare in quality to the true dry cure. The English fishing industry, concentrated in a few West Country ports, had a limited domestic market and salt supply, and so favored the dry process. When the Spanish market opened up after the defeat of the Armada, English West Country fishermen were equipped to meet this new demand. London merchants soon became important middlemen, sending out *sack ships* to buy up the surplus Newfoundland catch and take it to the Mediterranean. But by 1600 the French fishermen of the Biscay ports were also dry processing in earnest and were in competition with the English for a foothold in Newfoundland (Innis 1940:51–52).

Two significant developments in the early 17th century were the expansion of the cod fishery into Acadia and New England, and the beginning of sedentary fishing at semi-permanent installations occupied throughout the year. Bartholemew Gosnold, in his 1602 exploration of the Gulf of Maine and New England shores proclaimed "better fishing and in as great a plentie, as in Newfoundland" (Burrage 1906:331–332). Such reports induced seasonal fishermen to travel another 1200 km. (746 mi.) or so beyond the Grand Banks of Newfoundland to exploit the new fishing grounds. Thereafter, the coasts of Maine and Acadia were contested by the French and English until the middle of the 18th century. Christopher Levett, one of the Council of New England, recommended the "more profitable course" of permanent fishing stations over seasonal fishing voyages after his 1624 visit, and his advice was well taken (Levett 1847:105). Damariscove, for example, was first established in order to monopolize the cod fishery by controlling the harbors and land necessary to set up fishing stations. In addition, the Damariscove employees were to compete with the licensed seasonal fishermen and so provide a second source of revenue for their employer. Even though the licensing strategy failed for lack of enforcement, most settled fishing businesses in Maine prospered as efficient alternatives to seasonal fishing. The best known of these was at Richmond's Island on Cape Elizabeth, Maine, and was first operated for a Sir Robert Trelawny by his agent, John Winter, from 1633 to 1644 (Baxter 1884). Similar ventures were attempted by the French in Acadia in the middle of the 17th century, but according to Denys, they were unsuccessful (Ganong 1908:559–560).

The principal reason for the success of the sedentary fishery practiced in New England was its potential as a winter occupation. In many areas, as at Richmond's Island, the best fishing was in the months of January and February (Baxter 1884:26), whereas spring and summer fishing was the rule in Newfoundland and Acadia (De la Morandière 1962:163; Ganong 1908:562). Apparently in the winter the cod approached closer to the Maine shore to spawn (Woodbury 1880:23–26). Thus, after about 1620, fishing became a suitable employment for New England planters, giving a stronger basis for permanent settlement (Innis 1940:75–76). In Acadia, however, seasonal expeditions were still relatively cheaper. The employees were housed and provisioned for only eight or nine months of the year and were returned to France to spend the winter months on their own (Ganong 1908:559–562).

The New England winter fishery developed markedly in the 17th century, and the Massachusetts Bay Colony took ever increasing advantage of the carrying trade which it generated, so that by the end of the century the colony was becoming a powerful commercial force in competition with England itself (Innis 1940:197–198). The study of the mixed farming and fishing economy represented in the archaeology of sites such as Damariscove is thus truly of regional significance in considering the process of early colonial settlement in New England. In order to understand the archaeological manifestations of this economy, it is not sufficient to study just the procurement of the fish as has been done by Mousette (1979). One must examine the complete dry curing process in the seasonal and sedentary fisheries and its implications.

Dry Cod Processing in the Seasonal Fishery

A striking feature of the primary documents describing the complex dry cod process is the agreement between the French and English accounts, suggesting that the fishermen of both countries practiced essentially the same techniques throughout the early history of the cod fishery (De la Morandière 1962:161). A comparison of the 17th century Denys and Yonge accounts with Du Monceau's 18th century work shows them to be all but identical in key respects and in substantial agreement with Knight's description of the cod fishery practiced in the Gulf of St. Lawrence in the mid–19th century (Knight 1867:87–89). Variants of this curing method are still practiced in Newfoundland (Morison 1971:474).

A large crew was required for each ship engaged in the seasonal fishery, and each man was assigned shares in the value of the catch according to his duties and experience. While Denys places the minimum crew size at 50 for a 200-ton vessel, Du Monceau, writing a century later in the 1770s, puts the minimum figure at 120 for the larger 300-ton vessels then commonly in use. The latter crew included, besides the captain, a chaplain, two surgeons, and more than 100 workers specializing in various aspects of the fishery, many of whom had secondary roles as seamen during the voyage. Twenty men trained as stage and flake makers, carpenters, and caulkers were employed principally for the construction and maintenance of the land–based facilities. Sixty fishermen were assigned to 12 boats in crews of five each, three actually to fish, and two to tend flakes and mend equipment on shore. Eight to 10 additional fishermen were employed just to supply small bait fish for the cod fishermen. Ten headers and 10 splitters were employed to clean and split the fish while from eight to 40 young boys assisted in the numerous chores at the fishing station (De la Morandière 1962:162).

Much of the food for the lengthy voyage came from the fishery itself in the form of cod and mackerel. Produce was obtained from small gardens, and meat and eggs came from poultry. The ship had to be stocked with large quantities of provisions. Denys emphasizes wine (to be cut with water), pork, pickled herring, biscuit, peas, beans, vinegar and oil or butter (Ganong 1908:527, 548–549). Invoices from an English fishing station of 1634 include the same staples of biscuits, peas, beans, and vinegar and oil, but they also show several hogsheads of beef in addition to the pork and fish, with sack, aquavite and beer as beverages rather than wine (Baxter 1884:147–148). Supplies and equipment for the fishery were numerous and often bulky; therefore, they included only items that could not conveniently be made from native materials at the fishing site. These same English records include several hogsheads of pitch and tar for waterproofing and protecting boats, lines, and clothing. Also listed are sails, shrouds, anchor lines, mooring cables, lead, oakum, hardware fittings, and bait nets for outfitting and caulking the fishing boats (Baxter 1884:147–149). In the seasonal fishery, the boats themselves had to be imported, and Denys describes partially prefabricated boats which were stowed aboard ship for the voyage and then pieced together at the fishery (Ganong 1908:538–541). Salt, however, was the required item of greatest bulk, even in the dry fishery, and seasonal fishermen used their ship's hold as a floating salt bin (Ganong 1908:544).

Fishing tackle was prepared *en route* to the fishing grounds. Six hand lines were allotted to each boat crew, two for each active fisherman. The lines were first stretched and dragged astern to untwist and untangle them. A barbed but eyeless hook, with a flattened shank end for attachment, was then bound to each line. Lead sinkers were prepared from cast bar stock, and weighed 1.3 kg. to 1.8 kg. (3 lbs. to 4 lbs.) apiece. Among the most likely artifacts of the fishery to survive in the archaeological record, lead sinkers may prove to

have diagnostic forms, as suggested by Denys' description of French types:

> The bar is cut into three or four pieces according to its size; each piece makes one lead. Some make them round, others make them square, and they are much larger at one end than the other. The slender ends are flattened a little at the tip. They are pierced, and . . . tied with sail thread so that they cannot get off. Some give more ornamentation than others, in order to show their skill (Ganong 1908:275–276).

This work was not always performed under ideal conditions, for in the 17th century the voyage was undertaken at breakneck speed in order to arrive at the most favorable harbors first and establish the ship's captain as admiral. It was the admiral who had the choice of areas to set up his base camp and who directed the subsequent use of the harbor and reuse of the stages, flakes and other structures left in previous years (Ganong 1908:530–531; Poynter 1963:55–56). In the Newfoundland fishery, where early arrivals might be expected in March, the passage was sometimes extremely hazardous. John Yonge, surgeon aboard the *Marigold* in 1670, relates in vivid detail the hazards of winter storms, entrapment in seemingly endless ice floes, and attempts to manage frozen sails and rigging while the master and the mate turned to heavy drink (Poynter 1963:124–125).

The ground plans of many seasonal fishing stations probably resembled the French settlement of 1686 at L'Île Bonaventure, south of the mouth of the St. Lawrence (Figure 3). Here are clusters of temporary structures, stages and flakes, generally in about the same number as the larger ships represented. The compactness of settlement is probably not exaggerated, for the drying process required ready access to the stage area. Note the two gardens, probably belonging to the admiral and vice admiral, and the permanent structure surrounded by crosses, which was probably a mission.

Yonge describes succinctly the procedure of setting up a fishing station in Newfoundland (Figure 4):

> As soon as we resolve to fish here, the ship is all unrigged, and in the snow and cold all the men go into the woods to cut timber, fir spruce and birch being here plentiful. With this they build stages, flakes, cookroom and houses. The houses

FIGURE 3. Detail of dry cod fishing stations at L'Île Bonaventure, south of the mouth of the St. Lawrence River, ca. 1686. (courtesy of the Bibliothéque Nationale, Paris).

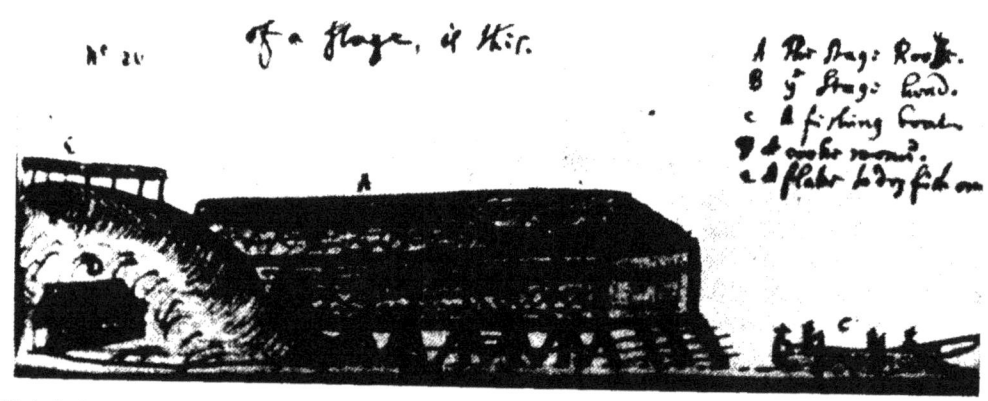

FIGURE 4. A sketch from John Yonge's Journal, 1670, showing components of a seasonal dry cod fishing station in Newfoundland. His key shows: A, "The Stage Rooffe;" B, "ye Stage head;" C, "A fishing boate;" D, "A cook roome;" E, 'A flake to dry fish on" (after Poynter 1963: Plate 4; courtesy of Longmans Group Ltd).

are made of a frythe [wattle] of boughs, sealed inside with rinds [bark], which look like planed deal [sheathing] and turfs of earth upon, to keep the sun from raning [ruining?] them. The stages are begun on the edge of the shore, and built out into the sea, a floor of round timber, supported with posts, and shores of great timber. The boats lie at the head of them as at a key, and throw up their fish, which is split, salted &c (Poynter 1963:56–57).

Denys' description of cookhouse construction, made independently from Yonge's, is very similar:

The steward with some of the boys, works to build the kitchen, which is covered with large turfs arranged like tiles one upon another, so that the rain cannot enter. And from the roof downwards, there are fir branches all around, interlaced [between pickets 30 cm. (1 ft.) apart] like the others. These the boys bring from the woods, as well for this as for all the rest of the lodgings (Ganong 1908:532).

Denys, like Yonge, makes reference to stripping the ship "as if she were in harbor in France to pass the winter" (Ganong 1908:532). The purpose, he explains, was to provide rigging and sails to make the other buildings in the camp—the *fishermen's quarters, captain's storehouse* and the *stage*—which were tent–like, rather than sod– or bark–roofed.

The fishermen were housed in rectangular barracks with walls made of pickets driven into the ground at about 30 cm. (1 ft.) intervals and interwoven with fir branches, rising on the sides about 1.5 m. (5 ft.) high. The sail roof was supported by a smooth ridge pole set on posts spaced at about 2.0 m. (6.6 ft.) intervals running down the center of the structure. This frame tent was high enough so that two tiers of fishermen could be suspended in rope hammocks between the posts. Each hammock served two fishermen, who were apparently separated from each other by a cross brace running underneath the hammock and connecting to the central row of posts. Denys notes only that the size of these quarters depended on the size of the mainsail. From his description, however, it is evident that four fishermen were housed for every 2 m. (6.6 ft.) of building length, and that at least 24 lineal meters (78.7 ft.) of structure would be needed to house most of the 50 members of the ship's company in Denys' time. This may have called for more than one barracks.

The captain's house, built of similar wattle and sail construction, was divided down the central axis with a solid palisade partition fitted with a door and lock. This separated the captain's quarters from the stores (Ganong 1908:531–532). Where not hopelessly complicated by seasonal rebuilding, it should be possible to distinguish the captain's quarters from the barracks by their footprints. While remains of support posts in the crew's housing should leave post molds spaced at 2 m. (6.6 ft.) intervals, the central partition of the captain's quarters should be a palisade interrupted only by a doorway.

The key structure of the dry fishery was, of course, the *stage* where the fish were dressed and salted, the construction of which Denys illustrates in detail (Figure 5). This was a covered rectangular building with an open triangular platform at one end which jutted out into the water. The entire building was erected upon a framework of stout pilings which, according to the tide differential, were as high as 6 m. (19.7 ft.) The pilings were set out at low tide and shored and cross–braced to make them rigid. From side to side across these underpinnings, floor joists were placed at about 2 m. (6.6 ft.) intervals. These joists in turn supported a flooring of small, round poles, as in Yonge's description above. The remainder of the superstructure resembled the housing facilities in its wattle and sail construction, except that the uprights were fastened to the underpinnings rather than driven into the ground. Also, the end wall at the stage head was elevated above the floor, leaving a 60 cm. (2 ft.) gap through which the fishermen passed their catch inside to be dressed. Built into the interior of the stage was the *splitting and cleaning table*, a *chute* for placing the cleaned fish, and a large *salt bin*.

Denys illustrates some of the paraphernalia associated with the stage activities, reproduced here in Figure 6. Two kinds of *train vat* were known, one of which was a planked structure about 2 m. (6.6 ft.) square, lined with pitch and elevated on legs, while the second was a specially modified barrel. Both had mat–like partitions near the front which served as strainers. Cod livers were thrown into the larger compartment and allowed to "melt" in the sun. Fluids then passed through the strainer into the smaller compartment. Two taps on the front of the device allowed the liquids to be drained periodically, the upper tap for the oil or *train*, the lower tap for blood and rainwater. Old, well–pitched boats were often rigged with strainers to serve as train vats as well (Ganong 1908:535–536).

Also shown in Figure 6 are the *roller barrows* used to drag the fish from the splitting area to the

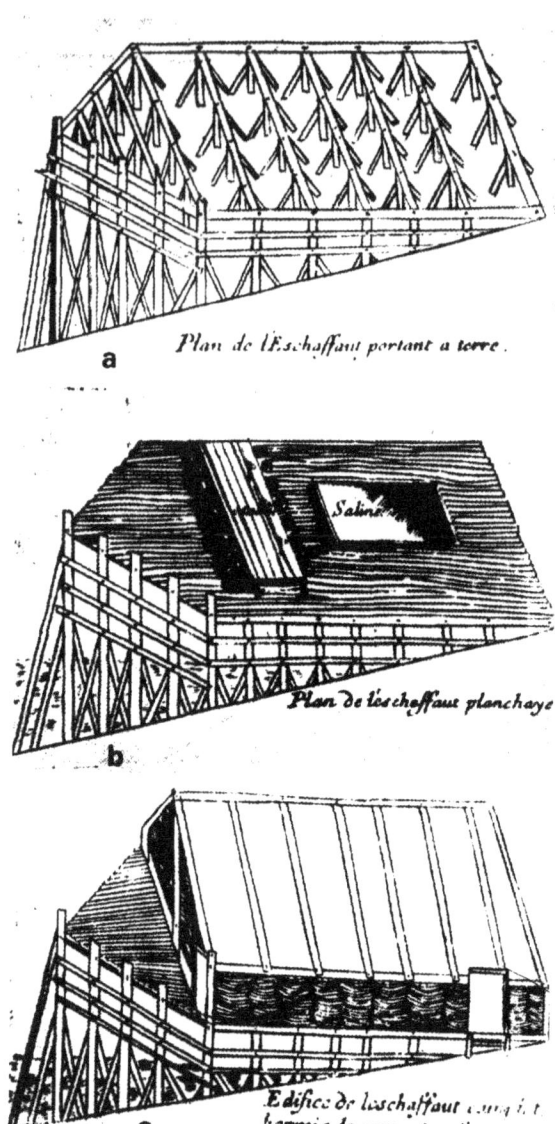

FIGURE 5. Construction details of a stage type used in the seasonal fishery in Acadia ca. 1672; a, pilings, shoring, and floor joists; b, pole flooring with built–in splitting table [établie] and salt bin [Saline]; c, wattle wall and tent roofing of the finished stage (after Denys in Ganong 1908:284).

salting area at the other end of the stage. Another carrying device (not shown) was a *wicker litter*, used to carry the fish from the stage to the beach to be washed. The 3 m. (9 ft.) square *cage*, into

which the fish were tossed after the salt was washed out of them, was built like a child's crib. Thereafter the fish were taken by litter to the *draining platform* (not shown) which was a miniature version of the stage itself, having a pole floor set up on pilings and covered with an arbor of interwoven branches which acted as a sun shade. Some were rectangular, measuring about 2 m. by 4 m. (6.6 ft. by 13.1 ft.) and oriented parallel to the shoreline, while others were double–sized platforms, measuring 3.7m to 4.6m (12 ft. to 15 ft.) square.

The most extensive structures of the dry fishery were the *flakes*, drying racks supported on small poles, 1.7m (5.5 ft.) long, which were driven into the ground so that the drying surface stood waist high. These simple structures were about 1.5 m. (5 ft.) wide, the supporting poles being spaced in pairs at 1.8m (6 ft.) intervals to form long, parallel rows. Side rails and cross braces were lashed to these uprights, and then covered with stripped branches to support the cod, allowing them to be dried from underneath as well as from above. Denys estimates that from 30 to 50 of these long and narrow flakes were needed for each ship, depending on its size, making the flake area the most extensive component of the fishing station. His approximate figures for the length and breadth of this area suggest that from 400 m.^{2} to 2000 m.^{2} (4,301 ft.^{2} to 21,505 ft.^{2}) were required for each vessel's flakes (Ganong 1908:536–537; Knight 1867:88).

Finally, a place along the beach was required to lay out the dried fish and then place them in piles, in order to make room on the flakes for fresh catches. Generally this was done on a gravel beach, especially cleaned and prepared for the purpose and lying well above high tide. To keep them dry, fish were piled on stone platforms 2 m. to 4 m. (6.6 ft. to 13.1 ft.) in diameter (Ganong 1980:537, 557; De la Morandière 1962:177). Remains of such structures have been reported in Labrador by Tuck and Grenier (1981:188).

The fishing itself was done from small boats propelled by oar and sail and manned by a crew of three fishermen. Provisioned with biscuit and watered wine (in the French case), the fishermen

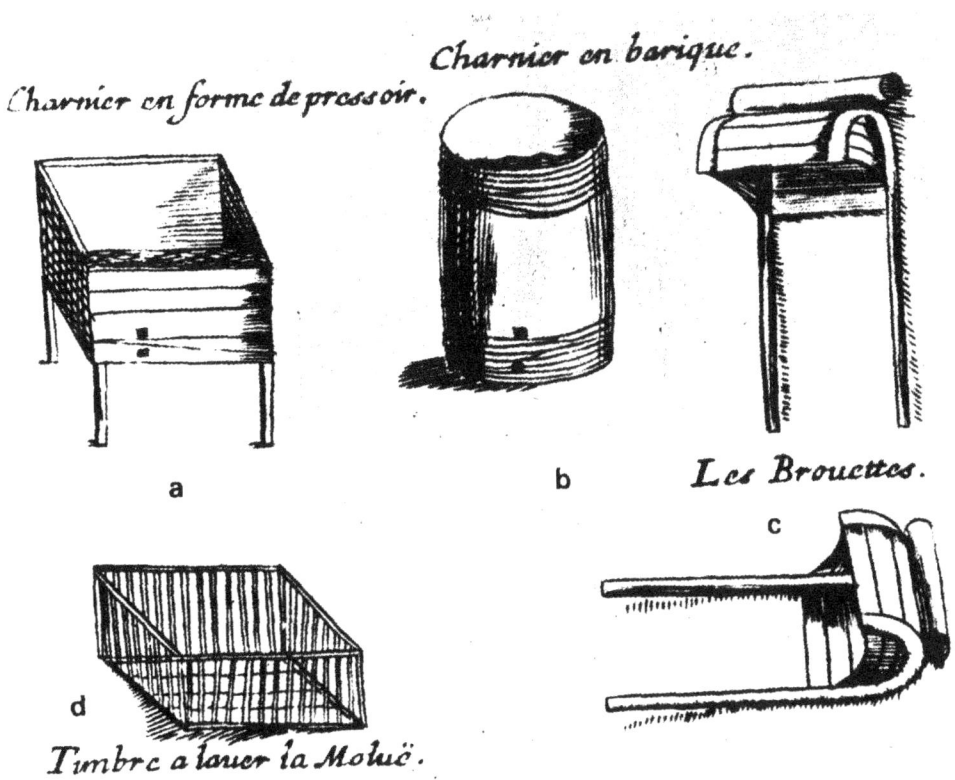

Charnier en forme de pressoir.

Charnier en barique.

Les Brouettes.

Timbre a lauer la Moluë.

a

b

c

d

FIGURE 6. Equipment used in the dry cod process in Acadia ca. 1672: a and b, "wine press" and "barrel" train oil vat forms; c, two views of roller barrows used to drag the cod along the pole floor of the stage; d, cage for washing excess salt from the cod (after Denys in Ganong 1908:288).

carried out the day's work within 5 km. to 8 km. (3 mi. to 5 mi.) or two to three hours, of their camp. Each fisherman set out his two handlines, one on each side of the boat. Cod entrails, shellfish, or any number of different kinds of small fish were used as bait. Fishing about 1.8m (6 ft.) above the bottom, they were able to work first one line and then the other, on good days bringing in the cod as fast as they could haul in the lines and rebait the hooks. In the summer fishery they worked until about 4:00 p.m. in order to return to the stage head by 6:00–7:00 p.m., allowing time for the shore crew to clean and salt the fish (Ganong 1908:542–544).

The land–based operation is carefully illustrated in an inset from Hermann Moll's map of North America (Moll ca. 1713), which shows a seasonal English station in operation in Newfoundland early in the 18th century (Figure 7). Discrepancies with Denys' description include the orientation of the splitting table and the number of salt bins, but otherwise these French and English depictions agree in detail.

Boats were tied up at the stage head, and the cod hoisted onto the platform using curved iron *pikes* about 30 cm. (1 ft.) long and fitted with long wooden handles. In managing the larger cod, they were assisted from above by boys using *gaffs*. The fish were then slid under the partition into the splitting room.

The cleaning process required three specialists, a *throater*, a *header* and a *splitter*. The fish was first passed to the throater, dressed in a heavy apron and protective sleeves, who opened the belly

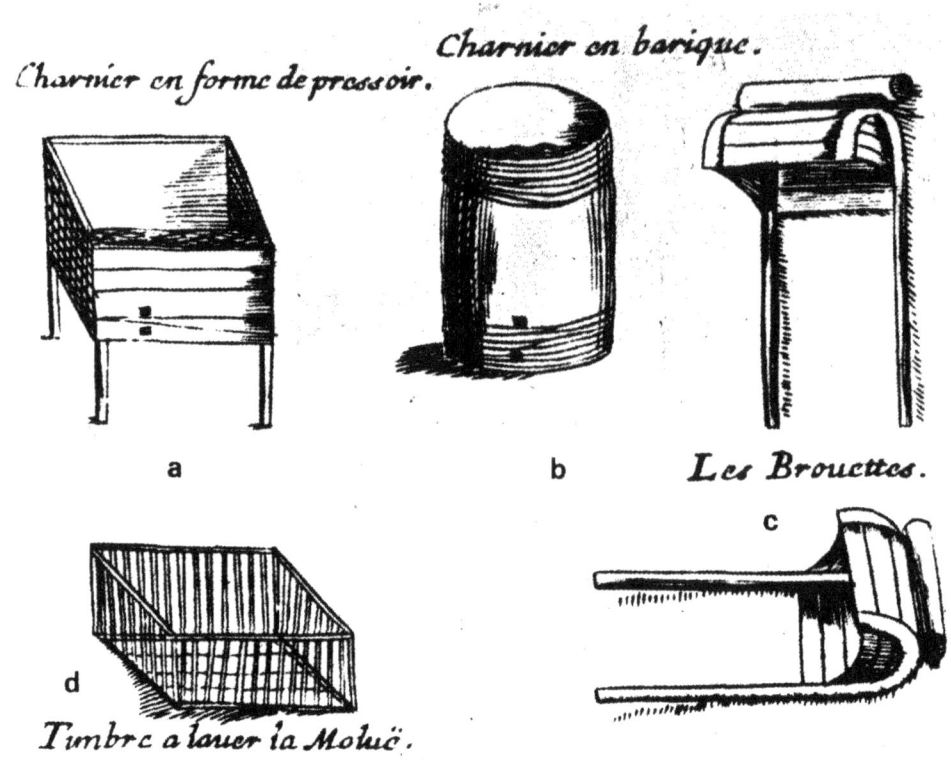

Charnier en forme de pressoir.

Charnier en barique.

Les Brouettes.

Timbre a laver la Moluë.

a

b

c

d

FIGURE 6. Equipment used in the dry cod process in Acadia ca. 1672: a and b, "wine press" and "barrel" train oil vat forms; c, two views of roller barrows used to drag the cod along the pole floor of the stage; d, cage for washing excess salt from the cod (after Denys in Ganong 1908:288).

carried out the day's work within 5 km. to 8 km. (3 mi. to 5 mi.) or two to three hours, of their camp. Each fisherman set out his two handlines, one on each side of the boat. Cod entrails, shellfish, or any number of different kinds of small fish were used as bait. Fishing about 1.8m (6 ft.) above the bottom, they were able to work first one line and then the other, on good days bringing in the cod as fast as they could haul in the lines and rebait the hooks. In the summer fishery they worked until about 4:00 p.m. in order to return to the stage head by 6:00–7:00 p.m., allowing time for the shore crew to clean and salt the fish (Ganong 1908:542–544).

The land–based operation is carefully illustrated in an inset from Hermann Moll's map of North America (Moll ca. 1713), which shows a seasonal English station in operation in Newfoundland early in the 18th century (Figure 7). Discrepancies with Denys' description include the orientation of the splitting table and the number of salt bins, but otherwise these French and English depictions agree in detail.

Boats were tied up at the stage head, and the cod hoisted onto the platform using curved iron *pikes* about 30 cm. (1 ft.) long and fitted with long wooden handles. In managing the larger cod, they were assisted from above by boys using *gaffs*. The fish were then slid under the partition into the splitting room.

The cleaning process required three specialists, a *throater*, a *header* and a *splitter*. The fish was first passed to the throater, dressed in a heavy apron and protective sleeves, who opened the belly

FIGURE 7. The dry cod process in Newfoundland: detail from a map of North America prepared for the British Privy Council by Dutch cartographer Hermann Moll, ca. 1713 (courtesy of the Maine State Museum).

of the cod from the throat to the anus. Denys describes the throater's knife as long and pointed, the cutting edge curving toward the point, perhaps like a modern filetting knife. The fish was then passed to the header, similarly dressed, whose job it was to remove the entrails, save the roe and liver in baskets, and then to break off the head and throw it into the sea through an open hole in the floor at his feet. Finally, the fish was handed to the highly skilled splitter, who stood in a barrel near the end of the table, his apron draped outside the barrel to keep himself clean. His knife was much heavier than that of the throater, being straight, squared off at the end, and thickened along the back. The splitter grabbed a lateral fin in his mitted left hand, and steadied the fish against a batten nailed to the table. He then removed the flesh from one side of the spine, working from the fin to the

tail, cut through the backbone at the tail, and then worked up the other side. Thus the entire ribs and spine, except for a few caudal vertebra, were removed intact through the ventral opening, leaving a single piece of flesh opened to the tail. The spinal column was discarded through a hole in the floor as before (Ganong 1908:545–546; De la Morandière 1962:177; Knight 1867:88). Just such fish cleaning remains have been recovered underwater at various fishing sites in the Maritimes (Cuumba 1981), which may allow a complete faunal analysis of the cod, giving species, size, and season, as well as establishing a diagnostic record of fish dressing techniques.

The cleaned fish was tossed into a chute, from which it was loaded into roller barrows and dragged to the other end of the stage to be salted. The first of the day's fish were placed head by tail on

Maritime Archaeology

the floor with the skin side down. A thin layer of salt was spread over them using a *flat shovel,* and then additional fish were added to the pile. Larger cod, which required more salt, were treated and stacked separately. The process continued until the entire day's catch was salted in piles, where it would remain for a day and a half. The basket of livers was carried off to the liver vat, and added to the top of the already rotting mass of livers from previous days. Finally, the roe was placed in a nook in the salt bin and lightly salted (Ganong 1908:545–546).

The land crew continued the curing process on the following day while the fishermen were at sea. Here, Denys' description is corroborated in every important detail by the account of John Downing, an English fishermen from Canso, writing in 1676 (Baxter 1889:372–376). The cod from two days earlier were carried to the water, washed in the cage to remove excess salt, and then taken to the draining platform. When thoroughly drained, they were placed head to tail on the flakes, skin side up. After a few hours, the flesh side was turned up. Care was taken, however, not to give the flesh too much exposure to the midday sun lest it become reddened or cooked so that it fell to pieces. At night the fish were turned skin up to protect them from the dew or rain, for if ever the fish were rewetted once the drying process had begun, they would spoil. The highest quality fish were those dried uniformly to a translucent white. Rainy weather put a halt to the drying process and meant a backlog of salted, unwashed fish which were left in piles on the stage until conditions improved. Depending on the weather and management of the land operation, from 6% to 20% of the catch might be second quality *refuse* fish. Usually four or five fair days were required on the flakes for cod of ordinary size to complete the first stage of drying, although the largest cod took somewhat longer (Ganong 1908:554–555; Baxter 1889:375; Knight 1867:89).

After initial drying, the fish were taken from the flakes and placed on the beach, first in little piles and then in larger ones as the drying progressed. When the larger piles began to "sweat" moisture, usually after about two weeks, they were taken

apart, the cod allowed to dry on the beach for a few hours, and then restacked. This procedure was then repeated at about monthly intervals to keep the moisture to a minimum and evenly distributed throughout the pile. Eventually the fish were placed high on the beach on the circular stone platforms, skin down to prevent them from taking up moisture from underneath. The largest cod, or else some large, flat *pressing stones* were placed on top, their weight extracting the last bit of moisture from the pile. The final stack, now ladder high, was covered with sails until time for embarkation (Ganong 1908:557–558; Baxter 1889:375–376; Knight 1867:89). At the end of the season there was insufficient time to dry the last of the catch, which had to be cured green to become *corfish* (Baxter 1889:376). Any salt remaining in the hold of the ship was removed and stored on shore under a layer of bark and turf for future use (De la Morandière 1962:67). The hold was then partially filled with branches to serve as bedding for the cod, keeping it dry for the return trip (Ganong 1908:558).

While there may have been some variation from this model of the seasonal dry fishery, very few discrepanices are evident in the literature. De la Morandière (1962:170) alleges that the English in the Newfoundland fisheries used smaller hooks, which were inferior because they could be swallowed whole, but does not specify hook dimensions or time period. He also notes a distinction between the early French and English cod dressing practices, asserting that until the 18th century the French made *round cod,* splitting the fish only to the anus, so that the region of the tail was still round in section and prone to spoil for lack of adequate drying. The English carried the incision all the way through the tail to make *flat cod,* which could be more evenly salted and dried (De La Morandière 1962:156). This difference might well be detected in analysis of caudal vertebrae from stage sites. Various shortcuts also were attempted in the laborious dry curing process by both the French and the English (De la Morandière 1962:170; Knight 1867:42), but it is not likely that they were widely adopted.

The construction and reconstruction of the temporary, seasonal camps year after year, and the resulting deforestation should be of considerable archaeological interest in considering environmental changes along the coast during the 17th century. One 1622 English source noted that in Newfoundland there were no woods within 1.6 km. (1 mi.) of shore, and that substantial timber damage had been done by barking trees for roofing material (Innis 1940:63). Denys, writing 50 years later of Acadia, claimed that it was necessary to travel 15 km. to 30 km. (9.3 mi. to 18.6 mi.) and more to secure building materials for the dry fishery (Ganong 1908:532).

Besides the wasteful outlay of labor and materials inherent in this annual rebuilding process, the seasonal strategy had the added disadvantage of lax security. Fishing boats left hidden in the woods were liable to be stolen by the first to come in the following season, and the owners' marks removed. Stages were cannibalized for timber or burned; stored salt was stolen; train vats were destroyed, and other acts of theft and vandalism were carried out to minimize competition between fishermen, regardless of nationality (Innis 1940:67). These problems were somewhat better controlled by the sedentary fishery.

In the long run there may have been a distinct advantage in making only temporary facilities, which helps explain why seasonal fishing continued long after the advent of the sedentary fishery. From decade to decade there were major changes in the migration habits of the cod and the food fish on which they depended (Baxter 1889:372–373). Captains in the seasonal fishery usually chose their base of operations carefully after having tested the fishing grounds, and they even made provisions for setting up subsidiary camps if the fishing near the base camp suddenly failed (Ganong 1908:551–552).

The Sedentary Fishery

The term *sedentary fishery*, as it applies to New England, refers to a number of different fishing strategies, all of which used resident labor. In the first half of the 17th century, sedentary fishing was commonly financed by European investor-patentees such as Gorges and Trelawny, who sought to maintain licensed monopolies over the fishing grounds. These gave way to companies under local authority, as in Maine at Pemaquid and Damariscove. Eventually, as settlement progressed, indentured fishermen earned their freedom and the right to fish for themselves. By the 1670s the cod fishery was conducted by a number of locally based enterprises of varying size, run for the most part by independent fishermen (Josselyn 1865:153–164). In many cases, such as at the Isles of Shoals and at the islands and peninsulas around Damariscove, the smaller enterprises were numerous, each owning or sharing its boats, stage, flake area, and perhaps a fish house for storing the catch and supplies (Robert L. Bradley 1982, pers. comm.).

Unlike most of the patentees, these new independent enterprises seldom controlled the marketing of their product, and they were often badly used by the Massachusetts Bay merchants who served as middlemen. It was apparently common for a merchant to contract for the season's catch and then so obligate the fishermen to him that their wages would often be little or nothing. At the time of reckoning the merchant would appear with "a walking tavern, a Bark laden with the Legitimate bloud of the rich grape," and give out a few free samples (Josselyn 1865:161). Starved for entertainment, the fishing crews would often embark on a drunken bout lasting several days, only to find in the end that their wages had vanished, and in some cases that their plantations were now mortgaged to the merchant (Josselyn 1865:162).

While this was the general pattern for the operation of the sedentary fishery along the coast of Maine, other New Englanders, principally from Massachusetts, would regularly exploit these same fishing grounds, much in the same manner as was done by the seasonal European fishermen (Essex Institute 1919:263). Also, some of the local fishermen on the Maine coast, who fished their own waters in winter, spent the rest of the year in voyages to the coast of Acadia and Newfoundland (McFarland 1911:69–70).

The most complete historical record of the sedentary fishery in New England, as practiced for the early patentees, is for the Trelawny station at Richmond's Island. Originally conceived as an entrepôt for commerce with settlers, traders, and Indians around Casco Bay, its economic strength was principally as a fishing station (Baxter 1884:25–34). From 1633 to 1643 John Winter, Trelawny's agent, employed a crew of about 40 persons at the station, most of them indentured young males. A few were engaged to raise crops of maize, peas, "English grains," and other produce, or to tend cattle, goats, and pigs in an effort to make the enterprise more self–sufficient and even to produce a modest surplus for market. The majority, however, were set to fishing, regardless of their aptitude, inclination or experience (Baxter 1884:50, 123–124, 164–165).

The facilities Winter describes were far more substantial than those recorded for the seasonal fishery:

> I have built a house heare at Richmon Iland that is 40 foote in length & 18 foot broad within the sides, besides the Chimnay, and the Chimnay is large with an oven in each end of him, & he is so large that we Can place our Chittle [kettle] within the Clavell pece. We can brew & bake and boyle our Cyttell all at once in him . . . [In] another house that I have built under the side of our house . . . we set our Ceves & mill & morter In to break our corne & malt & to dres our meall in, & I have 2 chambers in him, and all our men lies in one of them, & every man hath his close boarded Cabbin [bunk] . . . & in the other Chamber I have Rome Inough to put the ships sailes into and all our dry goods which is in Caske, and I have a store house in him that will hold 2 tonnes of Caske which we put our bread and beare into, and every one of these romes ar Close with loockes and keyes unto them (Baxter 1884:31–32).

One would expect more permanent stages to be used in the sedentary fishery, such as the board–roofed stages described by Downing in 1676 (Baxter 1889:374). However the Richmond's Island inventory for 1638 lists a "Store of Stayge Sayles," suggesting that temporary construction methods may still have been used at that date. The only other fishing structure mentioned at Richmond's Island was probably more permanent: a "house to put our fish in," capable of storing 50,000 dried fish for export (Baxter 1884:169).

Other details of the station include "4 or 5 akers" of garden fenced with "pales of 6 fote heighe" planted in "Corne [maize?] and pumpkins," and a "house for our pigs" (Baxter 1884:32). Like Damariscove, Richmond's Island was originally fortified although the defenses were not described. Winter evidently took some unspecified measures to improve security in 1636 in opposition to the French military build–up at Fort Pentagoet at the mouth of the Penobscot River, some 150 km. (93.2 mi.) to the northeast. The inventories of arms show many different pieces of ordnance, as well as obsolete hand weapons (Baxter 1884:86, 179–180).

The footprints to be expected in the excavation of Richmond's Island structures, therefore, include not just patterns of post holes associated with temporary frame tents, but also buildings with cellars and chimney remains, and possibly stone foundations as well. With its 10 years of early 17th century accounts and invoices dealing with the material culture of the station, Richmond's Island provides one of the most complete images of the early sedentary fishery available. However, the physical layout of the station remains to be examined archaeologically, and is currently "off limits" to excavation. For now, the preliminary work at Damariscove provides the best alternative image, one which pertains to the small, independent enterprises as well as to the early businesses of the Gorges and Trelawny type.

Survey and Test Excavations at Damariscove

Unlike Richmond's Island, Damariscove has a long history of activity in various economic pursuits and has changed accordingly. Here, in 1622, was a fortified fishing camp designed to regulate a considerable seasonal English fishery while engaged in the sedentary fishery itself. The year–round business was operated by an all–male crew of 13, working for an absentee English nobleman. By 1646, however, the island was inhabited by groups of independent fishermen, some with families, who worked for local fishing masters. Non–resident fishermen by this time were principally from Massachusetts Bay, and both residents and non–residents were obliged to pay "a certain acknowledgement" to the new patentees residing in nearby Pemaquid. In 1660, one resident had, in addition to his house and stage, a "considerable estate in fish and cattel," indicating that the mixed fishing and farming economy had become well–established (Faulkner and Faulkner 1981:11). In 1672, 15 Damariscove families petitioned the Massachusetts General Court for government. When this was granted in 1674, Damariscove was as prosperous as any settlement in this region, its tax assessment equalled only by that of Monhegan (Faulkner and Faulkner 1981:1–11).

This thriving community was abandoned in 1676 as a result of Indian attacks during King Philip's War. Thereafter, small groups of fishermen–farmers occupied the island intermittently until the final cessation of hostilities with the Indians ca. 1726. Fishing and sheep raising were continued on a small scale through the remainder of the 18th century with a brief interruption on the eve of the American Revolution when the single resident family was burned out by a British naval party, and all the stock in sheep and pigs confiscated (Faulkner and Faulkner 1981:11–20).

In the 19th century the number of dwellings on the island ranged from one to three, and the population probably never exceeded 40 individuals. Granite quarrying was practiced commercially early in the century, much of it going into nearby construction on the mainland. After the establishment of a summer colony on nearby Squirrel Island in the 1870s, the Damariscove farm business turned from sheep raising to dairying and supplying the summer visitors with milk, produce, meat, and fish. By this time the dry cod fishery had long been abandoned, and smaller fish, particularly mackerel, were of greater importance. At the end of the century, an attempt was made to turn Damariscove itself into a resort, but it soon proved unsuccessful. A major addition to the community was the establishment of the Life Saving Station on the island in 1896, which now stands in ruins on the island (Griffin and Faulkner 1982:28–33).

It is apparent that Damariscove, although abandoned and barren today, is a complex multi-component site, and that it is not possible to examine the 17th century fishing component in isolation. This condition surely holds for most fishing sites in Maine and probably applies to many other areas as well.

Survey Methods

The purpose of the 1979–1980 field work on Damariscove Island was to delimit structures, features, and centers of activity for all periods. About half of the known structural remains were located first through false color infrared aerial photographs taken in early May when vegetation growth patterns were most distinct (Figure 8). Comparatively recent structures were also evident in collections of early snapshots, and their functions were clarified through interviews with former residents (Griffin and Faulkner 1982). Together these procedures accounted for the location of nearly 80% of the structures identified.

The remaining 20% were found on foot in the process of preparing a detailed contour map of the island. The ground surface was examined systematically and in as much detail as the dense ground cover (predominantly bayberry and wild roses) would permit. On the more hospitable western lobe of the island, with its comparatively low relief, contours were taken at 0.5 m. (1.6 ft.) intervals, whereas on the much steeper eastern side a 2.0 m. (6.6 ft.) interval was adequate to insure thorough coverage of the landscape and to record the topography.

Test excavations conducted on this survey were limited in scale and in most cases were intended simply to identify areas of 17th century activity although a few tests were made of later structures and features. These excavations were made in 31 separate locations, chosen to give a representative sample of a variety of topographic situations. Several additional factors entered into the test site selection process, however, including the depth to bedrock, exposure to wind and tide, and the wishes of the resident lobster fishermen and current landowners.

FIGURE 8. Detail from an aerial view of Damariscove harbor, showing remains of 19th and 20th structures. Original in false color infrared.

The mantle of marine silts and sands which covers Damariscove is thin, a situation which predominates on virtually all of the island sites in this region. Where eolian redeposition has covered archaeological remains, culture–bearing strata are rarely as much as 40 cm. (15.8 in.) in depth, and accumulations of 25 cm. (9.8 in.) or less are more usual. Thus the natural mixing of components is frequent, and complete separation of occupations is rarely possible. Therefore sites for test pits were chosen after having been checked with a probe to see that they would yield at least 30 cm. (11.8 in.) of deposits.

The universe sampled by the survey was limited to the southern two–thirds of the island, the area covered in Figures 9 and 10. Although the area omitted from the survey boasts a large, shallow pond, the area generally is low–lying, and subject to submersion during severe storms. As a result, the water in the pond is quite brackish, much of the surrounding area being wetlands, and so was considered to be too swampy to be the focus of 17th century activity. Similarly, no pits were placed on the wet lowlands of the western half of the western lobe of the island, which is regularly flooded in high seas.

The eastern lobe of the island, which is rugged and rises to more than twice the height of the western lobe, was given relatively little attention beyond surface inspection during the mapping process. Its rocky eastern side receives the brunt of wave action and is nearly denuded. On the other side of this lobe, where the land slopes steeply towards the harbor, there are no suitable sites for boat landings, and the land appears to be more useful for gardening and pasture than for activities associated with the waterfront. Only three test pits were placed on this side. The remaining test excavations were located on the knobby terrain of the western lobe, in the general vicinity of Damariscove's small harbor. In spite of these restrictions, great differences in land use were apparent from the test excavations, as will become apparent.

Finally, some of the prime areas for study were off limits, as they were currently in use by the present–day lobster fishermen as camp sites, equipment stockpiles, and recreation areas. Also,

The Nature Conservancy, which owns the island and manages it as a nature preserve, declined certain test sites because they were thought to endanger various wildlife habitats. In both of these cases, however, it was possible to find alternative test sites which were comparable.

Considerable pains were taken in the 1979 season to grid off and survey some of the more open areas of the western lobe by proton magnetometry. Unfortunately, the anomalies discovered upon excavation all proved to be 19th and 20th century agricultural implements and related iron materials, and the procedure was abandoned in the following season.

Structural Remains

The majority of structures with surface indications were, understandably, from the most recent occupations. Most of the 69 structures and macrofeatures identified can be attributed to 19th and 20th century occupations of the island (see Figures 9, 10). These include remnants of permanent dwellings (2), barns (3), smaller agricultural outbuildings (7), stone fences (6), and an isolated cellar—probably all features of the farmstead. One permanent dwelling, a fish house, fishing camps (2) and stone landings (4) were associated with the fishery. Other structures and features include granite quarries (6), summer cottages (3), the Life Saving Station complex (18), and various wells, waterholes and other structures used by the entire island community (9).

Of all these structures only two, the stone footings for back–to–back stage heads at the northwest side of the harbor (see Figure 9), can be attributed to the 17th century fishery. Note, however, that the majority of this surface evidence is concentrated on the western side of Damariscove harbor, where, as has been noted, the land is of low relief and is protected from the prevailing southeast winds by the higher eastern lobe. The advantages of the western side of the island were surely as obvious and compelling in the 17th century as in later periods.

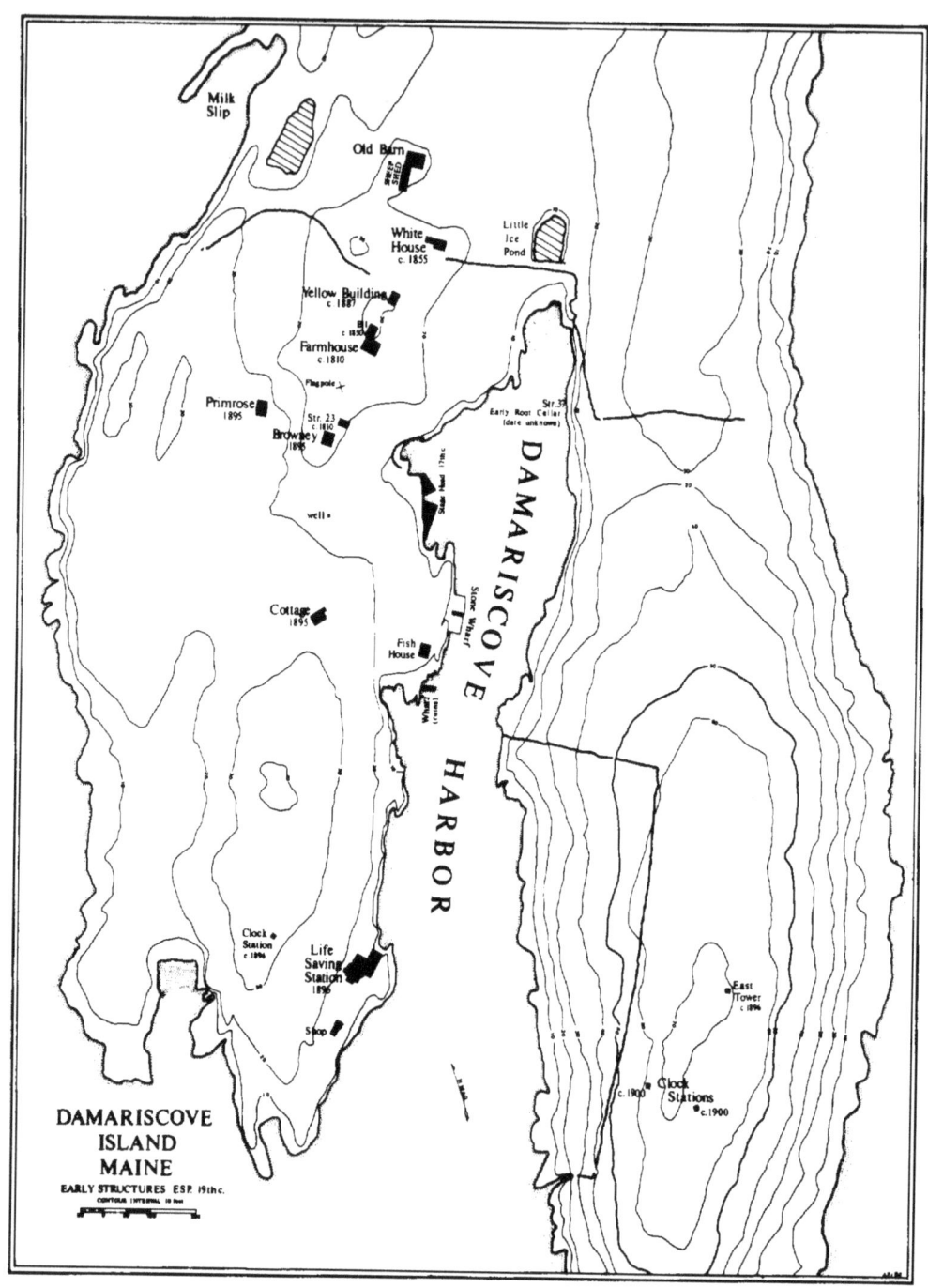

FIGURE 9. Structures on Damariscove Island prior to 1900.

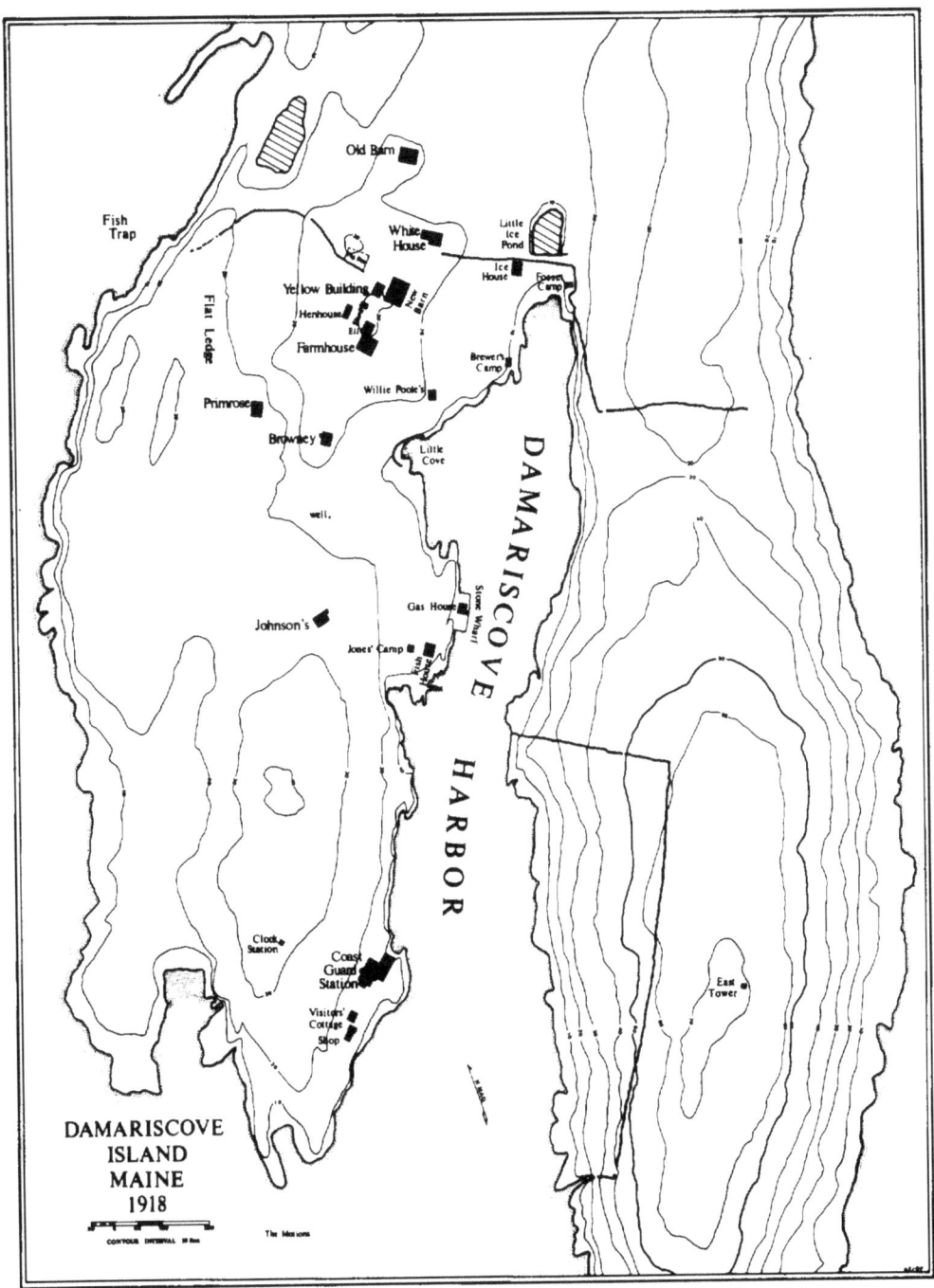

Fish Trap

Old Barn

White House

Little Ice Pond

Ice House

Forest Camp

Yellow Building

New Barn

Flat Ledge

Henhouse

Barn

Farmhouse

Brewery Camp

Willie Poole's

Primrose

Little Cove

Brownley

well.

DAMARISCOVE

Johnson's

Gas House

Stone Wharf

Jones' Camp

Fish Shack

HARBOR

East Tower

Clock Station

Coast Guard Station

Visitors' Cottage

Shop

DAMARISCOVE
ISLAND
MAINE
1918

CONTOUR INTERVAL 10 feet

The Motions

FIGURE 10. The Damariscove Island community in 1918.

Test Excavations

Excavations were made in 31 separate locations, most of which are shown in Figure 11. Outside this area were eight relatively unproductive units, five of which were located near the southern tip of the western lobe in the vicinity of the Life Saving Station (J,K,N,Y and AA), and three of which were situated on the eastern lobe of the island (V, CC and DD). In the main, test units consisted of 1 m. by 1 m. or 1 m. by 2 m. (3.3 ft. by 3.3 ft. or 3.3 ft. by 6.6 ft.) pits taken to bedrock although in more promising areas some of these units were expanded. More extensive excavations were conducted to test three of the structures previously identified from surface indications, the principal farmhouse (Unit G, Str. 11A), a permanent fisherman's dwelling (Str. 23) and a small, isolated, stone–lined cellar which was apparently a storage facility having no superstructure (Str. 37). As the first two structures proved to have no direct bearing on the 17th century fishery, they will be omitted from discussion. The cellar, measuring approximately 1.4 m. by 2.2 m. by 1.7 m. (4.6 ft. by 7.2 ft. by 5.6 ft.) deep, was laid up dry in rounded field stones, set into the steep bank of the eastern side of the harbor. While it may well have been connected with the cod fishery rather than the farm complex, no diagnostic artifacts or faunal materials were recovered in or around this structure. Its age and function, whether root or fish cellar, remain to be determined.

With the notable exception of clay tobacco pipes, the test excavations at Damariscove produced only a few artifacts diagnostic of the 17th century, let alone its fishery. Fragments of North Devon Gravel Tempered and North Devon Sgraffito earthenwares, and Bellarmine and early Westerwald stonewares were found, but in total these 17th century ceramics numbered less than 25 (Figure 12). Metal objects (Figure 13) included a serrated lead disc, resembling in an unfinished state the toy "whizzers" found nearby in 17th century contexts at Pemaquid (Camp 1975: Figure 34, no. 18). Also recovered were the head of a seal top spoon and a brass marlin spike.

Clay tobacco pipe fragments, however, were present in abundance, many having the rouletted "belly–bowl" form or large stem bores common during the first three quarters of the 17th century (Figure 14). These pipes show a dramatically different geographic distribution from pipes left in later occupations, as is apparent from a study of their bore diameters. Redware pipes of rouletted belly–bowl form made up nearly 13% of the total sample, but are omitted from tabulation as their origin and temporal limits are not known. The remaining white clay pipes can be presumed to be mainly of English origin and therefore amenable to dating by bore diameter (Binford 1961).

Shown in Table 1 are the dramatic differences in pipe bores between test units located by the harbor-side and units at higher elevations. The division occurs at a break in topography separating the gentle slopes near the harbor from the inland knolls and can be established, for the sake of convenience, at the 4 m contour (see Figure 11). Comparable excavation areas were opened above and below this elevation, and the overall densities of pipe fragments encountered were nearly identical. Yet it is remarkable that the pipe bore frequency distributions show practically no overlap (Figure 15). The 19 tests conducted below the 4 m contour produced 7, 8, and 9 bore pipestems almost exclusively, and yielded mid–17th century dates. Above that elevation, the 12 remaining tests produced nearly all 4 and 5 bore pipestems which may date to any period after ca. 1750 when bore diameters no longer decrease regularly. These upland sites could be dated independently, however, by abundant ceramic data. With the exception of test units H and X, which yielded a few white saltglaze and Westerwald stoneware fragments of 18th century date, the tests at the higher elevations represented occupations spanning the 19th century.

Taken as a whole, the pipestem data suggest that 17th century occupation was concentrated in the area of the stages, landings, and beach at the harborside, and that the flakes were tightly clustered on the gentle slopes nearby. The relative dearth of 6 bore pipestems (see Figure 15) is characteristic of many sites in Maine, and reflects the reduced activity on the island during the Indian

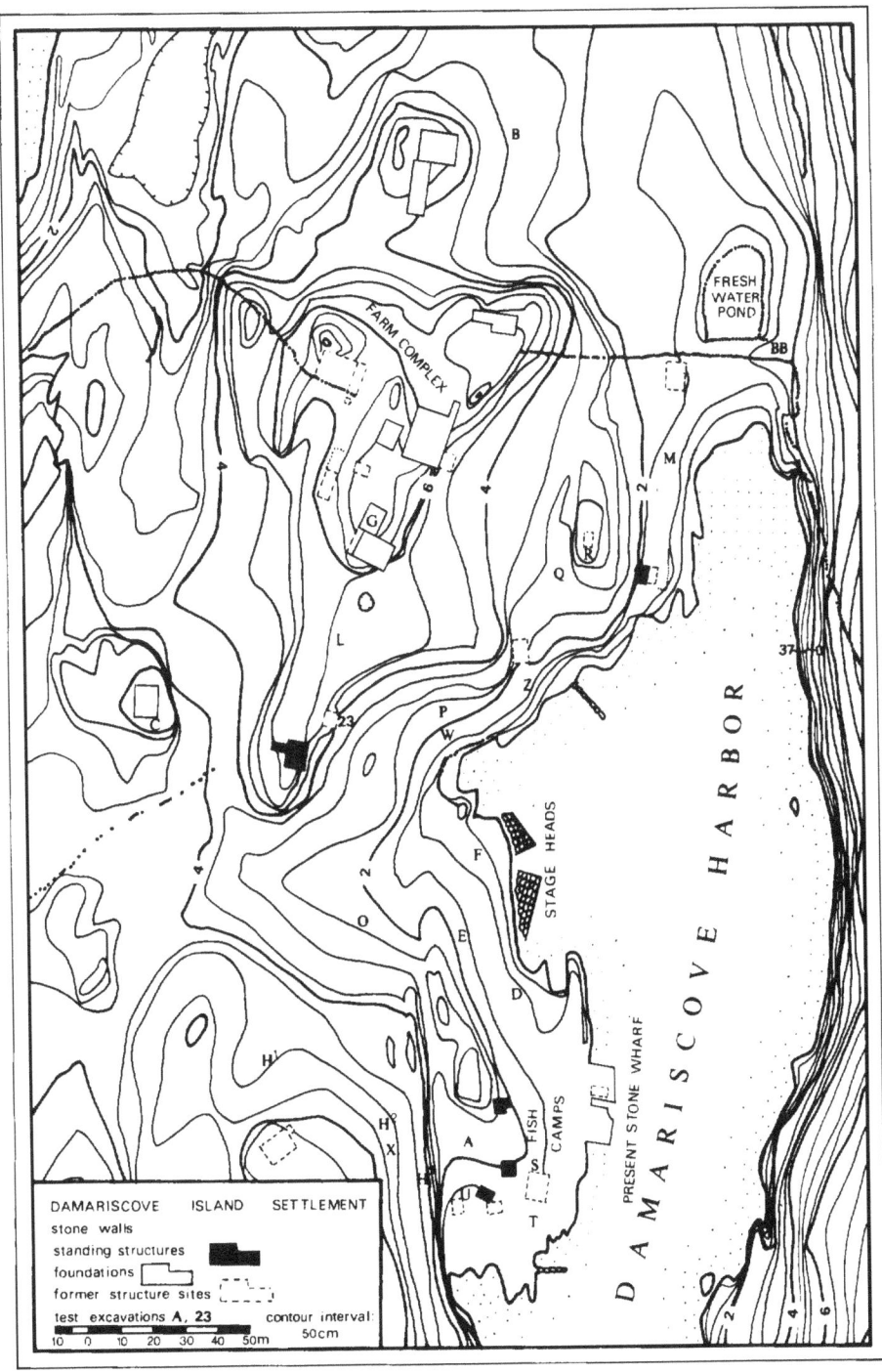

FIGURE 11. Location of Damariscove test units, 1979–1980.

TABLE 1

DISTRIBUTION OF WHITE CLAY TOBACCO PIPE STEMS AT LOW AND HIGH ELEVATIONS DAMARISCOVE ISLAND

	Test units	m² of excav.	Number of stems	Density stems/m²	3	4	5	6	7	8	9	Mean bore	Binford form. date[a]
Below 4m contour	A	6	74	12.3	1	3	2	7	36	22	3	7.05	1662
	D	1	0	0.0									
	E	1	1	1.0		1							
	F	2	108	54.0		8	8	2	59	28	3	6.93	1667
	J	1	2	2.0				2					
	M	3	8	2.7					3	3	2		
	N	3	2	0.7				1	1				
	O	4	0	0.0									
	P	4	1	0.2						1			
	Q	2	0	0.0									
	R	2	0	0.0									
	S	2	3	1.5					3				
	T	2	11	5.5					2	7	2	8.00	1626
	U[b]	4	4	1.0		1	2	1					
	W	1	32	32.0					9	18	5	7.77	1635
	Y	1	0	0.0									
	Z	1	3	3.0					3				
	AA	1	0	0.0									
	BB	1	0	0.0									
All units	4m −	42	249	5.9	1	12	13	13	115	79	15	7.12	1659
Above 4 m contour	B	3	0	0.0									
	C	2	0	0.0									
	G/11A	6	35	5.8		8	25	1	1			4.86	n/a
	H	7	27	3.9		8	15	1	1	2		5.03	1739
	K	2	0	0.0									
	L	8	0	0.0									
	V	3	0	0.0									
	X	1	3	3.0			3						
	CC	1	0	0.0									
	DD	1	0	0.0									
	23[c]	22	306	17.6		131	137	15	15	8		4.79	n/a
	37	10	0	0.0									
All units	4m +	66	371	5.6		147	180	17	17	10		4.82	n/a

[a]Binford 1961.

[b]Refuse from in front of an early 20th century fish camp.

[c]An early 19th century fisherman's dwelling at the edge of the 4m contour.

Wars of 1676 to ca. 1725. Later settlements were concentrated on higher ground, and it is likely that the dry cod fishery, with its constant tending of flakes and fish piles in the harborside area, had ceased. Certainly the fishing equipment from Structure 23 (Figure 16), a fisherman's dwelling occupied in the first quarter of the 19th century, suggests a shift to smaller fish such as mackerel, which would generally have been pickled in barrels (McFarland 1911:207–208, 297–298). Whatever use the harborside may have seen, the focus of 18th and 19th century settlement was

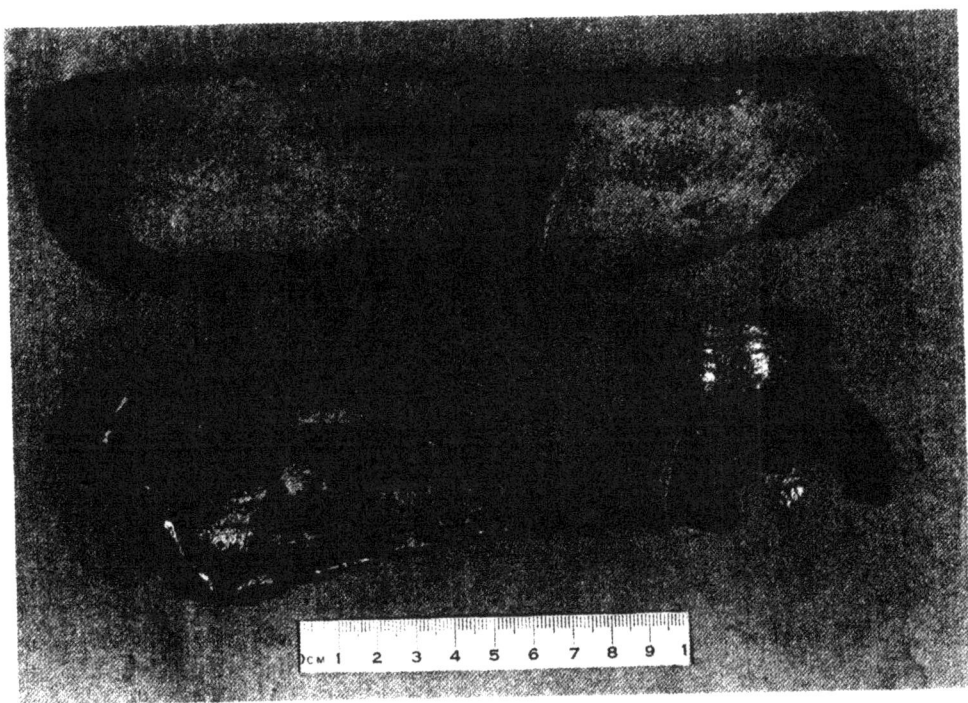

FIGURE 12. Ceramics associated with the Damariscove fishery: a and b, interior and exterior rimsherds of a tamarind jar from an early 19th century fisherman's dwelling, Structure 23; c, North Devon Gravel Tempered sherd, with pale yellowish brown glaze on the interior, from a 17th century context at Unit A; d, mottled brown glazed gray stoneware bottle neck of Bellarmine or similar type, from a 17th century context at Unit W.

determined by a nucleus of agricultural buildings, many of which were built into the side of the knolls to facilitate the construction of cellars.

Refuse and debris from late 19th and 20th century fishing shanties does indeed occur by the harborside as encountered in Unit U, a test for 17th century materials which accidentally exposed a portion of a recent fisherman's camp. However, these materials are found in pockets, generally in front of shanty sites, a pattern of refuse disposal and equipment storage still practiced by the lobster fishermen on the island. Interestingly, it is possible to select excavations sites directly behind these shanties, as in Unit A, and recover relatively uncontaminated 17th century materials.

Structural Remains of the Cod Fishery

Of all the structures that might be expected of the fortified cod fishing settlement at Damaris-

cove, only two have come to light at this time; these are the remains of the back-to-back stage heads noted above (see Figure 11). These two triangular fieldstone projections probably represent more permanent versions of the cross–braced underpinnings for stages noted for the seasonal fishery. The stone footings are difficult to examine, as only the top courses are exposed even at lowest tide, but they were laid up carefully in rounded boulders, 75 cm. (29.5 in.) in diameter and larger. The sides of these structures are still nearly vertical and are sharply defined, giving access to a boat drawing 80 cm. (31.5 in.) or less even at low tide. Nothing of the landward portions of these structures survives, as the immediate area is nearly all bare rock, but it is apparent from the submerged stonework that the stages were oriented at nearly right angles to each other. Adjacent to the stages is a shallow cove set off by a retaining wall of unknown date, an area which may well have pro-

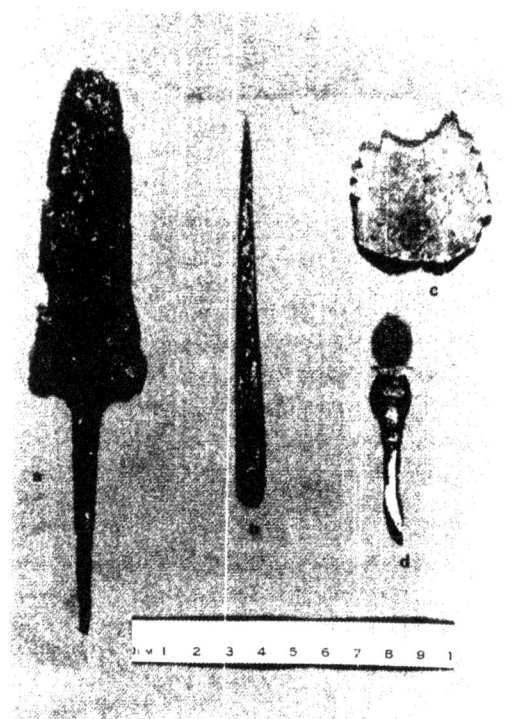

FIGURE 13. Metal objects associated with the Damaris-cove fishery: a, iron lance found west of Structure 23, of unknown date; b, bronze marlin spike, from a 17th century context at Unit E; c, serrated lead disc, tentatively identified as an unfinished "whizzer," from a 17th century context at Unit A; d, brass seal top spoon handle, from a 17th century context at Unit W.

vided the space required by this model for washing the cod after salting. It may also have served as a landing where smaller fishing boats could have been drawn up on shore.

Archaeological support for these inferences comes from the excavation at test Unit F (see Figure 11). Here, between the presumed stages, was found the highest concentration of early tobacco pipes, having a density of 54 per m², and giving a Binford (1961) formula date of 1667. Since the unusual bimodal distribution of bore diameters was surely caused by the separate occupations of the site before and after the Indian Wars, this estimate can probably be improved by eliminating the 4 and 5 bore stems from the sample. The revised date, 1651, seems to be a reasonable estimate for the median date of the cod fishery practiced at Damariscove.

At this time, no patterns of flakes have been recognized at Damariscove through aerial photography or subsurface testing, but as yet no broad areal excavations have been conducted. However, isolated intrusions, which may have been postholes for flakes or other structures, have been recognized at test units W and F (Figure 17). In other circumstances evidence for flakes can be distinct and long lasting, as shown in Figure 18, an aerial view of Grassy Island, off Canso, Nova Scotia. Essentially a single component site occupied from ca. 1713 to 1744, Grassy Island was a British fishing settlement and military outpost (Parks Canada 1981:1; Robert Ferguson 1981 pers. comm.). Here paths created by the fishermen in tending the flakes have had such a severe impact on the soil and vegetation that the layout of distinct sets of flakes is still visible.

The fortifications established in 1622 by Ferdinando Gorges and during the Indian Wars have not yet been identified on Damariscove. But the total absence of 17th century materials noted in test excavations and exhaustive foot survey of the peaks and promontories suggests that the military strategy invoked did not make use of this high ground. This was also true of other 17th century settlements in Maine, particularly the Clark and Lake Company trading post on Arrowsic Island in the Kennebec River, and Fort Pentagoet, a French outpost located at the mouth of the Penobscot River. Probably at Damariscove it was the low-lying area around the stages, flakes and boat landings that was enclosed for protection, in spite of being commanded by higher elevations. It is likely that these early defenses were intended primarily to discourage raiding parties, rather than to endure a sustained attack. Moreover, it seems to be generally true of Maine's pioneer fishing and trading settlements that protection of access to water routes took precedence over the defense of real estate.

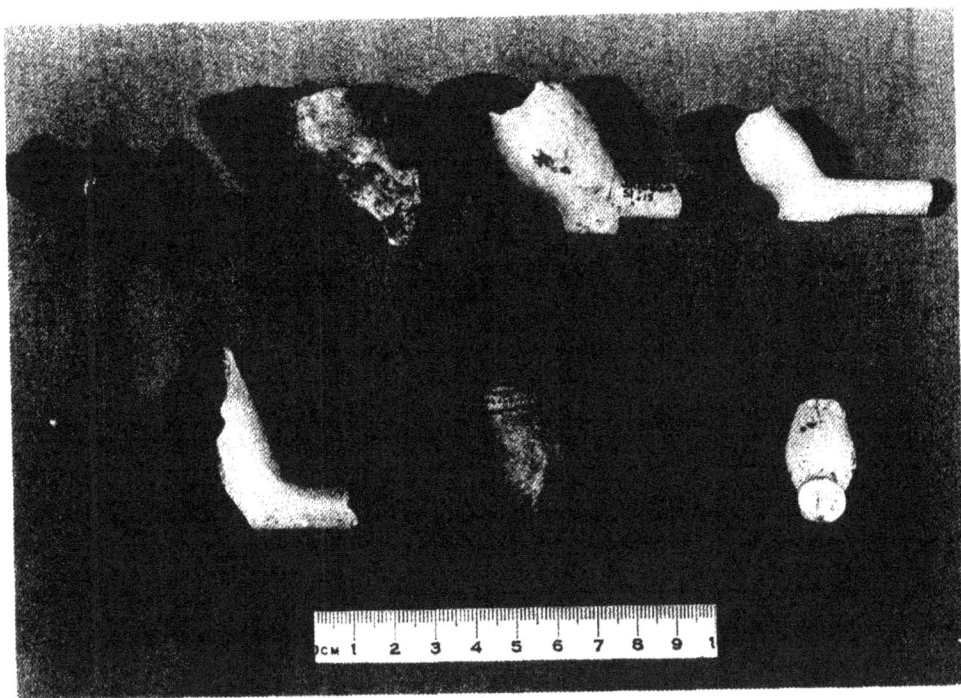

FIGURE 14. Clay tobacco pipes from 17th century contexts at Damariscove: a, red, oval heel, 7/64 in. bore, a surface find from the beach area at the head of the harbor; b, white, rouletted from Unit A; c, white, rouletted, round heel, 7/64 in. bore from Unit W; d, white, rouletted, cordiform heel, 7/64 in. bore, from Unit A; e, white, rouletted, no heel, 7/64 in. bore, from Unit A; f, white, relief moulded in "huntress and Crusader" motif, apparently Dutch (Camp 1975:57, 78), from Unit A; g, white, rouletted, "PE" heel (probably Philip Edwards I, ca. 1650-ca. 1669), 6/64 in. bore, from Unit J at the mouth of the harbor near the Life Saving Station.

Conclusions

As the Damariscove research was a survey, and not a full-scale excavation, it gives only a taste of the kinds of questions of historical and anthropological interest which can be addressed by the archaeology of the cod fishery. To date, one of the most useful aspects of the survey work has been setting bounds to the historically derived image of this settlement. A goal too often demeaned by archaeologists unwilling to be servants of history, it is often one of their most important contributions.

For example, based admittedly on negative results of an intensive survey, it is reasonable to conclude that Gorges' palisaded fortification was not located in a strategic upland site, but more likely somewhere in the vicinity of the head of the harbor. It is also apparent that the area used by the 17th century fishermen could sustain at most only three or four fishing crews of 40 or more men, the size Denys considered typical. The distribution of pipestems suggests that far from covering the island, the fishing activities were limited to an area of no more than 2 ha. (4.9 a.) in the immediate vicinity of the stages. Just four areas were identified where stages could be suitably located, and evidence was found only for two. Thus the 1622 observation that there were "30 sail of ships" engaged in the cod fishery at Damariscove (Young 1841:292–293) implies that they were not all based on the island proper. Many of these must have

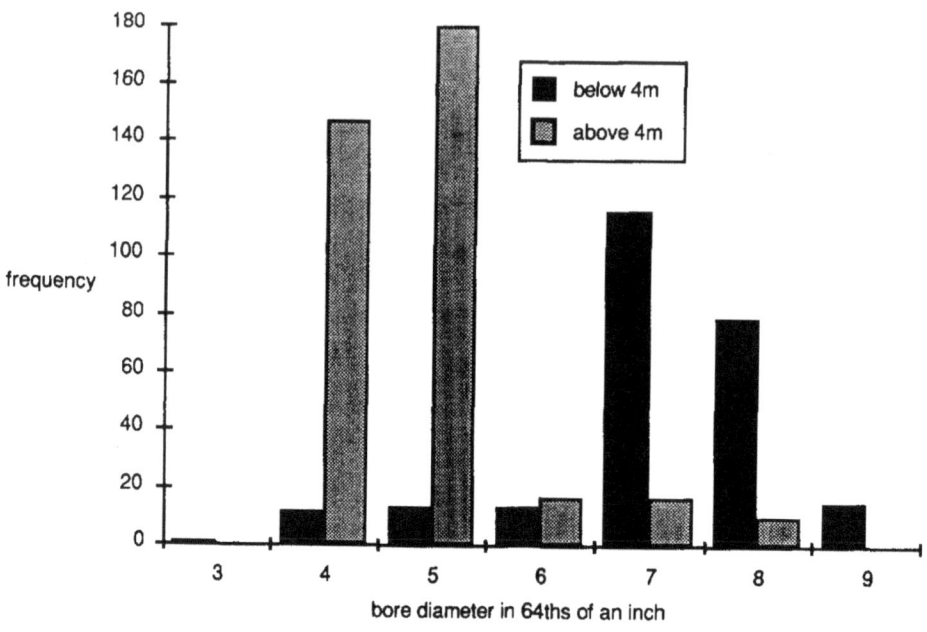

FIGURE 15. Pipestem bore diameter distribution from test excavations below and above the 4 m contour, showing marked separation of 17th century harborside activities and later use of the uplands.

been located on neighboring islands and peninsulas, which suggests a direction for future survey work. Damariscove was a convenient rendezvous for English fishermen and the supply vessels of the first settlers of New England and Virginia and the focus of the local fishery, but its ability to support fishing facilities has been exaggerated.

It should be apparent from this review of the cod fishery that far more is known historically about the seasonal cod fishing strategies than is known about the sedentary fishery. One would expect that the sedentary fishery would lack the homogeneity of the seasonal practice, as it was apparently practiced as part of a mixed economy, say, with lumbering, agriculture, or trading. When, for example, the budding English fishing settlements were neglected during the English Civil War, it is reasonable to suspect that they developed independent methods to insure their survival. Surely these adaptive responses are reflected in the physical layout of the fishing settlements of this time, and one would hope that they can be studied archaeologically.

One of the most fascinating hypotheses, accepted uncritically in the foregoing description of the sedentary fishery, is the presumed role of the winter fishery in promoting first settlement in early New England. Details of the actual conduct of the winter fishery remain obscure. It has been alleged that the fish cured in the winter were of superior quality to those cured in the summer sun (McFarland 1911:306). If true, the details of this process have some significance. Denys (1908:110) states that on the islands of the Maine Coast the fish were actually dried by freezing, but he does not describe the process, and it is difficult to imagine drying by sublimation. If, however, the catch was cleaned and salted in the winter, but dried in the early spring, one would expect some form of storage facility to keep the fish at an even temperature in the intervening period. Perhaps the cellar at Damariscove, which it has not been possible to tie directly to the fishery, served such a purpose. If this was the case, the "fish cellar" might prove to be a feature common to New England fishing sites. Indeed this may be the function of some of the

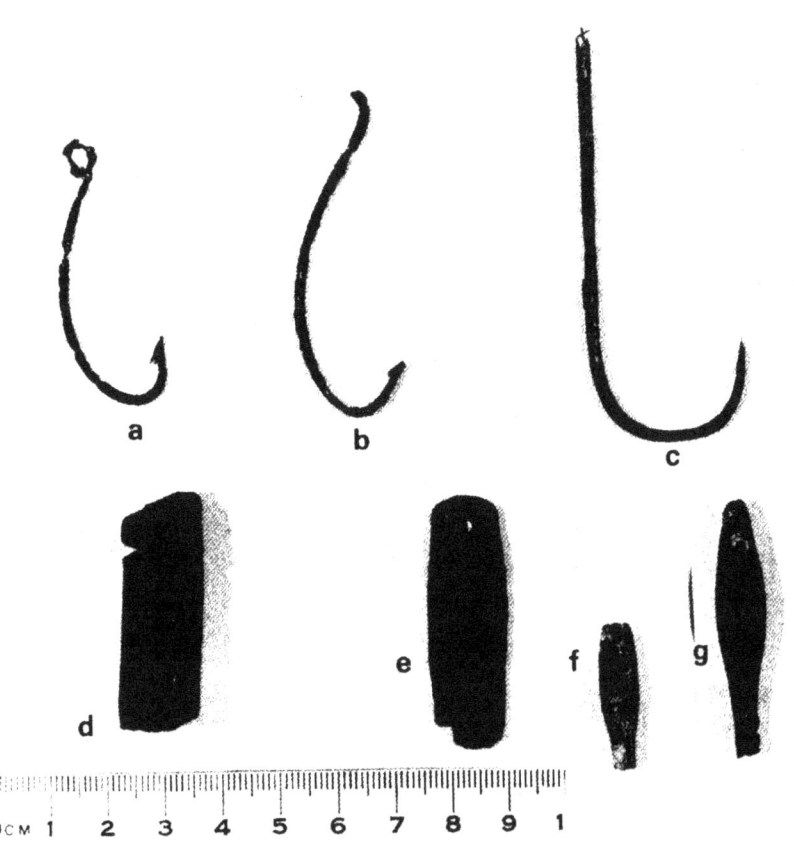

FIGURE 16. Early 19th century fishing equipment from Structure 23 at Damariscove: a–c, iron fish hooks; d–e, lead sinkers; f–g, lead jigging lures.

other "cellars" occasionally mentioned in early documents from coastal New England sites such as "Watts' Cellar" in Newburyport, Massachusetts (Faulkner et al. 1978:91–94).

Steven Cuumba (1982 pers. comm.) has predicted that well–preserved fish remains may be found in abundance off the sites of former stages in New England, as has been the case at certain sites in the Maritimes. Such faunal remains obviously could elucidate the nature of the winter fishery, providing they can be closely dated and identified. It should be possible, for example, to establish whether or not the "small cod" purported to be the mainstay of the winter fishery, were actually of a separate species, or were in any way physically distinct from those of the Acadian or Newfound-land fisheries. Faunal analysts may also be able to determine the season of the catch directly, discovering what proportion was actually caught in the winter months. Data from different periods should show changes in fish populations and migration habits which are sure to have affected the early fishing economy. While a few records exist for the export of groundfish such as hake, haddock, and pollack in addition to cod (Baxter 1884:135), their proportion in the actual catch might determine whether certain species were saved for local distribution. Further comparisons could be made with the domestic refuse of the fishermen found on land, to reveal what use the fishing population made of their own product.

Finally, it should be apparent that the primary

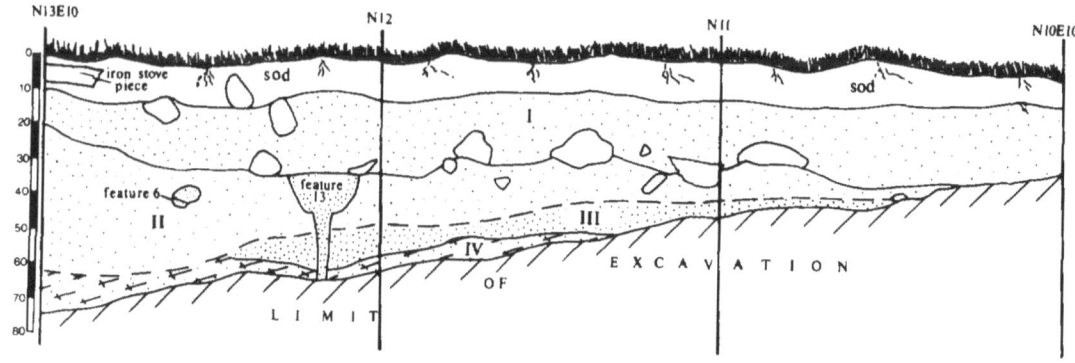

TEST EXCAVATION F, EAST WALL

FIGURE 17. Profile showing typical strata and post hole at Unit F, where the highest density of 17th century tobacco pipes was found: I, 10YR3/1 very dark gray (moist) fine sandy loam, containing charcoal and 17th, 19th and 20th century materials; II, 7.5YR3/1 dark brown (moist) fine sandy loam, containing 17th century materials; III, 10YR4/4 dark yellowish brown (moist) find sand, sterile; IV, 10YR5/4 yellowish brown (moist) sandy clay loam, sterile; Features 6 and 13, 7.5YR3/1 dark brown (moist) silt loam, containing charcoal flecks, organic matter, redware and clay tobacco pipe fragments.

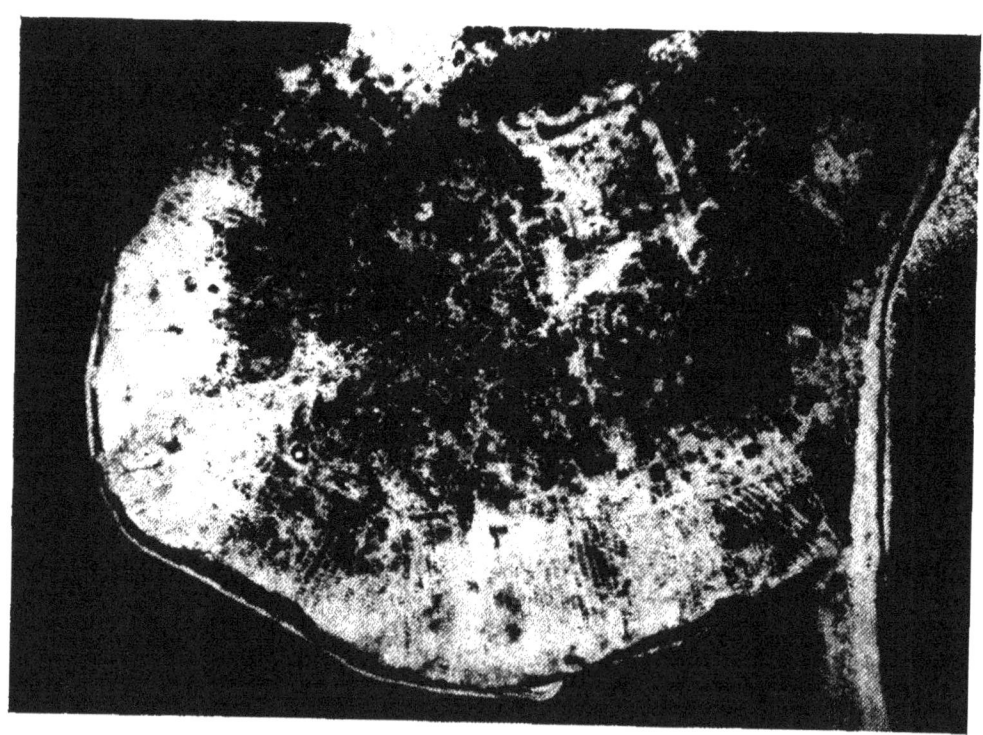

FIGURE 18. Aerial view of the fortified 18th century English fishing site at Grassy Island, off Canso, Nova Scotia, showing in addition to the four-bastioned fortification, the patterns of flakes established along the shoreline (courtesy of Robert Ferguson).

literature on the fisheries, although obscure, is abundant, and the effort made in its retrieval is worthwhile. Certainly the scant archaeological remains available so far at these kinds of sites would make little sense without this kind of documentation. This historical model of the dry cod fishery gives a detailed framework based on contemporary accounts against which new archaeological data can be compared.

ACKNOWLEDGMENTS

Funding for the Damariscove Survey was provided by the Maine Historic Preservation Commission (MHPC) and the National Park Service. The author is especially indebted to Robert Bradley of the MHPC for helping make field arrangements with the landowners, for continued support and advice throughout the project, and for contributing materials used in this article. The Nature Conservancy, which owns the site and maintains it as a nature preserve, deserves thanks for allowing test excavations to be conducted in selected areas of the island. Thanks are also due to Robert Ferguson of Parks Canada, Halifax, for sharing his information on the Grassy Island Fishery in Nova Scotia and providing the photograph used in Figure 18.

The historical research has been facilitated by the cooperation of the Centre d'Études Acadiènnes, Université de Moncton, where some of the primary sources used in this work were found. Also appreciated is the reproduction of the inset from Moll's Map of North America provided by the Maine State Museum. Finally, Gretchen Faulkner deserves special recognition for her part in assembling the historical documentation on the Damariscove fishery and for drafting many of the figures which appear in this work.

REFERENCES

BAXTER, JAMES P. (EDITOR)
1884 The Trelawny Papers. *Documentary History of the State of Maine* (Vol. III). The Maine Historical Society, Portland.
1889 Downing's Account of Fish. *Documentary History of the State of Maine* (Vol. IV:372–376). The Maine Historical Society, Portland.

BINFORD, LEWIS R.
1961 A New Method of Calculating Dates From Kaolin Pipe Stem Samples. *Southeastern Archaeological Conference Newsletter* 9(1):19–21.

BURRAGE, HENRY S.
1906 *Early English and French Voyages, Chiefly from Hakluyt, 1534–1658.* Scribner, New York.

CAMP, HELEN B.
1975 *Archaeological Excavations at Pemaquid, Maine 1965–1974.* The Maine State Museum, Augusta.

CUUMBA, STEVEN
1981 Archaeological Evidence of the 16th–18th C. Atlantic Cod Fishery. Paper presented at the fifteenth annual meeting of The Society for Historical Archaeology, New Orleans.

DE LA MORANDIÈRE, CHARLES
1962 *Histoire de la Pêche Française de la Morue dans l'Amérique Septentrionale* (Vol. I). Maisonneuve et Larose, Paris.

ESSEX INSTITUTE
1919 *Records and Files of the Quarterly Courts of Essex County Massachusetts, 1678–1680* (Vol. VII). Salem, Massachusetts.

FAULKNER, ALARIC, KIM PETERS, DAVID SELL, AND EDWIN DETHLEFSEN
1978 *Port and Market: Archaeology of the Central Waterfront, Newburyport, Massachusetts.* National Park Service, Inter-agency Archeological Services, Atlanta.

FAULKNER, GRETCHEN AND ALARIC FAULKNER
1981 A Documentary Chronology of Settlement on Damariscove Island, Maine: 1622–1918. Ms. on file, Historic Archaeology Laboratory, University of Maine-Orono.

GANONG, WM. F. (EDITOR AND TRANSLATOR)
1908 *The Description and Natural History of the Coasts of North America by Nicholas Denys.* The Champlain Society, Toronto.

GRIFFIN, CARL AND ALARIC FAULKNER
1982 *Coming of Age on Damariscove Island.* Northeast Folklore Society, Orono, Maine.

INNIS, HAROLD A.
1940 *The Cod Fisheries: the History of an International Economy.* Yale University Press, New Haven.

JAMES, SYDNEY V.
1963 *Three Visitors to Early Plymouth.* Plimouth Plantation, Plymouth, Massachusetts.

JOSSELYN, JOHN
1865 *An Account of Two Voyages to New-England, Made During The Years 1638, 1663.* William Veazie, Boston.

KNIGHT, THOMAS F.
1867 *Shore and Deep Sea Fisheries of Nova Scotia.* Provincial Government, Halifax.

LEVETT, CHRISTOPHER
1847   A Voyage Into New England 1623–24. *Collections of the Maine Historical Society* (Vol. II: 73–109), Portland.

LOUNSBURY, RALPH G.
1934   *The British Fishery at Newfoundland, 1634–1763.* Yale University Press, New Haven.

MCFARLAND, RAYMOND
1911   *A History of the New England Fisheries.* University of Pennsylvania, Appleton, New York.

MOLL, HERMANN
ca. 1713   *Map of North America.*

MORISON, SAMUEL ELIOT
1971   *The European Discovery of America.* Oxford University Press, New York.

MOUSETTE, MARCEL
1979   Fishing Methods Used in the St. Lawrence River and Gulf. *History and Archaeology* 22. Parks Canada, Ottawa.

PARKS CANADA
1981   *Grassy Island Historic Park* 1(2). Halifax.

POYNTER, F. N. L.
1963   *The Journal of James Yonge, Plymouth Surgeon, 1647–1721.* Longman's, Bristol, England.

TUCK, JAMES A. AND ROBERT GRENIER
1981   A 16th Century Basque Whaling Station in Labrador. *Scientific American* 245(5):180–190.

WOODBURY, C. L.
1880   *The Relation of the Fisheries to the Discovery and Settlement of North America.* Little and Brown, Boston.

YOUNG, ALEXANDER
1841   *Chronicles of the Pilgrim Fathers.* Little and Brown, Boston.

ALARIC FAULKNER
DEPARTMENT OF ANTHROPOLOGY
UNIVERSITY OF MAINE
ORONO, MAINE 04469

1986. Followup Notes on the 17th Century Cod Fishery at Damariscove Island, Maine—1622–1676,
Historical Archaeology 20(2):86 –88.

RESEARCH NOTES AND COMMENTS

ALARIC FAULKNER

Followup Notes on the 17th Century Cod Fishery at Damariscove Island, Maine

ABSTRACT

Exceptionally low tides in October 1985 revealed the stone footings of the 17th century fishing stages on Damariscove Island discussed in a recent article on the archaeology of the cod fishery. Photography shows two stage heads built of tabular granite and arranged side by side, part of a permanent fishing station which replaced the original seasonal facilities at the site. Such features can be taken as *prima facie* evidence of the development of the sedentary cod fishery, a settlement type characteristic of many sites on the coast of Maine.

As suggested in a recent article on the archaeology of the 17th century cod fishery (Faulkner 1985:57–86), the earliest structures left behind by seasonal fishing—temporary shelters with wattle walls and sail roofs—were ephemeral and only rarely left a recognizable pattern of post molds in the thin soils of the northeast coastline. Especially fragile is the evidence for *stages*—wooden shelters built on piers extending into the water—where the initial phases of processing dried cod were conducted (Faulkner 1985:64–65). Here, at the pointed ends of the stage, fishermen unloaded the day's catch from their boats, headed, cleaned and split the fish, and salted them down. Exposed to winter storms, these structures often had to be rebuilt on an annual basis.

One potential indicator of the transition from the seasonal fishery to the sedentary fishery is the evidence for establishment of more permanent fishing facilities. This change is important in the study of the early development of New England, as it demonstrates a commitment to settlement. Recent revisionist works devalue the significance of the fisheries in promoting early settlement and have questioned compatibility of fishing and farming as occupations (Vickers 1981:42–60; F. Harrington 1985, F. Harrington 1986, pers. comm.). They question the degree of integration of the two pursuits into a mixed economy, especially in Puritan Massachusetts Bay. Nevertheless, along the coast of Maine at least, there developed a series of small fishing plantations or communities between 1622 and 1676 in which an extractive industry, the cod fishery, was gradually supplemented by small scale agriculture. The best documented of these settlements include Richmond's Island and Spurwink, Pemaquid, and Damariscove (Baxter 1884; Churchill 1975:x–xv; Griffin and Faulkner 1980:17–20). To a greater or lesser extent, they all attained a degree of long term self-sufficiency.

In 1979 a University of Maine archaeology team identified a pair of stone footings jutting into a harborside at Damariscove Island, located about one third of the way "downeast" along the Maine coast. As reported earlier, the footings were aligned side by side on the edge of the harbor, their pointed ends canted towards each other (Faulkner 1985:73,79–80, Figure 11). These are interpreted as footings for permanent stages, reflecting a commitment by settled fishermen to a particular land base of operation—a concept foreign to seasonal fishermen from Europe who sought out new and more productive fisheries from voyage to voyage. Until recently, it had not been possible to photograph these submerged features. In October of 1985, however, the remains were exposed during an exceptionally low tide. The photographs in Figures 1 and 2 were taken from the middle of Damariscove's harbor and show the sharp lines of the pointed, seaweed-covered footings. Originally, the masonry was arranged around natural depressions in the folded schist, the principle bedrock, forming slips for the fishing boats. Later piles of rounded boulders were apparently dumped by farmers after

FIGURE 1. Exposure at extreme low tide of the footings of former stages associated with a 17th century fishing settlement at Damariscove Island, Maine. The source of the masonry was apparently an outcropping of jointed, tabular granite in a small cove in the background, far right.

FIGURE 2. Detail of the southern stage footings. The pointed, prow-like projection of these structures is typical of a tradition of stage construction which began in the 16th century and continued through the 18th century.

clearing their fields, and this debris now partially fills the slips.

The footings themselves were constructed of a tabular granite which appears to have been quarried from jointed beds in small cove or landing lying immediately to the north. Mid 19th century graffiti, carved on the bare ledge exposed by the quarrying, gives a *terminus ante quem* for that activity. That the features date to the 17th century is almost certain, as they were associated with an extremely dense concentration of 17th century tobacco pipes in an area essentially free of later materials. This collection of 108 pipe stems, from a 1×2m test pit on the landward side between the two features, yielded a Binford formula date of 1667 (Faulkner 1985: Table 1, Unit F). The prow-like form of the stage ends, together with their placement adjacent to one of the few areas of flat land suitable for setting up *flakes* or drying racks, support the interpretation of these features as 17th century stage footings.

REFERENCES

FAULKNER, ALARIC
  1985 Archaeology of the Cod Fishery: Damariscove Island. *Historical Archaeology* 19(2): 57–86.

BAXTER, JAMES P., ED.
  1884 The Trelawney Papers. *Documentary History of the State of Maine*, Vol. 3. Maine Historical Society, Portland, Maine.

CHURCHILL, EDWIN. A.
  1975 Colonial Pemaquid. In Helen B. Camp, *Archaeological Excavations at Pemaquid, Maine 1965–1974*, The Maine State Museum, Augusta.

GRIFFIN, CARL R. AND ALARIC FAULKNER
  1980 Coming of Age on Damariscove Island. *Northeast Folklore*, Vol. XXI, Northeast Archives of Folklore and Oral History, Orono, Maine.

HARRINGTON, FAITH
  1985 *Sea Tenure in Seventeenth Century New England: Native Americans and Englishmen in the Sphere of Marine Resources, 1600–1630*. Unpublished Ph.D. dissertation, Department of Anthropology, University of California at Berkeley.

VICKERS, DANIEL F.
  1981 *Maritime Labor in Colonial Massachusetts: a Case Study of the Essex County Cod Fishery and the Whaling Industry of Nantucket*. Unpublished Ph.D. dissertation, Department of History, Princeton University.

ALARIC FAULKNER
DEPARTMENT OF ANTHROPOLOGY
SOUTH STEVENS 44
UNIVERSITY OF MAINE
ORONO, MAINE 04469

2003. The Archaeology of Crisis: Shipwreck Survivor Camps in Australasia.
Historical Archaeology 37(1):128–145.

Martin Gibbs

The Archaeology of Crisis: Shipwreck Survivor Camps in Australasia

ABSTRACT

Shipwreck survivor camps are a neglected terrestrial component of maritime archaeology, usually being investigated purely as an adjunct to work on the associated wreck site. Most studies have considered these sites as individual and unique, molded by the particulars of the historic events that created them. However, by considering the history, anthropology, and archaeology of a series of Australasian survivor incidents and sites, this paper highlights common elements and themes, which allow examination of these sites within a comparative framework. These include the development of authority structures, social organization, salvage and subsistence strategies, material culture, short- and long-term rescue strategies, and the possible influences of crisis-related stress upon the decisions made by individuals and groups. Survivor camp studies are linked into the wider concerns of maritime archaeology and anthropology by placing them within the context of wreck formation models.

Introduction

The shipwreck survivor has been a recurrent theme in our literary heritage and iconography for more than 3,000 years from *The Odyssey* and *The Tempest*, to *Robinson Crusoe*, *Swiss Family Robinson*, *Lord of the Flies*, and even parodies such as *Gilligan's Island*. Consequently, we find ourselves familiar with the psychological trauma of the wreck crisis, the difficult dynamics of individual or group isolation, and the necessity for survivors to salvage the wreck and adapt to unfamiliar and potentially hostile environments. Strangely, while library shelves groan with analyses of these fictitious accounts, there has been limited systematic investigation of real shipwreck "survivor camps"—places where those who made it off a wrecked vessel gathered after the wreck event—either as archaeological phenomenon or for what they can tell us about human behavior in crisis situations. Because of the historical peculiarities of individual situations, existing studies have treated survivor camps as separate and unique, rather than as a class of site to be subjected to comparative study.

Part of the recent renaissance in Australian maritime archaeology has been an increasing interest in the development of appropriate theory, models, and research encompassing sites and activities, both below and above the waterline (McCarthy 1996, 1998; Veth and McCarthy 1999). Shipwreck survivor camps provide a particularly important opportunity to advance these aims. The first part of this paper analyzes a number of Australasian historical and archaeological investigations of survivor camps and proposes a framework for future comparative study. The second part examines the relationship between survivor camps and shipwreck sites, particularly the ways in which survivor activities and, hence, cultural factors embedded in these activities, affect shipwreck site formation. These relationships are discussed in relation to the site formation models originally proposed by Kenneth Muckelroy (1978).

Shipwreck Survivor Camps

Shipwreck survivor camps were common phenomena in the era of sail and steam. Depending upon circumstances, these camps might have been on an island, an isolated stretch of coast, or a riverbank, in any kind of environment ranging from familiar and well resourced, to alien and desolate. The duration of occupation could last anywhere from a few hours to many months, dependant upon the appearance or nonappearance of rescuers or the ability of the survivors to organize alternative means of deliverance.

The identification and investigation of shipwreck survivor camps is closely associated with the earliest phase of maritime archaeology in Australia. In the 1960s and 1970s, studies were made of sites associated with the 17th- and 18th-century wrecks of the Dutch East India Company (VOC) ships: *Batavia* (1629), *Vergulde Draek* (1656), *Zuytdorp* (1712) and *Zeewijk* (1727), lost along the Western Australian coast and nearby islands (Henderson 1986) (Figure 1). In the 1980s, several camps from the Australasian colonial period, including those of the British supply vessel *Sydney Cove* (1797) and the French whaler *Perseverant* (1841), were also recorded (Strachan 1986; Robinson 1988). The majority of these

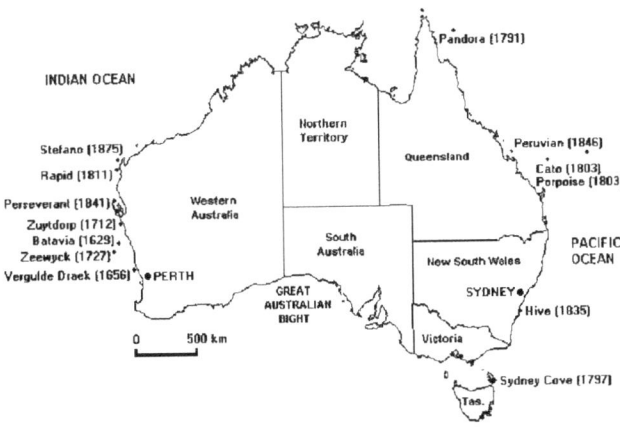

FIGURE 1. Australian shipwreck sites mentioned in the text.

studies were adjuncts to the wreck investigations and not problem oriented beyond confirming the relationship between ship and camp or attempting to correlate sites with activities described in the historical record. Surface collections and excavations were made at several sites, although these artifacts and assemblages have not been subjected to quantitative analysis or interpretation. More importantly, none of these studies has considered the individual site(s) within the wider historical, archaeological, and behavioral contexts of shipwreck survivor camps. A similar lack of comparison and contextual analysis was common throughout early maritime archaeological research.

Viewed collectively, the historical and archaeological data already available for Australasian sites suggests that, despite differences in the specifics of the disaster events, there are many commonalties (Piggin 1987; Hinton 1992), the majority of which are pragmatic in nature, a result of the fact that survivor camps are linked inextricably to the cultural and physical attributes of the ship. The starting point is, therefore, to understand the relationship between a ship and the culture of origin.

A ship is a cultural component that shares some conventions with the parent culture but is also a cultural entity in and of itself. Shipboard life is composed of behavioral patterns designed to effect a common, techno-intensive goal: the successful operation of a ship, completion of the mission, and survival at sea. The shipboard community is composed of groups with defined roles and duties, in a probable chain of command, which establishes hierarchy and certain patterns of interaction (Murphy 1983:67).

In the physical sense, a ship can be a specialized mechanism for carrying people and cargo to a destination, a platform for specific activities or tools, or a tool in its own right. The ship's structure and cargo comprise a subset of the material culture of the parent group. However, while some components of the cargo will have relevance to the operation of the vessel, the bulk of it reflects a diversity of intentions and activities associated with the destination rather than the voyage.

A "survivor group" was, therefore, a component of the original ship cultural subset, comprised of some or all of the elements of the ship's population: social, economic, and command structures, skills and abilities that remained available following the wreck event. The survivor camp was created as a product of whatever organization arose from this group, with a material culture comprised of what remained available of the ship's structure and cargo, supplemented by the resources of the surrounding terrestrial and marine environment.

Essentially, the study of survivors and survivor camps is an investigation of adaptation processes: whether and how people utilize their social and physical resources in order to endure. While there is a unique and complex series of relationships involved with each shipwreck and survivor situation, the initial constraints of the nature of the ship and population allow us to identify common themes for historical and archaeological investigation. The following are by no means exhaustive but probably represent the major categories for consideration in a comparative framework.

Authority, Social Structure, and Camp Organization

Because of the strongly hierarchical nature of shipboard life, a major question to be asked of survivor camps concerns the forms of authority and social organization that were established once on land. In many instances, the historical record indicates a direct transference of shipboard authority to the terrestrial setting. For instance, in the case of HMS *Cato* and HMS *Porpoise*, wrecked together on the Great Barrier Reef in

1803, Captain Matthew Flinders immediately took a firm hand in establishing control and maintaining the normal hierarchy (Austin 1964:188). He achieved this, in part, by the prompt and severe punishment of disorderly sailors as soon as the survivors were established on land. In contrast, the officers of the VOC ship *Zeewijk* (wrecked in 1729) remained only nominally in charge, with the crew actually controlling events on the island through a council, which made decisions and advised (van der Graaf 1727). The crew was contemptuous of the officers to the extent of openly stealing their food and water, while keeping them as figureheads, perhaps against the possibility of eventual rescue and return to civilization.

The transfer and acknowledgment of authority probably depended upon a range of variables, including who survived the disaster, their effectiveness during the crisis, and their ability to reestablish control and make decisions. The psychological stresses brought about by the disaster may have played a significant role in altering attitudes, possibly including perceptions that the captain or officers had lost the right to command by allowing the wreck to happen. The establishment or reestablishment of authority may also have rested on the personal charisma of the captain, surviving officers, or other individuals. Thus, a ship may have had passengers who had no role in the ship's hierarchy yet provided a focal point for subsequent command based on recognized abilities or qualities in the given circumstances.

The form of authority established on shore and the resulting survivor camp organization was influenced by whether a vessel was naval, merchant, passenger, or other as well as by the population size and the social, cultural, and ethnic mix. In the case of naval vessels, there was a recognized chain of command and mechanisms for rapid transfer of authority during time of war or crisis. Reestablishment of authority after a shipwreck might, therefore, have been relatively rapid and conformed to the recognized structure. Archaeologically, this might be expressed in a separation between officers and regular crew. However, there were alternative command structures, such as on VOC vessels (including *Batavia*). On these voyages, the captain controlled only the operations of the ship and the activities of the sailors. Supreme authority rested in the hands of the senior merchant or *commandeur*, who also commanded a small contingent of soldiers to guard any valuables aboard and, if necessary, to enforce this control. Such divisions suggest a more complex organization and archaeological signature once ashore.

A vessel that also carried passengers of different classes or other discreet groupings such as soldiers, slaves, or convicts may have offered greater opportunities for situational leadership, resulting in greater diversity in campsite organization. For instance, the convict vessel *Hive*, wrecked on the New South Wales coast, had 250 prisoners, 13 soldier guards, and 18 women and children, in addition to the normal complement of officers and crew (Nutley 1995). Once ashore, the need to guard the convicts may have altered the balance of authority away from the shipboard structure, demanding careful establishment of a camp that allowed observation and control. There would undoubtedly have been a different organization from that seen after the 1855 wreck of *Julia Ann* whose survivors were predominantly Mormon and who appear to have divided into family groups (Hundley 1996:10). Beyond the maintenance or creation of command, there is also the question of what happens to other social boundaries that were formerly in place aboard the ship. Whether or not distinct shipboard social groups do blur or become realigned in the survivor situation is an area for investigation.

The potential for radical changes into abnormal authority structures and social organization must also be considered. One example, which at first glance appears to embody such a dramatic shift, is the case of *Batavia*, a VOC ship wrecked in 1629 on the desolate Houtman Abrolhos Islands, 35 km off the Western Australian coast (Drake-Brockman 1963; Gibbs 1992, 1994). The historical record indicates that, following the wreck, the normal shipboard hierarchy was quickly reestablished by the officers. However, once the captain and senior merchant had departed in a boat to seek help in Jakarta, the junior officers, who had legitimately inherited command, instituted a increasingly dramatic series of changes (Drake-Brockman 1963). Intending to seize the rescue vessel and flee with the treasure from *Batavia*, the junior officers progressively shifted the basis of their authority away from the VOC and ship-

FIGURE 2. The mutiny and massacre of the *Batavia* survivors (Jansz 1647:fig. 3).

board hierarchies by creating new rules and a constitution (Tylor 1970). These legitimized extraordinary actions, including theft, rape, and the murder of 125 other survivors (Figure 2). One consequence of this restructuring was an increased mobility between other levels of passenger and crew as allegiances changed, based on who joined the rebelling officers or was subjugated to act as slaves or servants.

It is interesting to note that a group of soldiers from the *Batavia* who established themselves on a different island (West Wallabi) managed to survive by establishing their own command structure based on a military model. The ability to organize allowed them to endure, despite limited resources, as well as to resist attacks from the armed rebels and to ultimately contribute to the latter's demise.

The archaeological consequence of whatever authority and social structure emerges within a survivor group is the spatial patterning of the sites and artifacts that make up the survivor camp as a whole. Many survivor accounts do imply the division of groups into different areas, although they are not specific as to whether this involves clustering around a central camp or significant spatial separation (van der Graaf 1727; Drake-Brockman 1963; Strachan 1986: 91). At the *Perseverant* and *Batavia* sites, the archaeological record appears to indicate distinct camp areas, the former having sites separated by a sand dune, while the latter has sites at opposite ends of the main island (Robinson 1988; Gibbs 1992). The events surrounding *Batavia* are, again, interesting in that immediately after

the wreck, all survivors gathered on one or two islands. However, once the insurrection had started, the junior officers reorganized, placing small groups onto a series of tiny islands, ostensibly to prevent overcrowding but, actually, as a prelude to systematic mass murder. This action has potentially resulted in a wider dispersion of sites than might have been expected.

Archaeological identification of which social groups occupied particular sites or areas in the survivor camp may not be a simple matter of analyzing status-sensitive artifacts, such as applied in other terrestrial situations (Spencer-Wood 1987). In a survival situation, the mechanisms for sharing resources meant that social, economic, or shipboard hierarchical groups may not have retained exclusive access to their own goods or other items indicative of their status. Following the wreck of *Porpoise* and *Cato*, Captain Flinders recorded that several of the sailors who made it to shore were virtually naked. Using salvaged clothes, "Lt. Fowler had clothed four or five in lieutenants uniforms, and much promotion of a similar kind had also taken place amongst our own people" (Austin 1964:187). Such an action may well result in uniform buttons appearing within the campsites of ordinary sailors. Similarly, caution is necessary when supposing that there would be differential access to food, particularly in situations of scarcity. Mechanisms to ensure equality, such as the "share-out" used aboard ships, were probably implemented to reduce tensions.

The relative positioning of groups within a survivor camp and, in consequence, the nature of the sites created would, thus, be related to mechanisms beyond simple class differentiation. The need to observe, restrict, or control certain individuals, groups, or even the population as a whole might have seen strategic positioning of officers or other guards. The need to control access to scarce supplies, to boats, or to the wreck could have resulted in similar decisions about organization. In the case of *Batavia*, it is possible that it was the controlling group, initially officers and later renegades, who occupied the camp adjacent to the only beach on Beacon Island, which is also the closest point to the wreck. Historically we know that this was where the boats landed and the foraged and salvaged supplies were offloaded (Drake-Brockman 1963; Gibbs 1992).

Relationship between Wreck
Location and Camp Location

It is not inevitable that people abandoning a ship select either the nearest or the best land or refuge. A combination of prevailing currents, swell, light, visibility, perceptions of environmental conditions, and features and whether or not the survivors were in boats or swimming might have affected initial decisions and movement. Such physical factors may prove to be detectable and measurable through study of the relationship between wreck and land site. More difficult to ascertain might be whether or to what extent such judgments were affected by altered decision-making faculties resulting from the trauma of the wreck event.

In many instances, the Australasian survivor sites are located within relatively close proximity to the wrecks. However, the archaeologically visible campsite may not represent the initial landing place but a later movement to a more suitable location, once the immediate crisis phase had passed and the survivors had regrouped and investigated their surroundings. Even in this case, proximity to the wreck would surely remain an important factor, as the wrecked vessel would have performed several potential roles for the survivors. In the first instance, the wreck was an immediate source of familiar subsistence. It was also a large, visible, and immediately recognizable signal to potential rescuers. Finally, it was a familiar and reassuring symbol to the survivors, acting as a link to their homes and a source of emotional support in an unfamiliar environment. It seems unlikely that survivors would move a great distance away until perceived chances of rescue or salvage opportunities had greatly diminished or disappeared altogether.

Survivor campsites are commonly located close to the beachfront, sometimes directly behind the primary dunes, although this must have created difficulties in achieving shelter from winds and spray. On Beacon Island, which is less than 100 m wide, the archaeological sites associated with *Batavia* survivors are clustered on the eastern or lee side of the island, despite a relief of less than 2 m (Gibbs 1992). Examining the relative position of campsites to wrecks and taking into account the various topographic and other factors noted above may provide some insight into site selection and use. In addition to shelter, camp locations might have been determined by proximity to water or other resources or because they were conducive to some other form of longer term occupation. Positioning may also have had a defensive aspect against a real or imagined threat, whether from indigenes, hostile mariners, or other survivors. In the latter case, the soldiers from *Batavia* strategically positioned their camps so that the rebel attackers were forced to approach slowly and on foot across an expanse of razor sharp reefs (Drake-Brockman 1963; Bevaqua 1974c, 1974d). As will be discussed in a later section, the locations of survivor sites would also be affected by the formulation of different rescue strategies.

In the modern context, these beachside and coastal locations leave the survivor campsites vulnerable to destructive forces such as storm surges, dune mobility, and erosion as well as cultural factors associated with modern development and use of beach areas. The retreat of shorelines through progressive sand buildup can mean that former beach sites may now be situated a considerable distance inland (Cushnahan and Staniforth 1982). Dune mobility and artifact movements through unconsolidated sandy matrices may account for difficulties in locating some campsites, such as in the case of *Hive* and *Vergulde Draek*. In the case of a cliff top site, such as the possible *Zuytdorp* campsite, erosion of the cliff face may continue to destroy the archaeological signature of the survivors (Morse 1988; McCarthy 1990; Weaver 1994; Playford 1996).

Subsistence

The initial subsistence and material culture of survivors was presumably derived from the ship, either through what was removed at the time of escape, direct salvage of the wreck, or from a collection of flotsam and jetsam. Following or even concurrent with the salvage of the ship would be investigation of the surrounding environment, evaluation of the resources available, and implementation of a foraging strategy. Even in the case of the *Batavia* survivors, where the specifics of the insurrection and murders often overshadow all other aspects of the documentary record, there are clear indications of these subsistence behaviors.

The rapidity with which the survivors chose or were forced to exploit or adapt to the surrounding environment was determined by a variety of factors. The first of these was the proximity and accessibility of the wreck as well as whether the vessel remained intact, had broken up, or sunk completely and whether it could provide necessities for their continuing existence. Food, water, and shelter were the immediate necessities for sustaining life and, therefore, the items most probably sought in any initial salvage of the ship. However, most stores aboard ships, including the food and water, were contained in the lower hold areas that were susceptible to major damage and flooding during a wreck event. Many vessels also carried livestock on their upper decks as either food or cargo, although attempting to release panicked animals might have proved dangerous or difficult. Loss of some or all of these supplies would naturally force a more rapid shift to an external foraging strategy.

The second factor influencing the shift to foraging was the nature of the environment in which the survivors were stranded and their ability to identify and exploit potentially useful resources. Most shoreline, island, or reef situations provided some opportunity for fishing or collecting shellfish and crustaceans as well as catching birds, collecting eggs, and possibly hunting for marine and terrestrial animals. The need to reprovision ships during long-distance voyages meant that many sailors had some experience with foraging in unfamiliar environments. However, in the survivor situation, there remained the question of whether the group included experienced individuals and whether there were materials for fashioning hunting or fishing weapons. There were also instances where survivors found themselves with limited opportunities for salvage or foraging, such as the case of the *Invercauld*, wrecked on the Auckland Islands (south of New Zealand) in 1864. The documentary record describes an unsuccessful attempt to salvage the wreck, followed by 12 months of near starvation during which the original 19 survivors were reduced to a group of 3 (Allen 1997).

The discovery or collection of freshwater was usually the major subsistence priority for survivors, and the digging of wells or construction of a water catchment is described in most historical accounts. Several survivor camps have archaeological evidence of these efforts, ranging from modified rock holes (*Batavia*, *Zeewijk*) to more substantial well structures (*Sydney Cove*). Conversely, the Aboriginal wells known to have

been cleared out for use by the *Stefano* survivors are unlikely to have left identifiable traces. There is also the possibility of archaeological evidence of other forms of water supply. At the site of the *Perseverant* camp, situated on dry and barren Dirk Hartog Island, there is a row of barrel hoops along the dune edge, which is thought to represent a still or some other water purification system. Based on these remains, the site was initially identified as the site where an 1801 French scientific expedition, known to have visited the area, landed and set up a water-filtration plant (Marchant 1982; Robinson 1988).

Analysis of dietary remains can provide significant insights into the shift from salvage to foraging as well as into the nature and success of these adaptive strategies. Evidence of the use of salvaged foodstuffs, potentially detectable through bones from salted meats and other durable exotic items, can be contrasted to collection of local marine and terrestrial resources. It would also be of interest to see whether the emphasis in local exploitation remains oriented towards marine resources, perhaps suggesting reliance on the more familiar food types rather than potentially unfamiliar terrestrial resources. Of course, in survivor (or other initial colonization) situations, experimentation may be a necessity (Kirch 1980).

Management of food and water resources may also be archaeologically detectable, since preparation, butchery, or cooking areas leave distinctive concentrations of material. Mechanisms for livestock management, food storage, and food preservation are mentioned in some historical survivor accounts, such as for *Sydney Cove* where a smokehouse was constructed to salt and dry bird and kangaroo meat (Strachan 1986: 90). Survivors also built a pen for chickens and breeding pigeons. On Beacon Island (*Batavia*), early investigators reported that a seal skeleton was found beneath a large coral slab, possibly indicating an attempt to cache meat (Bevaqua 1974a, 1974b). In some instances, the controlling figures in the survivor group might have needed to restrict access to scarce food, water, or other resources, possibly by storing supplies in protected and potentially defensible areas.

Material Culture

The material culture of survivor camps starts as a subset of the ship's assemblage, derived from what was taken during the escape from the wreck, what was salvaged subsequently, and what was recovered as flotsam and jetsam. Over time, particularly with an extended occupation or where salvaged items were few, it would have been necessary to adapt salvaged materials to current needs as well as to manufacture items from materials in the surrounding environment. Items useful for survival would have been the primary focus of salvage, although there are numerous historical and archaeological examples of the recovery of nonessential and personal items. Studies of the material culture of survivors could consider issues of perceptions of property, ownership, sentiment, and the sharing or management of resources in such crisis or survival situations.

Although the study of material culture and notions of salvage and adaptation will form a significant part of future research on survivor camps, the limited analyses available make it difficult to provide good archaeological examples of these processes. The historical record contains various references to the adaptation of salvaged items, the most common being the use of sails for tents. A particularly interesting case is the group of soldiers from *Batavia* who successfully occupied West Wallabi Island and put up a resistance against the officer renegades. Originally intending only a brief absence from the main camp to search for water, this group had carried only limited supplies and was allowed no weapons. It is clear that the rebels hoped that the soldiers would perish or could be repulsed if they attempted to return. However, they not only found food and water but also improvised a variety of tools and weapons with which to survive and defend themselves (Drake-Brockman 1963). Analysis of this excavated assemblage may reveal archaeological evidence of adaptation of the limited resources available (Bevaqua 1974a).

Shelters and Structures

The construction of shelters is an aspect of material culture that has particular importance for archaeological study. Many historical accounts refer to survivors living in "tents," presumably constructed of canvas from the sails, which would also be one of the most readily accessible materials. However, there are instances, such as *Julia Anne*, where dwellings that were more substantial were constructed of salvaged timbers and local wood (Hundley 1996). In several cases, stone or coral structures have also been tentatively associated with survivor groups, such as the features on West Wallabi Island (*Batavia*) and Preservation Island (*Sydney Cove*) (Bevaqua 1974d; Strachan 1986). Alternatively, the *Stefano* survivors were forced to live in caves after their tents were destroyed during a cyclone (Rathe 1992).

The materials used for construction will naturally affect the archaeological visibility of any shelters. In most cases, it will probably be quite difficult to identify individual habitations. However, should evidence of structures survive, the materials, construction techniques, size, design, and evidence of internal layout may have wider implications for investigating the skills, activities, and social organization of the survivor group.

In addition to dwellings, there are other structures and features noted in historical accounts, such as the above-mentioned smokehouse and chicken coop associated with *Sydney Cove* survivors (Strachan 1986). When *Batavia* survivors were finally rescued, a small coral prison was constructed to confine the chief mutineers until their trial (Drake-Brockman 1963). Archaeological surveys of areas adjacent to survivor camps have also recorded a variety of other features, which may represent lookouts/windbreaks, marker cairns, fireplaces or signal fires (Bevaqua 1974c; Orme and Randall 1987). However, it is often hard to establish a clear association between these structures and the activities of the survivor group.

Health and Mortality

The health of the survivor population was related to a range of factors including subsistence and environment. Death could result from injuries sustained during the wreck event, from the attempt to reach land, or from other misadventure during the occupation. Medical problems and death could also be a consequence of starvation, dehydration, infection, disease, or other agents. General dietary deficiencies and, particularly, scurvy posed a significant threat, as was the case for *Perseverant*, while *Sydney Cove* survivors may have had problems from arsenic poisoning (Strachan 1986:91). For some time, the lack of potable water forced the survivors of *Batavia* to drink their own urine (Drake-Brockman 1963:265), although the medical consequences of this are unclear. The mental health of the survivor group, including the psychological effects of the various physiological problems and privations suffered, should not be underestimated either.

The main archaeological signature of mortality among survivors is the presence of burials, although most historical accounts are not specific as to how disposal of the dead was organized. The nature of burial may be indicative of the circumstances of the death, the social organization of the survivor group, or the physical well-being of the remainder, expressed by ability or inability to dig a proper grave. There are instances of execution within survivor groups by hanging (*Batavia*) or marooning on small islands (*Zeewijk*) as punishment for real, perceived, or even invented crimes, or as a result of foul play (van der Graaf 1727; Drake-Brockman 1963). In these cases, bodies were simply left to decay on the surface. Finally, it was possible that sole survivors or small groups could die without others to attend to them, resulting in a surface deposit of skeletal material.

Methods of body disposal or burial may also indicate efforts to control disease or maintain certain social or religious standards. Proximity of burials to the camp, depth and orientation of graves, inclusion of goods as well as evidence of trauma may provide further insights. In the case of *Batavia*, many of the burials discovered are shallow, haphazardly oriented, with skeletal evidence of trauma, suggestive of hasty and covert attempts to hide murder victims, rather than ritual interments (Gibbs 1994; Hunneybun 1995).

The bodies themselves are also a tightly controlled sample of a particular type of population and, therefore, an interesting source for investigation. Morphological studies and investigations of pathology and trauma as well as more sophisticated analyses may provide information on the life or identity of individuals, the effects of living at sea, and, potentially, the conditions suffered by the survivor group (Hunneybun 1995). In some instances, the possibility of cannibalism may need to be investigated, as it was not unknown for survivors *in extremis* to exploit the corpses of the deceased as a food source or to commit murder for this purpose. The best-known example of both scenarios is the survivors of the Nantucket whale ship *Essex* (1820), adrift in small boats in

the central Pacific after their vessel was sunk by a whale. Faced with certain starvation, they consumed the bodies of several shipmates who had died of natural causes and also drew lots to see who would be sacrificed as a means of allowing the others to live (Heffernan 1981).

Development of a Rescue Strategy

The survivor situation essentially presented several alternatives for salvation, with the decision as to how to approach rescue having obvious implications for the nature of activities on and around sites and, consequently, for their archaeology. The first option was to wait for rescue. This strategy presumably suggested that survivors perceived that rescue by others was possible, or it was an acknowledgment that a lack of resources, skills, or other factors precluded opportunities for self-deliverance. Even a passive approach to rescue might imply certain activities. Illustrations of survivor camps show flag posts erected from spars or other timbers, with the ensign hung upside down in the international code for distress (Jacob and Vellios 1987: 148). Construction of lookouts or beacons might also be considered, with Phillip Playford (1996) suggesting that a large hearth feature excavated on the cliff above the *Zuytdorp* wreck site may indicate survivors hoping to signal to other ships in the convoy.

The second possibility was to walk away from the site in the direction of safety. This strategy depended upon whether walking away was possible or essential (lack of food, water, or shelter) and the conviction that a settlement could be reached. In many instances, this was not feasible, although there were certainly cases, for example, the *Sydney Cove*, where mariners stranded in remote parts of Australia walked considerable distances, even hundreds of kilometers, to reach the nearest British colonies (Nash 1997). In some instances, survivors might attempt to reach special depots where supplies were kept for stranded mariners and that were often checked by passing ships (Delaney 1990).

A third option was to send a boat for help. In most cases, survivor groups sent one or more of the ship's boats to the nearest settlement for assistance. This sometimes required open-sea voyages of hundreds or even thousands of kilometers with limited supplies and only basic navigation equipment. Many such attempts were successful, although there was a significant chance of failure. For instance, while boats from *Batavia* and *Zeewijk* were both sent on the more than 2,000 km open-sea voyage from the Houtman Abrolhos to the nearest Dutch settlement at Jakarta, the boat from the former was successful, while the latter disappeared without trace (van der Graaf 1727; Drake-Brockman 1963).

Another possibility might be to repair the original vessel or to construct a new vessel. Both of these depended upon the condition of the wreck and the skills of the survivors. There are many examples of stranded groups constructing small vessels with which to rescue themselves. Survivors sometimes engaged in construction even if boats had been sent for help, possibly hedging against the loss of the messengers, while also providing the remaining survivors with a purpose. After the wreck of *Cato* and *Porpoise*, Captain Flinders directed the ship's carpenters to commence immediate construction of a rescue vessel, despite the fact that a cutter was being sent to Port Jackson to seek help (Austin 1964:188). Construction of even a small vessel required particular forms of salvage, a shipyard area, and possibly the establishment of a forge to make nails and manufacture or repair fittings. The scavenging of materials by *Zeewijk* survivors and the construction of their rescue vessel *Sloepie* is a well-documented example of this sort of activity (van der Graaf 1727). Location of this shipyard site formed the basis of C. Ingelman-Sundberg's (1977) archaeological investigations of the Gun Island (Western Australia) camp. There are numerous accounts of holed or damaged vessels being brought close to shore to be careened or repaired, although whether to include these instances as "survivor" situations is unclear. Certainly, the failure to repair a vessel had the same ultimate outcome as a more dramatic wrecking event and potentially demanded similar survival strategies by the stranded sailors. Further consideration might be given to whether there is an archaeological signature indicative of a failed repair versus a total wreck.

Yet another alternative was the "Swiss Family Robinson" strategy of establishing a new settlement (Birmingham and Jeans 1983). The long-term viability of the community would depend upon both the environment and the composition of the survivor group. Although not strictly a survivor site, the settlement of Pitcairn Island by HMAV *Bounty* mutineers and a group of Polynesian men and women (Nicholson 1965) shares some attributes of this class. Having chosen to destroy the vessel to escape detection by the British Navy, the survivors had stranded themselves as effectively as if they had been wrecked there. The final option, of integrating with an existing indigenous community, will be discussed in the following section.

The decision as to which rescue strategy(ies) to pursue in the short and long term, particularly with regard to self-rescue attempts, was also dependant upon factors other than immediate environment, access to resources, and the skills of the survivors. For example, to attempt a passage towards a settlement required knowledge of how to navigate to the destination; the presence of favorable winds, currents, and sea conditions; and even, in some areas of the world, the melting of ice and snow. Timing a rescue attempt for the most favorable window of opportunity may have required considerable delay, maybe of some months. The choice of rescue strategy might also depend upon who was in command and the ability of that person to determine an appropriate course of action. Presumably at least some of the basis for authority would derive from a real or perceived ability to bring about salvation.

Survivor Camp as Contact Site

The concept of the shipwreck survivor camp as a form of contact site has become increasingly important in the consideration of early relationships between Europeans and indigenous groups. In at least three of the four known VOC wrecks (*Batavia*, *Vergulde Draek*, *Zuytdorp*), there is a high probability that face-to-face contact between Australian Aboriginal populations and survivor groups (between 2 and 70 people) occurred. Because these survivors had disappeared before rescuers could locate them, it is not known whether the contact was in the form of conflict or cooperation.

From the colonial period, various accounts of Aboriginal-survivor interactions exist, usually of a positive nature. For incidents that are more recent, it may still be possible to obtain an Aboriginal perspective. In many cases, including those of the *Peruvian* (1846) and the *Stefano* (1875), survivors were cared for over a period of months until a passing ship could be signaled (Read 1954; Rathe 1992). However, survivors of the *Sydney Cove* (1797) received a variable reception from Aboriginal groups as they traveled by small boats northwards along the southeast Australian coast (Nash 1997:30). Presumably caution or outright avoidance of contact was the norm for survivors, given the potential risk of hostility. It would be interesting to speculate to what extent the survivor group size, age, and sex composition and their access to resources, including weaponry, may have determined the outcomes of contact encounters. As noted, real or perceived threats may also have had implications for the location and organization of campsites.

A debatable point is the extent to which wreck survivors, rather than mariners in general, may have directly influenced the indigenous Australasian populations with whom they came into contact. Playford (1996:228) has proposed that the survivors of the *Zuytdorp* (1712) left a genetic heritage, evidenced by the appearance of the rare genetic disorder *porphyria variegata* amongst some members of the Malgana people who traditionally lived near the wreck site. Medical studies have shown that modern sufferers elsewhere in the world all share descent from a Dutch couple, Gerrit Jansz van Deventer and Ariaantje Jacobs van den Berg, who were married in the Cape colony in South Africa in 1688. More radically, Gerritsen (1994) suggests that Dutch survivors from several wrecks had a significant cultural impact on the art, technology, and language of the Aboriginal communities of the Western Australian coast. However, this proposition has received little support from either linguists or archaeologists (Blevins 1998). The Western Australian Maritime Museum is currently undertaking a project to compile and analyze historical reports of a broader range of encounters between survivors and Aboriginal groups to determine what the extent of interaction may have been.

Later Aboriginal salvaging of survivor campsites (or wrecks) and the reuse of materials such as glass, ceramics, metal, or even ballast stone is a another form of contact site but does not imply face-to-face interaction of any kind. Material from the 1811 wreck of the *Rapid* near Point Cloates (Western Australia) has been found in Aboriginal sites throughout the area, although there was never a meeting between the survivors and the Djalendji people who lived in the area (Henderson 1983). Material from *Zuytdorp*, discovered hundreds of kilometers from the wreck site and camp, may well represent similar Aboriginal salvage rather than survivor movement (Playford 1996). David Nutley (1995) has also considered the possible *Hive* survivor camp as a contact site based on the conjunction of Aboriginal and European material. However, he is not specific as to whether this is a coincidental juxtaposition of sites, whether there are distinctive signs of Aboriginal utilization of the materials, such as flaked glass, or whether this could be a post-survivor occupation.

Salvage

Salvage of cargo and structure was an integral part of many survivor experiences and has, so far, been discussed in the context of other activities. However, the mechanisms by which survivors undertake such efforts also require study, as do the implications for the archaeological records of wreck site and campsite. Proximity and accessibility of the wreck, the extent of damage, the abilities of the survivors, and their real or perceived needs affected the nature of the salvage effort. Archaeological considerations of salvage processes are discussed in a later section of this paper.

Contemporary salvage of the camp by the survivors or rescuers was also a possibility, depending, in part, upon the nature of the rescue strategy. If the survivors constructed a small craft, the range of items removed was limited by the size of the boat and the object's utility during or after what might be a long, hazardous, and possibly crowded voyage. The latter might have included ships' logs or records, required to substantiate innocence or culpability for the wreck and subsequent events. A greater variety of items could be removed if a substantial rescue vessel arrived. When the senior merchant of *Batavia*, Francisco Pelsaert, returned with a rescue ship, he was also under explicit orders from the governor-general of *Batavia* to recover "as much money and goods as can be found" (Drake-Brockman 1963:257). Pelsaert, probably hoping to mitigate his own culpability in the loss of the ship, attempted to recover everything of possible value from both land and sea. This included inconsequential items such as barrel hoops from the wreck and casks of vinegar that had washed up on nearby islands. Finally, in repentant tones, he reported his decision to depart, "wholly convinced that nothing more is to be found ... seeing that all has been searched through and dived over" (Drake-Brockman 1963:221). In this instance, the extensive salvage undoubtedly has consequences for the archaeological record, although in most other survivor accounts, the efforts to retrieve material from land and sea do not appear to have been as comprehensive.

The Psychology of Crisis

While the themes described above provide a framework for the historical and archaeological investigation of survivor camps, it must be borne in mind that wreck events and survivor situations were associated with humans who were often under extreme stress. Wreck events varied in their severity and potential to produce psychological trauma, as did the circumstances of the stranding. The psychological well-being of the survivors was also influenced by other physiological and environmental conditions. Given these factors, we should not expect that all people thought or acted in normal ways or were capable of making rational decisions all of the time. Behavior during the crisis aboard ship and then as survivors on land may, in some instances, have been unusual or unexpected, and their outcomes may have potentially influenced the nature of the archaeological record of both wreck and campsite.

Although such crisis-inspired behaviors and psychology might seem elusive, a well-established body of literature which demonstrates that individuals and groups respond to disaster events in patterned and relatively predictable ways (Dynes and Tierney 1994; Leach 1994). This predictability and the resulting models of crisis response offer interesting opportunities for the analysis of behaviors during wreck events and survivor situations as well as the relationship of these to the archaeological record. Although it is not possible within this current essay to expand upon the role of psychology in wreck and survivor camp analyses, they are discussed in another paper (Gibbs 2000).

Jettisoning, Salvage, and Site Formation Processes

One way to understand the relationship between wreck and survivor camp, including the flow of items between them, is to view these sites as the products of a continuum of behaviors associated with the contemporary removal of material. This view also allows us to integrate the terrestrial activities into established models of wreck-site formation processes, especially Muckelroy's (1978) flowchart for the evolution of a wreck (Figure 3). Muckelroy depicted shipwreck sites as the result of cultural and natural formation processes, which he characterized as either "extracting filters" (which removed material) or "scrambling devices" (which affected the distribution of material) (Muckelroy 1978; Hardy 1990). While embraced by many maritime archaeologists, the model was simplistic with little explanation of what these processes consisted of or what were the implications for wreck analysis and interpretation. In particular, Muckelroy emphasized natural forces over cultural influences, representing the latter as "salvage in antiquity," without elaborating or discussing possible effects of these processes on later parts of the site formation sequence.

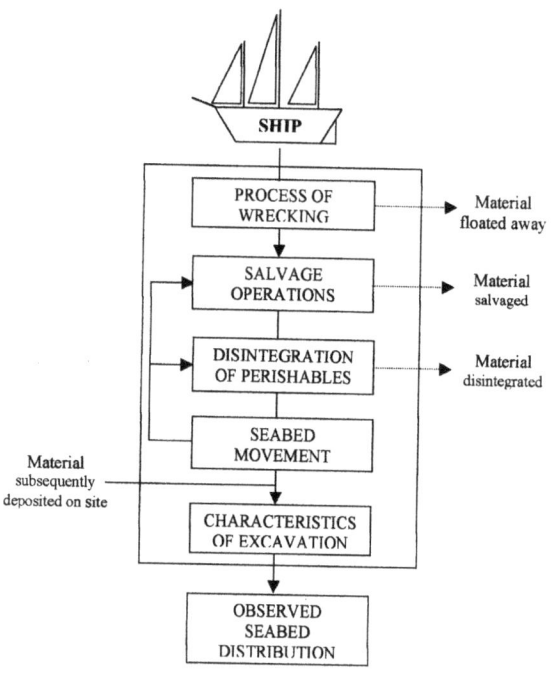

FIGURE 3. Evolution of a shipwreck (Muckelroy 1978).

Recent work by Australian archaeologists has better defined the physical, chemical, and biological factors acting on marine shipwreck sites, expanding upon Muckelroy's original model and introducing a predictive element to considerations of wreck disintegration (McCarthy 1996; Ward et al. 1999). However, this work does not diminish the need to understand the impact of human activities both during and after a wreck event. Put simply, if most of the cargo, contents, and structure is removed soon after wrecking occurs, then naturally these items will not be found at a later point, regardless of intermediary physical site formation processes. Following Muckelroy's lead, these cultural processes might still be considered under the heading of "salvage activities."

Muckelroy (1978:169) identifies the first cultural influences on the formation of the wreck site as beginning after the physical mechanics of the "process of wrecking" has taken place. However, decisions and actions taken before and during the wreck event will naturally have affected the eventual disposition of the ship and, ultimately, the site. In the long term, not only the physical capabilities of the ship but also the psychology of the crisis response need to be considered. However, for this discussion, the focus will be limited to the removal of items, before, during, and after the wreck event.

The first step towards understanding how material is taken away from a vessel is to create a broad framework for conceiving the physical nature of a ship and its contents. Although the following categories are flexible, four basic divisions might be determined from the relative ease with which items can be removed and how they relate to the integrity of the vessel (Figure 4). These classes are not, however, strictly hierarchical, as a large, bulky cargo item or one situated in the lower hold of the ship might be substantially more difficult to access and remove than fittings or structural elements situated elsewhere. The first category, of cargo and contents, consists of non-fixed items that were not associated with the mechanical operation of the ship and were meant to be removable. This would include the ship's boats and life rafts. Second were the fixtures and fittings, including minor fixed items, fittings, yards, ropes, and minor mechanical items and equipment. Anchors and cannon might also be included in this group. A third

CATEGORY	MATERIALS
Cargo and Contents	Non-fixed items not associated with the mechanical operation of the ship and that were meant to be removable, including the ship's boats and life rafts.
Fixtures and Fittings	Minor fixed items, fittings, yards, chains, ropes, anchors and cannon, minor mechanical items and equipment.
Minor Structural	Items not normally removed, but whose removal would not compromise the integrity of the hull, such as bulkheads, decks, masts, superstructure, major mechanical items, and equipment.
Major structural	Elements of the ship whose removal would affect the integrity of the vessel, including hull planking, ribs, and other structural items.

FIGURE 4. Categories of materials comprising a ship.

class of material was the structural items whose removal would not compromise the integrity of the hull, such as the bulkheads, decks, masts, superstructure, and major mechanical items and equipment. Fourth, there are the major structural portions of the ship, including the hull planking, ribs, and other structural items whose removal would affect the integrity of the vessel.

In turn, major cultural actions and salvage events can be broadly divided into five major types: jettisoning, crisis salvage, survivor salvage, opportunistic salvage, and organized salvage (Figure 5). During the warning period, where disaster was imminent and recognized (Leach 1994), sailors may well have engaged in activities aimed at rescuing the ship or mitigating the effects of the disaster. Such actions included cutting away the masts or jettisoning anchors, cannon, and other heavy fittings or cargo items that might have allowed the vessel to avoid impact or refloat. If successful, it was possible that such items might be recovered, although frequently they were left and so independently entered the archaeological record. If wrecking actually occurred, then jettisoning may explain the presence of some items away from the main site or in an unusual spatial relationship. Although not a salvage event, this first phase is a significant cultural factor in wreck formation and site interpretation.

The second phase, that of crisis salvage, involved the removal of items at the height of the wrecking process, that is, before and during the impact stage, including launching of the ship's boats. Normally limited to readily accessible cargo and contents and, presumably, oriented towards survival, there is clear historical evidence for irrational removal of nonessential items. The third phase was survivor salvage, which occurred

SALVAGE TYPE	PHASE	PURPOSE	MATERIALS REMOVED	ARCHAEOLOGICAL SIGNATURE
Jettisoning	Immediately before and after the wreck event (impact).	Preventing impact, mitigation of the effects of impact, or rescue of the vessel.	Cutting away of masts, jettisoning anchors, cannon, and other heavy fittings or cargo items that might allow the vessel to avoid impact or refloat.	Jettisoned items may be archaeologically visible but displaced from the main wreck site. If the strategy is successful, may result in there being a debris trail, but no wreck.
Crisis Salvage	Height of the wrecking process, once the decision has been made to abandon ship. Dependent upon the nature and severity of the impact and the time available before sinking or wrecking.	Focused on retrieval of survival-oriented materials.	Readily accessible cargo and contents, as well as launching of the ships boats.	Because of limited nature of crisis salvage, it may not be possible to detect the absence of items on the archaeological wreck site. However, salvaged items may be visible within the survivor campsite, either intact or in modified form.
Survivor Salvage	Return to the vessel after initial crisis phase. Dependent upon accessibility of wreck; the size, composition, and capabilities of the survivor group; and the nature of the survival or rescue strategy.	Primarily retrieval of a wider range of survival and rescue oriented materials.	Cargo and contents: foodstuffs, water, tools, and utilitarian survival items. Personal goods, valuables, or more extensive cargo removal may be attempted. Minor structural salvage for materials for housing, fuel, or construction of rescue vessel.	More extensive removal of cargo, fittings, and minor structural materials may be detectable archaeologically through absence on wreck. Salvaged items may be visible within the survivor campsite, either intact or in modified form.
Opportunistic Salvage	Usually after the crisis and/or survivor phases, but may precede or follow Systematic Salvage. Dependent upon accessibility, technology and perceived returns. Likely to be short duration, sporadic, and involving a number of persons over a period of time.	Recovery of readily removable materials perceived to have use, collectable, or monetary value.	Generally a nonsystematic removal of contents, accessible fixtures, fittings, and minor structural elements.	Variable archaeological visibility. May range from non-detectable to significant and obvious absence of cargo, fittings and structure. Salvaged materials likely to have been removed completely from site.
Organized Salvage	After the crisis and/or survivor phases, but may precede or follow Opportunistic Salvage. Dependent upon accessibility, technology, and perceived returns. Sustained activity over longer periods, usually be a single group.	Systematic removal or professional salvage of all materials that have use or monetary value.	Removal of cargo, fittings, minor and major structural elements, which may include 'breaking' the ship.	Probable high archaeological visibility with absence of all classes of material and major structural items. Archaeological wreck site may represent post-salvage discard or storage. Salvaged materials likely to have been removed completely from site.

FIGURE 5. Forms of wreck salvage and associated archaeological signatures.

after the initial crisis had passed. This phase assumed that all or part of the wreck was accessible and, depending upon the size, composition, and capabilities of the survivor group, further materials might be removed as necessary to sustain survivors while they waited for or organized rescue. This phase was primarily oriented towards foodstuffs, water barrels, tools, and utilitarian items necessary for survival, although the removal of personal belongings, valuables, or more extensive cargo may have been attempted. Minor structural salvage may also have occurred in order to use materials for housing, to provide fuel, or to attempt to construct a rescue vessel. Other materials from the wreck that had been removed and washed ashore by natural processes might also be collected and used.

The fourth or opportunistic salvage phase may have occurred sporadically over a long period. It was dependent upon proximity to land and settlements as well as on the situation and accessibility of the wreck. It generally occurred after the survivor salvage phase, although in the case of deliberate wrecking, it may even have preceded it. During this phase, there was nonsystematic removal of contents, accessible fixtures, fittings, and minor structural elements by visitors to the site who were not necessarily the owners or the survivors of the wreck. The fifth and final phase, organized salvage, was implicitly but not necessarily carried out by the owners of the vessel or their authorized agents. It involved the systematic removal or professional salvage of cargo, fittings, minor and major structural elements, which may have included "breaking" the ship. This was likely to be an intensive effort and associated with either eventual recovery or total abandonment.

The categories are partially defined by the time, effort, and equipment required, so that a group of survivors is unlikely to be able (or want) to effect recovery of major structural elements. However, it is conceivable that opportunistic salvers may attempt such an act, given sufficient incentive.

Figure 6 attempts to model the cultural processes affecting wreck formation in the same style as originally used by Muckelroy (1978), expanding upon his original concept. It also parallels Ingrid Ward's amplification of the natural

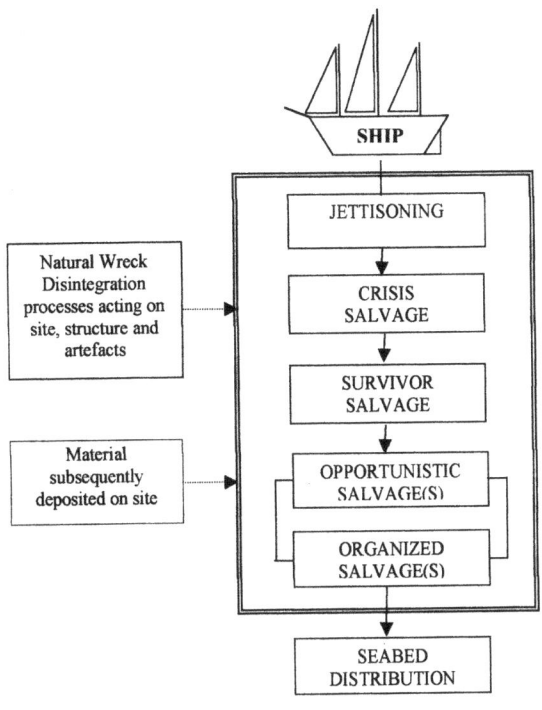

FIGURE 6. Cultural processes acting in the formation and disintegration of a shipwreck site.

process aspect of Muckelroy's model (Ward et al. 1999), so that all three could ideally be viewed together. However, reality is unlikely to have a simple linear relationship as represented here. While jettisoning, crisis salvage, and survivor salvage are bound in a fixed order to the wreck event and the immediate post-wreck period, opportunistic salvage and organized salvage may occur in several cycles, through both the contemporary setting (antiquity) and in the modern setting. A wreck may be subject to one or all of these cultural processes, not experience certain stages, or sustain repeated salvage efforts, depending upon historical, location, and environmental factors. In addition, natural processes are dynamic and, ultimately, result in the disintegration or transformation of material at varying rates, depending upon the wreck environment and the nature of the artifact (Ward et al. 1999). This process affects what was/is available to the salver, contemporary or modern, opportunistic or organized (Figure 5). Although archaeological excavation is essentially a form of organized salvage, it has been given a separate category because the model is an attempt to examine what remains to the archaeologist after

other cultural and natural processes have taken place on the wreck site.

Part of the significance of the study of survivor behavior and survivor camps is that these studies may provide detail as to the nature of the first and second phases of the wreck salvage process. Materials removed from wrecks by survivors stand a high probability of having been returned to whatever campsite has been established. For example, the site of the French whaler *Perseverant*, wrecked in 1841, has recently been discovered buried on a beach on remote Dirk Hartog Island, Western Australia. The survivor camp, where the crew spent 10 weeks before attempting to sail longboats to Jakarta, is situated in the sand dunes immediately adjacent. There is no record of later opportunistic or organized salvage of the ship or campsite, with the latter appearing to be remarkably undisturbed (Robinson 1988). Comparison between the contents of the wreck and camp may, therefore, provide significant insights into the cultural processes of crisis and survivor salvage. It may also provide a yardstick by which to evaluate the effects of subsequent natural formation processes.

Unfortunately, the mechanics of ship and wreck salvage of all four kinds are imperfectly understood, and it was not possible to find specific studies of the sorts of salvage processes discussed above. There have not yet been investigations of what people are likely to take with them during the panic of the wreck (crisis) event, just as what kinds of items are salvaged for use by survivors have not been established. Similarly, there are no studies of how or to what extent vessels are taken apart (either by opportunists or professional breakers) to retrieve useable structural or mechanical elements before abandonment, nor have there been published studies of the range of items removed by modern divers. Historical and ethnographic studies may provide clues, as would comparative studies between archaeological wreck sites known to have been salvaged.

Sources for Research

The introduction referred to the rich heritage of literary accounts and images of wrecks and survivors, and that analysis has focused on the fictitious or fictionalized. However, a diverse range of documentary records of real shipwreck events and the travails of their survivors also awaits examination. Particularly for wrecks within the last 400 years, such records include criminal trials, courts-martial, insurance investigations, and other inquiries dealing with the details of the wreck events. These frequently document the responses or actions by individuals and groups. There are also newspaper accounts, letters, journals, and memoirs in published and unpublished form, offering first-person accounts. While in some instances, attempts are made to deceive or to sensationalize, general patterns of how such events proceeded still should be detectable. These records can be analyzed for specific details and in the light of models of crisis response.

In addition to written documents, there are numerous contemporary images of wreck events and survivor camps, such as those of *Pandora* (Gesner 1991) and *Cato* and *Porpoise* (Jacob and Vellios 1987:148), to name just three Australian examples. Such images can provide critical details of relationship to the wreck, location and structure of the camp, the nature of dwellings, and other activities on and around the sites (Delaney 1988, 1990).

The second area essential for further research is the location and investigation of the archaeological literature of survivors. Although there are as many as a dozen published archaeological reports that either record or identify survivor camps in Australasia, undoubtedly a far greater number of sites is reported in the gray literature or on government registers. More are potentially locatable from historical or informant sources. Reanalysis of existing sites and collections as well as new research based upon well-considered questions are both desirable and necessary. The sorts of questions and themes that might be directed at these sites have been addressed above, although naturally there is a need for the refinement and development of specific questions for particular sites. As noted previously, one area of concern is the coastal nature of the sites and their vulnerability to disturbance by natural and cultural processes. As with wrecks, the survivor camps are highly susceptible to damage through "fossickers," people who pick over abandoned sites in the belief that they will yield treasure or valuables. The sites of *Batavia*, *Zeewijk*, and *Zuytdorp* survivors all have long histories of damage by collectors as well as by early nonprofessional investigators (Henderson 1986; Gibbs 1992; Playford 1996).

While disturbances by fossickers may potentially destroy or seriously compromise the integrity of the survivor sites, this does not necessarily mean that a disturbed site or area has lost all research potential. First, despite disturbance, issues of location and spatial organization may still be addressed purely through the distribution of sites and artifacts on the landscape. Second, most camps were occupied for only a short duration and, because of limited stratigraphic development, would appear archaeologically as single events in many respects. Although stratigraphic integrity is not ideal, disturbance and redeposition of material a short distance from the original context may not completely compromise its potential. Finally, most fossickers direct their attentions at only a limited range of items, primarily metal objects or other distinctive items. Dietary remains such as bone and shell almost certainly do not figure as collectibles, therefore providing researchers the potential to still address certain questions regarding diet, foraging strategies, and adaptation (Gibbs 1992).

Conclusions

Intersite comparison, pattern recognition, and model building are areas in which maritime archaeology has been lacking. That considerations of behavior in analysis and interpretation should only now be introduced is remarkable, given that it has been 15 years since the publication of Richard Gould's (1983) *Shipwreck Anthropology*. However, as paradigms and interests change, we should expect to see a broadening of the framework of maritime archaeological analysis and a move towards some of the concerns that motivate other areas of archaeological research.

The development of models of survivor behaviors and archaeology will ultimately increase our understanding of the many survivor situations where historical records are incomplete or lacking or where archaeological sites either cannot be located or are difficult to interpret. For example, of the early Dutch wrecks on the Western Australian coast, *Batavia* and *Zeewijk* are two well-documented survivor situations that also have substantial archaeological deposits. In contrast, *Vergulde Draek* and *Zuytdorp* have no documentary records, and there is uncertainty as to the fate of the survivors. In the former instance, 70 men were last seen standing on the mainland

Australian shore, waiting while a boat was sent to Jakarta for help. By the time a rescue vessel had returned, these men had vanished, and almost no archaeological trace has been found of them. In the *Zuytdorp* case, there is no documentary record of the wreck, and whether the artifacts and sites found on the cliff edge above the wreck indicate survivors or salvage by Aboriginal people is ambiguous. Deriving behavioral and archaeological patterns from the documented sites may inform us about the possible locations or natures of the latter sites.

This paper has presented a case for the comparative study of survivor camps as well as proposed linkages to other aspects of maritime archaeological analysis. In many respects, the structure set out above is deliberately simplistic. It emphasizes that certain commonalities must exist because of the physical nature of ships, the environmental constraints of life at sea, and the predictable norms in the command and social organization on vessels. The psychological or crisis aspect of disaster situations also seems to be a common link; at the extreme, it becomes a fundamental human response rather than a cultural response. On this basis, the structure proposes that survivor sites are likely to exhibit certain patterns of location and use that introduce a predictive element to archaeological research. However, the framework also recognizes that there may be other modifying factors. These include variations in the authority structure depending upon the type of vessel, (naval, merchant, etc), cultural origins, religious and ethnic backgrounds, social and economic variables, population mix, the cargo and contents of the ship, and the nature and severity of the wreck event. There may also be differences in behavior between different time periods. The possibility of differing responses is not an impediment but a fruitful area for investigation within a comparative framework.

ACKNOWLEDGMENTS

Thanks to Jeremy Green and the staff of the Western Australian Maritime Museum for allowing me to work on the Beacon Island *Batavia* sites in 1992 and 1994, where the ideas for this paper first emerged. Thanks also to the many people who discussed or commented upon the various ideas or drafts of this paper as it went through numerous changes, including David Roe, Peter Veth, and Nigel Erskine of the Department of Archaeology at James Cook University; Michael McCarthy of the Western Australian Maritime Museum; Wendy Bradshaw of the Western Australian Museum; and the several anonymous reviewers in Australia and elsewhere.

REFERENCES

ALLEN, MADELAINE
1997 *Wake of the* Invercauld. Exisle Publishing, Auckland, New Zealand.

AUSTIN, K. A.
1964 *The Voyage of the* Investigator *1801–1803: Captain Matthew Flinders R.N.* Rigby, Adelaide, SA, Australia.

BEVAQUA, BOB
1974a Archaeological Survey of Sites Relating to the *Batavia* Shipwreck. Report to the Department of Maritime Archaeology, Western Australian Maritime Museum, Fremantle, Australia.
1974b Report of a Test Excavation on Beacon Island. Report No.1, Department of Maritime Archaeology, Western Australian Maritime Museum, Fremantle, Australia.
1974c Archaeological Survey of Sites Relating to the *Batavia* Shipwreck. *Early Days*, 7(6):50–78.
1974d The Slaughter Point Site: An Archaeological Investigation of a Site Associated with the *Batavia* Shipwreck. Report No. 2, Department of Maritime Archaeology, Western Australian Maritime Museum, Fremantle, Australia.

BIRMINGHAM, JUDY, AND DENNIS JEANS
1983 The Swiss Family Robinson and the Archaeology of Colonisations. *Australian Journal of Historical Archaeology*, 1:3–14.

BLEVINS, JULIETTE
1988 A Dutch Influence on Nhanda? Wanyjidaga Innga! *Australian Aboriginal Studies*, 11(1):43–47.

CUSHNAHAN, STEVE, AND MARK STANIFORTH
1982 Magnetometers for Wrecksite Location: A Case Study at Bunbury, Western Australia. *The Bulletin of the Australian Institute for Maritime Archaeology*, 6: 62–80.

DELANEY, WARREN
1988 Wreck Reef Controversy: Unanswered Questions. *The Bulletin of the Australian Institute for Maritime Archaeology*, 12(1):21–27.
1990 Booby Island: The European Presence. *The Bulletin of the Australian Institute for Maritime Archaeology*, 14(2): 49–54.

DRAKE-BROCKMAN, HENRIETTA
1963 *Voyage to Disaster.* Angus and Robertson, Sydney, NSW, Australia.

DYNES, RUSSELL, AND KATHLEEN TIERNEY
1994 *Disasters, Collective Behaviour, and Social Organization.* University of Delaware Press, Newark, NJ.

GERRITSEN, R.
1994 *And Their Ghosts May Be Heard.* Fremantle Arts Center Press, Fremantle, WA, Australia.

GESNER, PETER
1991 *Pandora: An Archaeological Perspective.* Queensland Museum, Brisbane, QLD, Australia.

GIBBS, MARTIN
1992 "*Batavia's* Graveyard": A Report on Archaeological Survey and Excavations on Beacon Island, Wallabi Group, Houtman Abrolhos. Report No. 59, Department of Maritime Archaeology, Western Australian Maritime Museum, Fremantle, Australia.
1994 Report on the Excavation of Skeleton SK5: A Victim of the *Batavia* Massacre of 1629, Beacon Island, Western Australia. Report No. 112, Department of Maritime Archaeology, Western Australian Maritime Museum, Fremantle, Australia.
2000 Behavioral Models of Crisis Response As a Tool for Archaeological Interpretation. In *Natural Disasters, Catastrophism, and Cultural Change*, John Grattan and Robin Torrence, editors. One World Archaeology Series. Unwin Hyman, London, England.

GOULD, RICHARD
1983 *Shipwreck Anthropology.* University of New Mexico Press, Albuquerque, NM.

HARDY, DEBBIE
1990 A Century on the Sea-Bed: The Centurion. *The Bulletin of the Australian Institute for Maritime Archaeology*, 14(2):23–34.

HEFFERNAN, THOMAS
1981 *Stove by a Whale: Owen Chase and the Essex.* Wesleyan University Press, Middletown, NY.

HENDERSON, GRAEME
1983 The *Rapid* Excavation at Point Cloates in 1982. In *Proceedings Second Southern Hemisphere Conference on Maritime Archaeology*, Bill Jeffery and James Amess, editors, pp. 243–248. South Australian Department of Planning, Adelaide, Australia.
1986 *Maritime Archaeology in Australia.* University of Western Australia Press, Perth, Australia.

HINTON, P. (EDITOR)
1992 *Disasters: Image and Context.* Sydney Studies in Society and Culture, Sydney, NSW, Australia.

HUNDLEY, PAUL
1996 Captain Coffin and "*Julia Ann.*" Signals: *The Quarterly Magazine of the Australian National Maritime Museum*, 35:9–11.

HUNNEYBUN, BERNADINE
1995 Skullduggery on Beacon Island. Bachelor's (honours) thesis, Department of Archaeology, University of Western Australia, Perth, Australia.

INGELMAN-SUNDBERG, C.
1977 The VOC Ship *Zeewijk* 1727: Report on the 1976 Survey of the Site. *Australian Archaeology*, 6:18–33.

JACOB, TREVOR, AND JAMES VELLIOS
1987 *Southland: The Maritime Exploration of Australia.* Western Australian Ministry of Education, Perth, Australia.

KIRCH, PATRICK
1980 The Archaeological Study of Adaptation: Theoretical and Methodological Issues. In *Advances in Archaeological Method and Theory 3*, Michael B. Schiffer, editor, pp. 101–156. Academic Press, New York, NY.

LEACH, JOHN
1994 *Survival Psychology.* Macmillan, Sydney, NSW, Australia.

MARCHANT, LESLIE
1982 *France Australe.* Artlook Books, Perth, WA, Australia.

MCCARTHY, MICHAEL
1990 *Zuytdorp.* A Report on the Situation to Date. Report No. 42. Department of Maritime Archaeology, Western Australian Maritime Museum, Perth, Australia.
1996 *SS Xantho*: An Iron Steamship Wreck—Towards a New Perspective in Maritime Archaeology. Doctoral dissertation, Department of Archaeology, James Cook University, Townsville, QLD, Australia.
1998 Australian Maritime Archaeology: Changes, Their Antecedents, and the Path Ahead. *Australian Archaeology*, 47:33–38.

MORSE, KATE
1988 An Archaeological Survey of Midden Sites near the *Zuytdorp* Wreck, Western Australia. *The Bulletin of the Australian Institute for Maritime Archaeology*, 12(1):37–40.

MUCKELROY, KENNETH
1978 *Maritime Archaeology.* Cambridge University Press, Cambridge, England.

MURPHY, LARRY
1983 Shipwrecks as Data Base for Human Behavioral Studies. In *Shipwreck Archaeology*, Richard Gould, editor, pp. 65–90. University of New Mexico Press, Albuquerque.

NASH, MICHAEL
1997 *Cargo for the Colony: The Wreck of the Merchant Ship* Sydney Cove. Braxus Press, Sydney, NSW, Australia.

NICOLSON, ROBERT
1965 *The Pitcairners.* Angus and Robertson, Sydney, NSW, Australia.

NUTLEY, DAVID
1995 More Than a Shipwreck: The Convict Ship *Hive*—Aboriginal and European Contact Site. *The Bulletin of the Australian Institute for Maritime Archaeology*, 19(2):17–26.

ORME, ZUSANA, AND NUALA RANDALL
   1987   A Survey of the Historical Limestone Structures on West Wallabi Island, Houtman Abrolhos. *The Bulletin of the Australian Institute for Maritime Archaeology*, 11(2):25–31.

PIGGIN, S.
   1987   Disasters. In *Australians: A Guide to Sources*, D. H. Borchardt, editor. Fairfax Syme and Weldon, Sydney, NSW, Australia.

PLAYFORD, PHILLIP
   1996   *Carpet of Silver: The Wreck of the* Zuytdorp. University of Western Australia Press, Perth, Australia.

RATHE, GUSTAVE
   1992   *The Wreck of the* Barque Stefano *off the Northwest Cape of Australia in 1975*. Cannongate Press, Edinburgh, Scotland.

READ, FRANK
   1954   *The Romance of the Great Barrier Reef*. Angus and Robertson, Sydney, NSW, Australia.

ROBINSON, KEVIN
   1988   *Perseverant* Survivors Camp. Report No. 34, Department of Maritime Archaeology, Western Australian Maritime Museum, Fremantle, Australia.

SPENCER-WOOD, SUZANNE M. (EDITOR)
   1987   *Consumer Choice in Historical Archaeology*. Plenum Press, London, England.

STRACHAN, SHIRLEY
   1986   The History and Archaeology of the *Sydney Cove* Shipwreck (1797): A Resource for Future Site Work. *Occasional Papers in Prehistory No. 5, Research School of Pacific Studies*. Australian National University, Canberra, ACT.

TYLOR, PETER
   1970   The *Batavia* Mutineers: Evidence of an Anabaptist "Fifth Column" within 17th-Century Dutch Colonialism. *Westerly*, 4:33–45.

VAN DER GRAAF, ADRIAAN
   1727   *Journal of the Understeerman Adriaan van der Graaf*. The Hague, ARA, VOC Archives, Zeeland, series no. 1691, C. de Heer, translator. Western Australian Maritime Museum, Fremantle, Australia.

VETH, PETER, AND MICHAEL MCCARTHY
   1999   Types of Explanation in Maritime Archaeology: The Case of the *SS Xantho*. *Australian Archaeology*, 48: 12–15.

WARD, INGRID, PIERS LARCOMBE, AND PETER VETH
   1999   A New Process-Based Model for Wreck Site Formation. *Journal of Archaeological Science*, 26:561–570.

WEAVER, FIONA
   1994   Report of the Excavations of Previously Disturbed Land Sites Associated with the VOC Ship *Zuytdorp*, Wrecked 1712, Zuytdorp Cliffs, Western Australia. Report No. 90, Department of Maritime Archaeology, Western Australian Maritime Museum, Fremantle, Australia.

MARTIN GIBBS
DEPARTMENT OF ARCHAEOLOGY
JAMES COOK UNIVERSITY
TOWNSVILLE, QUEENSLAND 5001 AUSTRALIA

Franklin H. Price
Nathan Richards

Conflict and Commerce: Maritime Archaeological Site Distribution as Cultural Change on the Roanoke River, North Carolina

ABSTRACT

For centuries, the transportation provided by the Roanoke River, North Carolina, has played a vital role in the economic and military history of the area. The Civil War illustrated the importance of the waterway as a military consideration, when both the Union and the Confederacy strove to control the river. The conflict inflicted grievous harm upon the region's maritime transportation. Taken as a whole, the shipwrecks and abandoned vessels of the river provide an exceptional vantage point regarding questions of technology and economy, both in times of peace and when these tranquil periods are juxtaposed against warfare and upheaval. This research uses statistical and geo-spatial analyses of the shipwrecks and abandoned vessels of the Roanoke River in an attempt to discern anthropological patterns. Both historical and archaeological data are the subject of investigation. Three major themes: manner of loss, trade, and technology, are explored primarily to interpret how cultural change is reflected in the assemblage of shipwrecked and abandoned vessels of the waterway. The trends that emerge are often interwoven among these themes, and through them, this paper attempts to explain such diverse phenomena as shifting trade patterns, wreck clustering, vessel dimensions, and the dichotomy of behavior between times of war and times of peace.

Introduction

This article represents a synopsis of a comparative study of 62 watercraft historically or archaeologically documented as wrecked or abandoned on the Roanoke River, North Carolina, from the river mouth to the fall line at Weldon (Figure 1). Using statistical and geo-spatial analyses, the major aim of the research was to ascertain whether trends regarding cultural change could be gleaned from such an assemblage. The study aimed to answer how the archaeological resources of the Roanoke

River reflect cultural change. Lines of enquiry addressed what the maritime historical and archaeological resources of the Roanoke River reveal about the topics of circumstance of loss, technology, and trade within the region.

A study of an assemblage of shipwrecks and abandoned vessels by necessity is obligated to use a comparative approach. Numerous archaeologists have stressed the importance of such work. For example, the contributions of Gould (1983), Lenihan (1983), and Murphy (1983) in *Shipwreck Anthropology* called for broad theoretical approaches to maritime archaeology. Overall, this work is comparative and generalist, placing the sites within the framework of historical and anthropological trends. Far from a refutation of the historically particularist approach, a comparative study undertakes the task of synthesizing particularist studies into the larger framework of anthropology and history. This approach is applicable to lost watercraft because their archaeological value is greater than what can be learned from a particularist study alone (Richards 2002:49).

Several authors have produced significant works in the realm of riverine and/or regional shipwreck and watercraft discard research. Notable examples include studies in the United States (Shomette 1982, 1995; Kenderdine 1994a, 1994b, 1995a; Babits et al. 1995; Babits and Kjorness 1995; Shomette and Eshelman 1998; Parker 2000), in Australia (Coroneos 1997; Coroneos and McKinnon 1997; Duncan 2000; Foster 1987-1990; Jordan 1995; Kenderdine 1995b; Doyle 2000; Richards 2002, 2003), and Northern Ireland (McElrean et al. 2002). Like these, this research investigated and analyzed an assemblage of vessels in one geographic area.

As a comparative study of the shipwrecks of the Roanoke River, this article deals with an over-arching view of the region. Since a large measure of this interpretation concerns the relationship between the lost vessel assemblage and the physical landscape, this analysis must consider landscape archaeology, particularly work in Cultural Landscapes by Hoskins (1955), Sauer (1963) and especially

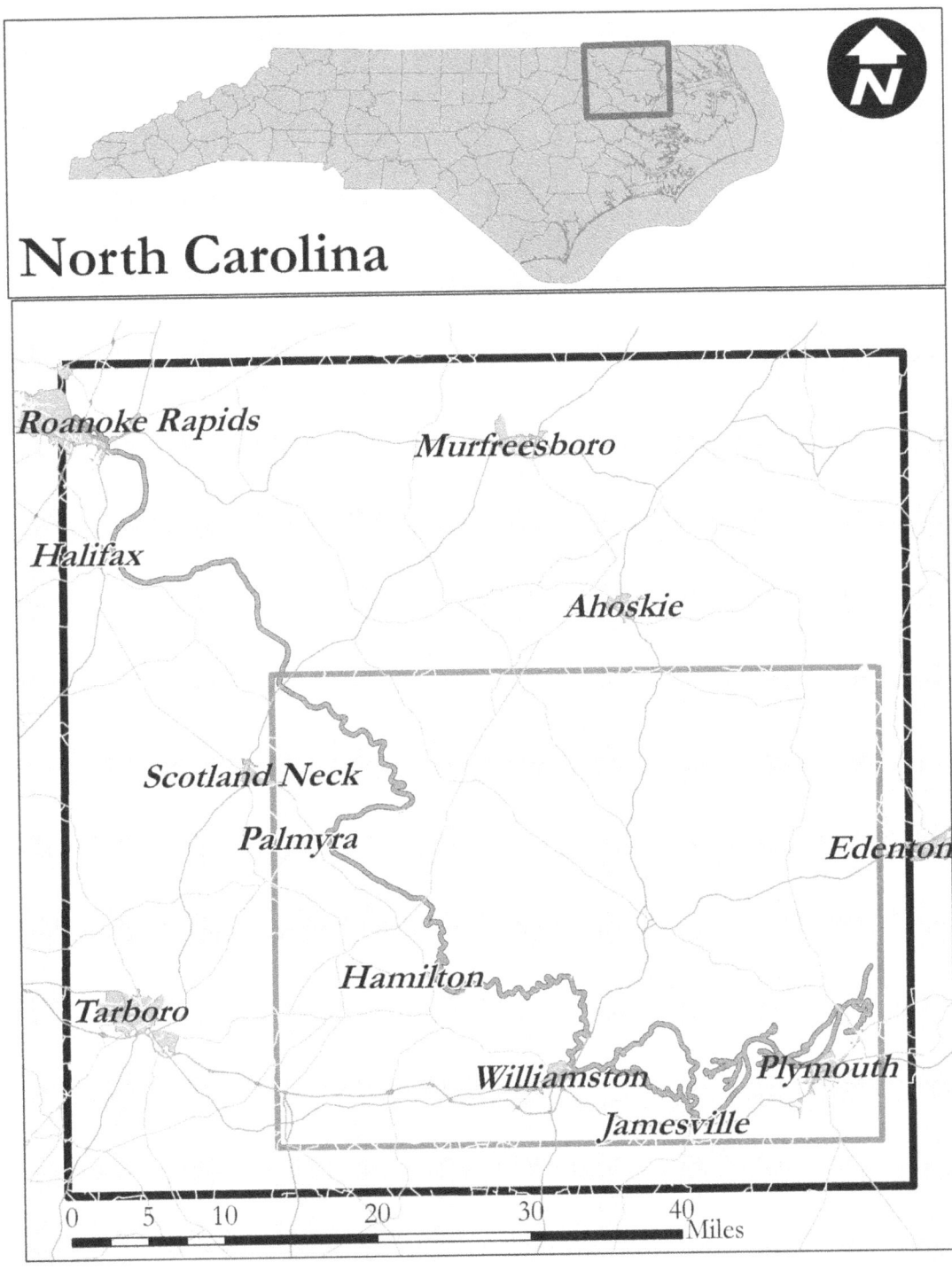

FIGURE 1. The Roanoke River and study area, inset. (Drawing by N. Richards.)

Christaller (1966). Maritime Cultural Landscapes Theory is a selection of geographically-based, anthropologically-informed paradigms that was also helpful in interpreting the Roanoke River assemblage (Westerdahl 1992; Jasiński 1993; Parker 2000; McElrean et al. 2002; Flatman 2003).

Methods included the consultation of historical sources and archaeological records pertaining to vessels lost between Weldon and the mouth of the river, and fieldwork including remote sensing in the spring of 2005 and the identification and exploration of sites and sonar anomalies on the river between Jamesville and Plymouth, North Carolina in the summer of 2005. Due to time and budget restrictions, upper Roanoke River ports (such as Weldon) could not be surveyed (see Friedman 2008 for details regarding an expanded remote sensing coverage). During this phase, investigators rediscovered three wrecks, two landings, and documented three above-water abandoned vessels. The final phase of the project included processing and analyzing data by consolidating it into Microsoft Access and interpreting it geospatially with ESRI *ArcMap GIS*.

Historical Background

The history of the Roanoke River may be divided into five chronological periods: Pre-Columbian to Colonial, Antebellum, Civil War, Late 19th-early 20th Century, and 20th Century. Each period contains defining characteristics. The river's history illustrates two main themes, the destructive nature of the Civil War and trends in vessel design. Historically, transportation patterns on the Roanoke River changed from the paddled vessels of Native Americans through sail to steam, and onward to the self-propelled barges of the 20th century. It was not until recently that the river itself lost its role as the region's primary transportation avenue. Although the river now lies relatively quiet, the detritus of past activity can be found in and around the waterway. This evidence yields a wealth of information regarding the Roanoke River and those who plied its course in trade and in war.

On the North Carolina portion of the river, the only archaeological example known from before European contact is the Rhodes Site, a Native American site consisting of a terrestrial component eroding into the river (Burke 1982:1). No canoes, dugouts, or other native watercraft have been discovered. The Colonial period (1650-1776) also exhibits an absence of wrecked vessels in the historical and archaeological records. Colonial settlement of the river basin, with accompanying maritime trade, would suggest that there should be wrecked vessels present. For example, the towns of Williamston and Hamilton sold lucrative pine products in exchange for the rum, salt, and molasses of the West Indies as early as the 1770s (Manning and Booker 1977a:74, 1977b:60,165). The river also provided a direct conduit for tobacco from as far as Virginia, brought downstream in flatboats (Manning and Booker 1977b:2; Dobbs 1984:89-90). The lack of vessels from the Colonial period is especially puzzling considering the importance of Halifax as the state capital and a center of trade. One would assume that numerous vessels would have been lost as they connected this important town with the outside world.

During the Antebellum years (ca. 1820-1861), use of steam power began its slow transformation of the region's transportation patterns. The adaptation of the steam engine to both terrestrial and marine environments affected regional traffic before 1820 (Watson 1982:43). Experiments with economically viable steam power came relatively early to the lower Roanoke. By the third decade of the 19th century, the Roanoke witnessed regular steam service (*Carolina Observer* 1827).

In the middle of the century, tar, pitch, turpentine, milled lumber, and fishing comprised the major industries on the river (Watson 1982:58). Hamilton had at least two steam lumber mills in the 1840s and 1850s (Manning and Booker 1977b:173). The importance of turpentine and tar remained vital to the region's economy for decades. Of naval stores, it has been written: "...the heart of coastal North Carolina pumped pine sap" (Cecelski 2001:131).

There is a complete lack of shipwrecks in the historical record before the 1831 loss of the Virginian steamer *North Carolina* (Emmerson 1949:133; Whitfield 2004:45). This is puzzling, with the documented economic activities in the region of trade, fishing, and even shipbuilding predating this substantially (Cornell 1833:1; Francis M. Manning Papers 1848:4-5). In the years leading to the Civil War, the schooner *Lady of the Lake* was lost in 1851 at the mouth of the Roanoke, and the steamer *Liberty,* "burned to the water's edge" at Plymouth in April of 1857 (*Tri-Weekly Commercial* 1857; Angley 1995:100). The lack of reported shipwrecks in the historical record should not lead to the assumption that few wrecks occurred along the Roanoke before the Civil War. Instead, as was observed in a Swedish case study, the absence of documented shipwrecks could be a function of the lack of a developed system to record these tragedies (Cederlund 1980:97). In the region, the appearance of periodicals occurred rather late. In Martin County, for example, the populace was not served by a newspaper until 1855 (Manning and Booker 1977a:265).

A sober assessment of the damage incurred during the years of the Civil War reads as a case study in the havoc that warfare can inflict upon a maritime transportation system. Widespread destruction resulted from the struggle between the United States and the Confederacy over control of the waterway.

The Roanoke River was the key to achieving a major strategic objective: the railroad at Weldon (Frankle 1900:93; Barrett 1963:31-32). With this supply line cut, the Confederate forces would be in a severely weakened position. The Confederacy, well aware of the river's strategic value, attempted to keep Union forces as far away from the railroad as possible. The epicenter of this drama for control rested over Plymouth, the first major settlement upstream, a town that changed hands in 1862, and twice in 1864. Most naval losses on the river took place near the town, or in attempts to defend it.

The Union first took Plymouth on 14 May 1862, with a flotilla of Federal gunboats, and held the town until the spring of 1864 (Barrett 1963:123). The US Navy had the initiative along the river, and the situation appeared grim from the Confederate perspective.

The Confederates turned to nineteen-year-old Gilbert Elliott, providing him with a contract to build the iron-clad ram *Albemarle,* completed in the spring of 1864 (Still 1971:91). Through intelligence sources, the US Navy became aware of something strange and powerful in the upper reaches of river (Flusser 1921:474-475).

In an attempt to block the vessel's passage, the Union sunk a series of vessels at Broad Creek during the late winter and early spring of 1864 (Lawrence 2002:1). This produced the largest cluster of wrecks along the river, referred to collectively as the Broad Creek Blockade. The vessels *Isabella Ellis,* CSS *Comet, Long Shoal Light Boat,* as well as light ships and other schooners that have as yet to be identified, were intentionally sunk to hinder downstream navigation, particularly in the hopes of stopping the ram CSS *Albemarle* (Flusser 1899:609-610). Unfortunately for the Union Navy, the Broad Creek obstructions failed in their objective

and the ironclad passed over them in an unseasonable freshet (Feuer 1989:50-52).

CSS *Albemarle* provided pivotal support for the Confederate capture of Plymouth, sinking the Union gunboat USS *Southfield,* and driving off the USS *Miami* on 19 April 1864 (United States Department of the Navy 1976:570). This facilitated the fall of the town, including the last Union holdouts in Fort Williams, on 20 April 1864 (Wessels 1891:296-301; Morrill 2002:378). *Albemarle* was already proven in battle as a force in and of herself. The vessel did not need other ships in order to engage the enemy; it could fight on its own and operated un-attached to any squadron (Still 1961:340). The ironclad "threatened Union control of the North Carolina Sounds" (Still 1971:229). This turn of events was of great concern to the Union (Peck 1891:288; Taylor 1998:222). In the Roanoke River, the advantage shifted into the hands of the Confederacy.

This initiative lasted until the night of 27 October 1864 when, after an aborted attempt at capturing *Albemarle,* an expedition led by William B. Cushing sank the ironclad with a spar torpedo (Morrill 2002:383). Although Cushing lost the steam launch under his charge, he escaped with his life and made it back to Union lines. With the ironclad out of the way, the United States Navy seized the advantage and re-captured Plymouth on Halloween of 1864 (Macomb 1900:12-15; Carbone 2001:19). In order to defend the town, Confederate forces submerged a variety of obstructions downriver, but these were as ineffective as Union attempts to halt the progress of *Albemarle* some months before. The Union Navy merely bypassed the obstructions by sending the flotilla up the Middle River (English 1900:19).

Although they held Plymouth, the Union had trouble in proceeding into the upper reaches of the tributary. The Confederates had turned the river into a dangerous nest of mines, known then as torpedoes (*North Carolina Times* 1864). These mines sunk the USS *Otsego,* a *Sassacus* class gunboat over 200 ft. in length, and the 70 ft. tug *Bazely,* near Jamesville in December 1864 (*North Carolina Times* 1864; *North Carolina Presbyterian* 1865; Marsh 1921:43; Canney 1990:313) (Figure 2).

The end of the war produced examples of scuttling and sabotage as Confederates strove to

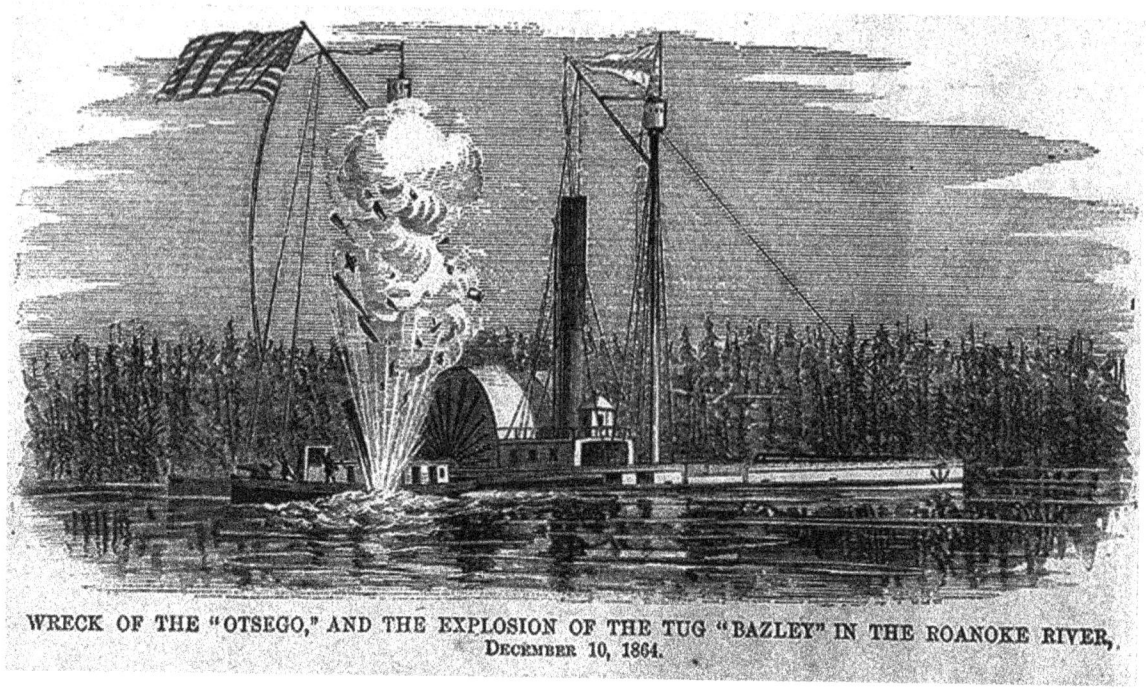

WRECK OF THE "OTSEGO," AND THE EXPLOSION OF THE TUG "BAZLEY" IN THE ROANOKE RIVER, DECEMBER 10, 1864.

FIGURE 2. "Wreck of the 'Otsego,' and the Explosion of the Tug 'Bazley' [sic] in the Roanoke River." (*Harper's Weekly*, 21 January 1865, p.44.)

keep resources out of Union hands. As the war drew to a close, Confederates scuttled a steamer, a lighter, and cut loose an unfinished vessel to be claimed by the torpedoes (Howell 1901:164-165; Silverstone 1989:209). Other vessels lost in the war included a floating battery "sunk in a sand bar" in April 1865 at Gray's Landing between Plymouth and Jamesville and the Roanoke Light Ship sunk off Willow Bend in 1862 (Brown et al. 1837:1; Franklin 1901:108; Lawrence 2003:15).

The Civil War led to the sinking of a large proportion of the vessels reported lost along the Roanoke River. Put into perspective, the losses during four years are comparable to the total number of vessels known to have been lost throughout the remainder of the river's history.

Passenger and freight service resumed not long after the war, and railroads began to connect towns by land. Steamer routes connected Windsor and Plymouth, Elizabeth City and Williamston, Williamston and Edenton, and Plymouth and Franklin, Virginia (*The Morning Star* 1875; *Wilmington Star* 1879; *Tarboro Southerner* 1880; Watson 1982:43). Although the western part of the state was joined with the ocean by rail in 1856, it took more than 30 years for service to come to Jamesville and Plymouth (Watson 1984:225). Decades passed before the economy of the area recovered. A look at the advance of the railroads to the region reveals that most roads were not finished until the 1880s. It was not until 1882 that the Wilmington and Weldon spur line ran to Scotland Neck, reaching Kinston by 1890 (Prince 1966:13). Tarboro and Williamston were also connected in 1882 (Manning and Booker 1977b:47-48). The Seaboard and Raleigh Railroad completed a line to Williamston in 1883, and extended it to Plymouth via Jamesville in 1889 (Prince 1966:13). Jamesville and Washington, as well as Hamilton and Tarboro, were joined in 1887 (Manning and Booker 1977b:76,80-82). As will be investigated below, the resultant shift in transportation patterns had a nearly immediate impact on the distribution of shipwrecks and abandoned vessels on the lower river.

On the Roanoke, the main characteristic of 20th century riverine trade is the dominance of the river barge. By mid-century, the barge entirely replaced the steamer in the archaeological record with the same completeness that the steamer had replaced sailing craft of the previous century. Investigators have identified the remains of numerous barges along the river. These include *Rodney Phillips McPhie, Jr.,* a barge of more than 150 ft. in length, and *Susan Preston McPhie,* of similar dimensions, both sunk in Plymouth in 1959 (United States Treasury Department 1959:701,710; Tidewater Atlantic Research 1990:13-15). Other archaeologically investigated examples include the 80 ft. long "Poplar Point Barge" and the 110 ft. by 30 ft. "Fort Branch Barge" (Wilde-Ramsing 1982a:4,8, 1982b:4,7). These vessels may be indicative of a shift in maritime trade away from the long distance transportation provided by earlier steamers, and toward a more localized trade characterized by barges. The presence of numerous 20th-century barges reflects a change in the nature of riverine transport, as affected by railroads and highways.

Commercial river traffic was phased out over the course of the century. Passenger boat service ended in the 1930s, and by the 1950s freight and passenger steamers were replaced by less frequent "oil and pulpwood barges" (Watson 1982:44). Despite the end of its heyday as a transportation medium, in the 1970s there was "considerable river traffic in wood products, fertilizer materials, oils and lubricants" (Manning and Booker 1977a:73). Slowly, however, land-based transportation replaced river borne commerce. Eventually "...river traffic all but ceased due to pressure from developing railroads and ultimately truck freight industries" (Tidewater Atlantic Research 1990:10). The rise of efficient, cost-effective railroads and automobiles forever changed the riverine transportation network, ending what had been a continuous pattern throughout the Roanoke River's history. From the distant past the river itself was the most important conduit for people and goods in the region. During the 20th century, land routes rose to prominence and the river became an avenue for slow local barge traffic.

Statistical and Geospatial Analyses

As previously discussed, this research is an attempt at a comparative work, with the aim of moving beyond particularism. One of the avenues available to undertake a comprehensive study is a statistical investigation of the entire assemblage. This method allowed the research to expose larger anthropological and historical patterns from the sample, in answer to the call of Gould (1983), Lenihan (1983), and Murphy (1983), and following the works such as those of Duncan (2000, 2004) and Richards (2002, 2004).

The most glaring problem with the statistical analyses is sample size. This entire study deals with 63 vessels. Of these, only 22 have build dates and 42 have loss years, presenting problems with the chronology and, by extension, the analyses generated from it. Numerous unknowns among categories such as manner of loss, state or nation of build, and propulsion type also hinder the research. Due to these factors, the analyses undertaken below represent tentative interpretations that have the potential to change with future research.

Statistical analyses present only one manner of interpreting the data. The various statistical analyses need to be grounded spatially in order to better understand the relationships between these variables and the landscape of the Roanoke River. The following section investigates these avenues of analysis in the hopes of providing more insight into the assemblage and the cultural life of the river.

Bridging statistics and the landscape, this section concerns itself with the geo-spatial patterns of vessel loss, while an assessment of the relationship between statistics and the river's geography was also undertaken. What follows are a sequence of statistical and/or geospatial analyses focused upon examinations of manner of watercraft loss, site chronology and distribution, trade and function analyses, as well as an examination of build location and technology.

Manner of Loss

The assemblage was divided into the categories of wrecked (catastrophically lost), abandoned (deliberately lost), and unknown manner of loss. Abandonment events themselves were further subdivided into vessels deliberately burned, sent adrift, beached, and scuttled. The shipwrecks, broken down into a larger array of causes of loss, represent eight separate circumstances. These include running aground, artillery, collision, fire, foundered, mine, torpedo attack, and unknown. The purpose of this analysis is to ascertain potential differences in wrecking and abandoning behaviors.

Abandonment was the largest cause of vessel loss on the river: 44% of the vessels lost on the river were abandoned, compared to 32% wrecked, and 24% of unknown fate. In Shomette's study of the Patuxent River, Maryland, abandoned vessels comprised 29% of the resource (Shomette and Eshelman 1998:332-333).

Abandonment events illustrate divergent wartime and peacetime behaviors. Warfare abandonment events comprise a surprisingly large percentage of all vessels lost on the river. It accounts for 30% of all vessels lost and 63% of abandonment events. Abandoning a vessel by scuttling often had a military purpose beyond keeping a vessel out of enemy hands; in the case of block ships they were in essence still in use as immobile barriers. A breakdown of wartime abandonment events illustrates the importance of strategic behaviors regarding watercraft discard during conflict. Almost two thirds of the vessels lost during the war were abandoned as block ships. This behavior is best termed "strategic discard," as strategic considerations trumped economic concerns regarding vessel abandonment during wartime on the river and often occurred within navigation channels. Peacetime methods for disposing of a vessel included beaching or scuttling out of the navigation channel. These represent a different motivation for abandonment than wartime events as discard occurred for economic reasons.

Shipwrecks account for nearly a third of the assemblage. Peacetime shipwrecks met their end due to fire, running aground, and foundering. Those sunk during war were lost via artillery, mines, torpedo attack, and intentional collision. The unknown in the category of cause of loss comprise 10%.

A look at wartime shipwrecks illuminates the essential difference between peacetime and wartime vessel losses on the river. During peacetime, economics and trade are the driving factors, while in wartime, strategy is paramount. Indeed, every vessel wrecked during the Civil War was related to a strategic concern. The Union vessels lost during the Confederate recapture of Plymouth met their end in a vain attempt to defend the town. Cushing sank CSS *Albemarle* to shift the advantage to the Union side. The torpedo nest that destroyed USS

Otsego and USS *Bazely* was designed to prevent the Union from capitalizing on their newfound advantage. War losses represent the utility of a selection of both offensive and defensive weaponry. Mines, torpedoes, artillery, and ramming all contribute as causes of loss.

Fire was the most common cause of shipwrecks; 40% of all wrecked vessels were lost to fire. The phenomenon could perhaps be related to steam technology as vessels propelled with steam engines appear more likely to burn. It could exemplify an inherent danger in the technology, at least during most of the 19th century, when problems with boiler explosions were compounded by an often lackadaisical attitude toward their inspection (Morrison 1953:591; Burke 1966:4). Kenderdine noted a similar trend among Murray River steamers in Australia (Kenderdine 1995a:169). Although the evidence linking fires with steamers is far from conclusive, numerous fire losses exist in the historical and archaeological records. *North Carolina* was lost in 1831, and the schooner *Liberty* in 1857. A series of steamers, *Commerce* (1883), *Ranger* (1896), and *Mayflower* (1920), burned in Williamston, Hamilton and Plymouth respectively (*The Morning Star* 1883; *Wilmington Messenger* 1896). *Rotary* (1882) and *City of Long Branch* (1892) burned at unknown locations on the river (*The Economist* 1882). The final vessel lost to fire also burned in the environs of a town. *Lucille Ross*, a diesel-powered vessel, burned and sank near the Jamesville pier in 1950.

When compared to other studies, evidence suggests that, at least statistically, this high proportion of fire loss may be regional. Shomette and Eshelman noted that 14.2% of the vessels in their study of the Patuxent were lost to fire (Shomette and Eshelman 1998:333). Nine of the 63 vessels, or 14.3%, on the Roanoke River perished in fires. In Australia, a different pattern emerged from their maritime shipwreck studies. Three studies of Australian shipwreck assemblages produced values between 7.6% and 8.3% that had been lost to fire (Jordan 1995:62; Coroneos 1997:102; Coroneos and McKinnon 1997:96). Potentially fire casualties may simply represent different working conditions, or could theoretically indicate differences in either technological developments in propulsion technology and variations in the degree of regulation of maritime transport between regions and nations.

Although urban site clustering did occur, from a geospatial standpoint abandonment events were more likely than shipwrecks to occur at various locations along the river's length instead of concentrated in towns (Figure 3). With time, abandonment events became progressively more likely to occur within the environs of the two downriver towns, an observation that is mirrored in the pattern of shipwrecked vessels.

In the case of Plymouth, commercial enterprise and watercraft discard apparently correlate. A plywood and veneer business, begun in 1912, may be associated with a substantial number of discarded barges (Tidewater Atlantic Research 1990:13). Previous literature agrees that abandonment events can have a relationship to businesses or to centers of trade (Shomette and Eshelman 1982:583; Kenderdine 1994a:71-72, 1994b:23; Richards 2002:231). This may be what

is witnessed in Plymouth. Discarded vessels on the Roanoke River were likely to be deposited at the bank of the main waterway, out of the navigation channel, corroborating the assumption that "perceived threats to navigation [will] define abandonment location" (Richards 2002:249; see also Babits and Kjorness 1995:28,76,78). Due to a variety of factors, wrecking events were even more likely to occur near towns than abandonment events. One cause could be a relationship between technology and ports, as steam vessels tended to wreck near population centers. These wrecking events occurred either as acts of war, such as actions carried out during the struggle for control of Plymouth, or during peacetime largely as the result of fires.

An analysis of the vessels lost, comparing wartime and peacetime vessel deposition, reveals two very different sets of behaviors (Figure 4). Wartime vessels were not always lost in areas of battle; in fact, as elucidated above, they were

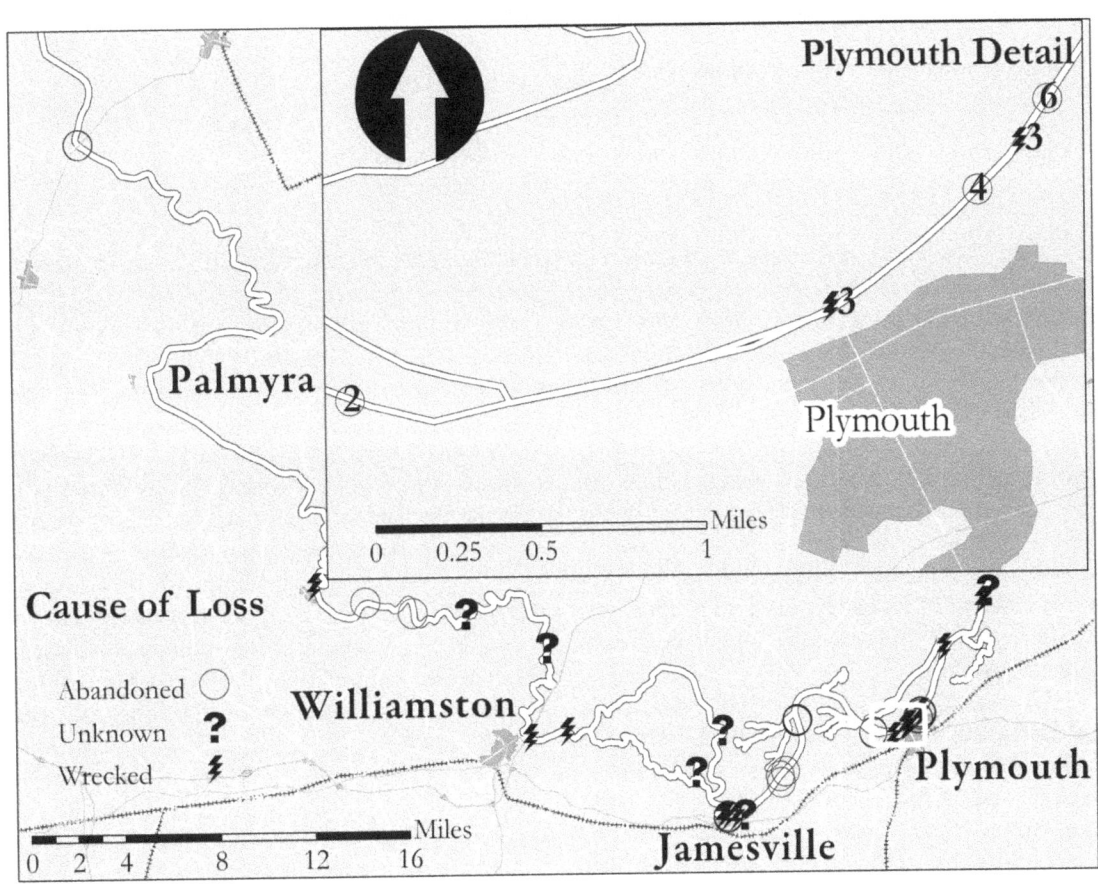

FIGURE 3. Cause of loss. (Drawing by N. Richards.)

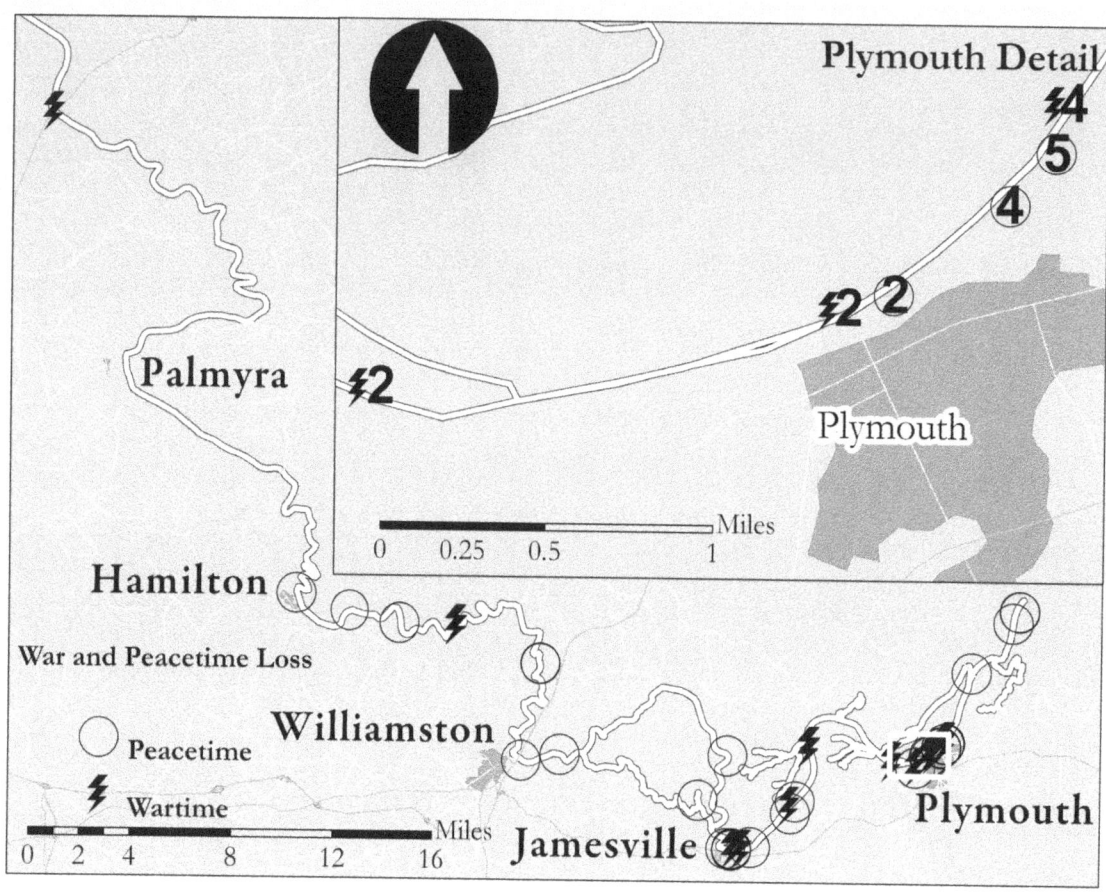

FIGURE 4. Vessel loss during war and peace. (Drawing by N. Richards.)

not even more likely to be lost in combat. The wartime loss assemblage can be further subdivided into the categories of shipwrecks and abandoned watercraft. The shipwrecks from this assemblage occur in the major areas of contention, Jamesville and Plymouth, at times when these areas were in a state of flux or combat. The abandonment events occurred due to the two situations discussed already, they were either abandoned in order to prevent capture, such as the scuttled floating battery, or they were sunk as block ships, such as *Comet,* but they were never abandoned without some greater strategic purpose.

This strategic purpose can be graphically represented as a reaction to shifting initiatives during the war. As discussed in the historical background, after the Union began to lose momentum, they consolidated their gains by blockading the channel at Broad Creek and Tallow Island in 1864. Block ships, as with the

Confederate defenses that followed, represent geographic markers of control and initiative. Once a side perceived that it was losing momentum it set up obstructions to prevent a counter-attack. After Lieutenant Cushing sank the CSS *Albemarle,* the Confederates exhibited the same behavior and placed a series of schooners around the wreck of the USS *Southfield* to prevent the Union from using its newly seized initiative to recapture Plymouth. Blockading the river is a strategically bankrupt idea for a navy considering an offensive, as a blocked channel would make it impossible to continue advancing. Strategically abandoned watercraft are, in the above cases, the material embodiment of the loss of initiative.

Peacetime behavior, however, reveals no such military concerns, and is instead governed by economic situations. Vessel loss locations, when examined as peacetime events, fail to provide any pattern other than persistent clustering

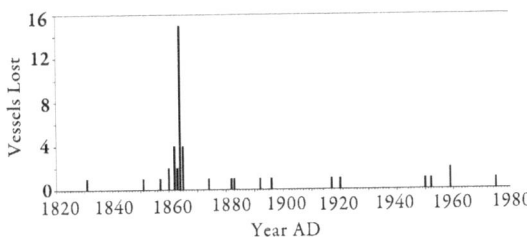

FIGURE 5. Number of vessels lost by year (n=41). (Drawing by N. Richards.)

at centers of trade on the lower river, itself indicative of economic concerns.

Chronology and Distribution

The largest chronological pattern involved the clustering of wrecking and abandonment events around the Civil War, highlighting a huge numerical discrepancy in vessels lost between 1861-1865 and all other times (Figure 5). The war was unequivocally the largest single cause of loss during the study period, driving home the magnitude of the conflict's destructiveness. Furthermore, a numerical correlation between the number of wrecks lost in 1864 and the Confederate capture, and subsequent Union recapture of Plymouth during that year, exhibits a direct link between a rise in military activity and vessel loss. In 1864 alone, 15 vessels were lost, 24% of the total, more than are documented as occurring on the Roanoke River than in any other year. These losses directly correspond to an increase in military action on the river, and illustrate the destruction wreaked upon the eastern portion of North Carolina. In the span of a few years, the river witnessed nearly as much destruction as in its entire history. At least 12 of the 1864 losses were block ships, while most of the remainder consists of vessels lost in combat: CSS *Albemarle*, USS *Bazely*, USS *Bombshell*, USS *Otsego*, and USS *Southfield*. An observation of the Patuxent River holds true in the case of the Roanoke River as well, "military activity provided a number of targets for investigation" (Shomette and Eshelman 1982:578). In Shomette and Eshelman's study of the Patuxent, they observed a lower percentage, 19%, of loss during wartime (Shomette and Eshelman

1998:333). Peacetime witnessed few specific spikes in wrecking or abandonment activity.

Arguably, the most obvious geo-spatial pattern is the concentration of vessels on the lower river. The available evidence suggests that watercraft were apparently lost, with limited exceptions, downriver from Hamilton. Both the historical and archaeological records lack the evidence to contradict the apparent absence of wrecking and abandonment events on the upper river. The importance of Jamesville and Plymouth, serving as the first two population centers encountered upstream from the mouth of the river, may be related to this phenomenon. Their roles as points of entry for incoming maritime traffic may explain the clustering. Previous studies provide two potential reasons.

Kenderdine noted that there were more wreck sites near the Murray River's mouth as vessels tended to be abandoned after their last voyage downstream (Kenderdine 1994a:72-73). It could be hypothesized that the Roanoke River witnessed a similar situation, but this would only hold true for abandoned vessels. The aggregation on the lower Roanoke includes all known vessels, whether shipwrecked or abandoned. Shomette provided an interesting observation in his studies of the Patuxent River that may have bearing on the question. He noted that submerged cultural resources were "generally buried much deeper in upriver sections" than downriver and might be more difficult to discover (Shomette and Eshelman 1982:573). It could be hypothesized that some of what remains has not been discovered because of siltation. The archaeological bias could come from a variety of causes, including the location of fieldwork and the use of side-scan sonar, which fails to detect significantly buried sites. The clustering of vessel remnants on the lower river is likely due to a variety of factors.

The second major pattern is the clustering of vessel loss near the population centers of Jamesville and Plymouth. This urban clustering is characteristic of both abandoned and wrecked vessels, more notably the latter. The phenomenon of a higher density of vessel loss at these towns is in tandem with the observations regarding wreck clustering on the lower river. This observation leads to an interesting hypothesis regarding transportation patterns and their effect upon shipwreck and abandoned vessel distribution that will be explored below.

Trade and Function

Extracting information relating to trade from the assemblage required several categories of analysis. Specifically, data regarding years of construction, tonnages, vessel function, and build location were analyzed with the intention of gleaning information regarding trade and economic patterns. This analysis brought to light relationships between local and national trade patterns, the commercial nature of riverine traffic, and a potential maritime link between the Roanoke River and the Chesapeake region.

The assemblage consists mostly of vessels built in the 19th century, with none currently known to have been built after 1937. The shift from riverine traffic toward railroad and highway transportation made vessels less economically viable. Fewer vessels used in trade resulted in decreased riverine commerce, reducing the amount of vessels lost. Manning and Booker (1977a) and Watson (1982) noted a decline in riverine commerce on the Roanoke over the course of the 20th century. This change apparently manifested itself in the archaeological record.

Function at loss, divided into the categories of support (harbor assistance or infrastructure construction and maintenance), transport (transshipment of people and cargo), unknown, and warfare, reveal the economic nature of most riverine traffic (Figure 6). Nearly half of the resource consisted of transportation vessels that may be assumed to have been engaged in economic activity. Warfare, the next largest

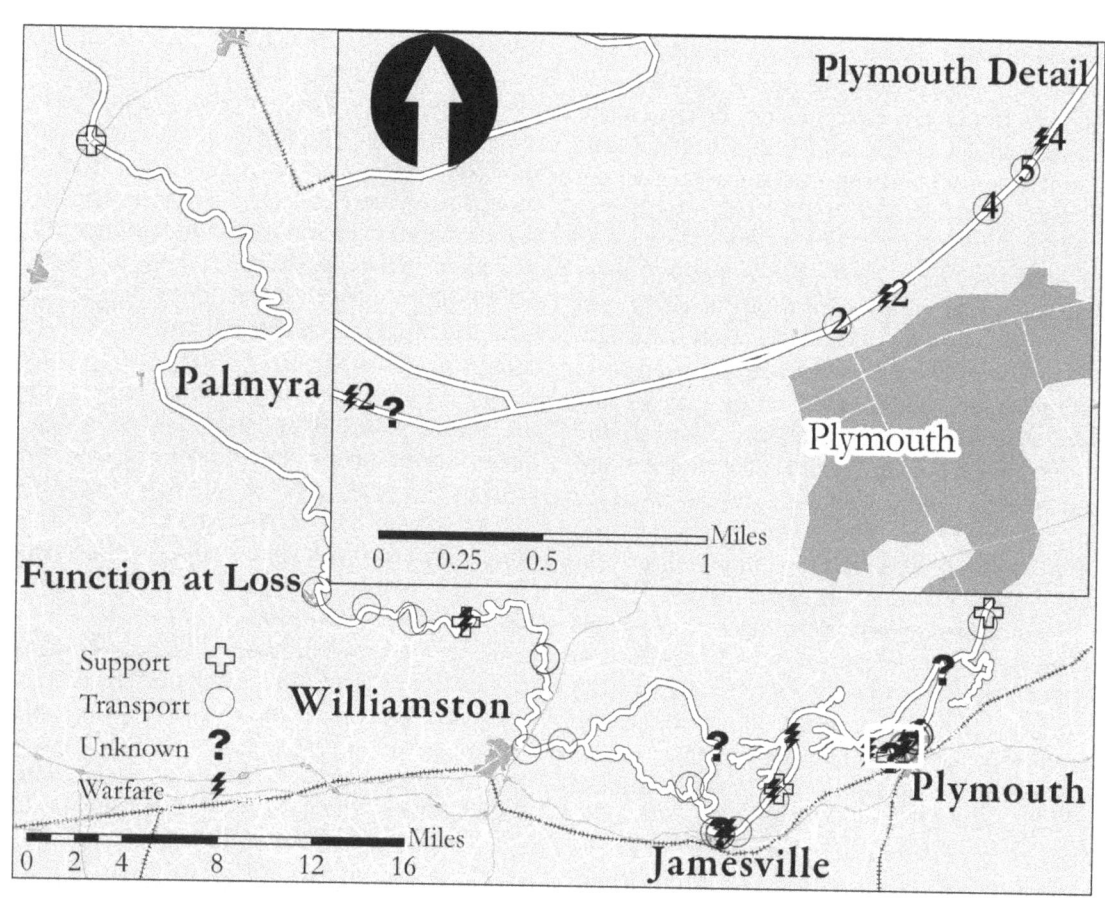

FIGURE 6. Function at loss. (Drawing by N. Richards.)

category, comprised 34% of the assemblage. Support vessels such as tugs, pile drivers, and lightships accounted for 10% of the resource. Other studies note similar trends in the dominance of trade as vessel function. Although Shomette's Patuxent River study (1995) does not have a similar breakdown of watercraft roles, studies in Australia tend to agree with the high percentages of transportation watercraft on the Roanoke River. Well over half the shipwreck assemblages of Encounter Bay and the Lower Yorke Peninsula contained vessels engaged in trade, and a study of shipwrecks at Port Philip notes that 80% of vessels were engaged in commercial activity at their time of loss (Foster 1987:21; Coroneos 1997:103; Coroneos and McKinnon 1997:98).

Surprisingly, vessels lost in warfare on the Roanoke River comprised the preponderance of known abandoned vessels, with 56% of all abandonment events occurring in merely four years. These include block ships, vessels sent adrift, and intentionally scuttled watercraft. Twenty-nine percent of abandonment events were transportation vessels, apparently involved in economic activity before they were discarded. These include vessels deposited in the environs of Plymouth and Jamesville mentioned above. Eleven percent of the remainder were support craft, and few were of unknown function.

Transportation was the function of 60% of wrecked vessels in the assemblage. This evidence appears to substantiate the notion that riverine traffic was primarily trade-related. Warfare, as a function, accounted for 25% of the vessels lost to wrecking events.

Investigations of shipping tonnages lost, loss by dimensions of vessel, function at build and loss, and chronological loss as they related to the landscape supplied the foundations for several analyses related to trade. The correlation between chronological loss and proximity to population centers was the most striking feature of this part of the geo-spatial analysis, and brought to light features of a correlation between railroads and the location of vessel loss. Although the geo-spatial relationship between the chronology of loss and trade is not immediately apparent, the analysis below supports its inclusion in this section.

The relationship between urban areas and the tonnages of lost vessels shows that larger watercraft were more likely lost near towns, as illustrated in Figure 7. As will be explored further, the clustering of wrecking events has a chronological component related to transportation patterns. With the exception of the schooners and light boats that composed the Broad Creek Blockade, the environs of Plymouth and Jamesville are the only locations along the river with more than three lost vessels of any significant tonnage. Using the criteria of vessel tonnage, the importance of the two population centers of the lower Roanoke River as centers of vessel loss continues to be brought into sharp contrast with ports further inland such as Williamston and Hamilton.

Build Location

Paralleling a paucity of chronological data, a large portion of this sample, 54%, has an unknown build location. Of those that remain, one expected pattern emerges; North Carolina produced slightly over half. New York shipyards built the second largest number of vessels lost on the Roanoke (five vessels), followed by Delaware, Maryland, Virginia, Mississippi, New Jersey, and Pennsylvania. With the exception of Southern Kraft No. 3, built in Mississippi, all vessels lost on the river were either locally built or were constructed north of the state. This could be partially explained by a combination of factors. The wartime losses of northern-built ships including the USS *Bazely,* USS *Bombshell,* USS *Otsego,* and USS *Southfield* weigh the numbers toward northern-built watercraft. The economic devastation faced by the southern states during the Civil War may have contributed to the trend, but this would only account for a small part of the total time period in question. A continuing bias in the assemblage toward local or northern-built vessels may suggest stronger trade links with the north than with states to the south.

After removing the Civil War vessels from the assemblage, an analysis of peacetime vessel losses is more likely to illuminate trade patterns. The figure may indicate a trend already extant during colonial times, that the region had strong trading ties with northern cities. For lost vessels with a known build location, Pennsylvania, Maryland, Delaware, Virginia, and New York comprise 75% of the contributions

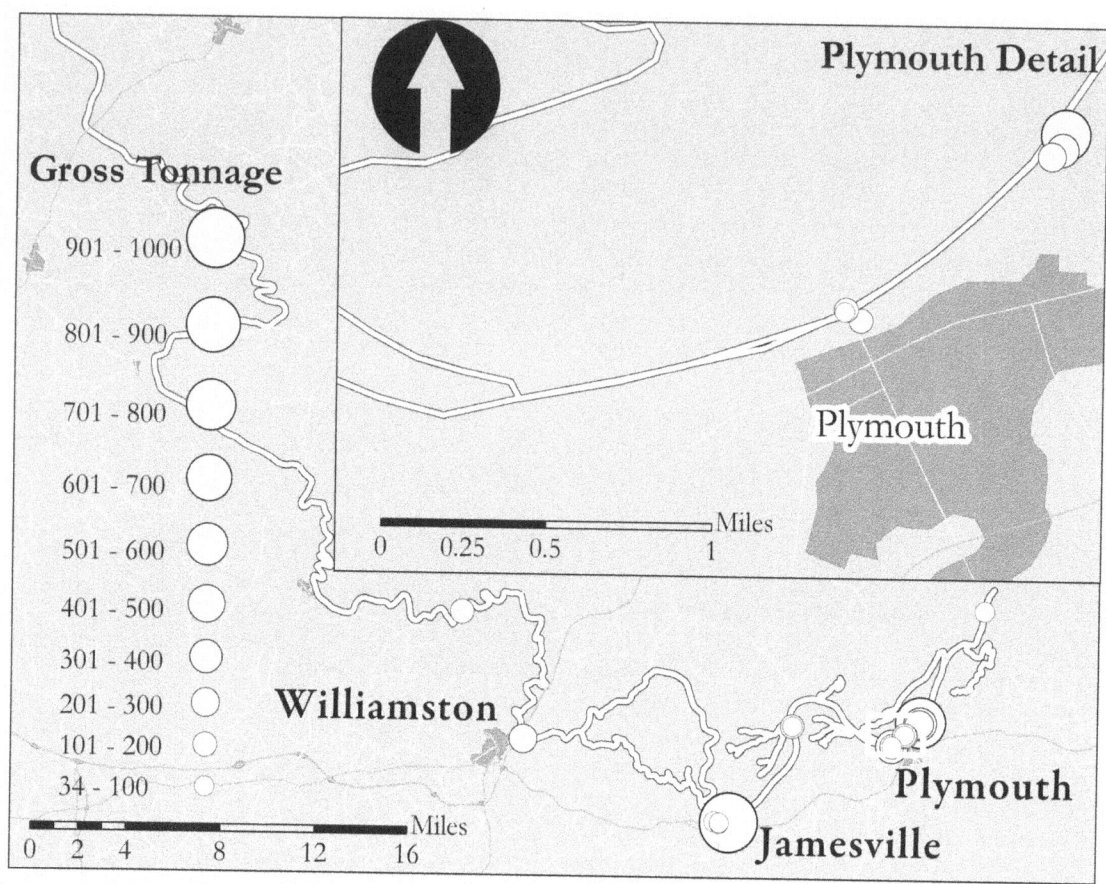

FIGURE 7. Gross tonnage of vessel at time of loss. (Drawing by N. Richards.)

to the archaeological and historical records. The figures may suggest robust maritime trade contacts between the Roanoke River and points to the north in keeping with previous research that classifies the Albemarle Sound area as part of the "Chesapeake region" (Babits et al. 1995:2).

Technology

An examination of the assemblage by propulsion subdivided into causes of loss illustrates the large difference between abandonment behavior and wrecking events. Sailing craft were more likely to be abandoned than any other vessel type. It may have been more affordable to dispose of sailing craft than to discard steam or oil driven vessels. Steamers account for the largest portion of wrecked vessels on the river.

Propulsion type is directly correlated with chronology. Historically, propulsion technolo-

gies on the river changed in a relatively orderly fashion from sail to steam to barges. The last wreck of a sailing vessel occurred in 1870, and the final documented steamer loss took place in 1920 (Manning 1870:1,3; Berman 1973). After this incident, all wrecks were either un-powered flats, barges, or oil screw vessels.

Sailing vessels were more likely to be lost outside of town environs than either steamers or oil screw vessels (Figure 8). On the Roanoke River, vessels powered by steam or oil were likely to be lost in or near population centers. The strength of the pattern is surprising. Among steam vessels with a known loss location, all but two were lost near a population center. This cannot be said of vessels in any other category except for those with an oil engine, which may suggest that chronology had a role in this aspect of geographic distribution. A breakdown of vessel loss years provides clues to a hypothesis that vessel losses near population centers

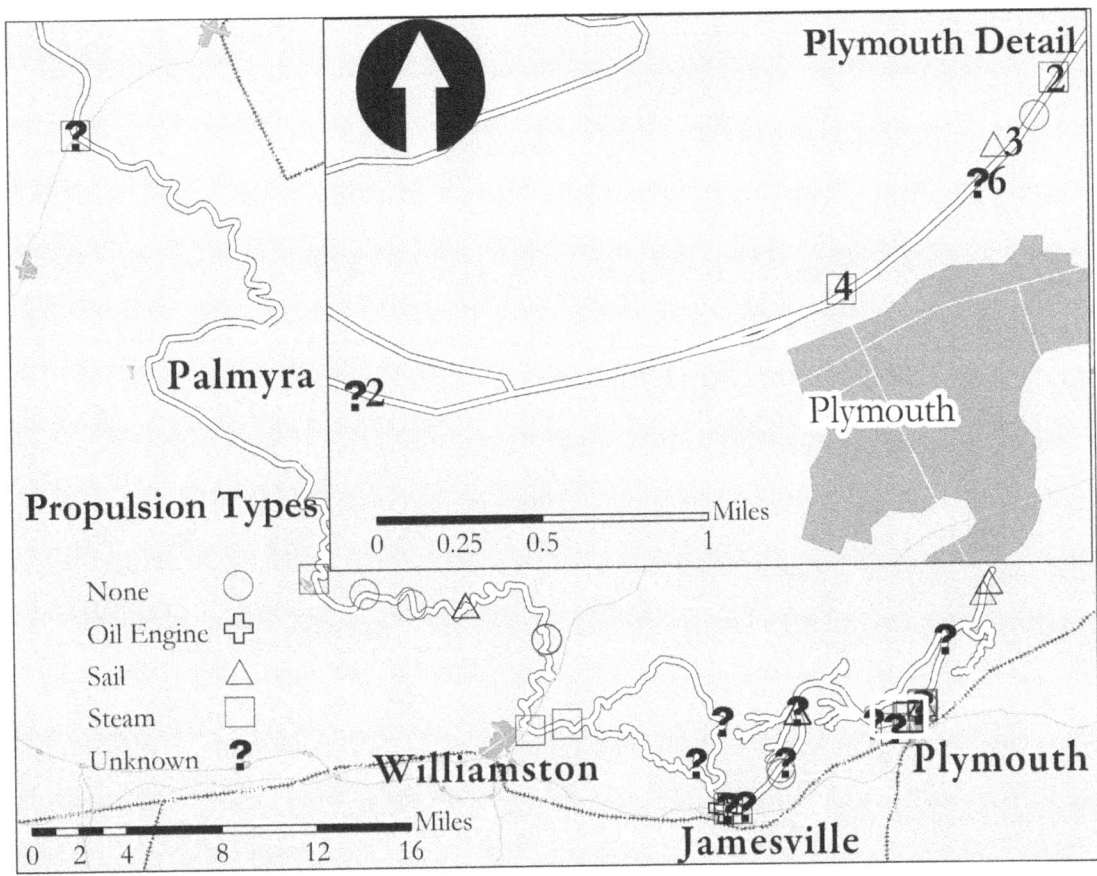

FIGURE 8. Lost vessel propulsion types. (Drawing by N. Richards.)

increased with time. The correlation, however, may go deeper than merely chronological causes, and is examined below.

While more than half of the river assemblage have unknown hull materials, of those with known hull material, all but two had wooden hulls, the exceptions being one ferrous-hulled and one armored wooden vessel. With more than half of the assemblage of unknown hull material, it is difficult to make any blanket statement. Two factors may have been responsible for the continued use of wooden hulls on the river. First, the United States did not witness a boom in the construction of metal-hulled vessels until the early 20th century (MacGregor 1984:10). The second reason may be logistical. Australian archaeologist Kenderdine also noted a low number of metal hulls in her study of the River Murray, where they comprised 10% of the River Murray's sites in South Australia (Kenderdine 1995a:148). She noted that "Iron

hulls were avoided because of the difficulties of finding leaks between riveted plates and conducting repairs in remote locations" (Kenderdine 1994b:25). There may be a similar situation between the Murray and the Roanoke in this regard. The Roanoke River was not known for any iron works, or for iron shipyards other than at Edward's Ferry.

The investigations above suggest that, as time advanced, wrecks tended to cluster near towns, especially around Plymouth and Jamesville, rather than around other parts of the river (Figure 9). At first, this phenomenon appeared to be related to technology. Steam vessels were more likely to be lost in the environs of population centers than sail vessels. Correlating the dates of vessel losses with the years that the railroads reached each town suggests that railways shifted river transportation patterns away from the numerous landings and to the rail hubs, causing a higher frequency of river traffic

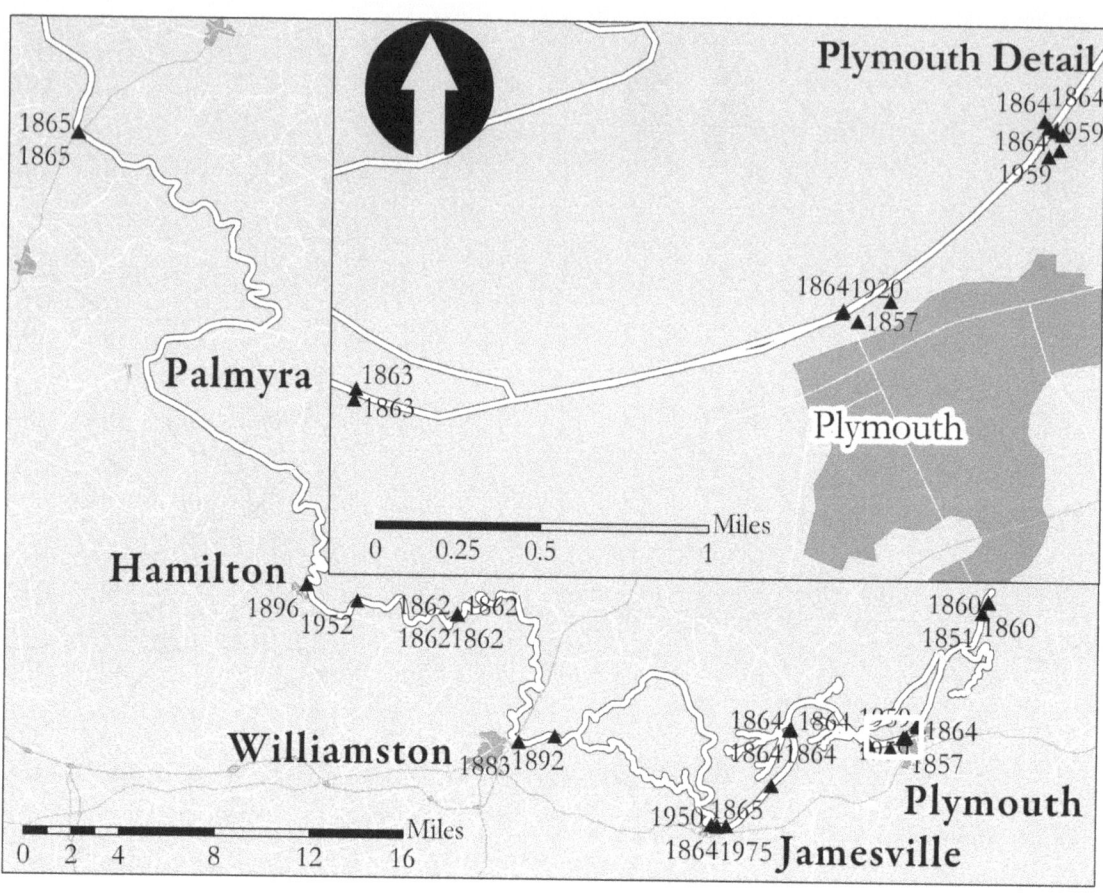

FIGURE 9. Year of loss. (Drawing by N. Richards.)

in the towns and resulting in a higher incidence of vessel loss in the environs of towns.

Although some degree of clustering occurred around the major ports, the wrecking and abandonment events over the greater part of the 19th century were more evenly distributed along the river's length than vessel losses after the 1880s. This may be reflective of a different perception of the importance of place along the river. Before the arrival of the railroads, landings held great economic importance for the populace of river communities (Brush 1953:394). In order to reach scattered settlements, before improved roads, and especially before rail travel, numerous landings filled an important role in the infrastructure. Each landing catered to its respective area, resulting in diffuse localized trading centers and a lack of centralization. As the railroads changed the nature of commercial transportation, river landings declined in importance until they lost their economic value as vessels concentrated their

traffic to the rail hubs at Plymouth, Jamesville, and further upstream. In time, new forms of transportation eclipsed river traffic entirely.

When vessel location is examined chronologically, one of the most striking trends in the entire assemblage emerges. Vessels lost after 1880 are nearly all in the environs of population centers, specifically Jamesville and Plymouth. When considering this characteristic, it is important to note that numerous vessels were difficult to date due to either the cursory nature of investigations or the lack of concrete evidence that would place the loss date with accuracy. Some vessels were excluded from these statistics even though they were likely lost in the 20th century, such as the Cut Cypress Wreck, the Unidentified Skiff, and the Unknown Tug 2 at Gray's Fishery. Since these vessels could not be placed with absolute certainty into any decade of the 20th century, they did not receive a loss date. This decision has ramifications on the number of vessels categorized as lost in the 20th century, and as a result may skew data into appearing that almost all vessels were lost near towns. This decision, however, also affected numerous late 19th- or early 20th-century vessels lost near towns, such as the *Cable Barge* and seven unknown flats. Regardless of whether or not a few of the excluded vessels were lost outside of towns, the striking characteristic of the 20th century is that the preponderance of vessels lost were either wrecked or abandoned near population centers. Without taking the above cases into consideration, all eight vessels lost in the lower river after the introduction of railroads occurred in close proximity to towns. If the above vessels are included, then 16 of 19 vessels were lost near a populated area.

With this phenomenon tentatively established, the question remains: why is vessel loss after 1880 characterized by its proximity to population centers? The answer appears to be a localized consolidation of trade over time as spurred by technological change. Watson has written (1982:43): "The nineteenth century brought spectacular changes in transportation in the United States, particularly by the adaptation of steam power to water and land travel." This pattern of change continued into the 20th century. As posited above, it may be hypothesized that as the railroads of the region grew in prominence and replaced landings, the former figured more prominently in the greater scheme of riverine commerce. This led to a concentration of traffic where vessels could more readily find markets for their cargoes, where the railroad provided ready access to transshipment points, such as Jamesville and Plymouth (Figure 10).

Wrecking events appear to have followed the railroad. The railroad network reached

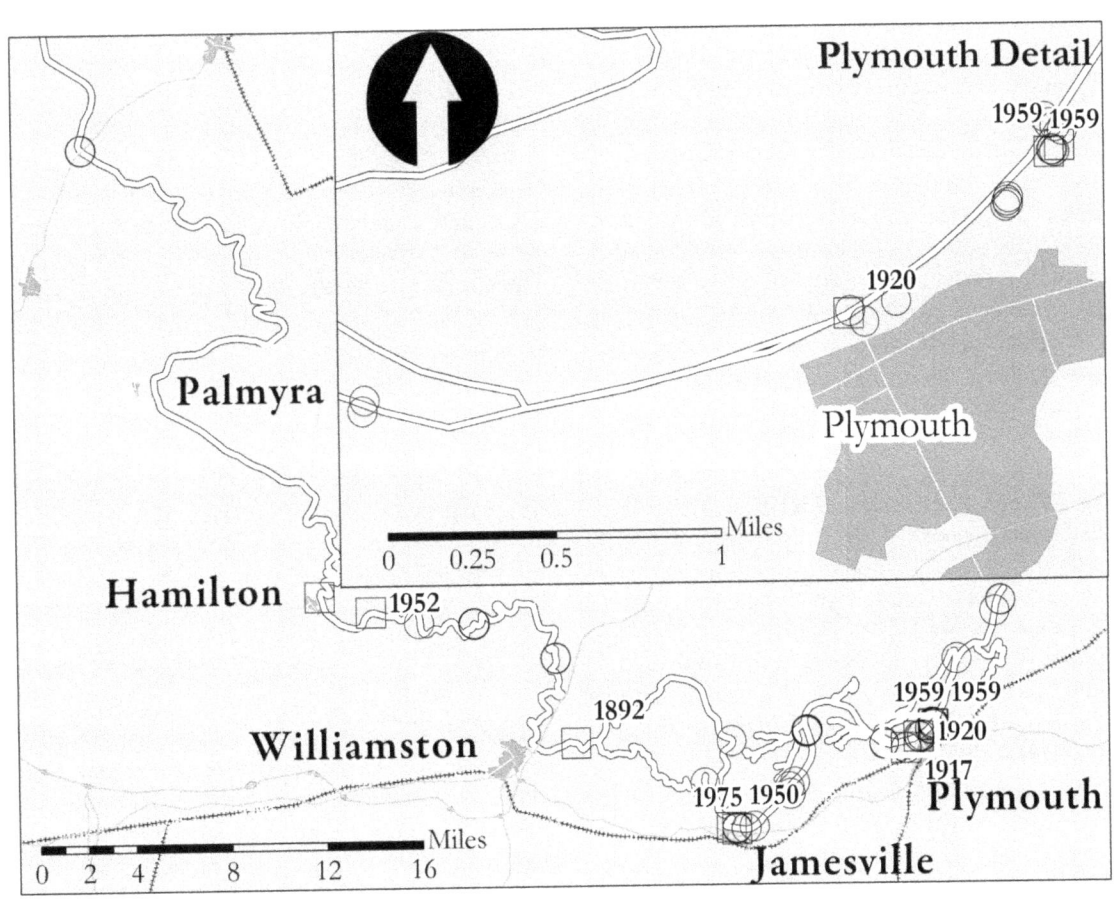

FIGURE 10. Vessel loss after the introduction of railroads. (Drawing by N. Richards.)

Williamston in 1883. The first shipwreck after the installation of the railway was the steamer *Commerce,* burned at Williamston that year (*The Morning Star* 1883; Prince 1966:13). *Ranger* wrecked at Hamilton in 1896 (*The Wilmington Messenger* 1896). After the railroad arrived, wrecks occurred near both Jamesville and Plymouth, as late as 1950 in the former and 1959 in the latter (Tidewater Atlantic Research 1990:13-15; Berman 1973).

The eclipse of the surrounding region as a center for trade and commerce may be explained using Walter Christaller's Central Place Theory. Christaller, in *Central Places in Southern Germany* (1966), explored the reasons why cities and towns thrive at specific localities. He posits that the relative importance of a location compared to its environs can be measured, and he provides a reason for the rise of population centers at certain locations. His ideas are directly applicable to explain the phenomenon of wreck clustering. The introduction of the railroad essentially expanded what Christaller would term the "centrality" of the municipalities of Hamilton, Williamston, Jamesville, and Plymouth (Christaller 1966:18). Centrality is, as Christaller defined it, "the relative importance of a place with regard to the region surrounding" (Christaller 1966:18). He has also written, "The greater the surplus of importance of the central place, the greater the size of its complimentary region" (Christaller 1966:18). This statement may explain the influence Plymouth and Jamesville exhibited to draw river traffic from their surroundings, away from the landings.

Christaller observed that the introduction of railroads changes the dynamic of a region's central places by adding to the centrality of the rail hub (Christaller 1966:105). Railroads in the lower Roanoke River towns changed trading patterns by overshadowing the importance of the previously essential river landings. Instead of using landings, watercraft visited the larger towns because the railroads raised the relative importance of these centers by easing product transportation and movement. This increase of centrality may have led to a higher frequency of vessel traffic in and around the major towns, translating to a higher incidence of both shipwrecks and watercraft discard.

Part of this hypothesis rests on the perception of the inhabitants of the river. Rippon stated "in order to truly understand the landscape, we must study it using the territories that were perceived as significant by past communities themselves" (Rippon 2004:19). This approach is especially applicable when assessing the data regarding shipwreck patterns on the Roanoke River. As the inhabitants of the region perceived Plymouth and Jamesville to be of greater value as centers of trade, the frequency of vessels at those locations rose, and along with it the frequency of vessels lost.

Another question emerges: if this pattern of vessel loss is the model, then why is this not the case for Weldon? The inland city was a hub of trade for the Wilmington and Weldon Railroad. During the Civil War, it was also part of a transportation network, albeit mostly terrestrial, that was a lifeline of the Confederacy. If the introduction of the railroad raises the relative importance of a town, then it would follow that Weldon should have witnessed an increase in its importance. Following the pattern of Jamesville and Plymouth, this should have led to an increase in the number of vessels lost in Weldon's vicinity. The research thus far indicates that this is not the case. Reasons for this could be that Weldon was too far up the river to benefit from the level of riverine traffic that Plymouth and Jamesville enjoyed, or that Weldon functioned economically as a terrestrial hub and not a port. Waterborne commerce through the Albemarle & Chesapeake Canal, coupled with the statistics of the place of build for the vessel assemblage, suggest strong trading ties with the Chesapeake region. Due to their proximity, it would follow that the ports of Plymouth and Jamesville would be more likely destinations for this trade, especially after the arrival of railways, than Weldon. In addition, as discussed above, the lack of fieldwork upriver could be a reason for this phenomenon, and wrecks may be waiting undiscovered near Weldon.

Conclusion

This study of the lost vessels of the Roanoke River builds upon previous works in archaeology, anthropology, and history, using a comparative regional approach to arrive at numerous observations, among them conclusions regarding behavior and watercraft distribution. The primary question of this study is: how do the archaeological resources of the Roanoke River, North Carolina, reflect cultural change? This paper has attempted to provide a comparative and generalist approach to the study of an assemblage of shipwrecks and abandoned vessels. Through historical, statistical, and geo-spatial investigations, patterns of human behavior emerged from the database. These patterns reveal the dichotomous nature of behavior during war and peace, as well as the direct correlation between shifting patterns of transportation and watercraft deposition. The assemblage of lost watercraft on the Roanoke River, when examined from archaeological and historical evidence, provides a glimpse into the life of an important waterway, a glimpse that owes much of its richness to the comparative approach employed during the course of the research.

Acknowledgments

The authors would like to thank Larry Babits and Wade Dudley of East Carolina University, Frank Cantelas of the National Oceanic and Atmospheric Administration (NOAA) Oceans Exploration, Larry Murphy of the National Parks Service, Richard Lawrence and the staff of the North Carolina Underwater Archaeology Branch, Harry Thompson of the Port O' Plymouth Museum, the Ruritan Club of Jamesville, North Carolina, and students from the ECU Program in Maritime Studies who helped collect data in the field. Associate editor Della Scott-Ireton is thanked for the article's reviews.

References Cited

ANGLEY, WILSON
    1995   *North Carolina Shipwreck References from the New York Shipping and Commercial List, 1815-1873.* North Carolina Department of Cultural Resources, Raleigh, NC.

BABITS, LAWRENCE, ANNALIES CORBIN KJORNESS, AND JEFF MORRIS
    1995   A Survey of the North Shore of the Pamlico River: Bath Creek to Wade's Point. East Carolina University, Greenville, NC.

BABITS, LAWRENCE E. AND ANNALIES CORBIN KJORNESS
    1995   Final Report on an Archaeological Survey of the Western Shore of the Pungo River from Wades Point to Woodstock Point. East Carolina University, Greenville, NC.

BARRETT, JOHN G.
    1963   *The Civil War in North Carolina.* The University of North Carolina Press, Chapel Hill, NC.

BERMAN, BRUCE D.
    1973   *Encyclopedia of American Shipwrecks.* Mariner's Press, Boston, MA.

BROWN, S., RALPH HOWLAND, M. ROBINSON, AND R.S. HALL
    1837   Contract for the Construction of the Long Shoals Light Boat, August 15, 1837. Long Shoal Light Boat File, North Carolina Underwater Archaeology Branch, Kure Beach, NC.

BRUSH, JOHN E.
    1953   The Hierarchy of Central Places in Southwestern Wisconsin. *Geographical Review* 43(3):380-402.

BURKE, JOHN G.
    1966   Bursting Boilers and the Federal Power. *Technology and Culture* 7(1):1-23.

BURKE, TOM
    1982   Rhodes Site. North Carolina Prehistoric Site Form II, Archaeology Branch, North Carolina Archives and History, Raleigh, NC.

CANNEY, DONALD L.
    1990   *The Old Steam Navy, Volume I: Frigates Sloops and Gunboats 1815-1885.* Naval Institute Press, Annapolis, MD.

CARBONE, JOHN S.
    2001   *The Civil War in Coastal North Carolina.* North Carolina Department of Cultural Resources, Raleigh, NC.

THE CAROLINA OBSERVER
    1827   No title. *The Carolina Observer,* 22 November. Fayetteville, NC.

CECELSKI, DAVID S.
    2001   *The Waterman's Song: Slavery and Freedom in Maritime North Carolina.* University of North Carolina Press, Chapel Hill, NC.

CEDERLUND, CARL OLOF
    1980   Systematic Registration of Older Sinkings and Wrecks in Swedish Waters. *The International Journal of Nautical Archaeology* 9(2):95-104.

CHRISTALLER, WALTER
    1966   *Central Places in Southern Germany,* Carlisle W. Baskin, translator. Prentice-Hall, Englewood Cliffs, NJ.

CORNELL, JOHN
    1833   Letter to Uncle, 8 February. North Carolina Underwater Archaeology Branch File ROR Shipping/ Miscellaneous, Kure Beach, NC.

CORONEOS, COSMOS
1997   *Shipwrecks of Encounter Bay and Backstairs Passage, South Australian Maritime Heritage Series No. 3.* Department of Environment and Natural Resources, Adelaide, South Australia.

CORONEOS, COSMOS AND ROBERT MCKINNON
1997   *Shipwrecks of the Lower Yorke Peninsula, South Australian Maritime Heritage Series No. 4.* Department of Environment and Natural Resources, Adelaide, South Australia.

DOBBS, ARTHUR
1984   Report of Governor Arthur Dobbs to the Board of Trade, 1755. In *The North Carolina Experience: An Interpretive and Documentary History*, Lindley S. Butler and Alan D. Watson, editors, pp. 88-91. The University of North Carolina Press, Chapel Hill, NC.

DOYLE, COLEMAN
2000   An Examination of Associations between Significant Historic Events and the Loss and Discard of Vessels in the Townsville Catchment (1865-1981). Master's thesis, James Cook University, Townsville and Cairns, Queensland, Australia.

DUNCAN, BRADLEY
2000   Signposts in the Sea: An Investigation of the Shipwreck Patterning and Cultural Seascapes of the Gippsland Region, Victoria. Honors thesis, James Cook University, Townsville and Cairns, Queensland, Australia.

2004   Risky Business, the Role of Risk in Shaping the Maritime Cultural Landscape and Shipwreck Patterning: A Case Study Application in the Gippsland region, Victoria. *Bulletin of the Australasian Institute for Maritime Archaeology* 28:11-24.

THE ECONOMIST
1882   No title. *The Economist*, 28 November. Elizabeth City, NC.

EMMERSON, JOHN C.
1949   *Steam Navigation in Virginia and Northeastern North Carolina Waters: 1826-1936*. John C. Emmerson, Portsmouth, VA.

ENGLISH, EARL
1900   Report to W. H. Macomb, 31 October 1864. In *Official Records of the Union and Confederate Navies, Series I, Volume 11*, John D. Long, editor, pp. 19. U.S. Department of the Navy, Washington, DC. Reprinted in 1987 by Historic Times, Harrisburg, PA.

FEUER, A.B.
1989   The Life and Death of a Confederate Ram. *Civil War* 16:49-57.

FLATMAN, JOE
2003   Cultural Biographies, Cognitive Landscapes, and Dirty Old Bits of Boat: 'Theory' in Maritime Archaeology.

The International Journal of Nautical Archaeology 32(2)143-157.

FLUSSER, C.W.
1899   Report to S.P. Lee, 12 April 1864. In *Official Records of the Union and Confederate Navies, Series I, Volume 9*, John D. Long, editor, pp. 609-610. U.S. Department of the Navy, Washington, DC. Reprinted in 1987 by Historic Times, Harrisburg, PA.

1921   Report to Rear Admiral S.P. Lee, 17 January 1863. In *Official Records of the Union and Confederate Navies, Series II, Volume 2*, C.C. Marsh, editor, pp. 474-475. U.S. Department of the Navy, Washington, DC. Reprinted in 1987 by Historic Times, Harrisburg, PA.

FOSTER, LEONIE
1987   Port Philip Shipwrecks Stage 1: An Historical Survey. Victoria Archaeological Survey, Melbourne, Australia.

1988   Port Philip Shipwrecks Stage 2: An Historical Survey. Victoria Archaeological Survey, Melbourne, Australia.

1989   Port Philip Shipwrecks Stage 3: An Historical Survey. Victoria Archaeological Survey, Melbourne, Australia.

1990   Port Philip Shipwrecks Stage 4: An Historical Survey. Victoria Archaeological Survey, Melbourne, Australia.

FRANCIS M. MANNING PAPERS
1848   Ledger. Francis M. Manning Papers, Special Collections, Joyner Library, East Carolina University, Greenville, NC.

FRANKLE, JONES
1900   Report to W. H. Macomb, 24 November 1864. In *Official Records of the Union and Confederate Navies, Series I, Volume 11*, John D. Long, editor, p.93. U.S. Department of the Navy, Washington, DC. Reprinted in 1987 by Historic Times, Harrisburg, PA.

FRANKLIN, CHARLES L.
1901   Report to Commander John C. Febiger, 9 April 1865. In *Official Records of the Union and Confederate Navies, Series I, Volume 12*, John D. Long, editor, p.108. U.S. Department of the Navy, Washington, DC. Reprinted in 1987 by Historic Times, Harrisburg, PA.

FRIEDMAN, ADAM
2008   The Legal Choice in a Cultural Landscape: An Explanatory Model Created from the Maritime and Terrestrial Archaeological Record of the Roanoke River, North Carolina. Master's thesis, East Carolina University, Greenville NC.

GOULD, RICHARD A.
    1983   Looking Below the Surface: Shipwreck Archaeology
           as Anthropology. In *Shipwreck Anthropology*, Richard
           A. Gould, editor, pp. 3-22. University of New Mexico
           Press, Albuquerque, NM.

HOSKINS, W.G.
    1955   *The Making of the English Landscape*. Reprinted
           1985, Penguin Books, London, UK.

HOWELL, J.C.
    1901   Report to Report to Gideon Welles, 27 June 1865.
           In *Official Records of the Union and Confederate
           Navies, Series I, Volume 12*, John D. Long, editor, pp.
           164-165. U.S. Department of the Navy, Washington,
           DC. Reprinted in 1987 by Historic Times, Harrisburg,
           PA.

JASIŃSKI, MAREK
    1993   The Maritime Cultural Landscape, An Archaeological
           Perspective. *Polish Archaeology (Archeologia Polski)*
           38(1):7-21.

JORDAN, D.J.
    1995   *East Coast Shipwrecks: A Thematic Historical Survey*.
           Heritage Victoria, Melbourne, Australia.

KENDERDINE, SARAH
    1994a *Historic Shipping on the Murray River: A Guide to the
           Terrestrial and Submerged Archaeological Resources
           in New South Wales and Victoria*. Department
           of Planning, NSW, Department of Planning and
           Development, Victoria Murray Darling Basin
           Commission, Sydney, Australia.

    1994b Revelations about River Boats and 'Rotten Rows': a
           Guide to Wreck Sites of the River Murray. *Bulletin of
           the Australasian Institute for Maritime Archaeology*
           (18):17-28.

    1995a *Historic Shipping on the river Murray: A Guide to
           Terrestrial and Submerged Archaeological Sites in
           South Australia*. State Heritage Branch, Department
           of Environmental and Land Management, Adelaide,
           Australia.

    1995b *Shipwrecks 1656-1942: A Guide to Historic Wreck
           Sites*. Western Australian Maritime Museum,
           Fremantle, Australia.

LAWRENCE, RICHARD W.
    2002   Archaeological Investigations of the Broad Creek
           Blockade: 1990 and 1991 Field Seasons. North
           Carolina Underwater Archaeology Branch, Kure
           Beach, NC.

    2003   Underwater Archaeological Investigations of the
           Roanoke River in the Vicinity of Plymouth, North
           Carolina, August 2001. North Carolina Underwater
           Archaeology Branch, Kure Beach, NC.

LENIHAN, DANIEL J.
    1983   Rethinking Shipwreck Anthropology: A History of
           Ideas and Considerations for New Directions. In
           Shipwreck Anthropology, Richard A. Gould, editor, pp.
           37-64. University of New Mexico Press, Albuquerque,
           NM.

MACGREGOR, DAVID R.
    1984   *Merchant Sailing Ships 1850-1875: Heyday of Sail*.
           Naval Institute Press, Annapolis, MD.

MACOMB, W.H.
    1900   Report to D. D. Porter, 1 November 1864. In *Official
           Records of the Union and Confederate Navies, Series
           I, Volume 11*, John D. Long, editor, pp. 12-15. U.S.
           Department of the Navy, Washington, DC. Reprinted
           in 1987 by Historic Times, Harrisburg. PA.

MANNING, CHARLES G.
    1870   Custom House Correspondence, 28 September. ROR
           Unknown Scows File, North Carolina Underwater
           Archaeology Branch, Kure Beach, NC.

MANNING, FRANCIS M. AND W.H. BOOKER
    1977a *Martin County History, Volume I*. Enterprise
           Publishing Company, Williamston, NC.

    1977b *Martin County History, Volume II*. Enterprise
           Publishing Company, Williamston, NC.

MARSH, C.C.
    1921   *Official Records of the Union and Confederate Navies
           in the War of the Rebellion. Series II, Volume 1*. U.S.
           Department of the Navy, Washington DC.

MCELREAN, THOMAS, ROSEMARY MCCONKEY, AND WES
FORSYTHE.
    2002   *Strangford Lough: An Archaeological Survey of the
           Maritime Cultural Landscape*. The Blackstaff Press
           Limited, Belfast, Northern Ireland.

THE MORNING STAR
    1875   No title. *The Morning Star*, 24 January. Wilmington,
           NC.

    1883   No title. *The Morning Star*, 14 December. Wilmington,
           NC.

MORRILL, DAN L.
    2002   *The Civil War in the Carolinas*. The Nautical and
           Aviation Publishing Company of America, Charleston,
           SC.

MORRISON, JOHN H.
    1953   *History of American Steam Navigation*. Stephen Daye
           Press, New York, NY.

MURPHY, LARRY
    1983   Shipwrecks as a Database for Human Behavioral
           Studies. In *Shipwreck Anthropology*, Richard A.
           Gould, editor, pp. 65-89. University of New Mexico
           Press, Albuquerque, NM.

NORTH CAROLINA PRESBYTERIAN
  1865 No title. *North Carolina Presbyterian*, 4 January. New Bern, NC.

NORTH CAROLINA TIMES
  1864 No title. *North Carolina Times*, 15 December. New Bern, NC.

PARKER, A.J.
  2000 A Maritime Cultural Landscape: The Port of Bristol in the Middle Ages. *The International Journal of Nautical Archaeology* 29(2):289-299.

PECK, J. J.
  1891 Letter to Headquarters of the Army, District of North Carolina, April 25, 1864. In *The War of the Rebellion: A Compilation of the Official Records of the Union and Confederate Armies, Series I, Volume 33*, Robert N. Scott, editor, pp. 288. U.S. War Department, Washington, DC. Reprinted in 1985 by Historic Times, Ann Arbor, MI.

PRINCE, RICHARD E.
  1966 *Atlantic Coast Line Railroad: Steam Locomotives, Ships, and History.* Wheelwright Lithographing Company, Salt Lake City, UT. Reprinted in 2000 by Indiana University Press, Bloomington, IN.

RICHARDS, NATHAN
  2003 *Unfit for Further Use: A Guide to the Waterfront Discard Sites of Tasmania (1808-1977).* Tasmanian Heritage Office, Hobart, Australia.

  2004 The Role of Geo-politics in Cultural Site Formation: A Case Study from the Northern Territory. *Bulletin of the Australasian Institute for Maritime Archaeology* (28):97-106.

RIPPON, STEPHEN
  2004 Historic Landscapes Analysis: Deciphering the Countryside. In *Practical Handbooks for Archaeology No. 16*, Council for British Archaeology, pp.14-100. Armatura Press, York, UK.

SAUER, CARL ORTWIN
  1963 The Morphology of Landscape (1925) in *Land and Life: A Collection of the Writings of Carl Ortwin Sauer*, John Leighly, editor, pp. 315-350. University of California Press, Berkeley, CA.

SHOMETTE, DONALD G.
  1982 *Shipwrecks on the Chesapeake: Maritime Disasters on Chesapeake Bay and its Tributaries, 1608-1978.* Tidewater Publishers, Centreville, MD.

  1995 *Tidewater Time Capsule: History Beneath the Patuxent.* Tidewater Publishers, Centreville, MD.

SHOMETTE, DONALD G. AND RALPH E. ESHELMAN
  1998 A Developmental Model for Survey and Inventory of Submerged Archaeological Resources in a Riverine System. In *Maritime Archaeology: A Reader of Substantive and Theoretical Contributions*, Lawrence E. Babits and Hans van Tilburg, editors, pp. 232-335. Plenum Press, New York, NY.

SILVERSTONE, PAUL
  1989 *Warships of the Civil War Navies.* Naval Institute Press, Annapolis, MD.

STILL, WILLIAM N, JR.
  1961 Confederate Naval Strategy: The Ironclad. *The Journal of Southern History* 27(3):330-343.

  1971 *Iron Afloat: The Story of the Confederate Ironclads.* Vanderbilt University Press, Indianapolis, IN.

TARBORO SOUTHERNER
  1880 No title. *Tarboro Southerner*, 13 August. Tarboro, NC.

TAYLOR, JOHN W.
  1998 Potomac Flotilla: A Gunboat Captain's Diary. In *Raiders and Blockaders: The American Civil War Afloat*, William N. Still, Jr., editor, pp. 214-223. Brassey's, Washington DC.

TIDEWATER ATLANTIC RESEARCH
  1990 An Underwater Cultural Resource Survey of a Proposed Barge Landing Site on the Roanoke River near Plymouth, North Carolina. Tidewater Atlantic, Washington, NC.

TRI-WEEKLY COMMERCIAL, WILMINGTON, NC, 1857
  1857 No title. *Tri-Weekly Commercial*, 23 April. Wilmington, NC.

UNITED STATES DEPARTMENT OF THE NAVY
  1976 *Dictionary of American Naval Fighting Ships, Volume VI.* U.S. Department of the Navy, Washington, DC.

UNITED STATES TREASURY DEPARTMENT
  1959 *Annual List of Merchant Vessels of the United States 1959.* U.S. Department of Commerce, Washington, DC.

WATSON, ALAN D.
  1982 *Bertie County: A Brief History.* North Carolina Department of Cultural Resources, Division of Archives and History, Raleigh, NC.

WATSON, HARRY L.
  1984 "Old Rip" in a New Era. In *The North Carolina Experience: An Interpretive and Documentary History*, Lindley S. Butler and Alan D. Watson, editors, pp.217-226. The University of North Carolina Press, Chapel Hill, NC.

WESSELS, H.W.
  1891 Letter to J. J. Peck, 18 August 1864. In *The War of the Rebellion: A Compilation of the Official Records of the Union and Confederate Armies, Series I, Volume 33*, Robert N. Scott, editor, pp.296-301. U.S. War Department, Washington, DC. Reprinted in 1985 by Historic Times, Ann Arbor, MI.

WESTERDAHL, CHRISTER
  1992 The Maritime Cultural Landscape. *The International Journal of Nautical Archaeology* 22(1):5-14.

WHITFIELD, LIZ
  2004 *A Historical and Archaeological Examination of the Upper Roanoke River Valley from Hamilton to Weldon.* North Carolina Underwater Archaeology Branch, Kure Beach, NC.

WILDE-RAMSING, MARK
  1982a *Fort Branch Barge.* North Carolina Shipwrecks Data Entry Form, North Carolina Underwater Archaeology Branch, Kure Beach, NC.

  1982b *Poplar Point Barge.* North Carolina Shipwrecks Data Entry Form, North Carolina Underwater Archaeology Branch, Kure Beach, NC.

WILMINGTON MESSENGER
  1896 No title. *Wilmington Messenger*, 7 April. Wilmington, NC.

WILMINGTON STAR
  1879 No title. *Wilmington Star*, 13 May. Wilmington, NC.

FRANKLIN H. PRICE
FLORIDA BUREAU OF ARCHAEOLOGICAL RESEARCH
1001 DESOTO PARK DR.
TALLAHASSEE, FL 32301

NATHAN RICHARDS
PROGRAM IN MARITIME STUDIES
EAST CAROLINA UNIVERSITY
ADMIRAL ERNEST M. ELLER HOUSE
GREENVILLE, NC 27858-4353

2011. Wagging the Dog: Technology and Archaeology. In *ACUA Underwater Archaeology Proceedings 2011*, Filipe Castro and Lindsey Thomas, editors, pp. 29–32.

Wagging the Dog: Technology and Archaeology

Kimberly Faulk

During the first SHA Technology Committee Symposium in 2010 Dr. Lu Ann de Cunzo, the outgoing SHA President, asked whether technology was altering the research questions that archaeologists pose. This paper seeks to identify whether or not established, new, and emerging technologies are creating research questions in archaeology, or whether research questions posed by archaeologists are driving the technology. Can archaeologists ask better research questions with the available technology, or has technology begun "wagging the dog" and started to drive greater specialization?

Introduction

I attempted to pull together a list of emerging or new technologies that archaeologists are excitedly using to push the field further. As I constructed the list it became apparent that many of the "new" technologies were merely modifications or advancements of preexisting systems.

New And Emergent Technologies That Are Not So New:
Ground Penetrating Radar
Mixed Gas Diving
pXRF
3-D Mapping
Digital Photography
Silicon Oil Treatment
Multibeam Echo Sounder
ROV
ROV Drill
AUV
Marine Magnetics
CSEM: Control Source Electromagnetics
3D Laser Scanning
3D Modeling in a Virtual Forum
Silicon Oil Treatment

I came to the conclusion that despite believing that the things on the list above are "emerging" technologies or technologies that are now being re-purposed for our field, they have been around long enough for the people using them to think of them as every day tools. In an effort to better define what made something a new or emerging technology that could influence the research questions archaeologists are asking, I went back to the source. I started with the basic definition of technology. According to Merriam Webster's primary definition, technology is: "the practical application of knowledge especially in a particular area, for example in medical

technology". The second definition was somewhat more useful in this discussion, as it defines technology as "a manner of accomplishing a task especially using technical processes, methods, or knowledge" (that is, new methods for storing information). By combining the two definitions above with the third which defines technology as "the specialized aspects of a particular field of endeavor" (such as educational technology) there is suddenly a logical correlation between the list above and my view of them as "new" or "emerging."

If the definition of technology is the ability to apply the practical knowledge of something to the process being undertaken, and it considers the specialization of the field, then clearly the list above not only includes technologies that are established, but also technologies that for varying reasons are emerging or evolving. The question remains, however, do these technologies change the way we ask our research questions or do they drive the research?

To answer that question I would like to take a subsample of those technologies listed above and look at how they started, how they are used, and how they are influencing our work today, keeping in mind that what may seem like a new technology to one user group is a well entrenched technology to another.

Ground Penetrating Radar and Controlled Source Electromagnetics

For those of us working in an offshore or littoral environment, Ground Penetrating Radar (GPR) is one of those tools we have seen on television and read about in books, but rarely used. GPR is simply not a useful tool in a wet environment when moist or even wet soils can prevent the electromagnetic pulse from penetrating further than a few centimeters. The first GPR survey was performed in Austria in 1929 to sound the depth of a glacier, and while the survey was a success, its application was essentially dismissed until the 1970s when researchers in the earth sciences began building their own portable ground penetrating radars to image subsurface geological and hydrological conditions (Olhoeft 2010).

Although GPR is not an emerging technology after its use in the field for forty years, it is the precursor to an emerging technology in our field that has wide ranging potential – CSEM, or Controlled Source Electromagnetic remote sensing. Like CSEM, GPR is an electromagnetic remote sensing tool that utilizes electromagnetic waves to image the subsurface. It can be used in terrestrial applications to image foundations, wells, privies, and postholes, but in the marine environment GPR is not a viable tool.

Currently in the offshore industry a survey company is utilizing CSEM to image deeply buried hydrocarbon reservoirs. The technology utilizes a towed high-power source to create low frequency electromagnetic dipole waves. The source is towed over the seafloor where the electromagnetic waves are either dispersed or attenuated by seafloor soils. The highly resistive subseafloor geology where the electromagnetic waves are propagated instead of attenuated indicates subseafloor reservoirs (EMGS 2010). What possible tool could this represent for the underwater archaeological community if tuned properly? If the offshore oil and gas industry can use this tool to predict with 70% to 85% certainty a reservoir's location and type, archaeologists could likely refine this tool to identify buried shipwrecks in coastal environments because the vessels would be more resistive than the surrounding seafloor soils. CSEM could provide one more tool beyond the standard chirp subbottom profiler to search for buried vessels, but it would also open entirely new avenues of inquiry. Engineers, material specialists, and geophysicists would be able to provide clearer answers on why a particular shipwreck survived based on the electromagnetic signature of the surrounding sediments.

Digital Technology

Digital imaging and rendering technologies are another realm of technologies that are not necessarily new, but are emerging as powerful tools within the archaeological community. Technologies such as digital photography, multibeam echo sounders, high resolution side-scan sonars, three dimensional modeling programs, virtual reality constructs, and second life applications could be combined in the digital imaging category. While the technologies listed above have little in common, they are all used to image, visualize, and display archaeological data. Autonomous Underwater Vehicle's now have the ability to not only image a wreck site with side scan sonar, multibeam and subbottom profilers, but also with digital cameras. The digital photos can be stitched back together and then draped over the rendered multibeam and side scan sonar data to create a three dimensional image of the wreck site. If subbottom data was collected over the wreck, the subbottom data can then be draped beneath the seafloor imagery to provide a comprehensive view of the archaeological site. Once the data is stitched together, it is easy to work in three dimensional modeling software and fly through the wreck, over it, explode it, and rebuild it in virtual reality, allowing more people access to a remote site and allowing broader research questions to be asked.

The Colonial Williamsburg Foundation, in collaboration with the Institute for Advanced Technology in the Humanities, is using archaeological and historical data to virtually reconstruct Williamsburg property by property. Archaeologists are modeling individual buildings and the surrounding landscape to recreate the town as it looked in 1776. These three dimensional virtual models allow archaeologists to better understand a site's patterns of use and wear. Likewise, these virtual models provide visitors a holistic view of Williamsburg at one moment in time as compared to today's Historic Area, in which earlier and later buildings may sit side by side. Three dimensional modeling in this context provides an opportunity for archaeologists to ask new research questions, but also provides an exciting opportunity to engage technologically savvy children and adults.

Does digital imaging and rendering technology change the research design and questions we might ask as archaeologists? In some ways the answer is yes. Until we could render data in three dimensions on a computer screen and examine each data point we could not begin to ask whether it would be possible to build a true model of a site without raising a ship to the surface, completely excavating a land site or building a reconstruction. Now we can create a virtual reconstruction of a site that may lie thousands of feet below the water's surface or of a site that will be lost during a municipal project.

In the past we could not have imagined mapping a complex site in a few days with the use of computer applications and geophysical tools. With the ability to focus more heavily on the collected data than on collecting the data, we have more time to mine the data for answers to questions that would have been swept aside in the past for lack of funding, time or resources. All of this extra return for the time investment also means that we are specializing even more within the field of archaeology. We now have the ability to examine minute details of building or ship construction and site formation processes, which means that while we become better at the overall archaeology, we also have the ability to become more focused on our preferred topic of study.

3D Laser Scanning

Another exciting "new" technology is 3D laser scanning. While the technology is not necessarily new, it is new to archaeology. Like many technological tools, archaeologists had to wait for the technology to become financially feasible for our projects. Groups like CyArk, the University of South Florida's Alliance for Integrated Spatial Technologies, and the University of Louisiana's Geography and Anthropology department, to name a few, are using 3D Laser scanning to image sites around the world. These scans help to preserve a data archive of archaeological sites and illuminate features that might otherwise be lost to our eyes. From Alaska to Peru archaeological sites are being scanned, the point clouds are being processed, and the data analyzed. With a 3D laser scanner, archaeologists can image fastener patterns, tool marks, and individual construction features in ways that conventional mapping techniques do not allow. A 3D laser scanner also acts as micro-field team that allows two to three people to map a complex intact site or structure in a day or two instead of a field team of twenty working for years to image every aspect of a site. The generated point clouds can then be loaded into imaging software to allow three-dimensional imaging, fly-throughs, and detailed micro-mapping. 3D laser scanning is a technology that not only allows archaeologists to do more in less time, it also allows very detailed questions to be asked and answered.

Parametric Subbottom Profilers

An interesting "new" technology currently being exploited by marine archaeologists to micro-record sites is the parametric subbottom profiler. A parametric subbottom profiler combines two subbottom profilers of differing frequencies working simultaneously to create a high resolution image of shallow marine sediments. By combing two differing frequencies, the unit creates a very narrow, focused beam with no side lobe, allowing a clean image of the subseafloor environment ideal for locating prehistoric sites, glacial low stands, and potential sites of

interest. Currently parametric subbottom profilers have been used to map sites in Europe and New England. Although the technology has been available since 1997, the technology's use in marine archaeology is still relatively new. The potential for this technology within the archaeological community is high when one considers the impact of sea level rise on inundated archaeological sites around the world.

ROVDrill

A technology that is truly on the cutting edge and has not yet been tested for archaeology is the ROVDrill. The ROVDrill is a tool created by several geotechnical engineers and ROV engineers who believed they could create a tool that attached to an ROV to collect deepwater borings and sediment cores. In creating a tool that allows for seafloor sampling from an ROV, expensive drill ships and survey vessels can be eliminated when looking for subsea cores and borings. What possible application does this hold for archaeology? ROVDrill can drill and retrieve a 75mm core in excess of 100m long (Oil Voice 2010). This could provide geotechnical data that would allow archaeologists to look at climate change, local sea level changes, potential inundated sites and the changes accompanying their existence. Although ROVDrill is currently working in mineral extraction and oil and gas related fields, the potential application of this technology to underwater archaeological sites is exciting.

Wagging The Dog?

Where do these technologies leave us? Are we, as archaeologists, allowing the glitz and glamour of new technologies to drive our research questions? Do we allow fundamental research questions to go unasked because we are caught up in the newest technology? I do not believe that we are. Underwater archaeology, for example, has always been a technologically driven aspect of archaeology. Underwater archaeologists are always pushing the envelope seeking ways to stay on the site just a little longer whether through the use of mixed gas diving, rebreathers, robotics, or enhanced geophysical technologies. Terrestrial archaeologists on the other hand may have an easier time getting to their sites, but they too embrace new technologies for mapping rock art, restoring damaged rock art panels, mapping buried features with non-invasive technologies, and delineating site boundaries.

As with so many things in the archaeological field,

technology is simply a tool that we rely upon to frame our research. Archaeologists are here to answer the who's, what's, where's and when's of our collective past. The use of new iPhone applications for updating site files, or the use of silicone oil treatment on rope from the *Belle* shipwreck (which in turn revealed the bugs, textiles, and pollens trapped in the rope's fibers), or the use of CSEM and parametric subbottom remote sensing technologies simply allows us to do our jobs more quickly, efficiently, and in some ways better than we have ever done them before. Archaeologists as a whole are slow to embrace new technologies, perhaps because we spend our time looking to the past. Despite archaeology's slow move to embrace new technologies quickly, archaeologists as a whole are quick to recognize a technology's validity when it allows researchers to ask more detailed research questions or reveal research questions we have never considered. Simply put, I believe archaeology is finding new uses for technology, rather than technology revealing new uses for archaeology. As archaeologists we are bound by a common curiosity about people and things, technology simply allows us to carry our curiosity further and in many cases to share our story with a broader public.

Acknowledgements

This paper would not have been possible without the assistance of several individuals. Without Lu Ann de Cunzo's support, insight, and inspiration this paper would never have come to fruition. Without the SHA Technologies Committee's support this paper would not have been relevant to the SHA. Lisa Fischer of The Colonial Williamsburg Foundation provided editorial assistance, verification of facts, and her expertise on digital technologies. Last, but certainly not least, my husband Brent Faulk deserves a thank you for his never ending support, his willingness to read countless drafts of this paper, and his expertise in CSEM technologies.

References Cited

Olhoeft, Gary R.
     2010   Ground Penetrating Radar. http://www.g-p-r.com/ introduc.htm. Accessed November 2010.

EMGS
     2010   http://www.emgs.com/the_marine_em_method/. Accessed November 2010.

Oil Voice
     2010   Seafloor Geoservices Awarded Contract for Rovdrill. http://www.oilvoice.com/n/Seafloor_Geoservices_ Awarded_Contract_for_Rovdrill/75bf42957.aspx

Kimberly Faulk
Geoscience Earth & Marine Services, Inc.; a Forum Energy Technologies Company
10615 Shadow Wood Drive
Suite 200
Houston, TX 77043

ANNALIES CORBIN

Shifting Sand and Muddy Water: Historic Cartography and River Migration as Factors in Locating Steamboat Wrecks on the Far Upper Missouri River

ABSTRACT

Steamboating on the Missouri River began in 1819 and, by 1860 Fort Benton, Montana Territory was established as the world's innermost port. Between 1819 and the mid-1920s more than 1,000 vessels were lost and subsequently forgotten on the Missouri River. Missouri River migration is investigated as a primary factor in predicting, locating, and assessing inland river wreck sites today. The study examines three historic river surveys conducted in 1867, 1874, and from 1892 to 1897, plus modern aerial photography for clues suggesting the location of steamboat wreck sites and information useful in predicting site conditions and site formation processes prior to archaeological disturbance.

Introduction

The opening of the upper Missouri River region made possible such developments as the upper river fur trade, military operations, mining in the Rockies, and settlement in the various Plains regions along the river. Steamboating on the Missouri River began in May 1819 when the 98 ton (89,000 kg) *Independence* ascended 250 mi. (400 km) from St. Louis to Chariton, Missouri. In 1832, the American Fur Company's steamboat, the *Yellow Stone,* ascended as far as Fort Union at the mouth of the Yellowstone River (Jackson 1985; Corbin 1995). Almost three decades later, in 1860, the American Fur Company's *Chippewa* reached Fort Benton, the effective head of steamboat navigation on the Missouri, and offloaded 250 tons (227 t) of cargo. This trip set a new distance record in the history of steamboat navigation, as the *Chippewa* journeyed 2,285 mi. (3,675 km) above the mouth of the river, and established Fort Benton as the steamboat capital of the upper northwest region.

Steamboat traffic at Fort Benton quickly became commonplace, and with the discovery of gold in Montana in 1862, traffic along the upper Missouri River increased dramatically, as miners, speculators, and suppliers flocked to the Fort Benton area (Corbin 1996). Between the years of 1861 and 1885 steamboats delivered well over 100,000 tons (90,700 t) of freight to the Fort Benton levee. Although often overlooked by scholar's preoccupation with the fur trade, military activity, and the coming of the railroad, the steamboat era was one of the fundamental building blocks in the history of Montana and the upper Missouri River region.

Fortunately for archaeologists and historians alike, not all of the steamboats that plied the upper Missouri and Yellowstone rivers survived the journey. Current research indicates that there are a minimum of 37 historic wrecks, including steamboats, barges, ferries, and early motor vessels, located along the Missouri and Yellowstone rivers in Montana (Figure 1) with more than an estimated 1,000 wrecks along the Missouri down river from Montana. Few, if any, of these sites have been properly verified, recorded, or investigated, although these historic archaeological resources offer a variety of opportunities for interpreting steamboat traffic on the Nation's interior rivers (Corbin and Karsmizki 1997).

Missouri River migration is investigated as a primary factor in predicting, locating, and poten-

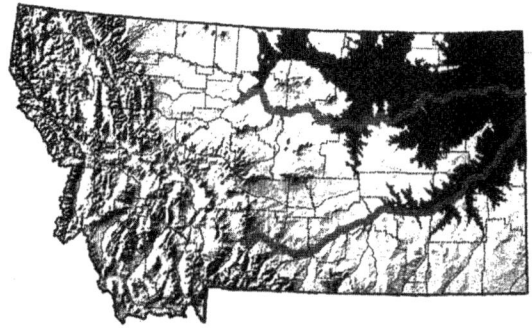

FIGURE 1. The Missouri-Yellowstone River drainage area in Montana (by the author).

tially assessing inland river wreck sites. Through careful utilization and examination of historic maps, documents, survey reports, and aerial photographs, changes in the course of the river over the past 138 years are clearly visible. Understanding changes in river migration through historic cartography is essential for accurately predicting wreck sites today. Historic maps provide the most important "first step" in developing a model for predicting inland river wreck sites. This work examines three historic survey projects, focusing on the manner and accuracy in which the surveys were conducted and asks if a predictive model for locating potential wreck sites is possible based a comprehensive examination of Missouri River migration. More importantly, will an appreciation of river migration help archaeologists determine aspects of the natural site formation processes before the site is investigated and subsequently disturbed?

Three Historic Upper Missouri River Surveys—Post 1860

Fortunately, the importance of the far upper Missouri River in the fur trade, the mining industry, and in the development of the United States military in the West spurred relatively consistent surveys of both the Missouri River and its tributary systems. These surveys were undertaken both during and after the steamboat era. The three most important surveys of the Missouri River drainage, pertinent to this study, were conducted in 1867, 1874, and from 1892 to 1897 (National Archives 1867, 1874, 1892-1897).

In 1867, Col. John M. Macomb of the United States Army authorized the first comprehensive survey of the far upper Missouri River, since Lewis and Clark, that included the Montana region. The field survey was conducted by Bvt. Major C. W. Howell, Captain in the Corps of Engineers. The "Sketch of the Missouri River from the Mouth of the Platte to Fort Benton" (Figure 2), provides the first detailed view of the river and the landscape through which it passed during the mid-19th century. The area was surveyed from the pilot house of the steamer *Minor*

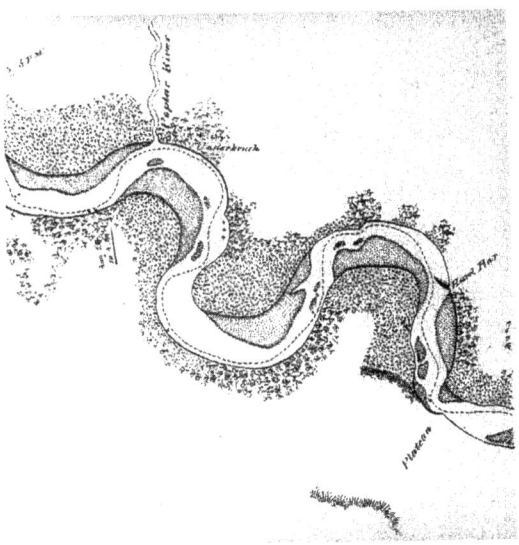

FIGURE 2. 1867 *Sketch of the Missouri River from the Mouth of the Platte to Fort Benton Montana*, map showing Hard Bar bend, the river channel, tributary streams, and landscape vegetation (National Archives 1867).

and the map was compiled with the aid of several Missouri River boat captains and pilots.

The "sketch" provides critical information on the riverbed including the course of the deepest channel, the location of snags and obstructions, and the placement of sand bars in relationship to the bends and curves of the river. Interestingly the survey also notes the location of the "Wreck of the *Trover* [1867]." This notation is both critical and curious. Present research suggests that by 1867, when the survey took place, a minimum of three steamboats had already sunk within the Montana section of the survey (Corbin and Karsmizki 1997). This raises the question of why the wreck of the *Trover* was the only wreck noted on the Montana area survey maps. Although Howell does not mention in his field notes that the wreck was visible from the surface, perhaps the wreck was still recent enough to be a considerable navigational hazard at the time of the survey and therefore was included on the survey maps. Documentary evidence suggests that wrecks prior to the 1867 survey were quickly absorbed into the environment.

The 1867 survey map also has several other important cartographic attributes. The maps name and illustrate the locations of tributary streams and creeks, note vegetation in great detail, and mark the locations of bluffs and other land forms adjacent to the river (National Archives 1867). But how can we better understand and therefore better utilize the information from these maps? The answers lie in the original field notes taken during the survey. Fortunately, Major Howell was a diligent note-taker.

Howell's notes provide information concerning the nature of the survey and how the survey was conducted. His original field notes document the landscape, the turbulence of the river, and the frequency of snags and steamboat wrecks. Most importantly, he details the river's influence on both the cultural and natural environment. Two vital pieces of information are provided. First, Howell noted the presence of wrecked steamboats (some wrecks were noted on the maps while others were only mentioned in the report but were not noted on the maps) in both the upper and lower river and their impact on the river environment.

As might be expected from the character of the river a great number of wrecks lie sunken . . . but the majority of them at present are not in the way and pilots are familiar with their positions. Many of them have been partially removed by the underwriters, leaving but the hulls and wheels, so the labor of cleaning them out of the channel has been greatly simplified. . . . (Howell 1868).

Second, Major Howell provided clues concerning the manner in which wreck sites are formed and are subsequently protected or destroyed by the natural environment:

The sand of which these bars are formed is of the nature of quicksand. Iron, stone or other materials too heavy to be moved by the current sink below the surface of the sand in a few seconds . . . This characteristic of the bottom makes it simply necessary for a boat when working through a bar, to push ahead with its spars and keep in position so that the current may wash under and around it (Howell 1868).

This same action, used in freeing a vessel from a sand bar, takes place when a vessel is snagged and sinks. The river quickly absorbs the obstruc-

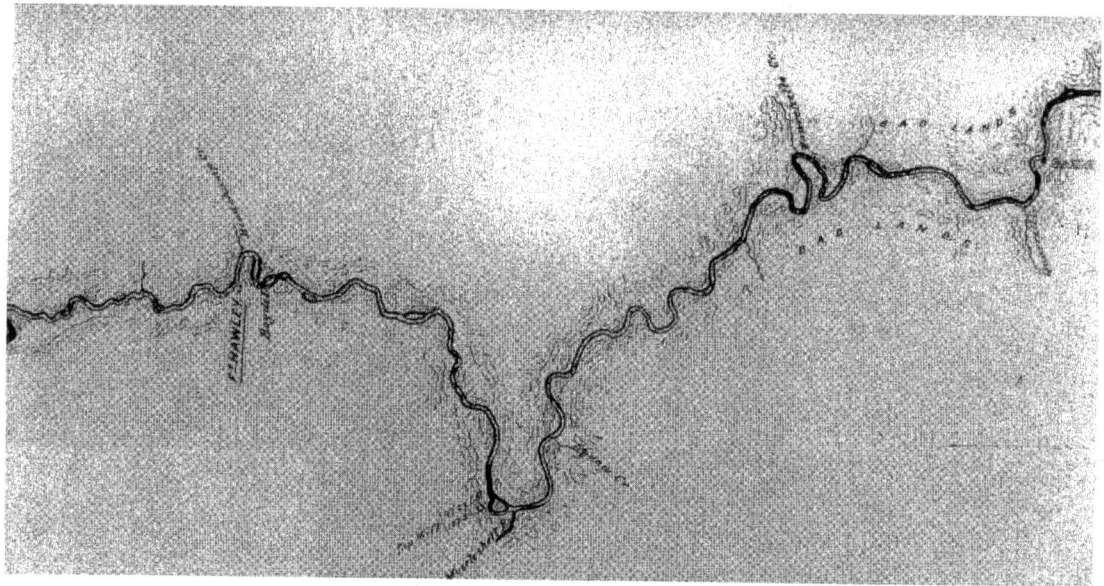

FIGURE 3. 1874 *Missouri River Boat Survey*, map showing the river channel, tributary creeks, land forms, and adjacent military posts (National Archives 1874).

tion, while simultaneously shifting around, under, and over it, forming an island around the wreck or simply shifting the current away from the obstruction entirely.

> Every bend of the river gives more or less emphatic evidence of this cutting action of the river at peculiarly susceptible points, shifting in a few weeks from 2 to 3 hundred yards into the bottom lands, and frequently cutting through the necks of bends[,] chang[ing] the whole channel for miles on either side . . . (Howell 1868).

By closely examining Howell's field notes we gain information vital for predicting site conditions, formation processes, and the potential for natural disturbance after the site was initially formed.

The second survey with its corresponding set of maps is the "Missouri River Boat Survey" (Figure 3), completed in 1874 by William J. Twinning of the United States Engineers Office and Lt. F. V. Greene, Chief Astronomer of the Engineers Office. Unfortunately this survey did not produce maps as detailed as the 1867 survey. The survey plots the course of the river and includes some information on channel composition, including depth, the prevalence of sandbars, and the names and locations of islands. No wreck locations are noted and few of the river bends are named. The names and locations of most of the larger tributary streams and creeks are present and river side military posts are also included. The overall topography is not as detailed as the previous survey, but the basic locations of bluffs and ridge lines are present. Noting the general land forms that are present proves crucial in evaluating the accuracy of this survey compared with modern topography. Further research revealed problems with the positional accuracy of the mapping. Twinning wrote, "I have compared the latitude with those of Captain Raynolds [1859/60 report and maps], and find no essential differences—the longitudes are however quite different in many places" (National Archives 1860; Raynolds 1860; Twinning 1875). Twinning's survey was a preparatory survey to

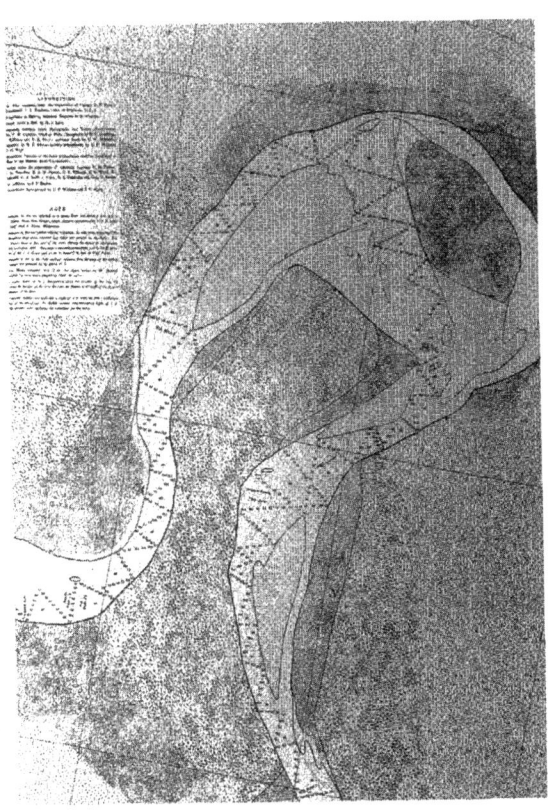

FIGURE 4. 1892-1897, *Missouri River Commission Map of the Missouri River from its Mouth to Three Forks, Montana*, 1:7,200. Hard Bar bend, location of the 1883 wreck of the steamboat *Big Horn* (National Archives 1892-1897).

be used in the logistical planning for the next big survey effort.

The Missouri River Commission's 1878-1895 survey (National Archives 1892-1897) which produced, "the Map of the Missouri River from its Mouth to Three Forks, Montana," is by far one of the most comprehensive historic surveys of the Missouri River. Most of the survey was conducted by Captains C. F. Powell and H. F. Hodges of the Corps of Engineers, with additional survey work in Montana conducted by Captain Hiram M. Chittenden of the Corps of Engineers.

Initially, two sets of maps were produced from the Missouri River Commission Survey. One set is large scale, 1:7,200, and a second set is a scale of 1:63,360. Although the two map sets cover the same geographical area, they provide slightly different information. For example, the larger set (Figure 4) provides river depths and soundings, bottom configuration, details of island composition, and vegetation of the land closely associated with the river channel. The smaller set (Figure 5) provides information about details further from the river bed and includes cultural information often left off the larger scale maps. Individual maps detail the location and depth of the river channel, and often illustrate areas with a high concentration of snags and other obstructions to navigation such as rapids and sandbars. Besides detailing the river channel, the survey also notes the surrounding natural landscape such as bluffs, tributary rivers, and canyons. Most notably, the Missouri River Commission maps illustrate the largest number of cultural features in the landscape. The names and locations of towns, individual homesteads, cemeteries, railroad lines and beds, and schools are often present on these maps. In addition, the cultural effects of long-term steamboating are present in the landscape and noted on the maps, with information such as river locations named for steamboats, steamboat pilots, and notable occurrences involving steamboat disasters. Although 19 wrecks had been reported by 1892 in the Montana area, the locations of only 3 wrecks are noted within the Montana section of the maps: the "wreck of the *Amelia Poe*" (1868), the "Wreck of the *Red Cloud*" (1882), and the "Wreck of the *Big Horn*" (1883) (Corbin and Karsmizki 1997).

The landscape and cultural information available on the 1892-1897 maps are an invaluable aid in predicting the location of wrecks in modern topography. Frequently, wreck locations are

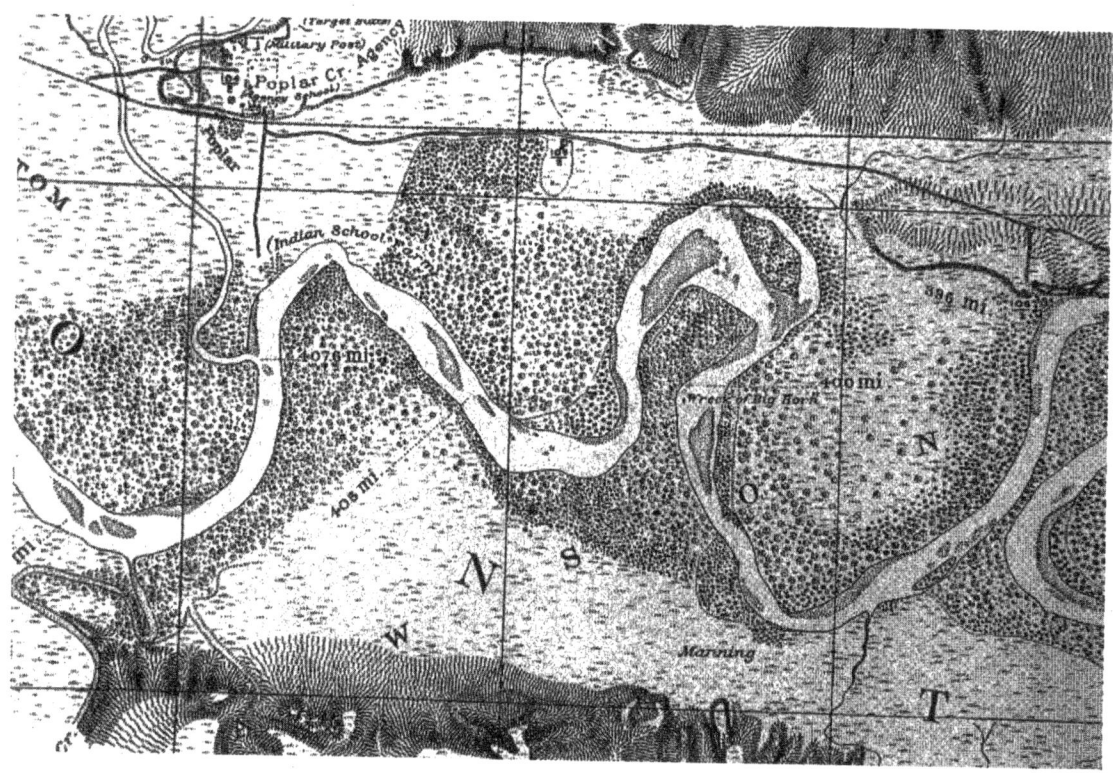

FIGURE 5. 1892-1897 Missouri River Commission *Map of the Missouri River from its Mouth to Three Forks, Montana*, 1:63,000. Hard Bar bend, location of the 1883 wreck of the steamboat *Big Horn*, note at this scale the wreck location is noted on the map (National Archives 1892-1897).

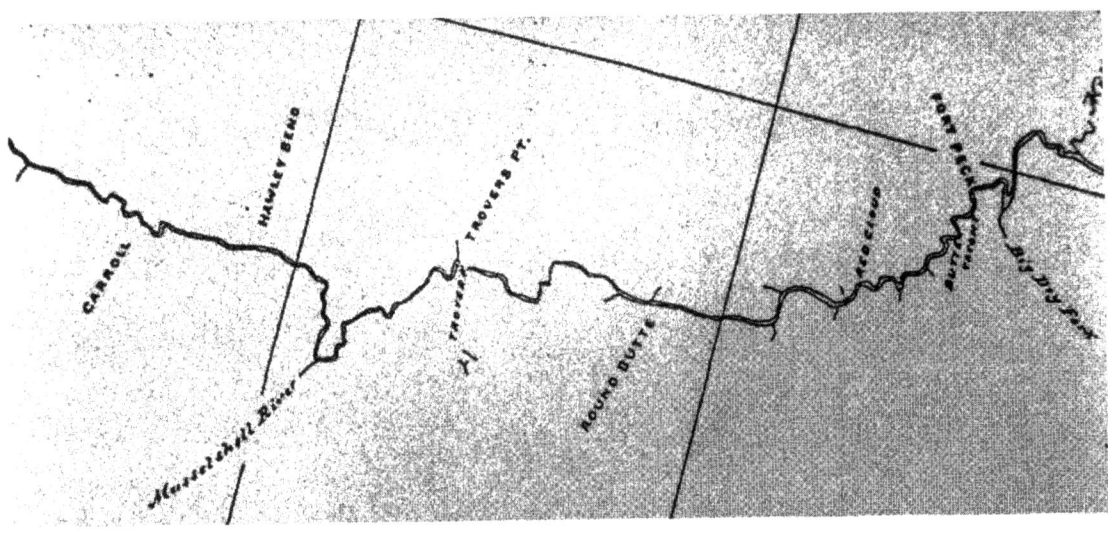

FIGURE 6. 1897 Chittenden map showing location of steamboat wrecks in Montana noted during the Missouri River Commission survey (Chittenden 1897).

noted by the use of a point or head of land, a bend in the river, or a proximity to a rural community. Often the only references to these places, frequently long forgotten, are on the historic survey maps. These historic place names become crucial when trying to relocate reported wreck sites today.

In addition to the original two sets of maps, Chittenden (1897) also produced a list of steamboat wrecks on the Missouri River and an accompanying map (Figure 6) derived from the Missouri River Commission survey. Chittenden's map only includes 47% of the Montana wrecks reported by 1897. His map, although sparse in landscape information, is the most complete mapping of Montana wrecks available in the historical map sources (Corbin and Karsmizki 1997).

Historic maps also provide significant data regarding stability and/or change at specific river locations over time, and thus provide an opportunity to evaluate site conditions prior to intrusive investigation. This is illustrated by examining the same point on the river on all three survey maps (Figure 7). An examination of the now familiar wreck of the *Trover* demonstrates that

the bend in the river where the boat sank becomes known as Trover Point by 1897. In examining the three maps, both the bend adjacent to the wreck and the shape of the point of land associated with the wreck changed through time. This shifting of the river is further illustrated by examining the 1882 wreck of the steamboat *Red Cloud*. When comparing visible river migration between the 1897 Missouri River Commission Map's site of the wreck of the *Red Cloud* and Chart 18 of the 1934 Fort Peck Reservoir survey (United States Engineers Office 1934), it is clear that the river channel moved south, away from the wreck of the *Red Cloud* (Figure 8). This is consistent with a *Helena Independent* (1920) news article in which Elmer Werner, a Montana local, claims to have found the wreck of the *Red Cloud* in an island formed as a result of the river meandering around the wreck. The 1934 survey shows that the island was absorbed into the surrounding landscape as a result of river migration (Corbin 1996; Corbin and Karsmizki 1997), thus verifying Howell's 1868 description concerning the formation of steamboat wrecks sites on the Missouri River.

The phenomenon of river migration is further illustrated by examining aerial photographs. Aerial photographs of "Hard Bar Bend" (Figure 9), location of the 1883 wreck of the *Big Horn*

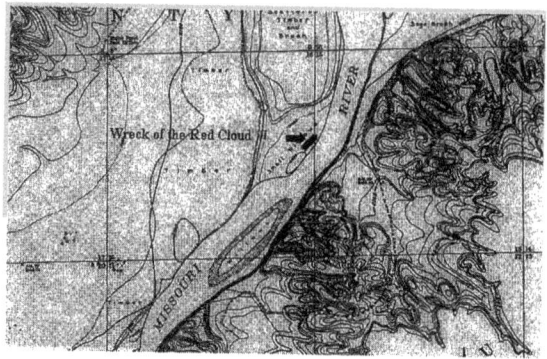

FIGURE 8. Chart 18 of the 1934 Fort Peck Reservoir Survey (U. S. Engineers Office 1934) with the wreck of the *Red Cloud* superimposed on it from an overlay of the 1892-1895 Missouri River Commission map (National Archives 1892-1897).

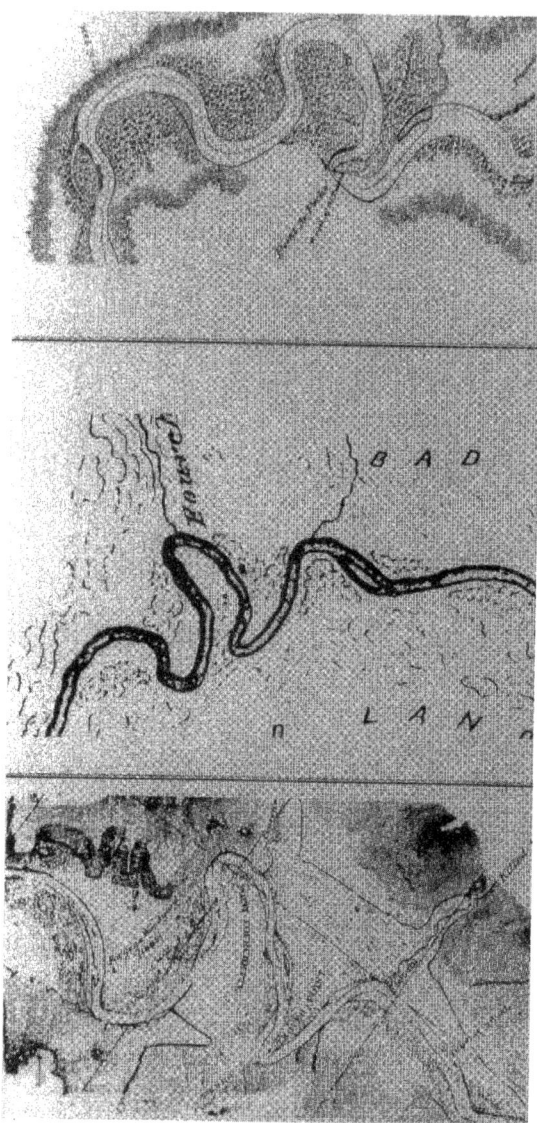

FIGURE 7. "Trover Point," site of the 1867 wreck of the steamboat *Trover* in all three upper Missouri River surveys; upper 1867, center 1874, lower 1897 (National Archives 1867, 1874, 1892-1897).

(Figure 10), document the changes in river bends, the formation and/or absorption of islands and sandbars, and the rate of erosion on the river landscape. Like changes that were noted in the 19th century maps, this particular bend of the river is still undergoing notable reconfiguration in the 20th century. In the 1956 photograph, the modern river (just south of the historic bend) splits around a large island in the south half of the photo. By 1991 this same island has been absorbed by the riverbank and now appears as a river scar much like the bend of the 1890s. Just as the 19th century Missouri River shifted continually to absorb or destroy cultural sites in the past, the same process is still observable today.

Conclusion

Investigating historic surveys and cartography is extremely important for understanding river migration of the upper Missouri River. This study has raised and subsequently answered several important questions concerning the use of historic cartography in evaluating the potential for locating archaeological sites. In 1979 Raymond Wood argued three important points:

FIGURE 9. 1956 (left) and 1991 (right) aerial photographs of "Hard Bar bend" area, location of the 1883 wreck of the *Big Horn*, on the Missouri River. Note the 1890s river channel scar north of the twentieth century river scars (National Archives 1956, 1991).

Maps are an important part of the interpretive program for any historic site. (1) First, because "maps are a precise index of geographical knowledge." . . . (2) Maps also preserve a variety of data relating to the locations of nearby features of importance to the mapmaker or his audience. . . . (3) Finally, maps preserve data on local ecology, information which is difficult [if not] impossible to reconstruct from written sources, but which is necessary in understanding the environmental setting of a site (Wood 1979).

Wood's arguments hold true for this study as well. Without a comprehensive cartographic evaluation of the migration of the Missouri River, it would be impossible to put together a predictive model for relocating lost steamboat sites along a volatile and unpredictable front. The Missouri River is one of the most historically turbulent rivers in the United States. Today, we often brace ourselves against the river leaving its banks during high flood years. We must not forget that long before modern dikes and levees, the river literally "ran wild," constantly altering its coarse at will. Understanding the meandering patterns of the Missouri and other river systems should be the basis of a well-informed archaeological investigation in any river basin and is, therefore, worthy of close scrutiny.

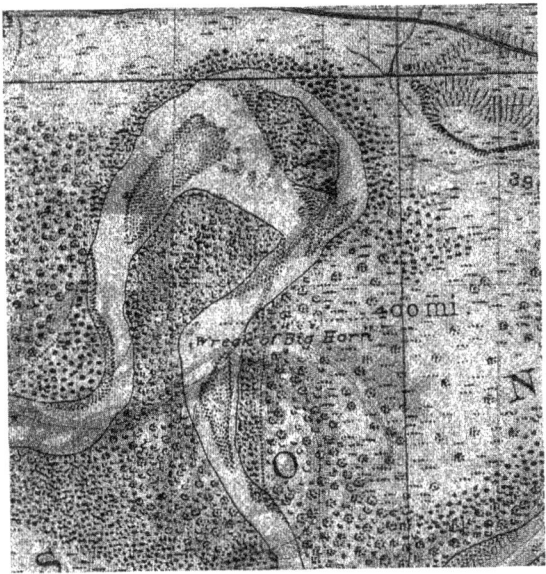

FIGURE 10. Predicted location of the 1883 wreck of the steamboat *Big Horn* in an old river scar just north of the present channel (by the author).

ACKNOWLEDGMENTS

The author thanks the University of Idaho's Honorable John Calhoun Smith Memorial Fund, Sons and Daughters of Pioneer Rivermen, which administers the J. Mack Gamble Fund, and the Museum of the Rockies for contributing funding for this research.

REFERENCES

CHITTENDEN, HIRAM M.
1897   List of Steamboat Wrecks on the Missouri River from the Beginning of Steamboat Navigation to the Present Time. *Annual Report of the Chief of Engineers, U. S. Army,* Serial Set 3631-3636. Washington.

CORBIN, ANNALIES
1995   Material Culture of Nineteenth Century Steamboat Passengers on the *Bertrand* and *Arabia*. Unpublished Masters thesis, Department of History, Program in Maritime History and Nautical Archaeology, East Carolina University, Greenville, NC.
1996   I. G. Baker & Co.'s Steamboat *Red Cloud*: Rediscovering a Forgotten Piece of Upper Missouri River History. Manuscript, University of Idaho, Department of History, Moscow, ID.

CORBIN, ANNALIES, AND KENNETH W. KARSMIZKI
1997   Steamboats in Montana: Wrecks of the Far Upper Missouri-Yellowstone River Drainage Area, Phase I—The Search for Historical Evidence. *Underwater Archaeology* 1997:61-68.

HELENA INDEPENDENT
1920   Location of Old River Steamer is Found in Jordan. *Helena Independent*, 8 June, p. 12. Helena, MT.

HOWELL, CHARLES W.
1868   Letter to General A. A. Humphreys from Colonel J. H. Macomb forwarding the Report of the Upper Missouri River conducted by Major C. W. Howell, in nine parts, January 14, 1868. Records of the Office of the Chief of Engineers, Correspondence of the Office Division, Entry 25, Letters Received, 1865-1870, Box 17-18, No. 641, Record Group 77, National Archives, Washington.

JACKSON, DONALD
1985   *Voyages of the Steamboat Yellow Stone*. Norman: University of Oklahoma Press.

KJORNESS, ANNALIES CORBIN
1995   See Corbin, Annalies

NATIONAL ARCHIVES
1860   Map of the Yellowstone and Missouri Rivers, U. S. War Department, Topographical Engineers. WDMC, 20, Record Group 77, National Archives, Washington.
1867   Sketch of the Missouri River from the Mouth of the Platte to Fort Benton, U. S. Corps of Engineers. Q137, Record Group 77, National Archives, Washington.
1874   Missouri River Boat Survey, U. S. Corps of Engineers. Q271, Record Group 77, National Archives, Washington.
1892-   Map of the Missouri River from its Mouth to Three
1897   Forks, Montana, in Eighty-four Sheets and Nine Index Sheets, Missouri River Commission. Civil Works Map File, 930 Portfolio Map, Record Group 77, National Archives, Washington.
1956   Aerial Photograph, Missouri River, Montana-ZV-3R-154. National Archives, Washington.
1991   Aerial Photograph, Missouri River, Montana-NAPP-3703014. National Archives, Washington.

RAYNOLDS, W. F.
1860   Topography and Hydrography of the Rocky Mountains and the Missouri River. Manuscript Q106-1, Subgroup b, Headquarters Map File, U. S. War Department, Record Group 77, National Archives, Washington..

TWINNING, WILLIAM J.
1875   Letter from Captain W. J. Twinning to the Northern Boundary Commission, 1 December. Records of the Office of the Chief of Engineers, Correspondence of the General Record Division, Entry 52, Letters Received, 1871-1886, Box 20, No. 2998, Record Group 77, National Archives, Washington.

UNITED STATES ENGINEERS OFFICE
1934   *Fort Peck Reservoir*, Chart 18. U. S. Engineer Office, Missouri River Division, Kansas City, MO.

WOOD, W. RAYMOND
1979   Notes on the Historical Cartography of the Vicinity of Fort Union, North Dakota. Manuscript, National Parks Service, Midwest Archeological Center, Lincoln, NE.

ANNALIES CORBIN
DEPARTMENT OF HISTORY
(HISTORICAL ARCHAEOLOGY)
UNIVERSITY OF IDAHO
MOSCOW, ID 83844-3175

1992 Using Remote-Sensing as a Tool for Middle-Range Theory Building in Maritime and Nautical Archaeology. In *Underwater Archaeology Proceedings from the Society for Historical Archaeology Conference: 1492-1992 500 Years of Change*, Donald H. Keith and Toni L. Carrell, editors, pp. 92–99.

SESSION

RICHARD J. ANUSKIEWICZ, MODERATOR

Technology, Theory, and Analysis

RICHARD J. ANUSKIEWICZ

Using Remote-Sensing as a Tool for Middle-Range Theory Building in Maritime and Nautical Archaeology

Introduction

This paper is presented to provide some guidance to the archaeologists working underwater contemplating using geophysical-prospecting data as a tool for middle-range theory building in maritime and nautical archaeology. The methodology and data presented herein are based on archaeological research conducted on and around St. Catherines Island, Georgia, and focus on the use of magnetometer remote-sensing. The research objectives were basically three-fold: first, to develop an historic maritime model for St. Catherines Island; second, to test this model by conducting comprehensive maritime and nautical archaeological studies of the waterways adjacent to and contiguous to the island; and third, to develop a correlation between remote-sensing signatures and the archaeological context for middle-range theory building. This presentation will specifically discuss the methodological approach used to develop a maritime model and how the model used nautical archaeology in middle-range theory building for St. Catherines Island.

Middle-Range Theory and How it Works

An example of how middle-range theory building works in historical archaeology can be drawn from a brief discussion of David Hurst Thomas' recent work (1987:67) at the Mission Santa Catalina de Guale on St. Catherines Island. Thomas was able to define linkages between the traditional archaeological concepts of walls, structures, and features and the way they are perceived remotely by sensors of geophysical prospecting, such as magnetometers (Anuskiewicz 1989:6).

Further, Thomas defines archaeological concepts as typically abstract categories employed by the archaeologist. In his research Thomas explored the archaeological context of 16th and 17th-century Spanish Florida, such as buildings, pits, graves, palisades, bastions, wells, etc., on St. Catherines Island. Therefore, effective middle-range theory relates these concepts to an unambiguously defined *class of empirically observed phenomena*; in remote-sensing these phenomena are the battery of signals and signatures that derive from nondestructive geophysical prospecting (Thomas 1987:66; Anuskiewicz 1989:7).

Constructing a correlation of remote-sensing signatures and the archaeological context *must* be viewed as middle-range theory building in archaeology. This is simply another way of assigning meaning to our empirical observations (Schiffer 1976; Garrison and Bray 1976; Binford 1977; Thomas et al. 1979; Hayden and Cannon 1984; Thomas 1986:238; Anuskiewicz 1989:7). Middle-range theory is how we *perceive* the past and is quite different from how we *explain* the past (Binford 1981:29; Thomas 1983a, 1983b).

Maritime Archaeology

The study of sunken watercraft on St. Catherines Island and their associated economic and cultural activities were subsumed under the general headings of historical and maritime archaeology. Muckelroy specifically defines *maritime archaeology* as:

The scientific study, through the surviving material evidence, of all aspects of seafaring: ships, boats, and their equipment; cargoes, or passengers carried on them, and the economic systems within which they were operating; their officers and crew, especially utensils and other possessions reflecting their specialized lifestyles

Chronological Periods - Spanish, British, Early American and Modern

Maritime Site Typology	Cultural Periods	Expected Site Factor Locational Indices	Expected Site Formation Processes	Expected Archaeological Indices	Expected Instrumental Indices
3.a.) SHIPWRECK Wooden hull, (continuous)	3.) Spanish, British, Early American	3.) "Loss traps", harbors, shoals, ocean-side beaches, shallows of navigable river and creeks.	3.) Poor navigation, natural-floundering, storms or hurricane, accidental-fire, economic-abandonment, warfare-scuttling or battle damage.	3.) Wooden debris and some metal fittings, nautical and personal implements, marine hardware, ship's cannons, sheathing and ballast stones.	3.a.) Bouyant hull pattern. A linear distribution of multiple anomaly peaks. A dipolar signature pattern oriented along the same heading as the long axis of the hull. Low to medium gamma intensity(10-80 gamma).
3.b. and c.) SHIPWRECK Wooden hull (discontinuous).					3.b.) Bouyant hull fracture pattern. Multiple dipolar anomalies radiating upslope and downcruuent from a more tightly clustered, high-intensity anomalies. Low gamma intensity(5-65 gamma).
					3.c.) Bouyant structure pattern. Non-clustered dipolar anomalies of varying intensities, scattered unevenly across the beach. Low gamma intensity(5-45 gamma).

TABLE 1. The St. Catherines Island Maritime Model

93

(Muckelroy 1978:6).

Maritime activity sites and sunken watercraft are a part of the archaeological resources. They were part of an active cultural landscape wherein maritime activities, processes, and the people who participated in them were part of a larger historical cultural context.

In my research, the use of nautical archaeology remote-sensing technology to evaluate the St. Catherines Island maritime landscape and waterways made it possible to discover and examine specific types of archaeological sites and materials of the historic period. By examining the physical characteristics and recent geological history of the island's landscape and waterways, this study was able to specify which waterways were navigable and to what size of vessel, and therefore predict the archaeological record for shipwrecks (Anuskiewicz 1989:11).

The St. Catherines Island Maritime Model

The maritime model for St. Catherines Island was developed to conceptualize archaeological expectations and to formulate and test a set of verifiable hypotheses. The model is represented by six major descriptive and analytical categories for data input, interpretation, and analysis (Table 1). The categories described in this model were developed from archaeological information initially derived by Thomas (1987, 1988) from the discovery and issuing studies of the Mission Santa Catalina de Guale.

Descriptive, Analytical Model Categories, and Expectations

Maritime Site Typology

This category identifies the types of specific maritime sites expected to occur on St. Catherines Island. These included a Spanish mission, a careening site associated with the mission complex, shipwrecks, and a ballast pile or marine dump site associated with the Spanish, British, early American, and modern periods of occupation.

Cultural Periods

This category is pretty much straight forward and represents individual cultural periods considered in this model. Each cultural period is matched with a maritime site type to provide specific site-type correlates for each period of the island's maritime history.

Site Factor Locational Indices

This category describes the expected geographic locations of maritime sites within the physiographic landscape of the island. These indices are specifically correlated with the *Maritime Site* and *Cultural Periods* categories to determine the most probable geographic location at which to search for a specific maritime site type.

The expected Site Locational Indices for shipwrecks on the island consist of the specific concept of "loss traps" as described by Schiffer (1976). These are specific areas where vessels are lost due to natural phenomena of storms, currents, and shoals. These loss traps are expected to be concentrated along open and unprotected areas of the eastern Atlantic coast and beaches of St. Catherines Island. Heavy shoaling areas located near the northeastern tip of the island and an inlet near the center of the island are also expected to be additional high probability areas for loss traps.

It is also expected that there is a direct correlation between the size of the vessel lost and the size of the loss trap or waterway in which it was lost. For example, the smaller, meandering creeks found on the island have historically been navigable only to smaller type vessels such as canoes, launches, sloops, skiffs, and smaller motor-powered recreational and sport fishing watercraft.

Site Formation Processes

This category describes how each type of maritime site was formed. For example, Thomas' recent work (1987) suggests the remains of the Mission Santa Catalina de Guale were formed as the result of the construction, destruction, and reconstruction sequence of the mission during the Spanish occupation of the island.

Site formations for shipwrecks are expected to be caused by poor navigation, natural foundering, accidental fire, economic abandonment, or mutiny, warfare, scuttling, or battle damage. The subsequent examination of the archaeological indices of individual wreck sites is expected to substantiate the site-specific shipwreck formation process. If a wreck is located in a "loss trap" and shows evidence of burning, one can assume that the vessel caught fire and ran aground.

Expected Archaeological Indices

This category represents specific archaeological features and material culture remains expected to be found in association with a particular maritime site type (Anuskiewicz 1982) identified in this model.

Wooden-hulled shipwreck sites associated with the Spanish, British, and early American period are expected to have the following archaeological indices: wooden debris, some metal fittings and fasteners, ballast rock, cannons, nautical implements, marine hardware, and personal items of the crew.

Wrecks of the later American and modern periods are assumed to contain more metal components associated with later construction techniques and the presence of the debris from these motor-powered vessels. Modern wrecks are expected to be constructed of materials such as steel, aluminum, and fiberglass and to be powered by diesel or gasoline engines (Garrison 1989).

Expected Instrumental Indices

This category is expected to produce correlative remote-sensing signatures for specific maritime features located during this study. These signatures and their verified archaeological correlates will form the foundation of middle-range

theory building for maritime sites associated with the island.

The Expected Instrumental Indices for a shipwreck associated with the island should vary with the particular historic period. For example, sailing vessels of the 16th, 17th, and 18th centuries were constructed mainly of wood and had relatively few associated ferrous metal fasteners and fittings. Some of these vessels are expected to have associated cannon, and all vessels should have associated anchor, ground tackle, and the crew's personal items as part of the ship's archaeological context. It is expected that historic period shipwrecks reflect specific wreck patterning and correlative magnetic signatures. In general, the magnetometer signature should reflect the lack of large quantities of ferrous components and produce low to medium amplitude dipolar anomalies.

Nineteenth- and 20th-century ships were, and modern ships are, constructed of more ferrous and steel components. These wrecks, and their specific wreck patterning, are expected to produce multi-point source, dipolar anomalies that are larger, sharper, and broader at a medium to high amplitude. These signatures would reflect the amount of iron or steel in the vessel's construction and the associated metal in the steam, diesel, or gasoline power train components.

It must be noted that the Expected Instrumental Indices represent only a general range of magnetometer readings for the periods identified in the St. Catherines Island maritime model. There are multiple variations of these instrumental indices for shipwrecks, variations caused by the wreck distribution pattern and the amount of ferrous material associated with the wreck.

The Archaeological and Material Cultural Expectations of Shipwreck Sites

Muckelroy wrote extensively on the expectations for shipwreck distributions and the preservation of specific elements of these sites (1978:157-225). His fundamental taxonomy divided shipwrecks into *continuous* and *discontinuous* types.

The continuous sites represent shipwrecks that, while undergoing varying levels of wrecking processes, are still relatively localized in their remains of the hull and any cargo or ship's fittings. The artifact distributions associated with these wreck have not been interrupted by sterile areas which do not have to be taken into account during the interpretation (Muckelroy 1978:182).

Discontinuous sites are those with elements of the ship widely scattered, with no single specific locus of the wreck site. These sites have been disturbed by the wrecking process. There is a total absence of any defining framework, making the reconstruction of such sites extremely difficult (Muckelroy 1978:196).

Clausen (1966) and Clausen and Arnold (1975) further discuss the discontinuous shipwreck patterns for shallow coastal wrecks:

> In the majority of cases, vessels of wooden construction lost on active, exposed coasts tend to break up and disintegrate under the influence of storm-generated waves and currents. Later, they may also be destroyed by intense attacks of various marine organisms and the effects of succeeding storms, scattering their components, ballast, and cargo over an area much larger than the dimensions of the original ship (Clausen and Arnold 1975:80).

Recent research in maritime and nautical archaeology has classified shipwreck patterning and developed Expected Instrumental Indices for specific wreck patterns, indices based on studies of the wreck's physical remains. Delgado et al. (1984) and Gearhart (1988a, 1988b) have further refined shipwreck patterning by developing distinctive site patterns using correlative magnetic signatures. They have designated these specific site patterns as buoyant hull, buoyant hull fracture, and buoyant structure. These wreck-type patterns and their correlative magnetic signatures were used as a basis to predict and develop shipwreck instrumental indices in this maritime model.

Development of Shipwreck Instrumental Indices Expectations

The *Buoyant Hull Site* is defined as a continuous wreck site in which the vessel comes ashore and settles in the sand relatively intact. Gearhart (1988b:40-43) reports that buoyant hull wrecks may differ from one wreck to the next because of materials used in their construction (e.g., wooden versus steel hulls). His expectations for this site type are characterized by two important magnetic patterns. First is a linear distribution of multiple anomaly peaks within the overall pattern produced by the remains of the intact hull. For a wooden-hulled vessel, one expects the anomaly patterns to exhibit a complex, elongated anomaly containing areas of high and low magnetic intensity within its boundaries. Further, the expectation is that the long axis of the anomaly pattern will be oriented along the same heading as the long axis of the hull. Finally, Gearhart suggests that the long axis of the anomaly pattern should be oriented parallel to the surf line because of the tendency of a drifting hull to turn broadside to the waves.

Buoyant Hull Fracture Sites are discontinuous wreck sites that occur when the hull of the ship comes ashore intact but breaks up on the beach and is dispersed by the surf. Therefore, the expected anomaly pattern for this wreck type would consist of multiple anomalies (i.e., wreck scatter) radiating upslope and downcurrent from an area of more tightly clustered, high-intensity anomalies (i.e., the area of hull breakup). This magnetic signature is produced as a result of the distribution of wreck parts (e.g., iron fittings or magnetic ballast material) that become scattered away from the main body of the wreck due to storms and wave action.

Buoyant Structure Sites are also discontinuous wrecks, formed when a vessel breaks apart offshore and washes onto the beach in pieces (Gearhart 1988b:40). This wreck type could leave a trail of wreckage scattered for miles along the beach. The magnetic signature would depend upon the size and quantity of associated ferrous debris that remained with the floatable materials that came ashore and the areal extent of their dispersal onto the beach.

This is a very complex wreck type because of the many variables to consider (e.g., distributional length of the wreck site, construction materials of the ship) when deriving expectations as to the magnetic signature pattern. Gearhart (1988b:43) expects such sites to consist of non-clustered anomalies of varying intensities, scattered unevenly across the beach.

Development of Specific Hypotheses

The specific information presented above has provided the necessary archival data and theoretical concepts to formulate working hypotheses to test the maritime, and nautical model for St. Catherines Island. From the maritime model, six working hypotheses were generated with respect to locating maritime sites and shipwrecks associated with the island. The hypotheses concerning shipwreck instrumental indices were easily evaluated using the St. Catherines Island data. The wrecks encountered, and their magnetic signatures, provided exhaustive data on the variety of expected site types discussed above. Certainly the data allow us to broadly classify sites based on the instrumental data. Evaluation of these hypotheses has led to the recognition of ancillary hypotheses. For example, the high correlation of wrecks with the "loss traps" of shoals and bars leads one to pose hypotheses concerning vessel type and size for other areas and to project probabilities for losses in those areas (Ervan G. Garrison 1992, pers. comm.). Even though several of these hypotheses are germane to this discussion, only one is presented below.

Results of Testing the Specific Hypotheses

What must be noted here is that state-of-the-art proton magnetometer instrumentation and underwater and terrestrial search techniques were used to test the specific hypothesis.

Hypothesis: Shipwreck sites will be concentrated at "loss traps"

This statement is true. The six shipwrecks inventoried during this research support the maritime model categories of the Expected Site Factor Locational Indices, Expected Site Formation Processes, Expected Archaeological Indices, and Expected Instrumental Indices developed for St. Catherines Island.

The Expected Site Factor Locational Indices category for shipwrecks in the model projected that wreck sites would be located in loss traps (Schiffer 1976). This study envisioned St. Catherines Island's loss traps at shoals and ocean side beaches. All of the shipwreck sites inventoried during this study were located in these areas. The wrecks exhibited various types of vessel damage prior to, or as a result of, the wrecking process. From the vessel damage, one could postulate the wrecking process and compare it with the Expected Site Formation Processes identified in the model. The debris observed at the wreck sites supported the Expected Archaeological Indices for modern-period shipwrecks. The magnetic signatures recorded for these wrecks also supported the Expected Instrumental Indices for modern wrecks as described in the model.

Middle-Range Theory Building for St. Catherines Island Using the Maritime Model

Maritime model building for St. Catherines Island through the use of archival research has developed sets of perceived archaeological indices for anticipated maritime sites and assigned correlative magnetic signatures to these expected sites. The testing of the maritime model through remote-sensing field work has developed sets of remote-sensing signatures that can be used as baseline reference information. These signatures have produced a framework for middle-range theory building for maritime sites associated with St. Catherines Island.

The shipwrecks studied and analyzed during the maritime study of St. Catherines Island are certainly specific to the island. The model building and testing by scientific inquiry for this study have provided sets of verifiable magnetic signatures. Therefore, this part of the research has provided the foundation for baseline geophysical signatures and the foundation for middle-range theory building for modern shipwreck sites associated with St. Catherines Island and similar physiographic sites throughout the southeastern United States.

Conclusion

The intent of this paper was to provide some guidance to archaeologists working underwater contemplating using geophysical-prospecting data, in particular from the use of the proton magnetometer, as a tool for middle-range theory building in nautical archaeology. This has been accomplished by presenting the methodological approach to building a maritime model. Further, this paper has shown that the systematic application of the scientific method and state-of-the-art instrumentation, along with a theoretical model, a sound methodological approach, and systematic field techniques, has provided the desired results in locating modern shipwreck sites associated with the island.

Using instrumental survey techniques in the service of well-defined theoretical expectations has eliminated many of the areas where many shipwreck sites could not occur. At a basic level of archaeological inquiry, this study has increased the discovery probability of locating these particular nautical sites with a continued application of this methodology.

This statement is particularly true if the specific theoretical expectations are manifest in discrete, archaeological indices. The archaeological indices are either the features and assemblages themselves or the observable instrumental correlates of these indices established by the application of middle-range theory building (Anuskiewicz 1989:228).

REFERENCES

ANUSKIEWICZ, RICHARD J.
1982 Site Reconstruction and Survey Methodology in a Blackwater Environment. Ms. on file, U.S. Army Engineer District, Savannah, Georgia.

1985 Three Dimensional Magnetometer Characterization and Marine Magnetic Distributional Analysis of the Hillsboro Beach Shipwreck: The Search for the *Gil Blas*, a 19th- Century Spanish Brig. Paper presented to the Broward County Historical Commission, Marine Archaeology Advisory Council, Ft. Lauderdale.

1989 A Study of Maritime and Nautical Sites Associated with St. Catherines Island, Georgia. Ph.D. dissertation, University of Tennessee. University Microfilms, Ann Arbor.

BINFORD, LEWIS R. (EDITOR)
1977 *For Theory Building in Archaeology*. Academic Press, New York.

1981 *Bones: Ancient Men and Modern Myths*. Academic Press, New York.

CLAUSEN, CARL J.
1966 The Proton Magnetometer: Its Use in Plotting the Distribution of Ferrous Components of a Shipwreck Site as an Archaeological Interpretation. *Florida Anthropologist* 19:77-84.

CLAUSEN, CARL J., AND J. BARTO ARNOLD III
1975 A Magnetometer Survey with Electronic Positioning Control and Calculator-plotter System. *International Journal of Nautical Archaeology* 4(2):1-88.

DELGADO, JAMES P., LARRY MURPHY, AND ROGER KELLY
1984 Shipwreck Survey of a Portion of Ocean Beach, Golden Gate National Recreation Area, San Francisco, California, to Locate the Remains of the U.S. Revenue Cutter *C. W. Lawrence*. National Park Service, Golden Gate Park National Recreation Area, San Francisco.

GARRISON, ERVAN G.
1989 A Diachronic Study of Some Historical and Natural Factors Links to Shipwreck Patterns in the Northern Gulf of Mexico. Paper presented at the First Joint Archaeological Congress, Baltimore, Maryland.

GARRISON, ERVAN G., AND ROBERT T. BRAY
  1976   Archaeological Investigations at George Washington Carver National Monument. Report prepared by the American Archaeology Division, Department of Anthropology, University of Missouri. Submitted to National Park Service, Midwest Region.

GEARHART, ROBERT L.
  1988a Cultural Resources Magnetometer Survey and Great Highway/Ocean Beach Seawall Project, San Francisco, California. Ms. on file, San Francisco Clean Water Program, San Francisco.

  1988b Marine Magnetometer Survey of a Proposed Sand Borrow and Sand Transfer Site Indian Rocks Beach Nourishment Project, Pinellas County, Florida. Ms. on file, Pinellas County Board of Commissioners, Clearwater, Florida.

HAYDEN, BRYAN, AND AUBREY CANNON
  1984   The Structure of Material Systems: Ethnoarchaeology in the Maya Highlands. *Society of American Archaeology Papers*, No. 3.

MUCKELROY, KEITH
  1978   *Maritime Archaeology*. University Press, Cambridge.

SHIFFER, MICHAEL B.
  1976   *Behavioral Archaeology*. Academic Press, New York.

THOMAS, DAVID HURST
  1983a The Archaeology of Monitor Valley: 1. Epistemology. *Anthropology Papers American Museum of Natural History*, 58(1).

  1983b The Archaeology of Monitor Valley: 2. Gatecliff Shelter. *Anthropology Papers American Museum of Natural History*, 59(1).

  1986   Contemporary Hunter-gatherer Archaeology in America. In *American Archaeology Past and Future: A Celebration of the Society for American Archaeology 1935-1985*, edited by David J. Meltzer, Don D. Fowler, and Jeremy A. Sabloff, pp. 237-276. Smithsonian Institution Press, Washington D.C.

  1987   The Archaeology of Mission Santa Catalina de Guale: 1. Search and Discovery. *Anthropology Papers American Museum of Natural History* 63(2).

  1988   St. Catherines an Island in Time. *Georgia History and Culture Series*. Georgia Endowment for the Humanities, Emory University, Atlanta.

THOMAS, D. H., AND CLARK SPENCER LARSEN
  1979   The anthropology of St. Catherines Islands: The Refuge-Deptford Mortuary Complex. *Anthropology Papers American Museum of Natural History*, (56)1.

RICHARD J. ANUSKIEWICZ
DEPARTMENT OF THE INTERIOR
MINERALS MANAGEMENT SERVICE
1201 ELMWOOD PARK BOULEVARD
NEW ORLEANS, LOUISIANA 70123-2394

2007. The Assimilation of Marine Geophysical Data into the Maritime Sites and Monuments Record,
Northern Ireland. *Historical Archaeology* 41(3):9–24.

Rory Quinn

The Assimilation of Marine Geophysical Data into the Maritime Sites and Monuments Record, Northern Ireland

ABSTRACT

Northern Ireland has been subject to significant maritime influences throughout its known 9,000-year human history. In 1997, the University of Ulster, in partnership with the Environment and Heritage Service, embarked on a program of seabed mapping in an attempt to record the submerged and buried archaeological resources. To date, the geophysical research program has imaged about 80 19th- and 20th-century wrecks and about 100 targets of further "archaeological potential." One method of integrating the results of geophysical surveys into the Maritime Sites and Monuments Record (SMR) is the use of the classification scheme CEBESSt, an alphanumeric wreck-site classification scheme based upon six site-specific variables: Composition of hull, Energy of wreck environment, Burial, Exposure, Structural integrity, and Substrate type, with t corresponding to time (the year of wrecking, if known). The classification is designed for use within a database scheme that allows for interrogation through character recognition and pattern matching.

Introduction

The northern Irish coastline, a predominantly high-energy environment on the North Atlantic, separated from Britain by the Irish Sea and Northern Ireland, has been subject to significant maritime influences throughout the last 9,000 years. Until 1992, when government accepted responsibility for the protection of wreck sites, archaeologists in Northern Ireland had a tendency to neglect the significance of maritime archaeology. Since that time, steps have been taken to record and protect the underwater cultural resource. Initial results, as reviewed in an interim statement by Colin Breen (1996), were encouraging, with the Maritime Archaeology Project culminating in the production of a computerized database of all known underwater sites in the coastal waters of Northern Ireland. This desktop survey was the first step in quantifying the potential resources. To date, the database contains details of more than 3,000 shipwreck sites.

The Built Heritage department of the Environment and Heritage Service (EHS) commissioned this research to assist implementation of The Protection of Wrecks Act 1973 and the Historic Monuments and Archaeological Objects (Northern Ireland) Order 1995. Although providing invaluable information, the major limitation in this approach was the lack of significant documentary information pertaining to pre-18th-century wrecks in Ireland. For this reason EHS, in partnership with the University of Ulster, embarked on a program of seabed mapping in an attempt to record submerged and buried archaeological resources (Quinn et al. 2000).

Large-scale terrestrial mapping of the island of Ireland began in the 1830s, and many of the visible archaeological sites on land have consequently been located and mapped. The program of marine geophysical investigation of the inshore waters of Northern Ireland is analogous to that process and represents an attempt to record maritime archaeological sites within their geomorphological context. A two-phase research program was designed: the initial phase (1998–1999) concentrating on reconnaissance mapping of sea loughs and embayments (Figure 1), and the second phase (2000–2003) focusing on individual sites such as natural harbors and navigation hazards around the high-energy coastline of Northern Ireland—areas selected through predictive analysis of the wreck inventory and the existing maritime landscape.

The coast of Northern Ireland measures approximately 1,000 km from Lough Foyle to Carlingford Lough (Figure 1). The geology and geomorphology of the coastal zone is varied but can be subdivided into three broad landscape types (Doody and Bleaky 1997). Rocky headlands and cliffs with local sand and gravel beaches characterize the northern and northeastern coastlines. The coastline to the east is of lower relief, with sand and gravel beaches predominating. The third coastline type is characterized by sea loughs or embayments (for example, Belfast and Larne loughs), dominated by fine sand and mud. Water depths

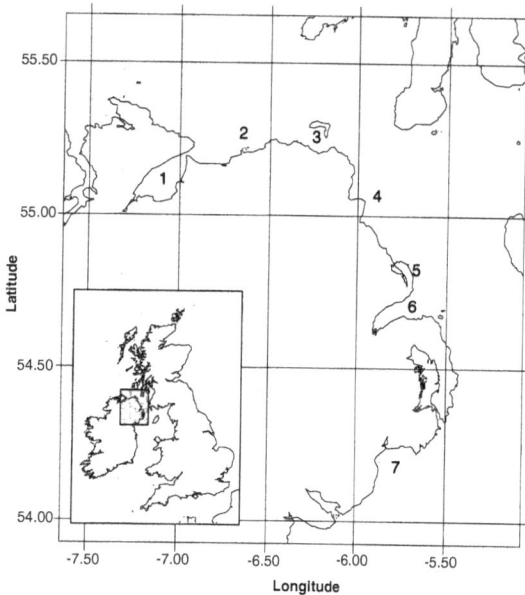

FIGURE 1. Locations of the field areas under investigation in the first phase of the marine geophysical research program: (1) Lough Foyle; (2) North Coast; (3) Ballycastle to Rathlin; (4) Red Bay to Carnlough; (5) Larne Lough; (6) Belfast Lough; (7) Dundrum Bay. (Drawing by author.)

within the field areas vary from a maximum of 200 m off the northern coast of Rathlin Island to 3 m within the sea loughs. Sand and gravel dominate nearshore substrate types, with gravel most common in North Channel where strong tidal currents prevent deposition of finer grained material (Atkins 1997). Two significant concentrations of nearshore sand deposits exist. One runs from Lough Foyle along the northern coast to Ballycastle Bay, while the other extends across Dundrum Bay. Nearshore mud deposits are confined to the sea loughs on the eastern coast.

The primary objectives of the marine geophysical research program are to

- locate the exact position (using a differential global positioning system, DGPS) and relative condition of wrecks; this information will make valuable additions to both the Maritime SMR and to the shipwreck database currently under consideration at the University of Ulster;

- present information on each archaeological site including site type, location data, water depth, site dimensions, seabed and subsurface conditions, sediment dynamics, and current or predicted site stability;

- produce wreck-prediction indices for the coastline of Northern Ireland based on site formation processes and site stability.

Research Program

The marine geophysical techniques most commonly applied to maritime archaeology are sub-bottom profiling, side-scan sonar, and marine magnetometry. The technology behind this instrumentation was primarily developed for military and commercial purposes, but it is being increasingly adopted in reconnaissance and site-specific underwater archaeological surveys (McGhee et al. 1968; Redknap 1990; Hobbs et al. 1994; Quinn et al. 1997, 1998; Arnold et al. 1999). The marine geophysical investigation of the inshore coastal waters of Northern Ireland employs the three techniques outlined above with the aim of providing comprehensive and detailed archaeological and geomorphological information on targeted areas around the coastline.

The nature and success of this type of research program dictates a multidisciplinary approach. In order to design each survey, relevant documentary sources are examined, and the known geomorphology of the area is considered. This information, in conjunction with data-resolution requirements, indicates the techniques to be employed at any given location. Palaeolandscape and wreck site evolution are of primary consideration, and the archaeology of coastal waters is being assessed within a geomorphological context. To facilitate the required multidisciplinary approach, the investigation includes researchers from a variety of backgrounds, including underwater archaeology, coastal geomorphology, and marine geophysics.

The University of Ulster geophysical survey suite comprises an EdgeTech Model SB-216S X-Star (Chirp) sub-bottom towfish, an EdgeTech Model 272-TD dual-frequency side-scan towfish, and an Aquascan AX2000 marine magnetometer. All data are logged as both hard copy and in digital format to facilitate offline processing. This suite of equipment is operated in association with a Litton Marine LMX 400 series DGPS system to provide real-time positioning.

To date, in excess of 1,100 km of trackline data have been acquired off the northern and northeastern coastlines, with survey speed at an average of 4 knots. The majority of the surveying was conducted in inshore waters, at depths ranging from 3 to 50 m. Surveys were primarily designed on a reconnaissance scale, with the side-scan sonar operated at 100 kHz (allowing swath widths of 200 to 300 m per channel) and a profiler line spacing of 300 to 400 m. When a wreck was imaged, the site was resurveyed with the side-scan sonar operating at 500 kHz, providing higher resolution data. One researcher is employed fulltime to acquire, process, and interpret data, also drawing on support from a number of archaeologists and geomorphologists.

At the time of writing, the geophysical research program has imaged about 80 19th- and 20th-century wrecks, and about 100 targets of further "archaeological potential." Once a site has been identified as being of archaeological potential, a contact sheet is completed for that site (Figure 2) and entered into the Maritime SMR (Sites and Monuments Record). Contact sheets provide details on position, water depth, substrate type, site dimensions, wreck identification, and a brief description of site dynamics and stability.

The following section outlines a case study of the Rathlin Island landscape project and demonstrates some of the lessons learned in conducting the seabed-mapping program. This is followed by a brief description of the CEBE-SSt classification scheme used for integrating the geophysical data into the Maritime SMR, currently under development at the Centre for Maritime Archaeology.

Case Study: Maritime Landscape of Rathlin Island and Ballycastle Bay

Introduction

The Rathlin Island case study is one component of the ongoing work reported in "Marine Geophysical Investigation of the Inshore Coastal Waters of Northern Ireland" (Quinn et al. 2000). The initial seafloor mapping survey around Rathlin Island was conducted during 1999, with the objective of mapping the location and current state of shipwrecks listed in the Maritime SMR. Rathlin Island was subsequently chosen for a diver-truthing exercise, as it offered a confined research area with high wrecking incidences and a large number of interpreted geophysical "anomalies." Diver truthing of the geophysical data was conducted during May 2000 to coincide with a visit by the Archaeological Diving Unit (University of St. Andrew) to the nearby protected wreck site of *Girona* at Lacada Point, County Antrim.

The success of any marine archaeogeophysical survey is largely dependent upon the experience of the surveyors and interpreters. While some research has been conducted on the geophysical signatures of manmade materials submerged and buried in the marine environment (Quinn 1997; Bull et al. 1998; Newell 1999), it remains a poorly understood subject. This often leads to the misinterpretation of acoustic data acquired for archaeological purposes. The only satisfactory method currently available for quantifying marine archaeogeophysical data is to physically ground truth any ambiguous reflectors, either through diver or remotely operated vehicle (ROV) investigations. With the increase in pre-development and research-orientated geophysical surveys (Quinn et al. 1997, 1998, 2002; Arnold et al. 1999; Momber and Green 2000; Simms and Albertson 2000), combined with initiatives to substantiate SMRs, a rapid and accurate method for ground truthing geophysical data is essential.

Natural Environment

Rathlin Island, L-shaped in outline, lies 10 km offshore from Ballycastle on the northern coast of Ireland and 22.5 km from the Mull of Kintyre, Scotland. The island measures approximately 4 km east to west by 2.6 km north to south, never exceeding 1.5 km across. Comprising tertiary basalt overlying cretaceous chalks, its perimeter is characterized by sea cliffs exceeding 100 m in places (Figure 3). Bathymetry is highly variable around the island, from 240 m off the northern coast to intertidal areas within Church Bay (Figure 3). On the northern coast of Ireland, the dominant winds are from the west, southwest, and south, each blowing for approximately 18% of the time, with winds from the northwest, east, and southeast blowing for 10% of the time (Atkins 1997). Tidal currents in the open sea during mean spring tides exceed 2 ms^{-1} (4 knots) off

ID Number	MGR0050	
Position	Latitude-Longitude[1]	6.2315°W 55.2165°N
	Irish Grid	435678E 203987N
Water Depth (m)	21m	
Seabed Type	Gravel-Sand	
Inferred Energy Conditions	High-energy	
Site Dimensions	50m x 30m	
Acoustic Return	High-energy backscatter with acoustic shadow	
Anomaly Desciption	Coherent structural debris	
Interpretation	Broken vessel	

Notes

Comparison of wreck with Maritime SMR and sports-diver reports indicates the wreck is *Templemore*, a coal steamer wrecked off Ballycastle in 1911. The remaining wreck-structure lies on a gravel-dominated substrate in a medium-to-high energy environment in Ballycastle Bay. The sonograph indicates the hull structure is fragmented, although structurally coherent. The acoustic shadow at the bow indicates the wreck structure lies approximately 3m off the seafloor at its highest part. Diver reports indicate the acoustic shadow towards the stern of the vessel emanates from the boiler.

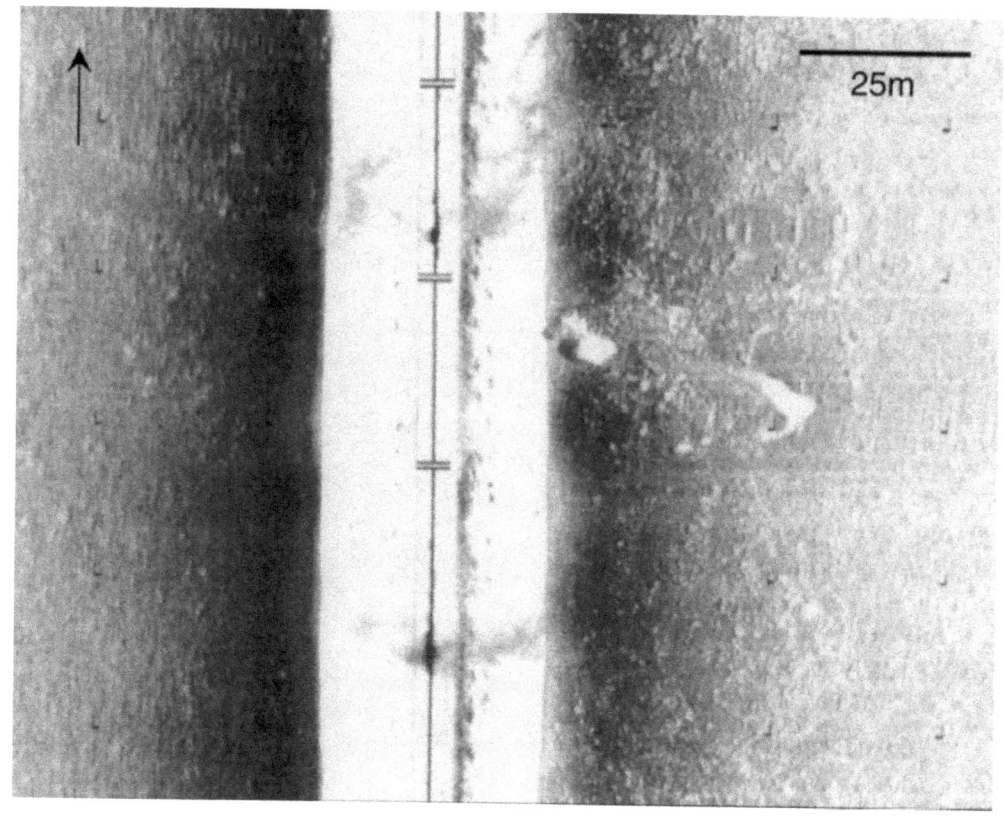

[1]Latitude-Longitude in WGS-074-84.

FIGURE 2. Sample contact sheet for the marine geophysical investigation research program. (Drawing and sonograph by author.)

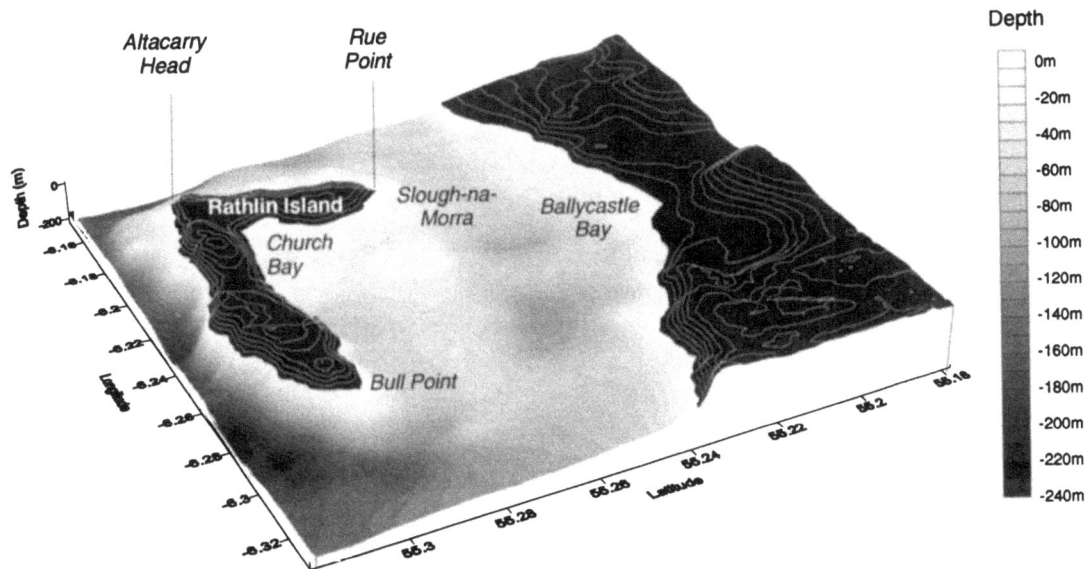

FIGURE 3. (*Top*) Digital terrain model of Rathlin Island and Ballycastle Bay; (*below*) Oblique aerial photograph of the lighthouse at Alticarry Head (Photo by Nigel McDowell; drawing by author.)

Ballycastle and Rathlin Island, where the North Channel is at its narrowest point. Tidal range is relatively low in the area, with a value of 1.0 m at mean spring tides (Atkins 1997). The sea around Rathlin Island is notorious for strong tidal forces, with variable and rapidly changing bathymetry combined with strong tidal currents producing a series of dangerous eddies around the perimeter of the island, most notably Slough-na-Morra (swallow of the sea) (Figure 3). The strong winds and variable tidal regime combine to make the Rathlin area hazardous for shipping.

Cultural Environment

Rathlin Island has a long history of occupation from the Late Mesolithic period to the present day (McCartan 2000). Archaeological evidence indicates that there was constant interaction between the island people and mainland Ireland and Scotland, with strongest evidence for this activity in the earlier periods of occupation. A Neolithic trading network, based on porcellanite stone axes, extended from quarries in northern County Antrim and Rathlin across Ireland and Britain (Sheridan 1986). Bronze Age burials and later promontory forts attest to continuity of set-tlement throughout prehistory. In the 2nd century A.D., the island appeared as Ricina in a gazetteer of the known world compiled by Ptolemy.

Within the last three centuries, 95 losses were recorded around the island (Figure 4). Of 50 strandings, at least 10 were refloated and 17 were reported as lost. Three recorded wrecks date to the 18th century, the earliest being a large, American three-masted vessel, which burnt and sank in Rathlin Sound in 1758. Sixty-seven vessels belong to the 19th century, and 25 belong to the 20th century. Of the 20th-century wrecks, nine were casualties of World War I, with eight armed vessels and the German *UB-82* falling victim to the conflict between October 1917 and March 1918. During World War II, a 1,375-ton Navy vessel, the *Duchess*, sank on collision with HMS *Barham* at Alticarry Lighthouse, with the loss of 129 men (Cecil 1990). Apart from the strong emphasis on naval vessels, more recent losses include schooners, brigantines, barques, fishing vessels, and steamers.

Much of the documentary evidence of shipwrecks in the Maritime SMR is rendered unsatisfactory by vaguely specified positions of loss. Thirty-nine of the ships listed for Rathlin Island are simply described as having foundered at Rathlin Island. Other positions are given in

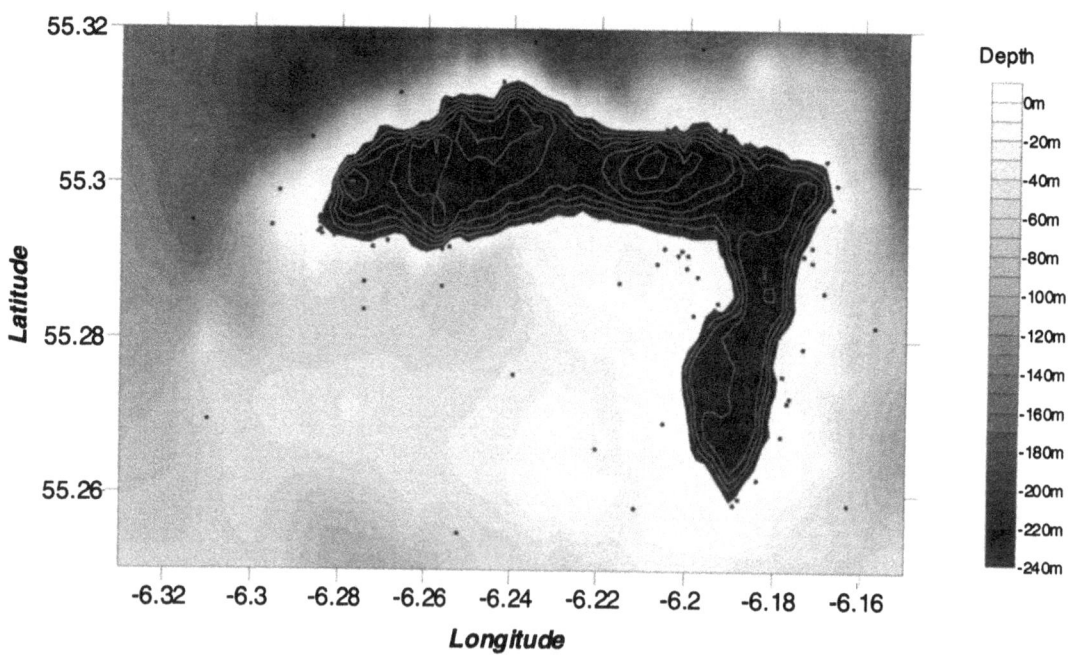

FIGURE 4. Maritime SMR for Rathlin Island plotted against contoured bathymetry. (Drawing by author.)

relation to bays or headlands, but few reveal accurate locations for confident ground truthing. There is a need for more exact and systematic survey techniques to accurately quantify the nature of the submerged cultural resource.

Geophysical Survey of Rathlin Island

The initial side-scan sonar survey of the seafloor around Rathlin Island was conducted over a four-day period in September 1999 from SV *Wandering Star,* using an EdgeTech Model 272-TD side-scan towfish in association with an EdgeTech Model 260-TH processor. Positional data was provided by a Trimble GeoExplorer II DGPS receiver. It was conducted at operational frequencies of 100 and 500 kHz with depth-dependent swath widths varying between 100 m per channel (Church Bay survey) and 200 m per channel (island perimeter survey). Water depths varied between 5 m and 200 m. No slant-range corrections were applied to the side-scan data during survey. Sub-bottom surveys in the region were conducted in 1996 and 1997 using an EdgeTech X-Star (Chirp) sub-bottom profiler operating at 2–10 kHz. Before diver-truthing exercises in May 2000 by

the Archaeological Diving Unit, high-resolution side-scan surveys were repeated over each target site using a LXT USBL (ultra short baseline) acoustic tracking system for accurate (±1 m) positional information. During these exercises, the real-time position of the diver was monitored using the LXT USBL acoustic tracking system. The position of the beacon attached to the diver was determined by interrogating three transducers housed in one unit on the side of the survey vessel and located immediately under the Trimble DGPS antenna. This was logged to screen in the wheelhouse, and the coordinates were overlain on the video image. Using this methodology, the diver was guided accurately to the feature of interest on the seabed, even where visibility was limited by suspended sediment and weed growth.

Results and Interpretation

The side-scan survey resulted in the identification of 46 anomalies deemed to be of archaeological potential based on geophysical signatures (Figures 5 and 6). These anomalies were further subdivided into three groups based upon their geophysical signature (dimensions, backscatter

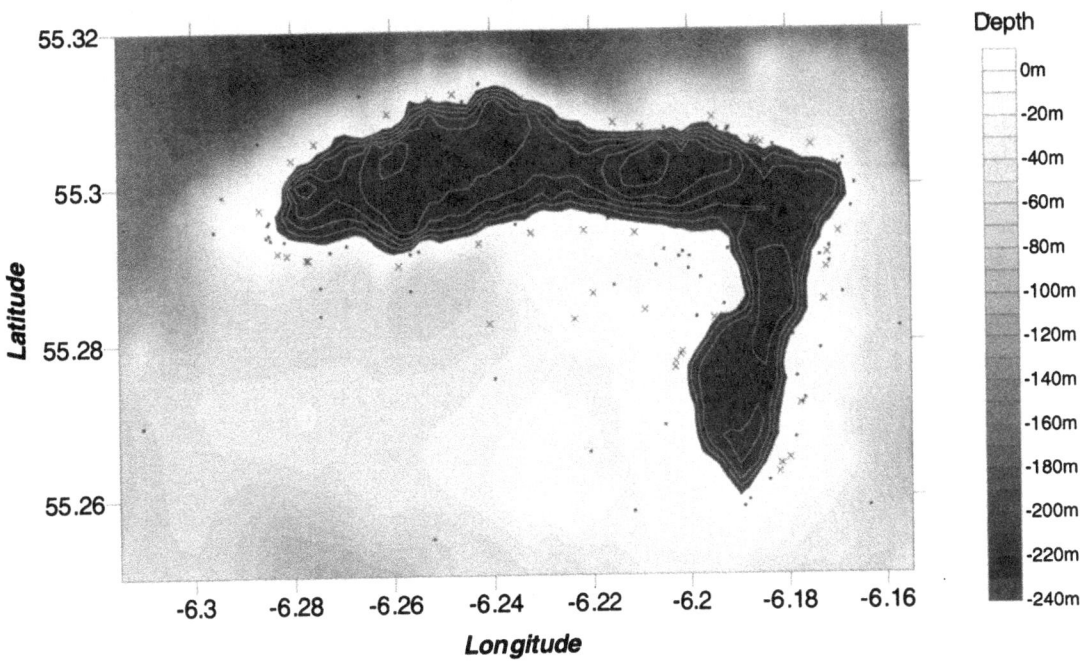

FIGURE 5. Side-scan sonar contacts (crosses) and Maritime SMR (dots) plotted against bathymetry for Rathlin Island. (Drawing by author.)

FIGURE 6. Examples of wrecks imaged in the side-scan sonar surveys around Rathlin Island. Tick marks on sonographs represent 25 m spacings. (Sonographs by author.)

characteristics, and morphology) and correlation with the Maritime SMR (Figure 5). These subdivisions are

Group 1: Definite wrecks

Group 2: Probable wrecks

Group 3: Possible wrecks (unclear whether the anomaly is cultural or natural)

Nine Group 3 anomalies were examined over a five-day period. The dive sites chosen were those that would best allow differentiation between natural and cultural reflectors. Of the nine sites dived, eight were natural features (predominantly bedrock), while the ninth was cultural—a 2.3 m Danforth anchor attached to 18 m of studded chain.

Examination of the point distribution in Figure 5 indicates the difficulty in directly correlating the results of the side-scan sonar survey (crosses) with the Maritime SMR (circles), since general patterns can be seen in each dataset. For example, there is no clear concentration of wrecks on any margin of the island, although there are local concentrations in each dataset around areas such as Bull Point and to the south of Church Bay.

CEBESSt: Wreck Site Classification Scheme

One challenge that faces the Centre for Maritime Archaeology and EHS after successful geophysical surveys and diver-truthing exercises is how to accurately assimilate the geophysical data into the Maritime SMR. Currently, the Maritime SMR is held as a digital database on a geographic information system (GIS) platform at the center. Researchers attempt also to integrate natural data (such as bathymetry, sediment types, etc.) with the cultural data, thereby aiding the development of wreck-prediction models through digital data processing and pattern matching. An obvious need exists for an elementary classification scheme to summarize the physical description of wreck sites interpreted from the geophysical data that can be integrated into SMR and GIS.

Classification scheme

The CEBESSt classification scheme is based upon six common wreck-site variables, which define sites by their physical characteristics: **C**omposition of hull, **E**nergy of wreck environment, **B**urial extent, **E**xposure to the marine environment, **S**tructural integrity, and **S**ubstrate type. The **t** in CEBESSt corresponds to time (the year of wrecking if known), which is not included as one of the standard variables, as the date of wrecking is not always known. Table 1

TABLE 1
CEBESSt CLASSIFICATION SCHEME

Variable	Description	Index
Var(1)=Composition of hull	Wood Metal Composite	W M C
Var(2)=Energy of wreck environment	High Medium Low	H M L
Var(3)=Burial extent	Clear Partially buried Buried	C P B
Var(4)=Exposure	Submerged Exposed Intertidal	S E I
Var(5)=Substrate type	Rock Coarse Medium Fine	R C M F
Var(6)=Structural integrity	Fully intact Hull partially degraded, with artifact scatter Hull unrecognized, artifact scatter	1 2 3
Numeric index=Time	Year wrecked (if known)	Subscript

summarizes the classification scheme, with each variable assigned a single character based upon the physical characteristics of sites. The result is a six-character, alphanumeric string of the form XXXXXX, which is a grading system providing information on site stability and site type.

Each variable is in some way dependent upon the other five. For example, the energy of the wreck environment, var(2), and the composition of the hull, var(1), are factors that obviously govern structural integrity, var(6).

Var(1): The composition of the hull is classed as wood, metal, or as a composite of the two.

Var(2): The energy of a wreck environment is dependent on many changing variables such as storm activity, wave-base interaction with the seabed and more constant factors such as bathymetry and surface- and bottom currents. In order to maintain the simplicity of CEBESSt, the energy variable is subdivided into three general states:

- Low-energy sites are considered as sites in which tidal currents and waves have minimal effect on the seabed. These sites are generally characterized by muddy substrates with consistent depositional rates.

- Medium-energy sites are defined within the classification as sites over which bottom- and wave-associated currents cause scouring of the substrate around the wreck (Caston 1979). Substrates at these sites typically comprise sand and gravel.

- High-energy sites are typified by a lack of sediment, with the majority of the seabed comprising exposed bedrock and scattered boulders. Such sites are often in open-water, swell-dominated environments.

Var(3): The third physical characteristic defined within the scheme is the burial of the wreck. This variable is in turn subdivided into three stages, with the two end members being sites that are completely buried and that are completely exposed above the seabed. Partially buried wrecks are defined as those with a minimum 10% of their hull structure buried in the seabed.

Var(4): The exposure of a site is defined as always submerged, always exposed, or alternately exposed and submerged (intertidal).

Var(5): Substrate types within the scheme are divided into rock and sediment. Sediment is further subdivided into coarse-, medium-, and fine grained according to the following grain sizes:

- Coarse grained refers primarily to gravel substrates with grain sizes less than -1ϕ (greater than 2mm). "ϕ" refers to phi-units, as used in the standard Folk classification scheme for sedimentary material (Folk 1954; Folk and Ward 1957).

- Medium-grained substrates, or sands, with grain sizes of -1 to 4ϕ (0.06 to 2.0 mm).

- Fine-grained substrates, clay or silt, with grains sizes greater than 4ϕ (0.001 to 0.06 mm).

Var(6): The degradation of the wreck structure over time is difficult to classify, as degradation rates and types vary significantly according to ship and boat construction. To maintain the simplicity of the scheme, structural integrity is only subdivided into three states of degradation:

- 1 = fully intact, with little to no erosion of super-structure

- 2 = partial hull and rigging degradation, with artifact scatter

- 3 = unrecognizable hull structure, with-artifact spread

This elementary classification scheme is designed with GIS and database management in mind, particularly as an aid to the production of digital SMRs. By using a character string to code the physical attributes of individual wreck sites, information can be sorted within a database according to individual or multiple variables by simple list or sort techniques. The uses and potential for CEBESSt are outlined below.

Individual CEBESSt Case Studies

Two contrasting sites have been chosen to illustrate the application of CEBESSt to the classification of wreck sites (Figure 7). The *Oregon* wreck site in Belfast Lough is typical of a nearshore modern site. *Oregon,* a single deck, twin-screw cargo motor ship of 4,774 gross tons ran aground on Wilson's Point in Belfast Lough in January 1945 (Figure 7). The fore- and after parts were subsequently refloated for scrapping, with the remaining wreckage lying off Wilson's Point (Wilson 1997). The shallow water depth over the site (4–8 m), together with its location within the path of strong northerly winds, contributes to the pounding the remaining wreck fragments receive (Figure 7). Additionally, there is an almost complete absence of sediment within the wreck area, with the majority of the remaining wreck elements lying directly on Silurian bedrock. As testament to the very high-energy conditions acting on the site, several pieces of wreckage were thrown above the high-water mark in 1997 and 2000 by severe storm-associated swell conditions (Newell 1999). The wreckage below the low-water mark is heavily rusted but structurally sound (Newell 1999).

In direct contrast, *La Surveillante* settled in 1796 in a very low-energy regime on a muddy substrate in 34 m of water in Bantry Bay (Breen and Forsythe, this volume) (Figure 7). Chirp sub-bottom profile evidence indicates that this composite wreck (oak hull, lined externally with copper sheathing) is buried to a depth of 2 m in uniform Holocene muds (Quinn et al. 2002). Side-scan sonar imagery (Figure 7) and divers' logs from the site indicate the wreck is degraded to its lowermost hull, with maximum exposure of the wreck at the bow and midships where the superstructure lies 4 to 5 m above the seabed. Diver surveys and geophysical data indicate good preservation of wood material on the buried portion of the remains of the hull. Tidal currents and wave base have little effect on the seabed in 34 m of sheltered water.

FIGURE 7. *(Top)* 500 kHz sonographs of the *Oregon* (1945) and *(bottom) La Surveillante* (1797) wreck sites. Tick marks on sonographs represent 25 m spacings. (Sonographs by author.)

The physical characteristics of both sites are in direct contrast. The modern (1945) metal-hulled wreck *Oregon* is located in a very dynamic environment, where the substrate is almost completely devoid of sediment. Conversely, the historic wreck *La Surveillante* is situated in a low-energy environment, with the buried hull remains protected from degradation by very fine-grained muds. The two case-study sites are ideal examples to test the application of the CEBESSt classification scheme. Table 2 summarizes the results for both sites, with *Oregon* classified as $MHCSR2_{1945}$ and *La Surveillante* as $CLPSF2_{1796}$.

Using a character string to code these physical site attributes, information can be sorted within a database according to individual or multiple variables by simple list or sort techniques. For example, if there is interest in composite wreck sites located in high-energy environments, the CEBESSt database is sorted by column 1 (hull composition) and then by column 2 (energy of wreck environment). This sorting procedure results in a list of wreck sites with the common variables.

Discussion

In the Republic of Ireland and the United Kingdom, increasing emphasis is being placed on national initiatives to quantify the maritime archaeological resource and compile accurate Sites and Monuments records (Ferrari 1995; Williams 1995; Breen 1996; English Heritage 1996). A key element in the identification and mapping of the archaeological resource is the use of geophysical survey. It provides a rapid, noninvasive survey technique, allowing large tracts of the seafloor to be surveyed in relatively short periods. The success of geophysics as a reconnaissance-mapping tool for maritime archaeology is dependent upon a combination of survey design, data quality, and the experience of the interpreter. Recognition of what constitutes an "archaeological anomaly" as opposed to a reflection from natural material is not always easy. When any doubt exists, the only effective means to clarify the origins of that anomaly are to ground truth the geophysical data through diver or ROV survey. The methodology presented above for diver truthing geophysical data is both accurate and time effective.

The side-scan sonar and diver surveys in Northern Ireland waters provide relatively accurate positional information for target sites, probably correct to within ±5 m when the accuracy of the DGPS (±1 m), WGS-84 ellipsoid Ireland (±2 m), and human error are taken into account. As noted above, however, the accuracy of positional information for sites in the maritime SMR is highly variable. Positional information in the record varies from word-of-mouth reports to DECCA and latitude-longitude readings from sources as varied as fishermen, sports divers, and the United Kingdom Hydrographic Office. Furthermore, for compatibility with the terrestrial SMR, these data are all converted to National Grid (in this case, the Irish Grid). These factors combine to introduce inherent inaccuracies in the

TABLE 2
CLASSIFICATION OF THE WRECKS *OREGON* (1945) AND *LA SURVEILLANTE* (1797)

Variable	*Oregon*	*La Surveillante*
Var(1)=Composition of hull	M	C
Var(2)=Energy of wreck environment	H	L
Var(3)=Burial extent	C	P
Var(4)=Exposure	S	S
Var(5)=Substrate type	R	F
Var(6)=Structural integrity	2	2
Numeric index=Time	1945	1796
CEBESSt classification	$MHCSR2_{1945}$	$CLPSF2_{1796}$

positional fields of the Maritime SMR. It is difficult, and sometimes impossible, to quantify this inaccuracy, and it is almost impossible to correlate the results from the side-scan survey to the maritime SMR on a one-to-one basis. Although a successful method for diver truthing the anomalies is now in place, the problem remains that this is a time-consuming and expensive exercise. To address this problem, all target sites are now being assimilated into the Maritime SMR using

TABLE 3
CEBESSt CLASSIFICATION FOR HISTORIC WRECKS

Variable	Desscription	Index
Var(1)=Composition of hull	Wood	W
	Metal	M
	Composite	C
Var(2)=Energy of wreck environment	High	H
	Medium	M
	Low	L
Var(3)=Burial extent	Clear	C
	Partially buried	P
	Buried	B
Var(4)=Exposure	Submerged	S
	Exposed	E
	Intertidal	I
Var(5)=Substrate type	Rock	R
	Coarse	C
	Medium	M
	Fine	F
Var(6)=Structural integrity*	Hull intact, mast & rigging upstanding	1
	Hull intact, partial mast & rigging	2
	Hull intact, collapsed mast & rigging	3
	Onset of hull degradation	4
	Stern & bow castle degraded to 1st deck	5
	Hull degraded to 2nd deck	6
	Hull degraded to lowest deck	7
	Hull degraded to lowermost section	8
	No hull, artifact scatter	9

* degradation

Numeric index=Time	Year wrecked (if known)	Subscript

Maritime Archaeology

contact sheets (Figure 2) so that with time, effective ground truthing exercises can be conducted in a systematic manner, perhaps aided in the longer term by student projects, sports divers, and predevelopment seabed assessments.

The resultant data may then be integrated into the CEBESSt classification scheme, which has a variety of potential long-term applications in the management of maritime sites in Northern Ireland. The six-string alphanumerics provide a basic but informative means of coding wreck sites for use in databases and GIS systems, which are increasingly being used for the analysis and management of archaeological data (Williams et al. 1990; Semeraro 1993). By integrating GIS with relational databases and data analysis tools, complex patterns result, which allow for spatial and temporal analyses. Amongst the most important applications of CEBESSt is its use as a predictive tool for highlighting areas of high potential in the coastal zone, by integrating wreck data with those from the natural environment (such as bathymetry and meteorological data). The results from predictive analysis can then be used for further geophysical investigations in selected areas.

One limitation of the basic CEBESSt scheme is that it allows minimal leeway for the classification of historic wrecks by their structural integrity. To address this shortcoming, the CEBESSt scheme may be extended by subdividing the sixth variable (structural integrity) into nine subdivisions that reflect the natural processes of structural degradation of wooden wrecks (Table 3). Using this classification scheme, *La Surveillante* is reclassified as CLPSF8$_{1796}$.

In summary, while the geophysical research program has successfully imaged some 80 19th- and 20th-century wrecks, the high-energy rocky coastline combined with harsh climatic conditions reduces preservation potential, especially for wooden wrecks. Preliminary findings indicate that modern wrecks are most readily located as meaningful images. Significant amorphous anomalies have also been identified on the seabed and *may* represent evidence of unrecorded wrecks. This has been the experience of researchers in the Centre for Maritime Archaeology in other parts of the world, where "seafloor mounds" identified from sonar data often betray the presence of older, less well-preserved wrecks. It is imperative that *all* geophysical anomalies are truthed with time.

Furthermore, to address the lack of understanding of the geophysical signatures of manmade artifacts submerged and buried in the marine environment, a control experiment was conducted in Belfast Lough in August 2001 as a collaborative project between the center, the Archaeological Diving Unit, and Management for Archaeology Underwater Ltd. A test site was laid out on the Lough floor, which was comprised of materials commonly found on historic wreck sites, including waterlogged timbers, leather, flint, gravel, glass, and ceramics. Side-scan sonar surveys were conducted over the site at different operating frequencies and ranges to assess the geophysical signatures of the anthropogenic materials. Initial results are encouraging and should allow for more accurate interpretation of sonar data in the future.

Acknowledgments

This research is funded by Environment and Heritage Service: Natural Heritage and Built Heritage, Department of the Environment for Northern Ireland. Many thanks to Brian Williams (Built Heritage) and Ian Enlander (Natural Heritage) for support. The following have offered logistical support and sound advice along the way: The Archaeological Diving Unit (University of St. Andrews); David Eccles and the crew of Fisheries Protection Vessel *Ken Vickers*; Geoff Farrow and the staff at the Centre for Maritime Archaeology; and the Coastal Research Group, University of Ulster, Coleraine.

References

ARNOLD, J. BARTO III, THOMAS J. OERTLING, AND ANDREW W. HALL.
  1999 The *Denbigh* Project: Initial Observations on a Civil War Blockade-Runner and Its Wreck-Site. *The International Journal of Nautical Archaeology* 28(2): 126–144.

ATKINS, W. S.
  1997 Offshore Geology. In *Coasts and Seas of the United Kingdom: Region 17 Northern Ireland*, J. H. Barne, C. F. Robson, S. S. Kaznowska, J. P. Doody, N. C. Davidson, and A. L. Buck, editors, pp. 23–28. Joint Nature Conservation Committee, Peterborough, England, UK.

BREEN, COLIN

1996   Maritime Archaeology in Northern Ireland: An Interim Statement. *The International Journal of Nautical Archaeology* 25(1):55–65.

BULL, J. M., RORY QUINN, AND JUSTIN K. DIX
1998   Reflection Coefficient Calculation from Marine High-Resolution Seismic Reflection (Chirp) Data and Application to an Archaeological Case Study. *Marine Geophysical Researches* 20(1):1–11.

CASTON, G. F.
1979   Wreck Marks: Indicators of Net Sand Transport. *Marine Geology* 33(2):193–204.

CECIL, TOMMY
1990   *The Harsh Winds of Rathlin*. Impact Printing, Coleraine, Northern Ireland, UK.

DOODY, J. P., AND R. J. BLEAKY
1997   Introduction to the Region. In *Coasts and Seas of the United Kingdom: Region 17 Northern Ireland*, J. H. Barne, C. F. Robson, S. S. Kaznowska, J. P. Doody, N. C. Davidson, and A. L. Buck, editors, pp. 13–19. Joint Nature Conservation Committee, Peterborough, England, UK.

ENGLISH HERITAGE
1996   *The National Inventory of Maritime Archaeology for England*. English Heritage and the Royal Commission on the Historical Monuments of England, Swindon, England, UK.

FERRARI, BEN
1995   Integrated Management of Archaeology in Coastal Waters. In *Managing Ancient Monuments: An Integrated Approach,* Andre Berry and Ian W. Brown, editors, pp.135–142, Clwyd County Council, Clwyd, Wales, UK.

FOLK, R. L.
1954   The Distinction between Grain Size and Mineral Composition in Sedimentary Rock Nomenclature. *Journal of Geology* 62(1):344–359.

FOLK, R. L., AND W. C. WARD
1957   Brazos River Bar: A Study in the Significance of Grain Size Parameters. *Journal of Sedimentary Petrology* 27(1):3–26.

HOBBS, C. H., D. B. BLANTON, R. A. GAMMISCH, AND JOHN BROADWATER
1994   A Marine Archaeological Reconnaissance Survey Using Side-Scan Sonar, Jamestown, Virginia, USA. *Journal of Coastal Research* 10(2):351–359.

MCCARTAN, SINÉAD
2000   The Utilization of Island Environments in the Irish Mesolithic: Agendas for Rathlin Island. In *New Agendas in Irish Prehistory: Papers in Commemoration of Liz Anderson,* Angela Desmond,

Gina Johnson, Margaret McCarthy, John Sheehan, and Elizabeth Shee Twohig, editors, pp. 15–30. Wordwell Ltd., Bray, Co. Wicklow, Republic of Ireland.

MCGHEE, M. S., B. P. LUYENDYK, AND D. E. BOEGMAN
1968   Locations of an Ancient Roman Shipwreck by Modern Acoustic Techniques: A Critical Look at Marine Technology. Paper presented at the 4th Annual Conference of the Marine Technology Society, Washington DC.

MOMBER, G., AND M. GREEN
2000   The Application of the Submetrix ISIS 100 Swath Bathymetry System to the Management of Underwater Sites. *The International Journal of Nautical Archaeology* 29(1):154–162.

NEWELL, PHILIP
1999   Ground-Truthing the Effective Resolution of Side-Scan Sonar Data. Master's thesis, School of Environmental Studies, University of Ulster, Coleraine, Northern Ireland, UK.

QUINN, RORY
1997   High-Resolution Marine Geophysics: Acquisition, Processing, and Applications. Doctoral thesis, School of Ocean and Earth Science, University of Southampton, Southampton, England, UK.

QUINN, RORY, JON ADAMS, JUSTIN DIX, AND JONATHAN BULL
1998   The *Invincible* (1758) Site: An Integrated Geophysical Assessment. *The International Journal of Nautical Archaeology* 27(3):126–138.

QUINN, RORY, COLIN BREEN, WES FORSYTHE, K. BARTON, S. ROONEY, AND D. O'HARA
2002   Integrated Geophysical Surveys of The French Frigate *La Surveillante* (1797), Bantry Bay, Co. Cork, Ireland. *The Journal of Archaeological Science* 29(1): 413–422.

QUINN, RORY, JONATHAN BULL, JUSTIN DIX, AND JON ADAMS
1997   The *Mary Rose* Site: Geophysical Evidence for Palaeo-Scour Marks. *The International Journal of Nautical Archaeology* 26(1):3–16.

QUINN, RORY, ANDREW COOPER, AND BRIAN WILLIAMS
2000   Marine Geophysical Investigation of the Inshore Coastal Waters of Northern Ireland. *The International Journal of Nautical Archaeology* 29(2):294–298.

REDKNAP, M.
1990   Surveying for Underwater Archaeological Sites: Signs in the Sands. *The Hydrographic Journal* 58(2): 11–16.

SEMERARO, GRAZIE
1993   The Excavation Archive: An Integrated System for the Management of Cartographic and Alphanumeric Data. In *Computing the Past: Computer Applications and Quantitative Methods in Archaeology,* Jens Andresen,

Torsten Madsen, and Irwin Scollar, editors, pp. 56–72. Aarhus University Press, Langelandsgade, Denmark.

SHERIDAN, J. A.
1986   Porcellanite Artifacts: A New Survey. *Ulster Journal of Archaeology* 49(1):19–32.

SIMMS, J. E., AND P. E. ALBERTSON
2000   Multidisciplined Investigation to Locate the *Kentucky* Shipwreck. *Geoarchaeology* 15(2):441–468.

WILLIAMS, BRIAN
1995   Coastal Zone Heritage Protection in Northern Ireland. In *Coastal Zone Management: From Needs to Action*, M. Carroll and K. Dubsky, editor, pp. 261–262. Trinity College, Dublin, Republic of Ireland.

WILLIAMS, I., W. F. LIMP, AND F. L. BRIUER
1990   Using Geographic Information Systems and Exploratory Data Analysis for Archaeological Site Classification and Analysis. In *Interpreting Space:*

GIS and Archaeology, Kathleen M. S. Allen, Stanton W. Green, and Ezra B. W. Zubrow, editors, pp.11–19. Taylor & Francis, London, England, UK.

WILSON, IAN
1997   *Shipwrecks of the Ulster Coast*, 3rd edition. Impact Press Ltd., Coleraine, Northern Ireland, UK.

RORY QUINN
CENTRE FOR MARITIME ARCHAEOLOGY
SCHOOL OF ENVIRONMENTAL SCIENCES
UNIVERSITY OF ULSTER
COLERAINE CO. LONDONDERRY BT52 1SA
NORTHERN IRELAND, UK

2011. Using Multibeam Bathymetry and Backscatter for Mapping and In-Situ Assessments of Deepwater Shipwreck Sites.
In *ACUA Underwater Archaeology Proceedings 2011*, Filipe Castro and Lindsey Thomas, editors, pp. 17–22.

Using Multibeam Bathymetry and Backscatter for Mapping and In-Situ Assessments of Deepwater Shipwreck Sites

Daniel Warren
Robert A. Church
Robert F. Westrick
Cheng-Wei Wu

Over the past decade multibeam echosounders have seen increasing use on underwater sites throughout the world. Since 2000, archaeologists at C & C Technologies, Inc. have utilized Autonomous Underwater Vehicles (AUVs) to collect high resolution acoustic data, including multibeam, and more recently camera imagery of deepwater shipwrecks. This paper discusses the use of multibeam bathymetry and backscatter data to document these deepwater shipwrecks. It shows how the data is used to map and assess sites, and examines the preliminary findings of recent research on the use of multibeam backscatter to assess site characteristics.

Introduction

For years, side scan sonars, subbottom profilers, and magnetometers have been the main tools for archaeologists to locate and initially assess shipwreck sites underwater. Underwater archaeologists have recently added multibeam technology to their repertoire of technologies for seeking out and documenting new shipwrecks. Multibeam bathymetry and backscatter provide high resolution, accurately positioned data that can be easily quantified, repeated, and integrated (Lawrence et al. 2004). Multibeam data allows three-dimensional (3D) viewing of archaeological sites in almost all water depths and visibility conditions.

Groundbreaking studies during the early part of the twenty-first century proved the viability of multibeam bathymetry and backscatter for underwater archaeology. Several innovative projects, including ScapaMap and RASSE, influenced the use of multibeam data in many areas of underwater archaeology, including deepwater archaeology. Deepwater archaeologists, many in offshore industry related fields, adapted multibeam data as part of standard methodology for deepwater shipwreck investigations. This paper explores the role multibeam bathymetry and backscatter play in deepwater shipwreck investigations.

Early Projects Using Multibeam on Shipwreck Sites

At the beginning of this century, several underwater archaeological projects employed multibeam systems for site documentation. Investigations on the Normandy Coast documented submerged features including lost vehicles, vessels sunk as artificial breakwaters, and Mulberry Dock remnants associated with the 1944 D-Day Landings (Mayer et al. 2003). In Italy, high resolution multibeam allowed mapping the submerged remnants of a Roman City at Baia and the Roman harbor at Porto Giulio (Wille, 2005). Two projects in the United Kingdom, RASSE, and ScapaMap keenly illustrated the potential for multibeam in shipwreck archaeology.

ScapaMap

At the end of World War I the German High Seas Fleet was interned at Scapa Flow in the Orkney Islands off the northern Scottish Coast. In 1919, 74 of the fleet's warships were anchored in the roads of Scapa Flow. The German officers and crew, isolated from news of the armistice, feared the British Royal Navy would seize their ships for use against Germany. This fear prompted the Fleet Commander, Admiral Von Reuter to send a prearranged signal to the Fleet on June 21, 1919. In short course, nearly the entire fleet, including 5 battlecruisers, 11 battleships, 8 cruisers, and 50 destroyers lay on the bottom. Recovery and salvage efforts over the previous half century have left only nine wrecks, or wreck remnants on the bottom. These wrecks form one of the world's most interesting underwater archaeological sites and its management and protection is a key concern of Historic Scotland, the agency overseeing the site (Forbes 2002).

Created by marine archaeologist Ian Oxley, ScapaMap's goal was to develop site management recommendations for Historic Scotland. ScapaMap was an integrated multi-disciplinary project. Its initial phase integrated data from various remote sensing systems, including side scan sonars and multibeam bathymetry systems, with diver based surveys to establish a baseline for site management and monitoring (Forbes 2002).

During the project, the use of multibeam systems alleviated most of the acoustic shadowing that typically obscured wreck site structure on side scan sonar records. The ScapaMap project results concluded that multibeam bathymetry combined with 3D visualization software was the best tool for documenting objects with high seafloor relief. The initial ScapaMap project did not utilize backscatter, but a subsequent study, part of the ongoing monitoring of the Scapa Flow wrecks, explored its usefulness (Forbes 2002).

ScapaMap2

ScapaMap provided an archaeological baseline for the remaining vessels of the German High Seas Fleet beneath Scapa Flow's waters. ScapaMap2 was developed based upon the recommendations in the original report for reassessment at the five year monitoring mark. In addition to reexamining the main wrecks, ScapaMap2 extended investigations to areas of previously salvaged vessels.

A RESON 7125 high resolution multibeam system collected bathymetry and backscatter data for ScapaMap2. Investigators found that when imaging high relief objects, acoustic shadowing in the backscatter data caused similar masking problems as those seen in side scan sonar data. The work found that backscatter data is a useful "collateral tool" for noting seafloor sediment change and "that it can help in the rapid-response and baseline mapping segments of archaeological sites investigation". The study further hypothesized that the ability of advanced multibeam systems to capture backscatter from the entire water column could increase resolution to allow identification of smaller seafloor targets (Forbes 2006).

Rapid Archaeological Site Survey and Evaluation (RASSE)

The Rapid Archaeological Site Survey and Evaluation study, RASSE for short, was a three-year study started in 2004 at the University of St. Andrews. RASSE's main goal was to devise a means of using geophysical remote sensing technology to quickly analyze underwater archaeological sites (Bates et al. 2007). It was designed to meet the need for a fast and accurate methodology for documenting shipwreck sites encountered in aggregate extraction areas in the waters around the British Isles. The project called for the assessment of wrecks using side scan sonar, single beam acoustic ground discriminating sonar, and ultra high resolution 3D multibeam bathymetry systems. The integration and quantification of data from these systems provides an accurate means of monitoring wreck sites (Bates et al. 2007:7).

Initial project testing was carried out on the Stirling Castle wreck site. Stirling Castle is a late seventeenth-century English warship lost in 1703 on the Goodwin Sands Banks off the eastern Kent coast. Stirling Castle was selected as a study site because it has seafloor morphology similar to those found in aggregate areas. RASSE project field work at the site used a RESON 8125 multibeam system combined with bathymetric and traditional side scan sonar systems (Bates et al. 2007:59).

RASSE concluded that multibeam sonar systems provided an effective means of quickly and accurately mapping shipwreck sites. The final 2007 RASSE report found that multibeam systems are valuable tools for detecting structural and sediment level changes at wreck sites over time, noting that remote sensing surveys and diver surveys are complementary rather than competitive to each other. The RASSE study recommendations argued for further trials to examine the feasibility of automated classifications using high resolution multibeam backscatter for wide area surveys (Bates et al., 2007:131).

Multibeam for Deepwater Shipwreck Studies

Deepwater archaeology is still a relatively new specialty in underwater archaeology. Many of the tools and technologies used for investigating deepwater shipwrecks have been adapted from offshore natural resources exploration industries. Although deepwater shipwreck study principles are still evolving, the subtle influence of early projects such as ScapaMap and RASSE can be clearly seen in current investigation methods, such as that put forth in Church and Warren's (2008) article "Sound Methods: The Necessity of High-Resolution Geophysical Data for Planning Deepwater Archaeological Projects". This methodology argues for the review and integration of all available remote sensing data for planning deepwater shipwreck investigations or excavations. Not surprisingly, this methodology makes extensive use of multibeam bathymetry and backscatter data for wide area site visualizations, site formation studies, and, more recently, site assessments.

Wide Area Visualizations

The development of wide area visualizations is a primary use of multibeam data for deepwater shipwreck studies. Deepwater archaeologists are unable to swim or walk over their sites (Church and Warren 2008). To gain a better understanding of the overall site deepwater archaeologists use 3D multibeam visualizations. This allows researchers the opportunity to understand site boundaries and seafloor topography, which is essential when planning ROV investigations and excavation projects. It can also illuminate spatial relationships among wreck components and artifacts that may not be readily apparent from other geophysical data. Archaeology relies upon the ability to discern spatial associations to accurately interpret and understand any archaeological site. Initially, only multibeam bathymetry was used for wide area 3D visualizations.

Deepwater archaeologists, however, are now incorporating backscatter into their 3D visualizations. Draping the backscatter over the bathymetry may illuminate, in addition to topographic and spatial data, subtle sediment differences within the site or site area. This is illustrated in Figure 1 showing bathymetry and draped backscatter imagery from the "Ewing Bank Wreck", the remains of a nineteenth-century sailing vessel discovered in 2006. The wreck site bathymetry in Figure 1A clearly shows the vessel's relief and the surrounding seafloor topography, but little else. Draping the backscatter over bathymetry (Figure 1B) reveals sedimentation differences within the wreck, most notably an area of high reflectivity within the wreck's interior that was also noted on the original side scan sonar data. Using this draped backscatter data archaeologists planned ROV surveys of the site in 2008 and 2009 that determined that the darker area of return on the backscatter was the vessel's ballast pile.

Site Formation Studies

Another way that multibeam bathymetry and backscatter data has been successfully used for investigating deepwater shipwrecks is in site formation studies, or how a site changes through time. Site formation studies examine the physical, biological, and chemical processes impacting a site over time (Quinn 2006:1420). Multibeam is used for impact analysis to provide important data regarding site formation, such as the direction and chronology of the initial wrecking or a wreck's disintegration. Multibeam visualizations allow researchers to view impact zone patterning that may be too subtle to discern, or may be masked by acoustic shadows on side scan sonar data.

Impact zone assessments at HMS Ark Royal, a World War II British aircraft carrier, only utilized multibeam bathymetry data to examine wrecking patterns. HMS Ark Royal was lost in 1941 to a single torpedo launched from a German u-boat. The wreck's remains were discovered during a 2002 Autonomous Underwater Vehicle (AUV) survey in the western Mediterranean Sea. The extensive seafloor relief of the main hull remains created extensive acoustic shadowing in the side scan sonar data that obscured much of the seafloor making it impossible to determine how the hull struck the seafloor (Figure 2A). To achieve a better view of the seafloor around the main hull section, the EM2000 multibeam data, but not the backscatter, over the site was processed. The resulting imagery (Figure 2B) enabled archaeologists to determine the direction of impact and calculated approximately how much of the hull had been buried beneath the bottom at impact. The directional sediment striations in Figure 2B, a result of sediment displacement from the hull's impact, indicate the direction at which the hull struck the bottom.

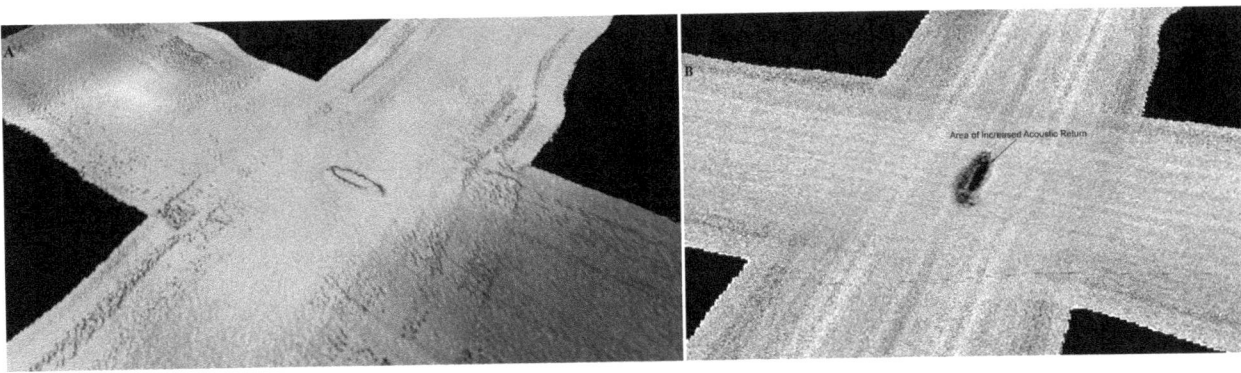

FIGURE 1. EWING BANK WRECK SITE (A) MULTIBEAM BATHYMETRY DATA, (B) MULTIBEAM BATHYMETRY DRAPED WITH BACKSCATTER DATA. (IMAGE BY AUTHOR, DATA COURTESY C & C TECHNOLOGIES, INC.)

FIGURE 2. HMS ARK ROYAL SHIPWRECK SITE (A) SIDE SCAN SONAR IMAGERY, (B) MULTIBEAM
BATHYMETRY DATA. (IMAGE BY AUTHOR, DATA COURTESY C & C TECHNOLOGIES, INC.)

Site Assessments

The integration of camera systems on AUVs is allowing archaeologists to use bathymetry and backscatter more effectively as part of their site assessments. In order to record images of the seafloor, camera equipped AUVs must survey at lower than normal altitudes, typically 8 to 10 meters above the seafloor rather than 20 to 40 meters above it. Flying this low increases the ensonification of the seafloor by the multibeam system. Initial visual comparisons of the bathymetry draped backscatter with AUV camera imagery revealed intriguing potential correlations.

In early summer of 2009, a shipwreck known as the "7,000 Ft Wreck" in the Mississippi Canyon Area was imaged with Woods Hole Oceanographic Center's Sentry AUV. The Sentry AUV collected not only camera imagery, but multibeam data from the onboard RESON 7125 high resolution multibeam system. Visual comparison of the camera mosaic and the draped backscatter data over the wreck noted areas of potential correlation. One area occurs at the port bow of the wreck (Figure 3). A linear area of increased acoustic return in the backscatter extending off the bow corresponds to an area of running rigging shown in the AUV camera images for the same location. It is hypothesized that the backscatter is reflecting an area of increased organics on the seafloor that represent the decayed or partially decayed mast

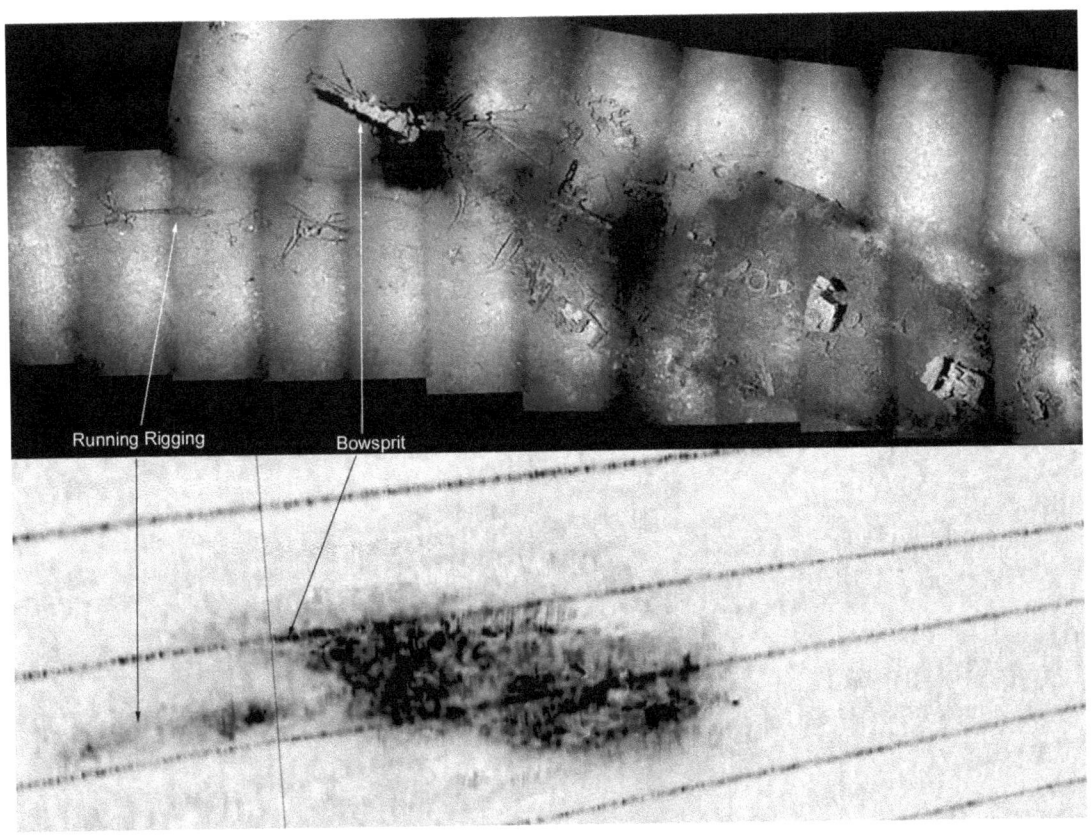

FIGURE 3. AUV DATA OF THE 7,000 FOOT SHIPWRECK SITE SHOWING THE CORRELATIONS BETWEEN CAMERA AND MULTIBEAM BACKSCATTER DATA. (IMAGE BY AUTHOR, DATA COURTESY OF WOODS HOLE OCEANOGRAPHICH CENTER AND THE LOPHELIA II PROJECT)

remnants that once held the rigging.

A second AUV survey, also conducted during the summer of 2009, imaged the remains of a nineteenth-century sailing vessel known as the "Ewing Bank Wreck". The survey, undertaken using C & C Technologies Inc.'s C-Surveyor IIITM AUV, collected camera images and EM 2002 multibeam data over the site. In September 2009, an ROV also surveyed the wreck in detail. Recent visual comparisons of the AUV camera and backscatter data from the "Ewing Bank Wreck" (Figure 4) appear to show subtle but distinct acoustic returns between areas identified in AUV camera and ROV imagery as copper sheathing, wood, and stone ballast. Although these two comparisons are far from conclusive, the results are tantalizing. Further research is necessary to determine whether these are valid correlations.

Conclusions

The first decade of the twenty-first century saw the use of multibeam systems grow in underwater archaeology, and especially in deepwater archaeology. Today, multibeam systems are a primary tool for deepwater archaeologists. Multibeam data plays an integral role in planning deepwater shipwreck investigations. Recent research in underwater archaeology and other associated disciplines shows potential for the further development

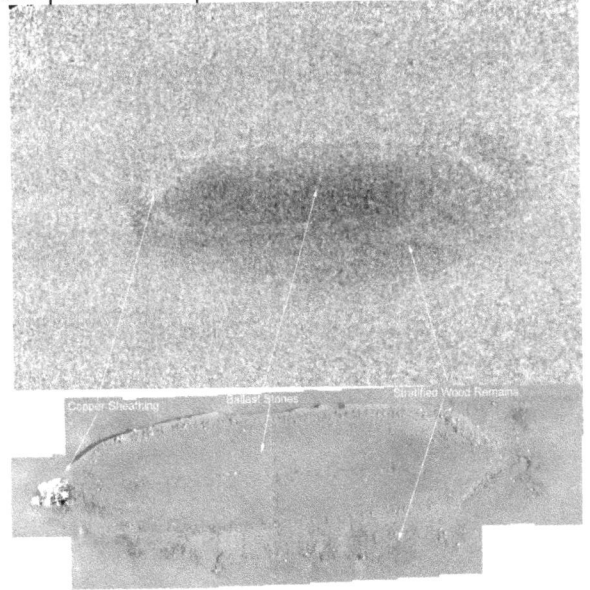

FIGURE 4. AUV DATA OF THE EWING BANK SHIPWRECK SITE SHOWING THE CORRELATIONS BETWEEN CAMERA IMAGERY AND MULTIBEAM BACKSCATTER DATA OF WRECK FEATURES. (IMAGE BY AUTHOR, DATA COURTESY C & C TECHNOLOGIES, INC.)

and use of backscatter data for archaeological assessments. But more research is necessary to confirm preliminary findings, improve backscatter processing software, and develop technologies and techniques for collecting backscatter. If the preliminary results hold true, then future advances related to multibeam bathymetry and backscatter may provide underwater archaeologists with a unique means of in-situ shipwreck analysis.

Acknowledgements

The authors would like to thank C & C Technologies, Inc., The Lophelia II: Rigs, Reefs and Wrecks Project Team, the Bureau of Ocean Energy Management Enforcement and Regulation, the National Oceanographic and Atmospheric Administration, the National Oceanographic Partnership Program, Woods Hole Oceanographic Institute, and TDI Brooks Inc., for their assistance and support. We would also like to express our gratitude the offshore AUV survey crews for their tireless efforts in collecting the data, without which this study would not have been possible.

References

BATES, RICHARD, MARTIN DEAN, MARK LAWRENCE, PHIL ROBERTSON, FERNANDO TEMPERA, AND SARAH LAIRD
2007   Innovative approaches to Rapid Archaeological Site surveying and Evaluation (RASSE). Final Report Submitted to English Heritage, Project Number 3837.

CHURCH, ROBERT AND DANIEL WARREN
2008   Sound Methods: The Necessity of High-Resolution Geophysical Data for Planning Deepwater Archaeological Projects. International Journal of Historical Archaeology 12:103-119.

FORBES, BOBBY
2002   ScapaMAP 2000-2002. Report Compiled for Historic Scotland on the Mapping and Management of the Submerged Archaeological Resource in Scapa Flow, Orkney (unpublished).

2006   ScapaMAP2 Marine Heritage Monitoring with High-Resolution Survey Tools: Scapa Flow 2001-2006. Final Report Compiled for Historic Scotland (unpublished).

LAWRENCE, MARK, IAN OXLEY, AND C. RICHARD BATES
2004   Geophysical Techniques for Maritime Archaeological Surveys. EEGS - Environmental and Engineering Geophysical Society Symposium on the Application of Geophysics to Engineering and Environmental Problems (SAGEEP) 17:156.

MAYER, LARRY, BRIAN CALDER, JAMES SCHMIDT, AND CHRIS MALZONE
2003   Providing the Third Dimension: High-resolution Multibeam Sonar as a Tool for Archaeological Investigations – An Example from the D-Day Beaches of Normandy. Center for Coastal and Ocean Mapping Joint Hydrographic Center, University of New Hampshire (unpublished).

QUINN, RORY
2006   The role of scour in shipwreck site formation processes and the preservation of wreck-associated scour signatures in the sedimentary record – evidence from seabed and subsurface data. Journal of Archaeological Science 33:1419-1432.

WILLE, PETER
2005   Sound Images of the Ocean in Research and Monitoring. Springer, Berlin, Germany.

Daniel Warren
C & C Technologies, Inc., Suite 100
10615 Shadow Wood Drive
Houston, TX 77043

Robert A. Church
C & C Technologies, Inc.
730 E. Kaliste Saloom Rd.
Lafayette, LA 70508

Robert F. Westrick
C & C Technologies, Inc.
730 E. Kaliste Saloom Rd.
Lafayette, LA 70508

Cheng-Wei Wu
C & C Technologies, Inc., Suite 100
10615 Shadow Wood Drive
Houston, TX 77043

2011. Testing the Efficacy of Synthetic Aperture Sonar to Locate Historic Shipwrecks in the Stellwagen Bank National Marine Sanctuary. In *ACUA Underwater Archaeology Proceedings 2011*, Filipe Castro and Lindsey Thomas, editors, pp. 23–28.

Testing the Efficacy of Synthetic Aperture Sonar to Locate Historic Shipwrecks in the Stellwagen Bank National Marine Sanctuary

Matthew S. Lawrence

Synthetic aperture sonar (SAS) has an area coverage rate several times conventional side scan sonar and a resolution of 3 centimeters. These advantages suggest that SAS can increase the efficacy of archaeological survey. Stellwagen Bank sanctuary partnered with Applied Signal Technology to evaluate SAS technology. The project undertook a survey on the approaches to Salem and Gloucester, Massachusetts, an area with nearly 400 years of maritime activity. Researchers found several shipwreck targets located on different seafloor varieties to analyze the SAS's target detection capabilities. This paper will discuss the project's results and the capabilities and costs of SAS.

Introduction

The Stellwagen Bank National Marine Sanctuary (SBNMS) encompasses 2180 km2 of seafloor astride the historic shipping routes used by mariners accessing some of America's oldest ports. Beginning with European colonization nearly four hundred years ago, much of New England's maritime traffic has moved through the sanctuary and over the centuries, collisions, fires, stormy weather, and human error have caused the loss of hundreds of vessels. Locating these shipwrecks is challenging; sanctuary depths range from 25 to 180 m and the offshore waters provide few geographic references for location. Lacking clearly defined vessel loss locations, this project sought to map the seafloor on the approaches to the historic ports of Gloucester, Salem, Marblehead and Boston. Sanctuary archaeologists believed that a large area survey was the best way to locate historic shipwrecks and that acoustic mapping would be the most effective method due to relatively low sedimentation rates in the area.

Archaeologists began inventorying the Stellwagen Bank sanctuary's shipwrecks in 2002 to meet the National Oceanic and Atmospheric Administration's (NOAA) mandates under Section 110 of the National Historic Preservation Act. Section 110 requires Federal agency preservation programs to identify historic properties under the agency's jurisdiction. Utilizing conventional side scan sonar and magnetometer methodology, surveys focused on discrete areas of the sanctuary that had been identified as having a higher likelihood of holding an archaeological site. Fishing hangs, historically reported vessel losses, and multibeam sonar anomalies have all been used to delineate survey areas. These efforts mapped seven percent of the sanctuary's seafloor and located 35 historic vessels, but surveys covering more than 20 km2 in area had not been undertaken. Investigating the sanctuary's entire seafloor with conventional marine archaeological remote sensing methodology was expected to require decades at its current pace. Fortunately, developments in synthetic aperture sonar technology began to surface for the archaeological community at events like AUV Fest 2008, a joint demonstration project organized by NOAA's Office of Ocean Exploration and Research and the U. S. Navy's Undersea Warfare Center. AUV Fest 2008 showcased the capabilities of mine-hunting autonomous underwater vehicles (AUVs) for archaeological research. While focused on AUV's, the sensors deployed on these vehicles offered exciting new research opportunities. In particular, the synthetic aperture sonar (SAS) developed by Applied Signal Technology, Inc. (AST) created very detailed sonar images at ranges beyond the capabilities of conventional side scan sonars. The Principal Investigator initiated discussions with AST to deploy a SAS for a large scale survey to test the sonar's real-world capabilities during an extended project, something the company had not yet done.

Synthetic Aperture Sonar Technology

Synthetic Aperture Sonar technology exemplifies recent advances in geophysical survey technology that will revolutionize seafloor mapping. SAS creates acoustic images similar to conventional side scan sonar, but the seafloor images are a constant, high-resolution over longer ranges. Conventional side scan sonars trade resolution for range or vice versa. Higher signal frequencies provide greater resolution, but signal attenuation limits the sonar's effective range. Lower signal frequencies suffer less attenuation, but have a longer wavelength and wider pulse width that prevents differentiation between closely spaced objects perpendicular to the sonar's path (Fish and Carr 1990:35). Conventional side scan sonar's ability to resolve small objects is further limited by beam spreading, which results in less resolution along track as across track, particularly as the sonar's range increases (Fish and Carr 1990:34). Side scan sonar's limitations are due to the length of its transducer arrays or aperture (Blondel 2009:25; McHugh 2000). Where most side scan sonars have an aperture less than 1 m long that uses a single transmit and receive cycle to create seafloor imagery, SAS combines multiple transmit and receive cycles using advanced signal processing to electronically create a 100 m long transducer array that maintains a constant resolution across its entire range (Sternlicht and Pesaturo 2004). Applied Signal Technology's synthetic aperture sonar, named PROSAS, operates at a frequency of 175 kHz, and can resolve objects as small as 3 cm2 out to the edge of its 150 m range at a speed of 4.5 knots. At this speed, PROSAS has a theoretical area coverage rate of 2.5 km2 per hour. In contrast, conventional side scan sonar technology in the form of an EdgeTech 4200 with 900 kHz transducers can resolve an object 18 cm along track and 1 cm across track (EdgeTech). When

operating at 50 m range scale and 4.5-knot tow speed, the Edgetech 4200 achieves a maximum area coverage rate of 0.83 km2 per hour. In reality, the area coverage rate is lower for both technologies as these rates do not include coverage of the nadir directly under the towfish. In addition to generating SAS imagery, PROSAS also operates as a multibeam side scan sonar creating interferometric bathymetry with 20 cm vertical and horizontal resolution. PROSAS's capabilities suggest dramatic advantages to using SAS technology.

AST combined their SAS with the MacArtney FOCUS-2 remotely operated tow vehicle (ROTV) to create an integrated towed acoustic mapping device, the PROSAS Surveyor (Figure 1). The FOCUS-2 towfish operates like an underwater box kite providing stability for the SAS multi-ping processing. Furthermore, the dynamically controlled towfish can maintain a precise altitude and track over varying topography and against currents. To create the "synthetic" transducer array, the precise heading, attitude, and speed of the towfish must be known by the SAS acquisition software. On the PROSAS Surveyor, a doppler velocity log and ring laser gyro inertial navigation system provide this information. As the sound velocity of the surrounding water is critical to the SAS processing, a conductivity, temperature, depth (CTD) instrument on the towfish continuously

FIGURE 1. THE PROSAS SURVEYOR TOWFISH BEING DEPLOYED FROM THE R/V SRVx (NOAA/SBNMS AND APPLIED SIGNAL TECHNOLOGY, 2010).

Perspectives from *Historical Archaeology* and *ACUA Proceedings*

provides salinity and temperature. Geographic positioning of the SAS data is derived from an ultrashort baseline (USBL) transponder system that calculates the range and bearing to the towfish from the research vessel's differential global positioning system. The FOCUS-2 vehicle utilizes an electric winch spooled with armored fiber-optic tow cable. While the FOCUS-2 ROTV weighs approximately 300 kg in air it is only slightly negative in water. More importantly, the winch weighs 3000 kg and requires a 440 VAC 3-phase power supply necessitating deployment on an appropriately sized research vessel.

The PROSAS Surveyor provides near real-time display of the SAS seafloor imagery. Like side scan sonar, SAS data is displayed in a waterfall; however, the display does not cascade at a consistent rate. SAS data is created in segments, referred to as SAS frames. Each SAS frame consists of a seafloor image covering an area 75 m along track and 150 m across track on both sides of the towfish. As the PROSAS software generates the SAS frames, it also produces a geo-rectified TIFF file for each segment. Data review and GIS analysis are greatly facilitated by this feature. The system's simultaneous multibeam side scan sonar provides a conventional waterfall display in real-time useful for responding to sonar glitches before they appear in the SAS data.

Survey Operations

The project's survey platform was the research vessel *SRVx*, operated by the Office of National Marine Sanctuaries. The *SRVx* measured 26 m long by 7 m in beam. Its stern well deck, spanned by an A-frame, proved to be an ideal launch and recovery area for the PROSAS Surveyor towfish. Mounted aft of the wheelhouse, the PROSAS surveyor winch could be locally controlled during launch and recovery or remotely controlled while surveying.

Sonar technicians controlled survey operations from the vessel's dry lab space. One station controlled the operation of the winch, towfish, and survey line navigation. The other station recorded and displayed the SAS and multibeam side scan data and allowed the team to log and study sonar contacts during data acquisition. The 10 person project team rotated shifts every 8 hours as survey operations ran 24 hours a day. Typically, two members of the vessel's crew and two sonar operators were on-duty at any given time.

Prior to beginning the survey, the project team developed a survey line plan to govern the path of the *SRVx*

and the PROSAS Surveyor. Using the known seafloor bathymetry in the survey area, the team plotted survey lines that followed the contours of the seafloor. The survey area was divided into two distinct line orientations to minimize rapid changes in bathymetry along any given line. When the project was initially conceived, AST intended to deploy a nadir gap-filling sonar array on the PROSAS Surveyor. The gap-filling sonar data was to be integrated into the SAS imagery creating a seamless 300 m swath. Unfortunately, data integration proved to be more difficult than the AST engineers anticipated and it was not ready in time. The project resorted to line spacing to ensonify the nadir. Survey lines were separated by alternating distances of 130 m and 280 m.

Project Results

The project set out to systematically survey the sanctuary's northwest corner off Cape Ann. Initial plans with the nadir gap-filling sonar estimated that 200 km2 per hour of seafloor could be covered during the time allotted; ultimately 169 km2 per hour were mapped (Figure 2). While data analysis has not been completed, over a dozen sonar targets with archaeological resource characteristics were found within the survey area.

Sonar targets ranged from identifiable vessel shapes to smaller objects that exhibited straight features or were at odds with the surrounding geology. Two examples of SAS targets with readily identifiable vessel features were detected at distances of 75 m to 125 m from the towfish. One target had a largely intact hull measuring

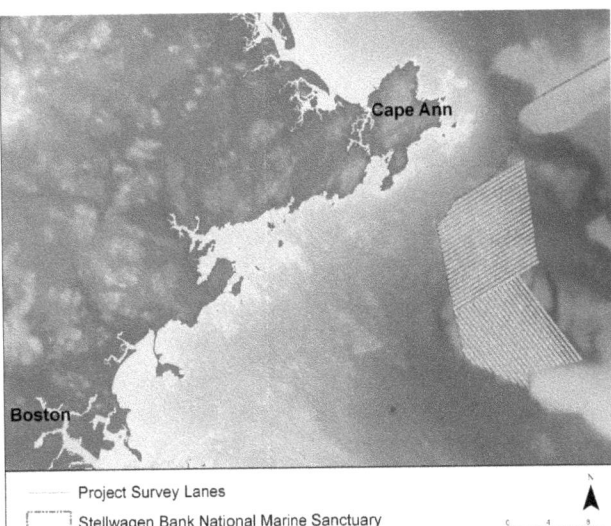

FIGURE 2. SURVEY LINES, COVERING 169 SQUARE-KM, COMPLETED DURING THE STELLWAGEN BANK SANCTUARY PROJECT (NOAA/SBNMS, 2011).

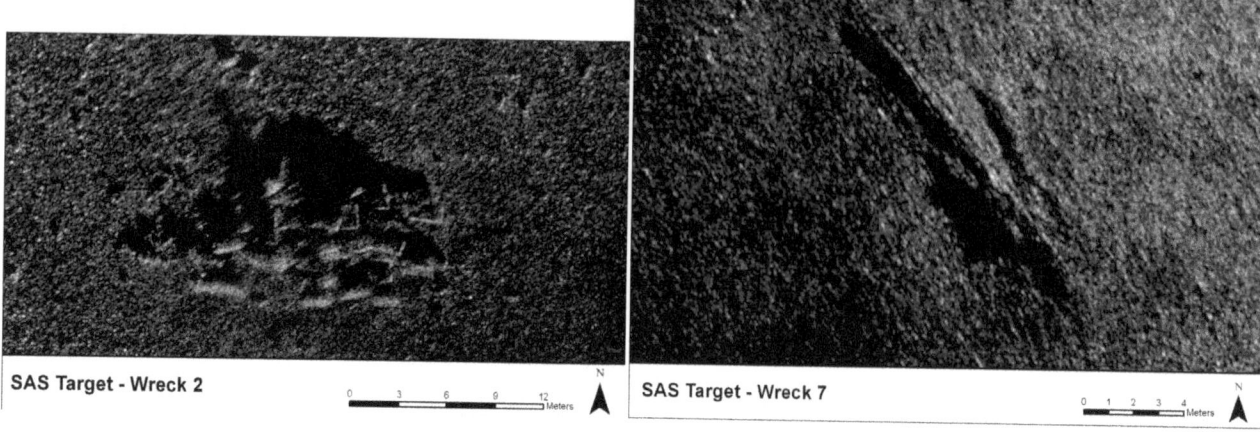

SAS Target - Wreck 2

0 3 6 9 12 Meters

N

SAS Target - Wreck 7

0 1 2 3 4 Meters

N

Figure 3. Two small sonar targets located with the PROSAS Surveyor. The top image, SAS Target – Wreck 2, was likely a shipwreck carrying a stone cargo, while the bottom image, SAS Target – Wreck 7, was the smallest shipwreck target located during the survey (NOAA/SBNMS and Applied Signal Technology, 2011).

26 m long by 6 m wide. The other target was a fragmented vessel with a sharply defined furrow extending outward from the vessel's remains. The furrow suggested that the shipwreck had been dragged across the seafloor. The overall site measured 33 m long by 7 m wide and included a ladder-shaped object. Side scan sonar would have detected both targets; however, close order side scan sonar surveys would have been needed to develop equally characteristic images.

Smaller, less obvious targets, depicted in Figure 3, included one that may be a shipwreck with a cargo of quarried stone that measured 19 m long by 8 m wide. Another small target appeared to be a partially buried keelson and frames measuring 13 m long by 4 m wide. These targets were imaged at a range of 50 m to 75 m from the towfish. The targets' small size and the similarity of the stone cargo site to the surrounding rocky seafloor emphasized the advantages of PROSAS's high resolution capabilities. Most surprisingly, two targets that looked like anchors were identified during data acquisition. Both measured 3 m long by 2 m across and were not in association with another sonar target. Remotely operated vehicle (ROV) survey will be required to confirm the identity of these targets, but the sonar images are convincing. The advantages of synthetic aperture sonar's constant resolution were further supported by several 20 m long sonar targets with archaeological resource characteristics that were identifiable to the edge of the PROSAS Surveyor's 150 m range.

In addition to locating new sonar targets, the project sought to evaluate the PROSAS Surveyor's ability to generate an easily identifiable shipwreck sonar target. Within the planned survey area, archaeologists had

previously located two shipwrecks. To evaluate the PROSAS Surveyor's performance, the line plan was not adjusted to better image these sites, nor was the project team given prior warning that a known site was going to be imaged during a particular survey line. The first test shipwreck was a wooden-hulled fishing vessel measuring 31 m long with 2 m of relief. Believed to be the fishing vessel *Olympia* that sank in 1964, previous ROV investigation revealed a partially intact engine-powered hull with fishing gear consistent with an eastern rig dragger. The PROSAS Surveyor generated a highly diagnostic sonar image of the *Olympia* shipwreck at a range of 120 m. Individual frames were identifiable and features imaged with the ROV could be discerned.

The second test shipwreck consisted of a coal cargo pile on top of lower hull remains 32 m long with 50 cm of relief. ROV site investigation yielded no ship's fittings or other artifacts and only a few frame ends protruded from underneath a gently mounded pile of coal. The identity of this vessel is unknown.

The coal pile wreck was less successfully imaged with the PROSAS Surveyor. The wreck fell almost exactly between two survey lines. Sonar coverage should have provided a 10 m overlap of the area; however, fixed fishing gear forced the survey vessel to deviate off one of the lines, creating a holiday (an area missed by the survey). Sonar imagery from the properly navigated survey line revealed a highly reflective smudge at the edge of the sonar's range that was not consistent with the background geology, but otherwise unremarkable. None of the project team marked the smudge as a contact during data acquisition and it is unlikely that the shipwreck would have been identified during subsequent data review.

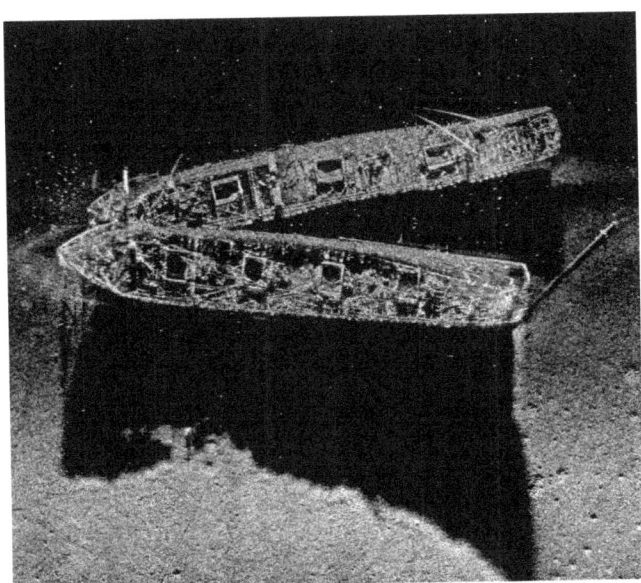

Figure 4. Synthetic aperture sonar image of the collided schooners Frank A. Palmer and Louise B. Crary (NOAA/SBNMS and Applied Signal Technology, 2010).

While the SAS accurately portrayed the seafloor, acoustic imaging systems are only as good as the operator making contact determinations based upon his or her knowledge of widely varying archaeological site signatures.

PROSAS Surveyor was also used to conduct close-order surveys of several sanctuary shipwrecks, to ascertain its directed imaging capabilities. Surveys of the largely intact steamship *Portland* and collided coal schooners *Frank A. Palmer* and *Louise B. Crary*, depicted in Figure 4, yielded excellent results. The sonar's SAS processing produced undistorted imagery across the sonar's range and its 150 m range allowed the project to image these large wrecks and their surrounding debris fields with fewer survey lines. Fewer survey lines result in more precise site mosaics as towfish positioning errors are not compounded. Furthermore, the sonar's range allowed gave the project's technicians a greater margin of safety for towing a sonar around very high profile wrecks with entangling derelict fishing gear.

PROSAS Surveyor Performance

The PROSAS Surveyor system operated as advertised by Applied Signal Technology with only a few minor computer glitches. It generated crisp seafloor imagery of rocky, muddy, and sandy seafloor and sonar targets on all three sediment varieties. Its performance as a turnkey system could not be assessed as AST's Chief Sonar System Engineer accompanied the PROSAS Surveyor on the cruise. The system's complexity would undoubtedly require a highly skilled operations team.

During the project, the towfish was in the water collecting data for approximately 130 hours of the 144 hours of actual survey time available. Dividing the survey area covered, 169 km2, by the hours spent collecting data resulted in a total survey area coverage rate of 1.3 km2 per hour. The difference between hours available and hours collecting data was due to fixed fishing gear entanglement. Nighttime operations and the density of fixed fishing gear in the survey area made these interactions inevitable. Nearly all of the fishing gear interactions ended with the successful disentanglement of the towfish without damage, but productive time was lost in each to recover the towfish and reset operations. Unfortunately, one buoyed line cut into the soft rubber wiring used at the tow cable's termination. Several hours were spent re-splicing and potting the damaged wires. AST is planning to better protect this vulnerable connection.

PROSAS seafloor image quality did diminish occasionally. The AST technicians described this data acquisition problem as "unfocused" data caused by towfish attitude or movement that was not properly calculated by the PROSAS software. The resulting images were slightly blurry as compared to the usually crisp imagery, but sonar target identification was still possible. Since the PROSAS Surveyor generates near real-time SAS data, the AST technicians were able to adjust the towing attitude of the towfish to "refocus" the imagery within a few SAS frames.

Applied Signal Technology quoted a price of $1.8 million for a turnkey PROSAS Surveyor in 2009. While purchasing a PROSAS Surveyor is beyond most organization's budgets, Applied Signal Technology leases the PROSAS Surveyor with a minimum seven day deployment. The equipment fits within a standard shipping container that can be transported worldwide. The total project cost was approximately $105,000.00 inclusive of equipment rental, shipping the PROSAS Surveyor to Massachusetts from California, *SRVx* operation costs, and personnel, but exclusive of the Principal Investigator's labor costs. Dividing the project cost by the square-kilometers mapped during this project results in a square-kilometer cost of $621.00.

In conclusion, maritime archaeologists are continually searching for new technologies to improve their research. Theoretical improvements in technology suggest possibilities for new research methodologies; however, real world application of these technologies is the true test. Oftentimes, technologies that work in a controlled lab setting cannot withstand the rigors of field deployment. This project's results indicated that the PROSAS Surveyor is a viable tool for large area survey and that SAS technology offers significant advantages over conventional side scan sonar survey.

Acknowledgements

The Principal Investigator would like to recognize NOAA's Office of Ocean Exploration and Research and Office of National Marine Sanctuaries' Maritime Heritage Program for providing project funding. Recognition for their attention to duty is due the crew of the R/V SRVx: Captian Robert Wallace, Dave Arch, Steve Kibner, and Chris Fosdick and the survey team from Williamson and Associates: Jay Larsen, Curtis Clement, and Kyle Fankhauser.

Special thanks are due to Steve Ruddy, Andy Wilby, and Matt Nelson of Applied Signal Technology, Inc. and Paul Igo from Oceanographic & Geophysical Instruments for making the project possible.

References Cited

BLONDEL, PHILIPPE
  2009   *The Handbook of Sidescan Sonar.* Springer-Praxis Ltd., Chichester, UK.

EDGETECH
  n.d.   4200 Series Side Scan Sonar System Brochure. West Wareham, MA <http://www.edgetech.com/docs/4200_series_brochure.pdf>.

FISH, JOHN P. AND H. ARNOLD CARR
  1990   *Sound Underwater Images, A Guide to the Generation and Interpretation of Side Scan Sonar Data.* Lower Cape Publishing, Orleans, MA.

MCHUGH, RON
  2000   The Potential for Synthetic Aperture Sonar in Seafloor Imaging. *Proceedings of the Annual ICES Science Conference.* Brugge, Belgium <http://www.ices.dk/products/CMdocs/2000/T/T-2000.pdf>.

STERNLICHT, DANIEL AND JOHN PESATURO
  2004   Synthetic Aperture Sonar: Frontiers in Underwater Imaging. *Sea Technology* 45(11).

Matthew S. Lawrence
Stellwagen Bank National Marine Sanctuary
175 Edward Foster Road
Scituate, MA 02066

2012 Integrating Data Sets: Results from the City of St. Augustine Seawall Phase I Archaeology Survey, St. Augustine, Florida.
In *ACUA Underwater Archaeology Proceedings 2012*, Brian Jordan and Troy J. Nowak, editors, pp. 101–107.

Integrating Data Sets: Results from the City of St. Augustine Seawall Phase I Archaeology Survey, St. Augustine, Florida

Bradley A. Krueger
Jean B. Pelletier

Disparate data types can be integrated using a synergistic approach for delineating complex, near-shore archaeological resources. This research focused on the identification of both onshore and offshore resources using magnetic data, side-scan sonar, ground penetrating radar, and excavation. It was necessary to integrate these data sets for the purposes of locating and documenting significant cultural material.

Introduction

In the spring of 2011, the Federal Emergency Management Agency (FEMA) contracted URS Group, Inc. (URS) to conduct a Phase I archaeological survey along a 1,200-ft. (365.8-m) section of the Avenida Menendez Seawall in St. Augustine, Florida (URS Group, Inc. [URS] 2011). The impetus behind this survey involved the proposed construction of a new seawall to better protect the city against storm-surge and localized flooding from the adjacent Matanzas River. An archaeological investigation was required before work could commence, as the seawall is a contributing component to the St. Augustine Town Plan Historic District, which is listed in the National Register of Historic Places and classified as a National Historic Landmark.

Given its placement at the interface between the commercial district of downtown St. Augustine and the intertidal zone, the St. Augustine Phase I Archaeology Project utilized a variety of survey techniques to locate and identify archaeological sites within the vicinity of the seawall. The project's Area of Potential Effect (APE) was not limited to the land and intertidal zone, however, and ultimately extended 40 ft. (12.2 m) out into the Matanzas River. This complex environment required URS archaeologists to divide the investigation into two separate components, terrestrial and marine. The project successfully completed both components and worked to integrate the different data sets from each phase to arrive at a more synergistic view of the area for the purpose of archaeological site identification.

Data integration was a key element to the interpretive portion of this investigation. While the techniques employed for data collection are standard for archaeology, it was how the resulting data sets coalesced that greatly enhanced understanding the context of both onshore and offshore cultural resources. To accurately show how this analytical procedure worked, the following discussion highlights the various investigative techniques employed, separated by phase, their results, and the data integration process. Attention is then paid to data interpretation and site identification, followed by concluding remarks.

Terrestrial Phase

The terrestrial phase of the project consisted of the examination of the land near and around the seawall, including the intertidal zone, to determine if archaeological resources were present and would be impacted by construction activities. URS archaeologists conducted this phase using four separate investigative techniques: pedestrian survey, ground penetrating radar (GPR), magnetometer survey, and mechanical trench excavation. Each method is described below.

Pedestrian Survey

The pedestrian survey commenced in the area inland of the Avenida Menendez Seawall. A thin strip of manicured earth, approximately 6 ft. (1.8 m) wide, is situated between the wall and Avenida Menendez. This strip houses several palm trees, parking meters, street signs, and utility structures (Figure 1). To create a detailed site map and identify features that could appear in other data sets, information was captured on all extant modern objects and structures in the area. This included photographic documentation and the collection of positional data via a handheld global position system (GPS) unit.

Pedestrian survey also took place in the intertidal zone on the shoals seaward of the wall. Much like the work that took place on the inland side of the wall, the goal was to identify objects that could potentially appear in other data sets. Additionally, archaeologists used this opportunity to look for traces of a historic pier. An 1885 map of St. Augustine depicts a pier extending into the river out from the St. Francis barracks, now the Florida

FIGURE 1. SEASIDE VIEW OF THE AVENIDA MENENDEZ SEAWALL. (PHOTO BY ALBEE, 2010.)

National Guard Headquarters. This area, which now contains an oyster bed, was inaccessible at high tide and could only be surveyed when water levels were low. The survey team cleaned any overlying sediment and attached oysters, photographed, and recorded the GPS coordinates of all encountered features.

Ground Penetrating Radar

The region along the inland side of the seawall was investigated with ground penetrating radar (GPR). This radar-based system detects buried features by continuously transmitting high frequency electronic signals into the earth to measure the soil's dielectric properties. The goal of the GPR survey was to locate and define a historic boat basin and gain a construction profile for the base of the seawall. The boat basin is featured in 19th-century depictions of the seawall and appears to date to the original construction of the seawall, between 1833 and 1844, but was abandoned and filled in during the 1890s (Halbirt 2005b). Furthermore, the GPR provided details about the types and density of sediments used to fill both the basin and the landward face of the wall.

The GPR survey was performed using a Sensor & Software, Inc., Noggin PLUS Smart Cart system with a 250 MHz scanning antenna. Data were collected in transects spaced 3 ft. (0.9 m) apart. The maximum vertical range of the device was 8 ft. (2.4 m), but was optimized to 5 ft. (1.5 m) based on the depth of water at low tide. Positional control was maintained using a Trimble Ag-114 GPS mounted atop the Smart Cart. Both the GPR and GPS data were automatically stored on the GPR system flash card, which was then transferred daily to a field computer.

Magnetometer Survey

A magnetic survey was conducted along both sides of the seawall and covered the entire length of the APE in order to detect ferrous anomalies beneath the ground. This is done by measuring disturbances within the Earth's magnetic field caused by the presence of iron alloys. The objective of the magnetometer survey was to discover potential cultural resources and discern the locations of modern disturbances, such as utilities and trash, as well as the historic boat basin at the southern end of the seawall.

Encountered anomalies were analyzed based on magnetic signature, duration, and intensity. Magnetic signatures refer to the shape of magnetic deflection caused by a ferrous object when compared to the surrounding ambient magnetic field. Signatures may be categorized as positive monopolar, negative monopolar, dipolar, or multi-component. The type of signature displayed depends on the orientation of the ferrous object relative to the magnetic sensor and whether the object's positive or negative pole is positioned closest to the sensor. The duration, or length per second, and intensity, or amplitude measured in nanoteslas, of the signature are also noted and interpreted by archaeologists to determine the presence of cultural material.

A Geometrics G-858G cesium-vapor magnetic gradiometer was used to collect data for this portion of the survey. Three 1,200-ft. (365.8-m) survey transects along the seawall were completed, in addition to another nine 200-ft. (61-m) transects over the suspected footprint of the boat basin. Two full and one half transects were also completed on the opposite side of the seawall in the intertidal zone. Magnetic data were collected simultaneously with positional data via a backpack-mounted GPS unit.

Trench Excavation

Following the pedestrian archaeological surveys, URS archaeologists excavated three test trenches. Guided by data collected in the magnetometer and GPR surveys, the primary aim was to locate the boat basin, determine if its northern wall was still intact, and to examine the western façade of the seawall to determine construction details. Excavation allowed archaeologists to validate their GPR and magnetic analysis and provided an opportunity to test the sediment from the bottom of the boat basin to potentially date its period of use (Figure 2).

Excavation of all three trenches was carried out using a Bobcat backhoe with a 24-inch (in.; 0.61-m) wide bucket. Depths of the trenches varied based on

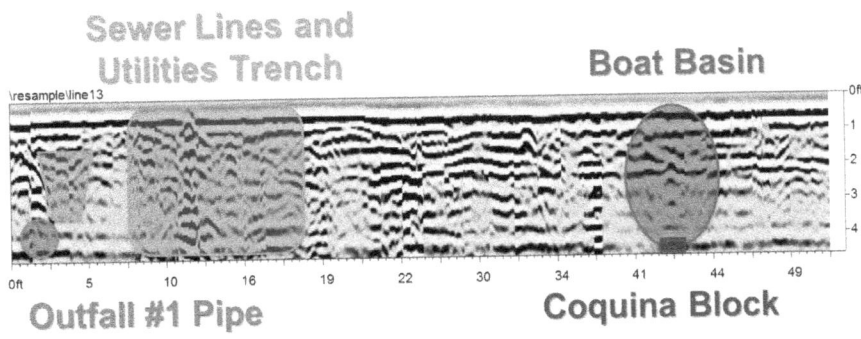

FIGURE 2. GPR TARGETS VERIFIED THROUGH THE RESULTS OF THE PEDESTRIAN SURVEY AND TRENCHING (DRAWING BY AUTHOR, 2012).

two factors: the overall objective of the trench and the stability of the trench walls. Due to the close proximity to the Matanzas River, water from the rising tide seriously weakened several trench walls and caused some of them to collapse. Given these conditions, archaeologists complied with OSHA safety standards to prevent potential accidents from happening. Following excavation, positional data for each trench was captured using a handheld GPS unit.

Trench 1 was excavated to sample the fill and potentially intact deposits within the historic boat basin. It was positioned in the project's southern area and oriented perpendicular to the seawall. The final dimensions of Trench 1 measured 12 ft. (3.7 m) long by 3 ft. (0.9 m) wide, and reached a depth of 5 ft. 10 in. (1.8 m).

The objective of Trench 2 was to uncover the northern boat basin wall, which appeared in maps and the GPR data. It was also situated in the southern portion of the project area and oriented parallel to the seawall. Additionally, archaeologists wanted to investigate the stratigraphy and obtain artifact samples from both the interior and exterior of the boat basin. The final dimensions of Trench 2 measured approximately 16.5 ft. (5 m) long by 3 ft. (0.9 m) wide, and reached a depth of 6 ft. 1 in. (1.9 m).

The excavation of Trench 3 sought to expose the western façade of the seawall so that its construction details could be examined by archaeologists. It was situated in the southern project area and oriented perpendicular to the seawall. The final dimensions of Trench 3 measured 6.5 ft. (2 m) long by 3 ft. (0.9 m) wide, and reached a depth of 5 ft. (1.5 m).

Marine Survey Methods

Following the completion of the terrestrial phase of investigations, archaeologists switched their focus

toward the Matanzas River. The APE for the proposed seawall improvement extended 40 ft. (12.2 m) into the river, on account of the presence of supporting toe features (or "pavers") running east from the base of the seawall (Halbrit 2005a). Composed of coquina blocks, historic documentation suggests that these features were lain during construction of the seawall on the surface of the intertidal flat and extended approximately 10 ft. (3.1 m) from the base of the seawall. As such, the waters adjacent to the seawall were subjected to a four-stage marine survey. Investigative techniques included: hydro-probe testing and manual trenching, a multi-component remote sensing survey, dredge testing, and geophysical core sampling. Each method is described below.

Hydro-probing and Manual Trenching

A series of hydro-probe tests were conducted in the intertidal zone beside the seawall to further investigate the supporting toe features. Previous archaeological investigations identified and recorded these coquina blocks, which extended 8 ft. (2.4 m) into the river (Halbrit 2005a). The pavers appeared to continue further out from this point, but the blocks were smaller and in poor condition. It was unclear where these features actually terminated, as the extremities could have been buried.

Twenty-one hydro-probing transects were established at intervals of 50 ft. (15.2 m) in the intertidal zone along the length of seawall's APE. Transects ran perpendicular to the wall for a length of 12 ft. (3.7 m), each one comprised of four tests spaced 3 ft. (0.9 m) apart. The hydro-probe itself consisted of a 6-ft. (1.8 m) long, 0.75-in. (1.9-cm) diameter copper pipe attached to a floating water pump via a 0.75-in. (1.9-cm) plastic hose. The upper end of the pipe ended in a T-handle, which served as a hand-hold, while water flowing out the leading end liquefied surrounding sediment, which let archaeologists reach greater depths.

To verify and build upon the results of the hydro-probing, nine manually-excavated trenches were placed at select locations between and parallel to the hydro-probe transects. The trenches attempted to identify stratigraphic layers encountered during probing. In the event coquina blocks were uncovered, trenching would provide a way for archaeologists to inspect and record these features. Trenching took place using shovels and began approximately 9 ft. (2.7 m) from the seawall. Dimensions of the trenches averaged 1 ft. (0.3 m) wide and reached a depth between 1 and 1.5 ft. (0.3 and 0.5 m).

Remote Sensing Survey

A multi-sensor marine remote sensing survey was conducted along the entire length of the project area. The goal of this survey was to identify cultural resources, as well as modern objects and structures, submerged within the river. To this end, archaeologists used four different types of equipment to map the river bottom. These included a GPS unit, side-scan sonar, a marine magnetometer, and an echo sounder. All of these devices were either mounted on or towed behind the project's 18-ft. (5.5-m) long pontoon boat. The range of the survey equipment, coupled with the boat's path of travel, meant that data were collected outside of the APE, which was also analyzed to better understand what type of objects were submerged in the river. Hydrographic and navigational controls were achieved using Hypack's Hypack Max 2010 hydrographic survey software. In total, the survey completed five track lines spaced 15 ft. (4.5 m) apart parallel to the seawall. A cursory explanation of the various components of the remote sensing survey follows.

Navigation and position control for the boat and equipment was maintained by means of a Hemisphere Crescent R130 differential GPS (DGPS). Positional information obtained by the DGPS was transferred in NMEA 0183 code to Hypack, which then displayed the survey vessel, sensors, and pre-plotted track lines. This ensured that the archaeologists knew their positions at all times and were where they needed to be during the survey.

Imaging of the river bottom took place using a MarineSonic 600-kilohertz (kHz) side-scan sonar unit. This system emits acoustic waves in a horizontal plane out from the device and produces high-resolution images with moderate ranges of a few hundred feet. Navigation fixes are embedded in the acoustic data, which allowed individual images to be georeferenced and side-scan mosaics to be created for analysis.

Magnetic data was collected with a Geometrics G882 cesium-vapor marine magnetometer. Much like the terrestrial equivalent, this device detects ferrous objects based on the localized disruptions they cause to the magnetic field. To avoid interference from the project boat's hull and electrical system, the magnetometer sensor was

towed a minimum of 2.5 times the length of the vessel from the transom. Output from the magnetometer was linked directly to Hypack, which enabled precise, real-time positions for recorded magnetic data.

The last piece of equipment used in the remote sensing survey was an Odom Hydrotrac digital fathometer, or echo sounder. The echo sounder recorded bathymetric data for each transect, which was transmitted directly into Hypack. This data set was used to better understand the geomorphology of the Matanzas River and how it affects the distribution of magnetic and acoustic anomalies, as well as to help delineate any features situated above the sediment surface.

Dredge Testing

To further examine the intertidal zone's subsurface region, certain areas were chosen for dredge testing. This was necessary because three new vortex vaults were to be installed along the seawall in the inter-tidal zone as part of the proposed improvement. Since this would require more ground disturbance, archaeologists had to determine if any significant cultural resources would be impacted at these locations.

Archaeologists investigated these vortex vault sites by excavating a number of dredge test pits (DTPs). DTPs use an induction dredge system to create a Venturi effect for removing sediment in a localized area. The system used the same floating water pump used during the hydro-probing. In place of a T-handle, however, was a hand-held brass tube connected to a 2.5 in. (6.4 cm) diameter plastic hose. Sediment was pulled up through the brass tube and discharged a short distance away. All excavated spoil material was sifted through a 0.25 in. (0.6 cm) mesh screen for small artifact recovery. DTPs were excavated to a depth of no less than 3 ft. (0.9 m) until progress ceased to be made. Two DTPs were initially placed at each vortex vault location along the northern and southern boundaries, and additional DTPs were added upon the discovery of cultural material.

Core Sampling

The final component of the marine survey was to capture the stratigraphic profile and determine the geomorphic processes of the intertidal zone through core sampling. Each core was collected in a 4-in (10.2-cm) diameter polyvinyl chloride pipe that was driven into the sediment. A gasket cover was then inserted into the test pipe to create a vacuum seal that facilitated sample recovery. The core sample tube was later opened and the sediments analyzed in a laboratory setting.

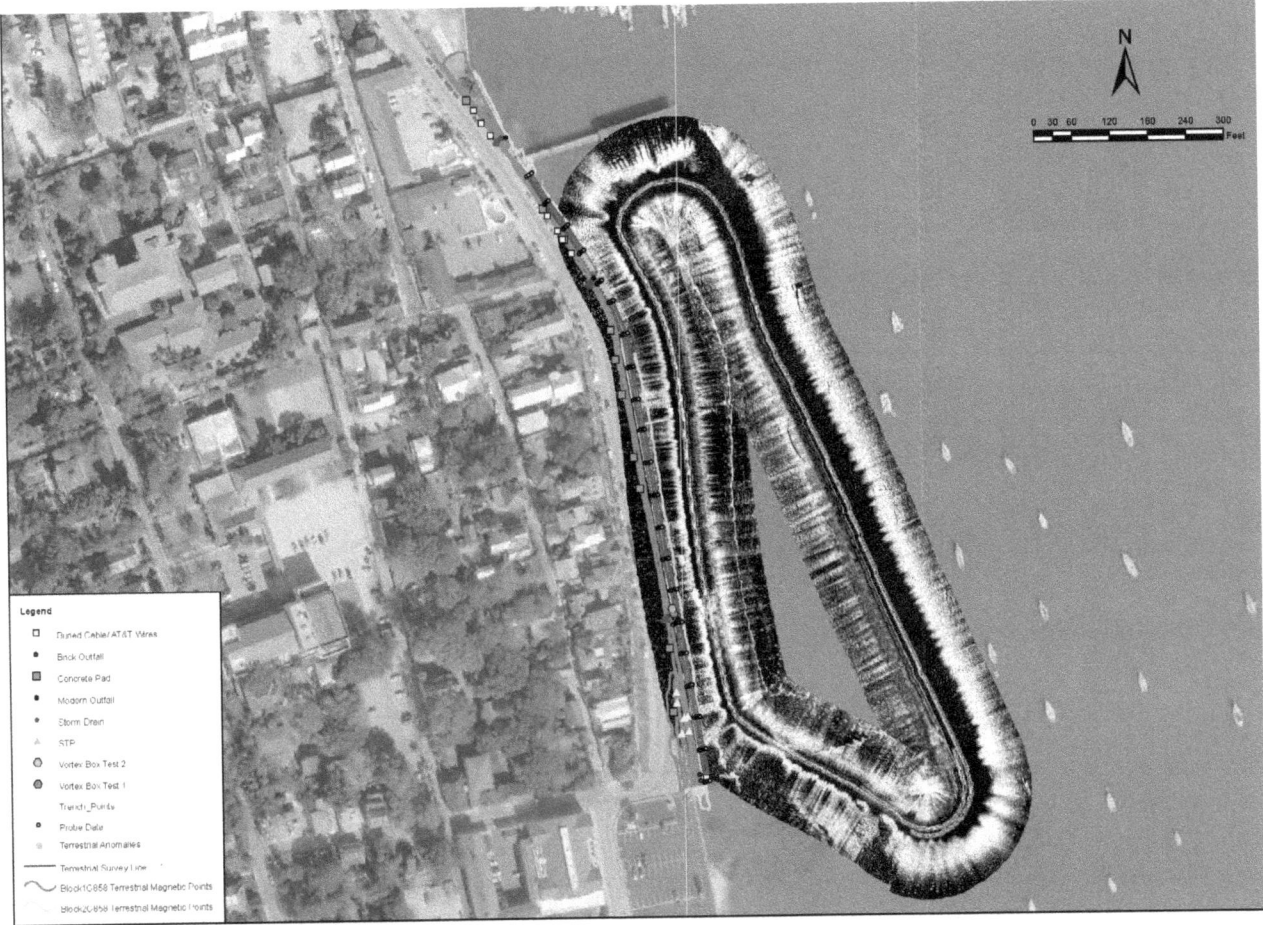

FIGURE 3. GIS MAP SHOWING THE COMBINED RESULTS OF THE PEDESTRIAN SURVEY, GPR TRANSECTS, EXCAVATION TRENCHES, DREDGE TEST PITS, AND REMOTE SENSING DATA (DRAWING BY AUTHOR, 2012).

Data Integration

The objective of the project was to identify potentially significant cultural resources within the vicinity of the seawall, as well as document construction details of the wall itself, to determine if the resources would be affected by the proposed improvements. Several unique data sets were collected during the archaeological investigation of the seawall. The process was complicated by the project area being located in an urban environment that has been consistently occupied since the 16th Century. To effectively analyze the archaeological setting of the study area, disparate data sets were combined into a single, unified view so that anomalous patterning could be seen by archaeologists, with the goal of recognizing culturally significant sites and structures.

Methodologically, this project was conducted in a linear fashion congruent with the layout of this article. Incoming data was processed in-field using a combination of Hypack and Golden Software's Surfer (Version 9). Together, these programs created geo-referenced overlays for particular data sets that guided later portions of the archaeological investigation. Following field investigations, final integration took place by entering all data sets into a geographic information system (GIS) program for improved visualization and analysis.

To highlight how the archaeologists integrated their data on this project, examples from both the terrestrial and marine phases will be considered. Starting with the terrestrial phase, two different sets of magnetics were collected, from the area atop from the seawall and from the intertidal zone. While both sets could have been reviewed separately, archaeologists found it much more effective to combine the data and then make interpretations. Synchronization of this type provided greater magnetic range (i.e., larger coverage) and a better understanding of continuous perturbations in the area, such as utility cables and pipes.

Similar integration took place for the data collection during the marine phase. After the remote sensing survey was completed, acoustic, magnetic, and bathymetric data were imported into Surfer and correlated using

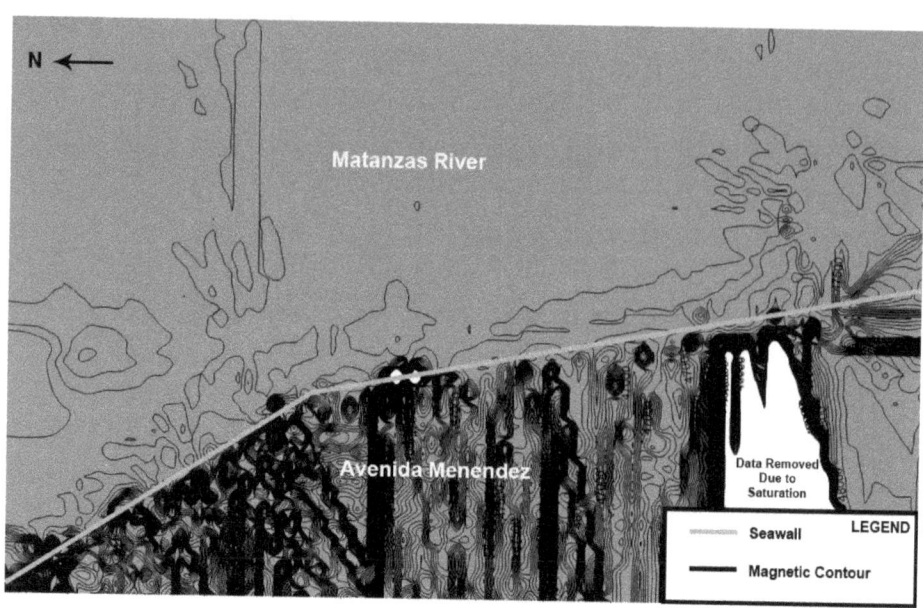

N ←

Matanzas River

Avenida Menendez

Data Removed
Due to
Saturation

LEGEND

∿∿∿∿∿ Seawall

▬▬▬ Magnetic Contour

FIGURE 4. COMBINED TERRESTRIAL AND MARINE MAGNETIC DATA FROM THE
AVENIDA MENENDEZ SEAWALL (DRAWING BY AUTHOR, 2012).

confirmed the interpretation of the GPR data and allowed for this portion of the boat basin to be more closely examined and documented. While not technically data integration, this process was incredibly valuable as it increased the overall accuracy of findings and reaffirmed assertions made regarding initial data interpretation.

After field investigations drew to a close, the project utilized GIS to spatially map out the locations and results of all survey methods. The only exception was the GPR data, the output of which could not be easily exported into a usable visualization layer. Once plotted, the final stage of the integration process included comparing the collected data to historic maps of St. Augustine. This greatly assisted the archaeologists in envisioning the former landscape, understanding how area has developed over time, and interpreting the finds from both the terrestrial and marine regions.

Problems can arise with data integration, so a word of caution must be offered. When done haphazardly, merging data sets can cause certain features or anomalies to become invisible. This can be illustrated by looking at the magnetic data for this project. Data from three different areas were collected and reviewed: from the land atop the seawall, from the intertidal zone at the bottom of the wall, and in the adjacent open waters. The results from the first two sets were comparable enough to combine together without issue, as they were collected with the same device, had similar parameters, and were, for the most part, detecting the same anomalies. When the marine magnetics were added to the combined terrestrial set, however, the resulting image was incredibly data rich to the point that certain features and objects on land could not be seen (Figure 4). The interval of magnetic contours was adjusted for optimization, but in doing so objects on the marine side became invisible while the terrestrial features became over-saturated. As such, only the combined terrestrial magnetics were used for analytical purposes.

There are ways to circumvent these issues and still obtain good, holistic data. Varying data sets can be

GPS markers. This was vital as the integrated data sets helped to more accurately define objects and structures than by individually reviewing any one set. For instance, telecommunications cables were seen crossing the river in both the side-scan and the magnetic imagery. These outputs showed the cables in different ways, but together they clearly outlined the object as a metal cable. Further integration took place when the remote sensing data were joined with the results of the pedestrian survey (Figure 3). Through the different data sets certain utility features could be traced from their origination points near the seawall to the opposite side of the river. Combining the terrestrial and marine data in this fashion bridged the information gap between these two zones and permitted the recognition of larger material distribution patterns.

Another benefit of this approach is that one method can be used to validate others while in the field. An example of this can be seen in the relationship between the GPR data and the excavation trenches. The data collected during the GPR survey assisted in directing where the trenches should be placed, but opening those trenches provided an opportunity to verify the results of the data analysis. Archaeologists could see certain features very clearly in the GRP profiles, such as outfall pipes and utility vaults, but other objects were more ambiguous. Such was the case with the boat basin, which appeared in the data stream, but its construction details were not readily identifiable. While the survey team knew that something was present beneath the surface, excavations geo-referenced to the same map, for instance, but reviewed separately. Alternatively, creating different layers in a GIS or program such as Surfer can allow individual data sets to be turned on and off, making data review much easier. For this project, archaeologists relied on experience and expertise to know what and when data should be combined.

Results and Site Identification

Three archaeological sites were identified during the St. Augustine Phase I Archaeology Project. This was achieved by integrating, reviewing, and comparing collected data against historic maps and documents. Additionally, archaeologists were able to identify the extents of the seawall's supporting toe features, which ranged from 2 to 10 ft. (0.6 to 3.1 m) in length. The three sites are briefly described below.

Historic Boat Basin
The historic boat basin, dating to the seawall's original construction between 1833 and 1844, was identified and delineated. The basin's foundation was discovered via GPR and magnetics and consequently exposed during mechanical trench excavations. Situated 6.5 ft. (2 m) below the top of the seawall, the foundation is made of cut coquina blocks, much like the seawall. The presence of an angled granite block adjacent to the foundation suggests that there was likely a stone ramp leading down to the wall of the boat basin. No artifacts or other cultural material were encountered that are associated with the boat basin.

St. Francis Pier Remains
The remains of a 19th century pier were discovered in front of the modern Florida National Guard Headquarters during the pedestrian survey and in the magnetic data. Five pilings, four arranged in two parallel lines and one off to the northeast, are likely the remnants of a pier depicted in front of the St. Francis Barracks on an 1885 Wellge map. The pilings are composed of metal-encased wood and are surrounded by disarticulated coquina blocks, which were likely served as footings for the pier.

Site 8SJ5511
Site 8SJ5511 is a multi-component site consisting of prehistoric, historic, and modern artifacts discovered in the vicinity of Vortex Vault 3 during dredge testing. This site yielded 311 historic artifacts, 364 faunal remains,

88 prehistoric artifacts, and 18 floral specimens. The prehistoric artifacts were mostly comprised of ceramic sherds dating to the Late Archaic, St. Johns I and II periods, and the Proto-Historic period. These artifacts were found in association with historic artifacts dating from the 17th Century through the present, suggesting previous site disturbance. Most of these materials were recovered from sands and gravels immediately below the seawall toe feature pavers, and as such are likely out of their original context, possibly deposited from a now destroyed site or storm event that washed terrestrial deposits into this reach of the river. This does not appear to be an intact archaeological site.

Conclusions

Data integration greatly added to the success of the St. Augustine Seawall Phase I Archaeology Project. In this study, the methods employed were successful in locating three distinct resources. As this article demonstrates, there is no one way to find cultural resources; several different methods exist that span the technological spectrum. Depending on site characteristics, some investigative methods work better than others, and it is important to know what data sets can be combined and when doing so is appropriate. While pitfalls do exist, there are numerous, successful techniques for effectively integrating and interpreting multiple data sets.

Acknowledgements

Our deepest thanks goes to the authors and contributors of the 2011 St. Augustine Seawall Phase I Archaeology Project final report: (in alphabetic order) Carrie Albee, Justin Bedard, Linda Mackey, J.B. Pelletier, Chris Polglase, and Anthony Randolph. Without their diligent work this paper would not have been possible.

References

HALBRIT, CARL D.

2005a   *Historic St. Augustine Seawall: Archaeological Investigations along the Seaward Side of St. Augustine Historic Nineteenth Century Seawall and National Historic Preservation Act Section 106 Report.* Report No. 11501; Florida Bureau of Historic Preservation, Tallahassee.

2005b   *Installation of Modern Latrine Facilities in the Old King's Bakery Florida National Guard Headquarters, St. Augustine, Florida.* Report prepared for the Florida National Guard. Report No. 12783; Florida Bureau of Historic Preservation, Tallahassee.

URS GROUP, INC. (URS)

2011   *Final Report: City of St. Augustine Seawall Phase I Archaeology Project, City of St. Augustine, St. Johns County, Florida.* Report prepared for the Federal Emergency Management Agency (FEMA) by URS, Germantown, MD.

· · · · · · · · · · · · · · ·

Bradley A. Krueger
URS Group, Inc.
12420 Milestone Center Drive, Suite 150
Germantown, MD 20876-7110

Jean B. Pelletier
URS Group, Inc.
12420 Milestone Center Drive, Suite 150
Germantown, MD 20876-7110

1992. Shipwreck in a Swimming Pool: An Assessment of the Methodology and Technology Utilized on the Yorktown Shipwreck Archaeological Project. *Historical Archaeology* 26(4):36-46.

JOHN D. BROADWATER

Shipwreck in a Swimming Pool: An Assessment of the Methodology and Technology Utilized on the Yorktown Shipwreck Archaeological Project

ABSTRACT

Between 1978 and 1988, the Yorktown Shipwreck Archaeological Project employed a wide range of technological tools during the location, assessment, and excavation of British vessels sunk during the Battle of Yorktown in 1781. The most unique aspect of the project was the utilization of a steel cofferdam and filtration system to offset adverse site conditions and assist the excavation team. The project also made use of remote sensing instruments, computer-aided drafting technology, and a new sonic measurement system.

Introduction

The Yorktown Shipwreck Archaeological Project, conducted between 1978 and 1988 under the auspices of the Virginia Department of Historic Resources, produced a wealth of archaeological data on 18th-century British warships and transport vessels. At the same time, the project provided an ideal test bed for the application and evaluation of a wide variety of technological tools, some of which had not been previously tested.

The Yorktown Project was a comprehensive, large-scale study of shipwrecks in the York River near Yorktown, Virginia. The project located and assessed the remains of nine British vessels sunk during the Battle of Yorktown, 1781, and culminated in the complete excavation of an extremely well-preserved British supply ship. The historical background and excavation results have been reported elsewhere (Broadwater 1980, 1988, 1989a; Broadwater, Adams et al. 1985; Broadwater and Morris 1991).

Beginning with initial surveys and continuing through the excavation phase, technology played a major role in the Yorktown Project. Adverse diving conditions in the York River—strong currents, near-zero visibility, dangerous power-boat traffic, and stinging jellyfish—necessitated the development of a research design which addressed this hostile work environment. As the project progressed, numerous opportunities arose for the application and assessment of technological equipment and methodology as tools for underwater archaeology.

This article presents a brief assessment of the methodology and technology employed at Yorktown in the hope that project results and conclusions will be of value to other underwater archaeologists. It is also hoped that non-diving readers will find the information to be clearly explained and of interest.

Remote-Sensing Surveys

Remote-sensing surveys conducted at Yorktown during the mid-70s involved the use of (then) state-of-the-art equipment, some of which was not commercially available. Remote-sensing technology has improved rapidly since that time; however, a brief summary of those early surveys is included, since many of the results and conclusions are relevant to current research.

For years, the primary remote-sensing instruments relied upon for locating submerged cultural resources have been the side-scanning sonar and magnetometer. The bottom-penetrating sonar, which can sometimes "see" objects beneath bottom sediments, is often utilized as a supplementary sensor in pinpointing and defining buried objects.

The Yorktown surveys utilized a wide range of survey equipment. In 1976, a remote-sensing survey of the Yorktown shoreline was conducted through the cooperation of the Magnetics Branch of the David W. Taylor Naval Ship Research and Development Center, Annapolis, Maryland, and the Virginia Institute of Marine Science, Gloucester Point, Virginia. The shallow waters of the York River along the Yorktown shore were surveyed with a Schonstedt high-balance gradiometer, operated from a small boat. Although the instrument performed well and was operated by extremely skilled personnel, few discrete sites could be distinguished from the high background "noise" resulting from the accumulation, over more than three centuries, of metallic debris. Further analysis revealed several strong, large concentrations of magnetic anomalies, which were charted and designated for further study (Andahazy et al. 1976: 19–22; Sands 1983:152–159).

The following year, the deep-water areas (as deep as 90 ft., or 27 m) were searched with a special Navy AN/ASQ 81 magnetometer, again through the assistance of the Navy and several state agencies. Eighty-eight magnetic anomalies were recorded and plotted on a large-scale map (Sands 1983:159–162).

In 1978, the Department of Historic Resources received a one-year survey grant from the National Endowment for the Humanities, thus formally establishing the Yorktown Shipwreck Archaeological Project, for which the author served as project director until its termination in 1988. The first project activity was an intensive survey of the York River near Yorktown, utilizing a Klein Associates Hydroscan 530 sonar which had both side-scanning and bottom-penetrating capabilities. Sixteen primary and 35 secondary sites were identified and plotted (Broadwater 1980, 1981; Sands 1983:165).

All remote-sensing data were correlated, and high priority assigned to those targets which possessed both magnetic and acoustic components. Because of site conditions at Yorktown—which are actually very typical of many coastal and riverine sites—target prioritization efforts met with limited success. The primary area of interest, the shallow river bottom just off Yorktown, was so littered with ferrous debris that locating specific shipwrecks by magnetometer was nearly impossible. Because the wrecks were almost completely buried in the soft river bottom, sonar, too, had limited effectiveness, although two of the strongest sonar targets were quickly verified to be shipwrecks. A subsequent survey in 1980 with a high-resolution Klein sonar revealed much more detail than the original survey.

The sub-bottom profiler was hampered by several factors: the shallow depths within the primary target area were nearly within the "dead zone," or minimum range of the profiler; the presence of tiny air bubbles imbedded within the silty bottom, a result of microbial activity, masked cultural remains (air bubbles are excellent sonar reflectors); and, except for stone ballast encountered at several sites, the shipwrecks proved to be relatively poor sonar targets, since the density of waterlogged wood differs very little from the surrounding water and silt.

Marine survey archaeologists are well aware that even recent improvements in remote-sensing equipment have not overcome the limitations imposed by many of the adverse site conditions encountered at Yorktown. An accurate generalization seems to be: the earlier the date of the site, the more difficult it is to detect. Earlier sites generally contain less ferrous material, making them less detectable to magnetometers; they also tend to be in a more advanced state of deterioration and more deeply buried than more recent sites. When searching for wooden shipwrecks and other early submerged archaeological sites, researchers should probably base survey strategies upon what could be termed the First Survey Corollary to Murphy's Law: The most significant submerged archaeological sites are the most difficult to find.

In fact, it is the difficulties and uncertainties encountered on marine surveys which underscore the importance of initial documentary research. Often a day in the archives can save thousands of dollars of field survey costs.

In spite of the above-mentioned limitations, the initial Yorktown surveys still provided both specific high-priority targets and high-probability survey zones. When remote-sensing data were combined with the results of historical research, it was possible to confidently designate survey zones for diver investigations. Diving surveys in 1978 resulted in the location and assessment of eight British shipwrecks from the Battle of Yorktown: six were located parallel to the Yorktown shoreline, while two lay in shallow water on the opposite shore, near Gloucester Point (Broadwater 1980, 1981; Sands 1983:164–165). In 1980, a sonar tar-

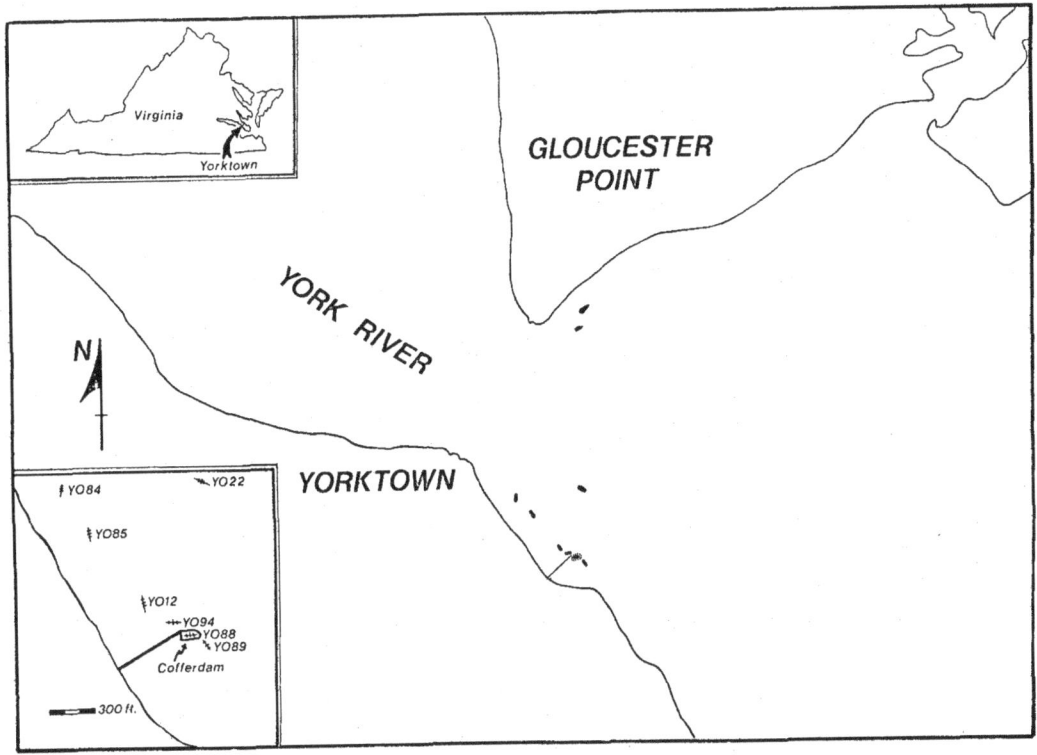

FIGURE 1. Location map showing Yorktown shipwrecks. (Courtesy of Virginia Department of Historic Resources.)

get in the deep water of the main river channel was verified to be a ninth British shipwreck (Figure 1).

Early Archaeological Investigations

During the same time that the project's early remote-sensing phase was underway, a revolutionary concept in underwater excavation was tested at Yorktown. During April–July 1976, a shipwreck located the previous fall was investigated in detail by the Institute of Nautical Archaeology (INA) (Bass et al. 1976; Johnston et al. 1978). The team found the poor diving conditions to be a severe impediment to the investigation. In order to overcome this obstacle, project director Dr. George F. Bass and his team developed a unique solution: a portable, water-filled cofferdam.

Drawing upon a concept first proposed by Nor-

man Scott for the excavation of the sunken iron-clad USS *Tecumseh*, Bass' team designed and built a cofferdam intended to facilitate excavation and recording (Bass et al. 1976:6). Unlike the fixed structure proposed by Scott, however, the INA cofferdam was a floating structure with a flexible kevlar skirt designed to isolate the water column directly over the bow of the shipwreck, thus diverting the strong river currents and permitting the enclosed water to be filtered and clarified (Figure 2).

The "portable cofferdam" ultimately proved to be no match for the powerful tidal currents in the York River, so the experiment had to be discontinued (Bass et al. 1976:6–9); however, the concept was eventually resurrected at Yorktown in a much-evolved form.

Following the comprehensive surveys conducted in 1978 and 1979, it was determined that

FIGURE 2. Temporary cofferdam tested at Yorktown in 1976. (Photo by John D. Broadwater.)

one of the Yorktown shipwrecks, archaeological site 44YO88, was in an excellent state of preservation. The project's archaeological team felt that complete excavation of the site would yield significant information on 18th-century ship construction, technology, and the naval aspects of the Battle of Yorktown. It was also determined that the site was threatened by further degradation from erosion, storms, commercial and recreational boating, and salvage. Therefore, as discussed more fully in other publications, complete excavation was recommended (Broadwater, Polk et al. 1985; Broadwater, Oertling et al. 1988).

The Yorktown Cofferdam

As planning for the excavation of 44YO88 developed, the team began considering options for combating the adverse environment of the York River. Although open-water excavation was deemed feasible, it was recognized that efforts would be hampered and slowed by site conditions and that photographic recording of the hull remains would be impossible.

As a result of planning studies during 1979, the project research design was revised to propose the use of a rigid steel cofferdam which would completely surround shipwreck site 44YO88; an associated filtration system would then be used to clarify the enclosed water. At first, designers considered a standard cofferdam, from which the water would be pumped to permit a dry-land excavation. Because of the water depth, however, costs for such a structure would have been prohibitive; in addition, maintaining the water over the site prevented the problem of site deterioration during excavation.

The Yorktown cofferdam was constructed in 1982, thanks to funding from a wide variety of sources (see Acknowledgments). The structure was unique. The cofferdam proposed by Scott was similar, but that cofferdam was never built. Cofferdams had previously been utilized on several shipwreck excavations in Europe, but all had been constructed in shallow water and the enclosed water removed to permit a dry excavation (Bass 1972: 128–129, 183–186, 200–201). The Yorktown cofferdam was the first to create a "swimming-pool" environment in a saline, silty, algae-rich river (Broadwater, Polk et al. 1985; Sands 1988: 156–168).

Another unique aspect of the Yorktown cofferdam was its public access. A wooden-pile pier connected the cofferdam with the Yorktown beach, and an observation platform along the north wall of the cofferdam permitted visitors to observe the excavation in progress. In a cooperative agreement with the Yorktown Maritime Heritage Foundation and the County of York, a historical interpretation program was established, with interpreters on-site during summer months to greet visitors and explain both the historical background and the ongoing underwater excavation. Thousands of visitors were introduced to underwater archaeology in this manner.

Initially, there was considerable concern about possible construction damage to the shipwreck. This concern was dealt with during the design and specification phase, and was included in project bid documents. At least one staff archaeologist was on site at all times during the construction phase. The contractor worked professionally and patiently with project archaeologists to ensure that no damage was done to the shipwreck within the cofferdam or to the shipwrecks on either side of the structure.

The first step, performed by the archaeological team, was to establish key reference points on the river bottom to serve as benchmarks for the cofferdam. Using these references, the contractor set pilings to support a "template," a steel frame which determined the exact placement of the cofferdam sheet-steel pilings. Positioning of each of the template pilings was personally checked by an archaeologist before the piling actually touched the bottom. Once the template pilings were set, there was almost no chance of damaging cultural resources; nevertheless, inspection dives were continued throughout the construction phase (Figure 3). No damage was observed.

The cofferdam was constructed of interlocking sheet-steel pilings to form an enclosure 97 ft. (29.4 m) long by 45 ft. (13.6 m) wide (Figures 4 and 5). With an average water depth of approximately 20 ft. (6.1 m), the cofferdam enclosed approximately one-half million gallons (nearly 2,000,000 l of water, which was clarified by commercial swimming pool filters donated by the Purex Corporation. Two separate, identical filtration systems were employed, each using an electric pump to circulate water through a bank of sand filters.

The system did not work as well as hoped. River water was freely exchanged with interior water through seams in the cofferdam walls and through the porous silt and clay of the river bottom. Incursion of river water introduced fresh silt and algae, thus limiting the effectiveness of the filters.

Various experiments were conducted for sealing the cofferdam walls, including marine epoxies, caulking compounds, and plastic liners. None of the methods completely eliminated water exchange between river and cofferdam, although flow rate

FIGURE 3. Yorktown cofferdam under construction. (Photo by John D. Broadwater.)

was eventually reduced to a manageable level. Various filtration procedures were also attempted, responding diligently and hopefully to suggestions from countless experts, some of whom, as it turns out, offered invalid or even inappropriate solutions. (Experience at Yorktown suggests an important axiom for underwater research: Be leery of all advice, but doubly so from those who profess to be experts. An equally pertinent, and more basic, axiom is: Murphy's Law works even better underwater!)

The first two seasons involved frustrating and excessive experimentation with the filters, which diverted an inordinate amount of effort and attention from the archaeological goals. Finally, in 1985, the Ecolochem Corporation of Norfolk, Virginia offered to contribute long-term assistance in

FIGURE 4. Aerial photograph of completed Yorktown cofferdam, 1988 (© 1988, Bates Littlehales, National Geographic Society).

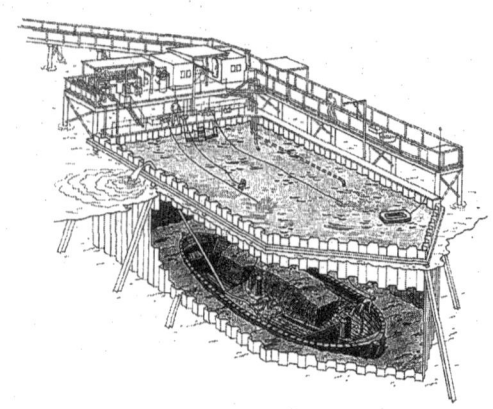

FIGURE 5. Yorktown cofferdam, 1988 (© 1988, Piere Mion, National Geographic Society).

finding a solution to the filtration problem. Ecolochem, the largest mobile filtration company in the world, conducted a series of tests, monitoring water conditions and filter output around the clock. Utilizing water purification technology developed by their company but modified for the unusual conditions within the cofferdam, Ecolochem engineers soon established a filtration procedure which dramatically improved diving conditions at the site (Broadwater, Morris et al. 1988; Adams 1989).

The principal criterion for filtration procedures was that none of the methods or chemicals should be harmful to divers or to the environment. Throughout the project, the primary methods used were those employed in the purification of drink-

ing water and the filtration of swimming pools. The procedure established by Ecolochem consisted basically of injecting alum into filter intake pipes, causing minute particles to precipitate into solids which could then be removed within the sand filters. Copper sulfate and chlorine were periodically injected directly into the cofferdam to kill blue-green algae and diatoms. This combination of treatments maintained a very acceptable level of visibility.

From late 1985 until the close of the project in 1988, average visibility in the cofferdam was better than 10 ft. (3 m), compared to near-zero in the open river. Visibility occasionally exceeded 30 ft. (9.1 m), providing excellent working conditions and permitting detailed photographic recording of the site. Unfortunately, the combination of depth, surface reflections, and turbidity made it impossible for visitors on the observation platform to discern details of the wreck. Had more funding and time been available, this secondary goal could also have been achieved.

Ironically, considering the efforts expended in developing an optimum filtration system, sometimes the clearest water was observed on days when the filters were not operating (although such clarity was never maintained for long without filtration). This suggests that under certain conditions cofferdams could be used to advantage as "stilling basins"—the appropriate term for the Yorktown structure, according to the design engineer—with no filtration system at all.

As is so often the case with first-time experiments, there were numerous problems, delays, and costs involved in testing the Yorktown cofferdam. Construction of the cofferdam cost $412,000 in 1982, nearly three times the original 1979 estimates. The cost increase was primarily due to a previously-unknown silt channel beneath the wreck which necessitated seating the cofferdam pilings as deep as 80–100 ft. into the bottom, and supporting the structure with additional exterior bracing consisting of I-beams as long as 170 ft. (Figure 3).

Evaluation of the cofferdam's cost-effectiveness is difficult. One of the major objectives of the project was to develop the cofferdam and test its effectiveness as an excavation tool. Because the cofferdam minimized the hazards and difficulties of working under water, it allowed the archaeological team to devote its attention more fully to the excavation. This advantage was especially important during annual field schools as well as the almost-daily utilization of volunteer divers who often possessed little or no archaeological experience.

Each year from 1982 to 1988, research projects were conducted at the site in cooperation with the Program in Maritime History and Underwater Research at East Carolina University (ECU), Greenville, North Carolina. The combination of a safe, efficient site and the presence of an extremely well-preserved wooden shipwreck provided an excellent training opportunity for students. In turn, the ECU teams provided much-needed skilled labor for the excavation. This cooperative research program was essential to the goals of the project.

Excavation and Analysis

For the excavation of site 44YO88, established archaeological methods and techniques were adapted for underwater excavation; in addition,

new methods were developed to take advantage of the unique cofferdam environment. Because of the complexity and long-term nature of the project, a project manual was developed which described all procedures and provided information on excavation, record-keeping, facilities, safety, personnel, and other project functions. A series of standardized recording forms simplified and expedited the enormous task of recording all site activities and archaeological data. The project manual, which was revised and updated several times during the course of the excavation, continually served as a guide for staff and volunteers alike.

The precise and regular shape of the cofferdam provided an ideal frame of reference for both horizontal and vertical control of the excavation. The cofferdam was exactly 45 ft. wide, making it suitable for division into 5-ft.-square units. A three-digit numerical grid designation was used because of its simplicity and adaptability to computer coding. The reference elevation datum was established from a permanent USGS survey benchmark in Yorktown.

Various types of grids were utilized during the excavation. The first system was made up of a series of steel cables stretched across the width of the cofferdam and tightened with turnbuckles attached to a carefully-positioned support frame attached to the cofferdam walls near the river bottom. This system provided a precise horizontal and vertical reference from which measurements could be made; it also served as a scaffold, keeping excavators away from the ubiquitous loose silt which continually threatened to obliterate the improved visibility. This system was replaced by a surface-supported grid and, finally, by bottom-supported grids as excavation progressed.

Sediment removal was accomplished in a standard fashion, utilizing 4-in. airlifts. Up to four airlifts could be used simultaneously, powered by a high-volume screw compressor on loan from Bauer Compressors. Overburden thus travelled up the airlift pipes and into the river outside the cofferdam. Care was taken to leave all artifacts in situ until mapped; however, a ¼-in. mesh bag was clamped to the airlift pipe at the outflow point to capture any artifacts which accidently escaped detection. The bag was removed and inspected after each level was excavated to insure proper provenience recording. Excavation proceeded in a "terraced" fashion which avoided deep trenches and minimized the possibility of collapsing walls.

Efforts were made to identify and follow natural stratigraphy during excavation, with each new layer, or zone, receiving a unique letter designation. Within each zone, or when no stratigraphy could be discerned, excavation was conducted in arbitrary 4-in. levels as a means of maintaining tight vertical control. The method proved particularly useful on this site where site profiles almost all contained a deep clay layer which was virtually free of cultural material.

Although this dual method of vertical control may seem somewhat redundant, recording both levels required little extra time, and it is recommended for its analytical value, especially during post-excavation analysis. By assigning artifact numbers containing both the zone letter designation and the 4-in. level designation (as well as the site and grid number, of course), it is possible to visualize at a glance the actual provenience within the hull of each object. Although stratigraphy within the hull of a shipwreck must generally be interpreted differently than that on a terrestrial site, relative depth within the hull is an important factor in site interpretation. An additional benefit is the ability to tabulate the number of 4-in. levels excavated within each 5-ft. grid square as a means of tracking excavation progress.

Several techniques were used for mapping and recording. Detailed underwater mapping was accomplished using waterproof mylar sheets taped to slates on which a grid was superimposed. When necessary, a sheet was drawn for each level of each square; in other situations, it was more efficient to record as many as 10 squares simultaneously on larger slates. These "mega-slates" were especially helpful in areas where large features or objects occupied multiple squares. An additional advantage to the use of standardized mylar sheets is that they provide permanent records which can be filed and retained.

Mapping of hull components, features, and significant artifacts was accomplished with a three-dimensional (3-D) measurement system devised by Charles Mazel and adapted to the cofferdam structure. Eyebolts were attached to the walls of the cofferdam at precise points to form adjacent rectangles. Surveyors' measuring tapes were stretched from three eyebolts to points to be measured and direct distances were recorded. These direct readings were converted by programmable calculator (later, a microcomputer) to rectilinear coordinates (x, y, z) which were then easily plotted onto the site plan.

The accuracy of the Yorktown 3-D measurement system was demonstrated to be within ± ½ in. Experience suggests one caution, however: accuracy depends on (a) the precision to which the reference points have been located, and (b) the care taken to obtain measurements. The cofferdam was an ideal fixed reference frame, but accuracy depended on careful double-checking of each measurement. Measurements were taken by two divers—one to hold the tape and the other to swim the length of the tape to ensure that it was not fouled on a float, grid, or other obstacle.

The 3-D system offers another, more powerful, method of verifying measurements. A tape can be pulled from the fourth corner of the reference rectangle, and the computer programmed to compare readings for several combinations of three readings. The computer can then compare the resulting point coordinates to see if all are within acceptable error limits. This extra step was used sparingly at Yorktown because the three-tape system had proven to be acceptable and because the four-tape method required extra time.

The same type of measurements can now be made electronically using the Sonic High-Accuracy Ranging and Positioning System (SHARPS). This device utilizes sonic transducers and associated computer hardware and software to locate objects quickly and with a very high degree of accuracy. In 1985, the Yorktown cofferdam provided SHARPS with its first field test. During a one-hour dive, the prototype system recorded several hundred data points on computer and plotted those points on a visual display—the equivalent of several weeks' work by divers.

Then, in 1987 the manufacturer, Marine Telepresence, Inc., brought one of the first production-model SHARPS systems to Yorktown to test a more ambitious field technique, one which promised to become the site recording method of the future. The plan was to use SHARPS on site to record the hull shape of shipwreck 44YO88, then, immediately following data collection, SHARPS data files would be transferred by phone link to a Prime minicomputer in Virginia Beach, where a computer-aided design and drafting (CADD) system would generate detailed drawings of the hull and other key features. This combination of electronic data-gathering and computer processing would provide a rapid and efficient flow of data from field to final drawings. SHARPS can now transfer data files directly into AutoCAD software for on-site review and analysis of data.

The system test worked well, but it proved to be preferable to pre-process the field data before entering them into the CADD system. Pre-processing removed spurious and redundant data points and separated data into discrete, more manageable files. A series of unexplained discrepancies was discovered in the resulting data, however, and as a result, measurements had to be re-checked by manual means. Field data from both data collection methods were then utilized in the preparation of a complete set of lines drawings for the hull (Caverly 1989).

It must be emphasized here that the CADD system was never envisioned as an expedient hull-lines-generation source. Rather, the CADD system was utilized as a tool for analysis, a function for which it proved to be invaluable. In addition to providing the means for generating detailed drawings which could be easily updated and revised, the CADD system became an ''electronic spline'' for the preparation of provisional hull lines. That is, all hull lines were generated on the CADD system directly from the raw field data (Caverly 1989).

A body plan was developed on the CADD system in exactly the same manner as if drawn by hand using splines and curves. Once the body plan was satisfactory, the other two projections were developed from the body plan. A limited amount of smoothing was then performed, but always

within the parameters of the field data. Remaining irregularities in the hull lines were assumed to be actual deformities in the hull itself (Caverly 1989; Broadwater 1989b; Morris 1991).

The significance of utilizing this method, rather than forming the lines from an automatic lines-generating program, is that the actual field measurements are retained—the baby has not been thrown out with the bath water. Resulting lines represent the as-found shape of the hull, and irregularities can be interpreted in terms of such factors as distortion over time, imperfections in the original construction, and so forth.

The final phase of the Yorktown Project included feasibility studies to consider options ranging from recovery, preservation, and exhibit of the hull to maintaining the cofferdam and filtration system as an underwater park and training facility. After exhausting all efforts to generate support for one or more of the proposed options, cognizant state and federal agencies recommended that the site be backfilled. In 1990, the hull was covered with river silt, which will provide excellent protection. Following backfilling, the cofferdam was dismantled, with the assistance of U.S. Navy Mobile Diving and Salvage Unit Two.

Summary and Conclusions

Although the Yorktown Shipwreck Archaeological Project utilized such ''hi-tech'' equipment as the cofferdam, SHARPS, and CADD, the project was, in many ways, a traditional archaeological excavation. Standard, well-accepted archaeological methods were employed during excavation, recording, analysis, and interpretation; technology was utilized when appropriate for facilitating these processes.

The most radical application of technology was the cofferdam. The cofferdam greatly improved site conditions and permitted more efficient excavation and more complete recording. Future researchers may find the method to be worth utilizing on appropriate sites, especially if materials and/or labor for a cofferdam can be obtained as donations (which was the original intent at Yorktown).

The ongoing research is expected to produce a comprehensive final site report which will present results of more than a decade of research at Yorktown, interpreting those results within the broader context of 18th-century political, economic, and technological factors. It is hoped that the technological methodology described in this article will be of value to others. The author would welcome comments and questions concerning the details of the project.

ACKNOWLEDGMENTS

Funding for the Yorktown Shipwreck Archaeological Project was provided by a broad cross-section of government, the historic preservation community, and the private sector. Principal sponsors were the National Endowment for the Humanities, U.S. Department of the Interior, Commonwealth of Virginia, County of York, National Geographic Society, and Yorktown Maritime Heritage Foundation. Numerous other corporate and private organizations, especially those mentioned in the text of this article, contributed invaluable assistance, both financial and in-kind. The Yorktown Project staff never exceeded six persons, and was usually only three except during the summer months. Harding Polk and Roni Hinote Polk were project archaeologists when the cofferdam was constructed; Robert Adams was assistant director during 1984–1985; John William ("Billy Ray") Morris III became assistant director in 1986 and continued in that capacity until the end of the project, becoming a very essential factor in the excavation and interpretation of the site; Marcie Renner served as assistant director for conservation throughout the excavation of 44YO88. Additional staff members deserving mention include Linda Brown, David Cooper, Bruce Terrell, and Eri Weinstein. Other temporary staff members, interpreters, and volunteers too numerous to mention, all made valuable contributions to the effort, and are remembered with fondness and gratitude.

REFERENCES

ADAMS, ROBERT M.
1989   Yorktown Shipwreck Archaeological Project: Results of the 1985 Season. *Archaeology in Solution:*

The 1986 Proceedings of the Conference on Underwater Archaeology, edited by James P. Delgado, pp. 214–220. Coyote Press, Salinas, California.

ANDAHAZY, WILLIAM J., DOUGLAS G. EVERSTINE, AND BRUCE R. HOOD
1976   Magnetometer Search for Shipwrecks from the Battle of Yorktown. *Sea Technology* 17(11):19–22.

BASS, GEORGE F. (EDITOR)
1972   *A History of Seafaring Based on Underwater Archaeology.* Thames and Hudson, London.

BASS, GEORGE F., I. NOËL HUME, J. O. SANDS, AND J. R. STEFFY
1976   The Cornwallis Cave Shipwreck. Report prepared by Institute of Nautical Archaeology, College Station, Texas. Submitted to the Virginia Historic Landmarks Commission, Richmond.

BROADWATER, JOHN D.
1980   The Yorktown Shipwreck Archaeological Project: Results from the 1978 Survey. *International Journal of Nautical Archaeology and Underwater Exploration* 9(3):227–235.
1981   Yorktown Shipwreck Project: Results from the 1978 Survey. *In the Realms of Gold: The Proceedings of the Tenth Conference on Underwater Archaeology (1979)*, edited by Wilburn A. Cockrell, pp. 33–45. Fathom Eight, San Marino, California.
1988   Secrets of a Yorktown Shipwreck. *National Geographic Magazine* 173(6):804–823.
1989a   Merchant Ships at War: The Sunken British Fleet at Yorktown, Virginia. *Underwater Archaeology Proceedings from the Society for Historical Archaeology Conference*, edited by J. Barto Arnold III, pp. 121–124. Society for Historical Archaeology, California, Pennsylvania.
1989b   Yorktown Shipwreck 44YO88: Stores and Cargo from a British Naval Supply Vessel from the American War for Independence. Unpublished M.A. thesis, Program in American Studies, The College of William and Mary, Williamsburg, Virginia.

BROADWATER, JOHN D., R. M. ADAMS, AND M. RENNER
1985   The Yorktown Shipwreck Archaeological Project: An Interim Report on the Excavation of Shipwreck 44YO88. *The International Journal of Nautical Archaeology and Underwater Exploration* 14(4):301–314.

BROADWATER, JOHN D., AND J. W. MORRIS III
1991   A Report on the Hull and Rigging of Yorktown Shipwreck 44YO88. Draft report on file with the authors.

BROADWATER, JOHN D., J. W. MORRIS III, AND M. RENNER
1988   The Yorktown Shipwreck Archaeological Project: An Interim Report on the 1987 Season. *Underwater*

Archaeology Proceedings from the Conference on Underwater Archaeology, edited by James P. Delgado, pp. 13–18. Society for Historical Archaeology, California, Pennsylvania.

BROADWATER, JOHN D., T. J. OERTLING, AND M. RENNER
1988   The Yorktown Shipwreck Archaeological Project: Results from the 1983 Season. *In Search of Our Maritime Past: Proceedings of the Fifteenth Conference on Underwater Archaeology*, edited by Gordon P. Watts, Jr., pp. 168–181. East Carolina University, Greenville, North Carolina.

BROADWATER, JOHN D., HARDING POLK II, AND MARCIE RENNER
1985   Yorktown Shipwreck Archaeological Project: An Interim Report on the 1982 Season. *Underwater Archaeology: The Proceedings of the Fourteenth Conference on Underwater Archaeology*, edited by Calvin R. Cummings, pp. 38–43. Fathom Eight, San Marino, California.

CAVERLY, ROBERT D.
1989   The Application of SHARPS and CAD Technology on the Yorktown Shipwreck Archaeological Project. *Underwater Archaeology Proceedings from the Society for Historical Archaeology Conference*, edited by J. Barto Arnold III, pp. 18–20. Society for Historical Archaeology, California, Pennsylvania.

JOHNSTON, PAUL F., JOHN O. SANDS, AND J. RICHARD STEFFY
1978   The Cornwallis Cave Shipwreck, Yorktown, Virginia. *International Journal of Nautical Archaeology and Underwater Exploration* 7(3):205–226.

MORRIS, JOHN WILLIAM III
1991   Site 44YO88: The Archaeological Assessment of the Hull Remains at Yorktown, Virginia. Unpublished M.A. thesis, Program in Maritime History and Underwater Research, Department of History, East Carolina University, Greenville, North Carolina.

SANDS, JOHN O.
1983   *Yorktown's Captive Fleet*. Published for the Mariners' Museum. University Press of Virginia, Charlottesville, Virginia.
1988   Gunboats and Warships of the American Revolution. In *Ships and Shipwrecks of the Americas: A History Based on Underwater Archaeology*, edited by George F. Bass, pp. 143–168. Thames and Hudson, London.

JOHN D. BROADWATER
MONITOR NATIONAL MARINE SANCTUARY
439 WEST YORK ST.
NORFOLK, VIRGINIA 23510

1978 Ship Reconstruction and Antiquities Conservation: Maximum Results from Minimum Remains. In *Beneath the Waters of Time: The Proceedings of the Ninth Conference on Underwater Archaeology*, J. Barto Arnold III, editor, pp. 53-54. Texas Antiquities Committee Publication No. 6, Austin, Texas. Reprinted with permission.

MAXIMUM RESULTS FROM MINIMUM REMAINS

by
J. Richard Steffy

Few excavations yield hulls as well preserved as Kyrenia (Katsev and Katsev 1974) or Brown's Ferry (Albright 1977). Nautical archeologists must face the fact that many of them will never encounter anything more than sparsely preserved hull remains. This does not mean they cannot contribute scholarly results, however. How often does one read "nothing could be learned about the hull, since only a few planks survived" or, "there was not enough wood left to warrant investigation"? The tragedy in these statements lies not in the fact that these wrecks were poorly preserved, but that their remaining fragments were totally ignored. The value of excavated hull remains has nothing to do with the extent of survival; it is the amount of information gleaned from each fragment which is important.

It is true that Kyrenia has provided hundreds of pages of new information, and Brown's Ferry can be expected to produce similar results. But for every revelation those ships make possible, a dozen new questions arise. For instance, it was not known whether planking on shell-built ships could be repaired or replaced until such replacements were discovered on Kyrenia. But now we are puzzled by such questions as what special tools must have been used, why that particular procedure was followed, and so on. Nearly complete old and ancient hulls do not solve all the mysteries. They only provide us with enough intelligence to notice new ones. Ironically, if only one planking fragment survived from a 4th century B.C. hull and that fragment belonged to a slightly different replacement strake of the Kyrenia type (a possibility, since the replacements are usually much better preserved), all the questions raised by the Kyrenia repairs might be answered. That single fragment, then, would have been far too valuable to ignore. There are similar discoveries to be made on many poorly preserved hulls, if only we take the trouble to carefully scrutinize them.

I do not infer that Kyrenia and Brown's Ferry wrecks are not important ships. Their value will be realized for years to come, and the fact that their abundant evidence raises new questions is an asset indicative of a higher level of understanding. It is the relative value of the extent of hull survival that is wrong in the minds of so many archeologists. A shipwreck with ten tons of extant wood is not necessarily forty times more valuable than one with only a quarter ton. The big wreck may be less valuable. Value depends on many factors — period, condition of the wood, extent of the excavation, which hull areas and related artifacts survived, and expertise of the investigators to name a few. Unless one has an intact hull with enough expertise, funding, and diplomacy to preserve it in a castle or museum, the extent of hull survival has little to do with the value of the project. At the present time, a poorly preserved wreck dated to the 9th century B.C. would be potentially more important to historians than a well preserved 30-ton merchantman from the 4th century B.C.

The quality and quantity of information to be gleaned from fragmentary remains is usually limited only by the ingenuity of the observer. Magnifying lenses and oblique lights can be used to reveal obscure marks made by carpenter's tools and equipment handled by the crew. Such marks identify tool sizes and types, the effects of rigging on fittings, and even the habits and expertise of the shipwright. Laboratory tests confirm wood species, the composition of metals, and the types of caulking, pitches and paints. Bilge matter, aptly called "gunk," is especially interesting because it is likely to contain samples of everything dropped into the hold during the life of the ship. Seeds, sawdust, and sand seem to be the most common bilge items, although our finds have ranged from coins to rats.

If the ship is not intended to be excavated, such features are more difficult to determine. But dimensions can be taken anywhere, even at zero visibility, and dimensions are the most important data of all. Thicknesses and widths of all timbers are important. So is their frequency, especially frame and wale spacing. The sizes and frequency of fasteners, the curvature of the hull — the list of items to examine and record goes on and on.

At what minimum level of preservation does one ignore the study of the hull? Even a single fragment may be valuable; its importance should certainly be investigated by the excavator. Two sparsely preserved wrecks, whose hull remains were recorded, exhibited different, but important results. One of these was the Cape Gelidonya wreck (Bass 1967), a Bronze Age trader excavated by Dr. George F. Bass in 1960. There were only five distinguishable fragments scattered among dunnage and ballast stones, yet 15 important dimensions were recorded. With today's improved techniques, that list might have been doubled. If a half dozen new Bronze Age shipwrecks are recorded in the future, each contributing only 15 new facts, we will be well on our way to understanding Bronze Age ship construction.

The Porticello wreck (Eiseman 1975) was little better preserved, but its few fragmentary remains were also documented. Again, there were only a dozen or so vital statistics concerning this 5th century B.C. vessel. By comparing these fragments with the slightly later Kyrenia ship, however, we were able to record pages of additional information regarding hull construction.

In both cases, hull survival was so sparse that ship finds might have been ignored, yet the recorded information proved helpful. Had those fragments been avoided, we would be lacking that much knowledge concerning two important maritime periods. Just as great cathedrals were built with nickel and dime contributions, so will small contributions from nautical archeology play an important role in the total description of man's past.

Limited budgets are no excuse for ignoring wood. Substantial knowledge of a particular vessel can be gained by making simple sketches and a few important measurements; even if there is no time or money to permit triangulation or photography, approximate provenience can be readily noted. Nor is the argument that it is morally wrong to remove hull remains a valid excuse for ignoring the ship completely. Ships do not have to be removed or disturbed to accomplish good hull interpretation. If it were morally right to expose the hull and excavate artifacts, however, then it is proper and necessary to record that exposed hull before backfilling. Archeologists can no longer ethically decide which part of a shipwreck is most important, regardless of their personal interests. Every part of a wreck is equally important because there are many disciplines interested in the results of an excavation.

In a sense, a sunken ship is an artifact — it is sometimes the most important artifact. Unlike representations, translations, and documents, it is primary evidence in three-dimensional form. Ships and pieces of ships bear tool marks, graffiti, and decorations. Anchors, fittings, and fasteners spell out the metallurgy of the period. Wood types, and their application, tell of forestry and the timber trade. Construction techniques indicate expertise, design reveals technology, and scantling determines hull size where much of the hull may be missing. Any old or ancient object so revealing, be it artifact, hull, or hull fragment, is far too important to be ignored.

By all means excavate cargoes and artifacts, but please don't stomp on the wood in doing so.

REFERENCES CITED

Albright, Alan B.
1977   The Brown's Ferry Vessel. *Proceedings of the North American Society of Oceanic History.* Salem.

Bass, George F.
1967   Cape Gelidonya: A Bronze Age shipwreck. *Transactions of the American Philosophical Society, New Series* 57:8. Phildelphia.

Eiseman, Cynthia J.
1975   The Porticello shipwreck. *AINA Newsletter* 2:4.

Katsev. S.W. and M.L. Katsev
1974   Last harbor for the oldest ship. *National Geographic* 146(5): 618-625.

ShipShape: Creating a 3D Solid Model of the Newport Medieval Ship

Toby N. Jones
Nigel Nayling

The mid-fifteenth-century, clinker-built Newport Medieval Ship represents the most comprehensively and accurately recorded large ship find in the United Kingdom. The ship timbers have been digitally recorded using a FaroArm three-dimensional contact digitizer and Rhinoceros modeling software. Using these precise and versatile digital records, a 1:10 scale model, complete with accurately modeled scarves, clench nail holes and treenail holes, has been produced using selective laser sintering technology. The completed 3D solid model is being documented, analyzed and compared to photogrammetry, site drawings and timber records in order to contrast the various shape states of the ship and provide a basis for determining the original hull form.

Introduction

In 2008, the University of Wales Trinity Saint David, in collaboration with the Newport Medieval Ship project and the Manufacturing Engineering Centre (MEC) at Cardiff University, received a substantial grant (ShipShape AH/G000905/1) from the United Kingdom Arts and Humanities Research Council (AHRC) to create a three-dimensional scaled physical model of the excavated ship remains. The subject of the study, a mid-fifteenth-century, clinker-built merchant ship, was found during the construction of a theatre alongside the tidal River Usk in Newport. The ship was excavated, disassembled and raised in the latter half of 2002, and the timbers were stored in large tanks of fresh water (Jones 2009a:111-116).

The ship timbers were subsequently cleaned and recorded using three dimensional contact digitizers. The archaeological team then created three dimensional digital solid models from each of the recorded timbers. The digital models were then used to create scaled physical solid models with a rapid prototyping technology called selective laser sintering. The model was assembled, piece by piece, using micro-fasteners. The shape of the research model was frequently documented during the construction sequence, using contact digitizing and laser scanning. The different shape states or phases of the model were then compared and analyzed in an effort to determine the original hull form (Nayling and Jones, forthcoming).

Documentation

The documentation phase of the Newport Ship project relied extensively on a variety of digital recording methodologies to record the structural ship timbers. The digital output of these methods, in the form of vector graphic drawing files, created a data set from which to construct digital and physical models. The documentation and digital and physical modeling processes are explained below.

In common with many rescue archaeology projects, archaeologists working on the Newport Ship excavation were under pressure to complete their investigations quickly. While they were able to document the position and context of artefacts and ship timbers with traditional hand drawings, photogrammetry, photography and videography, they were unable to record each timber in the detail required to create a reconstruction model of the ship. The reconstruction of the original shape of the hull form of an archaeological ship find is seen as a key research goal within nautical archaeology (Institute for Archaeology 2008). A decision was made to properly clean and record the timbers at a later date after the excavation.

During the brief lull between the end of the excavation in 2003 and the start of the post-excavation research in late 2004, the project managers were able to compare various recording methodologies and choose the most efficient, accurate and suitable system for recording the disassembled ship timbers. The pilot study compared laser scanning, one-to-one non-contact tracing and contact digitizing. The ideal solution proved to be the use of three dimensional contact digitizers to record the shape, surface detail, and fasteners of each ship timber and artifact (Jones 2009b:36-41).

The project initially acquired one 12 ft. Faro Advantage Arm contact digitizer and utilized Rhinoceros 3 digital

FIGURE 1. AN ARCHAEOLOGIST CLEANS CONCRETIONS FROM THE REBATES ON THE OUTBOARD FACE OF A JOGGLED FLOOR TIMBER (NEWPORT MUSEUM AND HERITAGE SERVICE).

modeling software to capture and display the output. Introductory training and example templates were provided by the National Museum of Denmark - Viking Ship Museum in Roskilde, Denmark. Subsequent expanded trials showed the contact digitizer was well suited to recording the waterlogged ship timbers, and a successful grant application to the Heritage Lottery Fund, specifically to clean and record the ship timbers, led to the acquisition of three more digitizers. The entire extant hull of the ship was cleaned and comprehensively recorded by archaeologists in two years using four identical digitizers.

During the initial training period, archaeologists were taught how to operate the equipment (both hardware and software), 'read' the timbers, and record important features like tool marks, fasteners and edges. Different features, like nails and wood grain, were recorded on separate layers and in specific colors. Template files were created for each hull component group, with template layers specifically tailored for characteristic clinker shipbuilding tradition timber types like lapstrake planks and joggled floors. A step by step timber recording manual helped to ensure quality and consistency in methods and interpretation among the large team (Jones 2011).

Before recording could commence, the ship timbers had to be cleaned. The surface detail was often obscured by layers of clay, tar, and iron concretion. Dental tools, toothbrushes, and large amounts of water were used to remove the softer concretions, while hammers and chisels were employed to remove the harder concretions that formed around the clench nail holes. The surface detail was well preserved, with clearly visible tool stop marks and intentionally inscribed carpenter's marks. During

the cleaning process, tar, iron and animal fiber samples were taken for future analysis. Sample locations were temporarily marked with Tyvek tags and pins, which were documented and removed during the recording process (Figure 1).

The recording process started by placing timbers on large, specially-constructed stainless steel tables, and stabilizing them with foam wedges to prevent any movement. Larger timbers were maneuvered by slinging and lifting them using padded straps, foam, and an overhead gantry. An adjustable framework of angle iron was clamped to the back of the table, from which hung flexible lights, an LCD monitor, and a counterbalance system to offset the weight of the digitizer (Jones 2011).

Control points, in the form of small stainless steel wood screws, were inserted into the edges of planks and along the inboard and outboard face of framing timbers. It was necessary to reference the heads of the wood screws with the contact digitizer probe tip when moving or rotating a timber (the points will remain in the timbers through the conservation process, and will provide a useful baseline against which distortion in the timber can be checked). After installation of control points, the archaeologist opened a read-only template file and labeled it according to the universal identifier number and timber function code. The digitization commenced by working through the layering system and recording all examples of each feature, such as rove impressions or treenail holes. The contact digitizer itself was fairly easy to use, with the operator grasping the end of the arm and lightly touching the probe tip against the surface of the ship timber while pressing the point acquisition button (Figure 2).

Nearly all of the digital data was generated using the following three tools in Rhino: single point, polyline, and DigSketch. The single point tool was used to record locations of samples, control points, and fastener centers. Polyline (which connects individually chosen single points with a line) was used to trace around fasteners and roves. The DigSketch tool was similar to polyline, except that points could be automatically taken at predetermined intervals, allowing the recorder to draw long edges accurately and quickly. When taking multiple points, wire frames were automatically constructed from the point data collected by the digitizer in real time. The resulting digital vector graphic drawing of each timber was an accurate three-dimensional (3D) wire frame drawing, which was saved as a read-only file in the proprietary Rhino 3dm file format and archived. Subsequent editing of the file required the user to save

FIGURE 2. AN ARCHAEOLOGIST RECORDS ONE OF THE NEWPORT SHIP TIMBERS WITH A 3D CONTACT DIGITIZER. THE DIGITIZERS ARE EFFECTIVE AND ACCURATE TOOLS FOR RECORDING SURFACE DETAIL AND ARTIFACT GEOMETRY (NEWPORT MUSEUM AND HERITAGE SERVICE).

the file as a copy.

Throughput was comparable to conventional 1:1 scale two-dimensional tracing methods in terms of time, with the benefit of increased accuracy and advanced modeling possibilities in the future. Typical file sizes range from 1 to 5 MB, with an average 3 meter plank using 2 MB of space, while a large floor timber would be 3-4 MB. File size was dependent on the sheer number of points (size of point cloud) taken during the recording process. Much of the data was captured by the DigSketch tool, which was set to acquire points with default 1 mm spacing. For smaller file size, the spacing setting could have been changed to a larger interval.

Contact digitizers have traditionally been used in quality control and reverse engineering applications, and are exceptionally precise tools. This precision allows surface details to be recorded in fine detail. However, accuracy can be degraded by inadvertently changing a particularly important setting in the Rhino software. When drawing with the DigSketch tool, there is an option to change the degree of the curve. Degree 1 curves are those in which the curve or polyline is drawn through each recorded point. Degree 2 and 3 (and higher) curves are smoothed or faired by the software, with the displayed curves merely passing near the actual points. Any degree setting other than Degree 1 causes areas where there is a sharp bend or corner to appear more rounded than they actually are.

Each digital drawing was checked by another archaeologist while the timber was still on the recording table. If mistakes or omissions were noted during the checking process, it was a straightforward process to reference the digitizer back to the original timber and record the missing features. After final checks, the digital drawings were saved as read-only files and archived for future analysis and modeling. The vast majority of timbers were subsequently examined by the archaeological consultant (NN) and compared with print outs of the Rhinoceros files and hand-written timber record sheets, and selective photographs requested. Requests for changes to the Rhinoceros files became increasingly rare as the recording team acquired a high level of competence and consistency in the recording process. The digital documentation methods were complemented by selective digital photography, hand-written timber record sheets, and laser scanning and casting of special features. Details about each timber, including function code, description and its progress through the documentation process were tracked in a Microsoft Access database.

There are currently a number of ship timber recording projects using contact digitizers and Rhinoceros modeling software throughout Europe and North America. Many of the projects are linked through the sharing of methods, templates and layering systems. The network has been named the Faro-Rhino Archaeological Users Group (FRAUG). There have been five meetings of the group, with the most recent occurring in March 2011 in Oslo, Norway. Goals of the group include further development of a common visual language for the 3D documentation of ship timbers, exploring publication methods for the 3D data, and effective archiving systems, the results of which will be publically available on a website that is currently under development.

Digital Modeling

The Newport Ship project developed a concise and effective methodology for turning the 3D digital timber records into digital solid models. The techniques were developed and evaluated through a series of small scale pilot studies. The final digital modeling process was divided into four distinct phases: simplification, surfacing, fastener modeling, and quality control. Developing a standardized method for the production of the digital solid models was necessary in order to achieve a consistent and accurate end product, given that a number of individuals were involved in the modeling effort, and potential scaled physical manufacture would leave little room for error. The results of the pilot studies were codified into a detailed step-by-step manual that was used to train staff and provide commentary (metadata) for subsequent data archiving.

To create a digital solid model, it was first necessary to reduce the detail and complexity of each vector graphic drawing. A vector graphic drawing of a typical lapstrake hull plank recorded with a contact digitizer consisted of long lines for the edges and scarfs, shorter lines for the ends, outlines of fastener holes, and various surface details, like construction marks and cracks. These lines were based on hundreds or thousands of points captured by the digitizer. The point spacing, while appropriate for the archived primary record, is excessive for digital modeling. For example, the upper edge of a typical three meter long plank might have been drawn with approximately 3000 points using the one millimeter point spacing setting. It was necessary to sample or decimate the number of points in a way that decreased the overall number without compromising the accuracy of the line. This task was rapidly achieved using the rebuild command in Rhinoceros 4.

The simplification process involves rebuilding the edges using the Rhino command Edit>Rebuild and selecting between 1-20% of the original points. The software would then redraw the line through the points remaining after the sampling. The end result would be a line with just enough points to accurately represent the edge geometry, and not the minute surface variations, of the timber. It was important to remember that if the digital solid model was to be scaled and physically manufactured, then much surface detail would be lost. For example, a two centimeter wide crack on a plank will show up as a 2 mm crack on a 1:10 scale digital or physical model. It is probable that whatever physical manufacturing technique was used, it would not be able to recreate the finer details at scale. The purpose of the modeling should also be considered when accounting for the level of required/necessary detail. If the ultimate goal was a scaled hull form reconstruction model, or a floating hypothesis, then small features, like the above mentioned crack, would be of little consequence. Finally, given that some shared edge lines were purposely duplicated on different layers during the recording process, it was only necessary to simplify one example of each line.

The second major step in creating a digital solid was surfacing the simplified vector graphic drawings. The most straightforward way of surfacing the wire frame drawing was a process called sweeping. Using the Sweep Two Rails command in Rhinoceros 4, the archaeologist selected two simplified long edges (for example, the upper and lower edges of the inboard face of a plank) and then selected a number of cross section curves that intersected both of these long edges. After executing the command, the software created a surface that was constrained by all of the edges and cross section curves. The process was repeated on each face or 'facet' of the timber. Complex areas, such as scarfs or damaged edges, were subdivided into smaller facets, which were individually simplified and surfaced. After the entire simplified wire frame drawing was surfaced, the surfaces were joined together using the Join command. The Join Command created a solid polysurface model, which was then converted into a polygon mesh. The resulting mesh file was checked for holes and naked edges; errors in the modeling process that would have made the final solid model invalid. Once a valid polygon mesh had been created and checked, attention was turned to modeling the fasteners.

The fastener modeling methodology consisted of creating correctly sized, angled and positioned digital models of the fastening holes and subtracting them from the polygon mesh solid, which created idealized but correctly positioned fastener holes. There were two main types of fastener holes that were recorded in the Newport Ship. One type of hole was created by the auguring of a round hole through two lapstrake planks. A square-shafted wrought iron nail measuring approximately 10 mm wide in cross-section was inserted into this hole. This nail was clenched over a sub-rectangular rove or metal plate placed on the inboard face of the planking, essentially creating a rivet to hold the planks together. There were thousands of these rivets and roves fastening the hull planking of the ship together. Both the nail head and rove left visible impressions in the surface of the planking. However, these features were not modeled. The key piece of recorded information was the centre of the fastener hole. In Rhinoceros 4, a polyline was used to connect the inboard and outboard fastener center points, with the resulting axis forming the basis for building a model fastener. Using the pipe command, a 10 mm diameter digital solid pipe was created for each clench nail hole. This process was repeated for all of the structural fasteners, from nails to treenails. The digital fastener solids were then automatically subtracted, using Boolean difference equations, from the solid model of the plank. The end result was a digital solid model of a plank with correctly sized and placed fastener holes. The process was employed on other structural elements, including frames and stringers, with only slight

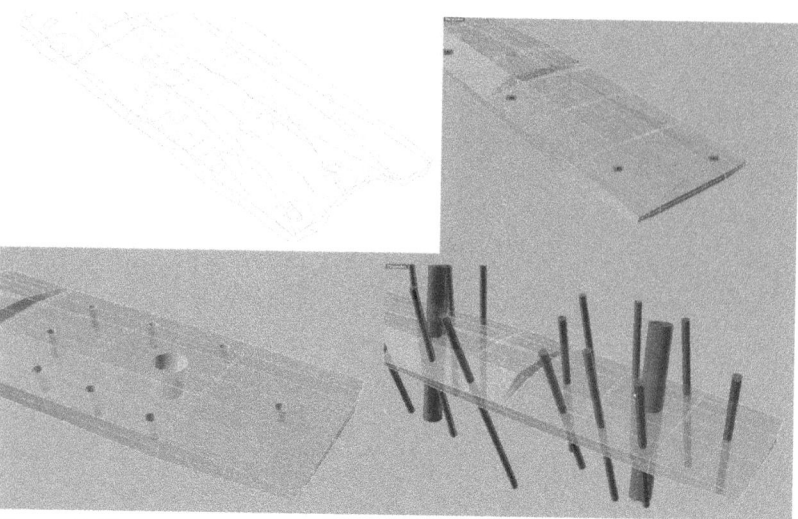

FIGURE 3. THE DIGITAL MODELING PROCESS. STARTING CLOCKWISE FROM TOP LEFT: THE VECTOR GRAPHICS OR WIRE FRAME DRAWING OF A TYPICAL HULL PLANK, CREATED WITH THE CONTACT DIGITIZER, A DIGITAL SOLID MODEL OF THE PLANK (WITHOUT FASTENERS, THE MODELED FASTENERS PRIOR TO THE BOOLEAN SUBTRACTION MODELING TECHNIQUE, AND THE COMPLETED DIGITAL SOLID MODEL (IMAGE BY THE AUTHORS).

modifications (Figure 3).

Each completed digital model was compared against the original wire frame drawing, and analyzed for accuracy. Programs like Rhinoceros and MiniMagics were used to check the integrity of the mesh and assess the models suitability for 3D manufacture. The digital model was then scaled to the desired level and saved as a 3D .pdf file and as an .stl file. The 3D .pdf version was suitable for archiving and was easy to share via email with colleagues, who could examine the 3D model using free viewing software (Abobe Acrobat Reader). The .stl (stereo-lithography) file is commonly used by rapid prototyping machines, and was the preferred format for the physical solid modeling procedure detailed below. In terms of time, an archaeologist, (once proficient in the technique developed) could model most structural timbers from start to finish in 1 to 3 hours using a standard laptop or desktop computer and Rhinoceros 4 software. At this stage, each .stl file could be imported into a master file and then oriented and aligned in order to create a 3D digital reassembly and an opportunity to create a digital reconstruction model of the ship.

Scaled physical modeling

The digital modeling phase of the ShipShape project created over 800 digital solid models of Newport Ship hull timbers. The next phase of the project called for the conversion of the digital solid models into scaled physical solids, from which a physical research model could

be constructed and analyzed in an effort to determine original hull form.

The locally based Manufacturing and Engineering Centre (MEC) at Cardiff University has a rapid prototyping division, which investigated and tested various innovative manufacturing technologies. Several parameters had to be considered when selecting an appropriate rapid prototyping technology. The various commercially available prototyping technologies have specific advantages and limitations. Some relate to properties of the model part material, such as flexibility or durability, whereas others relate to the maximum size of part that can be manufactured or the resolution with which fine features, like small holes, can be consistently created.

Investigations into rapid prototyping technology showed that the additive manufacturing process called selective laser sintering (SLS) was the most cost effective and accurate way of creating physical solids (model ship timbers) from the digital models. Unlike more familiar laser cutting or multi-axis milling machines, where material is removed from a solid block until the desired geometry is achieved, selective laser sintering is an additive manufacturing process whereby material is added or built up, until the desired geometry is achieved. The laser sintering process utilized lasers to melt successively deposited layers of finely ground plastic dust, a type of nylon called Polyamide-12, into complex shapes. Polyamide-12 was chosen because the end product was strong and flexible, and being a thermoplastic, capable of being reshaped when gently heated.

The nature of the SLS manufacturing process allowed for several important options, including the ability to shell the part, which meant fusing the plastic dust only near the edges of the part and around fastener holes. The thickness of the shelling could be adjusted, allowing for the desired degree of flexibility to be obtained through trial and error experimentation. Given that as the shell thickness increased, the flexibility decreased, the Newport Ship project used 2 mm shelling on all the framing timber models. An additional benefit of shelling was the decreased production time and cost. (Soe et al., forthcoming).

After several months of tests and adjustments, a consistent and repeatable manufacturing process was

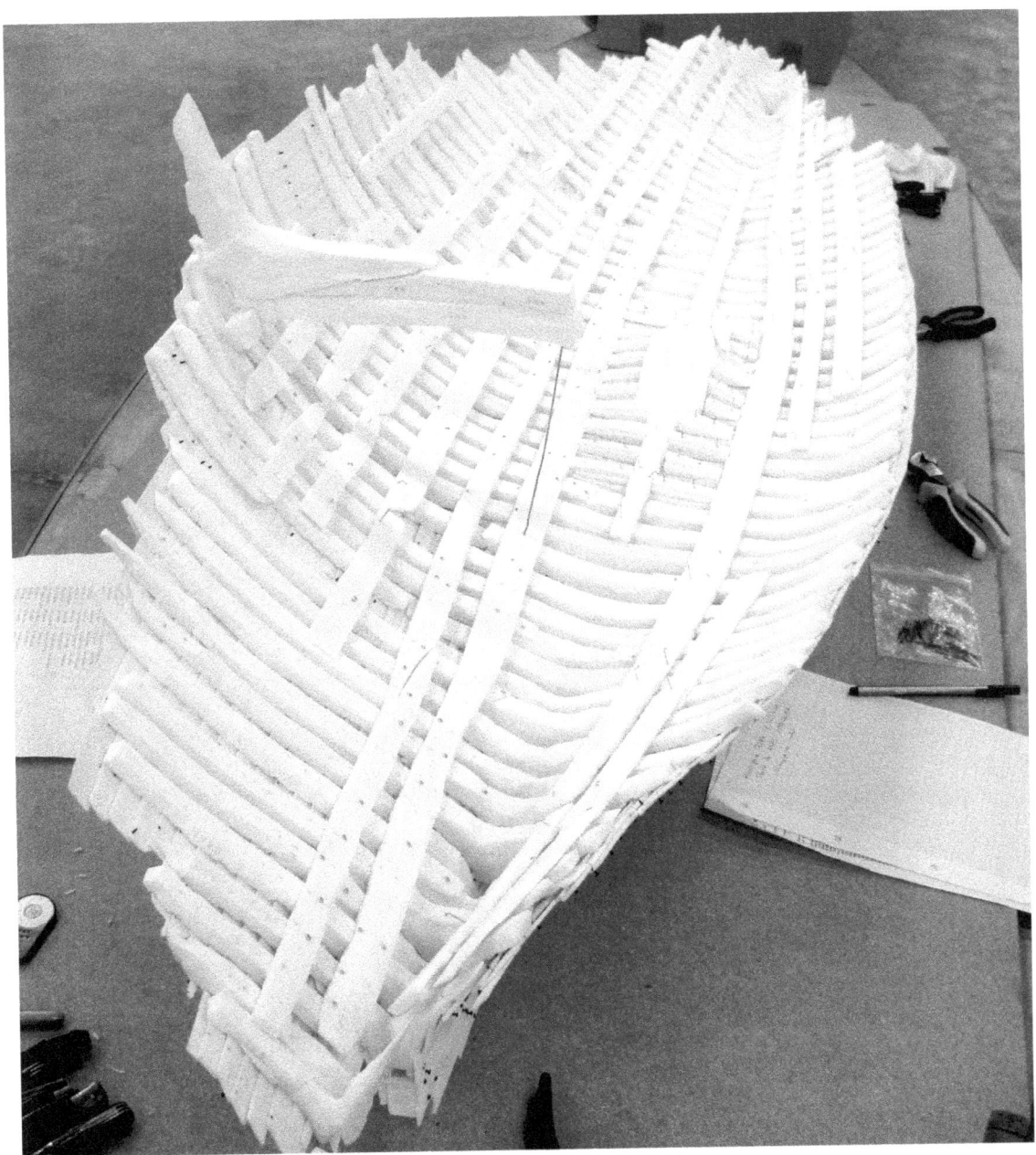

FIGURE 4. A 1:10 SCALE MODEL OF THE REMAINS OF THE NEWPORT SHIP, WITH THE INDIVIDUAL PARTS MANUFACTURED FROM POWDERED NYLON FUSED TOGETHER WITH SELECTIVE LASER SINTERING TECHNOLOGY. THE PIECES ARE HELD TOGETHER WITH METAL MICRO-FASTENERS WHICH ARE SPECIFICALLY DESIGNED TO CUT THREADS INTO THERMOPLASTICS (NEWPORT MUSEUM AND HERITAGE SERVICE).

developed and batches of digital solid models were sent electronically to the MEC, where they were then manufactured and posted back to the ship center. The individual laser sintered models of the ship timbers had the overall geometry, lands, scarfs, and major fastener holes recreated at the desired scale with exacting precision.

The model was assembled in the perceived original order of construction, starting with the keel, and then adding the garboards and lower hull planking. Floors and futtocks were added as necessary, but the focus was on letting the hull planking determine the original hull form. The model was held together using metal screws called micro fasteners, specifically designed to fasten thermoplastics. Archaeologists documented the shape state of the model through a series of time lapse photographs, laser scanning, and contact digitizing (Figure 4).

The completed model contained all of the articulated structural ship timbers found during the excavation. No attempt was made to create models for missing timbers. However, several hundred disarticulated timbers were found during the excavation, many of which resembled ship timbers. These were modeled and some, like a large crossbeam with an attached knee, were successfully attached to the model. The model helped both visitors and archaeologists to understand the size and complex construction sequence of the actual ship, and in the future will serve as a 3D blueprint when reassembling the original conserved hull in a museum. The public access and understanding that the model conveyed was especially important as the ship timbers have entered the conservation phase and will not be available for public viewing for some years.

During the modeling process, no attempt was made to flatten distorted timbers, although some areas of planking damaged by the concrete piles were ghosted in, with fastener locations being based on information gleaned from intact adjacent strakes. There was a conscious decision to model the timbers in their recorded 3D state, and not is any idealized way. When sections taken from the model are compared to sections taken from the excavation photogrammetry, the burial environment distortion is evident. However, this distortion has largely disappeared in the model. While the model is not a reconstruction, it does provide much insight into the probable hull form, with only minimal fairing required to create a convincing set of lines.

Conclusion

The completed 1:10 scale model of the excavated remains of the Newport Ship has proved useful in understanding and conceptualizing the construction sequence and hull form of the original vessel. The selection and utilization of selective laser sintering, coupled with polyamide-12, has created a realistic and durable research model, as well as a future museum display. The additive manufacturing technology is increasingly widely available and is becoming a cost-effective way of creating physical models of partial or complete hull forms. Further research strands include using the 3D digital solid models to create construction sequence animations and interactive 3D displays. The innovative offshoot project has been dubbed ShipShape 3D, and is also funded by the AHRC.

Acknowledgements

The authors wish to thank the UK Arts and Humanities Research Council for supplying the grant that made the ShipShape project possible. They are also grateful for support from the Newport Museum – Newport City Council, the Manufacturing Engineering Centre (MEC) at Cardiff University and the University of Wales Trinity Saint David. Additional recognition is due to Ben Jennings, Stuart Churchley and Erica McCarthy for doing much of the modeling work.

References

INSTITUTE FOR ARCHAEOLOGISTS
  2008   *Standards and Guidance for Nautical Archaeological Recording and Reconstruction.* http://www.archaeologists.net/sites/default/files/node-files/ifa_standards_nautical.pdf (accessed 04/26/2011).

JONES, T.
  2009a   "The Three-Dimensional Recording and Digital Modeling of the Newport Medieval Ship." In *ACUA Underwater Archaeology Proceedings 2009*, Laanela, Erika and Moore, Jonathan (eds.). Columbus, Ohio: PAST Foundation. pp. 111-116.
  2009b   'The Newport Medieval Ship: Her Three-Dimensional Digital Recording and Analysis.' *SKYLLIS Journal: Zeitschrift für Unterwasserarchäologie.* 9. Jahrgang 2009, Heft 1.
  2011   "The Newport Medieval Ship: Timber Recording Manual." Unpublished technical manual. Newport Medieval Ship Project. Newport, Wales, United Kingdom.

NAYLING, N., AND T. JONES
  (Forthcoming) "Three-dimensional Recording and Hull Form Modelling of the Newport Medieval Ship (Wales, UK)," In Nergis Günsenin (ed.), *Between Continents: Proceedings of the 12th international symposium on boat and ship archaeology, Istanbul 2009 (ISBSA 12).*

SOE, S., D. EYERS, T. JONES, AND N. NAYLING
  (Forthcoming) "Additive Manufacturing for archaeological reconstruction of a medieval ship," *Rapid Prototyping Journal.*

Toby N. Jones
Newport Medieval Ship Project
Newport Museum and Heritage Service
Unit 22, Maesglas Industrial Estate
Newport, Wales
NP20 2NN

Nigel Nayling
School of Archaeology, History and Anthropology
University of Wales: Trinity Saint David
Lampeter, Ceredigion, Wales
United Kingdom
SA48 7ED

2011. Maritime Experimental Archaeology: Trying the Impossible. In *ACUA Underwater Archaeology Proceedings 2011*, Filipe Castro and Lindsey Thomas, editors, pp. 49–53.

Maritime Experimental Archaeology: Trying the Impossible

Albrecht Sauer

In the scientific reconstruction of the seakeeping ability, the sailing performance, and the navigation of historical ships, model tests play an important role. Two categories of models can be differentiated: physical ones and numerical ones, both of them usually applied to specific, narrowly focused questions and based on thoroughly discussed conditions and validations. Considering replicas with reference to their application as physical models, there sometimes seems to exist a gap between the standards of examination of the specific test conditions and their concurrent constraints on the one side, and the standards of the reconstruction of the model itself and the rapid and broad acceptance of the test results as authentic knowledge in the scientific community on the other side. This paper demonstrates the cardinal constraints on the possibilities of valid results of tests in experimental archaeology with regard to the factors: "ship", "human", and "environment" – by category and by means of examples.

Introduction

Maritime experimental archaeology has been practiced for over a century. The first replicas of medieval or early modern ships – which are the main focus of this paper - sailed the seas at the end of the nineteenth century when Spain attempted to give the fleet of Christopher Columbus some kind of a tangible shape (Pastor 1992). From today's point of view these replicas represented mere crude and arbitrary pictures of the original ships – whose real designs even today are only vaguely known.

Evolving Principles in Maritime Experimental Archaeology

Since then a lot has changed. The last four decades especially have not only seen a lot of experimentation with physical small-scale and - more recently - virtual models, but also many full scale reconstructions and replicas, sailing the seas. At the same time there has been intensive discussion about the principles and methods of maritime experimental archaeology and about terminological conventions which should be agreed upon (McGrail 1977, Crumlin-Pedersen and Vinner 1986, Springmann and Wernicke 2008, Bennett 2009). Since it has been a multidisciplinary endeavor from the very first, the discussion reflects the differing methods of natural sciences, technology and the humanities. To give some few examples of the topics: there were – and still are – demands for projects to strictly follow the scientifically proven sequence of observation and enquiry – interpretation/hypothesis, tests, evaluation of the results, presentation, re-assessments and further research - set out by John Coates (1995:294), known from the Trireme-project OLYMPIAS (Shaw and Coates 1993). On the other hand, it was stressed that "the outcome of the experimental process is very much wider than the recorded quantified figures of speed potential, tacking ability and so on. It encompasses the whole range of problems related to such vessels in materials and techniques and the implication of these factors for our understanding of past societies." – quoting Ole Crumlin-Pedersen (1995:304), who – over almost half a century now – has significantly contributed to the establishment of a complex architecture of competence in medieval north European maritime history.

All in all, the theoretical positions differ as much as the projects do. However, what is common is the repeatedly postulated importance of having clearly defined aims from the beginning of the project, having clear questions, and working with scientific rigor and accuracy. Especially projects which plan to involve the use of replicas – with their immense costs – must be clear regarding their aims and should circulate their ideas at an early stage for criticisms from the multidisciplinary scene – as, amongst others, Sean McGrail has demanded (2009:17). He has also stressed that a further criterion for a scientific project should be that its outcome is a discernable contribution to our knowledge of ancient technology and seafaring. That undoubtedly includes a detailed publication of the results.

Categories of Replicas

All the contributions and discussions certainly show that maritime experimental archaeology has become an important and scientifically accepted segment of archaeology and historical research. In this context suitable categories were developed for all those replica projects whose aims were not scientific or at least not mainly scientific. In the Oxford Encyclopedia of Maritime History three main types of replicas are distinguished (2007:III,431-433): So called "Simple Interpretations" are replicas which are only a partial image of a historic ship, for example those for films, as attractions in tourist destinations and so on. The second category, "Hybrid Replicas", designates all those ships where the project follows "hybrid" goals: first that the replica looks as authentic as possible, second that it sails well, maneuvers satisfactorily, and fulfills today's legal regulations and requirements. The third category is "Scientific Reconstructions", whose dominating aim is to build the replica under scientific standards concerning historical correctness, with a maximum approximation to total conformity with the original historic craft. Among others, the Viking ships of the Roskilde Museum come under this category (Johansen 2009), as does the Kiel replica of the Bremen cog from 1380 (Baykowski 1991, Sauer 2003 and 2010). This paper deals with this last category, the "Scientific Reconstruction".

These reconstructions normally follow a certain sequence: In the first stages easy-to-build small-scale models for specific questions are made. For instance, preliminary

FIGURE 1. PRELIMINARY FRAME MODEL OF THE BREMEN COG (PHOTO DEUTSCHES SCHIFFAHRTSMUSEUM).

frame and working models as aids for the reconstruction process (Figure 1), as well as models for wind tunnel (Figure 2) or towing tank tests (Figure 3).

Highly visible, all of these models are built for a special purpose and their limitations are mostly, but not always obvious: as examples, models for wind tunnel tests lack the submerged underbody, models for towing tank tests lack the superstructure and rigging etc. According to good scientific practice these and other specific limitations are argued and discussed and are clearly indicated within the publication (Clausen 1988; Postel 1992). For instance, the results of the wind tunnel tests of this cog model were skeptically viewed, because the effects of the underwater hull were calculated with the help of a naval architectural software for modern hull designs, so its applicability was uncertain. Likewise, the towing tank test model with its numerous protruding nail heads presented uncertainties regarding a realistic appraisal of their effects. It goes without saying that the same is true for virtual models: here, too, a critical examination of all the parameters set, and of the general conditions, is indispensable.

If important questions regarding ship building details, stability, and performance cannot be answered by small-scale or virtual models – and the evidence is comprehensive enough – each maritime experimental archaeology team would be happy if a full size reconstruction or replica can be produced (Figure 4).

Its sea-trials should give all the answers that the previous experiments could not or only with uncertainties clarify. Compared with small-scale or virtual models the work that has to be done is much bigger, because building a replica involves much more research – fund raising, pictorial and literary sources, finds of similar tradition, and building methods, all have to be investigated. In short, every available source of information has to be consulted. Since a ship is a complex system

FIGURE 2. COG MODEL FOR WIND TUNNEL TESTS (PHOTO INGO CLAUSEN, KAPPELN, GERMANY).

FIGURE 3. COG MODEL FOR TOWING TANK TESTS (PHOTO HARRO POSTEL, KIEL, GERMANY)

of numerous parts and elements, which interact or are complementary, every single part has to be thoroughly and repeatedly checked and discussed. Any mistake can impact the whole system. Usually the evidence plus all other sources available do not provide the research team with all the information needed. Interpretations, most plausible solutions, "best guesses", simplifications, and additions have to be accepted. Probably, there is no scientific replica at sea without some "best guess", assumptions, and additions – even if scientifically corroborated.

Considering this, it is amazing how broad – and sometimes uncritical – the acceptance of the results of many sea-trials is. Whereas the results of small-scale or virtual model tests are usually judged with the necessary criticism, results of full-scale, "real" replicas seem to be mostly instantaneously accepted in the scientific community. Obviously the striking resemblance to the original, combined with exact and scientifically accurate measurements and equipment are the convincing elements.

Limitations

Limitations in the value of replica tests do not arise from lack of evidence or lack of knowledge in building

the replica alone. Determining factors come also from the test operators and the environment, so that we have three factors of influence: the "ship" (the replica itself), the "human factor" (the experimenters), and thirdly the "environment (sea and climate).

To give some examples for the first factor, the ship itself: as we all know, ship's underbodies are prone to fouling caused by fast growing animals and plants which severely reduce speed and maneuverability. Presumably no replica sails without a modern-antifouling. Historically tar and some resins were used, also sheathings with lead and later copper. Apart from the latter, none are very effective methods. So using modern antifouling instead of the authentic method represents a decision for protection of the investment but against authenticity. Clearly this decision is of relevance for all speed and maneuverability tests. The underwater part of the hull of any medieval ship – and of sixteenth- and early seventeenth-century ships as well – was typically not clean and smooth but fouled and rough, far from the hydrodynamic optimum.

A second point is the rigging. Des Pawson has recently thrown some light on the amazingly small amount of research conducted on medieval and early modern sails and ropes (2008:73). Tremendous uncertainties still exist about how they were woven, what profiles of the canvas surface we can assume, and how each rope was made for each purpose. Only a few replicas use natural materials instead of modern ones – but even these might be very different from the historical materials. For example, historical ropes prior to the invention of register plates in the early nineteenth century had to be much thicker than the cordage we know today. Of course this fact is not only important for the weight aloft, but also for the wind resistance of the entire rigging. Problematic and offering a wide field for assumptions is also the practical use of the running gear and other equipment used, since few of these things have come down to us. The same is valid for rudder or steering arrangements.

FIGURE 4. COG REPLICA HANSEKOGGE SAILING IN THE BALTIC (PHOTO DEUTSCHES SCHIFFAHRTSMUSEUM).

The human factor: most of the older traditions and knowledge of artisan ship building, rope and sail making, and seamanship were lost during industrialization and were replaced by modern learning and working methods. We all – craftsmen, sailors, academics - are theoretically and scientifically trained by school. We have a different way of thinking. We analyze and think about reality in abstract terms while our predecessors in the practical world did not. They were professionals, who learned their arts from childhood from experience. Compared to their profoundly practical education, we will always be amateurs – regardless of our own modern professionalism and skills in shipbuilding, sailmaking, and seamanship. There were no comprehensive reports about seamanship and life on board in those days, thus all of the important details are unknown to us. For example, was a cog sailed with a slight aft-or foretrim or level? And every seaman knows, how big a difference in the behavior of a ship can be with even slight modifications of trim – or rigging.

Human influence can also have another impact: successful fundraising for replicas very often generates certain constraints for the evaluation of a replica. Sometimes there is even an unexpressed political or commercial interest to produce the replica as a powerful and efficient craft. Then the experimenters are tempted – explicitly or unknowingly – to brighten the sea properties of their arduously financed replica. And sometimes historians are likewise tempted to gladly accept these bright results - instead of giving a sober scientific view of perhaps even poor sailing abilities. How often do we read "She sailed much better than expected".

The third source of value limitation comes from the maritime environment: firstly, numerous legal considerations have to be taken into account, vessels have to comply with conventions and rules for collision avoidance, and traffic regulations have to be observed. No less important are the SOLAS-rules for the safety of the crew and the passengers, as well as the MARPOL-regulations for the prevention of marine pollution from ships.

And it's not only the legal considerations that affect the outcome of tests, the biological state of the sea has probably changed, too – and therefore, for example, the propensity for fouling. Is the present bio-scene comparable to that of some 500 years ago? Climate, and therefore the physical conditions at sea, have similarly changed. The time of the cogs, for instance, coincided with the so-called "medieval warm period", with prevailingly modest winds. It is striking that the following period, "the little ice age" (Lamb 1995) in the fifteenth century, saw fewer

and fewer cogs at sea but rather new ship types such as the hulk and afterwards carvels. The comparatively calm seas may have been one important reason for the success of the cog type considering the poor craftsmanship of the joints between its floor timbers and frames. Today conditions at sea are different, and what has not yet been determined is the life of this replica if it were in continuous use for the whole shipping season from February to November.

In brief: building a replica involves lots of multidisciplinary efforts and expertise, and the result produced, the replica, may be beautiful, a "noble creation", and fascinating in its uniqueness. But we must not mistake it for the original. At the end of the day, the building process, the product, and its use at sea are just a special case of a model experiment – undoubtedly an experiment with great potential for the increasing our knowledge about our maritime past. But, since neither the replica, its operators, nor its environment are in any way "identical" to their historic prototypes or their "copies", the value of all conclusions derived from those experiments has narrow - and sometimes treacherous - limitations which have to be kept in mind.

References

BAYKOWSKI, UWE
1991   *Die Kieler Hansekogge. Der Nachbau eines historischen Segelschiffes von 1380*. RKE-Verlag, Kiel, Germany.

BENNETT, JENNY
2009   *Sailing into the Past. Learning from Replica Ships*. Seaforth Publishing, Barnsley, Great Britain.

COATES, JOHN, SEÁN MCGRAIL, DAVID BROWN, EDWIN GIFFORD, GERALD GRAINGE, BASIL GREENHILL, PETER MARSDEN, BORIS RANKOV, COLIN TIPPING, EDWARD WRIGHT.
1995   Experimental Boat and Ship Archaeology: Principles and Methods. *International Journal of Nautical Archaeology* 24(4):293-301.

CLAUSEN, INGO
1988   Die Segeleigenschaften der Bremer Hansekogge von 1380 aus Messungen im Windkanal. Thesis of the Institute for Shipbuilding, University of Hamburg, Germany.

COLES, JOHN
1977   Experimental archaeology. Theory and principles. In *Sources and techniques in boat archaeology. Papers based on those presented to a symposium at Greenwich in September 1976*. Sean McGrail, editor, pp. 233-243. *British Archaeological Reports, Archaeological series 1, BAR Supplementary series 29*. Oxford, Great Britain.

CRUMLIN-PEDERSEN, OLE

1995   Experimental archaeology and ships – bridging the arts and the sciences. *International Journal of Nautical Archaeology* 24(4): 303-306.

2006   Some Principles for the Reconstruction of Ancient Boat Structures. *International Journal of Nautical Archaeology* 35(1): 58-71.

CRUMLIN-PEDERSEN, OLE, AND VINNER, MAX

1986   *Sailing into the past: Proceedings of the International Seminar on Replicas of Ancient and Medieval Vessels, Roskilde 1984*, Crumlin-Pedersen, Ole, and Vinner, Max, editors. Viking Ship Museum, Roskilde, Denmark.

JOHANSEN, RIKKE

2009   The Viking ships of Skuldelev. In *Sailing into the Past. Learning from Replica Ships*, Jenny Bennett, editor, pp. 52-69. Seaforth Publishing, Barnsley, Great Britain.

LAMB, HUBERT

1997   *Climate, history and the modern world*. Routledge, London.

MCGRAIL, SEAN (EDITOR)

1977   Sources and techniques in boat archaeology. Papers based on those presented to a symposium at Greenwich in September 1976. *British Archaeological Reports, Archaeological series 1, BAR Supplementary series 29*, Oxford, Great Britain.

2009   Experimental Archaeology: Replicas and Reconstructions. In *Sailing into the Past. Learning from Replica Ships*, Jenny Bennett, editor, pp. 16-23. Seaforth Publishing, Barnsley, Great Britain.

OXFORD ENCYCLOPEDIA OF MARITIME HISTORY

2007   John Hattendorf et al., editors. Oxford University Press, New York.

PASTOR, XAVIER

1992   *The ships of Christopher Columbus – Santa Maria, Niña, Pinta*. Conway Press Limited, London, Great Britain.

PAWSON, DES

2008   Rope & sails, replicating and preserving old methods and materials. In *Historical boat and ship replicas. Conference-proceedings on the scientific perspectives and the limits of boat and ship replicas Torgelow 2007*, Maik-Jens Springmann and Horst Wernicke, editors, pp 71-76. Steffen, Friedland/Mecklenburg, Germany.

POSTEL, HARRO

1992   *Modellversuche zur Hydrodynamik der Bremer Hansekogge von 1380 und zum Kieler Nachbau*. Institute for Shipbuilding, University of Applied Sciences Kiel, Germany.

SAUER, ALBRECHT

2003   Segeln mit einem Rahsegel. *Die Kogge. Sternstunde der deutschen Schiffsarchäologie* Gabriele Hoffmann and Uwe Schnall, editors, pp. 18-33. Schriften des Deutschen Schiffahrtsmuseums, vol. 60. Convent, Hamburg, Germany.

2010   Sailing Performance of the Medieval Bremen Cog (1380). In *ACUA Underwater Archaeology Proceedings 2010*, pp 131-137.

SHAW, TIMOTHY, AND JOHN COATES (EDITORS)

1993   *The trireme project. Operational experience 1987-90.* Oxbow Books, Oxford, Great Britain.

SPRINGMANN, MAIK, AND HORST WERNICKE (EDITORS)

2008   Historical boat and ship replicas. *Conference-proceedings on the scientific perspectives and the limits of boat and ship replicas, Torgelow 2007*, Steffen Verlag, Friedland/Mecklenburg, Germany.

Albrecht Sauer
Deutsches Schiffahrtsmuseum (German Maritime Museum)
Hans-Scharoun-Platz 1
D-27568 Bremerhaven

1992. The Second Destruction of the *Geldermalsen*. *Historical Archaeology* 26(4):124–131.

GEORGE L. MILLER

The Second Destruction of the *Geldermalsen*

ABSTRACT

This review of C. J. A. Jörg's book on the Chinese porcelain from the Dutch East India Company ship *Geldermalsen*, which sank in 1752, addresses some broader questions involved in the destruction of shipwreck sites for commercial profit. These questions grew out of the issue of what relationship scholars should have with those who destroy sites and acquire objects from them. The first part of the article is a review of Jörg's book, followed by a commentary on the problems that collecting from looted sites raise.

Review

Christiaan J. A. Jörg. *The* Geldermalsen *History and Porcelain* (Groningen, Netherlands: Kemper Publisher, 1986). Cloth, 124 pages, 106 illustrations (86 in full color), bibliography, notes, 5 appendices, £25.00.

Christiaan Jörg's book on the history of and porcelain from the 1752 Dutch East India wreck *Geldermalsen* is amazing because it was put together in less than three months. Despite the limited amount of time, Jörg produced a credible study of this collection with excellent documentation of the wreck. In the spring of 1985, this wreck was mined for its valuables by English salvager, Capt. Michael Hatcher, who then shipped them to Christie's Amsterdam (Dyson 1986). Christie's cleaned and catalogued the collection for their auction in April 1986, just over one year after it was plucked from the wreck. Their catalogue for the sale was published in December 1985 (Christie's 1985).

In his Introduction, Jörg states that he was brought in to examine the porcelain by Christie's

This article first appeared in *The American Neptune*, 1987, 47(4):275–281. Reprinted by permission.

in December 1985 indicating that his research was an afterthought. Indeed, Christie's auction catalogue had no information on the identity of the wreck. In other words, Jörg had from December until the auction in April to study the collection. His Introduction is dated February 1986, suggesting that he wanted to have it published in time for the auction.

Despite the short time that he had to work with this collection of over 150,000 Chinese porcelain vessels, Jörg accomplished two important objectives. One, he clearly documented the wreck as being the *Geldermalsen*. Two, he produced a minimal record of the porcelain assemblage before it was dispersed around the world by Christie's and thus lost to future scholars as a collection.

Christiaan Jörg's accomplishment of the seemingly impossible was aided by his expertise in the Dutch trade with China, and the fortuitous existence and previously organized relevant documents. He is a recognized authority on the Dutch East India Company porcelain trade and is the author of a thesis titled *Porcelain and the Dutch China Trade*. In addition to his knowledge of the subject, he was given access to historian Peter Diebels' research notes on the Geldermalsen (Jörg 1986:6–7). Jörg uses this information to provide a lucid overview of the mechanics of the Dutch East India Company's involvement in the China trade.

From this background, Jörg focuses on the history of the *Geldermalsen* including purchase orders for 1751, and its wreck caused by navigational error. The ship's paper, including purchase orders, and 32 crew members survived the sinking. When those survivors reached Batavia, the company held an extensive inquiry to determine why the gold had not been saved. There was strong suspicion that the survivors had hidden the gold after the wreck. Jörg used these records very effectively to describe the wreck and explain the workings of the Dutch East India Company.

The rest of the book concentrates on those artifacts that Hatcher chose to pull from the wreck. In Jörg's words, "We can distinguish three categories—objects belonging to the ship's inventory, gold, and the collection of porcelain" (Jörg 1986:

51). Jörg makes comments throughout the book that mildly rebuke Hatcher for the destruction and skewing of information. Consider, for example, this passage from page 7:

> Besides, the underwater archives which are only just beginning to be discovered by man [sic], are very fragile and unique, and should be handled with utmost care. Future generations should also be able to profit from the information which is becoming available at present, and which can never be replaced.
>
> In this case most of the shards have remained at the bottom of the sea, while they might have told us even more about the variety of the assortment. The finds have not been registered systematically either, so that we cannot be sure whether, for instance, such a copper candlestick was part of the inventory of the cabin. Even the smallest detail can be of great value in a historical study (Jörg 1986:7).

Jörg's absence of anger does not make his criticism any less damning. Open criticism of Hatcher may not have been possible under the condition of his access to the ceramics. However, he left enough of a trail to show that he deplores the destruction that Hatcher wrought and that his first concern was to record the collection before the diaspora.

Using the original packing lists and purchase orders for 1750 and 1751, Jörg reconstructed the selection process for what became the *Geldermalsen's* cargo. By comparing the cargo list with the numbers of vessels Hatcher recovered, he is able to show the proportion recovered of the different types of vessels. In some cases a very high percentage was recovered. In others, a lower percentage was retrieved, such as cups and saucers— 32,500 were not recovered, which was about half of what was listed in the inventory. Along with information from the ship's inventory, there are excellent photographs, most in color, of the porcelain.

In summation, Jörg has provided a good documentation of the wreck of the *Geldermalsen* under conditions of extreme time constraints. Without his efforts, an extremely important wreck would have gone undocumented and the information completely lost to future scholars. This book will be an important one for anyone dealing with 18th-century Chinese export porcelain.

Commentary

Some archaeologists and nautical scholars will not have anything to do with looted materials and with those who destroy archaeological resources. An argument in favor of that position is that documentation and identification adds to the monetary value of the objects and thus encourages further looting. In this instance, however, the information on the *Geldermalsen* cargo would have been irretrievably lost had Jörg not recorded what he did in the short time available to him. Fortunately Jörg's research did not become part of the Christie's auction catalogue, and it is difficult to assess to what extent his book may have contributed to the extremely high prices the porcelain brought.

Given the quality of documentation related to the wreck and the excellent photographs in the book, Jörg has done a service in preserving some information from the *Geldermalsen* before its cargo was scattered to the winds. While the author disapproves of working with those who destroy sites and providing documentation for their artifacts which will increase their monetary value, one can appreciate Jörg's implicit position in rescuing the information. This issue leads to broader questions about wrecks and those who destroy such resources either by stripping the artifacts from them or making it profitable by marketing or purchasing objects from such operations.

First, look at Capt. Michael Hatcher and his history of destruction of underwater sites. Hatcher makes no claims to being an archaeologist. He is an English sea captain living in Singapore, who has salvaged cargos, such as tin and scrap metal, from World War II wrecks (Dyson 1986:111). *Geldermalsen* is the second historical wreck that he has scavenged. The first was a Chinese junk, which sank around 1640, from which he extracted 23,000 pieces of Chinese porcelain. According to Jörg, he donated over 50 vessels from that wreck to the Groningen Museum in the Netherlands and the rest was sole by Christie's of Amsterdam where the prices exceeded everyone's expectations and brought in over $2 million.

Clearly, Captain Hatcher had stumbled onto a good thing. He is like one of the bears of Yellowstone National Park. Once they find the easy living that the dumpsters can provide, they give up scavenging or in this case salvage work. *Geldermalsen* is the bear's second wreck. In a *Reader's Digest* article, John Dyson states that after sale of the porcelain from the 1640 wreck:

> Hatcher now decided that he would search only for historic shipwrecks. He invested his riches in a long-range working yacht, the *Restless M*, in which he could live on the job. He collected old maps and sent students hunting for details on wrecks through the archives of the Dutch East India Company (Dyson 1986:113).

Hatcher claims to have been looking for the *Geldermalsen* and that he resailed its last voyage before returning to the reef where the Chinese junk had been found, to look for other wrecks (Dyson 1986:113). It is not clear, however, whether or not Hatcher knew the wreck he found was the *Geldermalsen*. There would be good reasons not to know the name of the wreck, which will be discussed later.

Preservation on the wreck was excellent. A video film distributed by Christie's clearly shows divers reaching into crates of porcelain and removing the vessels. Some crates are also visible in some of the illustrations in Jörg's book. Some of the most damning comments on Hatcher's "excavation" techniques, or lack of them, comes from his own descriptions. When speaking of the speed of his retrieval operations, he indicated that "it was a race to get what they could before being interrupted by weather, rivals, pirates, or some government" (Dyson 1986:114). In Dyson's *Reader's Digest* article the scene is described:

> Using a big nozzle, chief diver Mohammed "Hash" Hashim sucked away thick debris and opened the lid of a crumbled crate. There sat row upon row of tiny blue-on-white teacups, shiny-bright (Dyson 1986:114).

As Jörg pointed out, "It is a pity that Hatcher has paid little attention to a detailed registration of his finds." The least competent of archaeologists would have recorded which porcelain vessels came from which crates. No attempt was made to save the crates let alone keep track of their contents. This is in sharp contrast to excavation of a 14th-century Chinese junk by the South Korean govern-

ment in 1976 which also contained an intact cargo of Chinese porcelain. Crates from that site had been stabilized and preserved. They are illustrated in an article in *National Geographic* (Kim and Keith 1979:236–237).

Some archaeologists might argue that *Geldermalsen* would never have been excavated by professional archaeologists because of the logistics involved. However, any wreck that produced $16 million at an auction could have been funded for legitimate excavation. The Korean government excavations clearly show that underwater archaeology can be done in that part of the world.

The last comment on Hatcher is that he recorded almost nothing about the ship and provided almost no conservation for the artifacts. After removal from the wreck, the "goodies" were packed into 1,400 large cartons and carried by a container ship to Amsterdam where it took six people a month to unpack and "clean" the 150,000 Chinese porcelain vessels (Dyson 1986:115).

Hatcher's strip-mining operation had nothing to do with archaeology other than it destroyed a significant site. He clearly understood the importance of this wreck. David S. Howard, an English expert on Chinese porcelain, gave a lecture on the *Geldermalsen* porcelain at the Colonial Williamsburg Antiques Forum in February 1987. There he explained Captain Hatcher's reasons why this wreck was so important and so well preserved. They were: (1) the wreck resulted from striking a reef, after which the ship drifted about 5 mi. and sank; thus, it was not broken up on the reef; (2) this occurred in calm weather, thus the ship remained intact; (3) there was a soft bottom into which the wreck settled; (4) the tons of tea above the ceramics settled in around them and provided a protective cocoon for the porcelain thus keeping them in superb condition; and (5) this remarkably well preserved wreck is accompanied by excellent records from the 32 survivors as well as the ship's paper which have survived in Dutch Archives. According to Howard, Hatcher doubts that he would ever in a thousand years of searching be able to find a wreck meeting all these conditions.

Hatcher's exploitation of shipwrecks for personal gain could not have been done without assistance. The second player, and perhaps the major force in the destruction of the *Geldermalsen* was Christie's of Amsterdam. Hatcher is only responding to opportunities that Christie's and other auction houses provide. The third player is those who purchase objects ripped from archaeological contexts. Without accomplices, he could not exist. *Auction News from Christie's* for April 1987 had an article titled "Shipwreck Sales at Christie's Amsterdam" which opens with the following sentence: "Over the years, Christie's Amsterdam has established itself as the most significant venue in the world for disposal at public auction of artifacts and cargos recovered from sunken vessels." Then the article goes on to describe the sale of objects from four different 17th- and 18th-century wrecks auctioned by Christie's Amsterdam (Christie's 1986). Such auction houses are the link between scavengers and the market. Attention needs to be focused on their role in the destruction of the world's archaeological resources.

Prior to the auctioning of the *Geldermalsen* porcelains, there was speculation about the impact that 150,000 pieces of mid-18th-century porcelain would have on the market. Some felt that the very quantity of the vessels would depress prices. The following comments from the antique dealers Ralph M. Chait and David S. Howard appeared in the *New York Times* in March 1986:

"The real charm of these objects lies in their provenance," Mr. Howard said. "Porcelain is not at all rare, rather it was standard everyday dinnerware made for the comfortable middle-class families of Europe." Mr. Chait calls the porcelain 'hotel crockery.' "Once you separate the wonderful romance of the discovery from the actual objects," he said, "you'll see that the pieces are nothing but a decorator's delight. It is the sheer volume that is overwhelming" (Vogel 1986).

Christie's promoted their auction under the name "The Nanking Cargo" and actively sought out an expanded elite clientele including embassies, department stores, restaurants, and interior decorators. Truly they had found the consumable past. A great archaeological assemblage was broken up before a detailed study could be made of it, to supply interior decorators with objects for yuppies' condos. Bloomingdale's, recognized as the arbiter of trendiness, purchased over 3,000 pieces of "The Nanking Cargo" and advertised that "it's a rare opportunity to bring museum quality artifacts into your home. Look for the Nanking Cargo Shop, starting today on the second floor" (Bloomingdale's 1986).

Christie's succeeded in enlarging the market beyond traditional collectors and museums. "The Nanking Cargo" had been expected to bring in $4.5 million (Vogel 1986). By dint of promotion alone they unloaded the largest assemblage to become available since the days of the Dutch East India Company for a cool $16 million. Many pieces brought from 10 to 15 times the estimated value in the Christie's catalogue (Austin 1986).

The high auction prices are perhaps the worst news that has come out of this whole sad affair. These inflated prices amount to a large bounty on any shipwrecks containing Chinese porcelain which will lead to a wholesale destruction of such wrecks. While Hatcher was the scavenger of the *Geldermalsen*, Christie's was the *agent provocateur* that made the salvaging possible and profitable. Their sale of the 23,000 vessels from the 1640s Chinese junk helped Hatcher decide "that he would only search for historic wrecks." With his cut from that sale, Hatcher was able to purchase a long-range working yacht and equip it with a $250,000 proton magnetometer for finding wrecks of which *Geldermalsen* was the first (Dyson 1986:113). Those who are concerned about the protection of shipwrecks would do well to direct attention, blame, and the harsh glare of publicity on auction houses such as Christie's of Amsterdam whose aggressive search for new sources of salable antiquities results in the destruction of archaeological sites.

Christie's and Hatcher's interest in the *Geldermalsen* was limited to what could be sold for a profit. Their auction catalogue is filled with color plates of the gold, porcelain, and those few other artifacts that Hatcher bothered to bring up. One of the most ironic lines in their catalogue is about Captain Hatcher which reads, "The Nanking Cargo is the result of exhaustive professionalism, which is the hallmark of Captain Hatcher and his team" (Christie's 1986). As they did not name the profession involved, perhaps they are right; however, they certainly were not talking about archaeology.

There are some aspects of Christie's involvement in this sale that raise interesting questions. Nowhere in their discussion of the wreck do they let on that they know its name or that it was a Dutch East India Company wreck. Given Hatcher's account in the *Reader's Digest*, it is difficult to believe that Christie's would not at least have considered the *Geldermalsen* as a probable candidate. None of the artifacts listed in the auction catalogue provides direct evidence that the ship belonged to the Dutch East India Company. However, a supplement to the catalogue adds two bronze cannons with Dutch East India markings to the auction. This supplement also has an illustration of the ship's bell which is dated 1747. Given this evidence, it would be reasonable to surmise that Christie's at least knew that the ship was a Dutch East India Company wreck.

Considering Christie's self-touted expertise in wrecks, it would not be unreasonable to surmise that they knew more but chose not to reveal their knowledge out of legal concerns. There may have been good reasons to be ignorant of the ship's identity. In 1798 the Dutch East India Company went bankrupt and all of its assets and liabilities were assumed by the Batavian Republic which became the Kingdom of the Netherlands in 1813. This government maintains a claim on all Dutch East India wrecks. For example, Dutch government claims to the *Amsterdam*, a Dutch East India wreck from 1748 on the coast of England, were recognized when that wreck was excavated in 1969 by Peter Marsden (1975:233–234).

Nowhere in the Christie's catalogue is there a mention of the name of the wreck or any claims that others may have to it. It is difficult to believe that Christiaan Jörg's research into the identification of the wreck was not known by Christie's by the time of the auction. Even their publication *Auction News from Christie's* for April of 1986 does not identify the wreck by name or mention its relationship with the Dutch East India Company. Given that Jörg's research was completed in February, it is inconceivable that they did not know that the cargo was from the *Geldermalsen*.

Beyond the claims of the Dutch government to the wreck is the issue of the wreck's location. Again there is no information in Christie's catalogue as to where the *Geldermalsen* was found. Was it in international waters or not? If it was not, who else may have a claim on the wreck? Hatcher apparently was aware of this possibility. His comment in *Reader's Digest* that "it was a race to get what they could before being interrupted by weather, rivals, pirates, or some government" clearly suggests that he was aware of probable claims from Indonesia (Dyson 1986:114).

There is currently a lawsuit by the Indonesian government concerning excavation of the *Geldermalsen*. If it turns out that the wreck was in Indonesian waters, then the wreck was illegally excavated, and the title of ownership of the artifacts will be clouded by claims of the Indonesian and Dutch governments. Customers normally expect a respected old auction house like Christie's to be very careful to make sure that they pass on a clear title to objects sold in their auction house.

In 1970 the United Nations adopted the UNESCO Convention on the means of prohibiting and preventing the illicit import, export, and transfer of ownership of cultural property. Many countries around the world have adopted this convention. Destruction of the *Geldermalsen* site and the complete disregard of archaeological and preservation principles are to be deplored on ethical and moral grounds. Besides, it may have been illegal by the terms of the UNESCO Convention of Cultural Property. If it turns out that laws were broken, then the artifacts could be subject to recovery and repatriation to Indonesia.

The third party to this destruction of the *Geldermalsen* is of course those museums, collectors, and others who purchased the artifacts. As was pointed out above, the size of this collection could have depressed the market for Chinese porcelain. Christie's knew this, so they hyped the sale to a wider universe of purchasers far beyond the circle of traditional porcelain collectors. Yuppies, interior decorators, and, indeed, most collectors do not have a great deal of consciousness concerning preservation principles. When they see an old, well-regarded firm like Christie's selling Chinese porcelain from a 230-year-old wreck and are presented the story of Captain Hatcher's finds, they do not think twice about possible ethical or legal problems.

Almost nothing has been done to educate the public to the fact that the sale of archaeological artifacts contributes directly to the destruction of sites. Laws and regulations related to the excavation of sites, particularly of shipwrecks, is presented in the news media as the government trying to come in for a free piece of the pie. Looters are pictured as David versus Goliath with the government as the bad giant. One of the problems in educating the public is that the agencies which should be preforming this task are some of the museums that most eagerly participated in the auctions and they show almost no concern for the sites being destroyed.

It is not uncommon for museum curators trained in an art history tradition to have little or no appreciation for preservation ethics. They commonly deal with intrinsic values of individual objects rather than with extrinsic relationships that can be extracted from an assemblage of artifacts. These curators need to wise up to the consequences of their purchasing artifacts from destroyed sites.

Fortunately, great strides are being made in terms of establishing codes of ethics for museum behavior in acquisition of objects, in recognition of the relationship between site destruction and the marketplace, and in recognition of the cultural property of other countries. This is directly an outgrowth of the UNESCO Convention.

In November of 1986, the International Council of Museums (ICOM) adopted its *Code of Professional Ethics*. Item 3.2 of that code, titled "Acquisition of Illicit Material," reviews the problems involved in importing objects with dubious titles. It stresses the importance of having clear title to ownership as well as avoiding objects that have been illegally imported. The discussion concludes with a paragraph related to the ethics of acquiring excavated material:

> So far as excavated material is concerned, in addition to the safeguards set out above, the museum should not acquire by purchase objects in any case where the governing body or responsible officer has reasonable cause to believe that their recovery involved the recent damage of ancient monuments or archaeological sites, or involved a failure to disclose the finds to the owner or occupier of the land, or to the proper legal or governmental authorities (ICOM 1986: article 3.2).

This statement deals with the spirit of compliance and calls unequivocally for attention to the circumstances under which the objects were recovered. If there is any doubt about the role that museums should play in this area, section 3.3 states flatly in "Field Study and Collecting" that:

> Museums should assume a position of leadership in the effort to halt the continuing degradation of the world's natural history, archaeological, ethnographic, and artistic resources. Each museum should develop policies that allow it to conduct its activities within appropriate national and international laws and treaty obligations, and with a reasonable certainty that its approach is consistent with the spirit and intent of both national and international efforts to protect and enhance the cultural heritage (ICOM 1986: article 3.3).

Archaeologists of course have been keenly aware of the problem for a long time because of the nature of their work and familiarity with the areas being plundered. Calvin Cummings (1983) presented a paper titled "A Matter of Ethics" at the Council for Underwater Archaeology meetings in 1983 which extracted positions taken by eight of the main archaeological societies in America. They all took positions against the selling of artifacts from sites for profit or to enhance personal collections. In addition to these general positions and ethical canons set out by various archaeological societies, there was a resolution relating specifically to destruction of the *Geldermalsen* that was published in the International Congress of Maritime Museums in October of 1986. It reads:

> Recently the firms of Christie's held a highly publicized auction of the cargo of the wreck of the Dutch East Indiaman *GELDERMALSEN*, whose cargo of Chinese export porcelain was the largest ever found. Since a number of museums purchased items from this collection, despite its poorly conducted excavation, it is felt worthwhile to bring to ICCM members attention the following resolution:

> "Members of the underwater archaeology group attending the PACT symposium at Louvain-la-Neuve, 17–19 April 1986, unanimously deplore the way the *GELDERMALSEN* was excavated.

> Such an archaeologically very important find as the *GELDERMALSEN* should have been excavated in a scientific way. Correlation of the rather well-documented information from the available archives and the excavation information

is of utmost importance. This means registration to find places within the wreck, details on the ship structure, environmental information, etc. Without such scientific standards, no excavation should take place in order not to lose the information which is very important for a historical point of view.

In fact, the cargo of the GELDERMALSEN has been looted without concern for context and its commercial sale will entirely destroy the wreck.

Thus, both the ship and cargo will be entirely lost to science. It is necessary to have international legislative regulations to prevent disasters like the looting to the GELDERMALSEN. Louvain-la-Neuve, 19 April 1986'' (ICMM 1986).

Considering all the support given the guidelines from the UNESCO Convention of Cultural Property, it is difficult to understand how museum curators can justify their purchase of the porcelains from the Geldermalsen. Some museums, such as the Rijks Museum of the Netherlands, boycotted the sale. Unfortunately, their ethical and moral position was ignored by other institutions.

When curators from otherwise respectable institutions purchase objects from such auctions, they help others to justify their own participation in such sales. They shirk their moral responsibility to, as ICOM states, ''assume a position of leadership in the effort to halt the continuing degradation of the world's . . . archaeological, ethnographic, and historical'' resources (ICOM 1986).

Awhile back on National Public Radio, there was a news item about some free-wheeling entrepreneurs who had purchased a number of Picasso paintings. They cut the paintings into 2-in. squares and offered them for sale. The objective they piously claimed was to enable more people to own a Picasso. Clearly they were destroying art to pander to the status-seeking ambitions of people with little understanding of the subject. People are making it profitable to destroy sites when they purchase artifacts such as the Geldermalsen porcelains. There is not much difference between the looter and his or her accomplices in auction houses, museums, and department stores.

ACKNOWLEDGMENTS

This review and commentary came about because of the purchase of some Chinese porcelain from the Geldermalsen by the Department of Collections of Colonial Williamsburg. I felt it was necessary to speak out concerning the destruction of an important archaeological site and to make an attempt at educating people concerning the ethical and legal questions related to such acquisitions.

My area of research is ceramics, and I do not have a background in maritime history or underwater archaeology. This article would have been difficult to write without the invaluable assistance and information provided by colleagues in underwater archaeology. Paul Johnston, formerly of the Peabody Museum, Salem, Massachusetts, provided assistance and pointed out several sources to me. I would also like to thank George Bass of the Institute of Nautical Archaeology and Dick Sweet of the Snow Squall project for information on and suggestions related to underwater archaeology.

James Wiseman of Boston University and Clemency Coggins of Harvard University both provided information on looting, legislation, and the ethics related to museum acquisition of archaeological artifacts. Ellen Hersher of the American Association of Museums provided information on museum standards related to the questions of collecting excavated materials.

At Colonial Williamsburg, I would like to thank Marley Brown and Cary Carson, director of research, for their support and for allowing me the time to research and write this article. Several colleagues read drafts and gave me helpful comments for which I am very grateful. They are Cary Carson, Marley Brown, Nancy Dickinson, Ann Smart Martin, Rob Hunter, and Kathleen Pepper. I would like to thank Gordon Fine and Catherine Hutchins for reading over drafts of this article and providing helpful comments. Finally, I would like to thank Julia Curtis of Williamsburg for information on Hatcher's earlier excavations.

REFERENCES

AUSTIN, JOHN
1986   Our New Dinner Service is 235 Years Old and Has Never Been Used. *Colonial Williamsburg News* 39(8):3.

BLOOMINGDALE'S
1986   Advertisement. *Boston Globe*, 21 November:11.

CHRISTIE'S
1986   Shipwreck Sales at Christie's Amsterdam. *Auction News from Christie's* 7(7):1–4. New York.

CHRISTIE'S AMSTERDAM
1985   *The Nanking Cargo: Chinese Export Porcelain and Gold, European Glass and Stoneware, Recovered by*

Captain Michael Hatcher from a European Merchant Ship Wrecked in the South China Seas. Drukkerij Onkenhout, Amsterdam.

CUMMINGS, CALVIN R.
1983 A Matter of Ethics. Paper presented at the Annual Meeting of the Council for Underwater Archaeology, Philadelphia.

DYSON, J.
1986 Captain Hatcher's Richest Find. *Reader's Digest* 129(10):111–115.

INTERNATIONAL CONGRESS OF MARITIME MUSEUMS (ICMM)
1986 *Geldermalsen* Resolution. Passed at the 19 April meeting of the International Congress of Maritime Museums, Louvain-la-Neuve, France.

INTERNATIONAL COUNCIL OF MUSEUMS (ICOM)
1986 International Council of Museums Subcommittee on Museum Ethics, in Accordance with Article 5 of the Statutes of ICOM. Revised draft, December 1985, adopted 4 November 1986.

JÖRG, CHRISTIAAN J. A.
1986 *The Geldermalsen History and Porcelain.* Kemper, Groningen, Netherlands.

KIM, E. H., AND D. H. KEITH
1979 The Yellow Sea Yields a Shipwreck Trove. *National Geographic* 156(2):230–243.

MARSDEN, PETER
1975 *The Wreck of the Amsterdam.* Stein and Day, New York.

VOGEL, C.
1986 Old Porcelain Up from Sea. *New York Times* 21 March:section F.

GEORGE L. MILLER
DEPARTMENT OF ANTHROPOLOGY
CENTER FOR ARCHAEOLOGICAL RESEARCH
UNIVERSITY OF DELAWARE
NEWARK, DELAWARE 19716

1990. After the Diving is Over. In *Underwater Archaeology Proceedings from the Society for Historical Archaeology Conference*, Toni Carrell, editor, pp. 11–13.

GEORGE F. BASS

AFTER THE DIVING IS OVER

For years we archaeologists have attacked treasure-hunters, chastised the press for glorifying and misrepresenting them, and tried to educate the public about the meaning of archaeology. Treasure-hunting is such a big, soft target it scarcely presents a challenge any longer. The greater threat today lies with those archaeologists of responsibility who lack the vision to understand the full potential of archaeology. They give meaning to the cliché: "a little learning is a dangerous thing."

I did not intend to present a paper here. I felt compelled to do so only after exchanges of disturbing correspondence with both federal and state archaeologists who rationalize their acquiescence in for-profit archaeology by asserting that it is "good archaeology." I can understand the ignorant treasure-salvor who lays a grid over his site and says on television and to the press that he is doing "good archaeology" because he "uses a grid." But for someone with an advanced degree in archaeology to equate good field techniques with good archaeology is frightening, and I have correspondence that reveals such naïveté among some who advise state governments.

Most of you remember the treasure-salvor's archaeologist who proposed, several years ago, that salvors should allow archaeologists three years to study their finds before selling any, thereby assuring "good archaeology." How ridiculous!

I've just returned from a term of research at the Institute for Advanced Studies in the Humanities at the University of Edinburgh. While in the United Kingdom I visited the impressive *Mary Rose* and *Mary Rose* Museum. The elderly guide told the children in my group that they and their children may see the *Mary Rose* completely restored, for it will be <u>decades</u> before the chemical treatment of its wood will allow the replacement of timbers even to begin!

A hull, some archaeologists might maintain, is different from small artifacts, especially duplicates, which are all right to sell, and thus the *Mary Rose* does not support my argument. But while in the U.K., I also attended an international conference on Bronze Age trade, held at Oxford University. I delivered my paper on shipwreck evidence for such trade on the second evening (Bass 1991). Yet before I spoke, a colleague pointed out to me that 80% of the speakers--Assyriologists, metallurgists, economic historians, and preclassical archaeologists--had already felt obliged to deal with my evidence, in advance, in their papers.

What evidence was so important to them? Largely the results of lead-isotope analyses of the copper ingots we excavated at Cape Gelidonya, Turkey, in 1960 (Bass 1967). Only days before, these analyses had confirmed that the ingots are of Cypriot copper (Gale 1991; Stos-Gale 1991). By comparing analyses of copper ingots we are currently excavating on another Bronze Age shipwreck in Turkey, at Ulu Burun, we have settled a long-standing academic debate that touches on the very collapse of Bronze Age civilizations in the Near East and Aegean. As lead-isotope analyses of the Cape Gelidonya bronze implements commence at Oxford, scientists at our National Bureau of Standards will analyze the wreck's lead fishing sinkers to determine if their metal came from Bronze Age lead mines that Aslihan Yener has recently discovered in southern Turkey (Yener et al. 1989). Neutron-activation studies of pottery from both Bronze Age wrecks are also being conducted, at this moment, by Manchester University, with the result that we already know that the pottery was not from mainland Greece as some archaeologists had believed. When the place of manufacture of the pottery is determined, we will know much more about the mechanics of second-millennium B.C. trade.

Why are we able to add revolutionary information to the study of ancient trade from a wreck excavated 30 years ago? Because all of the artifacts, many seemingly duplicates, have been kept together and are still being studied by archaeologists. In addition, with far better electronic detection equipment than was available 30 years ago, we return to the site at Cape Gelidonya annually, and have made major discoveries that support the date we originally proposed for the wreck--a date that is crucial to our understanding of the role of Cyprus in international affairs around 1200 B.C.

Between 1961 and 1964, Frederick van Doorninck and I excavated a seventh-century Byzantine shipwreck off Yassi Ada, Turkey (Bass and van Doorninck 1982). It carried as its cargo about 900 amphoras of two basic types. Because amphoras of each type seemed identical to one another, we were asked continually by well-meaning people what harm it would do if we sold some.

Here is the answer: After years of study, we published a "final report" on the Byzantine wreck in 1982. But a marvelous new book has just been published with a chapter by van Doorninck that offers important new insights about the amphoras (van Doorninck 1989). How? Because all of the amphoras remain together after three decades.

Twenty-nine years ago we did not have a paleobotanist sieving mud from each of the amphoras to determine what it had contained. Twenty-nine years ago we did not note the faint graffiti that appear on many of the amphoras. Twenty-nine years ago there were no neutron-activation studies of pottery to tell us if their clays came from one or more sources. One good thing we did twenty-nine years ago was to leave about 700 of the 900 amphoras on the seabed.

Professor van Doorninck has spent one semester plus a summer each year for the past several years conducting a detailed study of both the amphoras we raised twenty-nine years ago, and those we are now raising annually for him. He has identified over 40 sub-types, with different clays, among these seemingly identical globular amphoras. He has proved that the amphoras had been reused one or more times. What

was the mechanism by which they were collected from different places, including church property? Was it some kind of taxation involving the government, or was someone simply sailing around, gathering them up? Supplying food for troops on the border was important at that time. Was our ship involved? We are trying to sort all this out. With our collection of amphoras, of so many different fabrics, we have the potential, especially with neutron-activation, to determine where the centers of amphora production were, and the breadth of their geographic scope. Many scholars are working on this problem, trying to reconstruct the economic conditions of the Byzantine empire. The study of amphoras, which often tell us for the first time who was supplying whom with what, has truly revolutionized the study of Roman economics in the West. Now Byzantine amphora studies provide the only opportunity for doing the same thing in the Byzantine, or eastern Roman, empire.

Another wreck provides another example. During three brief summers, 1977 through 1979, our Institute of Nautical Archaeology excavated an eleventh-century shipwreck whose cargo included wine amphoras, three tons of glass, and thousands of other finds (Bass and van Doorninck 1978; Bass 1978). I was in Edinburgh last autumn to do library research on this site; I also visited Turkey to check details of the artifacts I was studying. Remember, this was ten years after the diving was over. During those ten years we have had a year-round staff in Turkey working on the wreck material: conservators, illustrators, a photographer, a cataloguer, and a ship reconstructor.

Each of hundreds of pieces of wood were soaked to remove marine salts, and were monitored for several years in vats of polyethylene glycol. Sheila Matthews traced every fragment at one-to-one scale, using color-coded symbols for tool marks. This allowed J. Richard Steffy, back at Texas A&M University, to build a series of research models (Steffy 1982) that in turn allowed Ms. Matthews to reassemble the actual hull. Next June, a decade after diving ended, the hull will be ready for display. Its publication will take years more.

What of its cargo? There was a ton of medieval Islamic glass--between half a million and a million bits (Bass 1984a and 1984b). We had raised this glass in plastic bags, each bag labeled with a four- or five-digit code signifying which 50-centimeter square of the wreck the glass in that bag came from.

It seemed reasonable to us to suppose that if we wanted to find joins among the shards, we would find them among pieces of glass that lay close together on the wreck. So we laid out all of the glass from one square meter and looked for joins. After weeks, we had found none. We slowly realized that we were not dealing with a cargo of glass vessels that had been broken by the impact of the ship as it was wrecked. Instead we were dealing with a cargo of scrap glass destined to be recycled, glass that had probably been shoveled into baskets and then tamped down to take up less space in the hold. So there was no order governing where associated shards might be found. Using the approach of the jig-saw puzzler who first separates pieces with green grass from those with blue sky, etc., we divided the glass into eighteen basic types of our own designation: plain glass, purple glass, green glass, green threaded rims, dimpled glass, purple dimpled glass, purple dimpled glass with green-threaded rims, and so forth.

As we would otherwise lose the provenience of any shard of glass once it left its labeled bag, we spent the winter copying onto each of the nearly million shards its four- or five-number provenience code. Then we selected one type--as an example, let us say purple. We piled the thousands of purple shards into a huge mound, which I then divided into two piles, one of darker purple and one of lighter purple. We stored away the lighter purple and divided the remaining pile into darker and lighter shades. Then we stored away the lighter pile and once more made such a division. Rather incredibly, this process eventually left on the work table the exact shards that could be joined together to form an entire vessel. The largest glass vessel surviving from antiquity is of nearly clear glass. Imagine finding its joining fragments out of a million. If you want to try your luck, smash three light bulbs on the floor, stir the pieces, and try to put them back together. We are doing just that with between 10,000 and 20,000 vessels.

We do not plan to mend all the glass vessels, but only a representative sampling of shapes. Already we have more than 200, many previously unknown. Of these 200 shapes, Joy Kitson Mim-Mack chose one, the beaker, as the subject of her M.A. thesis. During a year in the Bodrum Museum in Turkey, she identified over a thousand examples, many with intricately cut decorations. Several years of library research then led to a landmark study of ancient glass that will be part of the final publication of this remarkable collection.

In Edinburgh I was studying what one usually calls the "miscellaneous finds" of the site. I concluded that such a category may have no place in shipwreck reports, as nothing was taken aboard a ship, except quite accidentally, without a reason, and it is the duty of the archaeologist to ascertain that reason. Yet many of the finds I was studying did not exist until a year ago, almost a decade after the ship was excavated. All of you know that iron corrodes within its seabed concretion, but an iron object can be studied by cleaning out the resultant cavity in the concretion and casting a replica of its original form with epoxy or a similar material. Frederick van Doorninck, Joseph Schwarzer and others have spent years casting implements. But only last year did a razor and pair of scissors come out of concretion. Without them I would not have determined that wooden delousing combs on the ship were parts of more complete toiletry kits, and I would not have realized that the little piles of orpiment (a trisulfide of arsenic) found near them were probably for a male depilatory. Thus we would not have learned something of interest about hygiene on a medieval ship. Without those finds I would not have guessed that otherwise enigmatic marble fragments near the orpiment might have served as crude palettes for mixing the paste that removed body hair. And without those finds I might not have noted that spindle whorls on the ship were not items of cargo, but were found near the same personal pouches, which in two instances were left near where we have evidence that fishing nets were being mended. Although spinning in earlier classical times was almost totally a female occupation, I wondered if the whorls were used by the sailors to spin threads for their nets, as is done still today in some places. I ran across a twelfth- century Arab document that says it is all right for men to spin goat hair or sheep's wool, but not flax, for making linen is a woman's job. Because we still had the lead fishing sinkers, we could examine them for traces of hair, and learned that the nets were bordered with goat hair. So we may have learned something else new about shipboard life in the eleventh century--because we still had the artifacts.

Recently I received an enquiry from a newspaper reporter about a group that uses "hi-tech" to find shipwrecks in the Caribbean. She said that they want to do it right. They want to sell nothing, but to establish museums to recoup their expenses. They want to locate many, many sites. She didn't seem to understand when I tried to explain that it is not good archaeology to work site after site without the commitment to continue the project for as long as it takes. She said the group planned to hire archaeologists. I said that no true archaeologist would undertake the excavation of a site without being willing to commit as many years to it as necessary, even if it were that person's entire life.

In 1984 I began the excavation of the most exciting ancient shipwreck ever found in the Mediterranean (Bass 1986; Bass 1987). After directing its excavation for three summers, I realized that I was falling behind in my obligations to the medieval glass wreck I had excavated a decade ago. I therefore asked Cemal Pulak to assume the direction of the fieldwork so that I could devote more time to the publication

of the Glass Wreck. But I would now have nothing to study for publication had the finds been dispersed three years, or even a decade, after the excavation was completed.

It's what happens after the diving is over, not field technique, that turns archaeology into "good archaeology."

REFERENCES

BASS, GEORGE F.

1967   Cape Gelidonya: A Bronze Age Shipwreck. *Transactions of the American Philosophical Society* 57[8].

1978   Glass Treasure from the Aegean. *National Geographic* 163 (6):768-93.

1984a   The Million Piece Glass Puzzle. *Archaeology* 37(4):42-47.

1984b   The Nature of the Serçe Limani Glass. *Journal of Glass Studies* 26:64-69.

1986   A Bronze Age Shipwreck at Ulu Burun (Kas): 1984 Campaign. *American Journal of Archaeology* 90(3):269-96.

1987   Bronze Age Shipwreck Reveals Splendors of the Bronze Age. *National Geographic* 172(6):693-733.

1991   Evidence of Trade from Bronze Age Shipwrecks. In *Science and Archaeology: Bronze Age Trade in the Mediterranean.* Eds. N.H. Gale and Z.A. Stos-Gale, forthcoming.

BASS, GEORGE F. and FREDERICK H. VAN DOOR-NINCK, JR.

1978   An 11th Century Shipwreck at Serçe Liman,Turkey. *International Journal of Nautical Archaeology* 7(2):119-32.

1982   *Yassi Ada I: A Seventh-Century Byzantine Shipwreck.* Texas A&M University Press, College Station.

GALE, NOEL

1991   Copper Oxhide Ingots and their Relation to the Bronze Age Metal Trade. In *Science and Archaeology: Bronze Age Trade in the Mediterranean.* Eds. N.H. Gale and Z.A. Stos-Gale, forthcoming.

STEFFY, J. RICHARD

1982   The Reconstruction of the 11th Century Serçe Liman Vessel. *International Journal of Nautical Archaeology* 11(1):13-34.

STOS-GALE, ZOPHIA

1991   Sources of Metals and Trade in the Bronze Age. In *Science and Archaeology: Bronze Age Trade in the Mediterranean.* Eds. N.H. Gale and Z.A. Stos Gale, forthcoming.

VAN DOORNINCK, FREDERICK H., JR.

1989   The Cargo Amphoras on the 7th Century Yassi Ada and 11th Century Serçe Limani Shipwrecks: Two Examples of a Reuse   of Byzantine Amphoras as Transport Jars. In *Recherches sur la céramique byzantine.* Ed. V. Déroche and J.-M. Spieser *(Bulletin de correspondence hellénique,* suppl. 18:247-57).

YENER, K.A., H. ÖZBAL, A. MINZONI-DEROCHE AND
B. AKSOY

1989   Bolkardag: Archaeometallurgy Surveys in the
Taurus   Mountains, Turkey. *National Geographic
Research* 5(4):477-94.

GEORGE F. BASS
INSTITUTE OF NAUTICAL ARCHAEOLOGY
TEXAS A&M UNIVERSITY
COLLEGE STATION, TEXAS 77843-4352

1990 The World's Worst Investment: The economics of treasure hunting with real life comparisons. In *Underwater Archaeology Proceedings from the Society for Historical Archaeology Conference*, Toni Carrell, editor, pp. 6–10.

PETER THROCKMORTON

The World's Worst Investment: The Economics of Treasure Hunting with Real Life Comparisons

Introduction

The cost of undersea treasure hunts is double that of projects carried out by competent scientists. Only one in twenty salvage companies has any chance of making money. However, there is a way for investors to profit from shipwrecks.

Historic Preservation as a Public Issue

The American public has been exposed to a storm of rhetoric arising from the conflict between salvors and historic conservationists. Treasure hunters argue that their trade is good old American enterprise at its best and history and archaeology are boring and unnecessary pursuits carried out by a "bunch of bureaucrats feeding at the public trough" (Mel Fisher's attorney Paul Horan as quoted in *Time* Magazine in 1985). Extremist archaeologists say that compromise between business and science is impossible and seem to want to hide in their ivory towers while the salvors smash what they like.

The real issue is that American treasure hunting is destroying scant resources of desperately poor emerging Caribbean nations. Historic preservation in the Caribbean is an economic issue. Traditional sources of income for many Caribbean islands have declined in the past ten years. For example, the value of sugar exports from the Dominican Republic in 1987 were one-third of what they had been in 1977, and in the smaller islands they were about one-half. Jamaica's bauxite exports were down by over one-half in the same period. In contrast, tourism, two-thirds of it North American, has increased in all the islands. In Jamaica, the Dominican Republic, St. Kitts and Nevis, St. Lucia, Antigua, and the Cayman Islands it has doubled since 1980, and in St. Martin it has tripled. Today, tourism is rapidly becoming the treasure of the Caribbean.

Archaeology and Tourism

A recent study of the economic impact of the arts in Britain, by Mr. John Myerscough of the Policy Studies Institute, analyzed the economic impact of the arts, including museums, on Britain's economy. Foreign spending accounts for 37 percent of the turnover of the arts, compared to 27 percent of British manufacturing as a whole. The arts are the fourth biggest earner in Britain. Twenty-seven percent of tourism earnings are attributable to cultural attractions. A study by the Association of American Museums has shown that each tourist who visits a museum leaves about 10 dollars in the immediate local community's tax structure.

Archaeological resources are an asset to communities that create museums, because museums attract tourists. The ruined crusader castle in Bodrum, Turkey was converted into an archaeological museum in 1959. At that time the town's population was around 5000 and there was almost no tourism. Since then, George Bass and his group have been excavating shipwrecks and creating exhibit material. Today the museum is the second most visited in Turkey, after the National Museum in Ankara. The population has also tripled and local businesses are thriving. There are perhaps half a million visitors per year.

In 1967 Bass' group started excavating a fourth century BC ship off Kyrenia, a village well off the main tourist track at the southeastern end of the island of Cyprus. In 1967 Kyrenia Castle was the sixth most-visited archaeological site in Cyprus. By 1974, when the Turks invaded Kyrenia and put a stop to tourism on that end of the Island, there were over one hundred thousand visitors per year. and Kyrenia castle, with its ship exhibit, had risen to second in popularity.

The following table (courtesy Michael Katsev) illustrates the process:

TABLE 1

Visitors to Kyrenia Castle

1966	11,867	
1967	27,206	October survey of site
1968	29,791	First summer of excavation
1969	47,739	Second summer of excavation
1970	69,405	Begin preservation; temporary museum opened
1971	93,025	Continue preservation
1972	93,025	Begin hull reassembly
1973	113,500	Continue reassembly
1974	62,137	Visitors through mid-July; Turkish invasion

A significant part of the Caribbean's historical heritage is its dramatic history of buccaneering, privateering, slave trading and naval warfare. The islands were a cockpit for the conflicts of Europe for four centuries. The relics of all this are scattered over thousands of reefs and Cays and they are being mindlessly destroyed by treasure hunters. Americans are paying for this destruction twice. First, in the tax deductions granted to investors in salvage companies, and second in aid money given to impoverished governments. Tourist dollars paid to taxi drivers, hotel keepers, restauranteurs, store owners and the like, go directly into the local economy. Economies supported by tourism don't need our aid money.

Shipwrecks and the material in them, properly excavated, curated and exhibited in a museum are as valuable as historic houses, moldering castles or pre-Columbian ruins. When Caribbean countries barter away their historic shipwrecks in return for a percentage of an imaginary take, they lose tourist attractions that could produce income for all foreseeable time.

Opportunities like the one that existed in Bodrum 30 years ago are scattered all over the Caribbean. There are even suitable castles: St. Juan de Ulloa in Veracruz, English Harbor in Antigua, Sans Souci in Haiti, and Brimstone Hill in St. Kitts, to name a few. The treasures of the *Concepcion,* housed today in the old Governor's Palace in Santo Domingo, are the centerpieces of a spectacular historic restoration project and a thriving local boom, which brings the Dominicans much more money than if the collection had been sold. If the *Concepcion* had been professionally excavated the collection would be even more valuable.

Museum Economics

Digging into historic sites whether on land or under the sea usually produces material that has no value unless it has been intelligently excavated conserved, and exhibited. Shipwrecks are an extreme example. A few farseeing investors are beginning to understand that museums can pay. Several companies are now investigating financing archaeological projects that will result in museums, and building resorts around them. so that they acquire the long-term profit from the visitors attracted by the museum. If the museum is non-profit the excavations that produce the material can be done as 501(C)(3) projects through universities; this cuts costs in half. Investors are beginning to understand that archaeology is valuable, not because it produces "treasure", but because it brings in tourists.

A successful museum that might serve as a model for museums in emerging Caribbean countries is the Maine State Museum in Augusta, Maine, which was in part inspired by the National Museum of Mexico. The museum is free. Its attractive exhibits illustrate Maine's natural history and changing seasons, the disappearing world of nineteenth century Maine, and the 10 thousand year history of the state. It attracted 180 thousand visitors in 1978. The state legislature funds the museum according to annual visitation, figured at a rate of ten dollars per visitor per year. Half of this is spent for day-to-day operations, the other half for statewide educational programmes and development. Its director, Paul Rivard, says that people don't come to Maine specifically to see the museum, but stay longer in the state because of it.

Maine, with a population of 1.2 million, has about 4 million out-of-state visitors per year who spend 1.7 billion dollars. Like the Caribbean islands mentioned above, Maine's tourism is increasing at the rate of about 10 percent per year. Not so spectacular as some Caribbean islands, but still impressive. Maine's per capita income of 16 thousand dollars a year is not much higher than that of the most successful Caribbean tourist islands: the Cayman Islands per capita income is 12 thousand dollars, the Bahamas' is 9 thousand dollars.

Jim Thompson, of Maine's Department of Economic and Community Development, says that his office is investigating the relationship between amenities such as museums, theaters, concerts, fairs and festivals in order to establish how much such amenities effect the length of stay of visitors. The idea being that the longer you keep tourists in the state, the more money they will spend. Another aspect of providing cultural amenities is that their clientele will be more prosperous than, say, visitors to beaches or rock concerts.

Vasa, a battleship of 1628 salvaged intact from Stockholm Harbor in 1961, further illustrates the point. Conservation proved very expensive; there was an outcry against the project. Today, according to the Swedish tourist board, one million tourists spend an extra day in Sweden because of the *Vasa*. At about three hundred dollars per day per tourist, this amounts to several hundred million dollars per year added to Sweden's economy.

It appears then, that the best way to make real money out of old shipwrecks is to use them to create museums and then profit from the added revenue that follows the increase in tourist length of stay.

The Salvage Boom

Treasure hunting in Florida boomed in the early 1960s, with the discovery of the 1715 plate fleet off Vero Beach. What had been a relatively genteel weekend hobby as practiced in the Keys in the early days of SCUBA diving, became a gold rush, with its attendant cast of profit-minded adventurers. The best known, Mel Fisher, came in from California to work on the 1715 Plate Fleet, then moved to Key West for the famous search for the *Atocha* which he eventually found, to the acclaim of the American public.

Florida's policy towards its underwater antiquities has cost the state millions. The state's 25 percent share from the treasure grubbing of the past 20 years is a collection worth only about 5 million dollars today. The Florida state museum has in its possession approximately 1500 gold coins worth on the market about $2000 each, and about 20 thousand silver ones, worth $80 to $150 dollars each. This represents the state's 25 percent of all treasure recovered in Florida pre-1982.

The collection has cost more than its value to maintain, especially if one includes the cost of the continual legal cases that have resulted from the state's policy. If Florida had used state money, and invested 10 million dollars in two great maritime museums back in the 1960s, instead of giving leases to salvors, the state would be nearly half a billion dollars richer each year, if the Swedish example applies to Florida. The state's share of that sum in taxes would be not less than 25 million dollars per year. If the state was maintaining two museums at the Maine rate of 10 dollars per visitor there would still be a direct profit in tax money of 5 million dollars per year. It could even be argued that individuals and corporations who wanted to do legitimate work in searching for and excavating shipwrecks in collaboration with the state, would have profited. As things stand today in Florida, the state has set up such efficient barriers to stop treasure hunters, that even legitimate archaeology is inhibited.

The emerging economies of most small Caribbean islands can't even afford decent education systems and health care, much less archaeology and museums. As a result, they are wide open to the blandishments of salvors. As of the summer of 1988 there were five salvage companies working in the Bahamas and three or four in the Dominican Republic. A big one has a monopoly in the Turks and Caicos. Another, smaller, has rights to the British Virgin Islands. Mel Fisher has managed to get concessions from the Antiguan government for the reefs of Barbuda. Treasure hunters with millions of dollars behind them are working in the Marianas, the Philippines and the China Sea. In most cases the treasure hunters' contracts gives them exclusive rights, thus keeping out archaeologists. In 1988 I flew in a light plane over the east coast of Florida and spotted seven different salvage vessels industriously blowing sand with their mailboxes in the Vero Beach area where the 1715 fleet went ashore. These are said to be working under concessions from the Fisher organiza-

tion, which controls the leases. The hunt for antiquities has been reduced to the level of strip mining.

Florida treasure hunting sprang from a booming get-rich-quick society that has little historical past. Salvors tended to be working class midwesterners. Their divers were mostly typical products of the failed education system in this country, where one-quarter of the population can't read the directions on a can of soup and three-quarters don't read newspapers as often as once a week. According to a National Geographic Survey released in July 1988, one in four Americans can't identify the Pacific Ocean or the Soviet Union on a map, and 75 percent can't locate the Persian Gulf.

Today's salvors are no more aware of the cultural material they destroy than the peasant farmers who rob tombs for a living in Sicily or Columbia. Treasure investors are not well informed. Individuals knowing nothing about history or the ocean, with their sources limited to the national slicks and pulp "Treasure" magazines, are fair game for promoters. As P.T. Barnum said, "a sucker is born every minute."

When Mel Fisher won the Cobb Coin Case entrepreneurs turned treasure hunting into a nationally-financed industry. The passage of PL. 828 and the public confrontations that preceded it drew attention to the operations of salvors from environmental agencies, state and Federal prosecutors and the Securities and Exchange Commission. The promoters moved to the Caribbean. Like the drug trade that began with a bunch of happy-go-lucky hippies smuggling marijuana with sail boats, the treasure salvage industry has grown.

Today's treasure hunts are promoted on Wall Street and the Vancouver Stock Exchange. Their investors include some of the wealthiest men in the world. What we are seeing today is an assault on antiquity by an industry, not by a bunch of small-time adventurers. In scale it is larger and better financed than any assault on antiquities in history. About 25 treasure hunting companies are touted every year. About half get financed, for a total of up to 100 million dollars. This industry is equipped with big ships that have attached prop blowers that can blast away 500 tons of sand in 15 minutes, and open a hole in the sea bottom that is 15 feet around at the bottom and 50 feet across at the top. Sophisticated instruments can detect a cannon 100 yards away. Treasure salvage is now an industrial process.

While we deplore Lord Elgin's removal of the marbles from the Parthenon, we must admit that Europe's willingness to pay Turkish pashas good money for pagan statues saved a lot of statues from being smashed by Moslem fanatics. When dealers and governments paid adventurers to rob Egyptian tombs, they wanted the goodies because they cared about them. Today's investors are paying salvagers to take the valuables and smash the rest. The difference is one of scale. The modern salvagers of the *Geldermarsten* (the Nanking ship) are said to have dynamited the almost intact wreck after salvaging the Chinese blue on white porcelain so its location would remain unknown and the government from which it was stolen could not prove ownership.

The Government of the Turks and Caicos gave an exclusive contract to a professional industrial salvage company called TACMAR to rummage the shipwrecks in their territory for gold and silver in 1987. This is the moral equivalent of the Egyptian government giving Morrison Knutson a contract to bulldoze the Valley of the Kings in order to increase Egypt's gold reserves.

In the case of the Egyptian tombs, the salvaged material is now mostly in museums and the tombs themselves are mostly intact. While one can deplore destruction, a large percentage of their historical value survives. This is not so in the case of a looted shipwreck, where 90 percent of the interest lies in the ship itself and the artifacts that are ignored by the salvors, and destroyed, because they have been uncovered. One shipwreck like the *Geldermarsten* equals, in quantity of material destroyed, over 3,000 Etruscan tombs.

Now, in 1990 TACMAR seems to be going out of business. Nothing of value has been found and millions of dollars have been spent. The company's Wall Street investors have, perhaps. wearied of supporting a profitless project.

Evaluation of Some Undersea Archaeological Projects

Note that valuation of material recovered is based on today's estimated market value of the collection as a whole. In the case of expeditions that recovered material of important scientific, but little market value. the value of recovered material is given as $1 x $1. Value of collection to the host country is counted as $10 per visitor to the museum per year in the years since the exhibit became public. Money spent is the amount spent on the actual excavation calculated in todays dollars, calculated as 1960-67 x 3.4, 1977-87 x 1.7. All expeditions listed below are over 100 on the rating scale given below:

TABLE 2

Expedition/Year	Cost	Return	% Return
Cape Gelidonya 1960	$1,000,000		Museum x 11
Pelagos 1969	$ 50,000	$ 210,000	Market x 4
Torre Sgarrratta 1967-68	$ 100,000	$ 100,000	Market x 1
Kyrenia 1968	$ 120,000	$ 240,000	Museum x 2
Yassi Ada 1961-63	$ 370,000	$1,000,000	Museum x 3
Ulu Burun	$ 600,000	$ 1.000.000	Market x 2
Totals	$1,330,000	$3,550,000	Mixed x 2.6

Evaluation of a Group of Salvage Operations

Key to numbered items graded on 1 to 10 scale. 10 = excellent. The items below are broken down into ten questions for each heading. In the case that an item is not required. ten credit points are given.

1) Magnetometer
2) Research
3) The Expedition
4) The Ship
5) Equipment Shallow water
5a) Equipment Deep water
6) Archaeology
7) The Crew
8) The Company
9) Financing and Accountability
10) Political

This is a gross return of perhaps 35 million dollars. of which investors got less than 10 million dollars. However, the gargantuan *Atocha* project skews the figures. If one subtracts the approximately 13 million spent on the *Atocha*, we are left with 15 projects that cost a bit over 17 million dollars. which returned to their investors a total of between 3 and 4 million dollars. Only one project. *Concepcion II* returned any profit to the investors. This is a good deal less than donors got by supporting the 501(3)(C) non-profit tax organizations that did the non-profit projects listed. ie., 33 percent as opposed to 50 percent plus. Cost of the non-profit operations averaged about 5 thousand dollars per month. while salvage operations averaged nine thousand dollars. The most inefficient treasure hunt spent 500 thousand dollars for 16 days at sea.

TABLE 3

Project	Rating in Each Category 1 2 3 4 5 6 7 8 9 10										Total Rating	Cost Return for $1
Conception II 1987	10	10	7	10	9	0	8	10	9	9	92	$ 130,000x$18
Phoenix *	10	10	10	10	10	6	8	9	8	9	90	$ 2,000,000x$0
White Squall 1984	10	9	9	6	7	7	7	5	7	6	73	$ 100,000x$1
Accuro 1979	5	6	9	9	7	4	8	7	8	8	71	$ 375,000x$0
Seaview 1987-88	3	2	8	6	8	9	9	9	3	9	66	$ 1,250,000x$0
World Explor 1984	8	8	8	8	8	3	6	6	5	6	66	$ 250,000x$0
Concep 1978	2	10	5	7	9	8	8	9	2	6	66	$ 3,000,000x$1.5
Steed 1982	3	5	6	8	6	5	7	8	7	7	62	$ 210,000x$0
Rex II 1982-3	5	4	6	10	10	2	7	7	6	4	61	$ 275,000x$0
TACMAR * 1986-88	0	5	4	7	8	3	5	4	9	5	50	$ 4,000,000x$0
Atocha 1972-86	3	9	5	5	6	6	7	2	3	2	49	$13,000,000x$2.5
MAVL 1 1984-5	1	5	5	10	10	0	5	3	4	6	49	$ 350,000x$0
Baltimore 1982	0	3	5	6	6	4	6	6	5	5	46	$ 175,000x$0
Sea Search* 1987-81	0	4	8	7	6	0	6	3	1	3	39	$ 750,000x$0
James Bay 1978	3	0	3	5	8	0	5	3	5	4	36	$ 800,000x$0
NCR* 1985-88	0	0	2	8	5	0	2	2	2	5	26	$ 500,000x$0
Total												$27,165,000x$.30

*ongoing project

Notes: The grading system derives from experience with about fifty expeditions over the past thirty years in eight different countries. It is too lengthy to detail here. Amounts are approximate and are translated to 1988 dollars. Return is difficult to calculate due to the secretive nature of the salvage business. Returns of less than ten cents on the dollar have not been listed.

Trends

Pre-1985 Spanish treasure projects are relatively small time. The large industrial-type projects. ie., TACMAR. Phoenix, and two large projects in the Philippines (not listed), have appeared post the 1985 *Atocha* discovery and its attendant publicity.

Treasure hunting seems to be something that you can raise millions for doing even if your organization is incompetent. The old style investors didn't seem to care. When the *Miami Herald* put an investigative reporter onto Mel Fisher's operation. she found that a majority of Fisher's investors were satisfied because it had been an exciting adventure. and a much smaller percentage were suing because they felt conned. No one had any criticism of the inefficiencies of the project.

A grade of over 70 seems necessary for success. *Conception* I. although it returned $2 gross for $1 invested, went bankrupt, because the "take" was split with the Dominicans, which returned investors less than 50 cents on the dollar.

The *Atocha* project is the subject of much speculation. However the *Miami Herald* report shows that the luckiest Atocha investors probably didn't break even. The 3:1 return does not include investors. A low rated project such as Atocha can achieve something, if good money is continually thrown after bad, but is unlikely to return a profit.

Competent archaeologists are excavating shipwrecks and conserving what's worth saving for less money than the salvors spend ripping them up by the roots. Nearly all of the salvage projects being floated around the world today are doomed to failure because of the incompetence and ignorance of their principals. or because they are scams, designed only to benefit the promoters. No one seems to notice.

If investors understood that they cannot profit unless they employ professionals and professional societies could guarantee that the archaeologists are competent, and persuade host governments that they need cultural resource surveys, and need to protect shipwreck sites that can stock museums, there would be a better future.

It is not to the advantage of any salvor who wants to make money. to spend time wrecking sites that contain no treasure. It is not to the advantage of governments to allow cultural resources that might eventually benefit tourism, to be destroyed. It is not to the advantage of investors to be victims of the incompetence and chicanery that is characteristic of the treasure salvage industry today. Only archaeologists can prevent this.

Conclusion

Even a profitable barbarity, like the *Geldermarsten* project, would have paid its investors many times what it did if the project had been legitimate. Because the material was probably stolen, there was a chance that the country that owned it might sue. This caused a fast auction in Amsterdam. The porcelain sold is said to be bringing several times its auction price today. Even if the salvage company had gotten only half the porcelain, the investors would have made more money.

The only groups that have consistently performed in the shipwreck salvage business are a few salvors, and archaeologists using the systems developed by Penn Museum and their followers in the 1960s. If investors want to make money they need to turn away from the incompetents who infest the salvage business, and deal with professionals.

Governments of countries being exploited by salvors need to take a second look at what they are permitting and what it will cost the next generation. Archaeologists need to fulfill their professional responsibilities better. All of us who stand to benefit from reform of the salvage business, salvors, archaeologists. investors and the citizens of the countries being exploited should ask the people who control our foreign aid investment in the third world to take a hard look at the economics of museums and the tourist trade.

As things stand. investment in the salvage industry only benefits promoters and lawyers.

PETER THROCKMORTON
NOVA UNIVERSITY
8000 N. OCEAN DRIVE.
DANIA, FLORIDA. 33004

1992. The Ethics of Collaboration: Archaeologists and the *Wydah* Project. *Historical Archaeology* 26(4):105–117.

RICARDO J. ELIA

The Ethics of Collaboration: Archaeologists and the *Whydah* Project

ABSTRACT

The ethical dimensions of archaeological collaboration with treasure hunters are explored through a study of the *Whydah* salvage project. The *Whydah*, a pirate ship that sank off Cape Cod in 1717, has been the object of commercial salvage since 1982, which has resulted in intense ethical and legal controversy among treasure hunters, archaeologists, and public officials. The article describes the history of archaeological involvement in the salvage project and discusses the issue of collaboration from the perspective of the archaeologists who work for the treasure hunters and those in public agencies who regulate them. The ethical problems of archaeological collaboration are discussed in light of ethical standards of modern archaeology. The effects of archaeological collaboration in the *Whydah* project are assessed and the growing acceptance of commercial salvors in the management of underwater cultural resources is demonstrated with reference to recent projects in Boston Harbor.

Introduction

Since 1982, the commercial salvage of the 18th-century pirate ship *Whydah* has provoked controversy among those who are concerned about the ethical ramifications of archaeologists collaborating with treasure hunters. As the first major commercial salvage project involving the direct participation of professional archaeologists—both those engaged in the actual salvage and those in state and federal agencies who participate in the regulatory process—the *Whydah* project is likely to set important precedents, and possibly even serve as a model, for future commercial salvage projects involving historic shipwrecks.

The archaeologists who have worked for the *Whydah* treasure hunters include a past president of the Society for Historical Archaeology (SHA),

two active members of the Society of Professional Archaeologists (SOPA), and one current member of the Advisory Council on Underwater Archaeology. The salvage project has received permits from the Massachusetts Board of Underwater Archaeological Resources (MBUAR) and the U.S. Army Corps of Engineers and is operating under a Memorandum of Agreement whose signatories include the Corps of Engineers, the Massachusetts State Historic Preservation Office, and the Advisory Council on Historic Preservation.

Although a few opinions concerning the ethics of collaboration in the *Whydah* project have been published (e.g., Riess 1988; Roberts 1989; Wiseman 1989:442–443; Beaudry 1990; Bradley 1990; Elia 1990), most of the discussion has taken place behind the scenes, in board meetings of archaeological societies and committees engaged in evaluating professional papers. Professional attitudes are exemplified by the change in the status of the *Whydah* project at the annual Society for Historical Archaeology/Conference on Underwater Archaeology (SHA/CUA) meetings. In 1985, a paper was presented on the archaeological work (Riess et al. 1986) and in 1987, the *Whydah* project was featured in a symposium (Roberts 1987); in 1989, however, and each year since, papers based on research from the *Whydah* project have been rejected by the conference juries as being in violation of the SHA's ethical standards.

The *Whydah* project is an important instance of the ethics of archaeological collaboration with commercial treasure hunters and merits a full and open discussion. Is archaeological participation a necessary compromise, an imperfect but real-world solution that will ensure that archaeologists maintain at least some measure of control over salvage projects, even if the salable artifacts are eventually dispersed among the highest bidders? Or does archaeological collaboration lend a specious legitimacy to commercial salvage, one that increases the commercial value of recovered artifacts and contributes to the eventual destruction of data when artifacts are sold off? Are archaeologists striking a Faustian bargain by collaborating with treasure hunters, and in the process losing their souls?

Archaeological Involvement in the *Whydah* Project

The *Whydah* project began in late 1982 when treasure hunter Barry Clifford announced his intention of discovering and salvaging the wreck of the famous pirate ship that broke up in a storm and sank off Cape Cod in 1717. In the 10 years since, the *Whydah* salvage has involved continuous litigation; intensive, often acrimonious, involvement by regulatory agencies; a veritable "musical chairs" of collaborating archaeologists; and considerable attention from the popular media.

The site itself consists of an artifact debris field located 1,500 ft. off Marconi Beach in Wellfleet, Massachusetts. The artifacts lie in 20–30 ft. of water and beneath 16 or more ft. of shifting sand (Hamilton et al. 1990:2). When Barry Clifford sought title to the wreck in federal Admiralty Court in November 1982, the Commonwealth of Massachusetts claimed title to the site by virtue of its 1973 underwater archaeology law, which established a Board of Underwater Archaeological Resources (MBUAR) to oversee the survey and excavation of underwater sites (Massachusetts Underwater Archaeology Law 1973). Clifford initially refused to apply for a Board permit but later did so under protest pending the outcome of the litigation, which continued from 1982 to 1988, at which time the Massachusetts Supreme Judicial Court ruled in favor of the treasure salvors. This ruling effectively removed the site from the state's control (and also eliminated the salvors' requirement to pay 25 percent of the recovered value of the wreck to the state).

In 1983, testing at the site involved the removal of large amounts of sediment by prop-wash deflection, a technique that constituted dredging without a permit in the eyes of the Corps of Engineers. As a consequence of the Corps' investigation of this activity, the site was determined to be eligible for the National Register of Historic Places in 1985. A Memorandum of Agreement (MOA) was signed by the U.S. Army Corps of Engineers, the Advisory Council on Historic Preservation, and the Massachusetts Historical Commission. The MOA allowed excavation at the site but imposed conditions relating to the research design, performance standards, and coordination among parties. The MOA also stipulated that all analysis of recovered materials had to be completed before any artifacts were "sold or otherwise transferred to other parties" (Advisory Council on Historic Preservation 1985:3). Since 1985, the project has continued subject to the terms of the MOA.

Archaeological survey and testing of the *Whydah* site took place between 1983 and 1987. During this period, 23 test units totaling 2,784 sq. ft. were excavated and 71,107 artifacts and concretions were recovered. The 1988 and 1989 seasons were devoted to data recovery operations. In 1988, an additional 4,192 sq. ft. were excavated and 20,851 artifacts and concretions were recovered. The 1989 season involved the excavation of an additional 1,408 sq. ft. (Hamilton et al. 1990:66, 79–84).

For the first several years, the *Whydah* project was financed by private investments through Clifford's two marine salvage firms: Maritime Underwater Surveys, Inc., and Maritime Explorations, Inc. In 1987, a limited partnership called the Whydah Partners was established to conduct the project; the general partner is Whydah Management Company, Inc. In a 1987 private offering by EF Hutton & Company, Inc., the Whydah Partners sold shares in the venture, raising approximately $6 million. That same year, the Joint Venture made an agreement with Sotheby's for the identification, valuation, and sale of the *Whydah* artifacts.

In the earliest phase of the project, Barry Clifford hired as a consultant not a professional archaeologist, but a professional treasure hunter—Mel Fisher of Treasure Salvors, Inc. Fisher's involvement in the project seems to have been minimal, although there may be some dispute concerning Fisher's share of the profits that may yet lead to litigation.

The first archaeologist chosen by Clifford was R. Duncan Matthewson, who was rejected by the MBUAR because of his prior association with Mel Fisher. Clifford next hired Edwin Dethlefson as a consultant. Dethlefsen, then president of the SHA, was criticized by some of his archaeological colleagues and resigned in May 1983, not from the *Whydah* project but from the presidency of the SHA, complaining that the Society was becoming a "politically-activistic priesthood" (Dethlefsen 1983). Subsequently, Dethlefsen found that he had little actual control over the *Whydah* project, so he literally jumped ship, resigning from that endeavor in September 1983 (Dodson 1984:156–157).

The next year, Clifford's firm contracted with the Maritime Archaeological and Historical Research Institute (MAHRI). The professional team furnished by MAHRI for the 1984 testing season included Warren Riess as project archaeologist, SOPA member Michael Roberts as project manager, and Betty Seifert as project conservator. At the CUA annual meeting in January 1985, Riess and other MAHRI archaeologists presented a paper with the optimistic title: "The 'Whidah' Investigation: Satisfying Both Archaeological and Salvage Interests" (Riess et al. 1986:96–97). Once again, however, a dispute arose, this time over control of the project, funding, and excavation strategy, and led to MAHRI's withdrawal in 1985 (and to a lawsuit). At the next CUA meeting, in 1986, Riess publicly reversed his earlier position, organizing a symposium on "Ethics in Nautical Archaeology" (Ruppe et al. 1988) and speaking on the fundamental incompatibility between professional archaeology and treasure hunting. His concluding advice was, "You should not get involved, except to voice your objection" (Riess 1988:136).

Meanwhile, back at the wreck, Michael Roberts, who formerly worked on the MAHRI team, continued on as project manager, via a consultancy to Clifford's salvage firm. Roberts produced the report on the 1986 field season (Roberts et al. 1987) and chaired a symposium on the *Whydah* project at the 1987 annual meeting of the SHA/CUA in Savannah (Roberts 1987). He continued as project manager until mid-1987, when he left the project, according to the 1987 annual report, "due to disagreements with MEI [the salvage firm] concerning report production performance and deadlines" (Hamilton et al. 1988:7).

The current principal investigator for the *Whydah* project, Christopher Hamilton (a SOPA member), was hired by Clifford's firm in June 1987. Hamilton produced the final report on the 1984–1987 testing phase (Hamilton et al. 1988), as well as the reports of the 1988 and 1989 excavation seasons (Hamilton et al. 1989, 1990).

Other participants in the *Whydah* affair include Robert Cembrola, project archaeologist in 1984–1985; J. Robert Reedy, Jr., project archaeologist since 1986; Betty Seifert, who worked on the project as conservation consultant in 1984–1986; Sheila Charles, who was collections manager for the 1986 season; and David Muncher, the project's conservator and laboratory supervisor since 1988.

The Collaborators' Perspective

The justifications for participating in commercial salvage projects are well known. A typical defense of collaboration, culled from a selection of quotes from various archaeologists involved in the *Whydah* project, would form the following pastiche:

> I do not personally approve of or support the commercially-based excavation of archaeological sites . . . [but] our laws, in general, do not prohibit such activity. . . . Whether we like them or not, commercially based archaeological ventures are a fact; the question is how to deal with them (Bradley 1989:42–43).

> All archaeological work on the *Whydah* project is being performed in accordance with the [Section] 106 process. . . . Furthermore, material from the *Whydah* is being recovered in a setting controlled by a professional archaeologist and professional conservation personnel (Roberts 1989:1).

> As long as we control the whole investigation process, and have the right and duty to study the whole collection, we can glean most of the information from the site (Riess et al. 1986:97).

> The primary motive of archaeology is to gather information about archaeological sites and . . . the ownership of artifacts is a secondary consideration (Hamilton 1990b:5).

The current principal investigator of the *Whydah* project argues that archaeological involvement with commercial underwater salvage projects is a developing branch of cultural resource management (CRM) (Hamilton 1990a:8–9; 1990b:4ff.). The archaeologist who participates in these projects is simply helping to fulfill "the need to meet CRM regulations and guidelines as promulgated by the several review agencies" (Hamilton 1990b:4). In his view, the fact that private property laws give ownership of the artifacts to the treasure salvors should have no effect on the necessary presence of archaeologists in order to comply with CRM requirements. Worrying about ethical questions in this case is a waste of time, a non-issue (Hamilton 1990a:9).

Hamilton's equation of commercial salvage archaeology with CRM archaeology is as superficial as it is untenable. Surely there is a difference between a project concerned with an archaeological site that is threatened as an accidental consequence of a proposed development project and one that targets a historic shipwreck for commercial exploitation solely because it may contain objects of intrinsic value. The treasure hunter can hardly be equated with the developer who wants to build a house on top of what is, fortuitously, an archaeological site. Commercial salvage projects, in fact, violate one of the major principles that have gained broad acceptance in the past 20 years of CRM archaeology—namely, the conservation ethic, which treats archaeological sites as non-renewable resources that should be preserved whenever possible and only excavated if they are threatened (e.g., Lipe 1974; SOPA 1976; International Council on Monuments and Sites [ICOMOS] 1990). In most commercial shipwreck projects—the Whydah project included—there is no real threat to the site except from the salvage activities themselves.

An even more serious objection to Hamilton's linking commercial salvage with CRM archaeology is the relationship between the collaborating archaeologists and the treasure salvors. For, unlike most archaeologists working for clients on CRM projects, Hamilton and the other archaeological personnel working on the Whydah project are not independent archaeological consultants; they are, in fact, employees of the company that is conducting the salvage. Nor do they have complete control over all aspects of the archaeology, as an independent consultant would; for example, decisions about how much of the site will be excavated are controlled, ultimately, by financial considerations dictated by the general partner.

Also, the Whydah archaeologists have regularly engaged in activities that are directly related to publicity, promotion, and fund-raising. Recently, the current principal investigator has also been acting as the joint venture's advance person, promoting the idea of and soliciting support for a Whydah "themed attraction" as a way of keeping the collection together. The attraction would include a working conservation laboratory, museum, "pirate tavern," souvenir shop, and full-scale replica of the Whydah (Hamilton 1990b:5, 7–9). This promotion has, however, been rather misleading: the impression is given that the entire Whydah collection will be permanently curated when, in fact, no such guarantee has been made, and there is considerable evidence for believing that at least a part of the assemblage will be sold. And the practical consequence of promoting the "attraction" has been a cessation of reductions of concretions in the laboratory and the lay-off of laboratory personnel.

As for ethical scruples, Hamilton invokes as his philosophical authority not Immanuel Kant, or John Stuart Mill, but Noah Webster—more precisely, Webster's New World Dictionary of the American Language, whose definition of ethics Hamilton cites as "the system of morals of a particular person, religion, group, etc." (Hamilton 1990b:13). In other words, according to Hamilton, ethics is whatever any group decides it should be:

> Given that a project is legal, it is clearly ethical for business to make profits. . . . Like it or not, it is similarly ethical for treasure salvagers to salvage treasure; that is what they've done for many more years than archaeology has been a field of study and, I might add, with continued enthusiastic public support. It is also clear that it is ethical for archaeologists to meet the needs of the public by executing data recovery plans approved by regulatory agencies (Hamilton 1990b: 13).

By this absurd exercise in logic, it is ethical for robbers to rob and for murderers to murder. But by the same logic, it is ethical for professional archaeologists to establish their own ethical standards; the SHA did so in 1985 when it censured the commercial excavation of archaeological sites.

Some of the state and federal agency archaeologists who have been involved in the *Whydah* project as part of the regulatory process also share the viewpoint that commercial salvage archaeology must be treated as part of the existing framework of CRM compliance. This perspective is perhaps natural given the constraints faced by most agency archaeologists: it is, after all, their charge to work within existing laws and regulations, which do allow some control over archaeological procedures and standards on commercial salvage projects, but these legal strictures generally do not prohibit commercial salvage or the ownership of artifacts. Many states, including Massachusetts, actively encourage the commercial recovery of shipwrecks, and award a substantial percentage of the value of recovered finds (up to 90%) to the salvor (Giesecke 1989:36).

Thus, working within the existing CRM compliance framework, regulatory archaeologists tend to promote the granting of permits to commercial ventures as a way of exercising control and ensuring that some archaeological procedures are followed. James Bradley, a member of MBUAR from 1982 to 1990, has argued the advantages of this position. According to Bradley (1989:43), the best advice is "to make the power of the law work for us by permitting these commercial ventures and holding them to high standards rather than looking for ways to deny and exclude them." Bradley also asserts that the archaeology on the *Whydah* project has been done well, and even makes the extraordinary claim—one that the *Whydah* Joint Venture itself has never made—that no artifacts from the salvage are planned to be sold (Bradley 1990:22).

But compliance archaeology is not necessarily good archaeology, just as what is legal is not necessarily ethical, and some regulatory archaeologists seem to have become advocates of treasure hunting instead of regulatory enforcers (cf. Beaudry 1990; Elia 1990). There can be no doubt that an aura of legitimacy accrues to commercial salvage projects by virtue of their holding permits and being in compliance with various state and federal permit regulations. The treasure hunters,

even though they are forced against their will into complying with archaeological regulations, soon learn to take credit for doing all the archaeology that has been imposed upon them. And by treating commercial salvage projects as compliance archaeology, the regulatory agencies need only concern themselves with ensuring that the salvors meet the required level of compliance, however minimal. This in turn contributes to a general acquiescence in the status quo, and no effort is made to change existing laws in order to prohibit exploitative commercial salvage projects.

Bradley (1989:43) even claims that "what is most important is control of the process." But the process is clearly flawed with respect to commercial salvage; Bradley of all people should realize this after spending more than six years trying to regulate the *Whydah* project as a member of the state's underwater board, only to have the board's jurisdiction and control eliminated after years of litigation.

The defense of commercial shipwreck archaeology as CRM or compliance archaeology runs aground on several shoals. Commercial salvage excavations are *not* the same as development projects that accidentally affect archaeological sites, even though both may result in the destruction of cultural resources. CRM projects are generally evaluated within the framework of the conservation ethic; avoidance of threatened archaeological sites, rather than excavation, is generally the preferred approach. And archaeological collaborators are *not* independent consultants; they work *for* the treasure hunters, not *with* them, and the distinction is more than a grammatical nicety.

It is true, however, that commercial salvage archaeology does share a few points of similarity with CRM archaeology. Unfortunately, these similarities include some of the more negative aspects of the CRM field, including the tendency of some CRM archaeologists to play both ends against the middle—i.e., to act as the go-between for the developers/salvors on the one hand and the regulatory agencies on the other, telling each what they want to hear; and, also, the proclivity of practically everyone involved in the process to gloss over mistakes and, publicly, at least, make the compliance process appear to be completely successful. As Warren Riess (1988:136) remarked, after his experience with the *Whydah* project: "The state bureaucracy and the salvors will say that the cooperative effort is working even though it is not."

In terms of the *Whydah* project, one must await the completion of the project before making a final assessment of how well the archaeology was done. The work conducted to date, however, raises some disturbing questions. For example, in 1984, before MAHRI became involved in the project, a sizable portion of the center of the site was exposed through prop-wash blasting. This area covered approximately 2,700 sq. ft. (Roberts and Riess 1985: Fig. 1), or an amount roughly equal to the total area excavated (2,784 sq. ft.) during the 1984–1987 testing phase (Hamilton et al. 1990:66). The prop-washing exposed 18–20 cannon, a block, a deadeye, and numerous coins; in all, more than 3,700 unprovenienced artifacts were recovered (Roberts and Riess 1985:6; Hamilton et al. 1990: 66). Yet nowhere in the annual reports is there an adequate accounting of this work or an assessment of the likely disturbance to the site; the 1985 annual report glosses over the issue, describing the large-scale exposure as accidental and the disturbance as minimal (Roberts and Riess 1985:6).

Professional Ethics and Treasure Hunting

Is collaboration with treasure hunters consistent with ethical standards of modern professional archaeology?

The development of ethical standards in archaeology is a relatively recent phenomenon, and one that mirrors both the increasing professionalization of the field and the fact that cultural resource management has become an important element of public policy. Among the ethical principles that have achieved general acceptance among archaeologists, three are directly relevant to the issue of participation in commercial underwater salvage projects.

First is the so-called "conservation ethic," which has already been mentioned. Under the conservation ethic, archaeologists act as stewards of the archaeological resource base on behalf of the public. This responsibility includes avoiding exaggeration or misleading statements about, or taking actions that will result in harm to, the resource base.

Second is the explicit rejection of commerciality in archaeology and, specifically, of the buying and selling of artifacts for financial gain. This position was expressed in the by-laws of the Society for American Archaeology (SAA) as early as 1935 (SAA 1935:148) and continues to be an important standard of that and other groups, including the SHA, the Council of American Maritime Museums, and the International Congress of Maritime Museums (Johnston 1989).

A third standard, the logical consequence of the finite nature of the resource base and the inevitable loss of data resulting from the selling of artifacts, is the requirement that all recovered artifacts and project documentation be permanently curated (SAA 1961:137; SOPA 1976).

If artifacts are sold, the standard of permanent curation is obviously not being met. Those who support collaboration with treasure hunters often argue that they are more interested in data than objects. But objects *are* data. It is curious that those who object to the SHA/CUA ban on *Whydah* papers as censorship and an obstruction of the dissemination of scientific knowledge (e.g., Roberts 1989; Cohn 1989) do not seem to be bothered by the real loss of data that is occasioned when an artifact assemblage is auctioned. Is not scientific knowledge, after all, predicated on the requirement that research results can be replicated by other researchers? How can the analysis of the *Whydah* assemblage be verified, and how can additional analyses be conducted in the future (cf. Bass 1990), if the artifacts are sold?

With regard to the second ethical standard—the prohibition against commerciality in archaeology—it is evident that, despite the personal convictions of the collaborators, the mere fact of their participation in commercial salvage projects serves to promote those projects in very tangible ways. Given the present system of compliance archaeology, in many states a salvage project cannot take place without a professional archaeologist; therefore the archaeologist is making the project possible. If one adds to that the aura of respectability, professionalism, and official approval that accrues to the commercial project by virtue of its association with professional archaeologists, the conclusion is inescapable that collaborating archaeologists contribute to the commerciality of archaeology.

The fact that commercial salvage archaeology is absolutely inimical to the conservation ethic has already been discussed. The only way that collaborating archaeologists can claim that their involvement in commercial salvage enterprises protects the resource is by narrowly restricting their concerns to the specific site. Thus one constantly hears arguments like, "we must get whatever information we can;" "some information is better than none;" and "if we didn't get involved, the site would be looted." Such remarks, of course are a tacit admission that the salvors have no interest in the site other than commercial. Commercially-motivated excavations of non-threatened sites like the *Whydah* exploit, rather than conserve, the resource base, and no amount of sophistry can rationalize the selling of artifacts as conservation of the resource base.

Because the archaeologists who work for treasure hunters fail to live up to several of the most fundamental ethical principles of modern archaeology, how can anyone, especially those in public agencies, talk about ensuring "high standards of archaeology"? They may be referring to high standards of fieldwork and recording, although it remains to be seen on projects like the *Whydah* how high these standards in fact are. They cannot, however, speak about ensuring *high* archaeological standards, only *partial* archaeological standards, for without the core principles of the conservation ethic, permanent curation, and avoidance of commerciality, one is only talking about techniques, not the standards of a profession.

One of the essential elements of any profession is the notion of professional responsibility (Wildesen 1984:8–11) and for archaeology perhaps the most eloquent articulation of these responsibilities is the Code of Ethics of SOPA. Here the archaeologist's professional responsibilities are divided among three categories: those owed to the public (i.e., the resource), to colleagues, and to employers and clients (SOPA 1976).

The participation of several SOPA members on the *Whydah* project is especially intriguing. Whether right or wrong, their involvement extends SOPA's ethical imprimatur to the question of collaboration with treasure hunters. Yet the project appears to violate several of SOPA's ethical codes and standards. For example, 1.1.1(b) of the Code requires that archaeologists "actively support conservation of the archaeological resource base;" as has been noted, the *Whydah* site, like most targets of commercial salvagers, was not in any imminent danger but was selected for excavation solely for its treasure. Another apparent violation is number 5 of the Standards of Research Performance, which requires that "specimens and research records resulting from a project must be deposited at an institution with permanent curatorial facilities."

Implicit in the collaborating archaeologists' justification of their actions is their refusal to accept any responsibility for the motives and actions of their employer, the treasure hunter. A collaborating archaeologist might argue that, technically, these standards are being violated by the project sponsor, not the archaeologist. But this claim ignores another important element of the SOPA Code—that an archaeologist's professional responsibility cannot be isolated from the larger project of which he or she is a part. This is explicitly stated in 3.3.2(e) of the Code: "An archaeologist shall not recommend or participate in any research which does not comply with the requirements of the Standards of Research Performance" and in 3.3.1(a) of the Code: "An archaeologist shall refuse to comply with any request or demand of an employer or client which conflicts with the Code and Standards." Thus by acquiescing in the commercial motive of a salvage project, the collaborating archaeologist is shirking professional responsibilities.

While several SOPA standards clearly are at odds with the idea of archaeologists collaborating with underwater treasure hunters, SOPA does not explicitly prohibit such activity. In contrast, the Code of Conduct of the Institute of Field Archaeologists

(IFA), established in England in 1983, does address this issue. IFA's code, which was adopted in 1985 and amended in 1988, was modelled in large part on the SOPA Code and Standards, and contains four major principles with several rules for each principle. Principle 2 espouses the archaeologist's "responsibility for the conservation of the archaeological heritage" (IFA 1988:3).

The IFA Code of Conduct includes a series of notes on various rules. A note on Rule 1.6, which includes the statement that "an archaeologist shall not engage in, and shall seek to discourage, illicit or unethical dealings in antiquities," is particularly relevant:

> Archaeologists working on the foreshore and underwater may at times find themselves in difficulty regarding their association with commercial salvors and others engaged in exploiting the underwater cultural heritage. The underlying principles are (1) conserving the seabed heritage, (2) using it economically and in such a way that reliable information may be acquired, (3) dissemination of the results, and (4) professional permanent curation of the total site archive (IFA 1988:5–6).

The note goes on to say that archaeologists should "not knowingly permit their names or services to be used in a manner which may promote the recovery of archaeological material unless the primary objective of their work is to preserve the scientific integrity of the total site archive in a permanent professionally curated and publicly accessible collection." Moreover, archaeologists working on underwater sites should "not enter into any contract or agreement whereby archaeological or curatorial standards may be compromised in deference to commercial interests" (IFA 1988:6).

As is clear from the above, IFA has made explicit what SOPA only implies: "Professional permanent curation of the total site archive" is a fundamental principle of dealing with underwater salvors, and archaeologists should not enter into agreements if permanent curation is not guaranteed.

The Consequences of Collaboration

What are the effects of collaboration? Will it not lead the average person, who probably is not aware of the conservation ethic, to believe that treasure hunting is not only acceptable but must be a good thing? After all, why would so many archaeologists be involved? And will collaboration not result in further assaults on the archaeological resource base?

It is difficult to assess the effects of the *Whydah* project on the remaining resource base, but it is likely that it has stimulated interest in shipwreck salvage. It is interesting to note that between 1976 and 1982—the year Clifford received a permit from the state underwater board for the *Whydah*—fewer than 20 permits had been given for underwater projects in Massachusetts; between 1983 and 1990, over 65 permits were awarded (Victor Mastone 1990, pers. comm.). Certainly the project has generated a remarkable amount of publicity in the print and electronic media, and two popular books have so far appeared (Dethlefsen 1984; Vanderbilt 1986). The print media's coverage of the project includes 131 articles in the *Cape Cod Times*, 30 in the *Boston Globe*, 9 in the *New York Times*, and some 15 magazine features in publications like *People, Yankee, Time, Parade,* and *Boston Magazine*.

The national media reportage, which was sporadic but reached a wide audience, tended to focus on the more sensational aspects of the project. *People* magazine, for example, with a 1983 circulation of 2,600,000, carried a feature story with the headline "Barry Clifford's zany crew—including JFK Jr.—prove that way down deep, they're gold-diggers" (Ryan 1983:26). While most of the articles identify Clifford as a "treasure hunter" or "marine salvager," others use more colorful epithets, especially in the early years of the project. Thus Clifford is described as "a handsome, swashbuckling, 20th-century buccaneer" (Fee 1983:1), "the Cape Cod underwater salvage swashbuckler" (Ghioto 1984:17), and an "adventurer" (*Boston Globe* 1985). Clifford reached a new level of respectability in late 1988, when the *New York Times* (1988) referred to him as a "salvage entrepreneur."

Almost without exception, the print reporting has uncritically accepted the salvors' optimistic, if not inflated, estimates of the value of the treasure.

These estimates, of course, heighten popular interest in the project and serve to attract investors. The first estimate for the *Whydah*—"400 bags of gold and silver"—appeared in print in early December 1982 (Fee 1982a:1). A few days later, the figure was "$80 to $200 million" (Fee 1982b:1). This value was repeated in every story until July 1984, when the treasure was described as "probably worth $400 million" (Holmes 1984:1); this new figure, whatever its origins, was first announced by a sympathetic member of the MBUAR. From mid-1984 until the present, virtually every article in the local, regional, and national media has repeated the $400 million estimate.

The publicity surrounding the *Whydah* treasure reached a peak in a cover story in *Parade* magazine (White 1985:6–9). The cover shows a picture of Clifford against a background of silver and gold coins; the headline reads, "The man who discovered a $400 million pirate treasure," as if that much loot had already been recovered; in 1985, it should be noted, the circulation of *Parade* magazine was over 25,000,000. This article was one result of a national media campaign orchestrated by a New York public relations firm; can there be any doubt that the article played a role in the creation of the joint venture and the eventual infusion of $6 million into the project?

One certain consequence of the *Whydah* project, at least in Massachusetts, has been that commercial marine salvors are now respectably entering the mainstream of underwater archaeology, at least as far as public agencies are concerned. Two examples of this disturbing trend will suffice. On 27 October 1987, both of Boston's daily newspapers carried front-page stories reporting Barry Clifford's claim to have rediscovered the exact spot of the Boston Tea Party, and his intention to apply to the MBUAR for a permit to survey a segment of Boston Harbor with the eventual goal of salvaging tea chests. The site of the Tea Party incident—Griffin's Wharf—was never lost; it is, however, now several hundred feet inland as a result of landfilling since the 18th century. When this fact was pointed out at the underwater board meeting, Clifford quietly reapplied for a permit to survey a reduced area, now focusing on the waters off Long Wharf.

The targeted resource now was to be three scuttled ships and a quantity of military material dumped off the wharf by the British when they evacuated Boston in March 1776. In Clifford's permit application, a list of ships and supplies abandoned by the British was quoted to show what the salvors expected to find (Clifford 1988: Attachment C). Two sources were cited for the quoted list: a recent popular book (Birnbaum 1986:366–368) and an antiquarian history (Frothingham 1849:406–407). The original list is from a report of the Deputy Quartermaster-General of the Continental Army and contained an inventory of ships, supplies, and armaments that had *already been secured* by the Army (Frazer 1844 [1776]).

This documentation was presented to the MBUAR, which requires "demonstrable proof" of the presence of a resource before it can issue a reconnaissance survey permit (MBUAR 1985). When faced with a clear choice between historical evidence and pseudo-history, the Board, with one exception—the state archaeologist—still voted to grant a permit to Clifford's group. The vote confirmed the painfully obvious fact that the state underwater board, a body that includes representatives from the diving community as well as bureaucrats who are not archaeologists, is simply not competent to judge matters requiring archaeological expertise.

The second example shows that the legitimization of treasure hunters in Massachusetts is now nearly complete, thanks largely to the efforts of collaborating archaeologists. In late 1990, Clifford's marine salvage firm was awarded a public contract to conduct a CRM project—an underwater archaeological evaluation of a portion of Boston Harbor that will be disturbed as part of a multibillion dollar cleanup of the harbor. With Christopher Hamilton serving as principal investigator, the salvage firm employed commercial divers to identify and evaluate possible archaeological resources within the affected area. Public money is thus being paid to a marine salvage company in order to conduct an archaeological investigation that is required by federal preservation law. The unfortunate irony is that the salvage firm might discover underwater sites and, after the state agency avoids the sites in its construction (which is its stated intention), under state law there would be nothing to prevent the salvors from filing a permit to salvage the sites. Thus, federal preservation law and public funds can be used to give a private salvage firm an inside track to the commercial salvage of underwater archaeological resources.

Conclusion

Somehow it always seems to come down to money. The commercial value of some shipwrecks motivates treasure hunters and keeps underwater archaeological resources apart from other cultural resources in terms of treatment under the law, in public policy, and in the popular mind. And it is no coincidence that the most vocal advocates of collaborating with treasure hunters are those who themselves are currently receiving, or have received, substantial financial compensation from commercial salvage projects. There is also the fallacy—often used in the justification of commercial salvage projects—that only private-sector funding is used on such projects. In fact, public money is regularly being spent on these projects—in the form of the salaries and expenses of agency archaeologists and other public officials who must regulate them, and in the court system, which handles the incessant stream of litigation that seems to be a natural adjunct of commercial salvage projects.

Archaeologists must not lose sight of the fact that commercial treasure hunting is one of the last vestiges of an outmoded and outdated approach to the treatment of cultural resources. One can point to numerous examples in the past where a people's cultural patrimony was uprooted and carried off for the sake of its commercial, artistic, or historical value. In many cases this was accomplished through means that, at the time, were sanctioned by the force of law. One thinks of Lord Elgin's wholesale removal of the Parthenon Marbles in Athens on the basis of his *firman* from the Turkish government in Constantinople, or the removal of the Benin bronzes as spoils of war by the British in 1897 (Greenfield 1989:145–148).

Today, in this later and, one hopes, more enlightened age, notions about cultural patrimony have greatly matured. The international preservation movement has developed a much keener awareness about the importance of preserving cultural resources for the benefit of all people. This maturity is exemplified, most recently, by the unanimous adoption of a *Charter for the Protection and Management of the Archaeological Heritage* by the 59 national committees of the International Council on Monuments and Sites (ICOMOS 1990). The *Charter* fully espouses the conservation ethic as its guiding philosophy. To be sure, the profit motive still exists, as the flourishing international trade in illicit antiquities testifies, but, for the most part, the commercial exploitation of archaeological sites is an illegal and clandestine activity. When viewed from the perspective of the great strides that have been made in the preservation field over the past 20 years, commercial salvage projects like the *Whydah* are an outrageous and unacceptable anomaly.

The passage of the Abandoned Shipwreck Act in 1988 removed historic shipwrecks on state land from the jurisdiction of federal admiralty courts, which have traditionally treated shipwreck salvage as an economic, not an archaeological issue. Although the passage of the new law was a victory for preservation, it is only half the battle; now the states must manage their underwater cultural resources, and many are still doing so with regressive laws that encourage commercial salvage.

By actively participating in, or even acquiescing in, commercial salvage projects, archaeologists contribute to the exploitation of the resource base and the conversion of cultural patrimony into private gain. In so doing, they are abandoning the hard-won achievements of the past two decades and forsaking the ethical foundations of their young profession. Archaeologists study a finite and dwindling resource base whose preservation lies largely, though not solely, in their hands. If archaeologists do not speak for, and accept the responsibility for, these resources, can one expect anyone else to?

ACKNOWLEDGMENTS

This article is a slightly expanded version of a paper presented at the 1991 Society for Historical Archaeology Conference on Historical and Underwater Archaeology in Richmond, Virginia, 12 January 1991. Al B. Wesolowsky read several earlier versions of the paper and made many helpful comments and thoughtful insights. I have also greatly benefited from discussions with Paul Johnston, Marie Bourassa, Victor Mastone, and J. Barto Arnold III. Information on the print media's coverage of the *Whydah* project derives in large part from a class paper written by Boston University graduate student Claire Carlson. The opinions expressed herein are, of course, my own.

REFERENCES

ADVISORY COUNCIL ON HISTORIC PRESERVATION
1985   Memorandum of Agreement: The Wellfleet Site. Signed by Advisory Council on Historic Preservation; U.S. Army Corps of Engineers, New England Division; Massachusetts State Historic Preservation Office. On file, Advisory Council on Historic Preservation, Washington, D.C.

BASS, GEORGE F.
1990   After the Diving Is Over. *Underwater Archaeology Proceedings from the Society for Historical Archaeology Conference 1990*:10–13. Toni L. Carrell, editor. Society for Historical Archaeology, California, Pennsylvania.

BEAUDRY, MARY C.
1990   Looting by Any Other Name: Archaeological Ethics and the Looting Problem. *Society for Historical Archaeology Newsletter* 23(1):13–14.

BIRNBAUM, LOVIS
1986   *Red Dawn at Lexington: "If They Mean to Have a War, Let It Begin Here."* Houghton Mifflin, Boston, Massachusetts.

BOSTON GLOBE [Massachusetts]
1985   Sunken-Ship Hunters off Cape Get Permits. *Boston Globe*, 1 March:20.

BRADLEY, JAMES W.
1989   A Comment on Problems and Priorities for State Programs in Underwater Archaeology. *Underwater Archaeology Proceedings from the Society for Historical Archaeology Conference 1989*:42–43. J. Barto Arnold III, editor. Society for Historical Archaeology, California, Pennsylvania.
1990   A Reply to Beaudry. What Are We Really Here For? *Society for Historical Archaeology Newsletter* 23(2): 22–23.

CLIFFORD, BARRY L.
1988   Reconnaissance Permit Application, submitted to the Massachusetts Board of Underwater Archaeological Resources, 6 October 1988. Boston.

COHN, MICHAEL
1989   Comment. In Ethics and Treasure Hunting II, edited by Michael Roberts. *SOPA News* 13(4):1.

DETHLEFSEN, EDWIN
1983   "Letter of Resignation," 18 May 1983. *Society for Historical Archaeology Newsletter* 17(1):14–15.
1984   Whidah: *Cape Cod's Mystery Treasure Ship*. Seafarers Heritage Library, Key West, Florida.

DODSON, JAMES
1984   Not the Best of Times for Barry Clifford. *Yankee* (March):77ff. Dublin, N.H.

ELIA, RICARDO J.
1990   Dealing with Treasure Hunters: Regulate, Don't Collaborate. *Society for Historical Archaeology Newsletter* 23(4):7–8.

FEE, GAYLE
1982a A Treasure in Sunken Gold: Vineyard Man to Salvage Pirate Ship off Wellfleet. *Cape Cod Times*, 1 December:1.
1982b State Says Whidah Belongs to It, Too. *Cape Cod Times*, 3 December:1.
1983   Clifford Set to Reap the Whidah's Riches. *Cape Cod Times*, 24 July:1.

FRAZER, JOHN G.
1844   "Inventory of stores belonging to the king, and left in Boston; taken the 18th and 19th of March, 1776, by order of Thomas Mifflin, Esq., Quartermaster-General of the Continental Army," 20 March 1776. *American Archives: Fourth Series, Containing a Documentary History of the English Colonies in North America . . . etc.*, Vol. 5, edited by Peter Force, pp. 488–489. Published under authorization of an Act of Congress, Washington, D.C.

FROTHINGHAM, RICHARD, JR.
1849   *History of the Siege of Boston, and of the Battles of Lexington, Concord, and Bunker Hill*. Charles C. Little and James Brown, Boston.

GHIOTO, GARY
1984   Pirate Ship Whidah Is "Found" Again. *Boston Globe*, 25 July:17.

GIESECKE, ANNE G.
1989   States and Their Shipwrecks. *Underwater Archaeology Proceedings from the Society for Historical Archaeology Conference 1989*:35–41. J. Barto Arnold, editor. Society for Historical Archaeology, California, Pennsylvania.

GREENFIELD, JEANETTE
1989   *The Return of Cultural Treasures*. Cambridge University Press, Cambridge, England.

HAMILTON, CHRISTOPHER E.
1990a Managing Shipwrecks as Cultural Resources. *Sea History* (Forum on Marine Archaeology) 52 (Winter 1989–1990):8–9.

1990b   Shipwrecks and the Private Sector. Paper presented at the 44th National Trust for Historic Preservation Conference, Session No. 2, Maritime Track, "Shipwrecks: Preservation, Ethics, and Economics," Charleston, South Carolina.

HAMILTON, CHRISTOPHER E., D. A. MUNCHER,
JAMES R. REEDY, JR., AND KENNETH J. KINKOR
1990   The 1988 Annual Report of Archaeological Data Recovery. The *Whydah* Shipwreck: Site WLF-HA-1, Cape Cod, Massachusetts. Prepared by *Whydah* Joint Venture Laboratory, South Chatham, Massachusetts. Submitted to U.S. Army Corps of Engineers, New England Division, Waltham, Massachusetts.

HAMILTON, CHRISTOPHER E., JAMES R. REEDY, JR.,
AND KENNETH J. KINKOR
1988   The Final Report of Archaeological Testing—The *Whydah* Shipwreck: Site WLF-HA-1, Cape Cod, Massachusetts. Vol. 1, Text (December 1987, revised 1988.) Prepared by Maritime Explorations, Inc., South Chatham, Massachusetts. Submitted to U.S. Army Corps of Engineers, New England Division, Waltham, Massachusetts.

HAMILTON, CHRISTOPHER E., JAMES R. REEDY, JR.,
KENNETH J. KINKOR, AND D. A. MUNCHER
1989   The 1988 Annual Report of Archaeological Data Recovery—The *Whydah* Shipwreck: Site WLF-HA-1, Cape Cod, Massachusetts. Prepared by Maritime Explorations, Inc., South Chatham, Massachusetts. Submitted to U.S. Army Corps of Engineers, New England Division, Waltham, Massachusetts.

HOLMES, RICHARD
1984   Expert Calls Ship's Discovery "Biggest in North America." *Cape Cod Times*, 24 July:1.

INSTITUTE OF FIELD ARCHAEOLOGISTS (IFA)
1988   By-Laws of the Institute of Field Archaeologists: Code of Conduct (ratified and adopted 3 June 1985, amended 12 September 1988). Institute of Field Archaeologists, University of Birmingham, Birmingham, England.

INTERNATIONAL COUNCIL ON MONUMENTS AND SITES (ICOMOS)
1990   *Charter for the Protection and Management of the Archaeological Heritage.* International Committee on Archaeological Heritage Management, ICOMOS, Washington, D.C.

JOHNSTON, PAUL FORSYTHE
1989   Between the Devil and the Dark Blue Sea: Archaeology and the Council of American Maritime Museums. *Underwater Archaeology Proceedings from the Society for Historical Archaeology Conference 1989*:148–149. J. Barto Arnold III, editor.

Society for Historical Archaeology, California, Pennsylvania.

LIPE, WILLIAM D.
1974   A Conservation Model for American Archaeology. *The Kiva* 39:213–245.

MASSACHUSETTS BOARD OF UNDERWATER
ARCHAEOLOGICAL RESOURCES (MBUAR)
1985   Regulations of the Board of Underwater Archaeological Resources. State Legislative Code 312 CMR. Division of Massachusetts Executive Office of Environmental Affairs, Boston.

MASSACHUSETTS UNDERWATER ARCHAEOLOGY LAW
1973   An Act Establishing a Board of Underwater Archaeological Resources and Providing for the Preservation of Said Resources. (Chapter 989, Massachusetts *Acts* of 1973). On file, Massachusetts Historical Commission, Boston.

NEW YORK TIMES
1988   Salvager is Exploring Harbor for Boston Tea Party's Crates. *New York Times*, 18 December:A.

RIESS, WARREN
1988   Comment. In Symposium: Ethics in Nautical Archaeology, by Reynold Ruppe, Dan Lenihan, Larry Murphy, and Warren Riess. *Archaeology in Solution: Proceedings of the Seventeenth Annual Conference on Underwater Archaeology, 1986*:134–136. John W. Foster and Sheli O. Smith, editors. Sacramento, California.

RIESS, WARREN, WILLIAM A. BAYREUTHER, AND
ROBERT CEMBROLA
1986   The *Whidah* Investigation: Satisfying both Archaeological and Salvage Interests. In *Proceedings of the Sixteenth Conference on Underwater Archaeology*, edited by Paul Forsythe Johnston. *Special Publication Series* No. 4:96–97. Society for Historical Archaeology, California, Pennsylvania.

ROBERTS, MICHAEL
1987   Symposium: The Archaeological Testing Program for the Pirate Ship *Whydah*: The How and the What. *Underwater Archaeology Proceedings from the Society for Historical Archaeology Conference 1987*: 33–46. Alan B. Albright, editor. Society for Historical Archaeology, California, Pennsylvania.
1989   Ethics and Treasure Hunting. *Society of Professional Archaeologists Newsletter*, vol. 13, no. 1 (January 1989):1.

ROBERTS, MICHAEL, AND WARREN REISS
1985   Report on Archaeological Investigations off Wellfleet, Mass. for Maritime Explorations, Inc. Prepared by Maritime Archaeological and Historical Research Institute, Bristol, Maine. Submitted to Maritime Explorations, Inc., South Chatham, Massachusetts.

ROBERTS, MICHAEL, JAMES R. REEDY, JR.,
SHEILA CHARLES, AND LOUISE DeCESARE
  1987 Annual Report for the 1986 Permit Period—Archaeological Excavation at WLF-HA-1: The *Whydah* Site. Prepared by Michael Roberts for Maritime Explorations, Inc., South Chatham, Massachusetts. Submitted to Massachusetts Board of Underwater Archaeological Resources, Boston.

RUPPE, REYNOLD, DAN LENIHAN, LARRY MURPHY,
AND WARREN RIESS
  1988 Symposium: Ethics in Nautical Archaeology. *Archaeology in Solution: Proceedings of the Seventeenth Annual Conference on Underwater Archaeology, 1986*:134–136. John W. Foster and Sheli O. Smith, editors. Sacramento, California.

RYAN, MICHAEL
  1983 Barry Clifford's Zany Crew—including JFK Jr.—Prove that Way Down Deep, They're Golddiggers. *People*, 22 August:26–29.

SOCIETY FOR AMERICAN ARCHAEOLOGY (SAA)
  1935 By-Laws and Rules of Procedure of the Society for American Archaeology. *American Antiquity* 2:148–151.
  1961 Four Statements for Archaeology. *American Antiquity* 27(2):137–138.

SOCIETY OF PROFESSIONAL ARCHEOLOGISTS (SOPA)
  1976 Code of Ethics and Standards of Research Performance. *Directory of Professional Archeologists, 1981*:3–6.

VANDERBILT, ARTHUR T. II
  1986 *Treasure Wreck: The Fortunes and Fate of the Pirate Ship* Whydah. Houghton Mifflin, Boston.

WHITE, DAVID FAIRBANK
  1985 The Man Who Discovered a $400 Million Pirate Treasure. *Parade*, 27 January:6–9.

WILDESEN, LESLIE E.
  1984 The Search for an Ethic in Archaeology: An Historical Perspective. In *Ethics and Values in Archaeology*, edited by Ernestene L. Green, pp. 3–12. Free Press, New York.

WISEMAN, JAMES R.
  1989 Archaeology Today: From the Classroom to the Field and Elsewhere. *American Journal of Archaeology* 93:437–444.

RICARDO J. ELIA
OFFICE OF PUBLIC ARCHAEOLOGY
BOSTON UNIVERSITY
675 COMMONWEALTH AVENUE
BOSTON, MASSACHUSETTS 02215

1992. Is it Treasure or a Worthless Piece of Ship? *Historical Archaeology* 26(4):118–123.

PAUL FORSYTHE JOHNSTON

Is It Treasure or a Worthless Piece of Ship?

ABSTRACT

In response to a recent increase in treasure hunting ventures, and the ethical positions taken by professional archaeological associations, the Council of American Maritime Museums and the International Congress of Maritime Museums have developed specific guidelines and recommendations for the collecting and exhibiting of archaeological materials. In particular, objects from commercially exploited archaeological sites are prohibited, to reduce the market in these artifacts and prevent the perception that museums foster and/or condone the looting of archaeological shipwreck sites.

Introduction

For the past several years, the archaeological community has been struggling with the ethical problems relating to treasure salvage and the propriety of professional archaeological involvement with treasure hunting operations (Carrell 1988). Virtually every archaeological association with published ethical guidelines has condemned such activity (Cummings 1986, 1988), but a small minority of archaeologists has opted to work with salvors for a variety of reasons. One vocal member of that minority has obtained the official endorsements of the Advisory Council on Historic Preservation, the Massachusetts Board of Underwater Archaeological Resources, and the National Conference of State Historic Preservation Officers for the work he has undertaken in the waters of Massachusetts (Hamilton 1989, 1990; Beaudry 1990; Elia, this volume).

In response to the concerns of professional archaeologists, some of the largest national and international museum associations have developed positions on the issue, while other museums ignore or are unaware of the issues. This article discusses the various museum positions on treasure hunting and explores some of the issues and possible solutions to what is becoming one of the most significant and controversial topics in the profession.

Museum Types and Associations

As the largest category of collectors in modern society, museums represent the forefront of public policy-making on the issues of what should and should not be acquired, preserved, and exhibited on behalf of the public interest. Insofar as shipwreck materials are concerned, the museum type most often approached with offers is the maritime museum, as might be expected, with its focus upon collecting and interpreting the material culture from the nautical heritage. And so, from the late 1960s up to the mid-1980s, maritime museums around the world cheerfully acquired objects ranging in type from wet, rusty anchors from unidentified wrecksites in local harbors to coral-encrusted ancient Mediterranean amphoras, Caribbean cannons, and precious gold and silver objects from Spanish treasure galleons. Some of the sites were not obscure shipwrecks visited over weekends or vacations by sportdivers, but famous ships with names like *Geldermalsen* (alias "the Nanking Cargo Wreck") and *Atocha*, many of whose contents had been systematically salvaged by professional treasure hunters and sold at the most prominent auction houses in the world (Christie's Amsterdam 1986; Christie's New York 1988; Miller, this volume).

Should these items, representing valuable (if not unique) materials from our national or international maritime heritage (and often located on public lands), be purchased or accepted for donation by museums, or should they be declined on ethical grounds as archaeological materials which had been raised for personal profit and the artifact assemblages split up and sold? What had happened to the vast majority of the artifacts from these sites—especially the wood and other organic materials—which might not be monetarily valuable, but which were precious to historians and archaeologists who were trying to reconstruct the past from limited resources? In many cases, the archaeological contexts for these materials had not been carefully recorded by the divers or treasure salvors, especially those who were under financial pressure from their investors to raise the sea booty as quickly and efficiently as possible. Did art historians care whether an object was from the ship captain's personal sea chest, the vessel's cargo hold, or smuggled in a seaman's bag and stowed in the forecastle, as a scientific archaeological excavation might show? Or were the artistic aspects of the artifacts all that mattered? Some museum directors also questioned the wisdom of declining famous objects offered by wealthy or powerful donors, at the risk of offending them at a time when attendance and public support for museums in general have been declining.

In an effort to resolve some of these issues and formulate a set of guidelines acceptable to all of its member institutions, the Council of American Maritime Museums (CAMM), an association of 48 North American maritime museums, formed an Archaeology Committee of museum directors, curators, and historians. This group was charged with the responsibility for investigating current professional policies, ethics, and standards for archaeological collections. After more than a year of review and discussion, the committee developed a statement that was unanimously adopted by the CAMM membership as a by-law amendment at its Annual Meeting in 1987. The policy reads as follows:

> CAMM member institutions shall adhere to archaeological standards consistent with those of the American Association of Museums/International Congress of Museums (AAM/ICOM), and shall not knowingly acquire or exhibit artifacts which have been stolen, illegally exported from their country of origin, illegally salvaged, or removed from commercially exploited archaeological or historic sites (CAMM 1990).

In essence, the Archaeology Committee's review of professional museum and archaeological standards revealed the unanimous opinion that unscientific excavation for profit and the sale of the archaeological resources recovered were unacceptable, even though they might be permitted by law. It was felt that maritime museums were obliged to adopt a leadership role in this regard and avoid any prospect of supporting or condoning the private commercial exploitation of the public heritage, particularly when these shipwrecks or other submerged cultural resources were located in public waters (cf. AAM 1987). What was found on public property should belong and be available to the public, whether or not laws allowed the salvage to take place. The issue was perceived and handled as an ethical concern, not as a legal matter, and passage of the amendment by museum boards of trustees or the equivalent was made a condition of full voting membership status in CAMM in 1989. Along with the passage of the by-law amendment, CAMM was an outspoken advocate of the Abandoned Shipwreck Act of 1987, which was signed into law by President Reagan in April 1988 (Johnston 1989a, 1989b).

Survey Results

In late 1987, the Executive Council of the International Congress of Maritime Museums (ICMM) formed a Subcommittee on Maritime Archaeology to address many of the same issues. Founded in 1972, the organization now has a membership of ca.300 institutions worldwide, and is the largest professional association of maritime museums today. The ICMM subcommittee was formed of member museum directors, curators, and an academic archaeologist from different countries; its brief was to "complete a survey on existing policies as regards museum acquisitions of objects from underwater archaeological sites and set recommendations for ICMM's position with regards to the acquisition of these objects" (Henderson 1990). This task was completed in late 1989, and the results collated and tabulated for review by the Executive Council at the triannual ICMM meetings in 1990.

At the time of the survey, the ICMM had 284 members. Of that number, 226 members answered the questionnaire, for a response rate of 79.5 percent, although not all members answered all questions. However, the number of respondent institutions with maritime archaeological collections was 87, or 30.6 percent of the members. Some of the more significant results of the survey responses to the 27-item questionnaire are summarized below; all of the results will be published elsewhere.

Archaeological Collections

Of the ICMM museums that hold archaeological collections, 62 percent have 1–100 artifacts and 20 percent have 101–1,000 specimens. Only 13 percent have 1,001–10,000, and 6 percent have more than 10,000 artifacts. This indicates that even for those institutions with archaeological collections, those objects do not represent a major collecting category. The reasons for their collecting were (in descending order): display, research, to protect items from looters, educational purposes, and sale. Most of the items were received from donors rather than museum excavations or purchases. The most popular sorts of artifacts were ship parts and rigging elements, followed by samples of cargo, personal possessions (crew and passenger), "other," items dropped overboard, and lastly, materials from inundated shore sites. Nearly half (48%) of the institutions have published papers in academic or professional journals on their archaeological collections.

Legislative Questions

To the question of the existence of underwater archaeological legislation in various nations, 105 ICMM members responded in the affirmative, but more than one-fourth (n = 29) consider it ineffectual in protecting the resource. The same number (n = 29) stated that legislation did not affect their collecting policies for archaeological specimens. More than 10 percent of the responding institutions (n = 12) did not know whether their countries had legislation in place, or responded in the negative (n = 4). Eight reported that legislation was in preparation.

Internal and External Ethical Policies

Some of the most noteworthy responses came from the questions on internal and external ethical policies. When asked if their institutions had specific policies for collecting materials from cultural heritage sites, 75 of the 105 respondents (71%) stated that they either have no policy or no written policy. Only 30 (29%) have a written policy, and one institution among that number "does not refer to it."

A full third of respondent institutions were unfamiliar with the International Council of Museums' (ICOM) code of ethics, 68 percent were unaware of the International Council on Monuments and Sites (ICOMOS) charter (ICOMOS 1990), and 47 percent were ignorant of the 1970 UNESCO convention. No doubt the fact that 80 percent of the respondents (86 of 108) do not have archaeologists on staff is partially responsible for this lack of knowledge.

Recommendations to the ICMM

At the same time as the presentation of the survey results to the ICMM Executive Council, the subcommittee advised that an archaeological policy be adopted by the general membership of ICMM, forming its recommendations as the following draft resolutions:

1. That ICMM member museums should in regard to collecting policy follow the provisions of the ICOM Code of Professional Ethics, the ICOMOS Charter, and the UNESCO Convention.

2. That ICMM member museums should follow section 3.1 of the ICOM Code of Professional Ethics and that in particular, "each museum authority should adopt and publish a written statement of its collecting policy." Museums with collections derived from underwater archaeological sites should each adopt and publish either a written statement of their general collecting policy or a written collecting policy relating specifically to collections derived from underwater archaeological sites.

3. That ICMM member museums should follow section 3.2 of the ICOM Code of Professional Ethics as it relates to the acquisition of illicit material, and that in particular, "museum[s] should not acquire by purchase objects . . . where . . . their recovery involved the recent unscientific or international destruction or damage of . . . archaeological sites."

4. That ICMM member museums should follow Council of

American Maritime Museums (CAMM) policy and "not knowingly acquire or exhibit artifacts which have been stolen, illegally exported from their country of origin, illegally salvaged, or removed from commercially exploited archaeological or historic sites" in recent times. The words "in recent times" should be read as meaning "since the 1990 Full Congress of ICMM."

5. That ICMM members should report to the responsible authorities any illegal activities at underwater sites or auction or sale of artifacts from illegally excavated underwater sites in their countries.

6. That ICMM members should recognize that artifacts from underwater sites are integral parts of an archaeological finds complex which should stay together for research and display.

7. That ICMM should follow an active policy supporting the above-mentioned international codes on cultural heritage and report illegal activities at underwater sites to the responsible authorities.

8. That ICMM should explore ways whereby more member museums can involve students from tertiary institutions in the use of their underwater archaeological collections for study purposes.

These draft resolutions were presented at the 1990 ICMM Congress to the Executive Council, which recommended that they be followed by the general membership until they can be added to the ICMM by-laws at the next Congress. Still in draft form, it was clear that these guidelines needed some refinement, which was completed in June 1991. Nevertheless, in style and content they represent the strongest and most specific response to date on the matter of museums, ethics, and underwater archaeological resources. It is expected that these resolutions will generate some lively discussion at the next meetings of the ICMM in 1993 at Barcelona, particularly since there have been several recent and flagrant violations of the spirit of the guidelines by member institutions. These include the 1988 purchase of two astrolabes from *Atocha* by a prominent Portuguese maritime museum, and a collaborative agreement between treasure salvors and a British maritime museum, wherein the museum receives one of each artifact type, first refusal of the remainder, and records of the recovery. The salvor retains rights to sell the "unwanted" artifacts (Aked 1989, pers. comm.). And at least one history museum on Cape Cod (not

a CAMM or ICMM member) has just entered into an agreement to exhibit artifacts from *Whydah*, a pirate ship salvaged by treasure hunters beginning in 1983, despite being informed of the ethical issues involved (Colden 1990; Elia 1990, this volume).

Conclusions and Recommendations

It is clear that maritime museums with underwater archaeological collections have a long way to go in regard to their ethics, collecting policies, and international awareness. They must be more cognizant of their local, regional, and national regulations regarding archaeological materials (both maritime and terrestrial), as well as the broad concerns of the greater preservation community, sport divers, and treasure salvors. They need to know how to respond to the widely divergent approaches to submerged cultural resources that characterize these special interest groups, and develop written standards for their own collections and collecting. They will also need to communicate with non-maritime museums as well as the general audiences they serve and foster the preservation ethic through educational programming, exhibits, and publications. Hopefully, through the dissemination of the results of this survey to the general ICMM membership, and as a result of the discussions likely to ensue at the next full ICMM Congress, there will be far greater awareness of and sensitivity to the ethical concerns and policies currently under review for implementation among maritime museums.

There are other issues that will need to be addressed over the next few years, as salvage projects continue to be permitted, if not formally condoned by regulatory agencies. A disturbing new trend has surfaced in the United States, wherein salvors who have obtained permits to recover artifacts from significant shipwrecks later lose interest or financing prior to completing their projects, and simply abandon the ships and associated artifacts of little monetary value. This has happened in Delaware with the wreck of *De Braak*, a British warship, and in Massachusetts with the so-called *General Arnold*. Ownership of both of these wreck assemblages—which include large hull sections requiring extensive conservation—has reverted to the respective states, which are now forced to manage these resources without dedicated funding or staffing commitments. It is ironic that the general public, which has been so fascinated with the idea of treasure hunting and its characteristic free-wheeling spirit of capitalism, is now being forced to pay for the whims and misfortunes of the salvors. It may be anticipated that these artifact assemblages, or what survives of them, will be handed over to museums for collections management in the not-too-distant future, and the likeliest candidates will be maritime museums. How will these institutions respond to the issue of preserving these materials in the public trust, though they may be tainted by the brush of the treasure hunters?

And what of those objects that have already been collected by well-meaning institutions over the past two decades, prior to the recent expressions of concern and resultant ethical policy guidelines? Should they be repatriated to their state or nation of origin? If so, what if their provenance is unknown or unclear, or if there are specimens from several different nations in a single assemblage? And where might they end up if all the recipient museums in the affected countries subscribe to ethical standards as stringent as the CAMM or ICMM guidelines? Perhaps the specimens could be returned to the donors. But what if the donors have moved away, died, or taken tax deductions for their gifts? Alternatively, they might be used for an exhibition on treasure hunting, to display how the activity damages rather than preserves the resources. But here the host institutions for such an exhibit run the risk of public misinterpretation of the message, or antagonism from special-interest groups such as local sportdivers. The objects might also be retained for scientific analysis, possibly of a destructive nature, to learn more about their composition or origins, in an effort to recover at least some sort of useful information about them. In all likelihood, they will probably be shoved into a back corner of the museum's storage area and left for the next curatorial generation to manage. In

other words, they may be treated as some sort of second-class artifact unworthy of long-term preservation—as worthless pieces of ship. These and other issues must be addressed soon, if museums are to properly fulfill their public and professional obligations.

REFERENCES

AMERICAN ASSOCIATION OF MUSEUMS (AAM)
1987   Statement on H.R. 74, The Abandoned Shipwreck Act, 21 April 1987. Submitted by the American Association of Museums to the Subcommittee on Oceanography of the Committee on Merchant Marine and Fisheries, U.S. House of Representatives. (Serial Set No. 100–17:170–173.) U.S. Government Printing Office, Washington, DC.

BEAUDRY, MARY C.
1988   Looting by Any Other Name: Archaeological Ethics and the Looting Problem. *Society for Historical Archaeology Newsletter* 23(1):13–14.

CARRELL, TONI L.
1988   Ethics vs. Commercial Exploitation: What's It Worth to the Future? Paper presented at the 54th Annual Meeting of the Society for American Archaeology, Atlanta, Georgia.

CHRISTIE'S AMSTERDAM
1986   *The Nanking Cargo, Chinese Export Porcelain and Gold*. Christie's Amsterdam B.V., Amsterdam, The Netherlands.

CHRISTIE'S NEW YORK
1988   *Gold and Silver of the* Atocha *and* Santa Margarita. Christie's, New York.

COLDEN, ANNE
1990   Museum to Show *Whydah* Artifacts. *Cape Cod Times*, 3 December:1.

COUNCIL OF AMERICAN MARITIME MUSEUMS (CAMM)
1990   By-laws of the Council of American Maritime Museums, Inc. Article VI, Section 3: *Archaeological Standards*. Council of American Maritime Museums, Mystic, Connecticut.

CUMMINGS, CALVIN R.
1986   A Matter of Ethics. In Underwater Archaeology: The Proceedings of the Fourteenth Conference on Underwater Archaeology, edited by Calvin R. Cummings. *Special Publication* No. 7:v–x. Fathom Eight, San Marino, California.
1988   National Professional Standards and Guidelines for Underwater Archaeology. *Underwater Archaeology*

Proceedings from the Society for Historical Archaeology Conference 1988:46–52. James P. Delgado, editor. Society for Historical Archaeology, California, Pennsylvania.

ELIA, RICARDO J.
1990 Pirates Ahoy. *Boston Globe*, 10 September:1.

HAMILTON, CHRISTOPHER E.
1989 The Need to Clarify Ethical Issues Related to the *Whydah* Project. Statement presented 5 January 1990 to the SHA Executive Committee at the Annual Meeting of the Society for Historical Archaeology Conference on Historical and Underwater Archaeology, Phoenix, Arizona.
1990 Shipwrecks and the Private Sector. Paper presented at the 44th National Trust for Historic Preservation Conference, Session No. 2, Maritime Track, "Shipwrecks: Preservation, Ethics, and Economics," Charleston, South Carolina.

HENDERSON, GRAEME
1991 The Acquisition of Objects from Underwater Archaeological Sites. Draft Policy Statement and Report of the Subcommittee on Maritime Archaeology to the ICMM, 28 December 1990. Report on file with the author.

INTERNATIONAL COUNCIL ON MONUMENTS AND SITES (ICOMOS)
1990 Charter for the Protection and Management of the Archaeological Heritage. International Committee on Archaeological Heritage Management, ICOMOS, Washington, D.C.

JOHNSTON, PAUL F.
1989a Between the Devil and the Dark Blue Sea: Archaeology and the Council of American Maritime Museums. *Underwater Archaeology Proceedings from the Society for Historical Archaeology Conference 1989*: 148–149. J. Barto Arnold III, editor. Society for Historical Archaeology, California, Pennsylvania.
1989b Knowledge: The Real Treasure. *Sea History* 51:6–7.

PAUL FORSYTHE JOHNSTON
CURATOR OF MARITIME HISTORY
NATIONAL MUSEUM OF AMERICAN HISTORY
SMITHSONIAN INSTITUTION
WASHINGTON, D.C. 20560

1989. State and Their Shipwrecks. In *Underwater Archaeology Proceedings from the Society for Historical Archaeology*, J. Barto Arnold III, editor, pp. 35–40.

SYMPOSIUM

ANNE G. GIESECKE

States and Their Shipwrecks

The Abandoned Shipwreck Act of 1987 was signed into law on April 28, 1988. The purpose of the Act was to give states clear authority to control the excavation of state land for any purpose including shipwrecks. The impetus for the Act had come from two areas: one, a concern to protect historic shipwrecks, and the other, multiple-use conflicts in the coastal zone impacting sensitive natural habitats, fishing grounds, and mineral development.

The Act confirms the state's title to abandoned shipwrecks that are embedded in state submerged land, in coralline formations protected by the state, and those of National Register quality on or in state submerged land (Giesecke 1987a).

I drafted the bill in 1982. During the last seven years that I have worked on the bill, I have thought a great deal about existing state efforts and about implementation of the Act. This paper briefly lists some major concerns and considerations for states during the development and review of their historic preservation laws and submerged cultural resource management plans.

The paper is divided into five sections with a summary at the end: existing state programs, planning elements, program implementation, economics, and enforcement.

Existing State Programs

The number of administrative and management alternatives for submerged cultural resources has been as numerous as the states themselves. Some states manage submerged cultural resources as part of their general historic preservation legislation, and 30 states have legislation specific to cultural resources on submerged lands (Giesecke 1985).

All states include submerged resources in State Plans developed for the Department of the Interior. However, management of submerged resources in most states is only the minimum effort necessary to comply with state and federal legislation pertaining to development projects. Compliance efforts will not be discussed.

On the other hand, some states have developed management efforts or programs that highlight submerged resources. This emphasis is especially true in states where a particular find has prompted the program. The submerged cultural resource management alternatives used by states are on a continuum from decentralized volunteer programs to centralized administrative control. The following is a brief review of management alternatives.

State management efforts have included:
Volunteer based programs; South Carolina, Vermont
Preserve systems; Vermont, Michigan, Florida
Focus on one project; Virginia, Maine, Louisiana
Literature search and survey; Texas, California, Virginia
Administrative program; North Carolina
Commercial salvage; 18 states.

South Carolina revised its general salvage legislation in 1982 and established a permit system that has encouraged a volunteer sport diver program. Three types of licenses may be issued: Hobby Licenses for recreational diving; Search and Salvage Licenses for remote sensing survey and diagnostic artifact collection; and Salvage Licenses for excavation. Hundreds of Hobby Licenses have been issued, and the monthly reports sent to the state provide a growing picture of the state's resource base. The 1740 Brown's Ferry was identified through the license process, and the site became the focus for a major project that drew both state and private money. The state is in the position to maintain a leadership role with sport divers as volunteers doing state surveys.

Vermont has developed a more decentralized volunteer program for the study of its maritime heritage. The 1975 legislative mandate to preserve, protect and interpret the state's underwater historic resources did not include personnel or a budget. The result of state-sport diver cooperation was the Champlain Maritime Society, founded in 1980. The Champlain Maritime Society is a private not-for-profit tax-exempt corporation, and has, in cooperation with the Division of Historic Preservation, carried out the underwater research program of the state of Vermont. The organization is composed of historians, divers, lawyers, doctors, non-diving archaeologists, and other interested persons. The Society is funded through membership fees, state Department of the Interior Historic Preservation grants,

and donations. The program has been very successful, with a dozen projects to its credit, but recent fiscal concerns emphasize the need for a more stable economic base. The approach suits the size of the state, the type of resource base, and the interests of the population.

In 1985, Vermont instituted its Underwater Historic Preserve System. According to Arthur Cohn, three fully-documented shipwreck sites were selected and moorings were established. Divers tie up at surface moorings and descend to the wreck; a sign asks for their cooperation in diving safety and protection of the wreck. The mooring system prevents anchor damage to the wrecks, and the wrecks act as a focus of public education and as a tourist dollar attraction. Responsibility overshadows vandalism.

In 1980, Michigan passed legislation to establish Great Lakes bottomlands preserves for recreational or historical values. Although the state has not funded underwater archaeology, a system for the protection of shipwrecks has been established. The state Underwater Salvage Committee advises on policy and local committees advise on management. Committees for the five established preserves include representation of a wide range of interests including state and county management, history, parks and recreation, sport diving, charter boat operations, marinas, restaurants and hotels, and commercial salvage. Local enthusiasm encouraged by local economic benefit of the preserves has made the program successful.

Florida has five underwater reserve areas including John Pennekamp State Park and *Urca de Lima* Underwater Archaeological Preserve. Florida has been a draw for adventuring sport divers since the 1950's. The state is making an effort to balance the need for natural and cultural resource preservation with the need for recreation and tourism.

Virginia's legislation for underwater resources passed in 1976. In 1978, the Yorktown Shipwreck Archaeology Project began and has remained the focus of the state's underwater program. Underwater archaeology has received little or no state budget support for personnel or program. The Yorktown project has been funded by federal grants, private sector grants, corporate donations and two volunteer organizations. The volunteer organizations are The Yorktown Maritime Heritage Foundation and The Ship Committee. These organizations have helped raise money through donations and have produced publications about the project. Raising money for a particular project has been easier than for a general program or survey but has limited use in the evaluation of the state's resource base.

Maine followed much the same project-oriented pattern with limited state support for excavation of the Revolutionary Warship *Defense* during the late 1970's, and since then has maintained some level of effort. At about the same time, Louisiana responded to the discovery and excavation of the 18th century *El Nuevo Constante* but did not follow through with development of a program.

Texas, California, and Virginia have made significant efforts during the last five years to establish a data base from historical records of shipwrecks in state waters. California and Texas have recently made efforts to do field surveys and verify these site locations. The primary purpose of this approach is to facilitate planning and develop decision-making. An additional benefit is the ability to identify research priorities.

North Carolina, where legislation was passed in 1967, has taken an administrative approach to the management of underwater resources. The primary purpose of the Archaeology and Historic Preservation Section is to interact with other state agencies, such as the Attorney General and the Division of Purchase and Contract. While meeting state responsibilities under that National Historic Preservation Act for environmental review, National Register review, and permitting, the state has directed exceptional energy to the survey of submerged resources by state staff. Decisions about permits, port development, and dredging activities are made most efficiently when on-the-ground information is available. No other office or group has taken the responsibility to collect this information. As a result of its survey focus, North Carolina has evaluated more than 150 located wrecks as being historic. Although state money is the base for such an approach, that money has been supplemented by close cooperation with the National Park Service, Corps of Engineers, East Carolina University, and independent sport divers. This approach has been subject to disruption by state budget cuts.

Eighteen state laws specifically allow for the commercial recovery of state-owned shipwrecks. States without legislation specific to shipwrecks have issued commercial permits under their state contracting authority. Remember that not all state-owned shipwrecks are considered to have historic value. Some shipwrecks may be embedded but not historic, and some may be valued as artificial reefs, or may be located in areas where fishing or oil and gas development are more important.

Since 1983, commercial contracts have been written in 10 states: California, Delaware, Florida, Guam, Massachusetts, Michigan, New Jersey, Northern Mariana Islands, South Carolina, and Washington. The 10 additional states with authority are Louisiana, Maryland, Mississippi, Montana, New Hampshire, North Carolina, Puerto Rico, Rhode Island, Vermont, and Virginia. Commercial contracts are discussed under the subheading Economics.

Planning Elements

The creation or expansion of a state resource management system to consider shipwreck resources requires the administrator to apply basic planning concepts. The objective of the planning process is to provide an integrated, reasoned course of action whereby resource management problems and objectives are identified and prioritized. Resource management, then, is the sum total of a varying number of discreet activities, each of which demands the separate application of an organized thought process.

To develop a plan the administrator should state in as much detail as is possible:

a) methodology/methodologies to be used (how);

b) timing and frequency of action (what, when, how often);

c) responsibility (who);

d) personnel requirements (how many);

e) dollar requirements (how much and when);

f) information lacking and a statement of priority for information acquisition including methodology, anticipated benefits and cost (i.e. management studies);

g) requirement for training, safety, enforcement, or public/staff information programs;

h) an identification of decision points contained in the plan, the person having authority to make the decision, and guidelines for decision-making; and

i) how the plan's effectiveness will be measured and monitored.

The planning for a particular activity requires more detailed information. The activity might be the establishment of a state museum or a permit application for the excavation of a shipwreck.

In addition to the consideration of the above elements, a plan for a particular activity includes:

a) a statement of the problem or objective;

b) identification of an appropriate administrative level;

c) identification of relevant concurrent activities by state administrators or in the geographic area of the project;

d) procedures for public input and a statement of public benefit;

e) a design of the plan which considers:

1) the extent of the required information not already contained in a known data base;

2) the availability of required knowledge and technology;

3) the time available for the activity;

4) the availability of financial and personnel resources;

5) cost; and

6) factors including:

*required scale of information analysis;

*type of information required;

*required accuracy or confidence level;

*size of area to be surveyed;

*methodology selected for mapping and classification;

*time available for survey;

*length of field season;

*accessibility of site;

*logistic support requirements;

*availability of specialist expertise;

*monitoring requirements (decision points); and

*format and timing of intermediate and final products.

The detail and scope of the information required should fit the detail and scope of the proposed work. For example, the application for a permit to do a remote sensing survey using side-scan sonar should not require a discussion of the long term curation of artifacts because no artifacts will be recovered. Before a plan for a resource or project can be developed, the purpose of that plan or project must be clearly stated and justified.

Program Implementation

Passage of the Abandoned Shipwreck Act has raised people's level of awareness about the political process in the management of all submerged resources. This increased awareness, particularly in the sport diving industry and community, is reflected by new pressures on state legislatures. Historic shipwrecks have received much attention but related concerns are also receiving more attention. Some related concerns include: beach access for divers, more boat ramps, fishing rights, the use of dive flags, the creation of underwater parks for natural or cultural resources, and the creation of artificial reefs.

Managers can take advantage of this new awareness by anticipating demands and having well-planned proposals for action. By making the planning for the protection of historic shipwrecks an integrated part of the state's resource planning processes, the manager will strengthen the administrative and budget position of the program and the resource.

The more information that is available to the public about what resources are being protected and why, the broader will be the popular base that will help enforce the laws and protect the resource. A popular base is also important when arguing for state money for support activities such as the development of a state data bank or conservation laboratory.

Scarce resources will require that the manager use as efficiently as possible existing state systems for the dissemination of information about historic shipwreck resources. State permit and licensing programs may be useful. For example, boater registration programs and fishing licenses can provide mailing lists and mechanisms for the dissemination of information. Cooperation with the state Fish and Game Dept., or harbor police is important for effective enforcement. Working closely with other state programs such as port authorities or fishing and artificial reef programs may save time and resources.

The establishment of artificial reefs and the directing of sport divers to those areas may take pressure off historic sites or fragile natural resources while encouraging the development of the area's tourist industry. The state's artificial reef plan is a good place to start.

Considering shipwrecks as artificial reefs invites a question. When is a shipwreck no longer a shipwreck? One answer to that question is to say that the Abandoned Shipwreck Act took certain shipwrecks out of the admiralty system and distinguished between shipwrecks that are valued as part of modern commerce and those that are valued for environmental and historical reasons. Another level of answer to the question is that when a shipwreck has lost its integrity and provenience, it is no longer a shipwreck but a scatter of artifacts that may or may not have historic significance. That is to say, not all shipwreck sites are created equal. Not all shipwreck sites should be treated the same. What is historic and what is a shipwreck site require careful thought and decision-making. Once a decision has been made, planning for the protection or use of the site is necessary. Planning alternatives may be as varied as the sites themselves.

Survey and planning efforts are important parts of cultural resource management. Literature searches and field work collect the data that the manager needs to make decisions. Where and when one does research should depend on the anticipated benefit from that research. Research priorities might be set by many factors, including the planned disturbance of an area or its anticipated historic significance.

Research designs should match the scale of the research question. Reference to Corps of Engineers river basin studies might be the place to start in studying trade patterns, or local folklife studies might provide initial information about local shipbuilding.

Planners and managers should be particularly careful not to draw an imaginary line at the water's edge and exclude shore facilities from underwater studies and underwater areas from shore-based studies. Ships have always had ports, and ports have been known to sink below the surface.

Economics

In recent years the public funding of cultural resource projects has declined. However, some money is still available for underwater projects. Money is available from profit, not-for-profit, and publicly-affiliated organizations (Giesecke 1987b)

At the same time that federal and state funding programs have been cut, the demand for shipwreck resources has increased. Development has been very rapid, especially near water.

Two federal funding sources that have awarded money to not-for-profit groups are the National Science Foundation and the National Endowment for the Humanities. The National Science Foundation has funded work by George Bass in the Aegean Sea on wrecks dating back 3,000 years. The National Endowment for the Humanities has funded work by John Broadwater in the James River, Virginia on Revolutionary War wrecks. These agencies require that professional archaeologists head the projects and that the data collected on the shipwreck be used to answer research questions about the past.

State Endowment for the Humanities programs and State Historic Preservation Offices also have made grant funds available for shipwreck projects, with similar requirements for archaeologists and research questions.

As stated earlier, federal and state sources have less money to distribute now than they have had in the past. The result has been a number of important private sector initiatives. One of the most successful ways to finance the excavation of historic shipwrecks and recover the archaeological data necessary to tell the ship's story has been participant funding.

The best example of participant funding is the Center for Field Research and its affiliate Earthwatch. These are not-for-profit organizations which seek to increase public understanding and support of field research in the sciences and humanities. The Center receives proposals, conducts in-house and independent peer review, and recommends proposals to Earthwatch for support via participant funding, wherein qualified amateur volunteers who pay a share of the project's costs are recruited to assist in the gathering of field data.

Earthwatch is now the third largest source of private funds for research; the organization contributed $1.8 million to over 100 research projects in 1987. Earthwatch and the Center have supported some 20 underwater archaeology projects since 1971. According to Brian Rosborough of the Center,

> Volunteer field workers have responded enthusiastically to underwater archaeology projects. In addition to the obvious value of extra hands in the field, the financial, educational, and public relations benefits of participant funding have been well established by the success of the Center and Earthwatch.

The groups and projects that have been most successful have been those that understand and carefully market their product. There are some important questions to ask about a project before asking for support.

1) What is your product? Is it research, education, recreation, increased tourism, or economic profit?

2) How is your project priced compared with other projects or products? Are you competing with museums or amusement parks?

3) Does the project fit with the objectives, program, and structure of your organization? That is, will you be able to actually do what you propose?

4) What product (research, education, etc.) goes back to the participant, individual, business or community that helped?

Finally, private sector initiatives like those introduced here are finding the resources and making significant contributions to the study of maritime history. To continue to be successful, organizations will have to be accountable for the materials and services they receive. Reports must be written, popular articles published, and thank you's sent to acknowledge everyone's contribution. Participant funding and projects have a far greater potential for direct benefit than dependence on taxes collected and then given out as grants by state and federal governments.

As mentioned above, commercial profit private sector operations are legal in some states, and states have written contracts for the excavation of shipwreck sites. Contracts have been implemented in Delaware, Florida, Massachusetts, Michigan, Northern Mariana Islands, South Carolina, and Washington State.

Operations receiving these permits and hoping to make a profit excavating shipwrecks are often structured as limited partnerships. These operations have been characterized by less than 24 share holders investing less than $100,000 each. The government does not require these companies to make public disclosure statements. However, in the last few years the millions of dollars required to look for and excavate some historic shipwrecks have required these companies to go public. None of these companies has shown a profit, although a few investors, on one occasion in Florida, have gotten a positive return on their investments. Changing tax laws, environmental laws and increasing regulations will mean that profit operations will have to continue to adapt if they are to survive at all.

However, if contracts are written, they should carefully define what is to be kept by the state and what is to be kept by the salvor. After the state has given serious consideration to the site and its public benefit, it may be determined that the priority is to keep the collection of artifacts together for the purposes of study and conservation.

The sale of any public assets such as buildings or land, or the deaccessioning of any part of a museum collection, brings up a series of arguments for and against those actions. Consistency within the state system for the disposition of state property and the clear public benefit that must derive from the disposition are the manager's primary concern and responsibility.

Archaeologists are generally opposed to the sale of artifacts from historically significant sites, dry or wet. Museums, collectors, and the state treasurer are all interested parties. The manager should have a procedure for consulting with all interested parties before making a decision.

Financing alternatives to the division of the artifacts include: the sale by the state of copyrights for books, films, replicas, or logo; user fees; entrance fees; and the sale of slag products that result from conservation activities or of sediment recovered from the site.

Accountability to its citizens should be the state's primary concern when balancing the interests of any private party with the interest of the public as a whole. The public benefit of any state decision should be clear.

Commercial projects have recovered artifacts but have not been implemented so as to successfully recover archaeological or historical data. The application of private profit sector money to underwater projects is the most challenging issue that a manager will face.

Two areas where private money has been successfully applied are in the creation of museums and the development of the tourist industry.

The establishment of a museum is often spurred by a large private donation of a building, money, or artifact collection. The museum may then become a focus for other activities such as meetings or film festivals. These activities may also enhance the tourist economy of an area. Museums for underwater artifacts may also need conservation facilities.

Conservation requirements may be met in-house or by a state or regional laboratory. A commercial component of the laboratory operation will contribute to its financial stability. Work may be done for private individuals or for other states.

Public use of museum and laboratory facilities contributes to the public benefit and awareness of the state's efforts. The public will be more willing to contribute tax dollars or private donations when they see some personal benefit.

Just as museums are visible to the public, and so are parks. The preservation efforts in Florida, Michigan, and Vermont indicate the economic and historic preservation success of designating special use areas or underwater parks.

Underwater parks as described in the Program section may be large or small. The point is that parks become an economic focus. Tourist dollars can enhance the overall economy of the state, act as a source of private donations for projects, and provide an audience for the state's education efforts. The most successful preserve system is in Michigan.

Alger County is one example. As a result of the establishment of the Alger Underwater Preserve the gross revenue of Alger County went from $1.4 million a year to $6.8 million a year in 1984.

Benefits go to a variety of establishments including motels, cabins, camp grounds, restaurants, charter operators, dive shops, marinas, boat and equipment renters, and service stations.

The final and most basic economic consideration is the cost of state administration of a program. The type of permit program developed by a state should be dependent on what the state is willing to spend for administration and enforcement.

Enforcement

The keys to effective enforcement include: appropriate size of the administrative unit; consistent law; voluntary compliance; training; and trade.

Administrative Unit

At the national level the Abandoned Shipwreck Act delegated administration of certain shipwreck resources to the states. The state and state officers (usually from the Fish and Game Dept.) are the current administrative units. However, states vary considerably in size and population.

State laws, which require easy access to state officials such as in South Carolina, work because the state official can reasonably drive to anywhere in the state. However, a comparable state law in New York, Texas, or California would not work at the state level for two reasons. One reason it would not work is that the ratio of state officials (usually one) to the population is too great to allow access; the second reason is that the state is geographically too big to allow the official to be everywhere in a short time. Larger, more populous states may need to delegate authority to smaller administrative units such as counties.

Consistent Law

There are two areas where states should review their existing and proposed legislation for clarity and compatibility with the national Abandoned Shipwreck Act of 1987. Those areas are the definition of the resource using the concepts abandoned and embedded and giving public notice of the location of the state's shipwreck resources.

When reviewing the state system, the manager must keep in mind that there are three basic tools: laws, regulations, and guidelines. Laws are the most general, the least flexible, and the most difficult tools to change. Regulations also have enforcement potential, are easier to change than laws, and can provide the detail necessary to make a system work. Guidelines may provide even more detail including examples and explanation of the law and regulations, and may be written for a broad public audience. Guidelines may be issued at any time and without the formal public review required for laws and regulations. Guidelines may be used to reflect new thinking on a subject and be the first response to the public need for information about the state program.

In order for the delegation of authority from the federal government to the states to work, the delegation must be consistent with the overall state administrative and enforcement structure. In particular, the state's cultural resources laws should have an internal consistency. For example, to be enforceable, permit requirements and penalty provisions for wet and dry resources should be comparable.

Each system of state law is unique, but some of the areas of common concern may be given generic names. Take for example the state's Administrative Procedures Act, Freedom of Information Act, Environmental Protection Act, Wetlands Act, Water Right's Act, Contracting Authority, and Penalties Provisions. Inconsistency within the state system could result in a declaration by state court that the law is unconstitutional, or that all or some of the law and its procedures are invalid.

In addition to the internal consistency of state laws, state consistency with certain areas of federal legislation is necessary. For example, states must conform to the applicable regulations of the Corps of Engineers, Department of Transportation, Department of the Interior, and Department of Commerce. Inconsistency between state and federal law could result in a violation of federal law, a loss of federal funds, or the inability to enforce certain provisions of state law.

Florida experienced problems in 1987 when the state court found that the provisions of the state law written in 1967 describing the permit system for underwater exploration and excavation were not consistent with the state's Administrative Procedures Act or with the Corps of Engineers review process and permitting authority. The procedures were revised.

State administrators are advised to work closely with the state's Attorney General's office in the development of laws and regulations for the management of shipwreck resources to insure consistency and enforceability of the system. Consistency with adjacent states may also be critical to program management and effective enforcement.

Voluntary Compliance

The most cost-effective enforcement strategy is voluntary compliance. Voluntary compliance will work if people value what is being regulated and understand the purpose for regulating it.

Education is the key to voluntary compliance. Education has two components, the dissemination of information and training. The importance of the dissemination of information was presented in the Program section, and the importance of volunteer project financing was presented in the Economics section. Here we will briefly review the status of training.

The role of the non-archaeologist in the discovery and preservation of our nation's cultural heritage on land is impressive. The April 1985 Society for American Archaeology 50th Anniversary Issue cites many examples of private corporations and individuals such as John D. Rockefeller, Jr. and the Santa Fe Laboratory of Anthropology; Mr. and Mrs. Heard and the Heard Museum in Phoenix; and the work of the Amerind and Heye Foundations.

The role of less wealthy but more numerous individuals is exemplified by groups like the Archaeological Societies of Ontario and Manitoba in Canada and the societies of Arkansas, New Mexico, and New Hampshire in the United States. These three states have certification programs which recognize a variety of skill levels and responsibilities for individuals under the state's preservation programs. Land certification programs may provide appropriate precedents and information for use in the review and development of diver certification programs.

Today many groups give certificates for diving expertise and organize wreck diving and archaeological diving activities. Scouts have badges; colleges and universities run certification programs and field school projects; dive clubs, dive shops, and even individuals "certify" people. But the largest certifying organizations are the Professional Association of Diving Instructors (PADI), the National Association of Underwater Instructors (NAUI), and the Young Men's Christian Association (YMCA).

In general, all of the certification programs have the following components: classroom and hand-on experience; subject material including the history and structure of ships; laws; ecological and ethical values; mapping and recovery techniques; use of equipment; conservation of artifacts; safety; navigation; and special dive skills such as penetration and zero visibility work.

NAUI covers these subjects under two courses: underwater hunting and collecting and wreck diving. PADI covers these subjects under two courses: research diver and wreck diver. YMCA covers these subjects under two courses: archaeological diver and wreck diver. YMCA has the most formal and complete diver certification in these areas. However, for all three organizations, instructors for most archaeology diving courses have not had any formal training in archaeology.

Training is becoming an important management tool and component of state programs. For example, the Maryland legislation states in Chapter 503, 5-611.1(I)(1),

> The Trust shall establish an educational program for the training of interested members of the public in the identification and registration of submerged archaeological historic property, and certify those who have successfully completed such training . . .

However, a word of caution concerning the incursion of liability is necessary. The judicial trend is to hold states liable for the safety of their citizens and certifying organizations responsible for their instructors. According to Alan Cleveland, an attorney and sport diver,

> In 1985 alone, two lawsuits involving diver fatalities in separate incidents have led to out-of-court settlements of over $1.5 million each. Dive shops and instructors are now finding it difficult to obtain affordable liability insurance or coverage at any price. As a general proposition, once it is established that instructors in any activity or profession may be held liable for the (under) performance of their charges, certifying organizations are the next target for legal liability--especially if the organization has 'deeper pockets' than the individual instructor. I predict the time is not far off when organizations undertaking to award diver certifications will be called upon to legally defend their courses and methods of instruction and standards of safety in cases of diver

fatalities. And the larger one's role in this certification process, the greater the potential exposure to such claims.

Divers have certification programs with an interest in archaeology. The increasing interest in diving and the increasing recognition of a class of wrecks which are historic means that it is time to review certification programs and incorporate the activities of divers with their onshore counterparts in the study of local history. The threat of legal suit over liability means that the review and coordination of archaeological diving activities must be multidisciplinary enough to include all appropriate concerns. Good quality archaeological skills should be taught, but safety and good diving skills are as important.

The diving industry, archaeologists, and the states will need to work together to design certification programs that meet the needs and responsibilities of all parties.

Trade

As carefully as the historical or environmental value of shipwrecks may be taught, others will have different values for aesthetic or economic reasons. Hence, the domestic and international trade in cultural properties. Notably, the only claim against the United States under the Cultural Properties Act concerns Canada and may include some artifacts from the Great Lakes.

Education is again the best strategy, but enforcement is necessary. The prioritization of sites and geographic areas is important. Cooperative strategies among states and with Canada and Mexico should be planned and implemented. Effective enforcement will reinforce the state's accountability with its citizens as guardian of the public interest.

Summary

The purpose of this paper has been to highlight certain concepts that state managers should consider in the management of submerged resources.

State management alternatives should be considered after evaluating the size and administrative structure of the state, the type of resource base, and the interests of the population.

State managers must make clear statements of objectives and procedures. Project planning should be done in the context of other state cultural and natural resources. The questions of who, what, where, when, and why all need to be answered before planning and project evaluation can proceed efficiently.

State managers must build a popular support base for successful programs. At the state level they must work effectively with state managers responsible for tourism, fishing, boating, and other offices. Joint application of common planning concepts such as activity zones may help to integrate area planning. Outreach is necessary to state legislatures and the individuals in their districts who must understand the program before they will fund it.

The financing of an effective program is dependent on state philosophical as well as financial support. The key is a diversified funding base that may shift proportionally over time without disrupting the program. State, federal, volunteer, profit, and non-profit monies are all required.

To be enforceable, the state law must be consistent with the federal law, and, within the state, other parts of the state code. Compatible systems in adjacent states may facilitate program development.

The overriding test of the states' efforts will be the accountability of the states to the public. What have you done for them with their money? Cultural and fiscal responsibility are both necessary in the management of resources, especially submerged resources.

REFERENCES

GIESECKE, ANNE G.

1985   The Best in State Historic Shipwreck Programs. In *Proceedings of the Sixteenth Conference on Underwater Archaeology*, pp. 138-141. Boston

1987a   Shipwrecks: The Past in the Present. *Coastal Management* 15:179-196.

1987b   Creative Financing and Project Management. In *Underwater Archaeology Proceedings from the Society for Historical Archaeology Conference*, pp. 12-13. Savannah.

ANNE G. GIESECKE
1001 WILSON BLVD.
ARLINGTON, VIRGINIA 22209

1998. The Abandoned Shipwreck Act 1988 to 1998. In *Underwater Archaeology*, Lawrence E. Babits, Catherine Fach, and Ryan Harris, editors, pp. 111–114.

ANNE G. GIESECKE

The Abandoned Shipwreck Act 1988 to 1998

Introduction

The Abandoned Shipwreck Act (ASA) of 1987 became law in 1988; this review offers a then and now perspective. Current issues are briefly sketched in an effort to stimulate the reader's interest in helping to continue to improve shipwreck management. Issues are more complex today than in 1988, but the bottom line is that shipwreck management is much better now. A review of the 10 years that the Abandoned Shipwreck Act has been in place shows some commendable accomplishments. In 1988, the ASA clarified state entitlement to abandoned shipwrecks that are embedded, embedded in coralline formations, or eligible for inclusion in the National Register of Historic Places.

What we have seen since 1988 is that states with shipwreck programs in place before the law was enacted were able to enhance their programs. States that valued their underwater resources found that, with the increased legal certainty afforded by the ASA, they could put more money into programs for interpretation and protection and less into litigation. States with little interest in their shipwreck resources prior to 1988, conversely, maintained this indifference. Here, "state" is meant to include states, territories and possessions of the United States. Indeed, the fear of ASA opponents that states would go into the treasure hunting business to the loss of both resource protection and free enterprise proved unfounded. A primary function of the legislative debate proved to be the education of states and the general public about the value of the resource base. Some examples of the improved condition of the management and protection of submerged cultural resources follow.

In 1988, only 27 states had laws specifically addressing their underwater resources. Now, all states have evaluated their legal systems as they apply to underwater resources and, where necessary, have modified their laws. Only 18 state laws allow compensation for private sector recovery; notably 13 of those were in place before 1988. All states now include underwater resources in their state historic-preservation plans. In 1988, only 36 underwater sites were listed in the National Register of Historic Places, now there are 577. In 1988, only Florida had a state underwater park; now dozens of states have parks.

As to the cost of litigation, where states previously faced 30 to 40 salvor/admiralty claims a year before the ASA, the last seven years have seen the admiralty system deal with only three states and four cases. A selective chronology of critical events in the history of the ASA is shown below.

Chronology

In 1236, the English government developed the basis for what is today's admiralty law to reward salvors who recover ships, cargos, and lives from peril at sea with a payment from the vessel owner. In the 1960's, SCUBA equipment made underwater areas accessible to a broad range of people. George Bass and Peter Throckmorton began working to have shipwrecks recognized as legitimate archaeological sites. In 1960-1961, sport divers put two sites in Lake Champlain on the list of National Historic Landmarks: the American Revolutionary War ships sunk at Valcour Bay and the War of 1812 warships sunk at Plattsburg Bay.

In 1963 Colorado became the first state to pass a law specific to the ownership of abandoned shipwrecks on state submerged lands as part of a review of their water rights legislation. That same year, gold coins washing up on a Florida beach led to the discovery of the 1715 Spanish Plate Fleet. Four years later, Florida passed a law to manage shipwrecks.

In 1971 Mel Fisher and his company, Treasure Salvors, Inc., discovered the *Atocha* from the

1662 Spanish Plate Fleet. Seven years later, in 1978, Mel Fisher's company Cobb Coin, Inc., claimed the 1715 Spanish Plate Fleet in federal court. The following year, bills were introduced in the U.S. Congress to give the federal government ownership of shipwrecks buried in state land. Archaeologists largely settled their debate over the scientific merits of nautical archaeology and refocused their attention on the fight with salvors over cultural values and life-style issues.

In 1982, ownership of the *Atocha* was awarded to Treasure Salvors, Inc., by the Supreme Court because it sank beyond Florida state waters. At virtually the same time, the U.S. District court for the Southern District of Florida awarded ownership of the 1715 Plate Fleet to Cobb Coin, Inc., threatening the viability of state law. Anne Giesecke then drafted the Abandoned Shipwreck Act to decide the conflict of jurisdiction between the federal court and state governments in favor of the states.

In 1983, the U.S. Congress became the forum for resolving this conflict. Archaeologists and salvors continued their debate but did not control or own the resource as do the court and states. Anne Giesecke helped bring sport divers into the debate separate from salvors and archaeologists. Testimony was collected from groups representing about 2 million sport divers, about 200 underwater archaeologists and the few salvors.

In 1985, Dr. Robert Ballard proved new technologies and located the RMS *Titanic* sunk in 1912. Concerns were expressed about the management of shipwrecks in international waters as the era of deep-water technology and discoveries began. The *Titanic* Maritime Memorial Act of 1985 was passed in an effort to respect the integrity of the shipwreck.

Then in 1987, the *Central America*, which sank in 1857, was discovered. Concerns were raised about the management of shipwrecks in the deep waters of the United States beyond state waters. The Abandoned Shipwreck Act of 1987 subsequently became law in 1988. Abandonment was defined using the traditional admiralty standards — passage of time and a lack of effort to

maintain ownership. The National Park Service published its "Guidelines" for the management of shipwrecks in 1990. In litigation between the salvors and the insurance companies over the *Central America*, the federal court determined in 1992 that abandonment can only be found on the basis of an express renunciation of ownership — affirmative abandonment — and that technological possession of the wreck rather than physical possession is valid.

Discussion

Clearly, shipwrecks are now recognized as valuable cultural resources. Unfortunately, the law and management of shipwrecks have become a microcosm of the debates over greater social issues driven by coastal crowding and changing technology. The debates fall into three categories: environmental, technological, and territorial (property rights).

Environmental Management

The ASA was written because the states needed title to shipwrecks to control excavation of state land for any purpose. The states already had clear jurisdiction over the recovery of all natural resources including sand, gravel, minerals, oil and gas, and fishing including trawling. Treasure hunters were dynamiting coral reefs to look for wrecks and using prop-wash to blast sand; in the process they were destroying fragile fish-nursery areas. State resources were also threatened by the dredging of endangered species habitat, such as turtle nesting beaches, and by the dredging of recreational beaches, which endangered small children.

The state, as a land manger representing the public good, regularly balanced multiple-uses of the state's resources. The court, as an after-the-fact actor, is not in a position to be a land manager. Shipwreck resources cannot be managed in isolation from surrounding water and land environments. Current clean water legislative initiatives at the federal and state levels will highlight submerged lands and probably increase impact as well as protection. In 1988, the problem could be defined narrowly as a near-shore jurisdictional conflict. Today, the integrated problems of environmental management and development on a global scale are better appreciated and have substantially complicated the situation.

Technology

The technology issue has two components. The first is the availability of technology and the consideration of whether a wreck is abandoned if technology is unavailable for its location and recovery. The second involves the possession of a shipwreck by telepossession rather than by physical possession. Search and recovery technology is changing very fast. The traditional admiralty interpretation held that once a shipwreck was abandoned, ownership could not be reactivated.

Today we must consider that technology is available if it meets five criteria. (1) It must be commercially available, not just experimental. (2) It must also have cultural acceptance — for example, cloning humans does not. (3) The risk to human health and the environment must be acceptable. The Spanish diving bell of the 16th century was used to recover shipwrecks to a depth of 100 ft. (30 m), but the loss of life would be unacceptable today. Likewise, the use of prop-wash to move sand to the detriment of the environment and possibly the cultural value of the shipwreck is also unacceptable. (4) Furthermore, cost must be reasonable; that is, the technology should not be limited exclusively to national governments. (5) Finally, the technology must be available in a particular jurisdiction. The limitations of technology transfer and a broad range of trade sanctions may make technology unavailable. Perhaps a general rule for determining the availability of technology could be that if it costs less than $1 million and the expected loss of life is less than one in a million, then the technology can be considered available.

In the case of the *Central America*, the admiralty court introduced a new twist. They accepted possession on the basis of the electronic documentation of the wreck in lieu of actual in-hand recovery of ship and cargo. Telepossession is an interesting concept given our ability to manipulate technology for both public and private gain.

Property Rights

Traditionally, a shipwreck was considered abandoned if time passed and no effort was made to recover the wreck. The concept of affirmative abandonment for non-government ships was introduced in the *Central America* case. The definition of abandonment is still the most serious challenge to the ASA to date. During the last 10 years the ASA has with stood arguments that it is unconstitutional and a variety of challenges in several state courts. Currently, the United States Supreme Court is reviewing the case of the *Brother Jonathan*. The shipwreck was located by a salvor and claimed in federal court in 1991. The salvor, Deep Sea Research Inc., won lower court decisions to the effect that the 1865 wreck was not abandoned and belonged to them. The salvor bought the wreck from insurance companies, which had insured parts of the wreck. In short, it was concluded that the insurance companies had not "affirmatively abandoned" the shipwreck. The State of California argued that they were not obligated to show abandonment in a federal court.

Title under the ASA is dependent on the wreck being abandoned. The Supreme Court will probably clarify what, precisely, this constitutes. A traditional admiralty interpretation suggests that ownership be severed by the passage of time, the failure to maintain adequate documentation of ownership, and the failure to declare the asset for financial purposes. Implications of the court decision for the property rights of states, individuals, insurance companies and salvors are major.

Treasure salvors often talk about property rights and free enterprise. However, treasure salvors do not make money from abandoned shipwrecks. One fellow probably made a profit in the 1950s and another in the 1980s, but they are the exceptions and neither one was in the United States. Salvors argue for preservation of their life-style. Government has no social, legal or moral responsibility to preserve the salvor life-style. Government has a responsibility for protecting tolerance and free enterprise, not free lunches.

Conclusion

We cannot legislate values. We can legislate rules which direct behavior. Environmental and archaeological resources are managed at the most local level. An individual decides to dig a hole or not to dig a hole. The Abandoned Shipwreck Act and state laws implementing management programs protect many sites and expand the public's understanding of the value of these resources. The Abandoned Shipwreck Act is not an end point but an important success in the process of governance.

ANNE G. GIESECKE
1001 WILSON BLVD.
ARLINGTON, VIRGINIA 22209

2011. Shipwreck Protection: Federal and State Law—A View From Louisiana. In *ACUA Underwater Archaeology Proceedings 2011*, Filipe Castro and Lindsey Thomas, editors, pp. 66–73.

Shipwreck Protection: Federal and State Law – A View From Louisiana

Ryan M. Seidemann

Although strides have been made towards the legal protection of shipwrecks from salvage and looting in the United States, gaps in the coverage of federal and state laws persist. The passage of the Abandoned Shipwrecks Act of 1987 was a watershed event in the protection of maritime heritage. However, problems such as the protection of shipwrecks in federal waters and the protection of wrecks when a watercourse shifts remain. A review of the relevant law with examples from Louisiana is here undertaken to analyze what remains to be done to increase protections for shipwreck sites.

Introduction

What are the legal protections available for underwater cultural resources, particularly shipwrecks? On the whole, what protection exists is patchwork of federal and state laws that even at its best is not spectacular. When considering the law related to the protection of shipwreck sites in the United States, there is an important distinction between those resources located in state waters and those located in federal waters.

Protections in State Waters

In 1987 the United States Congress enacted the Abandoned Shipwrecks Act (ASA) (43 U.S.C. 2101-2106). With that law, Congress acknowledged the United States' sovereign ownership of all shipwrecks in the navigable waters of the nation (43 U.S.C. 2105(a)). In that same law, Congress relinquished the jurisdiction of all such resources to the individual states within whose boundaries the shipwrecks are located (43 U.S.C. 2105(c)). In essence, Congress created the federal authority for shipwrecks to be vested in state ownership if they are in navigable waters of a state, but then punted to the states for them to establish their own regulatory scheme to permit access to and protection of these resources. Although the ASA was a good starting point to establish baseline protection of shipwreck sites, there are real loopholes in the coverage of the law. Some of these loopholes have been filled by states acting in their sovereign capacity through their legislators, such as Louisiana (La. R.S. 1604-1605), which protects both shipwrecks as well as now-submerged terrestrial archaeological sites.

In order to understand some of the significant loopholes of the ASA, it is essential to understand the actual coverage of the law. The coverage of the ASA is tied to the federal definition of "submerged lands," which largely refers to the navigable waters of the states (and certain tidally influenced areas) at the time of their admission into the Union (43 U.S.C. 1301; 43 U.S.C. 2102(f)). Thus, the ASA defers to state tests of navigability for questions of whether particular wrecks are protected under the law.

In Louisiana, as in many other states, the State does not claim historically non-navigable waterways (La. C.C. Art. 450; 506). Thus, any wrecks in waterways that are unable to be proven to have been navigable in 1812 (the date of Louisiana's statehood) are not under the protective umbrella of the ASA. Although one would think that the discovery of a shipwreck in a waterway that is otherwise considered non-navigable would be a strong argument to the contrary, the law does not always favor logic. This is one loophole in the law. Certainly, there are archaeologically significant wrecks in waterways that do not meet the legal classification for navigability – these wrecks would not be protected under the ASA. In addition, in Louisiana, as elsewhere, the State has lost claims of navigability in the past (*Olin Gas Transmission Corp. v. Harrison*). These situations, which are decisions made by judges and juries, potentially place at risk shipwrecks located in the waters of what had once been thought to be navigable state waterways.

An example of the problems with shipwrecks being located in non-navigable waterways is the recent case of the unidentified vessel in Webster Parish, Louisiana. In 2010, the Louisiana Department of Wildlife & Fisheries received reports that a wooden vessel was poking out of the unusually low waters along Bayou Dorcheat in North Louisiana (Keith Cascio 2010 elec. comm.). Visual inspections by Wildlife agents and Louisiana's Northwest Regional Archaeologist, Jeff Girard, confirmed the reports. Although no detailed examination was possible, it is suspected that the vessel is either a shallow-draft ferry or a flatboat (George Castille 2010, elec. comm.). Due to the perishable nature of such vessels, their existence today is a rarity, making the discovery one of some scientific importance (George Castille 2010, elec. comm.). However, the riparian landowner was adamant that no one was to approach his property to view or salvage the vessel. The landowner's insistence was based on a 1920s Louisiana Supreme Court decision that had declared the particular reach of Bayou Dorcheat in which the wreck is located to be non-navigable (*Bodcaw Lumber Co. of Louisiana v. Kendall*), and the owner believed that the identification of a ship on the property would allow for a revisiting of the navigability issue from a legal perspective (an overturning of the 1920s case would threaten the landowner's title and mineral rights to the property). Thus, the riparian owner claimed that the wreck was on his private property and he had already begun to disassemble the wreck for his own purposes (Andrew Pistorius 2010, elec. comm.). Although Mr. Girard was ultimately able to convince the owner of the importance of this vessel and to dissuade him from further destruction (at least in the short term), this situation highlights the shortcomings of the reach of the ASA when wrecks are found in waterways that were once thought to be non-navigable. This matter has not yet been resolved and it is unclear on what legal basis such a resolution may be reached. Likely, there will be an agreement with the landowner for a conservation servitude over the vessel that will allow archaeologists to properly study and preserve the wreck.

Further limiting the scope of the ASA's protections, the law also constricts the concept of "navigable waters" by excepting from that term accretion, reliction, and dereliction (43 U.S.C. 1301(a)(1)). Thus, movement of the watercourse and the sloughing off or adding to of the banks of a waterway alters the coverage of protections afforded by the ASA (certain types of water course modifications – usually anthropogenic ones – are not excepted in Louisiana (La. Atty. Gen. Op. Nos. 06-0263; 07-0211). This exemption becomes especially acute in some of the inland rivers, streams, and bayous in places like Louisiana where the watercourses constantly shift (Seidemann 2009:118-129). Under this loophole, if a ship sinks in a navigable waterway, and that watercourse later shifts, causing the wreck to be partially or wholly stranded on dry ground, the ASA likely does not apply. This scenario has famously occurred in the Mid-West when sunken steamboats become stranded in cornfields when water courses shift (Corbin 1998; Hawley 1998).

The latter problem also has analogues in Louisiana, especially in situations in which the United States Army Corps of Engineers has undertaken straightening activities on waterways (Seidemann 2009). When the waterways are straightened, the water usually follows the easier route, leading to accretion in the originally-navigable channel. In these situations, anthropogenic activities have led to portions of navigable waterways drying up (usually at sharp bends), thereby stranding wrecks that had previously been in a navigable waterway. When these waterways completely dry up, the legal regime of ownership changes. Under Louisiana law, as accretion occurs, the newly accreted area inures to the ownership of the riparian owner (La. C.C. Art. 499). Thus, in addition to the ASA not applying due to its exception of accreted lands, most state protections of archaeological resources on state lands are also lost.

One example of this channel-shifting problem is highlighted by the wreck of the steamboat *Kentucky* in the Red River near Shreveport, Louisiana. The *Kentucky* sank on June 9, 1865, while transporting 900 passengers, mostly paroled Confederate soldiers, from Shreveport to New Orleans (Goodwin and Seidel 2004). It is estimated that 200 passengers lost their lives when the *Kentucky* struck a snag just south of Shreveport and sank quickly (Goodwin and Seidel 2004). At the time of the archaeological investigation of the *Kentucky*, the remains of the vessel were situated across three potential legal regimes of property ownership, two of which are likely exemptions to the ASA's coverage. Although it is not apparent that these legal issues were a problem for the interpretation of this vessel, the issues highlight the problems of the scope of the ASA.

When the *Kentucky* went down in 1865, it was in the navigable channel of the Red River. Over time, the River's course shifted, leaving a portion of the wreck in the original channel, a portion in the new channel, and a portion stranded beneath a newly-created island in the channel (Goodwin and Seidel 2004:Figure 21). It is clear that the portion of the wreck lying beneath the original channel of the Red River is covered by the ASA due to the fact that it is embedded in a navigable waterway. However, the portion that has become stranded under the newly-created island will belong to the owner of that terrestrial property (La. C.C. Arts. 482; 490). If the shift in the Red River that created the *Kentucky* scenario was occasioned by the Corps cutting a new channel to straighten the flow of the River, this new channel was likely (as is often the case) acquired by way of an easement (i.e., not in full ownership). In such cases, the property remains the private property of the landowner across whose land the channel now runs. Accordingly, assuming that the new channel was acquired by way of an easement, although it now carries the waters of a navigable waterway, it is privately owned and thus that portion of the *Kentucky* lying in the new channel is also privately owned and is not subject to the ASA. Further complicating the ownership of the *Kentucky* and its protection under the ASA is the fact that the old channel will slowly dry as the water follows the course of the new channel. As the old channel dries, the accretion formed by the drying inures to the ownership of the private riparian owners – thus exempting ASA and state property protections.

One possible partial solution to some of these loopholes, especially in the area of non-navigable waterways (i.e., those areas that do actually have water, but do not fit the legal definition for navigability) is for Congress to amend the ASA to incorporate concepts of regulatory control akin to those found in the Clean Water Act (CWA) (33 U.S.C. 1251-1387). Under the CWA (33 U.S.C. 1344), the government's regulatory authority extends the "waters of the United States," which, through court decisions that have been interpreted as providing regulatory jurisdiction over waterways based on a hydrological connection of attenuated waters to navigable waterways (*United States v. Riverside Bayview Homes*; *South Florida Water Management District v. Miccosukee Tribe of Indians*; Seidemann and Susman 2002; Seidemann 2005a) rather than the traditional test of navigability, which largely looks only to whether the waterway could support commerce (*Dardar v. Lafourche Realty Co., Inc.*; *Naquin v. Louisiana Power & Light Co.*). Under the CWA, the concept of waters subject to the regulatory jurisdiction of the United States is substantially broader, applying to non-navigable watercourses, wetlands, and marsh areas (Seidemann and Susman 2002).

Despite the shortcomings noted above, the ASA does provide substantial protection for shipwrecks that are in clearly navigable waterways within state waters. Unfortunately, this is only one part of the picture. The other part is federal waters, where the protections are more murky and sparse.

Protections in Federal Waters

The protections for shipwrecks in federal waters is, at best, a cobbled-together hodgepodge of laws with differing scopes and protections, and the coverage of these laws is far from comprehensive. The traditional terrestrial archaeological site protections available under the National Historic Preservation Act (NHPA) (16 U.S.C. 470-1-470x-6) and the Archaeological Resources Protection Act (ARPA) (16 U.S.C. 470aa-470mm), which are largely triggered by the National Environmental Policy Act (NEPA) (42 U.S.C. 4321-4370h), provide scant support for the protection of shipwrecks in federal waters (Seidemann 2003). Under these laws, protections for shipwrecks are only triggered when there is a federal action or a federal permit involved. Thus, in federal waters, these laws do not cover salvage operations – a gaping hole in the protection of shipwrecks in federal waters. In addition, the punitive provisions of these laws are not well tailored to counter the traditional dreams of shipwrecks full of gold that are the motivating factors for salvage companies. From the perspective of these companies, such penalty provisions are simply seen as a cost of doing business (Seidemann 2011). Thus, NEPA, the NHPA, and ARPA are fairly weak points in the protection of shipwrecks in federal waters.

Regardless of the weaknesses of NEPA, the NHPA, and ARPA, there are some strong points in the protection of shipwrecks in federal waters. The National Monuments Act (NMA) (16 U.S.C. 433) states that,

> Any person who shall appropriate, excavate, injure, or destroy any historic or prehistoric ruin or monument, or any object of antiquity, situated on lands owned or controlled by the Government of the United States, without the permission of the Secretary of the Department of the Government having jurisdiction over the lands on which said antiquities are situated, shall, upon conviction, be fined in a sum of not more than $500 or be imprisoned for a period of not more than ninety days, or shall suffer both fine and imprisonment, in the discretion of the court.

Although the plain language of this statute is powerful with regard to its coverage and what is restricted, the law only carries with it a $500.00 penalty provision. Admittedly, the NMA was passed in 1906, which may be an explanation for the minimal penalty provision, but the practical reality is that the strong enforcement language is undermined by the weak penal provision, thus limiting the law's utility, especially in the salvage context.

In *Treasure Salvors, Inc. v. Unidentified Wrecked and Abandoned Sailing Vessel*, the federal Fifth Circuit Court of Appeals held that the NMA is not limited to terrestrial settings and that it applies to federal waters in the same manner as it would to federal lands. Unfortunately, the court limited the protections afforded by the NMA to the 12 nautical mile extent of federal waters. In other words, the court refused to apply the law to areas beyond statutory federal waters where the federal government clearly exercises jurisdiction. This appears to be an incorrect interpretation of the law. As noted above, the NMA explicitly applies to "lands owned or controlled by the Government of the United States" (16 U.S.C. 433). Admittedly, when the *Treasure Salvors* case was decided in 1978, the volume of federal activity beyond the 12 nautical mile statutory limit of federal waters was less than it is today. However, there was activity beyond that limit. At a minimum, it seems that, based upon the volume of federal mineral leasing and regulation on the Outer Continental Shelf at the present time (which is largely beyond the 12-mile limit), a court interpreting the NMA today would have to seriously reconsider the *Treasure Salvors* 12-nautical mile limitation, as such areas are now clearly "lands owned or controlled by the Government of the United States."

Another law that protects shipwrecks in federal waters is the Marine Sanctuaries Act (MSA) (16 U.S.C. 1433-1445c-1). Unlike the NMA, the MSA contains strong penal provisions. The MSA specifically provides for the protection of cultural resources. In fact, the first marine sanctuary was created to protect the USS *Monitor* shipwreck off of the North Carolina coast (Chandler and Gillelan 2011). The penal provisions of this law are substantial: They include forfeiture of the equipment used to loot shipwreck sites, forfeiture of the ill-gotten material culture, prison time, and steep fines. However, the shortcoming of this law is its limited application. The MSA applies only to specifically-designated marine sanctuaries, which, in the grand scheme of things, are very small in area and there are only fourteen of them nationwide. If Congress would combine the penal provisions of the MSA with the geographic scope of the NMA, it is probable that the bulk of shipwrecks contained within waters controlled by the United States government would come under substantial protections from looting.

The most recent activity in this area by Congress is the Sunken Military Craft Act (SMCA) (Pub.L. 108-375, Div. A, Title XIV, §§ 1401 to 1408). This law provides virtually absolute protections for United States war crafts, including aircraft and space ships in United States waters. Thus, under this law, U.S. military crafts cannot

be salvaged in U.S. waters. In addition, the SMCA, makes it illegal to salvage U.S. military craft in the waters of other nations. Further, SCMA makes it illegal to salvage foreign military craft in U.S. waters. The law has a broad reach with fines of $100,000 per violation, per day. These types of restrictions are what are missing from the MSA and the NMA and they effectively make salvaging such craft too expensive to be considered a simple cost of doing business for salvage companies.

Further bolstering protections from the SCMA, unlike the ASA, this law does not distinguish between military craft located in the water and on land. The SCMA simply applies to sunken military craft, with no specification as to where the craft is currently located. Although this law has not yet been tested in the courts, it appears that a strong argument can be made, at least as to military craft, that the SCMA protections extend to such resources even when the sovereign waters in which they sank have now dried up or changed course. The threshold question with the applicability of this law appears to be whether the craft was sunken; not where it sunk and who now owns the property on which it sunk. Theoretically, the SCMA could apply to terrestrial sites that would otherwise be protected by private property rights (i.e., off limits to ASA and state law protections) may now fall under the "do not salvage" provisions of the SCMA if the subject craft was one of military use.

Between the ASA and state laws in state waters and the SCMA (and to a lesser extent, NEPA, NHPA, ARPA, NMA, and MSA) in federal waters, there emerges a complex legal scheme under which it is arguable that fairly substantial protections from looting should apply to a wide swath of vessels (especially military craft). In federal waters, what is now left largely unprotected are vessels whose use or origin cannot reasonably be identified or tied to the military. In state waters, non-military vessels located on private property (in either terrestrial or non-navigable settings) are left largely unprotected. Nonetheless, even some of those settings have some interesting law that applies.

Sovereignty and Insurance Claims

Although clearly not preservation-oriented, recent jurisprudence related to sovereignty and insurance claims on shipwrecks may serve as a deterrent to the salvage of these vessels. In a case in 2000 out of the federal Fourth Circuit Court of Appeals, two Spanish wrecks were the subject of a sovereignty battle between a salvage company and the Kingdom of Spain. The wrecks at issue in *Sea Hunt, Inc. v. The Unidentified Shipwrecked Vessel or Vessels* were permitted for salvage under the ASA by the State of Virginia. However, in rescinding the permit, the court found that Spain had never expressly abandoned these military vessels that were lost in 1750 and 1802. Another sovereignty matter was recently decided by the federal court for the Middle District of Florida. In *Odyssey Marine Exploration, Inc. v. The Unidentified, Shipwrecked Vessel*, a salvage company sought authority under admiralty law to be declared the owner of a wreck found in international waters off the coast of Gibraltar. This wreck, so claimed the salvage company, was a Spanish merchant vessel that had no identifiable owners. The Kingdom of Spain intervened in the lawsuit claiming that the wreck was actually a Spanish warship. The court refused to recognize the salvage company's claims and refused to exercise its jurisdiction over Spain. Although the court did not rule in a manner that would bind the parties in a court outside of the United States, the court did proclaim that,

> The ineffable truth of this case is that the *Mercedes* is a naval vessel of Spain and that the wreck of this naval vessel, the vessel's cargo, and any human remains are the natural and legal patrimony of Spain and are entitled in good conscience and in law to lay undisturbed in perpetuity absent the consent of Spain and despite any man's aspiration to the contrary.

This strong language from a federal court seems to suggest, when coupled with the Fourth Circuit decision noted above, that U.S. courts are now going the way of helping to protect submerged cultural heritage, even if that heritage is not in U.S. waters. Cases such as these are extremely expensive for salvage companies to litigate and it is expected that the continued success of sovereign nations in such suits may act as a deterrent to some salvage operations in the future.

Finally, in at least one reported case, *Columbus-America Discovery Group v. Atlantic Mutual Insurance Co.*, insurance companies that had issued policies to cover the gold cargo of the SS *Central America* in 1857 created yet another jurisprudential deterrent to salvage operations. The insurers in this case were successful in arguing that, because they had insured the cargo and had paid claims on the losses of the cargo when the ship sank in 1857, they had essentially purchased the cargo that had been salvaged from the wreck. Again, as with the sovereignty cases, when a salvage company has

to litigate cases such as this, it is a substantial financial burden. When, as here, the salvage companies lose some or all of their rights to the bounty of their efforts because of unrelinquished claims of former owners, the costs to their operations escalate significantly. Although these are not regulatory means for protecting shipwrecks and these types of cases do not guarantee that sovereign nations or insurers will make for better preservers of our cultural heritage than would salvors, the deterrent effect of the costs of these losses to the salvage community is important.

Recommendations for Future Protections

As noted above, although there seems to be a progression towards legislating and litigating for better protections for shipwrecks in state and federal waters in the United States, there are still gaps to fill in the law. The existing protections for non-military craft remain too weak. While it is often difficult to protect terrestrial archaeological sites due to the limitations on government action with regard to private property (where a large number of such sites are located) (D'Innocenzo 1997), in navigable waters – both state and federal – such private rights do not exist because this property is owned by the various governments in their sovereign capacity. The states have probably gone as far as is possible with the authority delegated to them under the ASA. In Louisiana, these ASA-derived laws apply to all navigable waterways. As noted above, a more CWA-style definition of "waters" would be helpful in extending state protections, but this authority will likely have to derive from federal legislation. There is little doubt that such an expansion of governmental authority will be met with fierce opposition by landowners, especially if the CWA wetlands protection cases are any indicator (*Solid Waste Agency of Northern Cook County v. U.S. Army Corps of Engineers; Rapanos v. U.S.*). However, with regard to the expansion of protections in waters under federal control (including the entire geographic area embraced by federally-permitted offshore mineral activity) no such private property concerns exist. In the absence of these concerns, Congress can enact protections for federal waters and not be subject to claims that such actions are takings of private property in violation of the Fifth and Fourteenth Amendments to the United States Constitution.

Another quick fix to some of the gaps in the federal legislation would be by way of the United States' accession to the United Nations Educational, Scientific and Cultural Organization's (UNESCO) Convention on the Protection of the Underwater Cultural Heritage (41 I.L.M. 40). If the United States accedes to this Convention, then the Convention's protections are automatically adopted into federal enforceable law (Vázquez 2008). Such a premade protective scheme has the added benefit of not needing to have Congress reinvent the wheel for such protections (Seidemann 2005b). Certainly, Congress could alter or strengthen the protections of the UNESCO Convention over time, but it would allow the United States to begin enforcing strict anti-salvage restrictions immediately upon accession.

Another possible mechanism for protecting non-military shipwrecks that have become stranded on private property, such as the *Kentucky*, is to apply human remains protection laws to the sites. Although it may be difficult to apply federal protections to these sites under the Native American Graves Protection and Repatriation Act (25 U.S.C. 3001-3013), because that law is specific to one ethnicity, namely Native Americans, most states now have non-ethnicity specific protections for sites containing human remains (Seidemann 2010). In the case of the *Kentucky*, which sank with 200 people onboard, a reasonable legal argument may be made that the site is now covered by human remains protection laws such as the Louisiana Unmarked Human Burial Sites Preservation Act (La. R.S. 8:671-681). Of course, such laws could only be applied to sites where it is reasonably possible to believe that people died onboard. However, the power of these laws is often broad and the protection of sites under them has been held by courts not to be a governmental taking of private property (National Trust for Historic Preservation 1990).

One final possibility is the use of the governmental power of expropriation to protect shipwreck sites located on private property. Especially in terrestrial settings where private property interests get in the way of the protection of shipwrecks, expropriation stands as a solid basis to simply take property in order to protect archaeological resources located on the property. All that is needed for the expropriation of shipwreck sites is monetary compensation to the landowner for the thing taken and a public purpose for the taking. The public purpose has been articulated in numerous laws – in fact, in Louisiana the protection of historic resources is part of the State's constitutional public trust mandate (La. Const. Art. IX, Sec. 1). The real limitation to the use of the power of expropriation to protect archaeological sites in general is the cost of paying the landowner for the value of the property. However, even this limitation could be minimized if the property is not taken in its entirety, but rather just the rights to the cultural resources are taken. In other words, the landowner could continue to use their property in any manner that does not impact the resources so long as the government is allowed to preserve and investigate the resources, as necessary.

Conclusion

Over the past few decades, federal and state protections for shipwreck sites have increased exponentially. With that said, there is still much to do to ensure the virtually universal protection of these irreplaceable resources. Some of these efforts may require action by Congress; others will require clever collaborations between archaeologists and lawyers to extend existing protections to cover factual scenarios that fall into the vague lacunae of the existing laws.

Acknowledgments

The author wishes to acknowledge the assistance of Tracy Poissot and Ericka Seidemann in the preparation of this manuscript. Thanks are also due to the organizers of the SHA symposium of which this article was originally a part – Kristen Vogel and Laura Gongaware – who extended the invitation for me to speak in Austin. Finally, thanks to Richard McGimsey, Trey Phillips, Louisiana Attorney General, James D. "Buddy" Caldwell, and the Louisiana Department of Justice for supporting this research and funding my trip to the SHA annual meeting in Austin.

References

Bodcaw Lumber Co. of Louisiana v. Kendall, 108 So. 664 (La. 1926).

CHANDLER, WILLIAM J. AND HANNAH GILLELAN
    2011   Designation of USS *Monitor* and Key Largo National Marine Sanctuaries. In Environmmental Law Institute [ELI], *Law of Environmental Protection*, § 20:29. ELI, Washington, D.C.

Columbus-America Discovery Group v. Atlantic Mutual Insurance Co., 974 F. 2d 450 (1992).

CORBIN, ANNALIES
    1998   Shifting Sand and Muddy Water: Historic Cartography and River Migration as Factors in Locating Steamboat Wrecks on the Far Upper Missouri River. *Historical Archaeology* 32(4):86-94.

D'INNOCENZO, PAMELA
    1997   "Not In My Backyard!" Protecting Archaeological Sites on Private Lands. *American Indian Law Review* 21:131-155.

Dardar v. Lafourche Realty Co., Inc., 985 F.2d 824 (C.A. 5 1993).

GOODWIN, R. CHRISTOPHER AND JOHN L. SEIDEL
  2004 Phase II and Phase III Archaeological Investigations of the Shipwreck Kentucky (Site 16BO358) at Eagle Bend, Pool 5, Red River Waterway, Bossier Parish, Louisiana. Report to U.S. Army Corps of Engineers, Vicksburg District, from R. Christopher Goodwin & Assoc., Inc., Frederick, MD.

HAWLEY, GREG
  1998 *Treasure in a Cornfield: The Discovery and Excavation of the Steamboat* Arabia. Paddle Wheel Publishing, Kansas City, MO.

LOUISIANA ATTORNEY GENERAL OPINIONS
  2006 La. Atty. Gen. Op. No. 06-0263.
  2008 La. Atty. Gen. Op. No. 07-0211.

LOUISIANA CIVIL CODE
  1978 La. C.C. Art. 450 (Public things).
  1979 La. C.C. Art. 482 (Accession).
  1979 La. C.C. Art. 490 (Accession above and below the surface).
  1979 La. C.C. Art. 499 (Alluvion and dereliction).
  1979 La. C.C. Art. 506 (Ownership of beds of nonnavigable rivers or streams).

LOUISIANA CONSTITUTION
  1974 La. Const. Art. IX, Sec. 1 (Natural Resources and Environment; Public Policy).

LOUISIANA REVISED STATUTES
  1989 La. R.S. 41:1604 (Responsibilities of the division).
  1989 La. R.S. 41:1605 (Archaeological finds on state land; state property).
  1992 La. R.S. 8:671-681 (Louisiana Unmarked Human Burial Sites Preservation Act).

Naquin v. Louisiana Power & Light Co., 768 So.2d 605 (La.App. 1 Cir. 2000).

NATIONAL TRUST FOR HISTORIC PRESERVATION
  1990 Minnesota Court Dismisses Inverse Condemnation Challenge to State Human Remains Statute. *Preservation Law Reporter* 9(12):1158–1160.

Odyssey Marine Exploration, Inc. v. The Unidentified, Shipwrecked Vessel, 675 F.Supp. 2d 1126 (M.D. Fla. 2009).

Olin Gas Transmission Corp. v. Harrison, 132 So.2d 721 (La.App. 1 Cir. 1961).

Rapanos v. United States, 547 U.S. 715 (2006).

Sea Hunt, Inc. v. The Unidentified Shipwrecked Vessel or Vessels, 221 F. 3d 634 (C.A. 4 2000).

SEIDEMANN, RYAN M.
  2003 Protection of Shipwrecks in Louisiana and Federal Waters. *Louisiana Coastal Law* 81:1-2.
  2005a Louisiana Wetlands and Water Law: Recent Jurisprudence and Post-Katrina and Rita Imperatives. *Loyola Law Review* 51:861-909.
  2005b What Does It Mean For Us? The United Nations Convention on the Law of the Sea. *The SAA Archaeological Record* 5(1):36-38.
  2009 Curious Corners of Louisiana Mineral Law: Cemeteries, School Lands, Erosion, Accretion, and Other Oddities. *Tulane Environmental Law Journal* 23:93-157.
  2010 NAGPRA at 20: What Have the States Done to Expand Human Remains Protections? *Museum Anthropology* 33(2):199-209.
  2011 Shipwreck Protection: Coverage of the Laws, Problems, and Suggestions for Broader Protection. Paper presented at the 2011 Annual Meeting of the Louisiana Archaeological Society, Alexandria, LA.

SEIDEMANN, RYAN M. AND CATHERINE D. SUSMAN
  2002 Wetlands Conservation in Louisiana: Voluntary Incentives and Other Alternatives. *Journal of Environmental Law & Litigation* 17:441-495.

Solid Waste Agency of Northern Cook County v. United States Army Corps of Engineers, 531 U.S. 159 (2001).

South Florida Water Management District v. Miccosukee Tribe of Indians, 541 U.S. 95 (2004).

Sunken Military Craft Act, Pub.L. 108-375, Div. A, Title XIV, §§ 1401-1408.

Treasure Salvors, Inc. v. Unidentified Wrecked and Abandoned Sailing Vessel, 569 F.2d 330 (C.A. 5 1978).

UNITED NATIONS EDUCATIONAL, SCIENTIFIC AND CULTURAL ORGANIZATION
  2001 Convention on the Protection of the Underwater Cultural Heritage (41 I.L.M. 40).

United States v. Riverside Bayview Homes, 474 U.S. 121 (1985).

UNITED STATES CODE
  1906 16 U.S.C. 433 (American antiquities).
  1953 43 U.S.C 1301 (Submerged lands).
  1966 16 U.S.C. 470-1-470x-6 (National historic preservation).
  1970 42 U.S.C. 4321-4370h (National environmental policy).
  1972 16 U.S.C. 1431-1445c-1 (Marine sanctuaries).
  1972 33 U.S.C. 1251-1387 (Water pollution prevention and control [CWA]).
  1979 16 U.S.C. 470aa-470mm (Archaeological resources protection).
  1987 43 U.S.C. 2101-2106 (Abandoned shipwrecks).
  1990 25 U.S.C. 3001-3013 (Native American Graves Protection and Repatriation).

UNITED STATES CONSTITUTION
    1791   Fifth Amendment.
    1868   Fourteenth Amendment.

VÁZQUEZ, CARLOS M.
    2008   Treaties as Law of the Land: The Supremacy Clause
        and the Judicial Enforcement of Treaties. *Harvard*
        Law Review 122:599-695.

Ryan M. Seidemann
Lands & Natural Resources Section
Civil Division
Louisiana Department of Justice
1885 North Third Street
Baton Rouge, LA 70802

1992. Threatened James River Shipwrecks and Historical Sites. *Historical Archaeology* 26(4):58–68.

KEVIN J. FOSTER

Threatened James River Shipwreck and Historical Sites

ABSTRACT

Historical records of shipwrecks in the James River indicate that large numbers of vessels were wrecked, abandoned, or scuttled there during the 18th and 19th centuries. These physical elements of maritime history are central to the history of Virginia and the United States and can yield valuable information, yet, many of these sites have been destroyed by looting and through regular dredging of the river. State and federal agencies have been largely unaware of the archaeological potential of the river and, until recently, unresponsive to notices that government inaction allowed important archaeological sites to be destroyed. This article describes several large archaeological sites: the wrecks of USS *Cumberland* and CSS *Florida* in Hampton Roads, the City Point wharves and anchorage, and two sunken fleets at Drewry's Bluff; discusses threats to the sites; looting, maintenance dredging, and channel widening projects; considers governmental responsibility and complex ownership issues; and finally makes recommendations for resolution of the management problems associated with shipwrecks in the James.

Introduction

The James River of Virginia has one of the richest histories of any North American river. Historical records of shipwrecks in the James River show that large numbers of vessels were wrecked, abandoned, or scuttled there during the American Revolution, the War of 1812, and the Civil War. Other vessels have been abandoned since the Civil War in out-of-the-way areas where tributaries meet the James. Recent archaeological projects on the shores of the James at Williamsburg, Jamestown, Bermuda Hundred, the Richmond waterfront, and many other sites have uncovered physical elements of maritime history. These sites are central to the history of Virginia and the United States and can yield valuable information.

Important historical and archaeological sites on the James are being destroyed because federal laws are being violated. Government agencies are failing to communicate with the public and with other agencies. Over the last six years a number of important maritime archaeological sites in or near the James River in Virginia have been destroyed through looting and through regular dredging of the river. Threatened sites are located the length of the navigable river channel. Artifacts from many sites have been appearing in Civil War gun and artifact collecting shows across the country. According to artifact hunters, archaeologists, preservationists, divers, historians, dredge crew members, and other interested individuals and organizations, the single largest reason for the total lack of effective preservation was a lack of communication. Artifact hunters, dealers, divers, and dredge crews have little idea that archaeological sites in the river are protected and owned by the Commonwealth or Federal government. Responsible government agencies appear unaware that the river holds historical material and thus have made no efforts to protect those resources. This lack of information exchange results in ignorance both by the agencies responsible and those destroying the sites.

Private archaeological surveys have located settlement and vessel remains in several places on the river. But major development projects from Richmond to Hampton Roads have taken and continue to take a toll of these important sites. Maintenance dredging of channels containing historical sites continues. Large-scale, illegal looting is occurring as indicated by the large quantity of James River artifacts on the antiquities market. Artifacts from James River sites have been shown for sale in at least five Civil War artifact shows, two antique shops, and one old book shop. The FBI recently seized allegedly looted material from an artifact shop, a small "museum," and one of Virginia's largest antique shops. And yet, in spite of preservation laws designed to protect such sites, there has never been a state or federally sponsored archaeological survey of any kind in the James River. Representatives of Virginia, the Norfolk District, U.S. Army Corps of Engineers, and the Port of Richmond could not identify any archaeological survey done on the James River channel. This article is intended to provide a starting point for such a study.

The most obvious examples of artifacts removed from state-owned shipwreck sites are United States and Confederate States naval objects from ships sunk during the American Civil War. These include both personal effects and material belonging to the ships. Objects have been exhibited and sold at shows in Atlanta, Georgia; Crystal City, Virginia; and even at the Ninth Annual Capital of the Confederacy Civil War Show in Richmond, Virginia, in late 1989. Most were coming from the James River. Looters and treasure salvors appear to be doing most of the surveying and all of the recovery work from shipwrecks in the James River.

Maritime Archaeological Sites on the James River

Maritime archaeological sites exist in abundance on the shores of the James River (Figure 1). Dwellings, camps, and communal structures of the inhabitants lined the water's edge. Native American habitation sites may have been inundated or were located on the river edges and may be silted over. Sites ranging from burials and garbage middens to large villages are known to have lined the river. Dugout canoes are likely to be found. They often survive long inundation or burial very well, but are fragile once removed from that stable protective environment. No prehistoric sites have been located on the James but two have been identified on the Lower York River, possessing points and pottery of the Late Archaic/Woodland period.

A great variety of prehistoric and historic period enterprises used the water for transportation, communication, defense, manufacturing, fishing, and recreation. All of these activities left tangible remains on shore and in the river. These sites were used for fish processing, ferries, brickyards, blacksmithies, and plantation landings, as well as large sites used as battlefields and major industrial locations (Goldenberg 1976:117–120). Many of these shore-side historical facilities may now be inundated due to changes in the river.

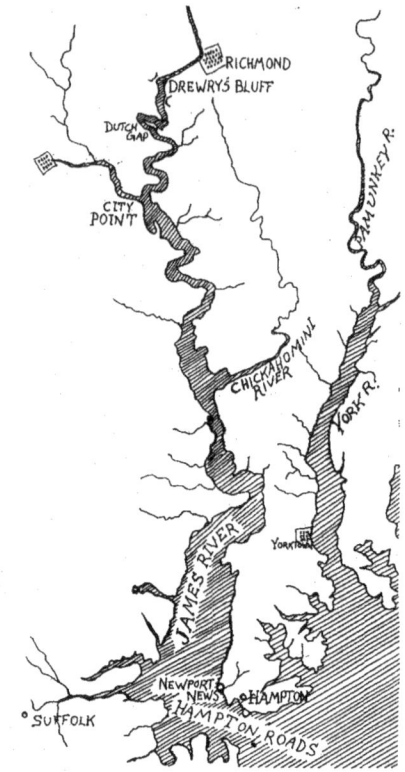

FIGURE 1. Map of James River, Hampton Roads to Richmond.

Only a few riverside historical sites have been archaeologically investigated. A colonial landing site near Williamsburg and portions of the Tredegar Iron Works site in Richmond have been partially excavated. Wolstenholme Towne, a colonial settlement site near Carter's Grove Mansion, has been investigated but failed to provide definitive information without more extensive offshore work (Colonial Williamsburg Foundation 1986:206). Most other colonial riverside sites have not even been surveyed.

Later historical sites exist as well. Reconstruction era and later structures include steamboat landings, fish plants, lumber yards, and shipyards. The James Trigg Shipyard operated below Richmond, between approximately 1890–1910. The yard built passenger screw steamers and warships for the U.S. Navy. The archives of the Mariner's Museum in Newport News hold a plan view of the shipyard.

Shipwrecks predating the Civil War also are present. A considerable colonial maritime trade existed at several locations on the James. Vessels ranged from bateaux and coasting schooners to large ocean-going vessels carrying on the tobacco trade and bringing immigrants. As an example of the size of the trade, the Governor of Virginia in 1670 reported that nearly 80 tobacco ships arrived annually in Virginia. No shipwrecks of this era have been identified in the river, although shipwreck fragments found in dredge spoil areas in the Richmond area suggest that they did exist until recently, and may still be found there (Goldenberg 1976:24–25).

Both sides which fought in the American War of Independence used ships and boats on the James River. A number of these were lost due to British action. Norfolk served as a major British base in the area. Both minor and major raids were made by the British into rebellious areas. The town of Hampton at the mouth of the James was destroyed, with its watercraft and shore-side buildings, in one such raid. The largest raid took place on 18 April 1781, when Benedict Arnold led a fleet of British warships on a raid against towns and settlements on the James and tributary rivers. They shelled, burnt, and destroyed property near the river and sank colonial vessels when they could not steal them. The expedition burnt the Virginia State Navy shipyard on the Mataponi River, a tributary of the James. Benedict Arnold's flotilla captured and burnt 11 ships at Osbornes' Landing on the James. Several other ships and shore installations were destroyed at the anchorage off Petersburg. Other vessels were destroyed in the James during the War of 1812. The ships sunk by Arnold's flotilla at Petersburg are in the same area as the vessels sunk by the Civil War explosion at City Point (Arnold 1781).

The largest group of vessel remains in the James dates from the Civil War. Examples of many important vessel types were lost in the river. These include warships such as steam and sailing frigates, sloops, ironclad rams, gunboats converted from merchant steamers, steam gunboats, transports and torpedo boats. Merchant vessels also were lost in the James. Known losses include whalers, a pilot schooner, coastal and cross-Atlantic steamers, canal boats, flatboats, and tugboats.

CSS Florida and USS Cumberland at Hampton Roads

The two most famous shipwrecks lie on the bottom of the James River off Newport News. The sailing frigate USS Cumberland, built in 1842, saw service in the Mexican War, the Mediterranean Squadron, the African anti-slavery patrol, and the Civil War, before being sunk by the Confederate Ironclad Virginia, the former USS Merrimack, in March 1862 (Naval History Division 1963). The other wreck is that of CSS Florida, the first Confederate commerce raider built in Great Britain. Florida sank near the wreck of Cumberland. A mystery that might be solved by archaeological survey could identify the cause and perpetrator of Florida's loss. Florida was built at Liverpool by William C. Miller in 1862, and voyaged to Mobile, Alabama, where the ship was armed and refitted to become a commerce raider. Florida captured 37 Union merchant ships before being captured in the neutral harbor of Bahía, Brazil. There, Florida was captured by the Union cruiser USS Wachussetts and towed to the United States. This violation of Brazilian neutrality raised a storm of diplomatic protest and might have resulted in the vessel being returned to Brazil. But before the offense against international law could be redressed, Florida "accidentally" sank due to clogged pumps (Owsley 1987). Whether the Union navy scuttled Florida to avoid releasing it remains to be answered by archaeology.

In 1984 Underwater Archaeological Joint Ventures (UAJV), a private Virginia company, sponsored by Clive Cussler's National Underwater Marine Agency (NUMA), located and identified the wrecks of Cumberland and Florida. The U.S. Navy and the Commonwealth of Virginia disputed jurisdiction over and ownership of the wrecks which resulted in little archaeological work being done (King 1989; Stehle 1989). The dispute also led to confusion concerning protection of the site from looters. Artifacts from both ships were on sale at the Ninth Annual Capital of the Confederacy Civil War show in Richmond in 1989 and were advertised nationally in a Civil War collecting magazine. The advertisement offered belt buckles made from brass recovered from CSS *Florida* and artifacts from *Florida* and *Cumberland* (*North-South Trader's Civil War* 1989).

The Confederate Naval Historical Society took action in early 1990 to bring attention to the matter. Without assistance from the State of Virginia Historic Preservation Office, the FBI and the Naval Investigative Service recovered a large number of items illegally removed from the wrecks of *Florida* and the nearby USS *Cumberland* (Townley 1989, 1990a, 1990b). Among the artifacts recovered were disassembled sections of several of the pumps reported clogged. They had been cleaned by the salvors, thus obliterating potential clues to uncover the cause of *Florida*'s loss (Townley 1990a).

City Point Docks and Anchorage

The most common artifacts from submerged sites at artifact collector shows are Union artillery, cavalry, and infantry equipment. These artifacts have appeared in gun shows, Civil War shows, and even in the shop of a rare book dealer in Richmond. When asked where the artifacts came from, the answer is usually a vague reference to the "City Point" area or just the upper James River. Most "City Point" artifacts are from the Civil War era, but a few date from the Revolution and the War of 1812.

City Point was the site of a huge federal supply base, built to support the forces of General Benjamin Butler in their campaign against Richmond. The base handled large amounts of supplies, using wooden and pontoon wharves to augment an old wharf site. Railroad tracks ran onto the wharves to speed supplies to the front. Steamers and sailing vessels of every type were hired to carry supplies

from the north to City Point. Even barges from northern canals were pressed into service (Calkins 1989).

At least three canal boats, in use as Army transports, were sunk in an explosion at City Point on 9 August 1864. The explosion tore into the *J.E. Kendrick*, an ammunition barge, spreading the cargo over a mile-wide area. The explosion also sank a number of other nearby vessels, including *General Meade* and *J.C. Campbell*. The wrecks and scattered cargoes of these vessels could provide data about canal boat construction, their adaptations for military use, and the lives of soldiers and mariners of the period. Although archaeology could provide such unknown information, unfortunately none has been attempted. Instead, material such as a complete set of artillery harness looted from this site has been available at artifact and gun shows across the country. On a recent visit to City Point, a section of low wooden railing with turned stanchions, similar to those used on some canal boats, was visible lying loose in shallow water. Other objects scattered at the water's edge appeared to be from the same period. Earlier visits had not shown such concentrations.

Looters have also been raiding the wrecks of several other Union Army and Navy vessels. Some Union Navy ship fittings, equipment, and personal affects have appeared at artifact shows. "From the James" is the general answer to questions of their source. When pressed one salvor answered, "from a Union armed ferry boat; I got it from guys who have a permit." According to Bruce Williams and John Broadwater of the Virginia Division of Historic Resources, a state permit to do preliminary reconnaissance of the *Commodore Jones* site was granted. This permit did not allow recovery of artifacts and has since expired. The U.S. Navy was apparently not consulted, although it still owns the wreck.

The converted ferry USS *Commodore Jones* was sunk by a mine in May 1864, at the junction of the James with Four Mile Creek. This was a 542-ton, sidewheel steam "Fulton landing" ferry from New York Harbor, converted and armed with six guns for service in the war (Young 1864; Bucknill 1889; Silverstone 1989). The wreck was tentatively located by a privately funded 1982 Underwater Archaeology Joint Ventures magnetometer survey (NUMA/UAJV 1982). Material identified as being from this vessel has been presented at several Civil War shows recently.

Other Union steamer wrecks apparently being looted are the Federal Army Quartermaster Corps transports *Greyhound* and *Thorne*. The 900-ton *Greyhound*, which had served as General Butler's flagship, was sunk in November 1864 by explosives camouflaged as coal (Bucknill 1889:3; Perry 1965). The *Thorne*, of 403 tons, was sunk by an ordinary mine in March 1865 (Bucknill 1889). Both of these vessels could provide valuable information on amphibious operations, Army seagoing activities, and Army equipment. *Greyhound* may have other "coal torpedoes" unexploded in the coal bin which can provide knowledge of sabotage methods and devices.

Another Union gunboat was sunk by a shore battery at Turkey Bend. USS *Shawsheen*, a converted sidewheel tugboat built in New York in 1855, had played an important part in the capture and early operations on the coast and in the sounds of North Carolina and later operated on the James and York Rivers. While clearing mines on the James, 6 May 1864, the gunboat was ambushed by Confederate Army forces, disabled, abandoned, and destroyed (Rushmore 1864).

Drewry's Bluff Fortifications, Obstructions, and Shipwrecks

A small but significant amount of Confederate Navy equipment, small arms, and personal affects have also been shown at Civil War shows. The material is vaguely referred to as from the Drewry's Bluff area. This section of the river saw several naval battles and holds ships sunk in battle. Other vessels were scuttled there by both sides to block the river.

Two sets of fortifications on the upper James River defined the Union and Confederate lines. Each army used a system of mutually supported forts and artillery batteries to overlook and guard a series of obstructions in the river. The Union ob-

FIGURE 2. Fort Darling and obstructions at Drury's (or Drewry's) Bluff.

structions and fortifications were designed to prevent the powerful Confederate ironclads from descending the river and attacking defenseless transports. Confederate obstructions kept the Union fleet from ascending the river and taking Richmond.

Fort Darling, atop Drewry's Bluff; Fort Harrison, atop Chaffin's Bluff; and Fort Brady, below Chaffin's Bluff, were large, log-reinforced, earthen forts. They anchored Confederate defensive lines on the James and prevented Union forces from using the upper river. Fort Darling is now part of Richmond National Battlefield Park. A number of smaller Confederate artillery batteries guarded the river below Chaffin's Bluff and tied the forts together into a defensive line. Each gun platform was protected by a log-reinforced earthwork. Several camouflaged earthworks on the riverbanks also protected the operators of electrically detonated underwater mines (Perry 1965).

Channel obstructions were placed between Drewry's Bluff and Chaffin's Bluff in the river by the Confederates and farther downstream by the Federals. (Figure 2). Obstructions were of several types. Scuttled vessels and heavy wooden cribs filled with large stones were the most common.

Sharpened wooden spars, called "Yankee catchers," were driven into the river bottom at an angle to impale Union ships venturing too far upriver. Some "Yankee catchers" were made doubly dangerous by mines attached to the upper end. Nearly 40 "frame" or "spar" torpedoes were placed across the river in November 1864. Several other types of underwater explosive devices were emplaced as well (Perry 1965:144).

One of these "Yankee catcher" torpedoes was offered in 1990 to a prominent museum by a relic dealer from Virginia. He said that the torpedo was recovered from the banks of the James "nowhere near the river" (sic) by salvors who wished to remain anonymous. The torpedo is one of only three known surviving examples of the type. It exhibited advanced corrosion similar to iron artifacts long under water and required conservation treatment.

Artifacts have also come from the wrecks of the ironclad rams CSS *Richmond, Fredericksburg*, and *Virginia II*. These three steam warships saw action against Union forces on the James and were the mainstay of the river defenses. When the lines protecting Richmond were breached, the ironclads were burned and sunk at the obstructions at Drewry's Bluff (Silverstone 1989). A map overlay in the collections of the Mariner's Museum of Newport News, Virginia, shows sunken vessel positions, including the rams, in relation to obstructions in the river at Drewry's Bluff (Obstructions 1871). This map was used in 1982 as a starting point by a NUMA/UAJV project seeking to locate wrecks of the James River Fleet. The project located several vessels and plotted their locations. No artifacts were retrieved, although locations of material concentrations were noted. At least one such concentration, an arms chest, was apparently destroyed by subsequent dredging. NUMA/UAJV provided a copy of the map to the State Office of Historic Preservation on 31 December 1982, as part of their report on the project (Figure 3). In 1988, when again alerted to the existence of historical shipwreck sites in the James, the Preservation Office stated that there was no record of any archaeological sites in the river (NUMA/UAJV 1982).

Another ironclad wreck possibly still in the river is the CSS *Virginia*. *Virginia*, the former *Merri-mack*, was one of the first ironclad warships to see combat. Following the loss of Norfolk to Union forces, *Virginia* was set afire near Craney Island at the mouth of the James to prevent capture by the North. The wreck was partially salvaged after the war but archaeological remote sensing work performed by Tidewater Atlantic Research indicates that the wreck may be intermittently exposed. Other Confederate ironclads may exist as well. A large, unnamed ironclad ram was burnt on the stocks (Still 1985).

Other shipwrecks located around Drewry's Bluff included: *Curtis Peck* and *Northampton*, Chesapeake Bay passenger sidewheel steamboats; and *Yorktown* and *Jamestown*, large oceangoing sidewheelers converted to naval use. The *Yorktown* became the CSS *Patrick Henry*, school ship for the Confederate Naval Academy. The *Jamestown* was armed as a gunboat and became the CSS *Thomas Jefferson*. The *Patrick Henry* was burned at a landing below Richmond at the fall of the city. The *Thomas Jefferson* was burned and sunk at the Drewry's Bluff obstructions on the same night. Both ships were reported salvaged several times, although portions remained in the river (Obstructions 1871).

The Army transport *Schultz* was sunk by a mine at Chaffins Bluff (Bucknill 1889:2). The steam gunboats CSS *Nansemond* and CSS *Hampton* were part of an early Confederate shipbuilding effort concentrating on building a number of steam gunboats for defense. They were sunk at Drewry's Bluff. Most Confederate states attempted to build these gunboats, designed by the brilliant Matthew Fontaine Maury. One of the wrecks in the river below Drewry's Bluff appears to be a "Maury" gunboat. Two Maury gunboat wrecks are known in other states, one in South Carolina was excavated privately in the 1950s, used as a roadside attraction, and scrapped. No records of that vessel appear to have been made (Still 1969).

The armed tugboats CSS *Roanoke*, ex-screw propeller tug *Raleigh*, and CSS *Beaufort*, an iron-hulled screw propeller tug, were burned at lower Richmond. Few wrecks of early iron-hulled vessels exist today. Much could be learned from *Beaufort* in iron technology and in the field of

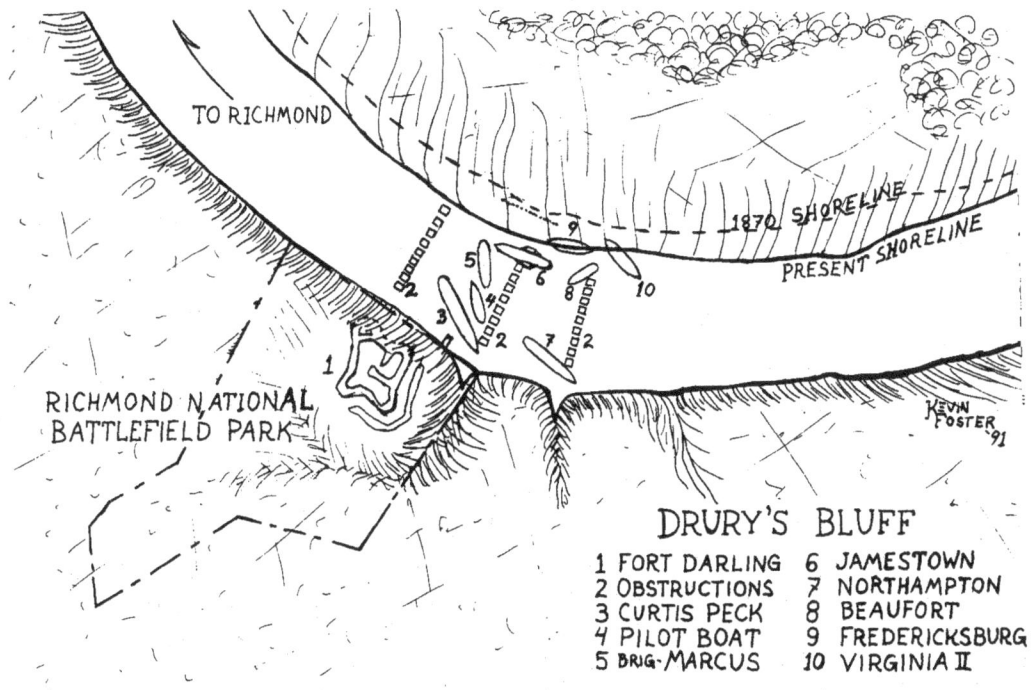

FIGURE 3. Drury's (or Drewry's) Bluff composite map of Fort Darling, shipwrecks, and obstructions.

steam engineering from both vessels. The fast steam torpedo launches CSS *Hornet*, CSS *Wasp*, and CSS *Bee* were built to attack large warships and transports using an explosive warhead attached to a long spar mounted ahead of the boat. They were probably scuttled at Drewry's Bluff or at Richmond. They are significant because they are among the first torpedo craft of any kind in maritime history. A pilot boat was also scuttled at the Drewry's Bluff obstructions. Most pilot boats were examples of the very best in naval architecture and construction technique. The pilot schooner shown on the obstructions map is undoubtedly a fast schooner built in the last age of sail power. It is probably from Norfolk, known for fine pilot schooners. No pilot schooner or Civil War era schooner has ever been excavated.

At least three flatboats, a type of sailing scow, were sunk at the obstructions at Drewry's Bluff. Sailing scows, built all over the United States, took a number of forms and were called by a variety of names. In Virginia they were often called

flatboats although they bore little relation to the flatboats in use on the Mississippi River. Little is known about any type of southern sailing scow. The Federal merchant brig *Marcus* was sunk at the Drewry's Bluff obstructions. *Marcus* had been owned in Maine until captured in Hampton Roads by the CSS *Thomas Jefferson*, ex-*Jamestown*.

Much could be learned from these vessels about their construction, fitting, armament, fittings, and crew lifeways. Documentation of the modifications made for military service could add to knowledge of adaptive behavior in wartime emergency conditions.

Dredging

The fort atop Drewry's Bluff, Fort Darling, has lost much of its riverside face due to erosion exacerbated by dredging of the channel below. State permits for (annual) maintenance dredging have not addressed the impact on Drewry's Bluff or the

City Point National Park sites. In 1989 the Port of Richmond proposed widening the channel. This action would have deepened the channel directly below the fort. Deepening would have increased the rate and extent of erosion and probably led to much greater loss of the fort's riverfront face. The Confederate Naval Historical Society raised concerns about the dredging given the lack of survey work. Rather than perform an archaeological survey, the Port of Richmond postponed the project. The Park management staff had not been consulted and was unaware that such a project was proposed.

Looting from the James is alarming, but federal dredging and channel widening without archaeological survey is irresponsible and illegal because it fails to comply with the Section 106 process (36 CFR Part 800). Relic hunters excused their actions by claiming that the "government did not care about the history and artifacts in the river—they dredge through wrecks all of the time." Several former dredge officers and crewmen were asked if that were true. They denied destroying wrecks. However, they also stated that the reason they avoided wrecks was that running into a wreck often broke the dredge. In fact, their dredge had been disabled several times after dredging through wreck sites. One pipeline dredge crewman recalled the glee of the crew when the dredge passed over a wreck. Some of the crew would race out atop the dredge pipeline to catch the cannon balls as they clanged through the pipe to the discharge end. Clearly, dredges have run over and damaged historic wrecks.

Maintenance dredging on the James is an annual affair. Permits for this activity have been granted by the state with no survey required because "there had always been regular maintenance dredging in the James." Bruce Williams of the Virginia State Historic Preservation Office; Pam Painter, Project Manager, and Gene Whitehurst of the Norfolk District dredging office of the Corps of Engineers all expressed a belief that there was nothing of any historic significance remaining in the James River navigation channel. The Corps of Engineers and the State Historic Preservation Office appeared to assume that because dredging had been carried on in the James prior to the National Historic Preservation Act of 1966, as amended, that further dredging could not harm sites that had already been dredged. In terms of navigation requirements, the State and the Corps know that channels meander, the banks erode into the river, and floods and droughts change channel navigation requirements. However, they did not consider that dredging to correct these hazards can increase channel bank erosion, uncovering and scattering archaeological material. Impacted sites include National Historic Landmarks such as Fort Darling. The National Park Service is concerned that the riverside face of the fort is eroding away, partly due to channel dredging removing the bottom of the slope (Morgan 1989; Waterway 1989).

Channel Widening

An even bigger threat to archaeological resources in the river than annual maintenance dredging was a major engineering project. In the late 1980s the Port of Richmond planned a major channel widening project to widen "critical bends" in the Upper James. The navigation channel on the upper river is narrow and today's large merchant ships can only make their way to the Port of Richmond with great care. The inability of large vessels to pass one another on turns was a particular concern. The project would allow larger ships to come up the river to Richmond. Larger ships and a safer passage would allow the Port of Richmond to compete more favorably with the ports of Baltimore and Hampton Roads.

The project required dredging to extend the river channel from 200 ft. to 300 ft. The Port of Richmond was to pay for the project and be reimbursed by the U.S. Army Corps of Engineers for 90 percent of the cost on completion. The project was surveyed by Waterway Surveys and Engineering, Ltd., of Virginia Beach, Virginia, between February and September of 1987. By January 1989, the plans for the project had been completed, the environmental review was finished, and survey stakes to guide the dredging had been placed in the river (Waterway 1989).

The Confederate Naval Historical Society heard

of the planned project and, recognizing that no remote sensing survey had been done, informed the Port of Richmond, the Corps of Engineers, and the Virginia State Historic Preservation Office that the project put known archaeological sites in the river at risk. The Confederate Naval Historical Society provided information about known and suspected archaeological sites to the Departmental Consulting Archaeologist of the Interior Department and the Maritime Initiative of the National Park Service. That information, plus advice on the requirements of Section 106 of the National Historic Preservation Act and the probable ownership of the shipwrecks, caused the project to be reevaluated. Neither the project nor an archaeological survey of the river has begun. A Port of Richmond manager said in early 1991 that the Port now plans to improve cargo handling facilities instead.

By far the largest and most visible group of vessel remains is a "ship graveyard" for old vessels at the confluence of the James and Appomattox Rivers, where vessels have been disposed of since the Civil War era. Aerial photographs show a number of large wooden and steel vessels scattered about in shallow water. Sidewheel ferries, three-masted schooners, and at least one large wooden ship or bark are badly dilapidated but recognizable. At least one group of schooners is surrounded by a line of pilings. This matches descriptions of the method used to dispose of excess wooden vessels after World War I so that floods would not send them wandering.

Who Is Responsible for This Material?
Who Owns It?

A number of different state and federal agencies have jurisdiction over Virginia Waterways. The State of Virginia owns all abandoned historic shipwrecks below state waters, due to the Abandoned Shipwreck Act of 1989. The State Historic Preservation Office reviews the projects permitted by the Corps of Engineers and ensures that they will not negatively impact archaeological sites. Virginia Fish and Game Police enforce laws dealing with state waterways. At present, the Fish and Game Police also grant permits for exploration of shipwrecks in state waters. The port of Richmond owns a considerable area of waterfront in the upper James and has an abiding interest in its safe navigation.

The U.S. Army Corps of Engineers is responsible for maintenance of navigable waterways. The Corps grants permits for all construction projects that might impact such channels. The Army has not taken responsibility for its wrecks. Last year the Army allowed private salvors in another state to libel a Quartermaster Corps' wreck from the Civil War and treat it under the Abandoned Shipwreck Act. The U.S. Navy owns the wrecks of its lost vessels and has also taken responsibility for, and possible ownership of, Confederate States Navy wrecks. The Navy also controls waters within its base limits. The U.S. Coast Guard owns the wrecks of its lost vessels. The Coast Guard is responsible for law enforcement, search and rescue, and environmental protection on rivers and coastal waters. Coast Guard and Coast Guard Auxiliary boat patrols are the most frequent government representatives on the river. The National Park Service owns property fronting the upper James River at Hopewell/City Point and at Drewry's Bluff. The City Point site is a unit of Petersburg National Battlefield. Fort Darling, atop Drewry's Bluff, is a unit of Richmond National Battlefield. Two external programs of NPS are also interested in archaeological sites in the James. The National Historic Landmarks Program and the National Register of Historic Places are designed to assess the significance of historical properties.

The Virginia State Historic Preservation Office apparently recognized in 1990 that a problem existed in underwater archaeological protection. The preservation staff attempted to meet legal and ethical requirements by upgrading submerged historic resource protection. The Yorktown Shipwreck Project was brought to an end to allow the maritime archaeological staff to head a broader underwater program. The Maritime Program would have met the needs and the legal requirements of historic preservation in Virginia State waters. Unfortunately, in late 1990, the governor not only cut funds for new equipment, but closed down the nascent program entirely. The maritime archaeological positions were eliminated. Virginia's severe budget deficit was given as the reason for the termination of state care for underwater resources.

Recommendations and Conclusion

Six recommendations, if followed, would do much to help care for the underwater resources on the James River. First, a baseline submerged cultural resources survey is vital for all existing periodically maintained river and harbor channels. Much of the confusion and delay which has confounded the James River channel-widening project can be attributed to the lack of any survey to prove or disprove the presence of cultural resources in the river. Second, information about archaeological protection law and purposes must be properly presented to the general public. Following the confiscation of artifacts looted from *Cumberland* and *Florida*, many people held a poor perception of preservation law as the press devoted more space to reporting unhappy looters and artifact dealers than it did to the loss of history and archaeology. Third, the state should educate sport divers on laws relating to underwater archaeological sites. A pamphlet or fact sheet distributed to local dive shops would be a start. Most sport divers are unaware that any law beyond "finders keepers" applies to shipwreck sites. Fourth, government agencies must communicate better with one another. Few agencies know what is being planned by others, and projects may overlap. The National Park Service was never consulted about dredging operations, permitted by the state and the Corps of Engineers, that would have impacted Richmond National Battlefield Park. Fifth, jurisdiction over the various types of shipwrecks and historical maritime resources must be clearly defined. New laws and newly applied interpretations of older laws have focused attention on underwater archaeological sites, but have not settled boundary disputes between jurisdictions. Sixth, the Advisory Council on Underwater Archaeology, the Confederate Naval Historical Society, and other interested organizations should help promote communication between individuals and agencies.

To conclude, the archaeological sites in the water and on the banks of the James River are significant to the history of the United States as well as the local area. Since 1966 Federal law has required that historical sites be evaluated through a prescribed process when they might be impacted by federal projects. Various forms and levels of mitigation then might be required. In the James River, federal and state dredging projects have been undertaken on an almost annual basis since protective legislation was enacted, yet no state or federal survey even lists the locations of historic sites in or near the James. Potential sites should be identified, known sites studied, and significant sites protected. These sites must not be lost due to bureaucratic inaction, incompetence, or ignorance.

ACKNOWLEDGMENTS

This article began as a listing of potential Civil War shipwreck sites near Drewry's Bluff on the James River. In researching the topic, sites were identified throughout the length of the river. Most appeared to be threatened by natural or human actions. A number of historians, archaeologists, archivists, and preservation specialists helped the author in gathering information for this article. Significant contributions were made by the following individuals: John Broadwater, R. Thomas Crew, Sam Margolin, Keith Morgan, John Sands, Bruce Terrell, John Townley, and Gordon Watts. Discussions with the following people were useful in gathering information: Chris Calkins, Keith Morgan, Pam Painter, Richard Waldbauer, Gene Whitehurst, and Bruce Williams. Several sources who asked to remain anonymous provided valuable information on dredging procedures, artifact looting, and marketing of artifacts.

REFERENCES

ARNOLD, BENEDICT
1781 Letter to Sir Henry Clinton dated 12 May 1781. Clinton Papers. Clement Library, University of Michigan, Ann Arbor.

BUCKNILL, JOHN TOWNSEND
1889 *Submarine Mines and Torpedoes as Applied to Harbor Defense.* Offices of Engineering, London.

CALKINS, CHRIS
    1989   Salvage Archaeology at the Site of the City Point
            Explosion, 9 August 1864, James River-Hopewell,
            Virginia–1989. Unpublished report and artifact list
            on file, Petersburg National Battlefield, Petersburg,
            Virginia.

COLONIAL WILLIAMSBURG FOUNDATION
    1986   *Toward a Resource Protection Process: James City
            County, York County, City of Poquoson, and City of
            Williamsburg*, Vol. 2. Second edition. Office of Ar-
            chaeological Excavation, Department of Archaeol-
            ogy, Colonial Williamsburg Foundation, Williams-
            burg, Virginia.

GOLDENBERG, JOSEPH A.
    1976   *Shipbuilding in Colonial America*. University Press
            of Virginia, Charlottesville.

KING, THOMAS F.
    1989   Letter to H. Bryan Mitchell dated 5 April 1989. On
            file, Advisory Council on Historic Preservation,
            Washington, D.C.

NATIONAL UNDERWATER MARINE
AGENCY/UNDERWATER ARCHAEOLOGICAL JOINT
VENTURES (NUMA/UAJV)
    1982   James River Survey 'The Last of the Confederate
            Navy.' Unpublished report on file, State Historic
            Preservation Office, Richmond, Virginia.

MORGAN, KEITH
    1989   General Development and Land Classification Plan,
            Fort Darling, Richmond National Battlefield Park.
            Park Map/Drewry's Bluff. Memorandum, dated 5
            April 1989, on file, Richmond National Battlefield
            Park, Richmond, Virginia.

NAVAL HISTORY DIVISION
    1963   *Dictionary of American Naval Fighting Ships*, Vol.
            2. Department of the Navy, U.S. Government Print-
            ing Office, Washington, D.C.

NORTH-SOUTH TRADER'S CIVIL WAR
    1989   Advertisement. *North-South Trader's Civil War*
            16(6):4. Fredericksburg, Virginia.

OBSTRUCTIONS
    1871   Obstructions at Drury's Bluff, James River, Va., Re-
            moved in 1871. Map overlay on file, Mariner's Mu-
            seum, Newport News, Virginia.

OWSLEY, FRANK LAWRENCE, JR.
    1987   *The C.S.S.* Florida: *Her Building and Operations*.
            Second edition. University of Alabama Press, Tus-
            caloosa.

PERRY, MILTON F.
    1965   *Infernal Machines: The Story of Confederate Sub-
            marine and Mine Warfare*. Louisiana State Univer-
            sity Press, Baton Rouge.

RUSHMORE, WILLIAM
    1864   Report of Acting Master's Mate William Rushmore
            to Gideon Welles, dated 19 November 1864. *Official
            Records of the Union and Confederate Navies in the
            War of the Rebellion*, Ser. I, Vol. 10. U.S. Govern-
            ment Printing Office, Washington, D.C.

SILVERSTONE, PAUL H.
    1989   *Warships of the Civil War Navies*. Naval Institute
            Press, Annapolis, Maryland.

STEHLE, NANCY S.
    1989   Letter to Thomas F. King, dated 14 March 1989, on
            file, Advisory Council on Historic Preservation,
            Washington, D.C.

STILL, WILLIAM N., JR.
    1969   *Confederate Shipbuilding*. University of Georgia,
            Athens.

    1985   *Iron Afloat: The Story of the Confederate Armor-
            clads*. University of South Carolina Press, Colum-
            bia.

TOWNLEY, JOHN
    1989   Inventory of Seized Articles from USS *Cumberland*
            and CSS *Florida*, dated 1989. Ms. on file, Confed-
            erate Naval Historical Society, White Stone, Vir-
            ginia.

    1990a   Looted Artifacts from CSS *Florida* and USS *Cum-
            berland* Seized by F.B.I. *Confederate Naval Histor-
            ical Society Newsletter*, 23 March 1990: special dis-
            patch. White Stone, Virginia.

    1990b   F.B.I. Seizures of CSS *Florida* and USS *Cumber-
            land* Artifacts Make Headlines. *Confederate Naval
            Historical Society Newletter* 4:1–2. White Stone,
            Virginia.

WATERWAY
    1989   Port of Richmond, Commission of the City of Rich-
            mond, James River, Virginia, Preliminary Plans for
            Dredging, Richmond Deepwater Terminal to
            Hopewell. Waterway Surveys and Engineering,
            Ltd., 31 January 1989: sheets 2 and 3 of 12. On file,
            U.S. Army Corps of Engineers, Norfolk District Of-
            fice, Norfolk, Virginia.

YOUNG, JEFFERSON
    1864   Letter to J. C. Beaumont, dated 12 May 1864. *Of-
            ficial Records of the Union and Confederate Navies
            in the War of the Rebellion*. U.S. Government Print-
            ing Office, Washington, D.C.

KEVIN J. FOSTER
NATIONAL MARITIME INITIATIVE
NATIONAL PARK SERVICE
P.O. BOX 37127
WASHINGTON, D.C. 20013

2011. ARPA and Site Damage Management Assessment Applicability to Offshore Underwater Cultural Heritage. In
ACUA Underwater Archaeology Proceedings 2011, Filipe Castro and Lindsey Thomas, editors, pp. 61–65.

ARPA and Site Damage Assessment Applicability to Offshore Underwater Cultural Heritage

Martin E. McAllister
Larry E. Murphy
James E. Moriarty IV

The Archaeological Resources Protection Act of 1979 establishes felony prosecution for unauthorized disturbance of archaeological resources on federal and tribal lands, and it has become an important and powerful legal deterrent. Incorporated into the Act and Uniform Regulations is the framework for a damage assessment methodology widely useful as a tested, legal model for other cultural resource protection laws. Currently, the Act is jurisdictionally limited from application to the extensive Outer Continental Shelf underwater cultural heritage. This discussion addresses the Act's damage assessment methodology and application, and a corrective amendment to the Act is proposed.

The Archaeological Resources Protection Act (ARPA; 16 USC § 470aa-mm) was enacted more than 30 years ago. Provisions of this federal statute are implemented by the 1984 ARPA Uniform Regulations (the Department of the Interior version of the regulations is referenced: 43 CFR Part 7). Together, the statute and the regulations establish a legal framework for a methodology to assess the harm caused by unauthorized damage to archaeological resources located on federal and Indian lands. The resulting methodology is the legal standard for all damage assessment in ARPA criminal and civil cases. This method is also used in criminal violations charged under other federal statutes that apply to the protection of cultural resources, such as those prohibiting theft and injury of government property (18 USC § 641 and 18 USC § 1361). This ARPA-based methodology provides a cultural resource damage assessment model tested in federal litigation for more than 20 years, and it is being incorporated into other federal legislation. In 2004, ARPA legal damage assessment concepts were incorporated into the Sunken Military Craft Act (10 USC § 113, 1401 – 1408). Recently, ARPA concepts were adopted for use in the new Paleontological Resources Preservation Act of 2009 (16 USC § 470aaa–1 – 11). (Implementing regulations, like the ARPA Uniform Regulations, that would provide further legal standards for the use of this methodology have yet to be adopted for either of these recent statutes.)

The ARPA damage assessment methodology is also being utilized in state cultural resource violation cases because state laws typically lack damage assessment provisions. Recent examples are cases in Arizona and California. In 2010, the California cultural resource protection statute was strengthened by an amendment that incorporates damage assessment provisions based directly on the ARPA methodology (California Public Resources Code § 5097.5 – 5097.993).

The ARPA damage assessment methodology has seen wide use in cases involving terrestrial resources. However, due to important jurisdictional issues, it has only been applied in very few submerged cultural resource cases. After reviewing ARPA's key jurisdictional, damage assessment provisions, and methodology, this paper proposes an amendment that would rectify ARPA's current jurisdictional limitations regarding its applicability to underwater cultural heritage and discusses the significant benefits of such an amendment.

ARPA's Jurisdictional and Damage Assessment Provisions

ARPA's provisions establish its jurisdiction and the requirement for archaeological resource damage assessment. These provisions are reviewed below.

Jurisdiction

ARPA's "Prohibited acts and criminal penalties" section states that:

No person may excavate, remove, damage, or otherwise alter or deface, or attempt to excavate, remove, damage, or otherwise alter or deface *any archaeological resource located on public lands* or Indian lands unless such activity is pursuant to a permit issued under section 470cc of this title, a permit referred to in section 470cc(h)(2) of this title, or the exemption contained in section 470cc(g)(1) of this title (16 USC § 470ee(a); emphasis added).

ARPA defines public lands as:

> (3) The term "public lands" means—
>   (A) lands which are owned *and* administered by the United States as part of—
>   (i) the national park system,
>   (ii) the national wildlife refuge system, or
>   (iii) the national forest system; and
>   (B) all other lands the fee title to which is held by the United States, *other than lands on the Outer Continental Shelf* and lands which are under the jurisdiction of the Smithsonian Institution (emphasis added).

Currently, ARPA's application to offshore underwater cultural heritage is limited to tribal lands and federal lands as defined above. However, ARPA's damage assessment methodology can arguably be used with other statutes that protect offshore cultural resources, such as the federal property statutes, the Sunken Military Craft Act, the National Marine Sanctuaries Act (16 USC § 32 1431- 1445), and applicable state statutes. The requisite legal elements for prosecutions under these statutes must, of course, be met, but ARPA's jurisdictional limit does not apply to them.

Damage Assessment

In addition to the first provision of the "Prohibited acts and criminal penalties" section of ARPA cited above, the Act states further that:

> Any person who knowingly violates, or counsels, procures, solicits, or employs any other person to violate, any prohibition contained in subsection (a), (b), or (c) of this section shall, upon conviction, be fined not more than $10,000 or imprisoned not more than one year, or both: Provided, however, That if the commercial or archaeological value of the archaeological resources involved and the cost of restoration and repair of such resources exceeds the sum of $500, such person shall be fined not more than $20,000 or imprisoned not more than two years, or both. In the case of a second or subsequent such violation upon conviction such person shall be fined not more than $100,000, or imprisoned not more than five years, or both (16 USC § 470ee(d)).

(The Criminal Fines Improvement Act of 1987 (see 18 USC § 3571(b)) increased the maximum fines for Class A misdemeanor and felony violations of federal law by individuals to $100,000 and $250,000 respectively and by organizations to $200,000 and $500,000.)

The three monetary measures of harm established by this section of ARPA, commercial value, archaeological value, and cost of restoration and repair, are defined in Section 14 of the Uniform Regulations:

> ... [T]he commercial value of any archaeological resource involved in a violation ... shall be its fair market value. Where the violation has resulted in damage to the archaeological resource, the fair market value should be determined using the condition of the archaeological resource prior to the violation, to the extent that its prior condition can be ascertained (43 CFR 7.14(b)).
>
> ... [T]he archaeological value of any resource involved in a violation ... shall be the value of the information associated with the archaeological resource. This value shall be appraised in terms of the costs of the retrieval of the scientific information which would have been obtainable prior to the violation. These costs may include, but need not be limited to, the cost of preparing a research design, conducting field work, carrying out laboratory analysis, and preparing reports as would be necessary to realize the information potential (43 CFR 7.14(a)).
>
> ... [T]he cost of restoration and repair of archaeological resources damaged as a result of a violation ... shall be the sum of the costs already incurred for emergency restoration or repair work, plus those costs projected to be necessary to complete restoration and repair ... (43 CFR 7.14(c)).

The restoration and repair determination should include all costs involved in examination of the damage, determination of the amount of monetary harm, and preparation of the damage assessment report (see 43 CFR 7.14(c)(6) and (8)).

It is important to note that:

> ... [A]ll cases that involve damage to *in situ* ... [archeological] resources require both archeological value and cost of restoration and repair determinations ... [but] ... may or may not involve a commercial value determination. Commercial value derives from collector interest in archeological resources. Archeological resources that have

collector interest will have a fair market value, while those that are not of interest to collectors will not have a market value. A commercial value determination is not necessary when the archeological resources involved in a violation are not of collector interest and do not have a fair market value. When there is collector interest in the resources and a resulting fair market value, then a commercial value determination is required. (Note that market value does not necessarily mean the exchange of cash, but can also include the exchange of goods, i.e., barter. For example, artifacts may be traded for drugs or other artifacts as well as for money) (McAllister 2007:9).

As established by the statute's criminal penalties section, felony charges in ARPA cases are possible if the amount of monetary harm exceeds the sum of $500.00. The statute mandates that this calculation must be based *either* on archaeological value and cost of restoration and repair *or* commercial value and cost of restoration and repair. Federal attorneys typically use commercial value determinations in ARPA trafficking cases. Criminal restitution and civil penalties in ARPA cases are also determined by one or the other of these two monetary combinations. Under the Cultural Heritage Guideline of the United States Sentencing Commission (2002), all three values can be considered by the judge in sentencing for criminal cases. Charges in cases involving other statutes protecting cultural resources also would be based on one of the two combinations of values deriving from ARPA relative to the amount of felony versus misdemeanor thresholds of the applicable statute or statutes.

The ARPA Damage Assessment Methodology

The goal of ARPA damage assessment methodology is to document the resource-based elements of the offense regardless of the statute being utilized in the case. (The senior author began to develop the methodology in a case that began in December of 1977, almost two years before ARPA became law and which led to the enactment of the statute; see McAllister 1981). As discussed fully in National Park Service (NPS) Technical Brief 20, *Archeological Resource Damage Assessment: Legal Basis and Methods*, these resource-based elements are: first, that the violation affected a protected archaeological resource; second, that it involved at least one statutorily prohibited act, and third, that for a felony violation the prohibited act or acts caused monetary harm to the

resource that exceeds the statute's felony threshold of $500.00 (McAllister 2007:4-5).

The ARPA damage assessment methodology that has been developed involves three basic steps:

1) Examination of the potential violation location to document that a protected archaeological resource has been affected and to identify the type and amount of damage;
2) Determination of the amount of monetary harm in terms of the relevant measures established by ARPA: commercial value, archaeological value, and cost of restoration and repair; and
3) Preparation of a damage assessment report documenting the findings of steps one and two that becomes part of the overall law enforcement case report for the violation.

NPS Technical Brief 20 describes the step one examination procedures as follows:

… [They are] carried out to obtain information about damage to an archeological resource or resources involved in a potential violation of ARPA or other applicable statutes. The assessment is conducted at the location of this damage and is part of the overall investigation at the scene of the violation. Typically, the damage location is an archeological site, but violations may occur that do not involve sites, such as theft of isolated artifacts or theft from curation facilities or museums. The resulting information about the damage will be used in both the value and cost determinations and in the archeological resource damage assessment report that will be developed as part of case preparation. Four operations must be completed in carrying out field damage assessment. The procedures use basic archeological data collection methods.

1. Identification of the … resource damage locations:
   a. Identify all damage locations.
   b. Attempt to distinguish new damage locations from old damage locations, if the latter are present.
2. Identification of the archeological resources damaged and the damage to them:
   a. Identify the … resources protected by ARPA or other statutes at the damage locations …
   b. Identify the damage to these resources in

458 Perspectives from *Historical Archaeology* and *ACUA Proceedings*

terms of the acts prohibited by ARPA …
[or other statutes] …

3. Measurement of the amount of archeological resource damage:

a. Make accurate tape measurements of the amount of damage, unless other, more sophisticated quantification methods are available (see 3b.) …

b. Use other more sophisticated methods to quantify the amount of damage, such as total station or 3D laser scanning [or other remote sensing]. More detailed measures such as these may be employed to complete an assessment, following the initial use of tape measurements.

4. Documentation of findings:

a. Take accurate and complete notes on all aspects of the field damage assessment process.

b. Photograph the damage locations, the archeological resources damaged and the damage to them.

c. Map the damage locations.

d. Documentation should be as detailed and objective as possible.

Results of this process provide basis for the second step in damage assessment methodology: determination of the amount of monetary harm in terms of the relevant ARPA measures, commercial value, archaeological value, and cost of restoration and repair. NPS Technical Brief 20 provides a detailed discussion of specific procedures for these determinations (see McAllister 2007:9-21). The Society for American Archaeology (SAA) recently adopted "Professional Standards for the Determination of Archaeological Value" (2003) and, as is stated in the technical brief, their use in the determination of archaeological value, is "recommended strongly" (McAllister 2007:14).

Procedures for the third and final step in the ARPA methodology, preparation of the damage assessment report, are also outlined in NPS Technical Brief 20 (see McAllister 2007:21 – 25). Topics typically included in the report are:

1) Introduction;
2) Resource Description;
3) Damage Examination Procedures;
4) Resource Damage;
5) Value and Cost Determinations; and

6) Summary and Conclusions.

The report content may vary depending upon the specific type of damage assessment work performed by the author. For example, commercial value determination reports have a different content format.

The ARPA Damage Assessment Methodology and Offshore Underwater Cultural Heritage

Several arguments support use of the ARPA damage assessment methodology in cases involving unauthorized damage to offshore underwater cultural heritage:

• ARPA has existed for more than 30 years, and its damage assessment methodology is more than 20 years old and has been accepted in federal court in many successful cases;

• The assessment methodology is applicable both to ARPA and to other federal and state statutes that protect cultural resources, and its conceptual language is incorporated into the Sunken Military Craft Act and the Paleontological Resources Preservation Act;

• It is based on the legal standards of the ARPA statute and the ARPA Uniform Regulations;

• It is the subject of professional standards, the SAA archaeological value determination standards and NPS Technical Brief 20.

• It is the subject of specialized training, a five-day advanced class on damage assessment for archaeologists taught on a regular basis by the firm of the co-authors of this paper.

Use of the ARPA damage assessment methodology in offshore submerged resources cases for any reason archaeological damage assessment is conducted will ensure that the damage is assessed according to firm legal and professional standards. Utilization of the ARPA damage assessment methodology obviously does not extend the full protection of the statute to underwater cultural heritage due to jurisdictional exclusion of the Outer Continental Shelf in the statute.

Amendment of the ARPA Definition of Public Lands

To remedy this situation, the ARPA definition of public lands should be amended to read as follows:

(3) The term "public lands" means—
  (A) lands which are owned or controlled and administered by the United States as part of—
    (i) the national park system,
    (ii) the national wildlife refuge system,
    (iii) the national forest system, or
    (iv) the Outer Continental shelf; and
  (B) all other lands the fee title to which is held by the United States, other than lands which are under the jurisdiction of the Smithsonian Institution.

This amendment does not state that the United States has fee title to the Outer Continental Shelf but does assert our nation's sovereign rights and exclusive jurisdiction over activities controlled by ARPA that occur there. As a result, this proposed amendment would appropriately extend ARPA jurisdiction to the Outer Continental Shelf and would improve and expand protection of the extensive underwater cultural heritage located there.

Summary and Conclusions

Public lands and Indian lands are specifically included in ARPA jurisdiction. As currently defined in the statute, public lands do not include the Outer Continental Shelf. The result is that ARPA's protection of underwater cultural heritage is significantly and unnecessarily limited.

An effective damage assessment methodology has been derived from the relevant sections of the ARPA statute and the ARPA Uniform Regulations that has broader applicability than the jurisdiction of the statute. The goal of the methodology is to document the resource-based elements of the offense in cases involving unauthorized damage to cultural resources. The ARPA damage assessment methodology involves examination of the damage, determination of the amount of monetary harm, and preparation of a damage assessment report. The long-tested and proven ARPA methodology is appropriate and should be used with other statutes that protect cultural resources on the Outer Continental Shelf such as the federal property statutes, the Sunken Military Craft Act, and the National Marine Sanctuaries Act.

However, protection of offshore resources should be expanded beyond the use of the ARPA damage assessment methodology in conjunction with other statutes because some of these other statutes are more limited in scope than is ARPA, which applies to any archaeological resource meeting the statute's definitions. To accomplish

the goal of expanding federal protection of archaeological resources in the large area of the Outer Continental Shelf, an amendment of the ARPA definition of public lands has been proposed. This amendment would make ARPA apply to lands that the United States owns as well as to lands that it controls and administers, which would include the Outer Continental Shelf.

ARPA is a powerful federal statute with provisions that impose felony criminal penalties, levy civil penalties and allow for forfeiture of all resources, vehicles, and equipment involved in an archaeological resource violation. ARPA applies not only to unauthorized damage of archaeological resources on federal and tribal lands but also to trafficking of resources obtained in violation of federal law, and to interstate or foreign trafficking of resources obtained in violation of state or local law. ARPA's protection should be extended to archaeological resources on the Outer Continental Shelf. The amendment of ARPA proposed here is an important step to increasing protection of our nation's underwater cultural heritage on a par with protection afforded terrestrial cultural resources.

References

McAllister, Martin E.
  1981   Smokey and the Looters: The Jones-Gevara Pot-hunting Case, December 1977 – June

  1980.   In *Cultural Resources Law Enforcement: An Emerging Science*, compiled by Dee F. Green and Polly Davis, pp. 44-49. USDA Forest Service, Southwestern Region. Albuquerque, New Mexico.

National Park Service
  2007   Technical Brief 20: Archeological Resource Damage Assessment: Legal Basis and Methods. <http://www.cr.nps.gov/archeology/pubs/techBr/TCH20.htm>. Accessed March, 2011.

United States Sentencing Commission
  2002   Guidelines Manual §2B1.5 Theft of, Damage to, or Destruction of Cultural Heritage Resources or Paleontological Resources; Unlawful Sale, Purchase, Exchange, Transportation, or Receipt of Cultural Heritage Resources or Paleontological Resources. <http://www.ussc.gov/Guidelines/2010_guidelines/Manual>. Accessed April, 2011.

Martin E. McAllister, Larry E. Murphy, and James E. Moriarty IV
Archaeological Damage Investigation and Assessment
4815 Larch Lane
Missoula, MT 59802

1996. Sovereign Immunity and the Management of United States Naval Shipwrecks. In *Underwater Archaeology*, Stephen R. James, Jr., and Camille Stanley, editors, pp. 98–104.

ROBERT S. NEYLAND

Sovereign Immunity and the Management of United States Naval Shipwrecks

Introduction

Over the last few years the Naval Historical Center has dealt with many policy issues involving U.S. Navy ship and aircraft wrecks and other government-owned wrecks that are entitled to sovereign immunity. This paper discusses the principle of sovereign immunity, addresses the extension of this principle to vessels of the former Government of the Confederacy, and clarifies the use of certain naval terms which are often misunderstood, such as "commission and decommission" and "stricken." However, I should add the disclaimer that I am an underwater archaeologist, not a lawyer. Therefore, the interpretations provided here are my own personal opinions based on my brief experience with these issues and do not necessarily represent those of the Department of the Navy.

The Department of the Navy retains custody of its ship and aircraft wrecks despite the passage of time and regardless of whether they are lost in U.S., foreign, or international waters. These wrecks are not abandoned but remain the property of the government until a specific formal action is taken to dispose of them and, thus, are immune from the law of salvage without authorization from the appropriate Navy authorities. This immunity is founded in long-existing, historic principles of maritime law. These properties are not considered "abandoned" in the Abandoned Shipwreck Act of 1987 (43 U.S.C. 2101-2106) and did not transfer to the states with adoption of the Act.

Navy custody of its wrecks is based on the property clause of the U.S. Constitution, Articles 95 and 96 of the United Nations Convention on the Law of the Sea (1982), and established principles of international maritime law. These laws establish that right, title, or ownership of federal property is not lost to the government due to the passage of time, or by neglect or inaction. Ultimately, abandonment of government-owned ships and aircraft occurs only through congressional action.

The principal law establishing ownership within United States' territorial waters is the property clause of the United States Constitution, Article IV, Section 3, Clause 2, which provides that only Congress and those persons authorized by Congress can legally dispose of United States property pursuant to the appropriate regulations.

The sovereign immunity provisions of admiralty law are well-established, founded in early principles of maritime law. In the United States, cases have supported this doctrine and established significant legal precedents in *Hatteras Inc. v. the USS Hatteras, her engines, etc. in rem and the United States of America, in personam* (1984 A.M.C. 1094, *aff'd*, 698 F.2d 1215, 5th Cir., [1982]) and *U.S. v. Richard Steinmetz* (763 F. Supp. 1293, 1294, [D.N.J. 1991]; *aff'd*, 973 F.2nd 212, [3d Cir. 1992] *cert. denied*, 113 S. Ct. 1578 [1993]), also known as the "Alabama bell case." The former is the most frequently cited legal precedent supporting the government's policy. It involved a claim against the wreck of the USS *Hatteras* and its associated artifacts by a private salvage company. The Court, citing numerous cases and well-established precedents, determined that neither the maritime nor the common law doctrine of abandonment was applicable, and stated, "It is well settled that title to property of the United States cannot be divested by negligence, delay, laches, mistake or unauthorized actions by subordinate officials" (1984 A.M.C. 1098).

Likewise, in *United States v. Steinmetz*, which considered ownership of the bell of the CSS *Alabama*, the wreck of the CSS *Alabama* was not considered abandoned by the mere passage of time. The court applied the doctrine of sovereign immunity to property formerly owned by the Government of the Confederacy and held that the United States rightfully succeeded to the property of the former. In so doing, the Court recognized that, in spite of the rhetoric used during the Civil War to describe Confederate raiders as pirates and the citizens of the rebelling states as traitors, the Union government had in its prosecution of the war dealt with the Confederacy as a sovereign nation, although an adversarial one (Poser and Varon 1995). This case also interpreted United States' ownership as unaffected by the passage of time or by failing to salvage the property.

Sovereign rights on the high seas are affirmed in Articles 95 and 96 of *The Law of the Sea Convention* (1982). These provide a legal basis for the sovereign immunity of sunken warships and government vessels on the high seas. Article 95 states, "Warships on the high seas have complete immunity from the jurisdiction of any State other than the flag States," and Article 96 continues, "Ships owned or operated by a State and used only on government noncommercial service shall, on the high seas have complete immunity from the jurisdiction of any State other than the flag State."

At present, there is no multilateral treaty governing the treatment of sunken warships and military aircraft. In the absence of such a treaty, the governments of France, Germany, Japan, The Russian Federation, The United Kingdom, Northern Ireland, and the United States issued a joint statement in September 1995 to be used as guidance when dealing with issues related to sunken state vessels and aircraft (Department of State [DOS] 1995). States with ownership of title are referred to as the "flag states," while those States with foreign-owned sunken vessels located in their waters and subject to their jurisdiction are identified as the "coastal states." The six nations acknowledge the property rights of the flag states over their vessels, that the sunken vessels under their jurisdiction are "historical artifacts of special importance and entitled to special protections," and acknowledge that "these ships and aircraft may be the last resting places of many sailors and airmen who died in the service of their nations." It is accepted that disturbance of a ship or aircraft wreck site is a destructive process and that these sites hold a special significance for scientific discovery. Thus, any proposed recovery or excavation must provide a research design, site surveys, minimal site

disturbance consistent with research requirements, adequate financial resources, preparation of professional reports, and a comprehensive conservation plan.

A coastal state does not acquire ownership of sunken warships even though the wrecks are "located on or embedded in land or the seabed over which it exercises sovereignty or jurisdiction." The coastal state does control access to those vessels and their associated artifacts that lie within their territorial or contiguous zones. The contiguous zone can extend a maximum of 24 miles beyond the territorial sea. The 1995 joint statement allows that most governments will honor requests from the sovereign states to allow visits to their sunken vessels and aircraft. Seaward of the contiguous zone, access to the submerged state vessels is subject only to flag state control.

The joint statement provides that salvage, or attempted salvage, of state vessels and their associated artifacts is prohibited, wherever located, without the express permission of the sovereign flag state. The only exception is "opposing belligerents" during the period of their conflict. In addition, vessels and aircraft containing human remains deserve special respect as war graves and are not to be disturbed; the flag state may use all lawful means to prevent disturbance or salvage.

For United States' wrecks within foreign territorial waters, this statement implies that protection or scientific investigation depends upon cooperation between the flag and coastal states. Management of the CSS *Alabama* is one example of such international cooperation. The CSS *Alabama* is the property of the United States, but the excavation of the site is carried out under the laws of the Republic of France (Dudley 1995).

Confederate Property and the Doctrine of Succession

The CSS *Alabama* and approximately 320 other Confederate naval vessels represent a special category of shipwrecks entitled to sovereign immunity. Confederate naval vessels are currently placed under the Administrator of the General Services Administration (GSA), a responsibility the GSA inherited from the Treasury Department. A Joint Resolution of Congress, signed 21 June 1870, enabled the Secretary of the Treasury to collect, "any moneys, dues, and other interests lately in the possession of or due to the so-called Confederate States, or their agents, and now belonging to the United States..." (Forty-first Congress, Session II, Res. 75, 1870). On 2 June 1965, this was incorporated into 40 U.S.C. 310 so that the Administrator of GSA is responsible for these sunken vessels.

United States' ownership of Confederate property is also supported by legal precedent. The United States Supreme Court developed the doctrine of succession concerning Confederate property in an 1872 Supreme Court decision, *United States, Lyon, et al v. Huckabee* (83 U.S. 414 1872). In 1862, C. C. Huckabee, with three other persons, constructed an iron works in Alabama which they later sold to the Government of the Confederacy. The factory was captured by Union forces in March 1865, and in 1866 it was sold to Francis Lyon. Huckabee made a claim to regain the iron works, alleging that he and his partners were forced to sell the factory to the Confederacy. The court ruled that

> Power to acquire territory either by conquest or treaty is vested by the Constitution in the United States. Complete conquest, by whatever mode it may be perfected, carries with it all the rights of the former government, or in other words, the conqueror, by the completion of his conquest, becomes the absolute owner of the property conquered from the enemy, nation, or state (83 U.S. 414 1872:435).

This opinion was upheld in a number of subsequent cases. In *Williams v. Bruffy* (96 U.S. 176 1877:188), the Court made a similar statement: "...the Confederacy failed and in its failure its pretensions were dissipated, its armies scattered, and the whole fabric of its government broken in pieces. The very property it had amassed passed to the nation."

Under the powers of Congress and the resolution mentioned above, the victor went about divesting itself of captured Confederate property and disposing of the wreckage of war. Prior to the 1870 resolution, the Department of the Navy took responsibility for removing and salvaging many Confederate naval vessels, blockade runners, and harbor obstructions in southern ports such as that of Charleston, South Carolina (United States Government Printing Office [USGPO] 1903:355). The principle of succession was applied to the wrecks of Confederate warships sunk during hostilities with *Leathers v Salvor Wrecking etc., Co.* (15 Fed. Cas. 116, No. 8164 [S.D. Miss. 1875]). This case considered the wreck of the steamboat *Natchez*, a vessel pressed into Confederate service and burned and sunk during that service. In this case, the Confederate Government compensated the owner, Leathers, for his loss. The Court stated that, because the owner had been fully compensated for his loss by the Government of the Confederacy, "... whatever was left of her hull and machinery belonged to that government, and, by consequence, became the property of the United States" (15 Fed. Cas. 116, No. 8164 1875:116). As was mentioned by the plaintiff in *Steinmetz v United States*, the Court did not rule on the issue of whether the wreckers acting under the full authority of the federal government would have been sufficient justification by itself for the transfer of title.

In a similar vein, the United States was recognized as the successor to the Confederate government under international law. In a case concerning the Confederate warship *Rappahannock, The Beactrice otherwise The Rappahannock* (36 L.J. Adm. 9 1866), the British Admiralty Court recognized U.S. ownership of title, but subject to the prior owner's lien upon the vessel for the remainder of its purchase price. In another case, the former USS *Harriet Lane*, which was captured by Confederate forces and later sold, was returned to United States Navy custody after negotiations with the government of Spain (Trexler 1931:109-123).

Government title can be lost, transferred, or given up. Under the rules of international law, government vessels and aircraft can be lost by capture during battle (before sinking), such as the Russian cruiser *Admiral Nakhimov* which sank one hour after being captured on 28 May 1905 by the Japanese Imperial Navy (29 Japanese Ann. Int'l L. 1986:185-187; Strati 1995:238). A second method is by international agreement or treaty, such as the Treaty of Peace with Japan, signed 8 September 1951, which provides in Chapter V, Article 14(a)2(I) that each of the Allied Powers "shall have the right to seize, retain, liquidate or otherwise dispose of all property, rights and interests" of Japan, "which on the first coming into force of the present Treaty were subject to its [the Allied Powers] jurisdiction" (DOS 1951). Another example is the United States' ships sunk during the Atomic Bomb test at Bikini and Kwajalein Atoll, the title to which was transferred to the Government of the Marshall Islands by international agreement in accord with Article 177 of the Compact of Free Association. Thirdly, an express act of abandonment, gift, or sale by the United States Congress can divest the government's title to property, such as was done with the War of 1812 ships *Hamilton* and *Scourge*. The procedures for abandonment of sunken United States warships and aircraft located outside the territory of the United States are set forth in 40 U.S.C. & 512 (1987 supplement V) and its implementing regulation 41 CFR Part 101-45 (1994).

In the case of transferring the *Hamilton* and the *Scourge* from the United States to the Royal Ontario Museum, the Secretary of the Navy W. Graham Claytor, Jr., used his authority under U.S. law (10 U.S.C. 7308) and the acquiescence of the United States Congress, as required by law, to donate the wrecks, provided that there was respectful treatment of any human remains that might be recovered. It was stipulated that the crew members' remains would be returned to the Navy and sent to the Armed Forces Institute of Pathology (Claytor 1979).

Terminology

The term "capture" indicates those cases in which the act of taking control immediately transfers the full legal ownership of that which is taken. By the act of capture, a vessel in the military service of an adversary becomes the property of the captor's government and title is immediately vested in the captor's government. It is unnecessary to send a captured public vessel into port for adjudication or to comply with the various formalities required when the case has to be prepared for a prize court (USGPO 1924:36; Smith 1959:126-127; Colombos 1967:801). Thus, a British gunboat captured during the War of 1812 could be used immediately in the United States fleet and, if sunk, would belong to the United States. Examples of acquisition by capture can be found in most naval wars in which the United States has been involved, including the American Revolution, the War of 1812, and the Civil War. Over the course of the Civil War, both the Confederacy and the Union captured and then deployed their respective prizes as warships. As a result of World War I and World War II, the United States received a number of German and Japanese naval vessels as war prizes.

Ships subject to capture during a conflict can be placed into four categories: (1) enemy warships, troopships, and other enemy vessels employed in the public service; (2) all ships, enemy or neutral, which take a direct part in hostilities on the enemy side; (3) "fleet auxiliaries," enemy or neutral, such as colliers and similar vessels, wholly engaged at the time in the direct service of the enemy or neutral, which take a direct part in hostilities on the enemy side; (4) "fleet auxiliaries," enemy or neutral, such as colliers and similar vessels, wholly engaged at the time in the direct service of the enemy armed forces (Smith 1959:126-127).

The terms "commissioned," "decommissioned," and "stricken" often create confusion but in fact have no relevance to title. Commissioning and decommissioning a ship refers only to making a ship a command or terminating that command. A commission is the fixed period of time in which a warship, with its full complement of officers and men, is allocated to particular duties anywhere in the world. After a ship is commissioned, she continues in that state until she returns to her home, or other port, to pay off, at which time her company is dispersed. At the end of a commission, a ship may recommission immediately with a new complement, may remain temporarily out of commission during a major dockyard refit, or if at the end of her active life may be laid up in reserve, or pending sale, or breaking up (Kemp 1976:118). A ship without a commission still remains government property under jurisdiction of the Navy, but it is simply no longer a command. For obvious reasons, Navy small craft, such as yard vessels, never receive a commission.

The term "stricken" frequently appears in Navy records in reference to the disposition of a ship or aircraft. Some individuals have inferred abandonment from the use of this term. Although a ship may "strike its colors in battle" to signify its surrender, the term "stricken" as in the Navy records refers to removing the aircraft or ship from active duty status. Logically, the last status reported for an aircraft or ship that is lost or missing is "stricken." A 1945 Navy memorandum lists six conditions under which "stricken" can be written into the record of an aircraft: lost or missing, damaged beyond economical repair, salvaged for essential equipment or parts, disposed of outside the United States pursuant to the policies of the Integrated Aeronautic Program, disposed of outside the United States as directed by the Commanding Naval Officer, or transferred from Navy custody (Gates 1945). More recently "stricken" is defined in OPNAV INSTRUCTION 5442.8 of 18 April 1995 as "The official action that removes an aircraft from the inventory and commensurate reporting responsibilities" (Chief of Naval Operations 1995:7). An aircraft or a vessel that is listed as "stricken" can, at a later date, be put back into active service.

There are several important reasons that continued United States' government ownership of its sunken warships and aircraft is important.

These are listed in the Navy's policy fact sheet *Sunken Naval Vessels & Naval Aircraft Wreck Sites* (Naval Historical Center 1995) and include compliance with federal preservation laws, protection of war graves, dangers to the public from ordnance and explosives, and the recognition that these wrecks represent valuable historic properties that are in the public trust.

Human Remains

Where human remains are concerned, United States Navy policy has been clear for some time:

> salvors should not presume that sunken U.S. warships have been abandoned by the United States. Permission must be granted from the United States to salvage sunken U.S. warships, and as a matter of policy, the United States Government does not grant such permission with respect to ships that contain the remains of deceased service men... (DOS 1986; UNESCO 1994).

This is not a new policy, as the Navy's involvement with the USS *Tecumseh* illustrates. *Tecumseh* was lost in 1864 during the battle of Mobile Bay with 93 men on board. In 1873, *Tecumseh* was sold for salvage by the Department of the Treasury to James E. Slaughter of Mobile for $50 (West 1995:27). After the purchase, Slaughter let it be known that he intended to use explosives to blast the wreck into salvageable pieces to recover iron and possibly the ship's safe. In 1876, the relatives of the men lost on the *Tecumseh* petitioned Congress to stop this salvage. Congress quickly passed Joint Resolution No. 23 on August 15, 1876, directing the Secretary of the Treasury to return the $50, with 6 percent interest, to Slaughter and empowered the Secretary of the Navy to assume control and protection of the *Tecumseh*. Congress stipulated that any salvage must provide for the removal and proper burial of the remains of the crew. Another example from the Civil War concerns the remains of the crew of the USS *Tulip*. A boiler explosion sent the *Tulip* and most of her crew to the bottom of the Chesapeake Bay. Only a few bodies were recovered, and these were buried on shore within site of the disaster. Correspondence in Navy files dating to at least three periods in 1929, 1951, and 1967 show continued Navy concern over the remains of both the crew members buried ashore and those carried down with the ship (Ellicott 1929; Heffernan 1951; [Eller] 1969). The Navy refused a 1967 request from a diving club for salvage rights to the *Tulip,* primarily on the basis of "nondesecration of crew members entombed in sunken naval vessels." Other considerations were ordnance still on board and damage to the historic and archaeological integrity of the site.

Conclusions

The refusal of permission to the salvage of the *Tulip* shows that as early as 1967, the Navy considered such wrecks to be war graves and of historic significance. The Navy staff involved were from the Naval Historical Center and the Navy JAG, Admiralty Division. The individuals in these Navy branches foresaw the importance of sunken ships and aircraft for interpreting the history of the United States and its Navy. Today, the Navy recognizes that it has under its jurisdiction some of the most significant historical properties within the United States. Many, if not all, of the Navy's sunken warships are eligible for listing on the National Register of Historic Places, for these are reminders of the actions and events that forged the nation. These sunken vessels and aircraft also represent the courageous actions of those Americans who have earned a permanent place in United States history and are the final resting place for many who sacrificed their lives for their country. Sovereign immune status is a key concept and doctrine for all those who seek to protect a nation's naval heritage, whether U.S. or foreign, from willful destruction and wrongful taking. It is also the *raison d' etre* for the Navy's policy concerning its ship and aircraft wrecks.

REFERENCES

CHIEF OF NAVAL OPERATIONS
   1995   OPNAV INSTRUCTION 5442.8. Management of the Naval Aircraft Inventory. Instruction dated 18 April 1995, on file, Department of the Navy, Washington, D.C.

CLAYTOR, JR., W. GRAHAM
   1979   Letter from Secretary of the Navy to the Chairman of the Board of Trustees, Royal Ontario Museum. April 27, 1979. Naval Historical Center, Washington, D.C.

COLOMBOS, C.J.
   1967   *The International Law of the Sea.* Longman Group Ltd., London.

DEPARTMENT OF STATE (DOS)
   1951   Treaty of Peace with Japan. 8 September 1951, *United States Treaties and Other International Agreements,* vol. 3, no. 3181.

   1986   Letter to Maritime Administration, dated 30 December 1980. *Digest of United States Practice in International Law,* 8:999, 1004. U.S. Government Printing Office, Washington, D.C.

   1995   Joint Statement on Sunken State Vessels and Aircraft. Cable to American Embassies Bonn, London, Tokyo, Paris, and Moscow. Unclassified naval message dated September 1995, on file, Naval Historical Center, Washington, D.C.

DUDLEY, WILLIAM S.
   1995   Submerged Cultural Resources in Peril: A Naval Perspective. *Underwater Archaeology Proceedings from the Society for Historical Archaeology Conference:*111-114. Paul F. Johnston, editor. Washington, D.C.

[ELLER, ERNEST M.]
   1969   Letter from Director of Naval History to the Judge Advocate General. Letter dated 28 February 1969, on file USS *Tulip* file, Ship's History Branch, Naval Historical Center, Washington, D.C.

ELLICOTT J.M.
   1929   Letter to the Secretary of the Navy. Letter dated 16 September 1929, on file USS *Tulip* file, Ship's History Branch, Naval Historical Center, Washington, D.C.

FORTY-FIRST CONGRESS. SESSION II RESOLUTION 75
1870 Joint Resolution to enable the Secretary of the Treasury to collect wrecked and abandoned property, derelict Claims, and Dues belonging to the United States. *Statutes at Large and Proclamations of the United States of America, from December 1869 to March 1871.* Vol. 26. George P. Sanger, editor. Little, Brown, and Company, Boston, Massachusetts.

GATES, ARTEMUS L.
1945 Memorandum from Acting Secretary of the Navy to the Chief of Naval Operations. 20 April 1945. Naval Historical Center, Washington, D.C.

HEFFERNAN, JOHN B.
1951 Letter to Captain Riddle, Commandant, Naval Gun Factory, Washington, D.C. Letter dated 31 October 1951, on file in USS *Tulip* file, Ship's History Branch, Naval Historical Center, Washington, D.C.

KEMP, PETER
1976 *The Oxford Companion to Ships & the Sea.* Oxford University Press, New York.

NAVAL HISTORICAL CENTER
1995 *Sunken Naval Vessels & Naval Aircraft Wreck Sites.* Policy fact sheet. Naval Historical Center, Washington, D.C.

POSER, SUSAN, AND ELIZABETH R. VARON
1995 *United States v. Steinmetz*: The Legal Legacy of the Civil War, Revisited. *Alabama Law Review* 46.3:725-762.

SMITH, H. A.
1959 *The Law and the Custom of the Sea.* Number 9, The Library of World Affairs. Stevens & Sons Ltd., London.

STRATI, ANASTASIA
1995 *The Protection of the Underwater Cultural Heritage: An Emerging Objective of the Contemporary Law of the Sea.* In Publications on Ocean Development. Vol. 23, edited by Shigeru Oda. Martinus Nijhoff Publishers, Boston, Massachusetts.

TREXLER, H.A.
1931 The *Harriet Lane* and the Blockade of Galveston. *Southwestern Historical Quarterly* 35:109-23. Texas State Historical Association, Austin, Texas.

UNESCO
1994 Buenos Aires Draft Convention on the Protection of the Underwater Cultural Heritage. Draft convention dated August 1994.

UNITED NATIONS
1982 *The Law of the Sea: Practice of States at the Time of Entry into Force of the United Nations Convention on the Law of the Sea.*

UNITED STATES GOVERNMENT PRINTING OFFICE (USGPO)
1903 *Official Records of the Union and Confederate Navies in the War of Rebellion.* Series I, Vol. 16. U.S. Government Printing Office, Washington, D.C.

1924 *Instructions for the Navy of the United States Governing Maritime Warfare, June 1917.* U.S. Government Printing Office, Washington, D.C.

WEST, WILSON W., JR.
1995 USS *Tecumseh* Shipwreck Management Plan. Report prepared by National Park Service-Maritime Initiative. Submitted to Naval Historical Center, Washington, D.C.

ROBERT S. NEYLAND
6113 QUEBEC PLACE
COLLEGE PARK, MARYLAND 20740

2008. Establishing Marine Protected Areas in the Dominican Republic: A Model for Sustainable Preservation. In *ACUA Underwater Archaeology Proceedings 2008*, Susan Langley and Victor Mastone, editors, pp. 52–61.

Establishing Marine Protected Areas in the Dominican Republic: A Model for Sustainable Preservation

Frederick H. Hanselmann
Indiana University Office of Underwater Science, 1025 E. 7th St., HPER 058, Bloomington, Indiana 47405

Charles D. Beeker
Indiana University Office of Underwater Science, 1025 E. 7th St., HPER 058, Bloomington, Indiana 47405

The establishment of Marine Protected Areas (MPA's) is the most effective way of preserving submerged cultural and biological resources for the future. Properly designed, interpreted and managed, MPA's not only protect resources, but also play a vital role in educating the current generations about their historical past and environmental present and can be used as a tool to further economic development. The development and establishment of a system of Marine Protected Areas in the Dominican Republic greatly enhances cultural heritage tourism in the country, provides a sustainable model for preserving the past, and serves as a tool for economic development.

Introduction

For centuries, man has used a wide variety of vessels to ply the oceans in search of discovery, conquest, and trade. Voyages, ships, and their captains have become the subjects of legend, history, and, most recently, tourism. Cultural heritage tourism is a growing activity and, due to the extensive global community of recreational scuba divers, shipwrecks and Marine Protected Areas (MPA's) are included on many tourists' to-do lists, along with places such as the Grand Canyon and the Great Wall of China. Many are drawn to see and attempt to experience history. Hundreds of shipwrecks litter the floor of the Caribbean. Marine Protected Areas preserve remnants of the past, as well as protect the biology associated with a wreck, and provide this experience of history by allowing tourists to dive shipwrecks. The Guadalupe Underwater Archaeological Preserve is the world's first underwater museum exhibit, a site that makes use of artifacts from a historical shipwreck to attract tourists to Bayahibe, Dominican Republic. The development and establishment of a system of Marine Protected Areas in the Dominican Republic, which incorporates the Guadalupe Underwater Archaeological Preserve, greatly enhances cultural heritage tourism in the country, provides a sustainable model for preserving the past, and serves as a tool for economic development.

Cultural Heritage Tourism

Cultural heritage may be seen as the attributes or objects inherited from those who preceded us. This can be both tangible and intangible. Cultural tourism involves a number of definitions. Some recognize it as a form of special interest tourism in which culture is the basis, or attraction, for tourists and the motivation to travel (McKercher and Du Cros 2002, Zeppel 1992). The World Tourism Organization defines cultural tourism as the culturally motivated movement of people essentially for participation in study tours, performing arts and cultural tours, travel to festivals and other events, visit to sites and monuments, travel to study nature, folklore, or art, and pilgrimages (World Tourism Organization 1985). From a business perspective, cultural tourism can also be seen as the development and marketing of sites and attractions for foreign and domestic

Perspectives from *Historical Archaeology* and *ACUA Proceedings*

tourists (McKercher and Du Cros 2002, Goodrich 1997). Archaeology focuses largely on the tangible attributes of heritage, which can be buildings, monuments, possessions, or, specifically, shipwrecks and their artifacts. Cultural attractions play an important role in tourism on a variety of levels. Cultural tourism has both positive economic and social outcomes; it preserves heritage, facilitates understanding, and furthers tourism (Gratton and Richards 1996). Cultural tourism focuses on the conservation of cultural resources, the interpretation of resources, visitors' experiences, and earned revenues, which demonstrates that an understanding of the impacts, benefits, and financial resources behind historical sites is crucial (Fladmark 1994).

Marine Protected Areas

Marine Protected Areas are a part of cultural heritage tourism. While shipwrecks are most widely associated with treasure and those who "hunt" it, more and more people are coming to view them as cultural resources. There are more profits to be found in displaying the artifacts than in simply selling them to the highest bidder (Throckmorton 1990). Archaeological resources are an asset to communities that create museums, which in turn attract tourists. In Bodrum, Turkey, a ruined crusader museum was converted into an archaeological museum in 1959; at this time, the town's population was approximately 5,000 people and there was relatively no tourism (Throckmorton 1990). Since then, a group of underwater archaeologists have been excavating significant shipwrecks and creating exhibit material for the museum. An estimated 500,000 visitors per year come to the museum, now the second most visited in Turkey next to the National Museum; the town's population has tripled, and local businesses are thriving (Throckmorton 1990).

The Marine Protected Area is a similar concept that tends to be more participative in nature. An excellent example of Marine Protected Areas is the United States' National Oceanic and Atmospheric Administration's (NOAA) creation of National Marine Sanctu-

aries, with the first established in 1972. Currently, there are thirteen national marine sanctuaries and one marine national monument, with sites found in areas surrounding American Samoa, the Florida Keys, and the Great Lakes. According to NOAA, the mission of the National Marine Sanctuaries is to "serve as the trustee for the nation's system of marine protected areas, to conserve, protect, and enhance their biodiversity, ecological integrity and cultural legacy" (NOAA 2006b). Under this similar rubric, NOAA's Maritime Heritage program functions to preserve "cultural and archaeological resources within the National Marine Sanctuaries...to protect, promote and explore our maritime heritage through a national program embracing heritage resources in our evolving coastal, marine and Great Lakes stewardship" (NOAA 2006c). Most importantly, NOAA also defines a Marine Protected Area as "any area of the marine environment that has been reserved by Federal, State, territorial, tribal or local laws or regulations to provide lasting protection for part or all of the natural and cultural resources therein" (NOAA 2006a). The keyword in this definition is "lasting," referring to a sustainable preservation of the sites for future generations.

Benefits of Marine Protected Areas

With the number of active scuba divers in the millions and continually rising, MPA's and underwater parks can see good deal of traffic and visitors. This creates a demand for both MPA's and underwater parks. Many of the existing parks are heavily used and more are needed. There are many benefits stemming from underwater parks. The Professional Association of Diving Instructors (PADI) listed the following advantages to increasing the number of underwater parks, which also detail many of the benefits associated with such sites including the following:

1) increased protection of precious, unique, and popular aquatic environments,

2) increased access for scuba divers to coastal and inland aquatic environments,

3) increased opportunity for local aquatic-oriented business near newly developed underwater parks,

4) increased opportunity for local business support such as hotels, restaurants, etc.,

5) increased income by state recreation departments and/or federal agencies from usage fees, concessions, etc.

6) the creation of new jobs (PADI 1984).

Studies have suggested that underwater parks are beneficial to divers, industry, and the community (Adams et.al. 2006, Alger County Underwater Preserve Committee 1980, Halsey and Martindale 1987, Whitehead and Finney 2003). Cost-benefit analysis of artificial reefs in Florida, many of which are shipwrecks and part of a national marine sanctuary, illustrate net benefits to society (Adams et al. 2006). These benefits involve an increase in economic activity related to the activities, such as expenditures, income, and jobs (Adams et.al. 2006).

Contingent valuation has also been used to place a value on underwater cultural resources. This is a method based on surveys of peoples' preferences that incorporate questions regarding how much they would be willing to pay to ensure a service such as an underwater park, or, conversely, how much they would be willing to accept in compensation to endure a welfare loss from the reduced service. Contingent valuation allows for an existence value. Existence values demonstrate how much people are willing to pay to ensure the existence of environmental services, such as the existence of the rain forest. Existence values, or the warm glow/good feeling effect, are also non-market benefits associated with the underwater park (Adams et.al. 2006). Such non-market value related to underwater cultural resources can be overlooked. One study examined the non-market value generated by management of shipwrecks as submerged cultural resources in North Carolina, which is well-known for

the variety of shipwrecks available to divers; the state directly and indirectly monitors approximately 5,000 shipwrecks (Whitehead and Finney 2003). In this case, contingent valuation showed that the majority of respondents were willing to pay money for protection of shipwrecks and preservation of these cultural resources as a public good (Whitehead and Finney 2003).

Establishing a Marine Protected Area: A Sustainable Model

In order to establish a successful Marine Protected Area, it is necessary to ensure that it protects the resources while allowing the public to enjoy the site and provides the scientific community the opportunity to conduct research within the protected area. Most importantly, the methods for establishing MPA's are sustainable and further the preservation of the archaeology and biology of the site for future generations. There are several steps that must be followed in order to successfully create a Marine Protected Area. The following are Indiana University's 10 Commandments of Underwater Park Establishment:

1) Proposal to governing bodies: includes all site data

2) Establish park boundaries

3) Install appropriate buoy system

4) Place an underwater plaque

5) Create an underwater guide

6) Create a land-based component

7) Publish a brochure or other materials

8) Organize a dedication ceremony

9) Establish site monitoring procedures

10) Encourage continuous public involvement

The first step in the process is to prepare a proposal for the establishment and development of the park. The proposal is a compilation of all the information gathered on the site. It should then be presented to the agency that will support and manage the park as well as representatives of the local community. This is the stage in which the parties involved address any potential problems foreseen in the site. Next, it is necessary to establish the park's boundaries. Said boundaries must encompass

470

all of the important archaeological and biological features of the site. They must also guarantee that the site is within the jurisdiction of the appropriate agency.

The site will then require the installation of an appropriate buoy system. Minimally, the sight should have one spar buoy and one mooring buoy. The spar buoy contains information on the identification of the park and the jurisdictional logo of the respective agency. The mooring buoy is used for boats to tie off to and is needed to prevent anchor damage and enhance the safety of divers visiting the site. Installation of a buoy system is very important for the protection of both the marine life and those visiting, or working on, the site.

Identification and education are important in an underwater park. An underwater plaque should be placed in a prominent location of the site. It should be a waterproof and marine environment resistant permanent plaque located underwater near the significant features of the site. The plaque should provide brief information about the origin of the site. The park also requires an underwater guide that is made available to divers and the non-diving public. The guide should contain a site map, historical information, safety concerns, and the rules of stewardship in the park. In addition, a land-based component of the park should be found within close proximity to the site. This component can be any of a variety of buildings or arrangements, such as a museum, a small building, or a kiosk. This is a method of educating the non-diving community about the site. Displays and exhibits can be set up as well, showcasing artifacts and providing brochures and literature regarding the site. A brochure or literature about the site is important because it is available to both divers and non-divers alike. It should be an expanded version of the underwater guide and should be available to the public through the administrative agency, local dive shops, and in the land-based component of the park.

Of crucial importance is the establishment of site monitoring procedures. The goals of site monitoring are to ensure that no harm occurs to any feature of the site, as well as to assess any changes. This is a key element to the park's success and entails periodic site evaluations. Site maintenance must be ensured by encouraging public involvement in the protection and monitoring of the park. Engaging local divers in recording and reporting observations is one method of acquiring the most up-to-date information. Using a combination of both local diver observation and periodic scientific site assessment by professionals, an MPA can be efficiently monitored and protected. Given the data that collected, scientists and park professionals may then decide how best to proceed with the management of the MPA. For example, if usage is deemed too invasive, the site can be placed on reserve status and closed to the diving public in order to allow the marine life time to regenerate. Yet, the point of public participation is to preserve the site and allow usage at the same time, in a sustainable manner.

Key to this process of establishment is fomenting local participation and ownership. An underwater park is important to a wide variety of stakeholders, on both a local and national level. In order to garner proper participation and foster site protection, stakeholder interest is crucial to creating a sense of local ownership. Community involvement seminars may be conducted to better gauge public perception and interest. The dive community can be involved in monitoring the site and educating divers about its importance. Local involvement is the key to the success of a marine protected area or an underwater preserve (Beeker 1991). The scientific community can use the site as a field resource for both students and professionals in fields such as archaeology, biology, ecology, and geology. The park is created in order for people to make use of it. Tourists are very important stakeholders in this process, insomuch that their interest plays a large role in which sites should be developed as MPA's. The visitors are the people that have a strong desire to experience the history of the associated sites and are also the main source of revenue to those with an investment in the MPA's. In finalizing the establishment of the park, it is very nice to organize a park dedication ceremony, to which should be invited the public and the diving, academic, and governmental communities. Press coverage is advantageous, as it can reach many that are interested in such activities.

The System of Marine Protected Areas in the Dominican Republic

Following the aforementioned guidelines, Indiana University professors, researchers, and students are establishing a system of Marine Protected Areas along the southeastern coast of the Dominican Republic, in the region of La Romana-Bayahibe (Figure 1). The model is based on the United States system,

which is used extensively by NOAA in its National Marine Sanctuary Program, and serves to protect cultural and biological resources from looting and treasure hunting, encourage local participation and ownership, provide public interpretation and educational resources, and serve as an economic development tool in furthering sustainable tourism. The goals entailed through the model are similar to that of NOAA, to preserve and protect the biological and cultural resources found in the waters of the given sites. Success has principally been achieved with the *Guadalupe* Underwater Archaeological Preserve and the St. George. The other four sites are still undergoing further development to become open to the public as MPA's.

Figure 1. Regional map which includes the systems of MPAs (Courtesy of Indiana University 2008).

The six potential MPA's are as follows:
- The 1724 *Guadalupe* Underwater Archaeological Preserve

- Padre Nuestro Cave Chicho Cavern
- Caballo Blanco Reef
- St. George
- Catalina Island Shipwreck

472

The difficulties associated with establishing this system stem from working in a developing country that does not have the same infrastructure as the United States or another, more-developed country. However, Indiana University has had much success with its work on the MPA's. A key aspect to the system's success is community involvement. The stakeholders involved in the system are on both national and local levels. Government agencies over culture, archaeology, and tourism are involved and play key roles in furthering the system. The local tourism and dive industry, including the hotel association and a number of dive operators have been crucial to maintaining and preserving the sites. The community in general is also very supportive, although people initially seemed skeptical. Archaeologists teach that there is more money to be made in residual income from using sites as an MPA, rather than a one-time profit from selling a looted artifact. The community is turning the corner, as local boat operators now communicate with researchers to make suggestions for site enhancement and protection, such as requesting additional mooring buoys. As the system progresses, so does its sustainability, as evidenced in the 1724 *Guadalupe* Underwater Archaeological Preserve.

1724 Guadalupe *Underwater Archaeological Preserve*

On July 13, 1724, the *Nuestra Señora de Guadalupe* set sail from Cádiz, Spain for Veracruz, Mexico, but never reached its destination. The galleon was constructed in 1702 in Campeche, Mexico and was specifically designed for transporting quicksilver for use in the King of Spain's gold and silver mines. The *Guadalupe* weighed over 1,000 tons, had 74 cannons, and could transport 250 tons of quicksilver. It could also carry passengers and their belongings (Borrell 1980).

The Guadalupe sailed with the *Conde de Tolosa*. Each carried 150 pounds (68.04 kg) of quicksilver and 600 people, including officials, sailors, soldiers, and settlers. After taking on fresh supplies in Puerto Rico, the vessels sailed towards Hispaniola, now the Dominican Republic. On the northeast coast of the island, disaster struck hammered by storms and wind, the *Guadalupe* ran aground on a shallow reef and gradually sank. More than half of the passengers were able to get safely to shore. The *Tolosa* was not so lucky and smashed against reefs in deeper water, quickly buried in forty feet of water. Almost all drowned, save a group of seven who remained in the main mast–which did not collapse–for 32 days and a group of six who managed to escape and reach shore by rigging a raft from the floating wood. The survivors of the wrecks made camp on the shore and a small group left to search for a village, trekking almost all the way to Santo Domingo before being discovered by a fisherman (Borrell 1980). The ships lay untouched until 1976 when the Dominican Republic's Underwater Archaeological Recovery Commission began archaeological work with Captain Tracy Bowden and his company, Caribe Salvage. Following a series of excavations that spanned the following years, many of the most important artifacts were conserved and then exhibited in several of the museums in Santo Domingo, with a majority of the artifacts kept in storage and others remaining unconserved due to lack of resources.

In 2002, Indiana University suggested that some of the unconserved artifacts could be put to better use as an underwater museum exhibit available to tourists. Following the guidelines for establishing a Marine Protected Area, the archaeologists returned with a multidisciplinary group of faculty and students to create the exhibit. The preserve is located off Dominicus Beach in Bayahibe, on the far southeastern stretch of the Dominican Republic's coastline, adjacent to the East National Park. The cannons were first transported via boom crane to Dominicus Beach. From there the cannons were moved into the ocean using a system of planks and poles as movement and placed in the water. They were then pulled by boat into deeper water. The site is located in front of the Viva Dominicus Beach Resort and is monitored and maintained in collaboration between the resort and its dive shop, the Aso-ciación de Hoteles La Romana-Bayahibe, the Dominican Republic's Oficina Nacional de Patrimonio Cultural Subacuático (ONPCS), and Indiana University. The original site was located in approximately 15 feet (4.57 m) of water. After a hurricane moved some of the artifacts, it was deemed necessary to relocate the site to deeper water. For a second time, the scientists moved the cannons into deeper wa-ter, where the site now currently sits at an ap-proximate depth of 26 feet, near a reef. The group chose the current site not only based on depth, but also based on the adjacent patch reef that is south of the exhibit. In this case, history protects biology. In the past few years, little damage has occurred to the artifacts and the integrity of the underwater museum ex-hibit has been protected. The artifacts are now experiencing growth as marine organisms make the site their new habitat. The Guada-lupe Underwater Archaeological Preserve brings many benefits to the area. The local dive industry utilizes the park on a daily basis. From the resort's point of view, it is an excel-lent marketing tool in regards to attracting new clientele and to be able to tell student di-vers that upon completion of their training, they will be able to dive on a location just off-shore that has authentic artifacts from a 1724 Spanish shipwreck. As the depth is minimal, it is also an excellent site for beginning divers.

The 1724 *Guadalupe* Underwater Ar-chaeological Preserve provides a sustainable alternative to the damaging side effects of treasure hunting. Treasure hunters often work on a percentage split with the host authority governing the waters and in order to maximize their potential profits, they need to recover as many artifacts as possible. Developing coun-tries rarely have proper conservation facilities. Even in the few less developed countries that do have the capability of archaeological con-servation, the resources to cover long-term treatment rarely exist. In essence, artifacts given to the appropriate host authority often fail to receive the required treatment and break down. Without proper conservation, the arti-facts would have been better left underwater.

The Guadalupe Preserve allowed for the placement of unconserved artifacts in the wa-ter for the purpose of public education and interpretation, thus preserving a part of history that could have been lost to future generations.

Padre Nuestro Cave and Chicho Cavern

Padre Nuestro Cave and Chicho Cavern are Taino water-gathering sites (Beeker et. al. 2002). While both are land-locked, their inclu-sion as MPA's further preserves submerged cultural resources and paints the picture of the cultural heritage of the Dominican Republic. Both sites have yielded hundreds of Taino ar-tifacts, mainly ceramic sherds and vessels used for gathering water (ibid). Two species of extinct sloths have also been found in Padre Nuestro. As Chicho is a cavern with little overhead environment, it is an excellent site for conducting open water dives. Padre Nuestro would be reserved for advanced di-vers only. However, each site is being devel-oped along the same lines as the *Guadalupe* Preserve following the aforementioned guide-lines. Indiana University archaeologists have arranged for the creation of museum quality replicas based on the artifacts recovered from the sites. These replicas will be housed and mounted at selected points of reference un-derwater in each site. Each site will also have its accompanying underwater guide. Also of importance are the preventative safety meas-ures that will be taken by placing signs warn-ing of penetrating into the submerged tunnels of the caves. These two sites will serve as un-derwater museum exhibits of the prehistory of the region.

St. George Artificial Reef

Originally known as M.V. Norbrae, the St. George was built in 1962, in Ardrossan shipyard in Strathclyde, Scotland. This 240 feet (73.15 m) long, transatlantic cargo freighter, which transported wheat and barley between Norway and the Americas, was aban-doned in Santo Domingo harbor after 20 years of service. Renamed after taking the full brunt

474

of Hurricane George, St. George was bought by Club Dominicus and sunk with the assistance of Indiana University on June 12, 1999, offshore of Dominicus Resorts.

Caballo Blanco

Caballo Blanco Reef has two sites that merit further research. Most importantly, it appears to be a 16th century grounding site, within which rest two iron anchors and two bombards. The remains of an 18th century wreck, such as cannons and anchors, are also found adjacent to the 16th century site. Once established as an MPA, the protection provided will greater further the future research of the shipwrecks of the area.

Catalina Island Shipwreck

The Catalina Island Shipwreck is the most recent inclusion to the system of MPA's. While full scale archaeological investigations are still to occur in the future, the site holds immense potential as an MPA and for sustainable tourism. Of very important note, the Dominican government contacted Indiana University about identifying the site and, more specifically, developing it as an MPA, which speaks to the benefits of MPA's and the popularity and success of the *Guadalupe* Preserve. Furthermore, initial research indicates that the wreck could possibly the *Quedagh Merchant*, which Captain William Kidd left on Catalina Island when he departed for New England to clear his name of piracy in 1699. This indicates a shift in the national paradigm regarding the protection and preservation of submerged cultural resources. For two years prior, a treasure hunting company searched for the Quedagh Merchant with no success. Shortly following the termination of the exploration and salvage contract, a local resident, Ferruccio Fiorucci, discovered a large quantity of cannons while snorkeling near Catalina Island. He contacted ONPCS, who in turn contacted Indiana University. The government could have easily renewed the treasure hunters' contract for a given sum of money, yet ONPCS has a long history of preserving and protecting cultural patrimony in Dominican waters and sought an alternative to treasure hunting. The shipwreck is located off of the eastern coast of Catalina Island, near La Romana. Based on the preliminary survey, the site boasts 26 cannons, 3 broken anchors, and a beautiful coral ecosystem that leads to a coral wall that drops to approximately 600 feet (182.88 m). Currently protected as a reserve, only authorized researchers are allowed to visit the site, which will be opened to the public following the completion of the fieldwork. The local tourism and dive industry highly anticipate the opening of the site, as its historical context has garnered international attention.

Conclusion

Cultural heritage tourism is a rapidly growing and vital aspect of global tourism and Marine Protected Areas have an exciting niche within this industry, which is very important to economic development in the Dominican Republic. Many other places exist in the Caribbean with more abundant marine life, better visibility, and better infrastructure. However, the Dominican Republic can be a hub of cultural heritage tourism. No other country can boast such history as the remains of Columbus' settlement at Isabela, the site of the first capital of the New World in Santo Domingo, or the variety of maritime cultural resources and museums available to the public. The Dominican Republic's first system of Marine Protected Areas furthers the sustainable use and public interpretation of this history: submerged prehistoric Taino sites, a 16th century Columbus-era grounding site, an underwater museum exhibit of an 18th century shipwreck, an artificial reef, and the possible wreck of Captain Kidd's *Quedagh Merchant* of 1699. As a part of this system, the 1724 *Guadalupe* Underwater Archaeological Preserve attracts a wide variety of tourists to Bayahibe and its resorts, even leading some to learn scuba diving for the first time. Most importantly, this system of Marine Protected Areas benefits the involved stakeholders, while preserving and protecting the historical and archaeological record of the Dominican Republic for future generations.

Acknowledgments

The authors would like to acknowledge their partners in developing the system of MPA's: Pedro Borrell, Francis Soto, and the staff of the Oficina Nacional del Patrimonio Cultural Subacuático of the Secretaria del Estado de Cultura, Wyndham Viva Dominicus Beach Resort, the Asociación de Hoteles La Romana-Bayahibe, the California Department of Parks and Recreation, and the various Indiana University faculty and students that have participated in the fieldwork over the past years.

References

Adams, C., B. Lindberg, and J. Stevely.
2006   The Economic Benefits Associated with Florida's Artificial Reefs. Document FE649 of the Food and Resource Economics Department and the Institute of Food and Agricultural Sciences, University of Florida.

Alger County Underwater Preserve Committee.
1980   An Evaluation of the Proposed Alger County Underwater Preserve. ACUPC.

Beeker, C.
1991   Recognizing a Renewable Resource: The Public and Shipwrecks. On file, Indiana University Office of Underwater Science

Beeker, C., G. Conrad, and J. Foster
2002   Taíno Use of Flooded Caverns in the East National Park Region, Dominican Republic. *Journal of Caribbean Archaeology*. 2:1-26.

Borrell, P.
1980   *The Quicksilver Galleons: The Salvage of the Spanish Galleons Nuestra Señora de Guadalupe and El Conde de Tolosa*. The Underwater Archaeological Recovery Commission.

Fladmark, J. (Ed.).
1994   *Cultural Tourism: Papers Presented at the Robert Gordon University Heritage Convention*. Donhead Publishing.

Goodrich, J.
1997   Cultural Tourism in Europe. *Journal of Travel Research*. 35(3):91.

Gratton, C. and Richards, G.
1996   The Economic Context of Cultural Tourism. In Richards, G. (Ed.), *Cultural Tourism in Europe*. CAB International.

Halsey, J. and J. Martindale
1987   Sacking the Inland Seas: Shipwreck Plundering in the Great Lakes. *Michigan History*. November/December, p.36.

McKercher, B. and H. Du Cros
2002   *Cultural Tourism: The Partnership Between Tourism and Cultural Heritage Management*. Haworth Hospitality Press.

National Atmospheric and Oceanic Administration, National Marine Protected Areas Center.
2006a   *Draft Framework for Developing the National System of Marine Protected Areas*. National Atmospheric and Oceanic Administration.

2006b Website on National Marine Sanctuaries. Retrieved November 2006 from: http://www.sanctuaries.nos.noaa.gov/.

2006c Website on Maritime Heritage Program. Retrieved November 2006 from: http://www.sanctuaries.nos.noaa.gov/maritime/welcome.html.

Professional Association of Diving Instructors.

1984 Development of a National Underwater Parks Plan. PADI Concept Report to President's Commission on the American Outdoors.

Throckmorton, P.

1990 The World's Worst Investment: The Economics of Treasure Hunting with Real-Life Comparisons. In Carrell, T. (Ed.), *Underwater Archaeology Proceedings from the Society for Historical Archaeology Conference.* Society for Historical Archaeology.

Whitehead, J. and S. Finney

2003 Willingness to Pay for Submerged Maritime Cultural Resources. *Journal of Cultural Economics.* 27:231-240.

World Tourism Organization.

1985 *The State's Role in Protecting and Promoting Culture as a Factor in Tourism Development and the Proper Use and Exploitation of the National Cultural Heritage of Sites and Monuments for Tourists.* World Tourism Organization, Madrid.

Zeppel, H.

1992 *Cultural Tourism in Australia: A Growing Travel Trend.* Material Culture Unit/Department of Tourism, James Cook University.

1996. Education versus Legislation. In *Underwater Archaeology*, Stephen R. James Jr. and Camille Stanley, editors, pp. 45–50.

ROBYN P. WOODWARD

Education Versus Legislation

Bordering the Pacific Ocean, British Columbia (BC) is Canada's westernmost Province. Virtually separated from the rest of the country by the Rocky Mountains, BC has more than 17,000 mi. of rugged coastline dotted with islands and punctuated with fjord-like, deep-water sounds, some more than 20 mi. in length. Buried beneath the silt and rocks lie representative examples of every era of coastal development from prehistoric settlements; First Nation's cultural remains; Spanish, Russian, and English explorers; fur-traders; and settlers.

Whether prehistoric sites were submerged by sea level changes or ships were lost due to storms, fire, collisions, misjudgment of navigational hazards, or drunken skippers, the coast and inland waters of BC have become a storehouse of a rich, yet fragile heritage resource. This resource, which until 20 years ago was little appreciated by any level of government, academia, or the general public, was being systematically pilfered and plundered by souvenir hunters and salvors.

Recognizing that the very shipwrecks which lend such drama to the Province's heritage were a finite resource which was disappearing at an alarming rate, a group of 20 divers who were taking a Continuing Education course in Maritime Archaeology at the University of British Columbia (UBC) formed the Underwater Archaeology Society of British Columbia (UASBC) in 1975. The UASBC is a non-profit, avocational organization dedicated to promoting the science of underwater archaeology and to conserving, preserving, and protecting BC's maritime heritage lying beneath our coastal and inland waters.

The task of protecting BC's submerged cultural resources is a daunting one. Despite its incredibly rich maritime heritage, BC has never had a provincial underwater archaeologist or a submerged cultural resource program. If the new Society were to succeed, its first task would have to be the establishment of a working relationship with the provincial government archaeologists and the education of various levels of government about the importance, extent, and fragile nature of their submerged cultural resources.

Starting with surveys of two wrecks of 19th-century sailing ships, *Panther* and the *Zephyr* in the Gulf Islands, the UASBC created a successful liaison with the provincial archaeologists. As the scope, complexity, and professionalism of our regional surveys have grown over the past 20 years, so has the provincial government's financial support of the Society. Core funding and specific project funding is now supplied in return for a pre-approved program of site surveys, inventory data, historical research, and management advice. Early on in this symbiotic relationship, the Province, prompted in part by financial constraints, made the decision not to establish its own division for submerged cultural resources but rather to rely solely on the input and assistance of this active avocational association. Through the years, as the expertise and competence of the UASBC increased, the provincial authorities have increasingly relied on the Society to advise on management decisions regarding the preservation of all underwater sites.

From the start, the UASBC recognized that the shipwreck resource had to be identified and quantified before it could be managed. Since 1980, the Society has completed shipwreck inventories in the Gulf Islands; Clayoquot, Nootka, and Barkley Sounds on the west coast of Vancouver Island; southern Vancouver Island (including Victoria); Howe Sound; and Burrard Inlet around Vancouver. Funding has just been received for a three-year project to inventory shipwrecks around northeast Vancouver Island, starting at Campbell River (Marc 1994:3). Additionally, we have an ongoing project in the Kootenay Region, in southeast BC, where, to date, members have surveyed and identified more than 50 sites of steamships, lake barges, and train wrecks in the interior lakes.

The UASBC's inventories do not just provide the provincial government with the names and locations of cultural sites and vessels, they also provide the history of each vessel, including details regarding its construction and unique features. Accounts of the vessel's wrecking (if known), salvage attempts (if any), and present location and condition are all documented. Site maps, video, and still photographic records are made of all visible features, and detailed computer data forms are completed. Finally, our recent inventory reports contain recommendations on further action that should be taken with regard to the management and preservation of each site.

Recommendations for the management of each site are developed based on the accessibility of the particular wreck, sport divers' knowledge of the site, historical significance, presence of collectible artifacts, or suitability for an underwater interpretive trail.

It is not, nor has it ever been, the intention of the UASBC to restrict public access to shipwreck sites; rather, we want to ensure that these sites are managed today so that they will survive for tomorrow.

If a wreck's location is widely known, if it is not of particular significance to the Province's maritime history, and if it lacks abundant collectible artifacts, we would normally recommend that no further action is required other than allowing for safe public access to the site. We may also choose to establish a mooring buoy or place a plaque on a site to identify the ship, as we did at the site of the *Del Norte*.

However, if there are some interesting structural remains left, we have recommended that an interpretive trail be developed for the public. This was done with the 260-ft. iron-screw steamer the *Bernard Castle*. Built in 1878 in England, the ship hit Race Rocks off Victoria and sank en route to San Francisco with a load of coal. There are eight plaques around the 131 ft. of extant hull identifying boilers, crankshafts, and other hull features, as well as cargo. Funding for the development of the trail and printing of the pamphlet (which includes a site map, history, and photo of the ship, plus diving safety tips) was provided by the BC Heritage Trust. Other interpretive trails are being planned for

two wrecks in Bedwell Bay, a popular local dive spot near Vancouver.

If a wreck site is not widely known, figures significantly in the maritime history of BC, or contains a wide variety of "collectible artifacts," the UASBC takes a number of different measures to protect the resource.

First, if the site is not readily accessible, we keep the location quiet, reporting it only to the provincial authorities and restricting our diving on it so as not to draw attention to the location. This approach was taken with the *Ericsson*, the first and only side-wheeled, caloric-powered ship, which ended its days as a clipper ship running aground in Barkley Sound in 1892. After surveying the vessel and tagging all important artifacts, we alerted the local community of Bamfield about their important and unique site. The community has since taken over responsibility for the protection of this shipwreck, reporting any suspicious activity to the local police. While our bright yellow survey tags may not totally deter souvenir collectors, they do send out a message that a site is being monitored and studied.

Although the UASBC has undertaken some small test excavations, it is our current policy to restrict this type of activity, and only diagnostic artifacts are removed from a site to confirm the identify of a vessel. To avoid theft, sensitive artifacts may also be removed. This is done only with the permission of the Provincial archaeologist and once we have mapped the site and arranged for conservation of the artifacts.

If a shipwreck features prominently in BC's history, we pursue the ultimate legislative protection by having it designated as an Underwater Heritage Site under the Heritage Conservation Act. This law makes it illegal to remove any object from the wreck without permission of the Archaeology Branch of the Provincial Government (Marc 1994:3). A plaque identifying the extant remains as a Heritage Site is placed on the wreck, if possible, or adjacent to the shore if the site is too deep, as is the *City of Anisworth*, a paddle-wheeler at 330 ft. in Kootenay Lake. This, however, is a lengthy process. To date we have designated six shipwreck sites and will be seeking similar protection for the Province's oldest train wreck site at Procter Point on Kootenay Lake.

Working in parallel with the provincial and professional archaeologists, the UASBC's efforts to elevate the status of submerged cultural resources were realized in 1994 when the Provincial Legislature passed the Heritage Conservation Amendment Act which affords the same protection to terrestrial and submerged cultural sites—including shipwrecks and aircraft older than two years. Lawyers who are members of the Society had a role in drafting parts of this legislation.

The UASBC's task of educating and liaising with government did not begin and end with the Archaeology Branch. Because of the intense development activity on the southern coast of the Province, members of the Society have made presentations to, and met with, many Ministries of the Provincial Government to apprise them of the significance of submerged cultural resources. Although not usually required by law, the Ministry of Lands and Recreation does send us notification of all foreshore lease developments and requests our input. This includes permits for logboom moorings, fish farms, and pipe and cable installations. The BC Ferry Corporation has consulted with us prior to constructing new docks at Bella Bella and Snug Cove. Likewise, the UASBC has developed a good working relationship with the major Federal Port authorities, who are now cognizant of the submerged cultural resources within their jurisdiction.

From its inception, the UASBC realized that governments and legislation alone would not protect cultural sites from indiscriminate salvage; there are simply too many sites to make this practical. Educating the public about their rich maritime heritage and its fragile, non-renewable nature would have to play a significant role in influencing public behavior. Education and public awareness campaigns have been a focus of the Society throughout its 20-year history. We feel strongly that if the local community is educated about the importance of their unique cultural resource, then they will be empowered to protect it for the next generation.

Through time the UASBC's public education program has taken many forms and has been tailored to suit the audience, venue, and available technology. Upon the completion of each regional survey, the UASBC has developed a slide show of its findings. Concentrating first on the schools, service clubs, and local historical societies in the area of the survey, members have detailed the significant finds, plus the aims and objectives of the Society. These presentations have been successful in promoting awareness of local maritime heritage and instilling a sense of community ownership and non-destructive appreciation of a resource. Our message that shipwrecks and submerged cultural sites are non-renewable resources of equal importance to the dwindling first-growth forests and fish stocks of the Pacific Northwest has been well received. With the assistance of our part-time archivist and members who are photographers, our public presentations can be tailored for any age and interest level.

Dive clubs and shops continue to invite us to speak with new divers. These presentations, as well as our annual SHIPWRECKS Conference, continue to generate new diving and non-diving members.

Four years ago the UASBC received a federal grant to develop a trade show display, with informational pamphlets, that could be manned by volunteers. This exhibit has been shipped all over the Province and set up in shopping malls, banks, museums, libraries, and schools. Additionally, it has been used at conventions and boating and diving trade shows.

The UASBC has rewritten, illustrated, and published three of its five survey reports into general interest publications. These reports are available through local libraries and bookstores. Members have also written a wide variety of articles for the popular press.

Our recently published *Wreck Diver's Guide to Sailing Ship Artifacts of the 19th Century* has been reviewed favorably by several international journals. Recent wrecks, with relatively intact hulls, are easy to explore and understand. Scattered remains are more challenging, and the in-

tent of the guide is to educate the general diving public and assist them to "read" wreck sites,
note the location of artifacts, and mentally reconstruct the original vessel. The conservation message runs throughout the book. Sales of this
book will assist us with our next publishing venture: *Wreck Diver's Guide to Steamships*.

Consistency and professional growth have
been key to the success of the UASBC over the
past 20 years. Education of our own members
has been instrumental in ensuring that we continue to attract a wide variety of lay-profession-
als, students, and archaeologists. We produce a
quarterly publication and a monthly bulletin, and
have established a computer-accessed bulletin
board system (BBS). Articles from our publications, site reports, scholarly papers, dive schedules, and Minutes of the monthly meetings held
in Victoria, Vancouver, and Nelson are made
available to our members on the BBS. This BBS
system is shared with other societies belonging
to the Underwater Council of BC, so it has a
dual purpose of keeping our own members informed while being accessible to a much wider
diving audience.

In the past, the UASBC has conducted its
own remote sensing and underwater survey
courses. Feeling the need for more in-depth and
structured courses, we successfully approached
the federal Minister of Heritage who assisted us
in purchasing the Nautical Archaeology Society
(NAS) training program from the UK and fly
two NAS instructors out to teach the NAS Level
I and the Tutors training course to 20 people.
The UASBC will be conducting its first Level I
course for our members in March 1996. Additionally, our next inventory project will enable
some members to work toward their NAS Level
II certificate. In the future, all NAS programs in
BC will be open to the public and conducted
under the auspices of the UASBC.

Over the years, the UASBC has chartered a
number of dive vessels for our projects. Enlist-
ing the charter-boat operators' support in preserving our maritime heritage has been crucial to
the success of our endeavors. We knew if they
could be encouraged to adopt strong conservation
ethics and educated all their diving patrons about

the importance and fragile nature of heritage
sites, then BC's shipwrecks would stand a better chance of survival. Our efforts in working
collaboratively with this sector were rewarded
two years ago when the newly formed BC Dive
Tourism Operators Association included in their
Code of Ethics a statement regarding their obligation to preserve shipwreck sites by not allowing any collection of artifacts or destruction of
cultural remains. This was a significant change
for many operators who had hitherto advertised
"port-hole collecting" dive excursions.

Another initiative started by members of the
UASBC was a series of artificial reefs made up
of modern shipwrecks. Working on the premise
that if there was an exciting, preferably large,
three-dimensional wreck on which to dive, sport
divers could be steered away from the more sensitive heritage wrecks. The Artificial Reef Society (ARS) started with a 150-ft. freighter, the *G.
B. Church*, and then graduated to 366-ft. Canadian Navy destroyer escorts: the HMCS
Chaudiere and HMCS *Mackenzie*. The ARS has
negotiated to sink two additional destroyer escorts in 1996. The program has been a financial
success for the communities and dive operators
adjacent to the new reefs and has diverted divers
away from cultural sites. Additionally, it has
helped us form collaborative relationships with
the marine science community.

Many of the submerged cultural sites and
several important shipwrecks lie within the jurisdiction of BC's Indian reserves or areas that are
currently subject to native land claims. While
some bands recognize the importance of archaeological evidence to support these claims, other
are very sensitive to any disruption or analytical
study of their cultural remains. The issue of
ships that may have been captured and sunk
during the course of the last century is understandably sensitive. Building strong relations with
various First Nations groups has been slow;
however, in the last few years we have received
permission to survey Friendly Cove, the first
Spanish site in BC and an active fur-trading
depot in the early 19th century. The band in
Bella Bella has invited members of the UASBC
to teach archaeological survey techniques to na-

tive divers so they could manage their own re-sources. We visited Bella Bella a second time last year to survey the areas adjacent to the Hudson's Bay Company's dock built soon after Fort McLoughlin in 1835. In each case, education and advice on responsible management of heritage resources have been the foundation for advancing and building strong relationships.

BC is fortunate to have maritime museums in both Vancouver and Victoria. Both institutions maintain excellent libraries and archival and photographic collections, and their staff provide invaluable assistance in our research. In return, we assist the museums by providing public lectures. The Vancouver Maritime Museum (VMM) also provides us with storage, conservation, and meeting space. Private sponsorship support has recently been secured to enable the VMM and UASBC to develop a science program on underwater archaeology for secondary school children.

The UASBC has maintained strong ties with UBC and Simon Fraser University (SFU). The UBC occasionally offers night courses in maritime archaeology through the Classics Department. SFU has offered third-year courses in nautical archaeology taught by UASBC members with post-graduate degrees in archaeology. SFU also invites the Society to present a seminar on submerged cultural resources to all historical archaeology classes. Some of our most active members come from these institutions.

From an academic perspective, it often appears that government cultural resource management is dictated by those operating the pile-drivers and bulldozers. Because professional archaeologists spend the majority of their time recording and protecting threatened sites, there are few opportunities to pursue research-driven archaeology (Robinson 1995:12). As an avocational society, the UASBC enjoys a degree of flexibility and independence not afforded the professional community. In the future we must develop the expertise to do more than just collect a "sea" of survey data; we must focus the collection of this data on a specific research design so as to interest the wider professional community in our work (Robinson 1995:12).

Five years ago the Society convinced the BC Heritage Trust to support a pioneering, research-driven project to locate and conduct test excavations of a prehistoric site in Montague Harbor on Galiano Island. The academic and government archaeological communities did not believe that the methods existed to get meaningful results from an underwater context. Sea level was 300 ft. lower immediately after the last Ice Age than it is today, therefore the earliest evidence of coastal settlements is underwater. The four-year project produced a wealth of paleo-environmental data regarding occupation patterns and sea level changes occurring 6,000 to 1,000 B.P. and proved that this method of investigation was worth pursuing. The results and methods developed at Montague Harbor have been the foundation for new underwater research programs on prehistoric sites in Canada.

Legislation is effective only if the jurisdiction has the resources and the manpower to enforce it. Faced with budget shortfalls and growing deficits, governments everywhere are decreasing, versus increasing, their support of heritage conservation initiatives. Educating and empowering the public to adopt the same conservation and protection ethic they now espouse to have with regard to the environment may be the only solution. Government agencies are not always well positioned or equipped to take on this task. Twenty years ago the government in British Columbia opened its door to a group of concerned sport divers who formed an archaeology society. They involved and empowered an avocational group to take ownership and responsibility for a unique resource. As a result, the avocationals are working in a collaborative and professional manner with the relevant government agencies, dive operators, academic institutions, and native bands, rather than in conflict or competition. A huge amount of work has been done for a relatively minimal investment on the government's part. Most importantly, the resources are now being preserved and managed in a manner that benefits the site, government and academic communities, as well as the sport diving population.

REFERENCES

MARC, JACQUES

1994   Protecting Shipwreck Sites. *Foghorn* 5(1):3. Steven
        Sproston, Newsletter Editor. Underwater Archaeology
        Society of British Columbia, Vancouver, British
        Columbia.

ROBINSON, KEVIN

1995   Sea of Data. *Foghorn* (6)2:12. Brian Cuthill, Newsletter
        Editor. Underwater Archaeology Society of British
        Columbia, Vancouver British Columbia.

ROBYN P. WOODWARD
UNDERWATER ARCHAEOLOGY SOCIETY
OF BRITISH COLUMBIA
1905 OGDEN AVENUE
VANCOUVER, BRITISH COLUMBIA
CANADA

2009 Innovative Approaches to Marine Heritage Management: A View from Across the Divide. In *ACUA Underwater Archaeology Proceedings 2009*, Erica Laneela and Jonathan Moore, editors, pp. 91–101.

Innovative Approaches to Marine Heritage Management: A View from across the Divide

Mark Dunkley

English Heritage, 1 Waterhouse Square, 138-142 Holborn, London, England EC1N 2ST, United Kingdom

In April 2008, the UK Government published a draft *Heritage Protection Bill* proposing new legislation to protect the historic environment in England and Wales. The Bill allows for establishment of a unified Register of Heritage Assets, creation of marine heritage sites, and protection of non-wreck marine heritage assets. Although the Bill was not brought forward in the current session, Government remains committed to introducing new legislation at the earliest opportunity. To prepare, English Heritage has implemented a Heritage Protection Reform program to improve the designation system. This paper outlines how heritage assets on, in, and under England's seabed are being managed in new ways to ensure their values are sustained for future generations.

Introduction

In April 2008, the UK Government published the draft *Heritage Protection Bill*. This innovative document proposes legislation to enable a wholesale revision of the existing laws that protect the historic environment in England and Wales out to the limit of the territorial sea. Provisions in the Bill allow for the establishment of a unified Register of Heritage Assets, the creation of marine heritage sites, and the protection of non-wreck marine heritage assets. As Parliamentary time was not available to take the Bill forward in the current session, introduction of new legislation has been delayed. However, Government remains committed to the historic environment and intends to introduce legislation at the earliest opportunity. In order to prepare the sector for change, English Heritage has implemented a series of initiatives through a Heritage Protection Reform program to commence improvement of the designation system without the need for primary legislation. This paper outlines how the now-static technological manifestations of conflict and trade on, in, and under England's seabed are being managed in new ways to ensure that their values are sustained for future generations to enjoy.

Background

English Heritage is the UK Government's statutory advisor on the historic environment in England and provides expert advice on all matters relating to the historic environment and its conservation, as set out in the *National Heritage Act 1983*. English Heritage works in partnership with other government departments, local authorities, voluntary bodies, and the private sector to conserve and enhance the historic environment, broaden public access to heritage, and increase understanding of the past.

English Heritage's functions relating to underwater archaeology derive from the *National Heritage Act 2002*, which redefined the term "ancient monument" to include ancient monuments in, on, or under the seabed within the 12 nautical mile limit of the UK territorial sea adjacent to England. Note that English Heritage has no statutory responsibility for archaeological sites beyond England's territorial sea.

The policy background to English Heritage's approach to the marine historic environment is framed by the UK Government's adoption of the Annex to the UNESCO *Convention on the Protection of the Underwater Cultural Heritage, 2001* as best practice for underwater archaeology in 2005 (Hansard House of Commons Debates, 24 January 2005 c2 109-17).

In March 2007, the UK Government set out a vision for a simpler, unified heritage protection system. Specific provision was made for proposed legislative change affecting the marine historic environment throughout territorial waters of the United Kingdom. This vision led to the *Heritage Protection Bill*.

Archaeological Potential of the English Seabed: Some Examples

In late 2007, an amateur paleontologist discovered 28 Middle Paleolithic hand axes in gravel deposits dredged from a discrete area off England's east coast, along with flakes, cores, and other Pleistocene materials. The hand axes date to a period when humans were believed to be absent from the northwestern European peninsula and have been described as the single most important find of Pleistocene material from the North Sea. The material is redefining knowledge of the extent of human occupation across northwest Europe during this period. Research is already underway to evaluate the source material in order to better manage the effects of offshore mineral extraction on archaeological and paleontological deposits.

At the other end of the technological scale, a German Dornier Do 17 light bomber was recently discovered off England's southeast coast during routine geophysical survey. Most likely lost in August 1940 during the Battle of Britain, the aircraft represents the only known airframe of this type anywhere in the world and is automatically designated under the *Protection of Military Remains Act 1986*.

The contrast between prehistoric remains and 20th-century military archaeology in terms of cultural significance is interesting. The prehistoric finds reflect a common European ancestry, while evidence of conflict on the scale of World War II leads towards concepts of independence and segregation. However, between these extremes lies evidence of past water transport comprising both military and mercantile interests throughout the ages.

The National Monuments Record (NMR) is the public archive of archaeological sites and monuments. The inventory is maintained by English Heritage and includes some 32,777 identified wrecks and recorded casualties within the territorial sea, with a cutoff date of 1945. The inventory was recently expanded to included aircraft casualties and submerged prehistoric archaeological sites and find spots. Limited records are maintained for sites in UK controlled waters.

Shipwreck concentrations around the British Isles are believed to be among the highest in the world owing to high volumes of shipping traffic, a long history of seafaring, and a high-energy coast. Some of these wreck sites, such as the Confederate paddle steamer *Iona II*, are afforded statutory protection on account of their historical, archaeological, or artistic importance.

Case Study: *Iona II*

Launched on 19 May 1863, the paddle steamer *Iona II* was built by J. & G. Thomson, for Hutcheson & Co., at the Govan shipyard on the Clyde. Following the general lines of its predecessor *Iona*, the luxurious saloon steamer *Iona II* was designed to ply between Glasgow and Ardrishaig at the southeast terminus of the Crinan Canal in Scotland. Specifically built for use in domestic internal waters, such river-class hulls had a distinctive knife-edge bow and a narrow beam relative to their length, in order to drive through the short seas of the Firth of Clyde (Graham 2006:107). *Iona II* is said to have attained a speed of 18 knots on trial, although some claimed the ship could make as many as 23 knots an hour.

Across the Atlantic, the American Civil War had created a demand in the South for swift ships capable of breaking the Federal blockade. Hutcheson & Co. took advantage of exceedingly high prices when they sold *Iona II's* predecessor *Iona* in 1855. After only one summer, *Iona II* was also sold in 1864 to run the blockade, registered in the name of D. Mc-Nutt and resold to Charles Hopkins Boster of

Richmond, Virginia. It is recorded that *Iona III* inherited the saloons and some of the furnishings from *Iona II*, since these items were still new and were not required for the service for which the latter had been purchased. Blockade running was the "lucrative business of running arms and luxuries in – and cotton out – from the beleaguered Southern ports in fast steamers. There were extraordinary profits to be made for those willing to gamble on such a venture – at the height of the war it was reckoned that two return trips paid for the vessel" (Graham 2006:1).

As the blockade tightened and Federal cruisers increased their stop and search missions during the spring of 1862, the runners out of Bermuda and the Bahamas sought to purchase smaller and faster craft. The Clyde's river-class paddle steamers, with their sharp lines and shallow draught, were ideal. The vessels were strengthened in the bow with diagonal struts, fitted with a "turtle" cover on their forward decks to shed broaching waves, and rigged as schooners to assist with the Atlantic crossings (Graham 2006:110). However, river-class steamers were not suited for the Atlantic swell and suffered badly in the crossing and during winter runs into the Confederacy (Graham 2006:107).

A narrow interpretation of neutrality allowed Britain to maintain its laissez-faire attitude towards the thinly disguised blockade-busting activities of the Clyde shipbuilders and owners until late in the Civil War. A pretence of peaceful trading had to be kept up, meaning specifically that the steamer was unarmed, sailed from the Clyde for a declared neutral destination under the command of a British master, and flew the union flag (Graham 2006:5). Runners were loaded with Welsh coal before making the crossing. However, after a U.S. consulate was opened in Cardiff to scrutinize coal ships, vessels were directed from the Clyde to Cork, from where communications with London took longer (Graham 2006:111).

Following a refit, *Iona II* departed the Clyde bound for Nassau, via Queenstown (now Cobh) in County Cork. Gunpowder was said to have formed a significant portion of the general cargo. In rough weather, *Iona II* sprang an unmanageable leak that was later attributed by the crew to strain caused by the vessel being so deeply laden. The ship sank off Lundy Island in the Bristol Channel on 2 February 1864. The loss was reported in *Lloyd's List* the following day.

Subsequently dubbed the "foundered Confederate steamer" by local newspapers, it was reported that the crew of *Iona II* later attempted to "bring away a large quantity of plate, spirits, and other valuable materials; but overloading the boat, she sank and all was lost." Additional contemporary salvage is also recorded.

Iona II was rediscovered accidentally in 1976 and partially excavated from the stern to the aft coal bunkers. Assessment by the Archaeological Diving Unit in 1989 concluded that:

> The iron built hull of the *Iona* survives to just above the turn of the bilges from stem to stern, with the boilers and machinery standing 4 m above the seabed.

> The ship's boilers, steam engines, and valve gear seem to be complete, except for some removable brass items which have probably been taken by divers since the site was discovered in 1976.

> The paddle wheels have collapsed but all the elements of the complex feathering system for the paddles seem to be there, with the exception of the wooden paddles blades. Similarly the massive horizontal crankshaft joining the two paddle wheel hubs is complete although one end has broken off and is displaced. (Archaeological Diving Unit 1989)

In 1986, the remaining structure was designated under the *Protection of Wrecks Act 1973*,

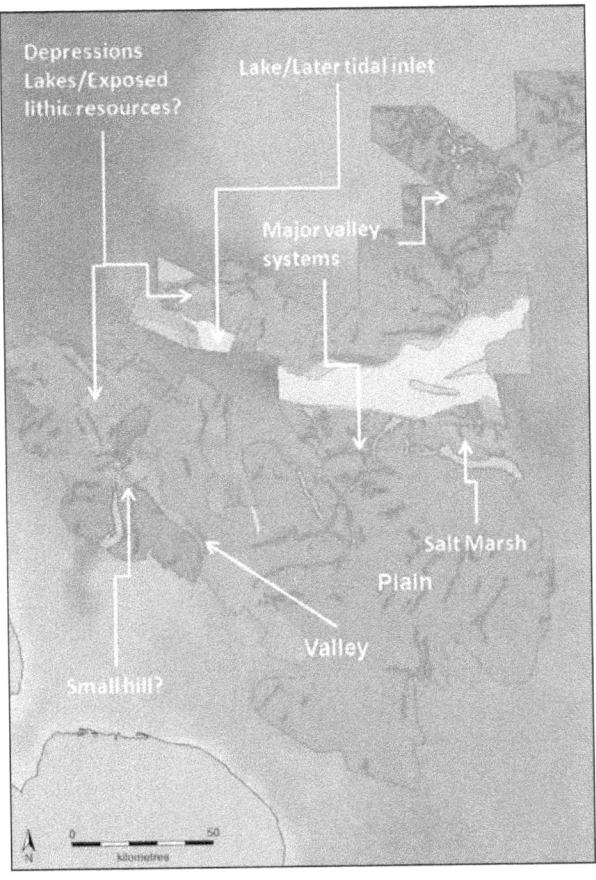

FIGURE 1. Major topographic features in the southern basin of the North Sea, identified using three-dimensional seismic data. (Gaffney et al. 2007; reproduced with permission.)

with management responsibilities falling to English Heritage from 2002. In 2008, the site was identified as being at high risk from unauthorized, and therefore uncontrolled, diver access and from significant natural decay. Enhanced visitor access has reduced unauthorized dives on *Iona II* and a full condition survey planned for 2009 will provide baseline information for developing conservation management policies.

Iona II remains the sole representative of the steam era among England's Protected Wreck Sites and requires careful management to ensure that the values and features of the wreck site can be conserved, maintained, and enhanced for future generations to enjoy.

Other Types of Maritime Heritage

In addition to fully submerged remains, buildings and monuments with maritime as-

sociations are afforded statutory protection where warranted, such as the early 19th-century Royal Navy dockyards, which were the largest industrial complexes in the country at the time of their construction. In 2007, English Heritage published the *Maritime and Naval Buildings Selection Guide* to provide advice regarding historic buildings on land that are associated with the sea (English Heritage 2007).

The National Register of Historic Vessels, maintained by the Advisory Committee on National Historic Ships, contains over 1,200 registered vessels, of which 250 are of special significance, including the Victorian sloop HMS *Gannet* and the 20th-century Royal Yacht *Britannia*, which are considered part of the National Historic Fleet. While English Heritage has no role in the administration of these historic vessels, we are seeking to determine exactly what inclusion on the Register means for heritage protection purposes.

Cultural Heritage beyond Territorial Waters

Extending beyond England's territorial sea and UK controlled waters, the North Sea is enclosed to the west by the British Isles and to the east by Norway, Denmark, Germany, and the Netherlands. Submerged prehistoric remains across the North Sea basin indicate a common background between the British Isles and continental Europe from at least the period known as the Cromerian Complex, around 700,000 years ago, as excavations in the east of England have shown. Recent work by Birmingham University has demonstrated that the North Sea covers one of the largest and best preserved prehistoric landscapes in Europe, and has been submerged since 5,500 B.C. (Figure 1).

For the recent past, the deployment and subsequent loss of British warships, particularly in the 18th-century, reflects the numbers of British warships operating overseas (including in UK controlled waters) and therefore beyond England's territorial sea and statutory protection. Blue-water strategies of the 18th century made trade the lifeblood of the nation, and led to the UK Government's emphasis on establishing overseas commerce and colonies. Foreign policy subsequently developed to avoid interference from other maritime powers, with the Royal Navy having a pivotal role in the defence of Britain's commercial interests overseas.

Where the remains of British vessels are discovered beyond England's territorial sea, English Heritage is often invited to provide advice, without prejudice, to Government and others, as in the example of the recent discovery of the HMS *Victory* in the English Channel (Hansard House of Commons Debates, 11 February 2009, c1997W).

Proposed Reform of Heritage Protection

Given the extent and range of maritime archaeological remains and the different types of designations that apply, commitment by the UK Government to reform heritage protection in the UK marine zone commenced in March 2004 with the jointly published consultation paper *Protecting the Marine Historic Environment: Making the System Work Better* (Department for Culture, Media and Sport [DCMS] 2004). The paper set out key issues and questions in relation to Marine Historic Environment (MHE) designation and proposed a legislative framework to enable positive, transparent, inclusive, sustainable, and effective management.

Following consultation, Government published the *Heritage Protection Review White Paper* in March 2007, which set out a vision of a simpler, unified heritage protection system (DCMS 2007a). Specific provision was made for proposed legislative change affecting the MHE throughout territorial waters of the United Kingdom, consistent with the current extent of the *Protection of Wrecks Act 1973*, to include:

- broadening the range of marine historic assets that can be protected;

- making designation decisions on the basis of special interests;

- publishing new selection criteria;

- establishing interim protection; and,

- introducing a new statutory duty for the Receiver of Wreck with regard to salvaged material.

The White Paper was accompanied by a Regulatory Impact Assessment indicating that costs from reform of the marine heritage protection system are expected to be negligible (DCMS 2007b:58).

Disappointment was expressed by the sector that the issue of salvage law had not been addressed within the White Paper. The Government's stated policy position was that they "do not intend…to make substantive changes to salvage law in relation to marine historic assets, as…this would be a disproportionate response" (DCMS 2007c:3.8.3).

At the same time, Scottish Ministers withdrew from the specific UK-wide marine applications of the proposed Bill in November 2007, preferring to legislate on the devolved issue in the Scottish Parliament (Philip Robertson 2008, pers. comm.).

Similarly, Northern Ireland withdrew from the proposed Bill in early 2008 after having decided that it had adequate provision under Article 38 of the *Historic Monuments and Archaeological Objects (NI) Order 1995* for the protection of wreck sites through scheduling. Northern Ireland also has a provision for the reporting of finds from the seabed under Article 42 of the same Order, though a review of this legislation is to have commenced in April 2009 (Rhonda Robinson 2008, pers. comm.).

Heritage Protection Bill

The draft *Heritage Protection Bill*, published in April 2008, proposed a wholesale revision of the existing law that protects the historic environment in England and Wales. The

Bill would also repeal several Acts, including the *Protection of Wrecks Act 1973.*

Marine Heritage Sites

Provisions in the draft Bill allow for the establishment of a unified list of all Heritage Assets, the creation of marine heritage sites, and the protection of non-vessel marine heritage assets, such as vehicles, aircraft and, for the first time, archaeological structures and sites located partly or wholly below the high water mark in English waters. The definition of English waters used within the context of the Bill extends to the seaward limit of UK territorial waters adjacent to England. The term "intertidal" is used to denote the area between the high and low water marks of ordinary spring tides. Archaeological sites or objects would be considered "marine heritage assets" if they are fully submerged or are located wholly or partly in the intertidal zone. All existing wrecks protected under Section 1 of the *Protection of Wrecks Act 1973* would be immediately added to the list as marine heritage sites.

Where a marine site containing heritage assets qualifies for statutory protection, future designation decisions would be based on special architectural, historic, archaeological, or artistic interest. Detailed principles of selection will define "special interest" in the marine environment, but in contrast to the procedure for the designation of terrestrial sites, the Secretary of State (SoS) for Culture, Media and Sport will be solely responsible for designation decisions following consultation with owners, local planning authorities, and other parties. Assets would automatically be afforded provisional protection during the consultation period.

Nevertheless, it is clear that for a site to qualify for protection, its special interest, location, and extent would have to be determined by assessing available evidence. In some cases, where further archaeological investigation is required, there is provision within the Bill to enable this. English Heritage or designated local authorities will be permitted to finance archaeological investigation, and English Her-

itage will have the authority to make grants and loans in respect of assets eligible for registration. However, specific management mechanisms for this have yet to be determined (Figure 2). Certificates of no intention to designate would be available in the same manner and basis as for terrestrial structures.

Enabling Access

English Heritage would be responsible for maintaining a publicly available list that would include all marine heritage sites. The list would be made available online through the Heritage Gateway (<http://www.heritage-gateway.org.uk>), which is expected to be the most publicly visible element of the proposed reforms.

Access to marine heritage sites would be controlled through the issuance of marine heritage licences by English Heritage. These licenses would define permitted activities and contain specific conditions. As under the *Protection of Wrecks Act 1973*, it would remain an offence to carry out certain activities without a licence. Some robust sites, however, could be designated as being suitable for low-impact diving activities, with access permitted under the condition that the site not be disturbed.

Revisions to the Merchant Shipping Act 1995

Section 2 of the *Protection of Wrecks Act 1973* enables the designation of prohibited areas around dangerous wrecks. With the repeal of this Act, responsibility for dangerous wrecks and cargo would be accommodated under the *Merchant Shipping Act 1995.* In addition, a new duty would oblige the Receiver of Wreck to communicate information relating to marine heritage to appropriate bodies.

Intertidal Structures

Dealing with structures and sites in the intertidal zone would require consideration of the most appropriate management regime. The SoS would first consider whether they should be registered as marine heritage assets. The SoS could reject such an application, leaving it open to English Heritage to consider whether

FIGURE 2. Archaeological investigation will continue to be required to assist in determining the special interest of candidate marine heritage sites, such as the 16th-century Swash Channel Protected Wreck Site in southern England. (Photo courtesy of Wessex Archaeology.)

registration as a land-based Heritage Asset is appropriate

Historic Environment Records

Another innovation would require local planning authorities to create and maintain an historic environment record (HER) for their area, or delegate that role to another authority. An historic environment record would contain a record of all marine heritage sites in the local planning authority's area.

Pre-Legislative Scrutiny

The House of Commons Culture, Media and Sport Select Committee (CMSC) undertook pre-legislative scrutiny of the draft Bill and published their results in July 2008 (Great Britain Parliament House of Commons Culture, Media and Sport Committee [CMSC]

2008). The Committee was not able to examine all aspects of the proposed legislation due to "existing commitments on other inquiries, coupled with the necessity to provide an assessment for DCMS prior to the summer redrafting of the Bill." In particular, the Committee regretted not being able to examine in detail the provisions relating to the protection of marine heritage (CMSC 2008:6). However, it is worth noting that among the marine issues raised during the inquiry, the Committee recommended a review of salvage law and the role of the Receiver of Wreck (CMSC 2008:18).

On the 20 October 2008, the Government published its response to the CMSC report. The response noted that the "draft Heritage Protection Bill takes forward the position set out in the White Paper, including the decision not to proceed with a wholesale revision of

FIGURE 3. The remains of the Confederate paddle steamer *Iona II* (1864) lie in England's first Marine Nature Reserve, offering socioeconomic benefits and opportunities for coordinated management. (Photo courtesy of Wessex Archaeology.)

Salvage Law" (DCMS 2008:20). As such, the Government does "not believe a further review of marine heritage protection is necessary before the introduction of the Heritage Protection Bill" (DCMS 2008:21).

Other UK Marine Policy

English Heritage was encouraged by the commitment made by the Government's Department for Environment, Food and Rural Affairs in *Safeguarding Sea Life* (Department for Environment, Food and Rural Affairs [Defra] 2005), the joint UK response to the Review of Marine Nature Conservation. The stated strategic goals of this initiative are "to increase our understanding of the marine environment, its natural processes and our cultural marine heritage and the impact that human activities have upon them."

In addition, the UK Government and Devolved Administrations recently set out a number of high-level marine objectives for the UK marine area as a whole, which precede development of a Marine Policy Statement (Defra 2009a). The long-term view promoted in this statement is that appropriate management of cultural heritage is a component of a "healthy, productive and biologically diverse" marine environment.

Marine and Coastal Access Act 2009

First published as a Bill in April 2008 (Defra 2008), this Act will facilitate more efficient and sustainable protection of all marine resources, including an improvement in the way the marine environment is protected and managed (Defra 2009b). Four areas of the *Marine and Coastal Access Act 2009* are most relevant

491

to the historic environment: planning and licensing; Marine Conservation Zones (objective-based statutory Marine Protected Areas); inshore fisheries and conservation authorities; and coastal access.

The term Marine Protected Area (MPA) has been used to describe any area of intertidal or subtidal terrain, together with its overlying water and associated flora or fauna, historical, or cultural features, that is protected by legal or other effective means (Parliamentary Office of Science and Technology 2008). Proposed Marine Conservation Zones (MCZ) will allow for the protection of nationally important habitats and species not presently subject to European protection (such as Special Areas of Conservation), and will take into account socioeconomic factors in site selection. English Heritage is currently determining how the conservation objectives of a MCZ might be used to secure coordinated management of cultural marine heritage both in the English territorial sea and in UK controlled waters (Figure 3).

Delay to Legislative Reform

Unfortunately, it was announced in November 2009 that Parliamentary time had not been found to take forward the *Heritage Protection Bill* in the current session. Introduction of the Bill has therefore been delayed. Despite this setback, Government remains committed to the historic environment and intends to publish a statement on its vision and priorities in 2009 and to introduce legislation at the earliest opportunity. Notably, the *Marine and Coastal Access Act 2009* may provide some level of protection for marine heritage in English waters.

Heritage Protection Reform

Despite Parliamentary delay of the *Heritage Protection Bill*, English Heritage believes that forthcoming initiatives provide a new focus for reform, and that many of the goals to improve the designation system, widen public involvement, and simplify protection process-es can be achieved without new legislation.

English Heritage has therefore set up a dedicated Heritage Protection Reform Team within the Heritage Protection Department to lead and coordinate delivery of the new system. This will ensure that the sector as a whole is adequately equipped to move the reforms forward in partnership. The marine aspects of the implementation strategy will be undertaken by a Maritime Designation Advisor, appointed to initiate and lead project planning and management to support and implement key maritime projects.

English Heritage's *Conservation Principles*, published in April 2008, provide the framework for consistent, well informed, and objective conservation decisions. Conservation is understood as the process of managing change in ways that will best sustain the values of a place in its contexts, while recognising opportunities to reveal and reinforce those values (English Heritage 2008a). At the same time, an innovative methodology for the risk management of Protected Wreck Sites will assist with strategic prioritisation (English Heritage 2008b).

In addition, English Heritage is working towards producing clearer designation records, termed designated asset descriptions, for marine sites to bring them into line with buildings and monuments. A selection guide for pre-industrial vessels is also being prepared to assist with future designation decisions.

For more information on the Heritage Protection Reform program, see: <http://www. english-heritage.org.uk/heritageprotection>.

Conclusion

Initially introduced as a private member's bill, the current law protecting wreck sites from unauthorized interference has always excluded other types of archaeological resources from statutory protection. England's rich and varied marine historic environment is a legacy for the future and we are responsible to future generations for ensuring it is protected and enhanced. The draft *Heritage Protection Bill* proposes, for the first time, to enable the unified protection of all types of archaeological sites, structures, and artifacts in English waters. Criteria to assist in the identification of special interest, as well as delivery of supporting policy and guidance documentation are now being developed with sector participation to support the proposed legislative changes, leading to an improved and unified system of heritage protection.

While it is disappointing that Parliamentary time was not available to take forward the *Heritage Protection Bill* at this time, English Heritage welcomes the Government's firm commitment to the historic environment. Although legislation is still required to create the unified list of all heritage assets and identify marine heritage sites on the basis of special interest, the Heritage Protection Reform program is already underway and it is estimated that more than two-thirds of the changes set out in the White Paper (DCMS 2007a) can be implemented without new legislation.

Whatever happens, changes to the way in which England's marine heritage is enjoyed, understood, valued, and conserved are in progress, and public engagement will be at the heart of this process.

References

Archaeological Diving Unit
1989   *Assessment of the Wreck of the Paddle Steamer Iona, Lundy, North Devon.* Manuscript, Archaeological Diving Unit, University of St. Andrews, Scotland.

Department for Culture, Media and Sport (DCMS)
2004   *Protecting Our Marine Historic Environment: Making the System Work Better.* The Stationery Office, London, England.

2007a   *Heritage Protection for the 21st Century – White Paper.* The Stationery Office, London, England.

2007b   *Regulatory Impact Assessment: Heritage Protection for the 21st Century.* The Stationery Office, London, England.

2007c   *Heritage Protection for the 21st Century: An Analysis of Consultation Responses.* The Stationery Office, London, England.

2008   *Government Response to the Culture, Media and Sport Committee Reports on the Draft Heritage Protection Bill and Draft Cultural Property (Armed Conflicts) Bill.* The Stationery Office, London, England.

Department for Environment, Food and Rural Affairs (Defra)
2005   *Safeguarding Sea Life: The Joint UK Response to the Review of Marine Nature Conservation.* Defra, London, England. <http://www.defra.gov.uk/environment/quality/biodiversity/marine/documents/rmnc-review-1205.pdf>

2008   *Marine and Coast Access Bill [HL].* The Stationery Office, London, England. <http://www.publications.parliament.uk/pa/ld200809/ldbills/001/2009001.pdf>

2009a   *Our Seas – A Shared Resource: High Level Marine Objectives.* Defra, London, England. <http://www.defra.gov.uk/environment/marine/documents/ourseas-2009update.pdf>

2009b   *Marine and Coastal Access Act 2009.* The Stationery Office, London, England. <http://www.opsi.gov.uk/acts/acts2009/pdf/ukpga_20090023_en.pdf>

English Heritage
2007   *Maritime and Naval Buildings Selection Guide.* English Heritage, London, England. <http://www.english-heritage.org.uk/upload/pdf/Maritime_and_Naval.pdf>

2008a *Conservation Principles, Policies and Guidance for the Sustainable Management of the Historic Environment.* English Heritage, London, England. <http://www.english-heritage.org.uk/upload/pdf/Conservation_Principles_Policies_and_Guidance_April08_Web.pdf>

2008b *Protected Wreck Sites at Risk: A Risk Management Handbook.* English Heritage, London, England. <http://www.english-heritage.org.uk/upload/pdf/Protected_Wreck_Sites_at_Risk_ACCESS_20081104114324.pdf >

Gaffney, Vincent, Kenneth Thomson, and Simon Fitch (editors)

2007 *Mapping Doggerland: The Mesolithic Landscapes of the Southern North Sea.* Archaeopress, Oxford, England.

Graham, Eric J.

2006 *Clyde Built: Blockade Runners, Cruisers and Armoured Rams of the American Civil War.* Birlinn, Edinburgh, Scotland.

Great Britain Parliament House of Commons Culture, Media and Sport Committee (CMSC)

2008 *Draft Heritage Protection Bill: Eleventh Report of Session 2007-08.* The Stationery Office, London, England. <http://www.publications.parliament.uk/pa/cm200708/cmselect/cmcumeds/821/821.pdf>

Parliamentary Office of Science and Technology

2008 Marine Conservation Zones. *POSTnote* 310. <http://www.parliament.uk/documents/upload/postpn310.pdf>

2007. Cooperative Approaches to Protecting Underwater Cultural Heritage: Emerging Themes and Trends. In *ACUA Underwater Archaeology Proceedings 2007*, Victor Mastone, editor, pp. 57–62.

Cooperative Approaches to Protecting Underwater Cultural Heritage: Emerging Themes and Trends

Sarah Dromgoole
School of Law, University of Nottingham, Nottingham NG7 2RD, UK

Although for some years most States have been required by international law to protect underwater cultural heritage in all sea areas and to act cooperatively in this respect, they have largely ignored this duty until recently. However, the process of negotiating the UNESCO Convention on the Protection of the Underwater Cultural Heritage 2001, itself an example of States acting in fulfilment of this duty, has also been the catalyst and inspiration for further types of cooperative action. This paper discusses a number of emerging themes and trends that indicate that States are increasingly recognising the benefits of a cooperative approach.

Introduction

In 2006, the author published an edited volume of national reports on the legal protection of the underwater cultural heritage (Dromgoole 2006). The volume contains perspectives on the law, policy and practice in 16 jurisdictions, written in light of the UNESCO Convention on the Protection of the Underwater Cultural Heritage 2001. The jurisdictions covered are Australia, China and Taiwan, Finland, France, Greece, Ireland, the Federated States of Micronesia, the Netherlands, New Zealand, Norway, Poland, South Africa, Spain, Sweden, the UK, and the USA.

This paper identifies some of the general themes and trends emerging from the various national reports, focusing particularly on examples of international cooperative action.

Background

From a legal point of view, the starting point for this discussion is Article 303(1) of the United Nations Convention on the Law of the Sea 1982. This provision of international law, binding on virtually all States, imposes on them a duty to cooperate to protect archaeological and historical objects found in all sea areas. The process of negotiating the UNESCO Convention 2001, and bringing it into force, is the ultimate paradigm of States acting to fulfil this duty, and, of course, the principle of cooperation is one of the core principles of the new Convention. Its regime is in fact dependent upon States cooperating.

Having now been ratified by 14 States as of 12 May 2007, it seems likely that the UNESCO Convention 2001 will come into force in the near future. Six further ratifications are required. However, its mechanisms for controlling treasure hunting and other activities will not be fully effective until the majority of major maritime States participate in its regime. It may be many years, if ever, before this happens.

A cross section of national viewpoints on the UNESCO Convention is represented in the reports in the 2006 collection: Spain, for example, was one of the first States to ratify the Convention; France, the Netherlands, the UK, and the US maintain strongly-held objections; and Norway was one of only four States that voted against the Convention at the UNESCO General Conference in 2001. Many of the other countries represented in the collection are broadly in favor of the Convention, but have yet to ratify it. Why is it that such States are holding back? Various reasons emerge.

Bill Jeffery points out that under the Australian Constitution (which is by no means unique in this respect), there is a need not only to institute a thorough review of all relevant legislation prior to ratification of any convention, but also to make any legislative amendments required to comply with the Convention prior to ratification. As in many States, but especially those with a federal system of government, there is a host of relevant legislation that needs to be reviewed In Australia, for example, Jeffery explains that there are eight federal and 17 State/territory acts which will need to be examined. It is not surprising, therefore, that there is a degree of reluctance to proceed with this preparatory work. Many countries, Ireland being one, have other legislative priorities due to commitments arising from the ratification of other international treaties, particularly the UNESCO Convention on the Means of Prohibiting and Preventing the Illicit Import, Export and Transfer of Ownership of Cultural Property 1970 and the European Convention on the Protection of the Archaeological Heritage (Revised) 1992. Some countries are simply adopting a 'wait and see' approach, in other words waiting to see if the Convention gains momentum before jumping on board if it does so.

One thing that comes across clearly from the collection of national reports is that there is widespread support for the Convention's objectives and general principles. The need for measures to be taken to protect underwater cultural heritage (UCH) situated extra-territorially, and for international cooperation to implement such measures, appears to be unquestioned. The Convention's starting point that preservation *in situ* should be the first option, its insistence that any interference with UCH must be conducted only in accordance with archaeological best practice and not for commercial gain, its focus on the need for proactive management of UCH by competent national authorities, and its recognition of the importance of public education and public access are all widely accepted. The Rules laid out in the Annex to the Convention appear set to become a globally accepted benchmark by which all activities directed at UCH will be judged. There is plenty of evidence throughout the collection that States are intending to apply the Rules within their territorial waters and in some cases further out to sea as well, whether or not they ultimately intend to ratify the Convention. Norway is a particular case to study.

Despite being one of the staunchest opponents of the Convention, Norway has apparently committed itself to applying the Rules in its territorial sea and contiguous zone, and in fact has also indicated an intention to apply them in respect of a shipwreck (the *Luise Horn*) found in 2005, 65 miles from the coastal baseline in its exclusive economic zone (EEZ). It is also interesting to note that many States are now taking action to declare a contiguous zone in order to exercise control over UCH out to 24 miles, turning to Article 303(2) of the Law of the Sea Convention to justify this action. Gwenaelle Le Gurun notes that the 'elaboration' of Article 303(2) by the UNESCO Convention: Article 8 has ended its 'somewhat clandestine existence'. Now that its existence has been recognized and in a sense legitimized by Article 8, many States are considering making use of it. France, Spain, Norway, South Africa, the Netherlands and Poland are among those that have used it, or are contemplating doing so.

The national perspectives also demonstrate that the UNESCO Convention 2001 is already having a profound impact, even in States such as Norway that have strongly held objections to its detailed regime. Many of the themes emerging from the national reports correspond to key features of the Convention, partly because the Convention enshrines modern thinking and therefore reflects developments that are already taking place and partly since the

496

Convention is directly influencing the approaches being taken at a national level.

Emerging Themes and Trends

The UNESCO Convention 2001 applies to UCH defined broadly to include 'all traces of human existence' underwater as written in Article 1(1) (a). The definition reflects the modern recognition that UCH comprises far more than just shipwrecks. Strikingly, those jurisdictions, which were the first to introduce legislation back in the 1970s, are now reconsidering their original approach, which focused on shipwrecks. The UK Protection of Wrecks Act 1973 and the Australian Historic Shipwrecks Act 1976, both pioneering statutes at the time they were introduced, are now under review. The present author reports that the UK is proposing to replace the 1973 Act, which relates only to 'vessels', with legislation applying to a much broader concept of 'marine historic assets', and Bill Jeffery reports that the Australian government intends to review the Historic Shipwrecks Act 1976 with a view to incorporating all aspects of maritime heritage, not just shipwrecks.

Another very clear trend emerging from the collection is the increasingly strong interest at the national level in the preservation of 20th century remains, particularly those from the two World Wars. Interestingly, this is one of the few national trends that run counter to the UNESCO approach, which adopts a temporal cut-off point of 100 years. One of the main reasons for the 100 year cut-off point in the Convention is that it avoids potential conflicts with the rights of private owners, which become increasingly identifiable the more recent the wreck. Several of the commentators in the collection illustrate examples wherein, attempting to protect recent shipwrecks, difficulties have arisen in balancing the rights of identifiable owners with the cultural interest. For example, Nessa O'Connor refers to an Irish High Court judgment in 2005, in respect to the *Lusitania,* which attempts to

reconcile the interests of the owner with the restrictions placed on the site by virtue of the fact that it is subject to an underwater heritage order under Irish heritage legislation. Significantly, the judge refers to the Rules set out in the Annex to the UNESCO Convention when discussing the standards that might be expected of the owner in undertaking work on the wreck. The case went on appeal to the Irish Supreme Court in March 2007, but the Supreme Court, somewhat disappointingly, did not find it necessary to pronounce on the substantive rights and responsibilities of the owner.

As is well known, the provision of UNESCO Convention 2001 for sunken warships and other State vessels is unacceptable to most maritime States because it interferes with what they believe to be their right to exclusive jurisdiction over these vessels, wherever they may lie. Nonetheless, almost certainly prompted at least in part by the negotiations at UNESCO, some of these States are now taking active steps to protect their sunken State vessels, and not just their own State vessels, but those of other States as well. The US Sunken Military Craft Act of 2004 seeks to protect all US sunken military vessels and aircraft wherever they are located and offers protection to the 'sovereign immune' vessels and aircraft of other States located in US waters. The comparable piece of legislation in the UK, the Protection of Military Remains Act 1986, was activated in 2002 to protect shipwrecks and now protects 48 vessels in total, including three German U-boats located in UK territorial waters. It is of interest to note that in the autumn of 2006, the English Court of Appeal upheld an earlier High Court decision that the World War II merchant vessel SS *Storaa,* which was torpedoed while carrying war supplies in convoy, was 'in military service' when she sank and is therefore eligible for protection under the 1986 Act. This decision, which will not be appealed further, considerably broadens out the potential scope of the Act. The nature of the US Sunken Military Craft Act and the

UK Protection of Military Remains Act in offering protection to the vessels of other States is commendable, and it is to be hoped that other maritime States will adopt similar legislation in the future. Formal reciprocal agreements can also be envisaged.

The assertion of State ownership rights with respect to a shipwreck or its cargo can be positive or negative from a cultural heritage perspective, depending on the circumstances and, in particular, the motivations of the State concerned. Generally speaking, the present trend seems to be positive, with many States claiming or asserting ownership rights for the specific purpose of protecting cultural interests. The US litigation in respect to the Spanish galleons the *Juno* and *La Galga* illustrates how a State can protect the cultural interest in shipwrecks by asserting its pre-existing ownership rights, thereby fending off salvage claims. This case, and others in the US and elsewhere, such as the *Vrouw Maria* in Finland in 2005, demonstrate a clear trend towards judicial recognition of State ownership and the right of the State, as owner, to prohibit 'unwanted' salvage. Interestingly, in the US report, Ole Varmer observes that it may well have been the fact that the US informed Spain about the case and inquired about its potential interest that played a significant part in prompting Spain to intervene.

Unfortunately, there are also examples of States asserting their ownership rights motivated entirely by the prospect of a windfall for their treasuries. Sadly, some of the most advanced and economically prosperous States of the world are the ones setting bad examples in this respect. The case of the 17th century British warship HMS *Sussex*, which lies in deep water off Gibraltar, readily springs to mind. In 2002, the British government negotiated a salvage contract with an American company for the recovery of gold coins from the *Sussex*. The contract caused outrage in the archaeological world and damaged Britain's political relations with the Spanish government, which believes the wreck may lie in its jurisdiction.

Cooperation between States may be a means of overcoming jurisdictional conflicts or uncertainties. One of the most obvious situations when a jurisdictional conflict will arise is when a sunken military vessel of one State is found in the territorial waters of another. Which takes precedence, the sovereignty of the coastal State over its territorial sea, or the exclusive sovereignty claimed by the flag State? The only way to resolve the uncertainty is through cooperative action. Even when, from a technical legal point of view, there is no strict jurisdictional conflict, sensitivities may arise, for example when a State-owned wreck that does not fall under the principle of sovereign immunity, which extends only to vessels on non-commercial service, is found in the territorial waters of another State. The Dutch East India Company vessels are a prime example. Domestic heritage legislation generally does not make provision for the notification of a flag State of the discovery, or potential recovery, of its UCH, be it a warship or other 'State vessel', a State-owned vessel, or simply a vessel originated from a particular State. A number of the national reports refer to this lacuna but make it clear that, in practice, consultation will take place. Problems will arise when the flag State's views on the future treatment of the UCH differ markedly from those of the coastal State. As Thijs Maarleveld has observed, tensions have arisen between coastal States and the Netherlands, as flag State of Dutch East Indiamen lying in various parts of the world. These tensions have manifested themselves recently in respect to the *Rooswijk*, a Dutch East Indiaman lying in UK territorial waters. The vessel had been designated under the UK Protection of Wrecks Act 1973 in February 2007.

Over recent years, it is apparent that there has been a general improvement in the regulation of illicit trade in UCH, and this improvement comes largely as a result of the ratification and implementation by many

498

States of the UNESCO Convention 1970 and, in some cases, of the complementary UNIDROIT Convention on Stolen or Illegally Exported Cultural Objects 1995. In his report on Australia, Bill Jeffery provides a specific illustration of the benefits that this can bring. In 2001, the Australian federal police, responding to a request by the Indonesian government, and acting under powers made available due to the implementation of the 1970 Convention, seized more than 70,000 pieces of porcelain from the trading ship *Tek Sing*, which had been recovered from Indonesian waters and illegally exported, and returned them to Indonesia. Although the *Dodington* coins case in South Africa in the late 1990s had a less happy outcome, the increasing influence of the 1970 Convention is undoubtedly having a positive impact. Apart from anything else, it requires States to cooperate. The more they do so, the more they will get into the habit of doing so, both at formal and informal levels.

One of the most formal types of cooperation between States is when they negotiate an inter-State agreement, which is essentially a mini convention or treaty. Article UNESCO Convention 2001: Article 6 encourages States to enter bilateral, regional, or other multilateral agreements, or to develop existing agreements for the preservation of UCH. The usefulness of bilateral agreements for overcoming sensitivities between flag States and coastal States in relation to wrecks found in territorial waters has been demonstrated on several occasions in the past (HMS *Birkenhead*, CSS *Alabama* and *La Belle* being well-known examples) and the emphasis placed on inter-State agreements by the UNESCO Convention 2001 will undoubtedly encourage further use of these agreements in circumstances when it would be politically difficult for one State to act alone in respect to a site. Unfortunately, there may be circumstances where sensitivities are so great that formal cooperation of this kind is virtually impossible. Wojciech Kowalski points out the plight of a number of German

vessels which sank off the Polish coast in 1945, with thousands of refugees from East Prussia and their valuables on board. These wrecks are now the subject of attention by recreational divers. In 2004, Poland designated two of the wrecks, the *Wilhelm Gustloff* and the *Goya*, as 'underwater cemeteries' under its domestic legislation and prohibited all activities in their vicinity. However, since the sites lie in Poland's EEZ, rather than its territorial sea, the prohibitions are not legally enforceable against foreign nationals. An inter-State agreement with Germany would be the best solution, but it seems that this is out of the question politically.

The situation is more positive in respect to another group of shipwrecks lying further westwards along the North European coast. There is some anticipation that the UK government will pursue the possibility of an inter-State agreement with the Danish and German governments with respect to the British and German vessels lost in the Battle of Jutland in 1916. Such an agreement would be quite remarkable; it would be the first to apply to a large number of wrecks, a whole battlefield in fact, and it would be the first agreement of its kind relating to sites that straddle several different maritime zones.

The Titanic Agreement is another interesting example of an inter-State agreement. It very clearly demonstrates how international cooperation can overcome jurisdictional limitations. While no State has direct territorial jurisdiction over the site, control can be exercised using other forms of jurisdiction, namely flag State jurisdiction and port State jurisdiction. Provided all those States whose flag vessels have the deep-water technology to access the site, and all those States with ports in the general geographical proximity of the site sign up to the Agreement, it could be very effective.

The UNESCO Convention 2001: Article 19 also places general duties upon State Parties to assist each other in the protection and management of UCH and the sharing of information, and it is apparent that such collaboration, especially between neighboring States, is increasingly taking place. For example, although the Baltic States have had difficulty in formulating a formal regional agreement, general cooperation has been taking place since 1997 under the banner of the 'Baltic Sea Heritage Co-operation'. The possibility that a State such as South Africa may be able to assist economically poorer neighbours is discussed by Craig Forrest, who points out that South Africans may well be responsible for some of the interference with UCH taking place in the waters of bordering States. There is also potential for collaboration between States with connecting historical ties. Mariano Aznar Gómez explains that Spain is embarked on a policy of endeavouring to conclude bilateral agreements with every Latin-American State with Spanish shipwrecks in its waters, and with the Philippines, but that tensions on the question of ownership have sometimes impeded progress. Thijs Maarleveld refers to the 'inheritance' of former Dutch imperialism and colonialism, and explains that the Netherlands has developed a concept of 'mutual heritage' to deal with the sensitivities that may potentially arise. Among other things, it has set aside a budget for projects with 'mutual heritage countries', including projects relating to UCH. Maarleveld cites instances when Dutch inflexibility on the question of ownership caused considerable offence and precluded the possibility of further co-operation. He suggests that the example provided by the Australia/Netherlands Agreement concerning Old Dutch Shipwrecks, when title was transferred to the State in whose waters the UCH lies, may be the best way to diffuse tensions and thereby allow for collaborative management.

Conclusion

Formally or informally, Cooperation between States in the interests of UCH is one of the keys to effective management. It can help to overcome strict jurisdictional limitations; it can help to overcome uncertainties about who has what jurisdictional rights; and it can help to overcome political sensitivities. The fact that the principle of cooperation lies at the core of the UNESCO Convention 2001 will undoubtedly be the catalyst and inspiration for further cooperative action, taken both within the Conventional regime, and outside it.

Acknowledgments

The author would like to thank Thomas Adlercreutz, Mariano Aznar Gómez, Piers Davies, Craig Forrest, Kuen-chen Fu, Bill Jeffery, Wojciech Kowalski, Frode Kvalø, Gwénaëlle Le Gurun, Thijs Maarleveld, Lyder Marstrander, Maija Matikka, Paul Myburgh, Nessa O'Connor, Anastasia Strati, and Ole Varmer for their valuable contributions to the 2006 collection.

Reference

Dromgoole, Sarah (editor)
2006   *The Protection of the Underwater Cultural Heritage: National Perspectives in Light of the UNESCO Convention 2001*, Martinus Nijhoff, Leiden, the Netherlands.